ABSOLUTE WAR

Absolute War

*Violence and Mass Warfare in
the German Lands, 1792–1820*

MARK HEWITSON

OXFORD

UNIVERSITY PRESS

Great Clarendon Street, Oxford, OX2 6DP,
United Kingdom

Oxford University Press is a department of the University of Oxford.
It furthers the University's objective of excellence in research, scholarship,
and education by publishing worldwide. Oxford is a registered trade mark of
Oxford University Press in the UK and in certain other countries

Published in the United States of America by Oxford University Press
198 Madison Avenue, New York, NY 10016, United States of America

British Library Cataloguing in Publication Data
Data available

Library of Congress Control Number: 2016945406

ISBN 978–0–19–878745–7

Printed in Great Britain by
Clays Ltd, St Ives plc

To my extended families,
old and new

Preface

Like many projects, this one has changed shape. The present volume is the first of a series on the violence of war, which is a subject that has been treated indirectly by a large number of scholars—military historians and many others—but which has only recently attracted attention on its own account, not least because the conjunction sounds tautological (but isn't). The significance of violence during military conflicts has varied enormously, as has its impact on combatants, in accordance with the means used, the intensity and scope of the fighting, and the proximity of wartime conditions to other aspects of life. The study of the violence of war in this extended sense requires a familiarity with social and cultural history as well as political, diplomatic, and military history. Because some of the relevant transformations (and reverses) are gradual, contrasting with outcomes of conflict—collapse, loss and acquisition of territory, political reform, and revolution—that are sudden, it also calls for the analysis of a long historical period, providing amongst other things a daunting opportunity to research the history of the late eighteenth and early nineteenth centuries, when early modern historians come face-to-face with modern ones. I have found this confrontation to be a bracing and stimulating experience. I owe a considerable debt to the editors and referees of *War in History* (especially Hew Strachan), the *English Historical Review* (Martin Conway in particular), and the *Historical Journal* (Andrew Preston), where drafts and offshoots of this study have been published, for giving useful criticism and for trusting in the (often obscure) purposes of the research, in the unwieldy form in which it first took shape.

I was able to start the basic reading and research for the project during an immensely enjoyable year at the Institute for Advanced Study in Princeton in 2010/11. I am very grateful to Joan Scott for helping to bring this period of leave into being and to Didier Fassin and all the members at the IAS that year for making it so intellectually rewarding. The distance, not just geographical, which our stay in New Jersey created has proved much more valuable than I realized at the time. Equally valuable, although quite different, was a second, extended period of leave facilitated by the award of an AHRC fellowship (under the aegis of the research leadership scheme), supplemented by a term of sabbatical at UCL. This leave allowed me to finish and write up a project which was expanding—at certain points—uncontrollably. I am thankful for the extra time permitted by the AHRC's new scheme before the publication of outputs is required. I was able to divide the first part of the project into two books as a result of such leeway—something that I would not have been able to do under the terms of previous schemes. I would also like to thank Christopher Wheeler and, more recently, Cathryn Steele at OUP for the same reason. Both have been willing to treat these metamorphosing studies in their own right, amending contracts and extending deadlines. Their flexibility has meant that I have been able to devote myself to writing up—perhaps more than I should—without distraction.

My principal and overwhelming debt in this respect is to my family: to Cécile, for covering, supporting, and distracting me as we have juggled the varying commitments of home and work (and work that comes home); and to Anna and Camille, who are now old enough to ask what we are doing and to criticize us for sitting for too long in front of a laptop. In addition to technical incompetence, they—along with our wider families and friends—have furnished the overriding reasons for turning the laptop off.

MH

London, April 2016

Acknowledgements

The author and publishers wish to thank the following for the use of copyright material:

Map 3. Central Europe, September 1809, from C. Esdaile, *Napoleon's Wars: An International History, 1803–1815* (London, 2007), xxvii, reproduced with the permission of Penguin Random House LLC.

Map 4. The Campaign of 1812, from D. Lieven, *Russia against Napoleon: The True Story of the Campaigns of War and Peace* (London, 2009), xviii–xix, reproduced with the permission of Penguin Random House LLC.

Figure 5.1. Caspar David Friedrich, *Huttens Grab* (1823–4), reproduced with the permission of Klassik Stiftung Weimar.

Contents

List of Figures   xiii
List of Maps   xv
List of Tables   xvii

Introduction: Theories of War and Violence   1

1. From Cabinet Warfare to Mass Armies   31
'Total War' and 'Military Revolution'   33
The *Levée en Masse* and Conscription   43
Patriotic and Cabinet Warfare   51
Tactics, Strategy, and Reform   60

2. Heroism and the Defence of the *Volk*   72
'Public Opinion' and the State   76
War and Peace   86
The Art of War   99
National, Patriotic, and Just Wars   104

3. The Violence of Civilian Life   125
Cultures of Violence and Death   126
The Sensibility of Suffering   131
Civilians and the Burdens of War   139
'War-time'   148

4. The Lives of Soldiers   159
War Stories   159
Hard Facts   164
Citizen-Soldiers   177
Surviving Invasion and Liberation   186

5. War Memories   204
1813: Festivals of Freedom, Liberation, and Sacrifice   205
The Politics of Memory   215
Histories of Liberation and the Post-War Order   225

Conclusion: A History of Remembering and Forgetting   244

Select Bibliography   253
Index   291

List of Figures

2.1. Caspar David Friedrich, *Der Chasseur im Walde* (1813–14)   100

3.1. A. W. Küfner, *Grossmüthige Aufopferung einer Tochter für ihre Mutter zu Frankenthal* (1795)   145

4.1. Christian Wilhelm von Faber du Faur, *An der grossen Strasse von Moshaisk nach Krymskoje*   195

5.1. Caspar David Friedrich, *Huttens Grab* (1823–4)   216

List of Maps

1. Central Europe on the Eve of the French Revolution   36
2. Central Europe at the Height of Napoleonic Power   54
3. Central Europe, September 1809   142
4. The Campaign of 1812   170

List of Tables

4.1. First Editions of Autobiographies and Memoirs by Publication Date 161

5.1. Accounts of the Revolutionary and Napoleonic Wars by Decade 238

Introduction
Theories of War and Violence

At the time of the Silesian War, in the eighteenth century, war was still a mere cabinet affair, in which the people (*Volk*) only took part as a blind instrument; at the start of the nineteenth century, the people on each side were significant in their own right. ...

Must not these different circumstances give rise to quite different considerations? Should they not in the years 1805, 1806 and 1809 have pointed to the extremity of disaster as a very close possibility, even a very great probability, and should they not at the same time have led to widely different plans and measures from any merely aimed at the conquest of a couple of fortresses or a paltry province?

They did not do so in a degree commensurate with their importance, although both Austria and Prussia, judging by their armaments, felt that storms were brewing in the political atmosphere. They could not do so because those relations at that time were not yet so plainly developed as they have since been in history. It is just those very campaigns of 1805, 1806, 1809 and later ones which have made it easier for us to form a conception of modern absolute war in its destroying energy. ...

Now we cannot conceal from ourselves the fact that the majority of wars and campaigns approach a state of observation rather than a struggle for life or death; that is, a struggle in which at least one of the combatants uses every effort to bring about a complete decision. Only the wars of the nineteenth century have this latter characteristic to such a degree that a theory founded on this point of view can be made use of in relation to them. ... Hence we shall commence with the case in which the desire of a decision permeates and guides the whole, therefore with *real*, or if we may use the expression, *absolute war*.

Carl von Clausewitz, Vom Kriege (1832)[1]

For Carl von Clausewitz, who later became the most famous theorist of the Napoleonic Wars, military conflict was more 'absolute' than his predecessors had claimed. As '*an act of violence (Gewalt) to compel our enemy to do our will*', war was 'a dangerous business', with a deadly logic:

---

[1] C. v. Clausewitz, *Vom Kriege*, 5th edn (Berlin, 1905), 615, 504.

Since the use of physical violence to its full extent in no way excludes the involvement of intelligence, whoever uses this violence ruthlessly, undeterred by bloodshed, will get the upper hand, if their opponent does not do the same. That side will force the other to follow suit; each will drive its opponent towards extremes.[2]

Although the logic of this position was merely an 'extreme' thesis 'in the field of abstract thought' and the starting point of Clausewitz's dialectic, it was nevertheless 'futile—even wrong—to try and shut one's eyes to what war really is from sheer distress at its brutality'.[3] The difference between 'civilized peoples', who were 'ruled by the mind', and 'savage peoples', who were 'ruled by passion', did not mean that the former could devise 'a kind of war by algebra': theorists of the eighteenth century 'were already beginning to think along such lines when the recent wars taught them a lesson'.[4] The difference between historical instances of armed conflict 'lies not in the respective natures of savagery and civilization, but in their attendant circumstances, institutions, and so forth', which did 'not operate in every case', even if they did 'in most of them'.[5] Abstract thought tended towards extremes, conceiving of objectives in 'absolute terms'.[6] In practice, war was impeded by friction and required constant limitation and adaptation. However, the Revolutionary and Napoleonic Wars had demonstrated to Clausewitz, a young Prussian officer who joined the Russian army in 1812, that military conflicts, which were imaginable in the realm of 'the absolute', were 'no pastime'.[7] It was in this context that absolute war had become conceivable.[8]

Over the century and a half or so after 1792, warfare was pushed in Germany, in particular, to extremes which even Clausewitz could not have imagined. German states have been the site or the source of a series of modern—or absolute—wars which have left a deep imprint on the history of the European continent. Such military conflicts not only altered the relations between what came to be known as the Great Powers; they also had a decisive effect on the territorial settlements and structures of government of the German lands. In important respects, the Revolutionary and Napoleonic Wars, which led to the institution of conscription and the development of forms of mass warfare different in kind from those of the eighteenth century, constituted the principal turning point of the long nineteenth century, with military states—or states which channelled most of their taxes towards armies—propping up a system of international relations in which the distinction between war and peace had become more discrete. This world of conscript armies, domestic pacification, state control of the means of violence, and irregular but

---

[2] Ibid., 3–4.   [3] Ibid., 4.   [4] Ibid., 5.
[5] Ibid.   [6] Ibid., 7.   [7] Ibid., 16–18.
[8] Andreas Herberg-Rothe, *Clausewitz's Puzzle: The Political Theory of War* (Oxford, 2007), shows how Clausewitz trusted more in extreme military violence on the battlefield during the early wartime era than during later years, whilst never renouncing the idea of extreme violence outright. Hew Strachan, 'Essay and Reflection: On Total War and Modern War', *International History Review*, 22 (2000), 343–5, shows how varying readings of Clausewitz have depended on the context of the Cold War: the emphasis on politics and limitation in Books I and VIII are at variance with the other sections of the work. Here, I rely on Book I, which was the only section actually finished; Y.-L. Zhang, 'Ideales denken, um Reales zu begreifen. Die methodischen Aspekte des Absoluten Krieges bei Carl von Clausewitz', *Zeitschrift für Politik*, 42 (1995), 369–82.

large-scale wars between European powers characterized the period between the 1800s and the 1940s. It forms the subject of these studies of the violence of warfare in Germany.

CONSCRIPT SOLDIERS, MASS WARFARE, AND THE POLITICS OF 'LIBERATION'

After the Napoleonic Wars, the subjects of German states faced the possibility of conscription in peacetime and the likelihood of military service during wartime. The meanings of words like 'citizen' or 'civilian' (*Bürger*), 'soldier' (*Soldat*), 'warrior' (*Krieger*), and 'the military' (*Militär*) remained in flux. Because of the perceived successes of mass warfare before 1815, however, the boundary between citizenship— or the varying statuses of different subjects—and soldiering had become more porous and less distinct. From the turn of the nineteenth century onwards, millions of men—and a smaller number of women—in the German lands looked forward, with differing degrees of trepidation and expectation, to individual acts of violence and collective upheavals during wars. Their responses were diverse, constituting a matter of subsequent historical dispute, yet they differed markedly from those of their predecessors. Here, I explore soldiers' and civilians' experiences of the changing conditions of warfare, as the *levée en masse* and conscription increased the size of European armies and transformed the ways in which those armies fought. Since the principal function of states in the nineteenth century remained the provision of internal and external order, such a transformation, together with the individual experiences of civilians-as-soldiers, had a significant impact on the emerging sphere of 'politics' after 1819/20, once the post-war system—or order— of the 'restoration' had been consolidated in the German lands through the issuing of the Carlsbad Decrees (20 September 1819) and the signature of the Vienna Final Act (15 May 1820).[9] This study examines the shifting relationship between subjects, politics, and states in respect of conscript armies and the menace of mass warfare. The reactions of modern citizens to twentieth- and twenty-first-century military conflicts can be traced, in specific instances (and not in others), back to the turn of the nineteenth century.

Unsurprisingly, there are varying emphases in the historiography. Scholars such as Michael Jeismann point to the close and enduring connection between national identification, stereotypes, and enmity which was established in the unprecedented conditions of the 'revolutionary' wars between 1792 and 1815.[10] Others such as Otto Dann have re-examined the nexus between citizenship and wars in the name of the nation, which contemporary commentators like Johann Gottlieb Fichte had

---

[9] The Carlsbad Decrees included a 'university law', the Confederal Press Law, and an 'investigatory law'; the sixty-five articles of the Vienna Final Act specified how the German Confederation would function.

[10] M. Jeismann, *Das Vaterland der Feinde. Studien zum nationalen Feindbegriff und Selbstverständnis in Deutschland und Frankreich 1792–1918* (Stuttgart, 1992), 382.

remarked upon at the time.[11] The majority of scholars of the revolutionary and Napoleonic periods, however, have been more sceptical about the significance of early nineteenth-century nationalism, taking issue with 'Borussian' and later historians who had contended—or were seen to have contended—that pre-existing national sentiments on the part of statesmen and a political public helped to bring about the wars against French hegemony in Germany.[12] Some have come to doubt, in the words of Jörg Echternkamp, whether a 'national awakening' took place during the Napoleonic period, even in Prussia.[13] They imply that Fichte's *Reden*

[11] O. Dann, 'Der deutsche Bürger wird Soldat', in R. Steinweg (ed.), *Lehren aus der Geschichte?* (Frankfurt, 1990), 61–84. On the wider debates surrounding this question, see D. Moran and A. Waldron (eds), *The People in Arms: Military Myth and National Mobilization since the French Revolution* (Cambridge, 2003).

[12] U. Planert, *Der Mythos vom Befreiungskrieg. Frankreichs Kriege und der deutsche Süden 1792–1841* (Paderborn, 2007), 19–20. She argues that Wilhelm von Sternburg, *Fall und Aufstieg der deutschen Nation. Nachdenken über einen Massenrauch* (Frankfurt, 1993), Horst Möller, *Fürstenstaat oder Bürgernation. Deutschland 1763–1815* (Berlin, 1998); Erich Pelzer, 'Die Wiedergeburt Deutschlands und die Dämonisierung Napoleons', in G. Krumeich and H. Lehmann (eds), *'Gott mit uns'. Nation, Religion und Gewalt im 19. und frühen 20. Jahrhundert* (Göttingen, 2000), 135–56; Peter Alter, *Nationalismus* (Frankfurt, 1985); and Hagen Schulze, *Der Weg zum Nationalstaat. Die deutsche Nationalbewegung vom 18. Jahrhundert bis zur Reichsgründung* (Munich, 1983) have all portrayed the Napoleonic wars as an 'initial trigger', with Schulze mistakenly drawing 'an unbroken line from the Prussian events after 1806 to the developments of the 1840s'.

[13] J. Echternkamp, *Der Aufstieg des deutschen Nationalismus 1770–1840* (Frankfurt, 1998), 216, referring to Prussia; K. Hagemann, *Mannlicher Muth und Teutsche Ehre. Nation, Krieg und Geschlecht in der Zeit der antinapoleonischen Kriege Preussens* (Paderborn, 2001), 49. For the more sceptical, see H.-U. Wehler, *Deutsche Gesellschaftsgeschichte 1700–1815* (Munich, 1987), vol. 1, 506–30; U. Planert, 'Wann beginnt der "moderne" deutsche Nationalismus? Plädoyer für eine nationale Sattelzeit', in J. Echternkamp and S. O. Müller (eds), *Die Politik der Nation. Deutscher Nationalismus in Krieg und Krisen 1760–1960* (Munich, 2002), 25–59; J. J. Breuilly, 'The Response to Napoleon and German Nationalism', in A. Forrest and P. H. Wilson (eds), *The Bee and the Eagle: Napoleonic France and the End of the Holy Roman Empire, 1806* (Basingstoke, 2009), 256–83; J. J. Breuilly, 'Napoleonic Germany and State-Formation', in M. Rowe (ed.), *Collaboration and Resistance in Napoleonic Europe: State-Formation in an Age of Upheaval, c. 1800–1815* (London, 2003), 121–52; D. Langewiesche, *Nation, Nationalismus und Nationalstaat in Deutschland und Europa* (Munich, 2000); D. Langewiesche, *Reich, Nation, Föderation* (Munich, 2008); M. Umbach, *Federalism and Enlightenment in Germany, 1740–1806* (London, 2000); D. Rogosch, 'Das Heilige Römische Reich Deutscher Nation und die Entstehung des deutschen Nationalgefühls', in H. Timmermann (ed.), *Die Entstehung der Nationalbewegung in Europa 1750–1849* (Berlin, 1993), 15–28; R. D. Billinger, Jr, 'Good and True Germans: The "Nationalism" of the *Rheinbund* Princes, 1806–1814', in H. Duchhardt und A. Kunz (eds), *Reich oder Nation? Mitteleuropa, 1780–1815* (Mainz, 1998), 105–39; J. J. Sheehan, 'State and Nationality in the Napoleonic Period', in J. J. Breuilly (ed.), *The State of Germany: The National Idea in the Making, Unmaking and Remaking of a Modern Nation-State* (London, 1992), 47–59. Broadly coinciding with Hagemann's stance are R. Ibbeken, *Preussen, 1807–1813. Staat und Volk als Idee und Wirklichkeit* (Cologne, 1970); B. v. Münchow-Pohl, *Zwischen Reform und Krieg. Untersuchungen zur Bewusstseinslage in Preussen 1809–1812* (Göttingen, 1987); O. Dann, *Nation und Nationalismus in Deutschland 1770–1990*; O. Dann and J. Dinwiddy (eds), *Nationalism in the Age of the French Revolution* (London, 1988); O. Dann (ed.), *Patriotismus und Nationsbildung am Ende des Heiligen Römischen Reiches* (Cologne, 2003); D. Düding, *Organisierter gesellschaftlicher Nationalismus in Deutschland 1808–1847* (Munich, 1984); D. Klenke, *Der singende 'deutsche Mann'. Gesangvereine und deutsches Nationalbewusstsein von Napoleon bis Hitler* (Münster, 1998); W. Hardtwig, *Nationalismus und Bürgerkultur in Deutschland* (Göttingen, 1994), 70–148; T. Nipperdey, 'In Search of Identity: Romantic Nationalism', in J. C. Eade (ed.), *Romantic Nationalism in Europe* (Melbourne, 1983), 1–16; E. Weber, *Lyrik der Befreiungskriege 1812–1815. Gesellschaftspolitische Meinungs- und Willensbildung durch Literatur* (Stuttgart, 1991); G. L. Mosse, *Fallen Soldiers* (Oxford, 1991); G. L. Mosse, *The Nationalization of the Masses: Political Symbolism and Mass Movements in Germany from the Napoleonic Wars through the Third Reich*

an die deutsche Nation (*Addresses to the German Nation*) in 1808 were not so much addressing a divided nation as no nation at all: at most, his addresses reached the small reading publics of separate and conflicting German states, in which the majority of subjects ignored or rejected his strictures.[14]

'The impact of nationalism during the so-called "wars of liberation" was limited to a small minority of Germans, especially German intellectuals, whose memoirs and historical accounts helped to create a mythic image of the national past', writes James Sheehan, referring to his seminal article, 'What Is German History?'[15] According to John Breuilly, there is almost 'universal agreement' amongst historians that, 'at a popular level, regional and local, religious and royalist sentiments mattered much more than any concern with German nationality or even state-wide identities in the conglomerate polities of Austria and Prussia'.[16] 'At the level of organised politics', too, recent historiography has emphasized the 'continued control of princes over the direction of affairs and their concern only to invoke national arguments if they served and did not threaten monarchical government and hierarchies of authority and prestige which were seen as integral to such government'.[17] The purpose of such critiques, as Breuilly rightly remarks, is 'to debunk the older notion of a strong national reaction against Napoleon combining, if only implicitly, ideas, discourses, sentiments and politics', as well as to outline 'a complex range of responses in which nationalism either does not figure, or is given a minor role'.[18] Nationalism was, in the view of Stefan Berger, 'at best a minority opinion in the wars of liberty'.[19] Against this background, most recent studies of nineteenth-century warfare have stressed the formative, causal role played by later conflicts—1859, 1864, or 1870–1—in establishing and consolidating a sense of national belonging.[20] For Frank Becker, only the national myths associated with 1870–1 allowed contemporaries retrospectively to add the contested earlier conflicts of 1864 and 1866 as 'preludes'.[21] What unites all such accounts, including those of Jeismann and Dann, is that they continue to focus largely on nationalism.

In an age of conscripts and mass warfare, the nature of the fighting and the wider ramifications of a campaign were more important for the majority of combatants than the aims or causes of a conflict. The obverse of German historians' focus on the relationship between war and nationalism, it can be held, has been their

---

(New York, 1975); H. Kohn, *Prelude to Nation-States: The French and German Experience, 1789–1815* (Princeton, 1967).

[14] G. A. Kelly (ed.), *Johann Gottlieb Fichte: Addresses to the German Nation* (New York, 1968), 123.

[15] J. J. Sheehan, 'State and Nationality in the Napoleonic Period', 47–59; J. J. Sheehan, 'What Is German History?', *Journal of Modern History*, 53 (1981), 1–23.

[16] J. J. Breuilly, 'The Response to Napoleon and German Nationalism', 262.

[17] Ibid., 262.   [18] Ibid., 263.

[19] S. Berger, *Germany: Inventing the Nation* (London, 2004), 37.

[20] W. Siemann, *Gesellschaft im Aufbruch* (Frankfurt, 1990), 190–306, which places emphasis on 1859; W. Siemann, *Vom Staatenbund zum Nationalstaat. Deutschland 1806–1871* (Munich, 1995), 415–25, which stresses the significance of 1864–6.

[21] F. Becker, *Bilder von Krieg und Nation. Die Einigungskriege in der bürgerlichen Öffentlichkeit Deutschlands 1864–1913* (Munich, 2001), 487–8.

emphasis on the continuity of combatants' and civilians' experiences of warfare itself: there was purportedly little need to justify war in national terms because the practices and patterns of conflict remained much the same as in the past (or the absence of new discourses about national interests and national survival permitted the continuance of such practices and patterns).[22] Ute Planert, in particular, has asked whether the wars of the French Revolution and Napoleon really constituted a transformation of the 'nature of warfare' and 'the realm of politics'.[23] In explicit opposition to the thesis put forward by David Bell, who has labelled the conflicts the first 'total war', she has questioned 'the importance of ideology', the existence of 'unlimited war aims that tend toward annihilation of the enemy, the development of unlimited destructive potential, the geographical expanse of military operations, the abandonment of moral and legal conventions, the deployment of mass armies, and the mobilization of civilian populations and economies for purposes of war'.[24] The waging and consequences of war, according to Planert, continued to follow an eighteenth-century pattern.

Much of the debate about the revolutionary and Napoleonic periods, which refers to long-standing controversies concerning the definition and character of 'total war', concerns the 'fusion of war and politics'.[25] Thus, even a critic of Bell such as Michael Broers 'acknowledges the intellectual and cultural presence of the concept of "total war" among the leadership of revolutionary France', not least because 'their sacred and profane intellectual baggage abounded in examples of "total war", defined in terms of "absolute enmity" as well as material obliteration', from the struggle of Rome and Carthage to Samuel's story of Saul and the Amalekites in the Bible.[26] Such conceptions were purportedly accompanied by 'absolute enmity' between opponents, with 'intense hatreds' 'spawned as much by the hard realities of fighting wars with mass peasant armies as by propaganda'.[27] What restricted warfare, preventing it from becoming total, in Broers's view, was 'the lack of effective technology' of killing and 'the survival of rulers still imbued with enough of the political ethos of the old order, and even of the Enlightenment,

---

[22] Historians have tended to focus on the limits of nationalism. Their preoccupation with this question has informed the ways in which they have conceived of war and its impact. For more on these emphases, see M. Hewitson, 'On War and Peace: German Conceptions of Conflict, 1792–1815', *Historical Journal*, 57 (2014), 447–83.

[23] U. Planert, 'Innovation or Evolution? The French Wars in Military History', in R. Chickering and S. Förster (eds), *War in an Age of Revolution, 1775–1815* (Cambridge, 2010), 69. Chickering and Förster have edited six volumes, all with 'total war' as the main theme.

[24] Ibid. Chickering argues in the Introduction of *War in an Age of Revolution*, 3, that changes in combat 'laid the moral and ideological foundations' of total war. D. Walter, 'Reluctant Reformers, Observant Disciples: The Prussian Military Reforms, 1807–1814', and Wolfgang Kruse, 'Revolutionary France and the Meanings of *Levée en masse*', ibid., 85–101, 299–312, agree with this position.

[25] See William Mulligan's review of Bell's study in the *Journal of Modern History*, 80 (2008), 912. Also, W. Mulligan, 'Total War', *War in History*, 15 (2008), 211–21. On the conflation of the terms 'total war', implying a total mobilization of resources, and 'modern war', resting on 'the fruits of indus-trialization and technological innovation', see H. Strachan, 'Essay and Reflection', 351.

[26] M. Broers, 'The Concept of "Total War" in the Revolutionary–Napoleonic Period', *War in History*, 15 (2008), 248, 256.

[27] Ibid., 253. Also, P. Geuniffey, *La Politique de la Terreur: essai sur la violence révolutionnaire 1789–1794* (Paris, 2000).

to hold in check the temptation to unleash all the forces they had'.[28] 'Power still rested in the hands of men of the old order, at least among the allies', he contends, meaning that states remained 'resolutely civilian in character, if not in purpose'.[29] The 'best test of the term "total war"' is therefore held to be, 'not whether it effectively mobilizes resources or how much damage it does, but how mass mobilization and prolonged campaigning are received by the populations subjected to them'.[30] Bell argues that both contemporary meanings of a *levée en masse*—a spontaneous, popular rising as well as an act of conscription, with 'the relentless imposition of the machinery of the bureaucratic state on hitherto seemingly unassailable hinterlands'—were characteristic of the revolutionary and Napoleonic eras, whilst Broers is more sceptical about a political dynamic tending towards total engagement and the abandonment of restraint.[31]

Partly in reaction to 'national' interpretations of the 'wars of liberation' and partly in response to Bell's case about the revolutionary impact of warfare between 1792 and 1815, which focuses above all on France but which has been extended— in modified form—to the rest of Europe and the United States through the work of Roger Chickering, Stig Förster, and others, recent historians of Germany have questioned whether the Revolutionary and Napoleonic Wars can be seen to have brought about a fundamental shift in the waging of war by the allies and enemies of Bonaparte.[32] The context of this debate about military continuity—and contemporaries' experiences of dislocation and continuity—is a much broader revision, not merely of the role of the 'wars of liberation' in the genesis of nationalism, but also of the impact of the French Revolution and of the 'French' wars in Germany.[33] Planert, Katherine Aaslestad, and others have asked to what degree civilians, particularly in the 'free' cities and in southern and western Germany, made a distinction between different sides and conceived of conflicts as patriotic or national struggles for survival and emancipation.[34] They have also, together with

---

[28] M. Broers, 'The Concept of "Total War"', 267.   [29] Ibid., 259, 265.

[30] Ibid., 253. This argument rests on Broers's extensive work on Napoleonic imperialism in Italy—in *Napoleonic Imperialism and the Savoyard Monarchy, 1773–1821* (Lampeter, 1997), *The Napoleonic Empire in Italy, 1796–1814: Cultural Imperialism in a European Context?* (Basingstoke, 2005), *Politics and Religion in Napoleonic Italy: The War against God, 1801–1814* (London, 2007)—and on banditry, in *Napoleon's Other War: Bandits, Rebels and Their Pursuers in the Age of Revolutions* (New York, 2010).

[31] M. Broers, 'The Concept of "Total War"', 247. D. A. Bell, *The First Total War: Napoleon's Europe and the Birth of Warfare as We Know It* (Boston, 2007), 8–9.

[32] U. Planert, 'Innovation or Evolution?', 69.

[33] E. Weis, 'Die aussenpolitischen Reaktionen der deutschen Staaten auf die französische Hegemonialpolitik: zwischen Widerstand und Anpassung', in K. O. v. Aretin and G. A. Ritter (eds), *Historismus und modern Geschichtswissenschaft* (Stuttgart, 1987), 185–200; M. Junkelmann, *Napoleon und Bayern* (Regensburg, 1985); V. Press, 'Warum gab es keine deutsche Revolution? Deutschland und das revolutionäre Deutschland', in D. Langewiesche (ed.), *Revolution und Krieg* (Paderborn, 1989), 67–86.

[34] On civilians, see U. Planert, *Der Mythos vom Befreiungskrieg*; U. Planert, 'Staat und Krieg an der Wende zur Moderne. Der deutsche Südwesten um 1800', in W. Rösener (ed.), *Staat und Krieg. Vom Mittelalter bis zur Moderne* (Göttingen, 2000), 159–80; K. B. Aaslestad, 'Lost Neutrality and Economic Warfare: Napoleonic Warfare in Northern Europe, 1795–1815', in Chickering and Förster (eds), *War in an Age of Revolution, 1775–1815*, 373–94; K. Aaslestad, *Place and Politics: Local Identity, Civic Culture, and German Nationalism in North Germany during the Revolutionary Era* (Leiden, 2005); K. B. Aaslestad, 'War without Battles: Civilian Experiences of Economic Warfare during the Napoleonic Era in

other scholars such as Peter Brandt, Michael Sikora, and Jörg Echternkamp, challenged the idea that soldiers were motivated by patriotic ideals, which had been believed to distinguish them from their eighteenth-century predecessors.[35] 'The master narrative of modern military history' has taken 'insufficient note of lines of continuity to early modern times' and has overlooked 'differences between the French Revolutionary and the Napoleonic wars themselves', encouraging 'a mistaken picture of developments during the nineteenth century', maintains Planert: 'From this perspective, the wars of the French Revolution fit in a long European tradition of state building by war that led from the early modern era to the nineteenth century.'[36] According to this reading of events, there are few, if any, grounds for discerning a fundamental or revolutionary change in the practices or consequences of warfare between 1792 and 1815. Such continuity supposedly affected the ways in which military conflicts were remembered and imagined during the nineteenth century.[37] By contrast, this study contends that the Revolutionary and Napoleonic Wars, as a consequence of compliance with French demands or imitation of French practices, ushered in a new era of war and peace resting on conscription, quicker movement, greater reliance on battles, and a more pronounced fear of the effects of military conflict on the part of decision-makers. The shift can be traced, at least in part, back to civilians' and soldiers' experiences of fighting.

Hamburg', in A. Forrest et al. (eds), *Soldiers, Citizens, and Civilians: Experiences and Perceptions of the Revolutionary and Napoleonic Wars, 1790–1820* (Basingstoke, 2008), 118–36; K. B. Aaslestad and K. Hagemann, '1806 and Its Aftermath: Revisiting the Period of the Napoleonic Wars in German Central European Historiography', *Central European History*, 39 (2006), 547–79; T. C. W. Blanning, *The French Revolution in Germany: Occupation and Resistance in the Rhineland, 1792–1802* (Oxford, 1983); M. Rowe, *From Reich to State: The Rhineland in the Revolutionary Age, 1780–1830* (Cambridge, 2003); U. Andrea, *Die Rheinländer, die Revolution und der Krieg 1794–1798* (Essen, 1994); G. Schuck, *Rheinbundpatriotismus und politische Öffentlichkeit zwischen Aufklärung und Frühliberalismus. Kontinuitätsdenken und Diskontinuitätserfahrung in den Staatsrechts- und Verfassungsdebatten der Rheinbundpublizistik* (Stuttgart, 1994); P. Sauer, *Napoleons Adler über Württemberg, Baden und Hohenzollern. Südwestdeutschland in der Rheinbundzeit* (Stuttgart, 1987); H. Berding, *Napoleonische Herrschafts- und Gesellschaftspolitik im Königreich Westfalen 1807–1813* (Göttingen, 1973); J. Engelbrecht, *Das Herzogtum Berg im Zeitalter der Französischen Revolution. Modernisierungsprozesse zwischen bayerischem und französischem Modell* (Paderborn, 1996); M. Hamm, *Die bayerische Integrationspolitik in Tirol 1806–1814* (Munich, 1996).

[35] On soldiers' motivations, see J. Murken, *Bayerische Soldaten im Russlandfeldzug 1812. Ihre Kriegserfahrungen und deren Umdeutungen im 19. und 20. Jahrhundert* (Munich, 2006); P. Brandt, 'Einstellungen, Motive und Ziele von Kriegsfreiwilligen 1813/14: Das Freikorps Lützow', in Dülffer (ed.), *Kriegsbereitschaft und Friedensordnung in Deutschland 1800–1814* (Münster, 1995), 211–33; P. Brandt, 'Die Befreiungskriege von 1813 bis 1813 in der deutschen Geschichte', in M. Grüttner et al. (eds), *Geschichte und Emanzipation* (Frankfurt, 1999), 17–57; J. Echternkamp, '"Teutschland, des Soldaten Vaterland". Die Nationalisierung des Krieges im frühen 19. Jahrhundert', in W. Rösener (ed.), *Staat und Krieg*, 181–203; M. Sikora, 'Desertion und nationale Mobilmachung. Militärische Verweigerung 1792–1815', in U. Broeckling and M. Sikora (eds), *Armeen und ihre Deserteure* (Göttingen, 1998), 112–40; K. Hagemann, 'Der "Bürger" als "Nationalkrieger". Entwürfe von Militär, Nation und Männlichkeit in der Zeit der Freiheitskriege', in K. Hagemann and R. Pröve (eds), *Landsknechte, Soldatenfrauen und Nationalkrieger. Militär, Krieg und Geschlechterordnung im historischen Wandel* (Frankfurt, 1998), 74–102.

[36] U. Planert, 'Innovation or Evolution?', 70–1.

[37] U. Planert, 'From Collaboration to Resistance: Politics, Experience and Memory of the Revolutionary and Napoleonic Wars in Southern Germany', *Central European History*, 39 (2006), 681–6.

ACTS OF VIOLENCE AND THE HORROR OF WAR

The dispute about the relationship between contemporaries' experiences of fighting and their disposition towards violence is an old one.[38] I argue in these volumes that a culturally and socially defined aversion to the perpetration and, especially, the suffering of injury and death affected a large and increasing number of German combatants in nineteenth-century wars. Their fear or apprehension of combat eventually played a part in governments' use of war as an instrument of policy. It also served to counter matter-of-fact accounts of the Napoleonic campaigns and the subsequent romanticization of warfare in the German lands, rendering the connections between patriotism, nationalism, and belligerence at once problematic and close. In these respects, historians' recent arguments in favour of military continuities and against the existence—or relevance—of a national rhetoric of war can be as misleading as earlier scholars' identification of national 'wars of liberation'.[39] Not least because of the death toll, cost, mass armies, and geographical scope of the Napoleonic Wars, soldiers and civilians struggled to make sense of the conflicts, despite continuing to believe that they were momentous. Their responses to military violence were historical and contingent.[40] In other words, the conditions in which they lived and exposure to violence and death in their daily lives affected how they reacted to war and, subsequently, how they understood and remembered it. Such linkages were rarely straightforward. They comprise the principal focus of this study.

Much of the recent literature on violence and warfare has overlooked the historical contingencies and conditions of individuals' attitudes and actions, public discourses, and collective decision-making. In Germany, historical sociologists, political scientists, and historians such as Wolfgang Sofsky, Herfried Münkler, and Jörg Baberowski have linked 'pre-modern' examples of violence, through the theoretical exposition of Thomas Hobbes, to the barbarity of the 'total wars' and 'new wars' of

---

[38] Hans Joas and Wolfgang Knöbl, *Kriegsverdrängung. Ein Problem in der Geschichte der Sozialtheorie* (Frankfurt, 2008), 24–92, go back to the radical break wrought by Thomas Hobbes, before showing how the nexus between liberalism and nineteenth-century social theory encouraged the separation of internal and external analyses of violence and social interaction. The consequent marginalization of war within sociology has been reversed over the last decade or so.

[39] U. Planert, *Der Mythos vom Befreiungskrieg*, 19–20, commenting on the linearity of post-Borussian historiography.

[40] The claim about the contingent, historically constructed nature of violence runs counter to much of the recent literature on it. The sociologist Wolfgang Sofsky, *Violence: Terrorism, Genocide, War* (London, 2003), 21, therefore offers an 'anthropological account', which is 'not cultural but universalist': 'It is more interested in social universals than individual cases, that is to say in those aspects of society that arise independently of one another and at times and places remote from each other. Historical events are not in the foreground; instead, such a study concentrates on the facts that lie behind all history.' Influenced by Sofsky and Trutz von Trotha, who has argued that violence is a form of emotional response and social order, historians such as Jörg Baberowski, 'Gewalt Verstehen', *Zeithistorische Forschungen*, 5 (2008), 5, have emphasized that 'Humans have always killed, tortured and burned. Violence belongs to the basic equipment of the human species.' T. v. Trotha, 'Zur Soziologie der Gewalt', in T. v. Trotha (ed.), *Soziologie der Gewalt* (Opladen, 1997), 9–56; T. v. Trotha, 'Die Zukunft der Gewalt', *Kursbuch*, 147 (2002), 161–73.

the twentieth and twenty-first centuries.[41] Amongst other things, they have been anxious to show that 'the world is as full of violence as ever' and that 'countless human beings are still busy torturing and killing their fellows by every conceivable means'.[42] Violence is not a deviation or an exception, but a norm, tying the purported ubiquity of casual violence in the medieval and early modern eras to the 'order of terror' of the concentration camp.[43] Although 'the twentieth century began with the highest of hopes', it 'ended in many parts of the world in pain and despair', claims Sofsky: 'We have woken from the dream that reason will prevail. … The great story of the improvement of *Homo sapiens* and his behaviour was only a fiction, a myth.'[44] Progressives' and modernizers' hopes that violence could be controlled or, even, eliminated have proved false.[45] Indeed, far from being a solution to the problem of violent excess, 'rationality' and 'civilization' have often been a cause. 'Experience teaches that violence did not disappear at all during modernity', writes Baberowski: 'The layer of civilization is clearly thinner than many believe and it is reasonable to reckon with the possibility of violence.'[46] Within the 'civilizing' actuality of modernity 'violence disappears', but then 'does not disappear'.[47] Viewed historically, '"civilized" war between states', in which military combatants were separated from a protected civilian population, remained 'the exception', 'an achievement of the nineteenth century' restricted to Central and Western Europe: '"unlimited" war' was 'the rule'.[48] Yet did this supposed geographical and historical exception merely constitute an interruption of a long and relentless history of human violence and, if so, why? Here, I take issue with this premise by examining the transition to and from 'civilized' warfare in the German lands between the late eighteenth and mid-twentieth centuries.

The historical overview provided by Sofsky, Münkler, and Baberowski is connected to a rereading of twentieth-century German history.[49] 'We may think of the terrors of war and persecution as nothing but occasional lapses, temporary setbacks within an otherwise unbroken development working towards state monopoly of the means of violence, control of our primitive instincts and the

---

[41] Herfried Münkler remains one of the best-known interpreters of Hobbes: H. Münkler, *Thomas Hobbes* (Frankfurt, 1993); H. Münkler, *Die neuen Kriege* (Reinbek, 2002); H. Münkler, *Der Wandel des Krieges. Von der Symmetrie zur Asymmetrie* (Weilerswist, 2006); and H. Münkler, *Kriegssplitter. Die Evolution der Gewalt im 20. und 21. Jahrhundert* (Berlin, 2012).

[42] W. Sofsky, *Violence*, 61.

[43] It is perhaps no coincidence that Wolfgang Sofsky's early work on this topic concerned *Konzentrationslager*, where 'human bestiality…appeared in many forms': W. Sofsky, *The Order of Terror: The Concentration Camp* (Princeton, 1997), 223. See also Christian Gerlach's *Extremely Violent Societies: Mass Violence in the Twentieth-Century World* (Cambridge, 2010), which follows on from a series of detailed studies of the Holocaust.

[44] W. Sofsky, *Order of Terror*, 223.

[45] J. Baberowski (ed.), *Moderne Zeiten? Krieg, Revolution und Gewalt im 20. Jahrhundert* (Göttingen, 2006), 7–11.

[46] J. Baberowski, 'Gewalt Verstehen', *Zeithistorische Forschungen*, 5 (2008), 8.

[47] J. Baberowski, *Räume der Gewalt* (Frankfurt, 2015), 44–76.

[48] J. Baberowski (ed.), *Moderne Zeiten?*, 9.

[49] Also on this topic, see J. P. Reemtsma, *'Wie hätte ich mich verhalten?' und andere nicht nur deutsche Fragen: Reden und Aufsätze* (Munich, 2001).

taming of cruelty', contends Sofsky, but we would be wrong, allowing ourselves to be led towards a series of comforting delusions about a German 'special path':

> Even taking the fragility and psychological cost of the civilizing process into account, this late version of the idea of progress can ultimately see Auschwitz only as the result of a peculiarly German ideology, mentality and state history. The mass murders there took place because the national conscience was still underdeveloped, the state unstable and civilization incomplete. Animal instincts were not tamed and controlled by the bonds of social interdependency. The principles of self-discipline and independence, and an ability to take the long view, were not yet firmly enough anchored in human nature, and since the perpetrators of violence lacked inner backbone they sought support in leaders outside themselves whose dictates they obeyed to the letter. But did not many of them go about the work of killing extremely conscientiously, while acting on their own initiative? And can their countless collaborators and accomplices who did not hold German passports also be seen as peculiarly German? Obviously civilization is not strong enough to stand firm against personality changes, against the mutation of a cultivated individual into a mass murderer.[50]

The other hypotheses about civilization and violence which Sofsky challenges are not peculiarly German and 'modern'. They are global and contemporary. The first 'holds that the release of violence results not from the incomplete development of the modern world but from the overwhelming success of that development', given that civilization was 'bound to topple over into barbarism', 'modern science was bound to invent the nuclear bomb', and 'state bureaucracy was bound to be transformed into the practice of genocide as a public service'.[51] The second contends that 'modernity is a necessary but not a sufficient condition of terror'.[52] 'Civilization exaggerates both our creative and our destructive tendencies', making the Shoah into 'a genuine product of the modern world', not an historical lapse or accident, since 'there can be no barbarism without the modern state's programme of law and order, without the moral indifference of rationality, without bureaucracy'.[53] The 'last position states that there is no connection between civilization and barbarism because human behavior has never evolved at all': 'Belief in civilization is a Eurocentric myth in which the modern world worships itself. Human emotions and drives have not changed with the change in social conditions.'[54] Sofsky contests these hypotheses, not to demonstrate the historical contingency or development of violence, but to disprove the arguments put forward by Zygmunt Bauman amongst others about the 'rationalizing of violence'.[55] A similar case has been made by scholars of violence outside Germany.

To many post-Cold War political and social theorists in the United Kingdom and the United States, acts of violence and the horror of war have seemed inescapable. Nightmares of slaughter and conflict have been legion, especially since 9/11. Most theorists concentrate on acts of killing and they blur the distinction, against the

---

[50] W. Sofsky, *Violence*, 63–4. [51] Ibid., 64.
[52] Ibid. [53] Ibid., 64–5. [54] Ibid., 65.
[55] Z. Bauman, *Modernity and Ambivalence* (Cambridge, 1991), 18–52; Z. Bauman, *Modernity and the Holocaust* (Cambridge, 1989), 1–30, 83–116. The reference to the 'rationalizing of violence' comes from Baberowski, 'Gewalt Verstehen', *Zeithistorische Forschungen*, 5 (2008), 7.

backdrop of a generalized 'war on terror', between the 'internal' and 'external' contexts where violent actions occur. For John Gray, for instance, who is a critic of neo-conservatives as well as of liberals, what has defined the secularized political religions of the 'West' has been the millenarian belief that history has an 'end', in both senses of the word.[56] 'Since the French Revolution a succession of utopian movements has transformed political life', he writes at the start of *Black Mass* (2007): 'The alteration envisioned by utopian thinkers has not come about, and for the most part their projects have produced results opposite to those they intended.'[57] These utopians have included in their number 'liberal humanists, who see progress as a slow incremental struggle', since they, too, aim for an unrealizable 'telos'.[58] 'Nowadays "the West" defines itself in terms of liberal democracy and human rights', he declares: 'The implication is that the totalitarian movements of the last century formed no part of the West, when in truth these movements renewed some of the oldest Western traditions.'[59] The only thing binding the West together is supposedly 'the pursuit of salvation in history': 'What is unique to the modern West is the formative role of the faith that violence can save the world.'[60] Utopians and reformers at once ignore the fact that 'conflict is a universal feature of human life' and that their own 'pursuit of a condition of harmony' is an 'unreality', which they then attempt to impose by force.[61]

Even though they are usually framed against the arguments and actions of twentieth-century 'utopians'—communists and Nazis—and the post-Cold War optimism of Francis Fukuyama and other liberal democrats and supporters of capitalism, these accounts closely resemble the fearful premonitions of the Cold War, including Theodor Adorno's warning of history 'progressing' from the slingshot to the megaton bomb, amidst a mediatized world of advertising, propaganda, lies, and deceptions.[62] What such commentators often forget, however, is that the citizens of the West, and particularly of Europe (and Japan), have become less and less willing to go to war or, even, to countenance military conflict. For James Sheehan, the 'eclipse of violence in both meanings of the word'—declining in importance and concealed from view by something else (namely, the 'state's need to encourage economic growth, provide social welfare and guarantee personal security for its citizens')—'happened gradually' after 1945, 'when the United States and the Soviet Union imposed a new order on the continent, in what became a remarkably stable and peaceful system'.[63] In the following two volumes, I contend that the process was also connected to citizens in 'civilian states' rejecting the extreme violence of military conflicts. Although subject to contestation and contradiction, such rejection could be observed from a much earlier date than Sheehan's juncture of 1945, extending back to the 1850s in Britain and France

---

[56] For the full panoply of Gray's targets and the links between them, see J. Gray, *Heresies: Against Progress and Other Illusions* (London, 2004).

[57] J. Gray, *Black Mass: Apocalyptic Religion and the Death of Utopia* (London, 2007), 2–3.

[58] Ibid., 2.   [59] Ibid., 73.   [60] Ibid.   [61] Ibid., 17.

[62] F. Fukuyama, *The End of History and the Last Man* (New York, 1992). T. W. Adorno, *Negative Dialectics* (New York, 1973), 320.

[63] J. J. Sheehan, *Where Have All the Soldiers Gone? The Transformation of Modern Europe,* (Boston, 2008), xx.

and to the 1860s in Germany. Unless war could be made to seem like a game, as the upshot of media coverage (from the Crimean War onwards) or an imbalance of military technology (in colonial wars and 'new wars' or 'low intensity warfare' after 1990), significant sections of the public had become increasingly wary of it.[64] Only when conflicts were presented as distant 'newspaper wars' or, as one journalist observed in 1991 of the Gulf War, as a 'video war without victims' was public opinion reassured.[65]

Post-modern scholars are particularly sensitive to this game-like play of the senses and emotions in our imagining of violence. 'We are…caught in a kind of ethical illusion, parallel to perceptual illusions', writes Slavoj Žižek in his study of *Violence* (2008):

> the ultimate cause of these illusions is that although our power of abstract reasoning has developed immensely, our emotional–ethical responses remain conditioned by age-old institutional reactions of sympathy to suffering and pain that is witnessed directly. This is why shooting someone point-blank is for most of us much more repulsive than pressing a button that will kill a thousand people we cannot see.[66]

In order to avoid confronting violence directly, since 'the overpowering horror of violent acts and empathy with the victims inexorably function as a lure which prevents us from thinking', the Slovenian philosopher and cultural critic prefers to 'cast sideways glances' at violence and to keep it 'at a distance out of respect towards its victims'.[67] Although he distinguishes between '(factual) truth' and 'truthfulness', given that 'the very factual deficiencies of the traumatized subject's report on her experience bear witness to the truthfulness of her report', his threefold model of violence—subjective, symbolic, and systemic—is predicated on a 'stepping back' from the 'fascinating lure of this directly visible "subjective" violence, violence performed by a clearly identifiable agent', producing the 'obvious signals of violence' in the form of acts of crime and terror, civil unrest, and international conflict.[68] Like Lenin, his aim is to withdraw to a lonely place, where he can 'learn, learn, learn': 'And this is what we should do today when we find ourselves bombarded with mediatic images of violence. We need to "learn, learn, learn" what causes this violence.'[69] The principal causes are purportedly symbolic, 'embodied in language and its forms', and systemic, deriving from 'the often catastrophic consequences of

---

[64] See especially the literature on the Gulf War, regarded by Susan Carruthers, *The Media at War: Communication and Conflict in the Twentieth Century* (London, 2000), 133, as the 'first *real* "television war"'. The conflict was famous for round-the-clock coverage and 'surgical strikes': P. Virilio, *Desert Screen: War at the Speed of Light* (London, 2002); S. Jeffords and L. Rabinovitz (eds), *Seeing through the Media: The Persian Gulf War* (New Brunswick, 1994); H. Mowlana, G. Gerbner, and H. I. Schiller (eds), *The Triumph of the Image: The Media's War in the Persian Gulf* (Boulder, CO, 1992); M. J. Arlen, *Living-Room War* (New York, 1997). On the contested notion of 'new wars', combining state and non-state networks, see M. Kaldor, *New and Old Wars: Organized Violence in a Global Era* (Stanford, 1999); H. Münkler, *The New Wars* (Oxford, 2005); M. van Creveld, *The Transformation of War* (New York, 1991); and M. van Creveld, *The Changing Face of War: Combat from the Marne to Iraq* (New York, 2007).

[65] Konrad Ege, a German journalist living in the US, cited in G. Paul, *Bilder des Krieges, Krieg der Bilder. Die Visualisierung des modernen Krieges* (Paderborn, 2004), 367.

[66] S. Žižek, *Violence* (London, 2008), 43.

[67] Ibid., 4.   [68] Ibid., 1, 4.   [69] Ibid., 8.

the smooth functioning of our economic and political systems'.[70] It is possible to conceive of a symbolic normalization of wartime violence and a systematization of killing within armies, but Žižek offers no examples of how they might function. His 'explosions' of subjective violence seem to issue from the generic pressures of a malfunctioning system and media-generated illusions.

Whereas subjective violence is perceived to be a 'perturbation of the "normal", peaceful state of things' against the background of a 'non-violent zero level', objective violence—symbolic and systemic—is 'invisible since it sustains the very zero-level standard against which we perceive something as subjectively violent'.[71] The latter has to be taken into account if 'what otherwise seem to be "irrational" explosions of subjective violence' are to be understood.[72] Like other post-modern (and post-Marxian) scholars of violence, Žižek pays more attention to symbolic and structural violence than to actual ('subjective') acts of violence, coming close to Walter Benjamin's notion of 'history as a state of siege' or, even, the anthropologist Michael Taussig's claims concerning 'terror as usual'.[73] As a consequence, he gives little indication of how violent symbols or a violent system are translated into violent actions. Pierre Bourdieu's own studies of symbolic violence—defined as 'the coercion which is set up only through the consent that the dominated cannot fail to give to the dominator (and therefore to the domination) when their understanding of the situation and relation can only use instruments of knowledge that they have in common with the dominator' and which appear 'natural'—do not imply a minimization of the role of physical violence, making people forget that 'there are battered, raped and exploited women, or worse'.[74] He, too, though, tends to ignore the question of how symbolic violence (or domination) issues in physical violence or how violent acts, including those of wars, are affected by the 'instruments of knowledge'.

THEORIES OF VIOLENCE AND CIVILIZATION

The links between systemic, symbolic, and subjective violence are often understood in a psychological or psychoanalytical sense.[75] Violent acts, even when they stem from the order of an officer or a gangster boss, are individual. The reasons why individuals carry out violent actions—or fail to resist orders to do so—are complex but they typically involve strong emotions, earlier experiences, habituation, and, more occasionally, pathologies and neuroses. Many scholars, before and after Sigmund Freud, have emphasized instincts and drives. 'The gladly denied piece of

---

[70] Ibid., 2.   [71] Ibid.   [72] Ibid.

[73] W. Benjamin, 'Theses on the Philosophy of History', in *Illuminations*, ed. H. Arendt (New York, 1969), 253–64; M. Taussig, *The Nervous System* (New York, 1992). Taussig himself has worked on Benjamin: M. Taussig, *Walter Benjamin's Grave* (Chicago, 2006).

[74] The definition comes from P. Bourdieu, *Pascalian Meditations* (Cambridge, 2000), 170; also, P. Bourdieu, *Masculine Domination* (Palo Alto, CA, 2001), 34–42.

[75] Thus, Žižek's repeated references to Lacan, for instance: S. Žižek, *Violence*, 13, 45–6, 52–3, 56, 61–2, 76, 97, 99, 174–5, 194–6, 204.

reality lurking behind everything is that the human is not a gentle being in need of love, who at most may defend himself if attacked, but that he can also count a considerable share of aggressive tendencies amongst his drives', wrote Freud in *Das Unbehagen in der Kultur* (1930):

> As a result, his neighbour is not only a possible helper and sex object, but also a temptation for him to satisfy his aggression, to exploit his [the neighbour's] labour without compensation, to use him sexually without permission, to take possession of his goods, to humiliate him, to prepare to inflict pain on him, to martyr and to kill.[76]

Although it had later become 'fashionable to consider war as caused by the power of man's destructive instinct', contended Erich Fromm in *The Anatomy of Human Destructiveness* (1973), 'Freud himself took a much more realistic view':

> In his famous letter to Albert Einstein, *Why War?* (1933), he did not take the position that war was *caused* by human destructiveness, but saw its cause in realistic conflicts between groups which always have been solved by violence, since there was no international enforceable law according to which—as in civil law—the conflicts could have been solved peacefully.[77]

Nevertheless, Freud did believe it was 'a general principle... that conflicts of interest between men are settled by the use of violence', as he warned Einstein: 'This is true of the whole animal kingdom from which men have no business to exclude themselves.'[78] Violence between animals was akin to that of human conflicts, including wars, helping to explain why humans continued to go to war, despite the costs. The Viennese psychoanalyst had speculated during the First World War, which he had initially welcomed and later criticized, that the 'vast amount of brutality, cruelty, and lies which are able to spread over the civilized world' were tied to 'the mental constitution of mankind'.[79] His approach to such a mental constitution was individual, even if also prompting 'the most banal truths'—as he put it in a letter about *Das Unbehagen in der Kultur* in 1929—about collective action.[80]

The most useful sociological adaptation of Freud's study of civilization (*Kultur*) and drives—with aggression not only as the 'destructive [death] drive' directed 'against the external world and other living beings', but also as a set of behaviours controlled, regulated, and inhibited by societies and individuals—is arguably Norbert Elias's thesis about a 'civilizing process'.[81] In modern Western societies, in the sociologist's opinion, violent impulses are constrained and norms internalized. 'Socially undesirable expressions of instinct and pleasure are threatened and punished

---

[76] S. Freud, *Das Unbehagen in der Kultur*, in S. Freud, *Gesammelte Werke* (London, 1948), vol. 14, 470–1.

[77] E. Fromm, *The Anatomy of Human Destructiveness* (New York, 1973), 237–8.

[78] S. Freud, 'Why War?' (1933), in J. Strachey (ed.), *The Standard Edition of the Complete Psychological Works of Sigmund Freud* (London, 1953–74), vol. 22, 204.

[79] S. Freud, *Introductory Lectures*, cited in D. Pick, *War Machine: The Rationalisation of Slaughter in the Modern Age* (New Haven, CN, 1993), 246.

[80] Cited in U. Jensen, 'Gewalt als triebhafte Überwältigung? Sigmund Freud: *Das Unbehagen in der Kultur*' (1930), in U. Jensen et al. (eds), *Gewalt und Gesellschaft* (Göttingen: Wallstein, 2011) 155.

[81] S. Freud, 'Das Ich und das Es' (1923), in U. Jensen et al. (eds), *Gewalt und Gesellschaft*, 157.

with measures that generate and reinforce displeasure and anxiety', proposes the sociologist in *Über den Prozess der Zivilisation*: 'In the constant recurrence of displeasure aroused by threats, and in the habituation to this rhythm, the dominant displeasure is compulsorily associated even with behaviour which may be pleasurable.'[82] Thus, the sixteenth-century French practice of burning cats is now seen as revolting 'simply because normal conditioning in our stage of civilization restrains the expression of pleasure in such actions through anxiety instilled in the form of self-control'.[83] In a Freudian sense, aggression, together with other drives and affects, is inhibited and repressed. 'The pleasure of physical attack' is permitted 'to larger numbers only in exceptional times of war or revolution, in the socially legitimised struggle against internal or external enemies'.[84] Even in war, however, violence had become more 'impersonal', leading 'less and less to affective discharge having the immediacy and intensity of the medieval phase'.[85] Modern warfare had created 'invisible' enemies and 'a mechanised struggle demanding a strict control of the affects'.[86] Such control had been acquired at a high price, with the development of 'reason', 'conscience', 'ego', and 'super-ego', and 'the consequent curbing of more animalic impulses and affects', never constituting 'a process entirely without pain'.[87] 'Drive energies' can, in certain cases, be 'dammed up in a form that permits no real satisfaction'.[88] They tend to be either 'anaesthetised' or expressed in a pacified form as compulsive behaviour or eccentric predilections.[89]

As an instinct or emotion, aggression or violence is inextricably connected to other 'impulses' because the 'affect structure of man is a whole'.[90] The inhibition of violent behaviour—or any drive—is likely to have had an impact on other instincts:

> We may call particular instincts by different names according to their different directions and functions, we may speak of hunger and the need to spit, of the sexual drive and of aggressive impulses, but in life these different instincts are no more separable than the heart from the stomach or the blood in the brain from the blood in the genitalia.[91]

Everyday language gives the impression that a 'whole bundle of different drives' exists, as if a 'death instinct' and a 'self-assertive drive' were 'different chemical substances', but 'the categories by which these observations are classified must remain powerless in the face of their living objects if they fail to express the unity and totality of instinctual life, and the connection of each particular instinctual tendency to this totality'.[92] In 'simpler' or 'less differentiated' societies like those of medieval Europe or modern Ghana, 'both joy and pain were discharged more openly and freely'.[93] Partly, this fuller enjoyment of pleasures was the corollary of greater physical suffering and insecurity: 'At that stage people live in far greater insecurity than we do. They are exposed to much greater dangers—illnesses for

---

[82] N. Elias, *The Civilising Process: The History of Manners* (New York, 1978), vol. 1, 204. See also J. Fletcher, *Violence and Civilisation: An Introduction to the Work of Norbert Elias* (Oxford, 1997).
[83] N. Elias, *The Civilising Process*, vol. 1, 204.
[84] Ibid., 202.   [85] Ibid.   [86] Ibid.
[87] Ibid., vol. 2, 244   [88] Ibid., 243.   [89] Ibid.
[90] Ibid., vol. 1, 191.   [91] Ibid.   [92] Ibid.   [93] Ibid., vol. 2, 241.

example; the unexpected can happen to them much more than to us.'[94] Instinctive impulses, in such circumstances, were linked to personal survival. 'Rapine, battle, hunting of men and animals—all these were vital necessities which, in accordance with the structure of society, were visible to all', argues Elias: 'And thus, for the mighty and strong, they formed part of the pleasures of life.'[95] In Abyssinia or the tribes of the Great Migrations, where war was the normal state, uninhibited violence was necessary for the survival of the group and was cultivated through hunting and warlike rituals during times of peace.[96] Such free expression of aggressive impulses had a direct impact on the release of other interconnected affects and it permitted one individual to take pleasure in enforcing his will on—and to satisfy his urges at the expense of—another. As a result, 'much of what appears contradictory to us' about 'simpler societies'—'the intensity of their piety, the violence of their fear of hell, their guilt feelings, their penitence, the immense outbursts of joy and gaiety, the sudden flaring of their hatred and belligerence—all these, like the rapid changes of mood, are in reality symptoms of the same social and personality structure'.[97] Because of their centrality to survival, outbursts of violence were common and widely condoned. Some historians—most notably, Joanna Bourke—have suggested that this acceptance or enjoyment of killing has had a critical effect on the dynamics of modern wars.[98]

COMBAT AND THE FEAR OF DYING

Other sociologists who have investigated violence have rejected the thesis that humans enjoy killing, once social prohibitions and individual inhibitions have been removed.[99] Basing his conclusions *inter alia* on evidence about military training and combat (since 'military organization is the easiest place to trace the social techniques for overcoming our biological propensity not to be violent'), Randall Collins has argued convincingly that violent acts, across a diverse set of social situations, are difficult to perform: 'Micro-situational evidence . . . shows that violence is hard. No matter how motivated someone may be, if the situation does not unfold so that confrontational tension/fear is overcome, violence will not proceed.'[100] If anything, 'one's physiological hard-wiring' consists in 'the human propensity to become caught up in the micro-interactional rituals of solidarity'.[101] In competent acts of violence, 'one needs to cut out all one's sensitivity to cues of human-to-human ritual solidarity, to concentrate instead on taking advantage of the other's weaknesses'.[102] 'Joy of combat' appears only to affect a small minority of soldiers

---

[94] N. Elias, *Reflections on a Life* (Cambridge, 1994), 71.

[95] N. Elias, *Civilising Process*, vol. 1, 193.　　[96] Ibid., 192; also, 195.　　[97] Ibid., 200.

[98] J. Bourke, *An Intimate History of Killing: Face to Face Killing in Twentieth-Century Warfare* (London, 1999); see also M. van Creveld, *The Culture of War* (New York, 2008); and N. Ferguson, *The Pity of War* (London, 1998), 339–66.

[99] Erich Fromm also rejects this thesis in *The Anatomy of Human Destructiveness*.

[100] R. Collins, *Violence: A Micro-Sociological Theory* (Princeton, 2008), 20, 29.

[101] Ibid., 80.　　[102] Ibid.

and can be explained as an instance of pre-battle elation, distance from the fighting front, the thrill of firing guns (not hitting enemy targets), the slow build-up of tension and fear into an emotional adrenaline rush and overkill at the point of contact ('forward panic'), or distance from the victim (sharpshooters and fighter pilots).[103] More typical of combat, in Collins's opinion, has been a continuum of degrees and kinds of tension and fear:

> At one end is frozen incapacity, burrowing into the ground or childishly hiding from the sight of the enemy. Next is panic retreat. Next comes shitting and pissing in one's pants,…lagging back from the front line, seeking excuses to do something other than move forward, drifting away. Then comes moving forward but not firing;…then firing one's weapons but incompetently, missing the enemy. Finally, at the high end, there is accurate and well-timed firing, and other aggressive manoeuvres in combat.[104]

According to S. L. A. Marshall's study of separate confrontations in the Second World War, no more than a quarter of well-trained and battle-hardened troops fired, with three-quarters refusing to fire or to persist in firing at the enemy; in an average infantry company the figure for those firing sank to 15 per cent.[105] Russell W. Glenn produced higher figures from his interviews of Vietnam veterans, finding that 9 per cent of infantry fired rarely or never, 45 per cent sometimes, and 46 per cent virtually always.[106] Half of the veterans said that they had witnessed another soldier failing to fire.[107] From his own survey of 290 photographs of soldiers in twentieth- and early twenty-first-century wars, Collins concludes that 30 per cent show fear, 32 per cent show a range of expressions between tension and concentration, and 26 per cent seem calm or neutral.[108] A mere 6 per cent betray anger and 0.3 per cent joy, which can be seen in their smiling faces.

Collins's approach is situational and interactional, relying on heterogeneous sources or 'micro-evidence' (video recordings, photographs, interviews, surveys, observations, and reconstructions) relating to all manner of violent confrontations, from sports fixtures to serial killings and terrorist attacks. His principal finding is that violence normally results from the detached, competent actions of a 'violent few' or from different forms of 'forward panic', where a 'build-up of tension' is 'released into a frenzied attack when the situation makes it easy to do so' and when the perpetrators have the emotional support of others (a crowd, a regiment, or a criminal gang).[109] This thesis militates against cultural explanations, on the one hand, and theories of resistance, opportunity, and social control, on the other, all of which assume that 'violence is easy'.[110] The latter posit that criminal violence

---

[103] Ibid., 66–7.
[104] Ibid., 68. Collins relies on evidence concerning the US military presented by S. L. A. Marshall, *Men against Fire: The Problem of Battle Command* (New York, 1947); Samuel Stouffer et al., *The American Soldier* (Princeton, 1949), 2 vols; Dave Grossman, *On Killing: The Psychological Cost of Learning to Kill* (Boston, 1995); and Dave Grossman, *On Combat: The Psychology and Physiology of Deadly Combat in War and Peace* (Belleville, IL, 2004).
[105] S. L. A. Marshall, *Men against Fire*, 50–4.
[106] R. W. Glenn, *Reading Athen's Dance Card: Men against Fire in Vietnam* (Annapolis, MD, 2000), 37–9, 159–61, cited by R. Collins, *Violence*, 51–2.
[107] R. Collins, *Violence*, 51.   [108] Ibid., 68–9.
[109] Ibid., 89, 370–430.   [110] Ibid., 22.

can occur when there is a convergence of a motivated perpetrator, an available and unthreatening victim, and the absence of police (opportunity or routine activities theory) or they contend that violence can be a response to discrimination and unfairness from those in a lower class or racial ghetto (resistance theory).[111] The former (cultural theories) are 'almost always macro explanations', with a 'trans-situational culture...assumed to be the (necessary, and implicitly even sufficient) explanation of why the violence takes place'.[112] They regularly ignore the fact that

> the micro-situational realities of talking about violence fall into ritual patterns of bluster and bluff, and these rituals provide an ideology that covers up the real nature of violence—that it is hard to perform, that most people are not good at it, including those who are doing the bragging and swaggering.[113]

In attempting to link physical and symbolic violence, cultural theorists are prone to vacuity, in Collins's view: '"Symbolic violence" is mere theoretical word play; to take it literally would be to grossly misunderstand the nature of real violence. Symbolic violence is easy; real violence is hard.'[114] The American sociologist does not deny that 'factors outside the situation'—poverty, racial discrimination, family disorganization, abuse, stress, and the language in which they are described—are often 'necessary or at least strongly predisposing'.[115] Occasionally such factors are 'sufficient, giving violence a much more emergent quality than any other kind of human behaviour', but usually they are not.[116] 'Conflict, even quite overtly expressed conflict, is not the same as violence, and taking the last step is not at all automatic', Collins continues: 'Many, probably most, frustrated persons swallow their anger, or let it go with bluster and bluff.'[117] Although he is 'more inclined to see historical sequences in terms of a Weberian theory of multi-dimensional changes in the social organization of power', he believes that 'techniques for carrying out violence must always be fitted to the task of overcoming confrontational tension/fear; however extensive these organizations are at the macro and meso level, their effectiveness is always tested at the micro level'.[118] In armies at war, organizations—particularly when taken in conjunction with other 'background' conditions—appear to be the main 'cause' of violence, yet evidence about soldiers' unwillingness to shoot or about their varying readiness to commit atrocities, for example, suggests that situational factors also play an important part.

The institutional and discursive conditions in which individuals act do not simply permit or push them towards violence. In the nineteenth and twentieth

---

[111] For opportunity theories, see W. D. Osgood et al., 'Routine Activities and Individual Deviant Behaviour', *American Sociological Review*, 61 (1996), 635–55; M. Felson, *Crime and Everyday Life* (Thousand Oaks, CA, 1994); R. F. Meier and T. D. Miethe, 'Understanding Theories of Criminal Victimization', in M. Tonry (ed.), *Crime and Justice* (Chicago, 1993), 459–99. For a discussion of resistance theories, see P. Bourgeois, *In Search of Respect: Selling Crack in El Barrio* (Cambridge, 1995); L. Wacquant, 'Scrutinizing the Street: Poverty, Morality and the Pitfalls of Urban Ethnography', E. Anderson, 'The Ideologically Driven Critique', M. Duneier, 'What Kind of Combat Sport is Sociology?', and K. S. Newman, 'No Shame: The View from the Left Bank', *American Journal of Sociology*, 107 (2002), 1468–599.
[112] R. Collins, *Violence*, 23.   [113] Ibid., 23–4.   [114] Ibid., 24–5.
[115] Ibid., 20.   [116] Ibid., 20–1.   [117] Ibid.   [118] Ibid., 29.

centuries, they have more commonly prevented potential perpetrators from acting violently. Sociologists especially have emphasized, like Weber, the centralization of power by modern states and the pacification of civil society. Even those such as Michael Mann, who 'loosens' Weber's definition of the state as 'the monopoly of the legitimate use of physical force in the enforcement of its order' in favour of his own model of overlapping but autonomous networks of power (including a military network), accept that the modern state is a 'differentiated set of institutions and personnel embodying centrality, . . . a territorially demarcated area over which it exercises some degree of authoritative, binding rule making, backed up by some organized force'.[119] For Anthony Giddens, the spread of civil law, the enforcement of property rights, the control of production and the workplace, the commodification of goods and wage-labour, the necessity of rational behaviour and efficiency, the industrial transformation of humans' environments, more extensive surveillance as a result of changing means of communication, increased storage of information, democratization, and the participation of citizens within the political process have all reinforced processes of disciplining and internal pacification.[120] 'In nation-states surveillance reaches an intensity quite unmatched in previous types of societal order, made possible through the generation and control of information, and developments in communication and transportation, plus forms of supervisory control of "deviance"', the British sociologist claims in *The Nation-State and Violence* (1985): 'The successful monopoly of control of the means of violence in the hands of the state authorities is the other face of surveillance in the work-place and the control of deviance.'[121] Alongside this accretion of power within nation-states and capitalism, a separable control of and detachment from nature has occurred: 'The technological changes stimulated by the energetic dynamism of capitalist development involve processes of the transformation of the natural world quite distinct from anything occurring before', he goes on: 'In industrialized societies, and much of the rest of the world reached by the influence of industrialism, human beings live in a created environment distinct from the "given" world of nature.'[122] Subsequent 'transformations in the relations between the habits of day-to-day social life and the *milieu* in and through which they are ordered' have made the 'natural' aspects of warfare—hardship, the cold, injury, violence, and death—more alien to the 'civilians' of industrial nation-states.[123] These changing sensibilities and lack of experience of analogous actions and conditions in daily life seem to have consolidated Collins's barriers—including the need to overcome tension and fear—to the carrying out of acts of violence.

The marginalization of violence has not necessarily been intended by individuals, in Elias's view. Instead, the 'basic tissue resulting from many single plans and actions of men can', asserts the sociologist, 'give rise to changes and patterns that no individual person has planned or created'.[124] Yet these often unintended, interdependent

---

[119] M. Mann, *Social Sources of Power: The Rise of Classes and Nation-States, 1760–1914* (Cambridge, 1993), vol. 2, 55.

[120] A. Giddens, *The Nation-State and Violence* (Cambridge, 1985), 31–4, 122–221.

[121] Ibid., 311–14.   [122] Ibid.   [123] Ibid.

[124] N. Elias, *Civilising Process*, vol. 2, 230.

actions, which have produced civilization, create 'an order sui generis', or a 'social order', which in turn helps to condition future civilizing actions.[125] A civilized order is dominated by two principles, both of which demand and enforce pacification. The first concerns complex divisions of labour, competition and interdependence, requiring increasingly 'stable', 'differentiated', and 'automatic' actions.[126] The outcome of violence is too unpredictable and the cost of containing violence 'externally' by social means too expensive to allow the effective functioning of a complex society: 'The pressures operating upon the individual now tend to produce a transformation of the whole drive and affect economy in the direction of a more continuous, stable and even regulation of drives and affects in all areas of conduct.'[127] Norms have had to be internalized and made more routine because of the very complexity of modern social systems.

The second principle of civilization involves the growth of the state and its monopolization of violence. The implication of Elias's argument is that only powerful state structures could overcome the obstacles to pacification. This is the reason that the sociologist devotes much of the second volume of *Über den Prozess der Zivilisation* to state formation:

> The moderation of spontaneous emotions, the tempering of affects, the extension of mental space beyond the moment into the past and future, the habit of connecting events in terms of chains of cause and effect—all these are different aspects of the same transformation of conduct which necessarily takes place with the monopolisation of physical violence.[128]

Perhaps because such drives are part of a single personality structure, in Elias's opinion, the inhibition of violent impulses has helped to thwart the strong expression of other emotions. Nowhere has this process been more pronounced than amongst European aristocracies, which have been transformed from warrior castes into peaceable, etiquette-ridden courtly communities, increasingly preoccupied with forms of rationalization and psychologization more commonly associated with the bourgeoisie.[129] Implicitly, the pacification of the nobility owed most to the emergence of the state, that of the middling orders to the division of labour and spread of specialization. Yet both sets of processes have been closely connected: 'societies without a stable monopoly of force are always societies in which the division of functions is relatively slight', whereas 'societies with more stable monopolies of force, always first embodied in a large princely or royal court, are societies in which the division of functions is more or less advanced, in which the chains of action binding individuals together are longer and the functional dependencies between people are greater'.[130] What has given the West its 'special and unique character', the sociologist concludes, is 'the fact that here the division of functions has attained a level, the monopolies of force and taxation a solidity, and interdependence and competition an extent' which has not, 'in terms of physical space and of numbers of people involved', occurred anywhere else.[131]

---

125 Ibid., 230.   126 Ibid., 232.   127 Ibid., 240.   128 Ibid., 236.
129 Ibid., 281.   130 Ibid., 235–6.   131 Ibid., 247.

VIOLENCE AND POWER

If the modern West is so civilized, as states have renounced their former sovereign power of inflicting death in favour of 'the administration of bodies and the calculated management of life', why have wars 'never [been] so bloody as they have been since the nineteenth century' and why have regimes visited 'such holocausts on their own populations?' asks Foucault in *La Volonté de savoir* (1976).[132] His own answer is predictably paradoxical. Sovereign states which gave up the right to take the lives of subjects acquired new, more invasive powers to protect those lives: 'One might say that the ancient right to take life or let live was replaced by a power to foster life or disallow it to the point of death.'[133] Power over life evolved between two poles of development:

> One of these poles—the first to be formed, it seems—centred on the body as a machine: its disciplining, the optimization of its capabilities, the extortion of its forces, the parallel increase of its usefulness and its docility, its integration into systems of efficient and economic controls. ... The second, formed somewhat later, focused on the species body, the body imbued with the mechanics of life and serving as the basis of the biological processes: propagation, births and mortality, the level of health, life expectancy and longevity, with all the conditions that can cause these to vary.[134]

The organization of power over life occurred via the disciplines of the body and the regulatory controls of a bio-politics of the population. By taking charge of life, 'power'—in different *locales*—gained control over all spheres of existence. Thus, at the same time as economic improvements began to provide to all 'a measure of relief' from epidemics and famine—or 'the two great dramatic forms of this relationship [between biology and history] that was always dominated by the menace of death'—the state began to develop 'great instruments, as *institutions* of power', which served to maintain the relations of production and which overlapped with 'the rudiments of anatomo- and bio-politics as *techniques* of power present at every level of the social body and utilized by very diverse institutions (the family and the army, schools and the police, individual medicine and the administration of collective bodies)'.[135] States and other institutions had become more interventionist as they had become less sovereign.

What 'power'—often epistemic or discursive rather than institutional—has done to citizens in such circumstances has proved difficult to limit, in Foucault's opinion. 'Power would no longer be dealing simply with legal subjects over whom the ultimate dominion was death, but with living beings, and the mastery it would be able to exercise over them would have to be applied at the level of life itself', he declares: 'it was the taking charge of life, more than the threat of death, that gave power its access even to the body'.[136] Yet although the analysis of epistemes helps to explain how the powerful have used their power and why others have conformed to their will (or simply acted in accordance with widely held imperatives),

---

[132] Published in English as M. Foucault, *History of Sexuality* (New York, 1978), 135–44.
[133] Ibid., 138.   [134] Ibid., 139.   [135] Ibid., 141.   [136] Ibid., 143.

it does not itself explain why individuals carry out violent actions or threaten to do so. How has a control of bodies up to but not including death been translated into modern 'holocausts' of killing? Domestically, 'capital punishment could not be maintained except by invoking less the enormity of the crime itself than the monstrosity of the criminal, his incorrigibility and the safeguard of society', so that 'one had the right to kill those who represented a kind of biological danger to others', opening up the possibility—which Foucault does not explore—of executing 'deviants'.[137] Abroad, 'wars are no longer waged in the name of a sovereign who must be defended; they are waged on behalf of the existence of everyone; entire populations are mobilized for the purpose of wholesale slaughter in the name of life necessity'.[138] Foucault's conclusion is that regimes 'have been able to wage so many wars, causing so many men to be killed', precisely because they have acted 'as managers of life and survival, of bodies and the race'.[139] 'The atomic situation [of the Cold War] is now at the end point of this process[—]the power to expose a whole population to death is the underside of the power to guarantee an individual's continued existence', the philosopher declares:

> The principle underlying the tactics of battle—that one has to be capable of killing in order to go on living—has become the principle that defines the strategy of states. But the existence in question is no longer the juridical existence of sovereignty; at stake is the biological existence of a population. If genocide is indeed the dream of modern powers, this is not because of a recent return of the ancient right to kill; it is because power is situated and exercised at the level of life, the species, the race and the large-scale phenomena of population.[140]

The apparently 'natural' assumptions governing state action—what was later termed 'symbolic violence'—are linked directly by Foucault to the exercise and abuse of power and to acts of physical violence.

Foucault refrains from explaining individual acts of violence and from investigating possible distinctions between discourse, power, and violence. Why do individuals and groups countenance and carry out particular forms of violence, of varying intensity and scale, in different contexts, overcoming social prohibitions and psychological tension and fear? Perhaps the best-known reply to this type of question is that of Hannah Arendt. In her reflections *On Violence* (1969), she criticizes 'political theorists from Left to Right' for their assumption 'that violence is nothing more than the most flagrant manifestation of power'.[141] Thus, to the postwar 'New Left', it came to seem—following the maxim of Mao Tse-tung—that '[p]ower grows out of the barrel of a gun'.[142] The combination of a rejection of colonialism, 'the resistance movement against the war in Vietnam', and 'the weird suicidal development of modern weapons', giving the young in the 1960s a 'greater awareness of the possibility of doomsday', had reversed their earlier 'revulsion against every form of violence', which 'they inherited from their parents' generation' and which seemed to them to be a response to the 'massive intrusion of criminal

---

137 Ibid., 138.   138 Ibid., 137.   139 Ibid.   140 Ibid.
141 H. Arendt, *On Violence* (Orlando, FL, 1969), 35.   142 Ibid., 11.

violence into politics', manifesting itself in concentration and extermination camps, genocide, and torture.[143] It was now possible for Jean-Paul Sartre to declare, in his preface to Frantz Fanon's *Les Damnés de la terre* (1961), that 'to shoot down a European is to kill two birds with one stone', since 'there remain a dead man and free man': 'Sartre with his great felicity with words has given expression to the new faith. "Violence," he now believes, on the strength of Fanon's book, "like Achilles' lance, can heal the wounds it has inflicted." '[144] In Arendt's opinion (alluding to Marx), 'mad fury... turned dreams into nightmares for everybody', which were difficult to banish.[145] To think the contrary, in the manner of Sartre, was dangerous because violence and power are opposites: 'The extreme form of power is All against One, the extreme form of violence is One against All', with the latter 'never possible without instruments'.[146] Whereas the power of the government depends on numbers, being 'in proportion to the number with which it is associated' and making 'tyranny... the most violent and least powerful of forms of government', 'violence up to a point can manage without them because it relies on implements'.[147] Power requires legitimacy, with people acting in concert, and violence is associated with justification, where 'legitimacy, when challenged, bases itself on an appeal to the past, while justification relates to an end that lies in the future'.[148] For this reason, violence reinforces power only when the ends it achieves are seen to be legitimate. Often, it can destroy power or be destroyed by it: 'Where commands are no longer obeyed, the means of violence are of no use; and the question of this obedience is not decided by the command–obedience relation but by opinion, and, of course, by the number of those who share it.'[149] Governments' use of violence at home could be long-lasting, with 'terror... the form of government that comes into being when violence, having destroyed all power, does not abdicate but, on the contrary, remains in full control'.[150] Abroad, their exercise of violence tended to be justified by reference to legitimate ends, often linked to self-defence.

Individuals continued to act, despite their aversion to violence and its likely costs, because they were insulated, to a degree, from its consequences. In complex divisions of labour and chains of command, a functionary could always claim like the SS officer Adolf Eichmann, on whose trial in Jerusalem Arendt reported in 1961, that 'his guilt came from obedience, and obedience is praised as a virtue'.[151] According to his statement given to Israeli interrogators, when confronted with the thought of death in the gas chambers, Eichmann was 'horrified': 'My nerves aren't strong enough. ...Even today, if I see someone with a deep cut, I have to look away. I could never have been a doctor. I still remember how I visualized the scene and began to tremble, as if I'd been through something, some terrible experience.'[152] Reinhard Heydrich's subordinate continued to obey orders because he was able to

---

[143] Ibid., 14, 17.   [144] Cited ibid., 13, 20.   [145] Ibid., 21.   [146] Ibid., 42.

[147] Ibid., 41–2, citing *The Federalist* and referring to Montesquieu's view of tyranny.

[148] Ibid., 52.   [149] Ibid., 49.   [150] Ibid., 55.

[151] H. Arendt, *Eichmann in Jerusalem: A Report on the Banality of Evil* (London, 1963), 247.

[152] J. v. Lang (ed.), *Eichmann Interrogated: Transcripts from the Archives of the Israeli Police* (New York, 1983), 75–6.

cut himself off from their physical consequences. For Arendt, such insulation in totalitarian hierarchies underpinned the 'banality of evil' for crimes 'committed *en masse*, not only in regard to the number of victims, but also in regard to the numbers of those who perpetrated the crime', meaning that 'the extent to which any one of the many criminals was close to or remote from the actual killer of the victim means nothing, as far as the measure of responsibility is concerned': 'On the contrary, in general *the degree of responsibility increases as we draw further away from the man who uses the fatal instrument with his own hands*.'[153] By carrying out the Holocaust in the gas chambers of isolated extermination camps rather than by execution squads composed of reservists, the Nazi regime had attempted to separate the fatal instrument from the hands of its own men.[154] During wars, this separation seemed to have been accomplished by 'the implements of violence', which, 'like all other tools, increase and multiply human strength'.[155] Unlike the repression of undefended, scapegoated minorities within 'totalitarian' dictator-ships, however, wars continued to expose soldiers themselves to risk of injury and death, especially in conflicts between Great Powers, during which troops were victims of the technologies they were using to kill others. The culmination of the technology produced by the Cold War and 'the establishment of the military-industrial-labour complex', in Arendt's judgement, was the 'universal suicide' of a thermonuclear war, as the Soviet physicist Andrei Sakharov put it.[156] It also entailed the abandonment of Carl von Clausewitz's notion of war as 'the continu-ation of politics by other means' and Friedrich Engels's definition of 'violence as the accelerator of economic development'.[157]

This study investigates soldiers' responses to these dynamics of modern warfare during the period of mass conscription from the late eighteenth century onwards. For 'more developed industrial states', this was the point at which, as Elias recog-nized, 'the gradient between pacification within the state and the threat between states is often especially steep'.[158] At war, in contrast to the political violence used by small groups of paramilitaries, party men, and other perpetrators against defenceless targets within post-First World War regimes, millions of citizens were faced with the prospect of violence inflicted on their own bodies as well as on those of enemies.

UNDERSTANDING MODERN WARS

It is notoriously difficult to make sense of individuals' 'experiences' and to relate them to the experiences and actions of other individuals and, especially, to those of groups. According to Nikolaus Buschmann and Horst Carl in *Die Erfahrung des*

---

[153] H. Arendt, *Eichmann in Jerusalem*, 246–7. See also H. Arendt, *The Origins of Totalitarianism* (New York, 1951).

[154] See note 17 for further reading. The seminal work remains C. Browning, *Ordinary Men: Reserve Battalion 101 and the Final Solution in Poland* (New York, 1992).

[155] H. Arendt, *On Violence*, 53.   [156] Ibid., 9–10.   [157] Ibid., 8–9.

[158] N. Elias, *The Germans* (Cambridge, 1996), 177.

Krieges (2001), 'experiences' can be broken down into immediate sensations (*Erlebnisse*) and cumulative, longer-term understanding or even learning (*Erfahrung*), which is individual but also connected to social and historical practices and processes.[159] They can also be viewed through the lens of a sociology of knowledge—namely, as a type of constructivism, with reality as the product of a permanent process of communication—and as a temporal concept, existing in the interstices of a 'space of experience' (*Erfahrungsraum*) and a 'horizon of expectation' (*Erwartungshorizont*).[160] As a consequence, they are in constant flux, subject to the contradictory pressures of subjective expression—of personal feelings and sensations—and intersubjective communication, as experiences become objects of understanding and are made intelligible to others. It is unlikely, writes Reinhart Koselleck, that 'a common war' would 'be experienced in common', for combatants were drawing on a multiplicity of sensations (*Erlebnisse*), structures of events (*Ereignisstrukturen*), and 'numerous socializing conditions' (language, religious certainties, ideological conceptions of a party, class, or gender), which ensured that any transformation of consciousness brought about by war would 'take place with different ramifications on all levels at the same time'.[161] Wartime experiences were typically 'very local, limited, incoherent', in Edmund Blunden's words, describing and omitting time, place, and conditions in a fragmentary, unreliable fashion.[162] What was more, they came to depend on selective processes of recollection and remembrance, textual dissemination and reception, public debate and symbolism in accordance with the social interests and political imperatives of the post-war era.[163]

Soldiers' experiences seemed so impenetrable because they were interwoven with the visible and invisible threads of overwhelming, complicated emotions and physiological reactions. Fear prior to action was 'the body's preparation', wrote E. G. Boring and Marjorie Van de Water in the best-selling *Psychology for the Fighting Man* (1943):

> The heart pounds faster, pumping blood more rapidly to the arms and legs and brain, where the oxygen is needed. The lungs do their part by quickened breathing. ... Adrenaline, which is nature's own 'shot in the arm', is poured liberally into the blood to act as fuel for the human fighting machine. Subtle changes in body chemistry, automatically effected by powerful emotion, serve to protect the soldier in action in ways he would never think of, if he had to plan for himself.[164]

---

[159] N. Buschmann and H. Carl (eds), *Die Erfahrung des Krieges. Erfahrungsgeschichtliche Perspektiven von der Französischen Revolution bis zum Zweiten Weltkrieg* (Paderborn, 2001), 15–21. See also K. Latzel, 'Vom Kriegserlebnis zur Kriegserfahrung. Theoretische und methodische Überlegungen zur erfahrungsgeschichtlichen Untersuchungen von Feldpostbriefen', *Militärgeschichtlichen Mitteilungen*, 56 (1997), 1–30; K. Latzel, 'Kriegsbriefe und Kriegserfahrung. Wie können Feldpostbriefe zur erfahrungsgeschichtlichen Quelle warden?', *Werkstatt Geschichte*, 22 (1999), 7–23.

[160] N. Buschmann and H. Carl (eds), *Die Erfahrung des Krieges*, 15–21.

[161] R. Koselleck, 'Der Einfluss der beiden Weltkriege auf das soziale Bewusstsein', in W. Wette (ed.), *Der Krieg des kleinen Mannes* (Munich, 1992), 325–9.

[162] E. Blunden, *Undertones of War* (London, 1928), vii.

[163] R. Koselleck, 'Der Einfluss der beiden Weltkriege', 329.

[164] Cited in J. Bourke, *Fear: A Cultural History* (London, 2005), 201–2.

Other psychiatrists were not so sure. 'The psychiatrist inexperienced in evaluating combat reactions is likely to judge manifestations of fear and anxiety by civilian standards, in relation to which the combat normal is distinctly pathologic', wrote one in 1943:

> The untried soldier has never experienced fear-producing stimuli of such intensity as those he will endure in combat. …Both he and the inexperienced medical officer whom he may ask to review his case are often quite unprepared to recognize his symptoms as lying within the range of the normal reaction to combat fear and fatigue.[165]

The 'calamitous and horrifying situations produced by modern war machines penetrate deeper and more acutely sensitive levels', making it difficult for soldiers to understand and control their emotions or to associate them with the moral codes of peacetime, reported two more American psychiatrists a couple of years later.[166] Subjective feelings and their conjunction with the chemistry of the body, which were studied so extensively in the Second World War, were internal and, 'looked at historically', hidden from view, concedes Joanna Bourke.[167] The first psychiatric report on combat within a German army was published in 1885, using the 'theory of nervous diseases'—which was 'already a preferred field of scientific activity' outside military circles—only in hindsight, after the perusal and classification of the archival material of the Franco-German War more than a decade after the event.[168] In 1870–1, noted the report, 'the majority of doctors in general had not been given the opportunity, either in their university studies or afterwards, of gaining further insight into this specialized field, which was cultivated by very few at the time'.[169] During the first half of the nineteenth century, doctors had virtually no knowledge of or interest in the 'nervous diseases' of war at all.[170] Other eyewitnesses—journalists and artists, for example—were faced with the difficulty of interpreting individuals' emotions from the outside. This task was complicated by the fact, as Charles Darwin had pointed out in *The Expression of the Emotions in Man and Animals* (1872), that apes 'possess the same facial muscles as we do'.[171] What historians are left with, for the most part, are the ego documents of the soldiers themselves.

Such documents can be interpreted as texts or narratives but they also refer to physical and social worlds through whose filters their readers understood and

---

[165] *Bulletin of the United States Army Medical Department*, cited in J. Bourke, *Fear*, 203.

[166] E. A. Strecker and K. E. Appel, *Psychiatry in Modern Warfare* (New York, 1945), cited in J. Bourke, *Fear*, 204.

[167] Ibid., 6.

[168] Militär-Medizinal-Abtheilung des Königlich Preussischen Kriegsministeriums (ed.), *Traumatische, idiopathische und nach Infektionskrankheiten beobachte Erkrankungen des Nervensystems bei den Deutschen Heeren im Kriege gegen Frankreich 1870/71* (Berlin, 1885), i.

[169] Ibid.

[170] This is not to say that there was no interest in psychiatric conditions: Dirk Blasius, 'Reformpsychiatrie im frühen 19. Jahrhundert', in Dirk Blasius, *Umgang mit Unheilbarem. Studien zur Sozialgeschichte der Psychiatrie* (Bonn, 1986), 53, has—amongst others—noted 'a civic sensibility to the problem of the mad' in early nineteenth-century Germany.

[171] J. Bourke, *Fear*, 16: Darwin had criticized Guillaume Benjamin Amand Duchenne de Boulogne's *Mécanisme de la physionomie humaine* (1862), which showed photographs of an old man having his facial muscles contorted by electrical current to 'express' emotions.

discussed conflicts.[172] Although it overlapped with other genres (fairy tales, for instance), 'war literature', which was established during the course of the nineteenth century as the volume of memoirs increased, was at once uncertain, because of its novelty and its portrayal of unfamiliar scenes and feelings, and alienating, as a result of its examination of extreme situations and its breaking of taboos.[173] By the later nineteenth century, it had come to share common elements with travel writing, history, and autobiography, but it belonged to none of these genres, as Samuel Hynes rightly remarks. Although such narratives tell readers about unfamiliar lands, describing their physical features, they deliberately alienate them from the place of war, increasingly stressing its artificiality, its Gothic horror, and its emptiness, rather than making them feel at home there in the manner of travel writing. Despite the fact that soldiers' tales purport to obey—and contribute to— a chronology of historical events, they tend to ignore 'the exact location of events in time (they rarely put dates to actions) or in space (either [soldiers] never knew exactly where they were or they have forgotten the names)'.[174] They are also 'not concerned with *why*. War narratives are experience books; they are about what happened, and how it felt. *Why* is not a soldier's question.'[175] Yet this ahistoricity does not mean that war stories are autobiographies in the usual sense, notwithstanding their description of one individual's passage through time and his or her 'conversion' at a particular moment of time, since they rarely narrate continuous lives which are joined to 'the life the teller lives as he writes': 'Military service is a kind of exile from one's own life, a dislocation of the familiar that the mind preserves as life in another world'.[176] This absence of place, time, and a continuous, developing self in much nineteenth-century war literature stemmed amongst other things from the authors' intention to demonstrate that their texts referred to events and experiences which were historic and real, not literary fictions. The underlying similarities of soldiers' ego documents are arguably more significant than discrepancies of embellishment, hindsight, and political accommodation which separate memoirs from diaries and, especially, letters.[177]

The main question is how to treat such sources. 'Narrativity'—or an exclusive focus on the interpretation of texts and discourses—leaves 'the problem of

---

[172] I have written more extensively about such interpretation in '"I Witnesses": Soldiers, Selfhood and Testimony in Modern Wars', *German History*, 28 (2010), 310–25.

[173] This case differs from that presented by Leighton James in *Witnessing the Revolutionary and Napoleonic Wars in German Central Europe* (Basingstoke, 2013), 42–67, which stresses overlap between genres, narrativity, and continuity; see also Leighton James, 'Travel Writing and Encounters with National "Others" in the Napoleonic Wars', *History Compass*, 7 (2009), 1246–58; K. Moritz, *Das Ich am Ende des Schreibens. Autobiographisches Erzählen im 18. und frühen 19. Jahrhunderts* (Würzburg, 1990); F. S. Steussy, *Eighteenth-Century Autobiography: The Emergence of Individuality* (New York, 1996); D. M. Hopkin, *Soldier and Peasant in French Popular Culture, 1766–1870* (Suffolk, 2003); D. M. Hopkin, 'Storytelling, Fairytales and Autobiography: Some Observations on Eighteenth- and Nineteenth-Century French Soldiers' and Sailors' Memoirs', *Social History*, 29 (2004), 186–98; N. Ramsey, *The Military Memoir and Romantic Literary Culture, 1780–1835* (Aldershot, 2011).

[174] S. Hynes, *Soldiers' Tale: Bearing Witness to Modern War* (London, 1998), 11.

[175] Ibid., 11.   [176] Ibid., 8.

[177] These discrepancies are the starting-point for Alan Forrest's *Napoleon's Men: The Soldiers of the Revolution and Empire* (London, 2002).

causation', as Bourke puts it, unanswered.[178] Between the Second World War and Vietnam, there was a broad shift from a language of fear (of something in particular) to that of anxiety (or a generalized apprehension), influenced by psychoanalysis:

> Did the shift in the nature of war (factors such as greater distance between enemies and the killing of civilians) lead to increased anxiety or did changes in the labels with which men could 'make sense' of what was going on around them change the way they 'actually experienced' combat?[179]

In order to answer the question, a laborious cross-referencing of individual accounts of varying types and a detailed reconstruction of actions and events—and reactions to events—is necessary, not to work out what 'really' happened, but to be able to interpret, evaluate, and explain soldiers' and civilians' shifting experiences of warfare in conditions where the 'fleeting' and 'malleable' emotions associated with them have been forgotten, misremembered, modified, or repressed.[180]

Jan Plamper describes what form such procedures might take in the hypothetical case of an official account failing to explain why soldiers have fled a battlefield:

> As a first step, I could reconstruct the local culture of emotion of the specific case, as far as possible, in our example collecting information about genre rules of battle descriptions. I shall thus find that the depiction of anxiety, above all collective anxieties which end in panic, have been placed under a taboo in the battle descriptions of the First World War.[181]

The historian of emotions then goes on 'to find information about emotional constructs, where possible diverging in accordance with rank, religion and ethnicity'.[182] As a second step, he would examine the text of the officer again to discover whether euphemistic language or 'substitution' descriptions are deployed:

> Is the micro-logic of the text disturbed—is there an unexpected change of tempo, does a preposition suddenly appear which does not recur in the rest of the text or does the author upset the logic of his narration? In the event that other texts of the officer are available, the methods of literary criticism could be useful.[183]

There are bound to be gaps in this form of corroboration and reading-between-the-lines, constituting 'an analytical leap': 'But it would be a more transparent leap than that which most historians make when they unknowingly transfer the emotional concepts of their own time to the past and thereby lapse into anachronism.'[184]

This study posits that changes in the sensibilities of conscripts and volunteers, extending well beyond the ranks of the *Bürgertum*, affected the ways in which these soldiers experienced wars. They can be interpreted in part by examining the rules or norms governing expression (in the manner of 'emotionologists' such as Peter

---

[178] J. Bourke, *Fear*, 288.   [179] Ibid.
[180] The instability and impermanence of emotions is one of the three main theses of Ute Frevert, *Vergängliche Gefühle* (Göttingen, 2013), 7.
[181] J. Plamper, *Geschichte und Gefühl. Grundlagen der Emotionsgeschichte* (Munich, 2012), 347.
[182] Ibid.   [183] Ibid.   [184] Ibid., 348.

and Carol Stearns), in part by asking what the role of such language was in social interaction (Ludwig Wittgenstein), and in part by investigating the wider contexts—including exposure to death or the body—in which sensibilities were cultivated and transformed.[185] The study also contends, however, that these changing sensibilities and experiences had a long-term effect, helping to alter the terms of the debate about war. Subsequent volumes explore such effects. This volume investigates the more immediate impact of the first conflicts to involve masses of German conscripts.

[185] P. N. Stearns and C. Z. Stearns, 'Emotionology: Clarifying the History of Emotions and Emotional Standards', *American Historical Review*, 90 (1985), 813–36.

1

From Cabinet Warfare to Mass Armies

Most Prussian and Austrian officers seem to have expected the campaign of 1792, begun by France's declaration of war against Austria on 20 April, to be a 'promenade to Paris', in the words of one French émigré.[1] In the event, the fighting between revolutionary or Napoleonic France and the German states continued, with few interruptions, for the next twenty-three years. Around 5 million Europeans, out of a total population of 190 million (1800), were killed in combat or through war-related diseases. According to one estimate, 2,532,000 soldiers had perished on the battlefield or through wounding, making up more than 5 per cent of men of fighting age.[2]

Historians disagree about the nature, impact, and continuity of such warfare, but few question the fact that it constituted part of a revolutionary threat to the foundations of the Continent's *anciens régimes*, creating the impression or reality of rapidly changing social, economic, and political conditions, and that it menaced the very existence of states, transforming the map of Europe and, via overseas expeditions (Egypt, Syria, and Palestine, 1798–9) and the naval war with Britain (1793–1802, 1803–14/15), the wider world.[3] French revolutionaries and their allies had created the Batavian Republic from the United Provinces, Belgium from the Austrian Netherlands, the Helvetic Republic from Switzerland, the Roman Republic from the Papal states, the Cisalpine Republic from Habsburg possessions in north-eastern Italy, and the Parthenopean Republic from the mainland section of the Kingdom of the Two Sicilies. Their Napoleonic successors had annexed Belgium, the left bank of the Rhine, Nice, Liguria, and parts of Piedmont; they had replaced the Helvetic Republic with the Helvetic Confederation and the Republic of the Valais; they had established the Kingdom of Italy—of which Napoleon was made king—from the northern territories of Parma, Piedmont, Modena, Lombardy, and Venice; and they had created the Grand Duchy of

---

[1] T. C. W. Blanning, *The Pursuit of Glory: The Five Revolutions That Made Modern Europe, 148–1815* (London, 2007), 639.

[2] J. S. Goldstein, *Long Cycles: Prosperity and War in the Modern Age* (New Haven, 1988), 236–7. On the contentious nature of the figures, see Owen Connelly, 'The First Total War: Napoleon's Europe and the Birth of Warfare as We Know It', *The Journal of Military History*, 71 (2007), 920–1.

[3] See Maps 1 and 2. For a summary of historiographical differences of opinion, see R. Pröve, *Militär, Staat und Gesellschaft im Neunzehnten Jahrhundert* (Munich, 2006). On 'world war', see S. Förster, 'The First World War: Global Dimensions of Warfare in the Age of Revolutions', in R. Chickering and S. Förster (eds), *War in an Age of Revolutions, 1775–1815* (Cambridge, 2010), 101–16.

Warsaw, after the 'third partition' of Poland had divided the rump state between Prussia, Russia, and the Habsburg monarchy on 24 October 1795.

The German states, in particular, were profoundly and increasingly affected by the revolutionary and Napoleonic campaigns, with southern Germany subjected to a series of invasions, culminating in the *annus horribilis* of 1796. The Habsburg monarchy was at war with France between 1792 and 18 October 1797 (Treaty of Campo Formio), following Bonaparte's and Masséna's victories in northern Italy and their march to Vienna during the previous year, and between 1798 and 1801 under the auspices of the Second Coalition, which effectively collapsed with the Treaty of Lunéville on 9 February 1801 after Austrian defeats at Marengo (14 June 1800) and Hohenlinden (3 December 1800). Austria went to war again in 1805, 1809, 1813, and 1815, and Prussia in 1806–7 and 1812–15. The German territories on the left bank of the Rhine were annexed at the Congress of Rastatt in March 1798; on the right bank, 110 Reich cities and ecclesiastical and other small states were mediatized and secularized in accordance with the Franco-Russian scheme of 'compensation' worked out in June 1802, with 3 million subjects being assigned to another ruler. The same states—the new Kingdoms of Bavaria, Saxony, and Württemberg, and the Grand Duchy of Baden—were enlarged again, alongside the Napoleonic creations of the Kingdom of Westphalia and the Grand Duchy of Berg, after the dissolution of the Holy Roman Empire and the founding of the Confederation of the Rhine in 1806. Menaced or coerced by Napoleonic armies, the patchwork of German principalities within the Reich had been replaced forever by the larger states, which either became French vassals within the *Rheinbund* or which were dismembered or badly weakened. Prussia was forced to give up about half of its territory to Saxony, the Kingdom of Westphalia, and the Grand Duchy of Warsaw by the Treaty of Tilsit in July 1807. At Pressburg in December 1805, the Habsburg monarchy lost the Tyrol to Bavaria and Venetia to the Kingdom of Italy; at Schönbrunn in October 1809, it ceded Salzburg to Bavaria, Trieste, and part of Croatia to France, Tarnopol to Russia, and West Galicia to the Grand Duchy of Warsaw. The French wars had destroyed the majority of German states and brought most of the rest to the brink of collapse.

The effects of military conflict varied dramatically over time and in space, influencing contemporaries' experiences and conceptions of warfare. Austria saw its fortunes wax and wane in a succession of conflicts, having already been embroiled in a war—in support of Russia—against the Ottoman Empire between 1787 and 1790, which had subsequently triggered a successful secessionist revolt in the Austrian Netherlands (Belgium): Archduke Karl pushed the French, who had advanced to Bavaria, back across the Rhine in 1796, before failing to arrest their march through Italy, much of which was ceded to France, in 1797; Austrian troops under the command of Aleksandr Suvorov pursued the French across northern Italy to the Alps in 1799, only to be defeated in Italy by Napoleon's armies in 1800; Habsburg—and Russian—forces were quickly vanquished in 1805, but they inflicted early defeats in 1809 and helped to provoke an uprising against France and Bavaria in the Tyrol, which lasted until November; finally, Austrian armies played a decisive role in defeating Napoleon in 1813–14, having been at war for seventeen of the twenty-eight years between 1787 and 1815. By contrast, Prussia enjoyed an unprecedented period of peace, compared to the regular conflicts of the eighteenth century, between 1795 and 1806, followed by a disastrous defeat at Jena and Auerstädt, a precarious existence between French and Russian forces until 1812, victory at Leipzig in October 1813, and two successful advances to Paris in 1814 and 1815. For their part, southern and central German lands served as a battleground or billet for Coalition and French forces between 1792 and 1800, 1805 and 1806, and 1812 and 1815, with the Rhenish lands subjected to French hegemony by the Treaty of Campo Formio (1797) and with most princi-palities of the Reich made the object of French and Russian compensation by the Treaty of Lunéville (1801), before the surviving regimes became vassal states in 1806. Baden, Bavaria, Saxony, Württemberg, and other states were required to send soldiers to Spain in 1808 and to Russia in 1812, and they fought alongside France against Austria in 1805 and 1809, against Prussia in 1806–7, and against both in 1813.[4]

Witnesses gave different accounts of such conflicts, depending on where they were, when they were writing, whether they were civilians or soldiers, officers or from the rank and file, in the standing army, volunteer units or militia, noble or *bürgerlich*, urban or rural, young or old, revolutionary or not. The following chap-ters attempt to make sense of their contradictory testimony by assessing the extent to which warfare and armies had changed between 1792 and 1815, by investigat-ing how far conflicts were perceived to be 'national' or 'patriotic', by evaluating the impact of wars on civilians, and by examining the effects of combat on soldiers.

'TOTAL WAR' AND 'MILITARY REVOLUTION'

In the wake of Jena and Auerstädt in 1806, reform-minded Prussian officers like Gerhard Johann David von Scharnhorst and Hermann von Boyen regularly criti-cized the old system, which they held to be partly responsible for the kingdom's defeat.[5] To August von Gneisenau, later Quartermaster-General and a staff officer of the Prussian commander Prince Friedrich Ludwig Hohenlohe in 1806, Berlin had failed to 'awaken the common mood in Germany' of 'disgust against French oppression', which could have created 'a new Vendée' for the Napoleonic regime; instead, it had maintained the separation of military and national affairs, allowing South Germans to remain disinterested bystanders and obliging 'only a fraction of

---

[4] On the succession of wars, see H. v. Brandt (ed.), *Aus dem Leben des Generals der Infanterie z. D. Dr Heinrich von Brandt* (Berlin, 1868), vol. 1; F. M. Kircheisen, *Wider Napoleon! Ein deutsches Reiterleben 1806–1815* (Stuttgart, 1911), 2 vols; G. Muhl, *Denkwürdigkeiten aus dem Leben des Freiherrn C. R. von Schäffer* (Pforzheim, 1840); L. v. Wollzogen, *Memoiren* (Leipzig, 1851); W. v. Conrady (ed.), *Aus stürmischer Zeit. Ein Soldatenleben vor hundert Jahren* (Berlin, 1907); J. Schrafel, *Merkwürdige Schicksale des ehemaligen Feldwebels im königl. Bayer. 5ten Linien-Infanterie-Regiment* (Nuremberg, 1834), 44.

[5] K. Breitenhorn and J. H. Ulbricht (eds), *Jena and Auerstedt: Ereignis und Erinnerung in europäischer, nationaler und regionaler Perspektive* (Dössel, 2006).

the nation (*Nation*) to take up arms'.[6] The detachment of the army from civilian society was made worse by 'our system of recruitment, with all its exemptions', and Prussia's long period of military service, which necessitated strict discipline to keep unwilling soldiers in check, but which also permitted troops to marry, engendering homesickness and other burdens during long campaigns.[7] What was more, Prussia's artillery and weapons were in a 'poor state', its many soldiers were sent home untrained in accordance with an antiquated system of leave (*Beurlaubungssystem*), and its generals were marked out by their 'incapacity'.[8] The age of Duke Karl Wilhelm Ferdinand von Braunschweig, who had turned 71 on the eve of the battle of Auerstädt, left him with 'the indecision so characteristic of his years', aggravated by the 'disunity of the doyens of the General Staff'.[9] 'In summary, our self-conceit...does not let us keep up with the times', Gneisenau concluded.[10] The impression which he and other reformers gave was that Prussia's military system, widely thought to be the most advanced of its kind during the eighteenth century, had fallen behind the more flexible, national system of France by the 1800s.

Prompted by French victories and the expansion of French power, it seemed, in the language of the time, that *Fürstenkriege* and *Staatenkriege*, or princely and state wars, had been superseded by *Volkskriege*, or wars of the people or nation.[11] Later, in the mid-nineteenth century, the term 'cabinet war' (*Kabinettskrieg*), which has subsequently been adopted by the majority of historians, came to describe the supposed shift from the regular, limited, aristocratic conflicts of the eighteenth century to momentous, unconstrained wars of 'annihilation' during and after the French Revolution. The term derived from the councils or cabinets of generals and ministers, which were meant to guide the monarch as the nominal commander-in-chief of the army. It became synonymous with the concealed war aims, secret diplomacy, and self-serving nepotism of cliques of nobles surrounding the ruler. Even in Prussia, where a noble warrior caste had been created over the previous century and a half as a functional, state-serving elite, the structure of command had become opaque, indecisive, and top-heavy, wrote the young officer Carl von Clausewitz to his fiancée on 29 September 1806, a fortnight before the battle of Jena: it was possible to comprehend the difficulties facing Scharnhorst, his mentor and actual commander in 1806,

> if one realizes that *three* commanders-in-chief and *two* chiefs of staff serve with the army, though only *one* commander and *one* chief of staff ought to be there. ... How much must the effectiveness of a gifted man be reduced when he is constantly confronted by obstacles of convenience and tradition, when he is paralyzed by constant friction with the opinions of others.[12]

---

[6] A. W. A. N. v. Gneisenau, 'Über den Krieg von 1806', in G. Förster and C. Gudzent (eds), *August Wilhelm Anton Neidhardt von Gneisenau. Ausgewählte militärische Schriften* (East Berlin, 1984), 50.

[7] Ibid., 50–1.   [8] Ibid.   [9] Ibid., 50.   [10] Ibid., 51.

[11] See N. Buschmann, C. Mick, and I. Schierle, 'Kriegstypen: Begriffsgeschichtliche Bilanz in deutschen, russischen und sowjetischen Lexika', and F. Göse, 'Kabinettskrieg', in D. Beyrau, M. Hochgeschwender, and D. Langewiesche (eds), *Formen des Krieges* (Paderborn, 2007), 24–5, 121–47.

[12] C. v. Clausewitz to M. v. Brühl, 29 Sept. 1806, cited in P. Paret, *Clausewitz and the State*, new edn (Princeton, 1985), 124.

With hindsight, cabinet wars seemed to have been characterized by relatively small standing armies, which had been deployed often but for specific purposes, as an extension of dynastic and commercial policy. Their use relied on the emergence of a more or less stable international order of consolidated states, within the 'Westphalian system' after 1648, and those states' gradual monopolization of violence at home during the seventeenth and eighteenth centuries (see Map 1 for the continuing patchwork of states in Central Europe). 'The times are over', remarked Helmuth von Moltke, the Elder, in his history of the Franco-German war of 1870–1, 'when small armies of professional soldiers were deployed for dynastic ends, in order to conquer a city or a stretch of land, and then returned to their winter quarters or signed a peace'.[13] In effect, standing armies had become the instrument of dynastic states, or 'absolutist' ones, in the common nineteenth-century cognate of 'cabinet wars', removing warfare, with its attendant risk of rebellion, from 'civilian' (*bürgerlich*) life. Ideally, suggested Friedrich II, the civilian population should not notice that the state was at war at all.[14]

Reacting to the blood-letting of the Thirty Years' War (1618–48), which had combined the large-scale combat and levels of killing of a religiously inspired civil war and the constant fighting of a state of baronial anarchy, monarchs had harnessed the new potential of their centralizing states, tying aristocracies to the royal court, in the manner of Louis XIV, and to the officer corps of standing armies, which were used to quash opposition to royal power.[15] Conflicts were frequent in the eighteenth century, occurring every two to three years on average and blurring the distinction between war and peace, but they were less bloody than in the early seventeenth century, with the warring parties relying on an established system of Great Powers and a shared aristocratic code of honour to regulate conduct and bring wars to an end.[16] Whereas states had failed to control the violence of noble retinues, popular revolt, and religious conflict in the century after 1559, they had managed to do so by a variety of means—most notably by increasing tax revenue, disbursing favours to a court aristocracy, expanding administration, and creating standing armies with noble officers and mercenary, foreign, or dragooned troops—after that date.[17] Partly because of their domestic role as a police force and partly because of the cost of equipment and, especially, replacement soldiers, standing armies seemed increasingly to have concentrated on manoeuvring, informed by the enlightened 'science' of warfare, and on protecting elaborate supply lines, needed for a system of fortifications, sieges, artillery, and other weaponry, rather than on battles. 'Why risk battle?' the Duke of Brunswick (Braunschweig) asked the French envoy from Paris, whose offer of the command of French forces in January 1792 he had just turned down in favour of a similar invitation from Prussia:

---

[13] H. v. Moltke, *Geschichte des Deutsch-französischen Krieges von 1870–71* (Berlin, 1891), cited in F. Göse, 'Kabinettskrieg', 123.

[14] K. J. Holsti, *Peace and War: Armed Conflicts and International Order, 1648–1989* (Cambridge, 1991), 103.

[15] A. Gat, *War in Human Civilization* (Oxford, 2006), 665–6.

[16] On the frequency and limitation of warfare, see K. J. Holsti, *Peace and War*, 84–7.

[17] D. Kaiser, *Politics and War: European Conflict from Philip II to Hitler*, new edn (Cambridge, MA, 2000), 135–41, 197–202.

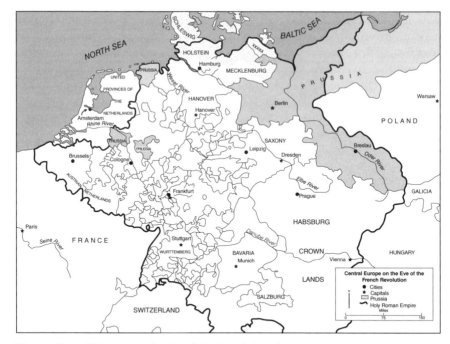

Map 1. Central Europe on the Eve of the French Revolution
Source: J. Sperber (ed.), *Short Oxford History of Germany, 1800–1870* (Oxford, 2004), 286.

If the French are the victors it will ruin us; if they lose they will still have other resources. My plan is to move numerous armies into your border regions, station them there for an extended period, have them take up unassailable positions, and await your defeat from internal troubles and bankruptcy.[18]

A great general, the official Saxon military manual of 1752 had declared, 'shows his mastery by attaining the object of his campaign by sagacious and sure manoeuvres, without incurring any loss'.[19] On the battlefield itself, losses in the most important clashes had already diminished from approximately 15 per cent for the victor and 30 per cent for the vanquished during the Thirty Years' War to 11 and 23 per cent respectively, for the period between 1648 and 1715.[20] Such losses continued to diminish until at least the Wars of the Austrian Succession between 1740 and 1748, in which the fighting was less intense than during the Wars of the Grand Alliance (1689–97) and Spanish Succession (1701–14).[21] Friedrich II, who was famous for contravening many of the mantras of eighteenth-century warfare and forcing his opponents onto the battlefield, conceded that, 'of the five battles which

[18] Cited in P. Paret, *Clausewitz and the State*, 23.
[19] T. C. W. Blanning, *The French Revolutionary Wars, 1787–1802* (London, 1996), 14.
[20] F. Göse, 'Kabinettskrieg', 128–9.
[21] J. S. Goldstein, *Long Cycles: Prosperity and War in the Modern Age* (New Haven, CT, 1988), 236–7.

my troops have joined', there were 'only three which I had planned'.[22] Even these battles, under the circumstances, he saw as a means of conserving men and supplies, asking in 1759 'whether it is not less dangerous to meet the enemy in battle and risk the danger of a small reverse' than to face the losses, through disease, hunger, and desertion, of a prolonged campaign.[23]

The costs and losses of eighteenth-century campaigns were still great, of course, comparable in many respects to those of earlier and later conflicts.[24] In contrast to the seventeenth century, wars became the preserve of the Great Powers in the Westphalian system, with Saxony, Bavaria, Sardinia, Venice, Naples, Holland, and Savoy—and not the myriad of other small states—involved only as minor powers: Russia played a major part in fourteen eighteenth-century wars, Austria and France twelve, Great Britain eleven, Prussia eight, Turkey seven, and Holland and Naples merely two.[25] Yet not all such conflicts were easily contained and, when they did escalate, they were likely to be bloody precisely because the Great Powers were involved. Furthermore, some wars concerned the very survival of states, as the first partition of Poland (1772) had proved, with the potential to break the precarious rules and practices of engagement. Most German contemporaries seem to have distinguished between major and minor wars, with the Thirty Years' War and the Seven Years' War their principal points of reference.[26] Certainly, officers, diplomats, ministers, and rulers—those most responsible for the outbreak of wars—were guided by memories and myths of Friedrich II's struggle for survival—or by Austria's and Saxony's confrontation with Prussia—between 1756 and 1763. For Hermann von Boyen, later Prussian War Minister (1814) and a member of the General Staff in 1806, the problem during the 1790s and 1800s was the gradual disappearance of the idiosyncratic but decisive generals 'from the times of the Seven Years' War' like his own commanding officer, who had barely been able to read and had given briefings in his kitchen, but who had 'maintained a certain independence at grave moments, which can only be won by a profound inner education, not by social forms'.[27] What would happen, Scharnhorst asked his audience at the Berlin *Militärische Gesellschaft*, which he had helped to found in 1802, 'when the men Friedrich II trained during the Seven Years' War are no longer with us?'[28] To such officers, the Prussian king had risked everything in 1756 in a war for the existence of Prussia, countenancing battles, the massing of troops, rapid marches, looting, living off the land, the further professionalization of the officer corps, promotion of commoners, and fuller exploitation of the cantonal

[22] F. Göse, 'Kabinettskrieg', 129.   [23] Ibid., 130.

[24] For the German case, see especially U. Planert, 'Innovation or Evolution?', 69–84; and U. Planert, 'Die Kriege der Französischen Revolution und Napoleons: Beginn einer neuen Ära der europäischen Kriegsgeschichte oder Weiterwirken der Vergangenheit?', in D. Beyrau, M. Hochgeschwender, and D. Langewiesche (eds), *Formen*, 149–62.

[25] K. J. Holsti, *Peace and War*, 84.

[26] On the long shadow cast by the Thirty Years' War into the nineteenth century, see K. Cramer, *The Thirty Years' War and German Memory in the Nineteenth Century* (Lincoln, Nebraska, 2007).

[27] H. v. Boyen, *Denkwürdigkeiten und Erinnerungen 1771–1813* (Stuttgart, 1899), vol. 1, 24–5.

[28] Cited in P. Paret, *Clausewitz and the State*, 67. Also, C. White, *The Enlightened Soldier: Scharnhorst and the 'Militärische Gesellschaft' in Berlin, 1801–1805* (New York, 1989).

system of conscription introduced in the 1730s. As a result, Prussia's army had increased from 39,000 men in 1710 to 260,000 by 1760.[29] The number of fatalities incurred in this perceived fight for survival was greater than that incurred in the revolutionary wars between 1792 and 1802—992,000 compared to 663,000—and the intensity of the fighting, or number of fatalities per head of population, was almost double that of the revolutionary conflicts.[30] With its 'geographical position and lack of natural and artificial defensive means', it seemed to Scharnhorst in April 1806, 'Prussia cannot wage a defensive war.'[31] In such conditions, the risk, cost, and bloodshed of war could appear undiminished and the distinction between civilians and combatants tenuous.

The 'taming' of eighteenth-century warfare, particularly from the point of view of north German onlookers, was less salient than historians have claimed.[32] Nonetheless, Prussian military reformers, most of whom emphasized the speed and all-or-nothing character of Friedrich II's campaigns, also underlined the fact that the Revolutionary and Napoleonic Wars were different in kind from earlier conflicts as a consequence of changes introduced by French regimes. War seemed, in Clausewitz's phrase, to have become 'absolute', transforming the significance of ideology, creating mass armies, giving a greater role to conscripts and public opinion, mobilizing civilian populations and economies, promoting unlimited war aims and wars of 'annihilation' (*Vernichtung*), and compromising moral and legal conventions.[33] Scharnhorst, who had transferred to the Prussian army from Hanover in 1801 and became the principal military reformer after 1806, had already indicated in his well-known essay on 'The Development of the General Causes of the Good Fortune of the French in the Revolutionary War' (Entwicklung der allgmeinen Ursachen des Glucks der Franzosen in dem Revolutionskrieg) of 1797 that the neighbouring state's victories had not been fortuitous: 'The source of the misfortune which struck the allied powers in the French revolutionary war must be deeply interwoven with its internal relationships and with those of the French nation.'[34] Tellingly, he began with the soldiers' new-found, nationally inspired motivation to wage war and ended with questions of military tactics and leadership, as if the former had informed or even produced the latter. In 1807, Scharnhorst was made the chair of the Military Reorganization Commission, created by Friedrich

[29] J. Black, *A Military Revolution? Military Change and European Society, 1550–1800* (Basingstoke, 1991), 7.

[30] J. S. Goldstein, *Long Cycles*, 236–7.

[31] Scharnhorst to E. F. v. Rüchel, 16 Apr. 1806, in P. Paret, *Clausewitz and the State*, 111.

[32] The term 'tamed Bellona' comes from J. Kunisch, 'Von der gezähmten zur entfesselten Bellona. Die Umwertung des Krieges im Zeitalter der Revolutions- und Freiheitskriege', in J. Kunisch (ed.), *Fürst—Gesellschaft—Krieg. Studien zur bellizistischen Disposition des absoluten Fürstenstaates* (Cologne, 1992), although he has himself pointed to important continuities, especially those relating to *kleine Kriege*, which adumbrated the mobility and flexibility of later conflicts; J. Kunisch, *Der kleine Krieg. Studien zum Heerwesen des Absolutismus* (Wiesbaden, 1973).

[33] U. Planert, 'Innovation or Evolution?', 70.

[34] M. Sikora, 'Scharnhorst und die militärische Revolution', in J. Kunisch and H. Münkler (eds), *Die Wiedergeburt des Krieges aus dem Geist der Revolution. Studien zum bellizistischen Diskurs des ausgehenden 18. und beginnenden 19. Jahrhunderts* (Berlin, 1999), 158. Also, M. Sikora, 'Scharnhorst. Lehrer, Stabsoffizier, Reformer', in K.-H. Lutz (ed.), *Reform, Reorganisation, Transformation* (Munich, 2010), 43–64; M. Sikora, 'Aneignung zur Abwehr. Scharnhorst, Frankreich und die preußische Heeresreform', in M. Aust (ed.), *Vom Gegner Lernen* (Frankfurt, 2007), 61–94.

Wilhelm III to investigate every capitulation and to receive reports from every senior officer implicated in Prussia's defeat. Five of the six members—by the end of 1807—were in favour of thoroughgoing change, encouraged by the king's 'Guidelines for the Reorganisation of the Army', drafted in July 1807, which had confirmed that 'it will neither be feasible nor advisable, after the experiences we have had until now, to put the army completely on its old footing after its rebirth'.[35]

Many Prussian officers, however, were opposed. It was 'not to be doubted that our officers still dream ("think" would be to say too much) of a great army on the old footing, and the propertied, the merchant and the farmer can pay and suffer', wrote Barthold Georg Niebuhr in a letter to Heinrich Friedrich Karl vom und zum Stein on 4 January 1808: 'Each limitation is an assault (so says von Kalckreuth).'[36] Initially, Friedrich Wilhelm III had appointed three of his own adjutants to the commission, plus another similar-minded officer, to create a conservative majority, only averted by Scharnhorst's subsequent manoeuvring.[37] Lieutenant-General Julius von Gravert, who was later appointed to command the Prussian forces in the *Grande Armée* in 1812 and whose division had been slaughtered at Jena in 1806 whilst using the traditional tactic of advancing slowly and volley-by-volley, wrote to the king from Breslau in September 1807 that 'the renown which the Prussian army had fought for in the whole of Europe during the Seven Years' War' had only been lost through the softening of the army during too long a peace and by 'the unfortunate revolution in France', which had nurtured ideas, 'especially among the civilian orders' (*Zivilstände*), which 'threatened to overthrow every previously existing order and constitution (*Verfassung*)'.[38] Correctives put forward by Grawert included emergency relief for impoverished officers, who had been falsely accused of a dereliction of duty in 1806, measures against 'immorality', such as the establishment of workhouses, and putting any 'burgher' who impugned the honour of an officer in chains.[39]

Other Prussian officers were more moderate, but remained cautious. Prince August, for instance, submitted a memorandum in June 1807, whilst still a prisoner of war in France, which backed Scharnhorst's proposal to combine infantry, cavalry, and artillery in separate divisions, improving their coordination, and which called for greater speed, partly by relieving soldiers of heavy equipment, better use of sharpshooters—a Prussian invention—and a more flexible system of supply.[40] He also demanded tactical alterations, most notably 'an intelligent combination of line with light infantry' which 'the French were the first to carry

---

[35] Friedrich Wilhelm III, July 1807, in R. Vaupel (ed.), *Die Reorganisation des Preussischen Staates unter Stein und Hardenberg* (Leipzig, 1938), part 2, vol. 1, 8.

[36] Cited in G. H. Pertz, *Das Leben des Ministers Freiherrn vom Stein* (Berlin, 1849–55), vol. 2, 82–4.

[37] P. Paret, *The Cognitive Challenge of War: Prussia, 1806* (Princeton, 2009), 86.

[38] J. v. Grawert memorandum, 27 Sept. 1807, in R. Vaupel (ed.), *Die Reorganisation*, part 2, vol. 1, 108–9.

[39] Ibid., 108–19.

[40] For the broader context, see D. Showalter, 'Weapons and Ideas in the Prussian Army from Frederick the Great to Moltke the Elder', in J. A. Lynn (ed.), *Tools of War: Instruments, Ideas and Institutions of Warfare, 1445–1871* (Chicago, 1990), 177–210.

out…on a large scale', securing 'important advantages', but he stopped short of fundamental 'French' innovations requiring greater independence and motivation on the part of nationally inspired troops: 'In modern times one generally cannot expect great results from patriotism. …In nearly all contemporary wars love of honour and ambition have been a greater influence and have often replaced enthusiasm or patriotism.'[41] In Vienna, Archduke Karl had arrived at a similar conclusion a decade earlier, in his treatise *Über den Krieg gegen die Neufranken* (1795): 'How was it possible that a well-equipped, balanced, disciplined army had been defeated by an enemy with raw troops, lacking cavalry, and with inexperienced generals?' His answer, like August's, concentrated narrowly on strategic and tactical questions: Austria had fought a defensive war, it had been preoccupied with its lines of supply, and it had fragmented and dispersed its forces in an easily punctured cordon of defence.[42] Although aware of military reforms carried out by Austria, after defeat in 1805, officers and ministers in other German states had fewer reasons and less opportunity, given the swingeing nature of French demands for money and troops from its allies in the Confederation of the Rhine, to implement changes on the Prussian model. They were, however, required to fit into Napoleon's military system, which—in former ecclesiastical territories, small principalities, and city-states—meant the imposition of military service for the first time.[43]

The scholarly debate about a metamorphosis of warfare during the revolutionary and Napoleonic periods rests on two connected controversies: one concerning a 'military revolution' and the other, 'total war'. The dispute about a 'revolution' has centred on a series of claims by historians of the early modern era that changes in military technology—either the introduction of muskets (Michael Roberts) or the construction of fortifications and new types of artillery (Geoffrey Parker)—required increases in the size of European armies and necessitated higher taxation and a larger state, with the greatest changes taking place in the first century or so of the period between 1500 and 1800.[44] Roberts contends that Gustavus Adolphus introduced linear formations of infantry with guns during the Thirty Years' War, in conjunction with more aggressive cavalry charges, which, in turn, pointed to the need for better-trained, more disciplined soldiers and a new system of drill, uniforms, and standing armies.[45] Parker extends and modifies Roberts's thesis, identifying the invention of new artillery fortifications in early sixteenth-century Italy (the *trace italienne*) as the cause of a shift towards defensive wars, sieges, and

---

[41] Prince August of Prussia, 'Vorschläge zur Verbesserung der preussischen Militair-Verfassung', 13 June 1807, in P. Paret, *Yorck and the Era of Prussian Reform, 1807–1815* (Princeton, 1966), 126–7.

[42] Cited in T. C. W. Blanning, *The Pursuit of Glory*, 639.

[43] U. Planert, 'Innovation or Evolution?', 75.

[44] A. N. Liaropoulos, 'Revolutions in Warfare: Theoretical Paradigms and Historical Evidence—The Napoleonic and First World War Revolutions in Military Affairs', *Journal of Military History*, 70 (2006), 366: the dispute about a 'revolution in military affairs' has been complicated, despite agreement about the occurrence of 'a radical change or some form of discontinuity in the history of warfare', in the words of one recent commentator, by a lack of 'consensus regarding how and when these changes or discontinuities take place, or what causes them'.

[45] M. Roberts, 'The Military Revolution, 1560–1660', in M. Roberts, *Essays on Swedish History* (Minneapolis, 1967), 195–225. See also C. J. Rogers (ed.), *The Military Revolution Debate* (Boulder, CO, 1995).

increased garrisons.[46] The 'culmination' of this revolution was purportedly the mid-eighteenth century, followed by innovations deriving from 'small wars' (*kleine Kriege*) such as light infantry and cavalry, the formation of self-contained divisions, the advent of standardized and mobile artillery, and—during the French Revolution—further increases in the size of armies: 'The scale of warfare was so totally transformed that it might be said that another "military revolution" had occurred.'[47] Parker's claim coincides with that of Peter Paret, alluding to the stand-ardization of parts for artillery under Jean-Baptiste Vaquette, comte de Gribeauval, and the formation of divisions under Victor-François de Broglie, following France's defeat at the battle of Rossbach in the Seven Years' War: 'The French Revolution coincided with a revolution in war that had been under way through the last dec-ades of the monarchy. Soon the two meshed.'[48] Despite leaving the question open, such changes are generally treated as the end-point of an ongoing military revolution.

More recently, scholars such as Azar Gat have questioned, not the fact that armies expanded and became permanent institutions nor that centralized and powerful monarchies were established in the sixteenth and seventeenth centuries, but that military innovations were largely responsible for the emergence of the modern state.[49] Rather, it is argued, the size of armies depended on the capacity of states to borrow and to raise taxes, which was sometimes accelerated by wars, the production of armament, and the professionalization of armies, but which was also linked to the growth of capitalist economies, the development of more efficient or reliable bureaucracies, and the creation of credit markets and central banks.[50] The implication of Gat's argument is that armies depended on 'modernization'— state-building, commerce, administrative techniques, finances—which continued to take place, often incrementally, in the eighteenth century. 'Contrary to the widely accepted view among scholars, it should be emphasized that revolutionary France was no more able than earlier states in history to keep over one percent of her population under arms for any prolonged period of time', he points out: 'No miracles were performed here. With a population of some 25 million, France

[46] G. Parker, 'The Military Revolution, 1560–1660: A Myth?', *Journal of Modern History*, 48 (1976), 195–214; G. Parker, *The Military Revolution: Military Innovation and the Rise of the West, 1500–1800* (Cambridge, 1988).

[47] Parker, *The Military Revolution*, 153.

[48] P. Paret, 'Napoleon and the Revolution in War', in P. Paret (ed.), *The Makers of Modern Strategy* (Princeton, 1986), 124. Other historians have examined changes in tactics and reorganization in a similar way: J. A. Lynn, *The Bayonets of the Republic: Motivation and Tactics in the Army of Revolutionary France, 1791–1794* (Urbana, IL, 1984); S. Wilkinson, *The French Army before Napoleon* (Aldershot, 1991); J. Black, *Warfare in the Eighteenth Century* (London, 1999), and J. Black, 'Eighteenth-Century Warfare Reconsidered', *War in History*, 1 (1994), 215–32.

[49] A. Gat, 'What Constituted the Military Revolution of the Early Modern Period?', in R. Chickering and S. Förster (eds), *War*, 21–48; M. van Creveld, *Technology and War* (New York, 1991). See also A. Latham, 'War Transformed: A Braudelian Perspective on the Revolution in Military Affairs', *European Journal of International Relations*, 8 (2002), 231–4.

[50] See D. Parrott, 'Strategy and Tactics in the Thirty Years' War: The "Military Revolution"', *Militärgeschichtliche Mitteilungen*, 38 (1985), 7–25; C. Jones, 'The Military Revolution and the Professionalisation of the French Army under the Ancien Régime', in M. Duffy (ed.), *The Military Revolution and the State, 1500–1800* (Exeter, 1980), 29–48; J. Black, *A Military Revolution?*.

reached a peak of 750,000 soldiers in 1794 only at a price of economic mayhem, and numbers fell to around 400,000 the year after, where they remained until the end of the decade.'[51]

Briefly, however, French regimes and those of their opponents did manage to raise unprecedented numbers of troops, albeit comprising a historically comparable percentage of the population. Prussia's troops constituted more than 5 per cent of its total population, although containing many foreigners, during the Seven Years' War (260,000) and 6 per cent, with fewer soldiers from other states and with part of its territory recently occupied by France, in 1813 (280,000).[52] The effort required to levy and support such numbers of soldiers, over a period of twenty-three years of sporadic conflict, has prompted historians like David Bell to label the Napoleonic Wars 'the first total war'.[53] The term, of course, was coined in the interwar era to describe an allegedly complete mobilization of societies' resources for the sake of the war effort. Bell argues that this mobilization was necessarily incomplete in the twentieth century and that the decisive shift towards an attempted mobilization occurred, not in 1914–18, but in 1792–1815. His case rests on four propositions: first, that there was a political dynamic, created by the revolution, towards total engagement and the abandonment of restraint; second, that there was a widespread fear in France of a 'war of extermination', waged by the Coalition, which fostered a demonization of the nation's enemies, including non-combatants, an escalation of French war aims on 'defensive' grounds, and a general radicalization of warfare; third, that it proved difficult to end wars, as their human and political costs and their expected economic and diplomatic benefits multiplied, especially under Napoleon, who was 'the product, master and victim of total war'; and fourth, that 'new understandings of war'—or a 'culture of war', separable from nationalism and revolutionary ideology, although deriving from the 'intellectual transformations of the Enlightenment' and 'the political fermentation of 1789–92'—developed their own momentum and justified more extreme or extensive forms of national sentiment.[54]

It was not the king who wages war on the king, 'not an army against another army, but a people against another people', wrote Clausewitz in 1812, admittedly in an attempt to justify his own desertion from the Prussian to the Russian army, after Friedrich Wilhelm III had decided to provide troops for Napoleon's war

[51] A. Gat, *War in Human Civilization*, 503.

[52] G. A. Craig, *The Politics of the Prussian Army, 1640–1945* (Oxford, 1955), 60.

[53] D. A. Bell, *The First Total War*; R. Weigley, *The Age of Battles: The Quest for Decisive Warfare from Breitenfeld to Waterloo* (Bloomington, IN, 1991), 290; T. C. W. Blanning, *The French Revolutionary Wars*, 101; W. Kruse, *Die Erfindung des modernen Militarismus. Krieg, Militär und bürgerliche Gesellschaft im politischen Diskurs der Französischen Revolution 1789–1799* (Munich, 2003); E. Fehrenbach, 'Die Ideologisierung des Krieges und die Radikalisierung der Französichen Revolution', in D. Langewiesche (ed.), *Revolution und Krieg. Zur Dynamik historischen Wandels seit dem 18. Jahrhundert* (Paderborn, 1989), 57–66.

[54] D. A. Bell, *The First Total War*, 8–9. See William Mulligan's review of Bell's study in *The Journal of Modern History*, 80 (2008), 912. Also, W. Mulligan, 'Total War', *War in History*, 15 (2008), 211–21. On the conflation of the terms 'total war', implying a total mobilization of resources, and 'modern war', resting on 'the fruits of industrialization and technological innovation', see H. Strachan, 'Essay and Reflection', 351.

against Russia.[55] His point was not only that nations demanded new kinds of loyalty, but also that wars had become a 'total phenomenon' or 'a self-contained whole', calling for and vindicating actions which would have been unimaginable in the princes' wars of the past.[56] Although such a conceptual rupture is confused by the anachronistic use of the label 'total war', which suggests a type and degree of economic and ideological mobilization lacking in the 1790s and 1800s, it did produce a new form of warfare, or 'people's wars' (*Volkskriege*), resting on unparalleled levels of popular enthusiasm, participation, and sacrifice: the intensity of fighting—the number and size of battles and the percentage of fatalities—increased progressively between 1803 and 1815, surpassing that of any other external conflict and leaving almost 1 million Frenchmen dead, or approximately 20 per cent of the adult male population.[57] The incidence and depth of popular involvement varied.[58] Nonetheless, the combination of the French Revolution and a perceived war of defence had created new types of national conflict in Europe, even if the revolutionary model was widely misunderstood and its measures—and its opponents' counter-measures—only partially implemented. The conflicts had historical antecedents, but inauspicious ones, recalling the communal violence of civil wars (*Bürgerkriege*), which had been kept separate by eighteenth-century theorists from the more controlled warfare of states.[59] Wars between nations and states, it appeared, had once again assumed some of the characteristics of internal conflicts or 'civil wars'.

THE *LEVÉE EN MASSE* AND CONSCRIPTION

The French *levée en masse* challenged contemporary assumptions about warfare. Although failing to recruit more than half the cohort—even in 1794—and later restricted by Napoleon through the reintroduction of 'substitution' and preferment for the propertied classes, the system had allowed the mobilization of 750,000–800,000 men (1794), after the National Convention had introduced conscription for an additional 300,000 soldiers in February 1793, of which about 75,000 were sent to fight in the Vendée. The French army in 1789 had numbered 180,000, but it had since shrunk as a result of desertion, the departure of foreign troops, and the flight of 60 per cent of active officers—6,000—into exile by the end of 1791. The 80,000 or so Prussians, Austrians, Hessians, and émigrés, who had crossed the French border in mid-August 1792, had met little resistance, taking the fortress of Verdun, the last major defence before Paris, on 2 September. The initial plan, drafted in

[55] C. v. Clausewitz, 'Bekenntnisdenkschrift', in W. Hahlweg (ed.), *Carl von Clausewitz. Schriften, Aufsätze, Studien, Briefe* (Göttingen, 1966), vol. 1, 750.

[56] The first reference comes from C. v. Clausewitz, *On War* (Princeton, 1976), 479; the second from Clausewitz's drafts of *Vom Kriege* from 1807–1812, in W. Hahlweg (ed.), *Clausewitz*, vol. 2, 67.

[57] J. S. Goldstein, *Long Cycles*, 236–7; D. A. Bell, *The First Total War*, 7.

[58] Ute Planert perhaps makes this point most forcefully, drawing on her detailed study of southern Germany, *Der Mythos vom Befreiungskrieg*.

[59] D. Beyrau, M. Hochgeschwender, and D. Langewiesche (eds), *Formen*, 11.

Potsdam in May, had been for a force of 42,000 Prussians to enter France through Luxembourg, with 56,000 Austrians entering through Belgium on its right flank, and about 20,000 Austrians attacking from the Breisgau—of a total force there of 50,000—on its left flank. It had been scaled down as a consequence of internal squabbling, with Vienna and Berlin not wanting to do the other's bidding, but also because of the Coalition's confidence that a smaller army would suffice to capture French fortresses, which was the military planners' main concern. The Allies were shocked, therefore, to be stopped by a superior number of republican troops under General Charles François Dumouriez—64,000, including reserves, against 34,000 Allies, depleted by dysentery—at Valmy on 20 September.[60] As Johann Wolfgang von Goethe, who witnessed the battle, recorded at a much later date, 'the French could not be shifted':

> The greatest consternation spread through the army. Only that morning all they had had in mind was skewering the French and eating them for breakfast. Indeed, it was this unconditional confidence in this army and its commander [the Duke of Brunswick] which had seduced me into joining this perilous expedition. But now everyone kept his own counsel, did not meet the eyes of his comrades, and if he did give tongue, it was only to curse or complain.[61]

Whether or not Goethe's claim that he had foreseen the beginning of 'a new epoch in the history of the world' was coloured by later events, Valmy at once reversed the Allied advance and demonstrated the effectiveness of the rapidly recruited French volunteers, which had been described by *The Times* as 'a very motley group', with 'almost as many women as men, many without arms, and [with] very little provision'.[62] One hundred thousand such volunteers had already reached the front by the spring of 1792, when war had been declared.[63] The French army had swelled to approximately 450,000 by autumn of 1792, falling to 350,000 by the start of 1793, from which a total of about 220,000 were 'effectives'.[64] Such forces far outnumbered those of the Coalition.

The Allies quickly recognized the value of France's numerical superiority, especially when combined with the patriotism of its soldiers, even if many Allied leaders refused to accept the consequences of French levies and conscription.[65] One Prussian observer from Valmy reported:

> The volunteers were not as straight as a die, as were the Prussians, and were not as polished, well-trained or skilled in handling a gun or marching in step; nor did they

---

[60] T. C. W. Blanning, *The French Revolutionary Wars*, 73–9. On the unpreparedness of the Hessian troops in 1794, see C. C. Zimmermann, *Geschichte des 1. Grossherzoglich Hessischen Dragoner-Regiments* (Darmstadt, 1878), 27.

[61] J. W. v. Goethe, 'Campagne in Frankreich' (1819–22); T. C. W. Blanning, *The French Revolutionary Wars*, 78.

[62] *The Times*, 10 Sept. 1792, in D. A. Bell, *The First Total War*, 131.

[63] T. C. W. Blanning, *The French Revolutionary Wars*, 85.

[64] The figures are inevitably estimates, because of the discrepancy between numbers on paper and in the field, T. C. W. Blanning, *The Pursuit of Glory*, 627.

[65] See, for instance, F. v. Varnbuler, *Beitrag zur Geschichte des Feldzugs vom Jahr 1796 in besonderer Rücksicht auf das schwäbische Korps* (Altona, 1797). More generally, see H. Händel, *Der Gedanke der allgemeinen Wehrpflicht in der Wehrverfassung des Königreiches Preußen bis 1819* (Frankfurt, 1962).

know how to tighten their belts around their tunics as the Prussians did, yet they were devoted to the cause they served in body and soul…Nearly all those I encountered at that time knew for whom and for what they were fighting and declared that they were ready to die for the good of their *patrie*.[66]

The poor training and equipment of French troops, and the difficulties of integrating volunteers in the standing army of the *ancien régime* and of coordinating new divisions—usually only 5,000 or so strong instead of the intended 15,000—meant that revolutionary armies often lost when their numbers were equal, but they won when they enjoyed a numerical advantage, which they regularly did. As a consequence of poor training and inexperience, revolutionary armies were less consistently victorious than Napoleonic ones, losing at Neerwinden in March 1792, Mainz in July 1793, and Kaiserslauten three times in 1793–4, but also— critically—winning at Valmy, Jemappes in November 1792 and Fleurus in June 1794, so that France's wars were, after 1792, conducted abroad rather than at home. In the border region of Baden, Wilhelm, one of the Margrave's sons, recounted that the 1790s had been characterized by flight from, and fear of, approaching armies, usually—in 1793, 1796, and 1799—French ones.[67] The early threat of defeat in 1792 seemed to have galvanized the French population and its revolutionary government, altering war-planners' expectations of combat. Scharnhorst wrote in 1797,

> The terrible position the French found themselves in, surrounded by several armies which sought (or so they believed) to enslave and condemn them to eternal misery, inspired the soldier with courage, induced the citizen to make voluntary sacrifices, gathered supplies for the army and attracted the civilian population to the colours.[68]

In a defensive and patriotic war, France had been able to recruit greater numbers of troops than its opponents, which—despite the initial scepticism of Allied commanders—had gone on to make a decisive difference in the revolutionary wars. 'Reduced to the defensive, we are continually harassed on two flanks of our positions in Flanders and on the Sambre by innumerable hordes who are in fact constantly defeated and repulsed,' lamented the Austrian leader Franz Maria von Thugut in 1794, 'but our army is vastly weakened by these partial victories while the enemy repairs its losses with the greatest ease.'[69] Although Bonaparte's later boast that he could afford 30,000 casualties per battle was an exaggeration, with the republican army's notional strength of 434,235 in 1799 concealing a deployable force of 181,000 once Allied, interior, expeditionary, and absent troops had been subtracted, France certainly proved able in the 1790s and 1800s to field and replace a larger number of soldiers than its enemies.

---

[66] Cited in T. C. W. Blanning, *The French Revolutionary Wars*, 87.
[67] Wilhelm Markgraf v. Baden, *Denkwürdigkeiten* ed. K. Obser, (Heidelberg, 1906), vol. 1, 2–15. Given Wilhelm's age, born in 1792, this early account was clearly influenced by other family sources.
[68] G. v. Scharnhorst, 'Entwicklung der allgemeinen Ursachen des Glücks der Franzosen in den Revolutionskriegen', *Neues militairisches Journal*, 8 (1797): the translation here is from T. C. W. Blanning, *The Pursuit of Glory*, 640.
[69] K. A. Roider, *Baron Thugut and Austria's Response to the French Revolution* (Princeton, 1987), 153–4.

German states' reaction to the *levée en masse* was slow and uneven.[70] Prussia had ended its war with France through the Peace of Basle on 16 May 1795 and had done little to reform its army before defeat at Jena and Auerstädt in 1806. The majority of middling and small states, although formally at war under the aegis of the Holy Roman Empire with its contingent of 40,000, continued to maintain smaller armies in the 1790s than they had had in 1700.[71] Attempts to introduce conscription and to organize militias failed.[72] Principalities such as the Electorates of Mainz and Cologne, with their 'armies' of 3,000 and 1,700, respectively, were mocked by Prussian observers for providing soldiers suitable merely for accompanying Corpus Christi processions.[73] Vienna's main response to France before defeat at Austerlitz on 2 December 1805, given that the cantonal system introduced by Joseph II in 1786 remained a dead letter because of exemptions (clerics, nobles, notables, officials, transport workers, miners, workers in manufacturing, artisans and apprentices, peasants owning land), was to pressure St Petersburg to enter the war and to redeploy its existing forces.[74] Its hopes of Russian support were dashed when the Tsarina, Catherine, who had just agreed to enter the conflict, died in 1796. The Foreign Minister Thugut in December 1796 wrote to Franz de Colloredo-Waldsee, the *Kabinettsminister* since 1792:

> Your Excellency can easily sense the incalculable consequences that could result from this fatal event, and in what embarrassment we might find ourselves in the midst of the great changes that might result: without an army, without finances, and with all of the internal disorder in the bureaucracy.[75]

Russia entered the war on 1 March 1799, after the formation of the Second Coalition in December 1798, too late to prevent the humiliating defeat of Austria in northern Italy in 1796–7. Left on its own in 1796, the Habsburg monarchy attempted, not to recruit more troops, but to move 25,000 of Field Marshal Dagobert Sigismund Wurmser's troops from Germany to Italy in order to stop Bonaparte's and Masséna's advance. When French forces continued to move across northern Italy, in spite of reverses, the most common Austrian retort, lamented Thugut, was 'the cry of all our marshals and the War Ministry that all is lost, that we are absolutely at the end of our rope, and that all that remains for us to do is to surrender'.[76] The Foreign Minister was more optimistic when Austria went back to war in 1799, after losing its Italian territories through the Treaty of Campo Formio (1797), but his feelings were not shared, in the absence of increased recruitment

---

[70] See R. Wohlfeil, *Vom stehenden Heer des Absolutismus zur Allgemeinen Wehrpflicht 1789–1814* (Munich, 1979).

[71] T. C. W. Blanning, *The Pursuit of Glory*, 608: Saxony disposed of 27,000 troops in 1702 and 22,900 in 1790, Hanover 18,000 and 17,000, respectively, and Bavaria 27,000 and 15,750 (despite the fact that the Elector of Bavaria had inherited the Palatinate in the meantime).

[72] M. Rowe, *From Reich to State*, 161. On militias, see U. Planert, 'Innovation or Evolution?', 74.

[73] M. Rowe, *From Reich to State*, 161. See also Wilhelm von Eberhardt's mockery of the '*Ländchen*' of Anhalt in M. v. Eberhardt (ed.), *Aus Preussens schwerer Zeit. Briefe und Aufzeichnungen meines Urgrossvaters und Grossvaters* (Berlin, 1907), 127.

[74] U. Planert, *Der Mythos*, 390.

[75] F. M. v. Thugut to F. de Colloredo-Waldsee, 10 Dec. 1796, K. A. Roider, *Baron Thugut*, 228.

[76] F. M. v. Thugut to F. de Colloredo-Waldsee, 21 July 1796, ibid., 213.

and army reform, by military commanders, as Karl von Schwarzenberg confided to his wife from the army's headquarters during a ceasefire in 1800: 'I still hope that we are not so utterly senseless as to start [fighting] again, especially with our means in even worse condition than at the time we felt compelled to renew a less than honourable armistice.'[77] Little over one month later, on 3 December 1800, Habsburg forces—under the command of an 18-year-old Archduke Johann, after Archduke Karl had refused to countenance what he predicted would be the inevitable destruction of the army—were routed at the battle of Hohenlinden and Austria was compelled to sue for peace.

The territories annexed by France and the states of the Confederation of the Rhine were forced to expand their armies before Austria or Prussia.[78] The revolutionary authorities, which controlled the left bank of the Rhine from the end of 1794 onwards, had elected not to impose conscription on the 'liberated' Rhinelanders and they had been unsuccessful in attracting volunteers, with Mont-Tonnerre (containing Mainz, Worms, and Speyer) furnishing a mere fifty-seven recruits in the first half of 1799, for instance, out of a population of 400,000. The attempt to establish a 'Legion of North Franks' in July 1799 was little more effective, counting approximately 2,000 volunteers at its height, including Belgians and others, and experiencing 1,800 desertions.[79] Formal annexation after the Peace of Lunéville (1801), however, permitted the introduction of conscription in 1802 and a rapid increase in recruitment in the Rhineland, with all those between 20 and 25 years old classified as 'conscripts'.[80] By 1810, the Rhineland was providing 5,554 conscripts per year, which was 42 per cent higher than the average for France as a whole, and amounted to 80,000 soldiers between 1802 and 1815 from a population of 1.6 million, or about 30 per cent of the eligible age groups, rising to almost 60 per cent in 1813.[81]

The states of the *Rheinbund* experienced a similar fate after 1806, going on to contribute approximately 190,000 troops in 1812 to Napoleon's armies.[82] In the 1790s, officials of the *Reich* had noted, in Württemberg and elsewhere, that 'the proclivity of subjects against the institution of a land's militia' was 'so great that they do not hesitate to voice their view openly'.[83] Yet such subjects were obliged to comply with the gradual introduction of conscription in the 1800s. In Baden, conscription for all those up to 30 years of age replaced a cantonal system in 1808–9, increasing the state's contingent from 6,550 to 8,000, then to 10,000 men; a new

---

[77] K. v. Schwarzenberg to his wife, 23 Oct. 1800, K. A. Roider, *Baron Thugut*, 357.

[78] J. Smets, 'Von der "Dorfidylle" zur preußischen Nation. Sozialdisziplinierung der linksrheinischen Bevölkerung durch die Franzosen am Beispiel der allgemeinen Wehrpflicht (1802–1814)', *Historische Zeitschrift*, 262 (1996), 695–738.

[79] M. Rowe, *From Reich to State*, 163–5.

[80] Wilhelm Göbbel, writing to his family on 14 July 1812, *Kriegsbriefe* Archive, Universitäts- und Landesbibliothek Bonn, gives a good impression of what such service was like, commenting simply that he was now a servant of a major, which meant that he had to clean his clothes and 'write French, which I really like doing'.

[81] M. Rowe, *From Reich to State*, 168.

[82] The figures rose from 63,000 in 1806 and 119,000 in 1809; T. C. W. Blanning, *The Pursuit of Glory*, 668.

[83] Cited in U. Planert, *Der Mythos*, 400–1.

conscription law in July 1812 ended most exemptions—nobles, civil servants, the educated, and commercial middle classes—in order to meet French demands for troops during the Russian and German wars in 1812–13, at the end of which the Badenese contingent was 16,000, supplemented by 10,000 men in the *Landwehr*, which had been formed in 1813 to match similar measures in Prussia.[84] Württemberg was asked to supply France with 6,300 soldiers by the terms of Friedrich's alliance with Napoleon in October 1805, and 12,000 troops, from an expanded territory and population, on entry into the *Rheinbund* in 1806, obliging the government to tighten the recruitment law of 1803, which had specified for the first time that all male subjects had a duty to serve in the army. Those liable for military service—eight years in the infantry, twelve in the cavalry during wartime—were not allowed to leave Württemberg and, in the case of evasion, they were stripped of political and legal rights, including the right of inheritance. Fathers could be punished in the absence of their sons. For its part, Bavaria had to provide 30,000 soldiers—double the number of its troops in 1790—for the French army as a condition of entering the Confederation of the Rhine, rising to 62,000 men in arms by 1809; 33,000 Bavarian troops were dispatched to the *Grande Armée* in 1812, from which only 3,000 returned, and a further 30,000 had to be found by the summer of 1813 in order to help Napoleon stop the advance of Prussia, Russia, and Austria in Saxony. Such levies went well beyond Napoleon's pledge, over dinner with the Grand Duke of Baden in 1806, to make 'the princes learn to defend their own lands'.[85]

Partly because of its long military tradition, impressing even Napoleon 'with the ancient glory' of its army (in Charles-Maurice de Talleyrand's estimation), Prussia had done little to expand its forces during the years of peace after 1795 in order to meet the French challenge.[86] With Saxony—disposing of 20,000 troops—as its sole ally, the Hohenzollern monarchy went to war in 1806 with an army of 245,000 men, half of them foreign mercenaries, and a field army of only 140,000, once Anton Wilhelm von L'Estocq's defensive contingent in East Prussia and garrison and depot troops were deducted.[87] The Napoleonic army, re-formed in the years of relative peace between 1801 and 1803, consisted of 265 infantry battalions, 322 cavalry squadrons, and 202 batteries of artillery, or about 300,000 men, supplemented by 63,000 troops from the states of the *Rheinbund*;[88] 160,000 French troops advanced to Saxony from Bayreuth and Bamberg in three columns in early October 1806. By 1807, after the remnants of the Prussian army had retreated to East Prussia to join the two Russian armies—with 90,000 troops in total—reconstituted from the defeated Russo-Austrian forces of Austerlitz (2 December 1805), the French army of observation in Germany and the *Grande Armée* in Poland—including foreign

[84] Ibid., 409–19; P. Saurer, *Napoleons Adler über Württemberg, Baden und Hohenzollern. Südwestdeutschland in der Rheinbundzeit* (Stuttgart, 1987), 110–33, 255–306.

[85] Wilhelm Markgraf v. Baden, *Denkwürdigkeiten*, vol. 1, 36.

[86] M. V. Leggiere, 'From Berlin to Leipzig: Napoleon's Gamble in North Germany, 1813', *Journal of Military History*, 67 (2003), 82.

[87] G. E. Rothenberg, *The Napoleonic Wars* (London, 1999), 96.

[88] C. J. Esdaile, *Napoleon's Wars: An International History* (London, 2007), 164.

troops—numbered 400,000, from a European total of 600,000.[89] Although many Prussian officers had forecast victory in 1806, with Gebhardt Leberecht von Blücher promising 'One successful battle, and allies, money and supplies are ours from every corner of Europe', Napoleon himself could barely believe in September that Berlin would declare war, given the balance of forces: 'The idea that Prussia could take me on single-handed is too absurd to merit discussion. . . . She will go on acting as she has acted—arming today, disarming tomorrow, standing by, sword in hand, while the battle is fought, and then making terms with the victor.'[90] The actual disposition of forces on the battlefields of Jena and Auerstädt on 14 October was more equal than such figures would suggest, with Napoleon commanding 55,600 at the former—with a further 40,300 ready to join in the early afternoon—against Hohenlohe's 40,000 men, and with Louis Nicolas Davout leading a corps of 27,300 against Brunswick's 50,000 retreating troops at the latter. Jean-Baptiste Bernadotte's force of 20,000 had been ordered to join whichever battle was nearest but remained suspended between both, and Ernst von Rüchel's 15,000 troops, who had been defending Weimar, arrived at Jena too late, during the afternoon. Together, therefore, France's battlefield forces numbered 143,200 and Prussia's 105,000. Arguably, however, the more important figure for the campaign as a whole, if Brunswick's army had not collapsed in the face of a force half of its size at the battle of Auerstädt, concerned the pool of trained replacement troops. Here, France enjoyed a clear advantage.

Prussian military reformers recognized France's numerical superiority in 1806 and took steps to increase the size of the kingdom's army. Such increases were prohibited by the Convention of Paris in September 1808, which limited the Prussian army to 42,000 troops for the next ten years at the same time as reallocating half of Prussia's territory to Saxony, Westphalia, and the Grand Duchy of Warsaw. To an extent, the provisions of the convention were circumvented, in spite of the French occupation of Prussia, allowing the early release of trained soldiers, whose records were kept, and the training of the next cohort. By August 1811, 74,413 trained soldiers were—if one estimate is to be believed—already available for immediate mobilization.[91] The most important measures, though, were discussed within the Military Reorganization Commission and concerned what was to happen after the French occupation, which appeared, as a consequence of Russia's uncertain stance, at least contestable. Early in 1810, the commission recommended the introduction of universal conscription without exemptions. It was opposed by Stein's successor as Interior Minister Alexander zu Dohna-Schlobitten; prominent reform-minded advisors such as Ludwig von Vincke and Barthold Georg Niebuhr, who denounced conscription as an enemy of culture; the commercial classes of cities such as Königsberg, who were the most ardent opponents, according to

---

[89] G. E. Rothenberg, *The Napoleonic Wars*, 103.
[90] G. L. v. Blücher to Friedrich Wilhelm III, cited in E. Henderson, *Blücher and the Uprising of Prussia against Napoleon, 1806–1815* (London, 1911), 10–11; Napoleon to C.-M. de Talleyrand, 12 Sept. 1806, in J. M. Thompson, *Napoleon Bonaparte* (Oxford, 1988), 290.
[91] P. Paret, *Yorck*, 139. G. A. Craig, *The Politics of the Prussian Army*, 49–50, is more cautious, claiming that only 65,675 officers and men were ready by 1813.

Friedrich Wilhelm von Goetzen; and much of the aristocracy, who saw universal conscription—in the words of one East Prussian petition—as 'the child of a revolution that had smashed all existing arrangements and conditions in France' and 'can be based only on the concept of universal equality', which would 'lead to the complete destruction of the nobility'.[92] As usual, the king was undecided. Having avowed the necessity of 'eine allgemeine Konskription' he refused to sanction its passage into law in December 1808 and blocked it again in 1810.[93] As soon as the French had withdrawn, however, after the catastrophic failure of the *Grande Armée*'s invasion of Russia in 1812, and before Prussia had formally declared war on France on 16 March 1813, the recommendations of reformers—within a new committee set up by the king in Breslau and led by Scharnhorst—were rapidly put into effect, notably: universal conscription for the army of the line on 9 February 1813; the establishment of volunteer *Jäger* detachments for the propertied classes, able to pay for their equipment and uniforms, on 3 February; the formation of a *Landwehr* for all men between 17 and 40 not serving in the regular army or *Jäger* on 17 March; and the creation of the *Landsturm*, or home-defence force, for all remaining men, either too old or physically unfit to serve in the *Landwehr*, in April 1813.

The Prussian forces brought into being by conscription in 1813 differed in kind from those of the old standing army.[94] While it is true that the *Kantonreglement* (1733) made military service compulsory in theory, it did so by assigning each regiment of the army a recruitment district, from which it found its quota of 'native' troops. All young males in the district were enrolled on regimental lists, but only a small proportion was enlisted and numerous exemptions were granted, covering the nobility, the clergy, civil servants, the educated and propertied, some prosperous artisans and peasants, and workers in industries of interest to the state. From a total population of 8.7 million in 1799, 530,000 men were exempt and 1,170,000 resided in Prussian territories beyond the cantons.[95] In the Teltow district of Kurmark, for example, there were twenty-nine resident soldiers in army service and 224 serving sons out of 5,552 enrolled men in 1750, and 216 resident soldiers and 235 serving sons out of 6,627 in 1801.[96] If an insufficient number of volunteers came forward, 'native' recruits were selected, after 1763, by a staff officer from the regiment and a rural commissioner, both of whom often came from, or were closely connected to, local noble landowners. They were joined by a large number of mercenaries from abroad, since the proportion of 'natives' to 'foreigners'—those recruited, frequently by guile or force, from outside the recruiting district, mostly also from outside Prussia—was deliberately kept roughly equal in order to maintain the domestic, largely agricultural labour force. Although on

[92] Cited in P. Paret, *Yorck*, 135–6.

[93] 'Regulativ über die allgemeine Konskription', 20 Dec. 1808, P. Paret, *Yorck*, 136.

[94] See D. Walter, 'Reluctant Reformers, Observant Disciples', 92; H. Händel, *Der Gedanke der allgemeinen Wehrpflicht*.

[95] K. Hagemann, *Mannlicher Muth und Teutsche Ehre*, 33.

[96] O. Büsch, *Military System and Social Life in Old Regime Prussia, 1713–1807: The Beginnings of the Social Militarization of Prusso-German Society* (Atlantic Highlands, NJ, 1997), 17.

active duty for only two months per year, in April and May, under the furlough system, soldiers served for life until 1792, when the period of service was reduced to twenty years. Such a system was unequal and authoritarian, resting on the discipline, often resented, of noble-dominated rural localities and of the noble-officered regiments: 'we have to fight over every recruit with his lord', wrote Yorck in August 1811, and 'miserable egotism is the only dominant passion'.[97] The system also led to the recruitment of those least able to resist, prompting officers' complaints about their poor 'quality'. Transgressions 'against discipline continue to be very frequent despite all efforts of the commanding officers, and this, too, is the result of the bad composition of the troops', Yorck had written to the king a year earlier: 'The *Kantonreglement* protects everyone who is not a complete vagabond or beggar.'[98] The reforms of 1813, which created a system of conscription—with the word itself being contrasted by reformers with the term 'canton system'—for all adult males without exemptions, transformed the Prussian army, creating 12,000 *Jäger*, who often replaced officers of the line, by the end of 1813, and 120,000 soldiers of the *Landwehr*, who were organized in separate regiments with their own uniforms but who fought alongside regiments of the regular army during and after the autumn of 1813.[99] Prussia's 270,000–280,000 mobilized troops in 1813 were added to those of Russia, Austria, and other Allies to create a combined force of about 800,000 or 570,000 in the field, compared to 600,000 in the French-led 'army of the nations', of which 410,000 could be used in battle.[100] Not only did such levies give the Coalition an overall numerical advantage for the first time since 1792, they also altered the individual armies and changed soldiers' experiences of warfare, with more than one in four adult males in Prussia sent into the field in 1813 alone.

PATRIOTIC AND CABINET WARFARE

The transformation of the German armies which occurred in the 1800s and 1810s was at once part of a broader movement of reform and a direct response to the changing imperatives of combat.[101] More and more soldiers entered the army and the relationship between civilian—particularly urban—society and the military became closer, at the same time as military institutions, codes, and traditions were collapsing or were being replaced. As Clausewitz revealed in 1813, in an essay

---

[97] Yorck to Scharnhorst, 22 Aug. 1811, in J. G. Droysen, *Das Leben des Feldmarschalls Grafen York von Wartenburg* (Berlin, 1851–2), vol. 1, 285.

[98] Yorck to Friedrich Wilhelm III, April–June 1810, cited by Scharnhorst, in P. Paret, *Yorck*, 137.

[99] H. v. Jordan, *Erinnerungsblätter und Briefe eines jungen Freiheitskämpfers aus den Jahren 1813 und 1814*, ed. Ludwig von Jordan (Berlin, 1914), 250.

[100] G. E. Rothenberg, *Napoleonic Wars*, 178–9.

[101] The best analysis of the tensions between the two is currently M. Sikora, 'Militarisierung und Zivilisierung. Die preussischen Heeresreformen und ihre Ambivalenzen', in P. Baumgart, B. R. Kroener, and H. Stubig (eds), *Die preussische Armee. Zwischen Ancien Régime und Reichsgründung* (Paderborn, 2008), 164–95.

comparing 1813 to 1806, even the most entrenched institutions and practices—in Prussia—had been shown by the Revolutionary and Napoleonic Wars to be flimsy:

> In the unfortunate days of Jena and Auerstädt, the Prussian army lost its glory; in the retreat it fell apart. Its fortresses were given up, the state was conquered, and after four weeks of fighting little was left of either state or army. ... The [armistice] completed the misery. ... Within a year, Prussia's glittering military state, a joy to all lovers of soldiers and war, had disappeared. Admiration was replaced by reproach and censure, homage often by humiliation. An oppressive sadness weighed on the army's morale. Finding confidence in the past was not possible; nor was hope for the future. Even that ultimate source for regaining courage, trust in particular leaders, was absent, because in the brief war no one had achieved prominence, and the few who had distinguished themselves were divided among factions holding different opinions.[102]

Having been captured in the 'various capitulations' of 1806 and then released, 'a great number of officers', wrote Grawert in September 1807, had been obliged to 'go back to the provinces' and, receiving nothing from the state, 'had to seek out a means of living, helplessly, for many months, without any support'.[103] Some soldiers had fled with Blücher towards Lübeck or with the king and much of the General Staff towards Silesia and East Prussia; others were captured and sent home, or—like Boyen—evaded capture and made their way back to Prussia clandestinely.[104] The impression which such insiders give is of an army—or 'remnants of an army', in Boyen's phrase—close to dissolution.[105]

Some officers, confronted by the need to reform existing practices, found themselves in the company of uncomfortable bedfellows. Gneisenau, writing to Friedrich Wilhelm III to resign his duties on the Military Reorganization Committee, complained that 'the necessary innovations in the army weigh us down with the hatred of all those who are bound, through habit or interest, to the old things'.[106] Yorck, who continued to work with Stein in 1813 in spite of rejoicing at his dismissal—as a chance of controlling 'mad heads' and removing 'nests of vipers'—in November 1808, was in favour both of radical measures such as the arming of a *Landwehr* in 1810–11 and of maintaining preferential noble access to commissions in the army—as an 'older privilege of the class that had borne this duty'—and of retaining serfdom, 'that so-called slavery of the peasants etc.', opposition to which was 'nothing but philanthropic babbling'.[107] Other officers, especially those from the *Rheinbund* states but also the 'French party' in Prussia, were forced to adapt to the demands and military conventions of their French overlord. Baden's '*Anschluss* with France' in 1805 had necessitated the dispatching of a corps of 3,000 troops to the French army, which was about to attack Austria, provoking several officers to resign and leaving 'the rank and file', who had

---

[102] C. v. Clausewitz, 'Der Feldzug von 1813 bis zum Waffenstillstand', in P. Paret, *The Cognitive Challenge of War*, 74–5.

[103] Grawert memorandum, 27 Sept. 1807, in R. Vaupel (ed.), *Die Reorganisation*, part 2, vol. 1, 110.

[104] H. v. Boyen, *Denkwürdigkeiten und Erinnerungen 1771–1813* (Stuttgart, 1899), vol. 1, 212–13.

[105] Ibid., 203.

[106] Gneisenau to Friedrich Wilhelm III, 14 Jan. 1808, in A. W. A. N. v. Gneisenau, *Ausgewählte militärische Schriften,* ed. G. Förster and C. Gudzent (Berlin, 1984), 91.

[107] Cited in P. Paret, *Yorck*, 227, 229.

been issued with French painted flags just before their departure, feeling 'that they had been sold out to France'.[108] As a result, 'desertion gained ground in a shocking fashion'.[109] Keeping their uniforms, which meant that they were occasionally shot at by their allies as 'Prussians', Badenese units subsequently fought alongside French ones, sometimes under direct French command, against Prussia in 1806 (8,000 troops), in Spain in 1808, against the Habsburg monarchy in 1809 (6,000 troops), as part of the *Grande Armée* in Russia in 1812 (6,766 troops), and against Prussia, Austria, and Russia in 1813.[110] In disarray, with soldiers 'very inadequately equipped' and an officer corps depending on '*Fremde*'—mainly from Kurhessen— 'because of the rapid expansion of our troops in this country', the Badenese army was bound, especially in 1806, to toe the French line.[111] Although the army had been consolidated between 1807 and 1811, acquitting itself well in 1809, it was destroyed in 1812, forcing Karlsruhe to rebuild it. 'The impression which I received was not the most favourable', recalled the Grand Duke's brother in August 1813: 'The three battalions were composed of raw, very young soldiers who had scarcely been in the service for three months; there was a great lack of officers and, especially, NCOs.'[112] The cavalry units which joined the Badenese infantry in Saxony had only just received horses and they 'could barely stay on them', presenting 'a pitiful picture' to their peers.[113] The same was true of other German armies.

The tutelage rather than enmity of France makes it difficult to compare the metamorphosis of the armies of the medium-sized and smaller *Rheinbund* states with that of Prussia or the Habsburg monarchy. There were attempts, before 1806, to awaken patriotic sentiments in newly expanded states such as Baden, Württemberg, and Bavaria, of which laws of recruitment to the army were part. In Karlsruhe, a decree of 23 March 1804, although perpetuating many exemptions, restated subjects' duty to serve in the militia and defined recruiting cantons along Prussian lines. A cadet school for officers was established in Ludwigsburg the following year. In Stuttgart, the law of 1803, which had first mooted general conscription, was replaced by a law on 6 August 1806, which purported to bring such conscription into effect, albeit with familiar exclusions for the nobility, officials, state industries, well-to-do merchants, and only sons. Having improved the system for replacing troops and having carried out manoeuvres in 1806, King Friedrich of Württemberg was able to raise an army of 8,000 troops and 3,500 reserves for the war against Prussia in the autumn of 1806 with little difficulty. As his army departed for Saxony, the monarch made an emphatic appeal for it to honour its king and fatherland.[114] In Munich, Max Joseph's call for support arguably derived from more reliable sources, drawing on anti-Austrian sentiment and popular acclamation, which had been evident at the time of his coronation as the first King of Bavaria on 1 January 1806.[115] The 'General Reglement on the Expansion of the Electorate's Army' on

---

[108] Wilhelm Markgraf v. Baden, *Denkwürdigkeiten*, vol. 1, 32.   [109] Ibid.
[110] Ibid., 32–275.   [111] Ibid., 41, 48.   [112] Ibid., 232.
[113] Ibid., 234.   [114] P. Saurer, *Napoleons Adler*, 112–13.
[115] F. Kramer, 'Bayerns Erhebung zum Königkreich', *Zeitschrift für bayerischer Landesgeschichte*, 68 (2005), 815–34. On anti-Austrian feeling in Bavaria, see M. Junkelmann, *Napoleon und Bayern* (Regensburg, 1985), 55.

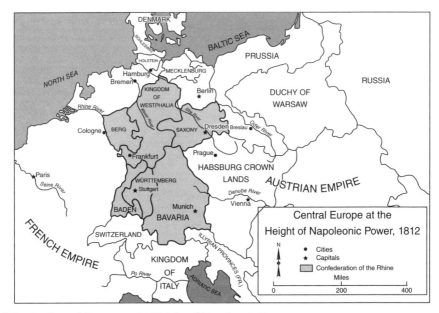

Map 2. Central Europe at the Height of Napoleonic Power
Source: J. Sperber (ed.), *Short Oxford History of Germany, 1800–1870* (Oxford, 2004), 287.

30 April 1804 had brought to an end Bavaria's reliance on mercenaries. It was supplemented by the establishment of military cantons on 7 January 1805 and a declaration that it was the duty of every fit male subject between 16 and 40 years old to serve in the military. Substitutions were still allowed and exemptions persisted, but the exclusion of foreigners and a formal oath to the Elector had created a fundamentally new conception of a specifically 'Bavarian' army.[116]

The idea of 'patriotic' or 'state' armies rather than the mercenary standing armies of princes could initially be held to be compatible with the close and one-sided alliances of the various states with France, not least because Napoleon Bonaparte enjoyed considerable support in southern and central Germany as a harbinger of peace and an enemy of the old order (for the new states see Map 2).[117] Over time, however, the Napoleonic Wars seemed to sever the connection between the states' armies and Bavarian, Saxon, Swabian, or Badenese patriotism.[118] The newly anointed monarchs and dukes of the Confederation of the Rhine, with their expanding territories and growing populations, remained beholden to the French Emperor. As early as 1799, Max Joseph, on becoming Elector, had professed his loyalty to the Directory, partly

---

[116] J. Murken, *Bayerische Soldaten*, 28.

[117] U. Planert, *Der Mythos*, 544–56.

[118] This is not to say that patriotism disappeared completely in the *Rheinbund* armies, but that it diminished. For one example of persisting patriotism even in the new creation of the Kingdom of Westphalia, ruled by Jérôme Bonaparte, see H. O. Wesemann (ed.), *Kanonier des Kaisers. Kriegstagebuch des Heinrich Wesemann 1808–1814* (Cologne, 1971), 90–1: 'It is in no way our intention to fight for Napoleon's affair, but we wanted to remain true to our oath to take up arms only for our fatherland.'

to expel occupying Austrian forces, massing to attack France, and partly as a scion—and former Duke of Zweibrücken—of the western German outpost of the Palatinate, which had provided Bavaria with its ruling dynasty in 1777: 'I was born in France, I beg you to take me for a Frenchman. ... After every victory of the French army I have felt myself to be a Frenchman.'[119] By 1806, though, the new king was already fulminating against his envoy in Paris, who had been forced by the French, 'against his instructions', to sign too compromising a set of acts of confederation. 'If he had come within my sight, I would have put a bullet in his head', threatened the monarch: 'The evil has happened. It is no longer to be prevented, notably because of the peace with Russia and because we have 150,000 Frenchmen in the country.'[120] The war of 1809 against the Habsburg monarchy divided the Bavarian population, with some Catholics supporting Vienna, and it destroyed the Bavarian army, with its best division losing 3,600 soldiers, or 60 per cent of its total, at Wagram—the largest battle up to that point, involving 340,000 combatants.[121] The invasion of Russia in 1812 proved much worse, with Bavarian divisions split up and some regiments put under direct French command, leading the First Minister Maximilian von Montgelas to complain of 'the most damaging influence' of the 'separation' on 'the morale of troops used to serving together'.[122] The same troops had then marched all the way to Moscow and back again, with about 9 per cent of soldiers, or 3,200 out of 35,799, returning to Bavaria alive. 'The campaign which has just finished has cost the army of the king 30,000 men, of which enemy fire has killed the smaller part', wrote Montgelas in February 1813: 'The greater part has succumbed to the cold, to hunger, and to the misery which is to be found at the hands of the enemy.'[123] King Max Joseph complained to Napoleon that the monarchy was barely able to continue: 'It is not the vertigo and the discontentment of the people, it is the exhaustion of the resources of the government which is giving me serious cause for concern.'[124] Nonetheless, he had little choice, given his—and his *Rheinbund* neighbours'—earlier decisions, but to remain in the French camp until the eve of the battle of Leipzig in October 1813.

Baden and Württemberg were in a weaker position than Bavaria. The government in Karlsruhe had had to build an army virtually from scratch after the turn of the century, having gone to war against Prussia in 1806 with a cavalry without horses and an infantry with looted guns and the wrong sort of ammunition.[125] On grounds of 'cleanliness and comfort', soldiers were no longer required to

---

[119] Junkelmann, *Napoleon und Bayern*, 51.   [120] Ibid., 147.

[121] U. Planert, *Der Mythos*, 556–72.

[122] R. Braun, 'Die Bayern in Russland', in H. Glaser (ed.), *Krone und Verfassung. König Max I. Joseph und der neue Staat, 1799–1825* (Munich, 1980), 260–71. For Montgelas, see J. Murken, *Bayerische Soldaten*, 31.

[123] Montgelas to Mercy-Argenteau, 18 Feb. 1813, J. Murken, *Bayerische Soldaten*, 40.

[124] Max Joseph to Napoleon, 3 Mar. 1813, J. Murken, *Bayerische Soldaten*, 41.

[125] P. Saurer, *Napoleons Adler*, 113. Wilhelm Meier, *Erinnerungen aus den Feldzügen 1806 bis 1815* (Karlsruhe, 1854), 4, gives a more positive account, although admitting the army was not prepared to fight in the French way.

wear—and powder—wigs.[126] Crown Prince Karl, who had shortly beforehand been
forced into a marriage with Napoleon's adopted daughter Stéphanie de Beauharnais,
had been put in charge of the Badenese forces, but he had been heavily criticized
by the French and distanced from the troops. Even his own subordinate officer,
Valentin von Harrant, had avowed that 'it would have been better, on the whole,
if the prince had stayed at home'.[127] 'Above all, this campaign was a salutary yet
hard lesson for the military', reported one of the Badenese army's surgeons.[128] By
comparison with that of its western neighbour, Württemberg's army had performed well in both 1806 and 1809, but it had done so under the direct command
of the French general Dominique Vandamme against the wishes of King Friedrich,
since it had been deemed too small to stand on its own.[129] In 1812, in order to
avoid the imposition of another French general, Crown Prince Friedrich Wilhelm
was chosen by the monarch to command the state's contingent, but he was soon
being accused by Napoleon, whom—his father was sure—he hated, of fomenting
revolt. King Friedrich wrote to caution him that 'I was put in a position to found
the state, of which you should one day be the ruler, by him [Napoleon] alone.'[130]

In a similar fashion, 20-year-old Graf Wilhelm von Hochberg, the Grand Duke's
younger brother, was put in charge of Badenese troops in 1812, yet his presence
did not prevent the contingent being incorporated into the Third Army Corps
under Marshal Michel Ney. Only 800–1,000 soldiers from Baden's contingent of
7,166 and 387 or so from Württemberg's force of 15,800 returned from Russia,
contradicting, in the most damaging way, King Friedrich's earlier prediction, in
1809, that 'We are with Caesar, and everything will go well.'[131] Although the monarch
was aware, as he wrote to his Foreign Minister at the start of 1813, that 'displeasure'
was increasing daily in Stuttgart and in the countryside 'with everything that is
French' and that 'calls to the people are being made, in different places, ... in which
a freeing from the yoke with the help of Austria is spoken of', he was obliged to
continue to assure Napoleon, despite the difficulties which he encountered in raising
a new army for the campaign of 1813, that he had done everything possible to fulfil
his treaty obligations to France over the previous eight years.[132] Grand Duke Karl
of Baden was even more explicit, as he wrote to Napoleon—his father-in-law—in
January 1813: 'My greatest ambition consists, as a consequence of my eagerness
and my unchanging subjection, in gaining the support of Your Majesty.'[133] 'I, who
am bound by the sweetest and holiest ties to the great fortune of Your Majesty and
of the house founded by you, am fully convinced of the necessity that all the allied

---

[126] P. Saurer, *Napoleons Adler I*, 114.   [127] Cited ibid., 115.

[128] W. Meier, *Erinnerungen*, 4.

[129] For an example of how Swabian contingents took orders directly from Vandamme, see
F. Schneider, *Erinnerungen aus den Feldzügen der Württemberger. 1806 und 1807 in Schlesien* (Stuttgart,
1866), 38.

[130] P. Saurer, *Napoleons Adler*, 264.

[131] Friedrich to his daughter, 19 Mar. 1809, P. Saurer, *Napoleons Adler*, 125. For the numbers, see
S. Fiedler, *Grundriss der Militär- und Kriegsgeschichte. Das Zeitalter der Französischen Revolution und
Napoleons* (Munich, 1976), vol. 2, 224–5.

[132] P. Saurer, *Napoleons Adler*, 268, 274.

[133] Karl to Napoleon, 4 Jan. 1813, P. Saurer, *Napoleons Adler*, 275.

states will also, for their part, make those efforts which the circumstances demand of them', he went on a month later.[134] It was more and more difficult for such rulers and their governments, confronted by popular scepticism and resistance, to pretend that their armies had a patriotic purpose.

The transfer of the states and armies of the Confederation of the Rhine to the Coalition against Napoleon in the autumn of 1813 proved to be painful for many of the participants, particularly officers and officials, and it was rarely accompanied by expressions of patriotic or 'German' feeling. Wilhelm, the commander of the Badenese contingent still trapped in Leipzig in mid-October, gave a vivid account of the travails of the remaining *Rheinbund* regimes. Told by Napoleon, whose forces had left the city on 19 October, that he no longer enjoyed French protection, the King of Saxony had already begun to negotiate with the Crown Prince of Sweden, who was acting on behalf of the Allies, when he heard a 'Vivat' outside the building in which the talks were taking place.[135] Thinking that it might be for Napoleon, the monarch went into the square to witness a crowd rejoicing at the arrival of Tsar Alexander: 'With sadness', recorded Wilhelm, 'I noticed how no one made way for the worthy old gentleman, who was now abandoned by everyone, after fortune had turned against him.'[136] The Tsar, ignorant of the King of Saxony's presence, acknowledged the crowd and left the square with the Crown Prince, who had not bothered to tell him of the Saxon monarch's plight. 'I shall never forget the impressions which this day left me with', wrote the later Margrave of Baden, having observed the Habsburg Kaiser ride into the market square, to a 'Vivat' from the Badenese troops, 'many of whom were former [Austrian] subjects': 'In the morning, I saw Emperor Napoleon and his army, made up of so many different parts, withdraw, and now I was confronted by the same colourful picture of diverse nations and peoples (*Völkerschaften*), as I viewed the Allied army.'[137]

Cut off from the French forces but without orders to switch sides from Karlsruhe, 'whose situation' was 'very difficult because of the proximity of the French border', Wilhelm surrendered and was taken prisoner by the Prussian army, which also took control of the Badenese soldiers.[138] On 21 October, he had an audience with the King of Prussia, who assured him that he understood 'the painful situation of the Grand Duke fully and [understood] that other states, too, [had] recently been in the same position, and he would, therefore, ensure that all possible allowances were made'.[139] On returning to Baden in December 1813, Wilhelm found that 'the mood' was an 'unusual' one:

> One was ill-disposed to anything French in its entirety, but people did not really trust themselves to voice their opinion, partly out of fear of a further turn in the fortunes of war, partly out of shame in front of the Grand Duchess. Everything which had to take place did so, therefore, but without enthusiasm for the so-called German business.[140]

[134] Ibid.
[135] For the context of these events, see R. Köpping, *Sachsen gegen Napoleon. Zur Geschichte der Befreiungskriege 1813–1815* (Berlin, 2001).
[136] Wilhelm Markgraf v. Baden, *Denkwürdigkeiten*, vol. 1, 258.
[137] Ibid.   [138] Ibid., 261.   [139] Ibid.   [140] Ibid., 273.

The government and army of Württemberg were in a similar predicament, caught after 8 October, as King Friedrich explained in a letter to Napoleon, between an advancing Bavarian and Austrian army and a retreating French one. Friedrich's decision to declare his state's neutrality did not mean, he assured the emperor, that his feelings had changed, 'but my steps have to be guided by unchangeable necessities'.[141] As in Baden, the king's decision seems to have produced mixed feelings among Württemberg's soldiers and to have met with few public expressions of patriotic sentiment.

Unlike other *Rheinbund* states, Bavaria concluded an alliance with the Coalition nine days before the battle of Leipzig, on 8 October, and its actions were justified by Max Joseph in patriotic and national terms for the well-being of the kingdom and in the name of 'German' culture.[142] About 6,000 volunteer soldiers and 230 volunteer officers eventually came forward, funded by 'patriotic' donations.[143] In this respect, the experiences of the Bavarian government and army were closer to those of Prussia, which had used the military reverses of 1806 to improve the motivation, independence, and mobility of its soldiers. The significance of such state 'patriotism'—not to mention German nationalism—varied, of course, with even Bavaria failing to enforce conscription in the newly annexed Tyrol after 1808–9 and with its internal troops arresting 7,800 Bavarian deserters and 5,100 fleeing conscripts, together with 43,500 'foreign' deserters, out of a total of 270,000 people arrested, between 1806 and 1815.[144] Likewise, Prussian authorities found it difficult to enlist conscripts in cities such as Berlin and Potsdam and in annexed or border regions like Westphalia, Silesia, and its Polish provinces. In 1813, 631 out of 2,800 soldiers in the Prussian *Landwehr* of the district of Münster deserted, yielding a figure—22.4 per cent—in excess of the French desertion rate of 10 per cent between 1803 and 1814 or that of the German-speaking territories of the left bank of the Rhine, annexed by and subjected to the conscription of France, where 14 per cent of recruits, or 5,000 out of 35,000, deserted between 1801 and 1810.[145] In the Prussian and Bavarian heartlands, however, desertion was much rarer, in spite of the makeshift nature of the two states between 1806 and 1815 and increasing levels of conscription, with Berlin doubling the size of its forces through the creation of the *Landwehr* in 1813 and with Munich disposing of 50,000 troops in October 1813, including 10,000 in the National Guard, and 60,000 in April 1815.[146] Although 'desertion'—which had been redefined by extension (Articles 1

---

[141] P. Saurer, *Napoleons Adler*, 278. Also, O. Gerhardt, *Die Württemberger im deutschen Befreiungskampf 1813–1815* (Stuttgart, 1938), 85.

[142] Few diarists referred to Bavaria's changing of sides: for instance, F. Mändler, *Erinnerungen aus meinen Feldzüge in den Jahren 1809 bis 1815,* ed. F. J. A. Schneidawind (Nuremberg, 1854), 126–8.

[143] U. Planert, *Der Mythos*, 600.

[144] C. Küther, *Räuber und Gauner in Deutschland* (Göttingen, 1987), 19–20.

[145] M. Sikora, 'Desertion und nationale Mobilmachung', 116, 120, 133. On the left bank of the Rhine, see also C. Hudemann-Simon, 'Réfractaires und déserteurs de la Grande Armée en Sarre 1802–1813', *Revue Historique*, 111 (1987), 11–45; J. Smets, 'Von der "Dorfidylle" zur preussischen Nation', 695–738.

[146] M. Junkelmann, *Napoleon und Bayern*, 326, 341. Also, K. Uebe, *Der Stimmungsumschwung in der bayerischen Armee gegenüber den Franzosen 1806–1812* (Munich, 1939). On the lack of desertion in the Prussian *Landwehr* from the Neumark and elsewhere, in contrast to that from Silesia, see B. v. Knobelsdorff-Brenkenhoff, *Briefe aus den Befreiungskriegen* (Bonn, 1981), 37.

and 6) as state 'treason' in the revised military code of 1808 rather than as an internal army matter—was endemic in the Prussian Lützower corps of volunteers, comprising 15 per cent of all troops and 25 per cent of infantrymen, as educated or prosperous idealists and a mixed group of other combatants experienced the realities of a campaign, the desertion rate for Prussia's *Freiwillige* as a whole—from 8,000 troops by June 1813 and 30,000 by mid-1814—was low, at between 1 and 5 per cent.[147] Notwithstanding much higher levels of recruitment, fewer exemptions, the transitional character of military and state institutions, and the changing meaning of 'desertion', which now included the flight of young men before actual enlistment, average rates of desertion in Prussia, Bavaria, and elsewhere in Germany in the 1800s and 1810s were lower than in the eighteenth century. During the last phase of its old system, Prussia had experienced 9,500 desertions during the mobilization of 1805 and the short campaign of 1806 alone.[148]

To Prussian reformers such as Scharnhorst, the Allies had lost and France had won primarily because the French had been more motivated than their opponents. 'The struggle was indeed too unequal: one side had everything to lose, the other little,' he had written in 1797: French soldiers, as well as officers, had believed in 1792 that they were threatened with subjugation and the disappearance of the state at the hands of their enemies, pushing civilians and combatants to make extraordinary sacrifices.[149] This sense of fighting for survival had combined with the desire for a free society and with a longer-standing national pride—'The French nation has always deemed itself to be the only people which is enlightened, intelligent, free and happy, despising all other nations as uncultured, bestial and wretched'—to create a new type of soldier and, as a corollary, new forms of combat: 'the reasons for the defeat of the allied powers must be deeply enmeshed in their internal conditions and in those of the French nation.'[150] When war recommenced on the continent in 1805–6, the Allies demonstrated that they had still not learned their lesson. Prussia had treated the conflict 'like an autumn manoeuvre', averred Scharnhorst from Hamburg on 13 November 1806: 'I was the only one who knew all the different parts of the great military machine, but I was transferred to Hanover with a small corps, as Quartermaster-General, and only then, when they could not help themselves, did I come to a larger army.'[151] Prussian soldiers and civilians had not realized, despite the revolutionary changes which had occurred in France in the 1790s, that they were fighting a 'national' war of survival:

---

[147] M. Sikora, 'Desertion und nationale Mobilmachung', 134; P. Brandt, 'Einstellungen, Motive und Ziele von Kriegsfreiwilligen 1813/14: Das Freikorps Lützow', in J. Dülffer (ed.), *Kriegsbereitschaft und Friedensordnung in Deutschland 1800–1814* (Münster, 1995), 211–33.

[148] M. Sikora, 'Desertion und nationale Mobilmachung', 117; M. Sikora, 'Verzweiflung oder Leichtsinn? Militärstand und Desertion im 18. Jahrhundert', in B. R. Kroener and R. Pröve (eds), *Krieg und Frieden. Militär und Gesellschaft in der Frühen Neuzeit* (Paderborn, 1996), 237–64.

[149] Scharnhorst, on 'The Development of the General Causes of the Good Fortune of the French in the Revolutionary War' (1797), cited in T. C. W. Blanning, *The Pursuit of Glory*, 640.

[150] Ibid.

[151] Scharnhorst to F. v. der Decken, 16 Nov. 1806, in J. Niemeyer (ed.), *Scharnhorst Briefe an Friedrich von der Decken 1803–1813* (Bonn, 1987), 114.

It was a great misfortune that no one knew that everything was in play—the indifference of the milieu of the king and of the king himself often made me melancholic, and often vexed, to the highest degree. 8 weeks before the outbreak of war, I sent a memorandum to the king and asked him for the general arming of militarily capable men, up to a 300,000-strong national militia (*Nationalmilitz*).[152]

Six-and-a-half years later, in a memorandum for Hardenberg of April 1813, Scharnhorst remained more convinced than ever that 'only an arrangement which employs the entire strength of the nation (*die Gesamtkräfte der Nation*) can secure the throne and our independence':

To entrust the security of the king and national independence to a standing army alone is always dangerous, especially against an opponent such as ours is, which stands before us, which risks everything in order to win everything. If chance should decide against us in a few battles, it will destroy us, insofar as we do not now muster the entirety of our national forces against it. Without such a development of all the institutions of defence available to us, which does not merely mean the standing army but also the physical and moral resources of the nation, we cannot vouch for success. On the other hand, if this development of our armed forces (*Streitkräfte*) in their full extent takes place, then we will never again be completely knocked down, and the operations of our armies can therefore be carried out with greater security.[153]

TACTICS, STRATEGY, AND REFORM

The Prussian 'articles of war' (*Kriegsartikeln*), or disciplinary code, issued on 3 August 1808 rested on Scharnhorst's patriotic principles, as the Auditor-General and author of the initial draft, Johann Friedrich von Koenen, spelled out in his gloss on the code on 26 May: 'The soldier was until now, especially in earlier times, kept in order here by means of invective, beatings in the stocks and other harsh corporal punishments', he explained for the benefit of the king, government, and army on behalf of the Military Reorganization Commission: 'This was necessary as long as the mass of soldiers came, for the most part, from the least educated class of natives and from raw, enlisted foreigners, who had run away in breach of their duties under oath.'[154] By contrast, he went on, 'how differently things will happen in future!'[155] Anticipating 'general conscription', which Koenen assumed was a matter of course, 'the estate of soldiers will unite a large part of educated people and the strongest, most promising sons of the fatherland', who had to be convinced that they were carrying out 'an honourable and worthy career in itself' and fulfilling their duties towards their ruler and 'their fellow citizens (*Mitbürger*)'.[156] Former soldiers would be able to acquit themselves of 'other duties to the fatherland' in the

---

[152] Ibid.
[153] Gneisenau and Scharnhorst memorandum for K. A. v. Hardenberg, Apr. 1813, in A. W. A. N. v. Gneisenau, *Ausgewählte militärische Schriften*, 254.
[154] J. F. v. Koenen report, 26 May 1808, in R. Vaupel (ed.), *Die Reorganisation*, part 2, vol. 1, 431.
[155] Ibid. [156] Ibid., 431–2.

knowledge that they would be honoured and trusted by other citizens, whom they had 'bravely and gloriously defended'.[157] In order 'to awaken this spirit and this mood in our youth', contended Koenen, routine, 'dishonouring' corporal punishment, in particular the stocks (Art. 2), should be abandoned.[158] This more humane form of military discipline, which was linked in supplementary discussions to French precedents, retained its emphasis on discipline and obedience, punishing the simple disobeying of orders with up to three years in gaol (Art. 8) and placing at the disposal of an officer 'every means to ensure that his order is obeyed' (Art. 4), including the right to 'strike down refractory soldiers', albeit in accordance with the *Kriegsartikeln*. The code sanctioned penalties of execution and 'severe arrest'— or two to three days of solitary confinement lying on bars nailed to the floor of a dark room in order to make it 'uncomfortable', followed by a long term of imprisonment—for contraventions such as talking to the enemy, actions or negotiations causing 'damage to the royal house, the army or subjects' or putting 'the state and the army in danger and insecurity' (Art. 6), threatening an officer with a gun (Art. 9), provoking a riot over conditions or lack of provisions during wartime (Art. 11), looting on home, neutral, or allied soil (Art. 12), abandoning a watch whilst at war (Art. 14), and fleeing from or going over to the enemy 'with a weapon in hand' (Art. 17).[159] Soldiers going over to the enemy in wartime or wounding an officer were to be broken on the wheel (Arts 9 and 17), those committing murder were to be executed by the sword (Art. 36), and those carrying out arson were to be burned, with 'the punishment sharpened if people actually died as a result' (Art. 50).[160] Despite such continuing harshness, however, the new articles of war were viewed at the time as a way of bridging the previous gulf between civilian society and the military 'estate', which was necessary because the army would encompass 'every subject, without any distinction of birth', and would be 'almost entirely composed of natives (*Einländer*)' (Art. 1).[161] There would always be 'individuals who cannot be kept to their duty other than by sensitive disciplining', wrote Gneisenau, who had given the main response of the Military Reorganization Commission to Koenen's draft, but 'it is not a logical conclusion to claim that, because *some* are worthy of a beating, *all* must be beaten'.[162]

The army, contended Gneisenau and other reformers, had to be made more 'civil', easing its expansion, improving its relationship with middle-class citizens, and permitting it to exploit the resources of the nation. Part of the process, which promised to make the military more effective, was the promotion of 'burghers' to the officer corps, as had occurred in France during the revolution, which had 'awoken all sources of strength and given each source an appropriate field of action'.[163] Likewise, in Prussia, Gneisenau continued elsewhere, using the same phrase which he had first applied to revolutionary France, it had become clear to an enlightened monarch that all the powers of the nation needed to be deployed: 'Birth gives no

---

[157] Ibid., 432.   [158] Ibid., 427, 432.   [159] Ibid., 410–17, 424.
[160] Ibid., 412, 415, 419, 423.   [161] Ibid., 410.
[162] A. W. A. N. v. Gneisenau, *Ausgewählte militärische Schriften*, 116.
[163] Gneisenau memorandum, July 1807, cited ibid., 75.

monopoly over services; if one concedes too many rights to it, a series of sources of strength in the very lap of the nation continue to slumber, undeveloped and unused, and the striving wings of the genius will be lamed by oppressive relations.'[164] Gneisenau barely troubled to conceal references to Friedrich II, who had promoted many commoners to officers during the Seven Years' War, and the unimpeded military genius of Napoleon Bonaparte, who was contrasted with the superannuated elite of the Prussian army. In 1806, four of 142 Prussian generals were over 80 years of age, thirteen over 70, and sixty-two over 60.[165] Nearly all were noble, with the small minority of 695 commoners, out of 7,000 officers, usually in the artillery, subsidiary branches, or lower ranks.[166] To reformers such as Karl von Grolman, who was asked to devise a new system of promotion in 1807, it was 'not necessary to belong to a special class in order to fight': 'The melancholy belief that one must belong to a special class in order to defend the fatherland has done much to plunge it into the present abyss, and only the opposite principle can pull it out again.'[167] Conservatives like Friedrich August von der Marwitz disagreed and decried a 'revolution from above', with Yorck warning the king that if he deprived 'me and my children of our rights', he would have no foundation for his own, yet their position was weakened by the support of the king for the investigation, instigated by the Military Reorganization Commission and carried out by a special commission of enquiry, into officers' misconduct in 1806–7, which eventually pronounced 208 men guilty.[168] Thirteen per cent of generals were cashiered and 3 per cent of captains, lieutenants, and ensigns.[169]

As in the case of the articles of war, reformers managed to push through a decree on promotion on 6 August 1808, which was opposed by much of the officer corps. 'A claim to the position of officer shall from now on be warranted, in peacetime by knowledge and education, in time of war by exceptional bravery and quickness of perception', ran the decree, presaging the introduction of examinations for promotions at all levels and the closure of the old, basic military schools and the opening of new ones in Berlin, Königsberg, and Breslau:

> From the whole nation, therefore, every individual who possesses these qualities may claim the highest positions of honour in the military establishment. All social preference which has existed until now is terminated in the military establishment, and everyone, without reference to his background, has the same duties and rights.[170]

The principle of seniority and privileges accorded to nobles were formally abandoned. Although the king retained the right to appoint commanding officers, other appointments were made in conjunction with the examining commissions and schools, with the upper class—the *Selekta*—of the Berlin military academy providing many of the young recruits of the General Staff. High-ranking noble officers kept overall control over promotions, and examining commissions were

---

[164] Ibid., 105.   [165] G. A. Craig, *The Politics of the Prussian Army*, 26.
[166] Ibid., 17.   [167] Ibid., 43.
[168] F. A. L. von der Marwitz, *Aus dem Nachlasse. Lebensbeschreibung* (Berlin, 1852), vol. 1, 275–312. K. Demeter, *Das deutsche Heer und seine Offiziere* (Berlin, 1930), 16.
[169] P. Paret, *Cognitive Challenge of War*, 85.   [170] Ibid., 15.

told to pay attention, not merely to a candidate's 'knowledge and scholarship', but to his 'presence of mind, ready perception, precision, correctness in his duty and propriety in his deportment', yet the hold of the old guard had been loosened, abetted by the forced retirement of officers as the army was reduced to less than a quarter of its former size in September 1808; 4,594 officers out of a total of 7,096, including 86 of the 142 generals, were pushed to retire 'voluntarily and honourably' between 1806 and 1813.[171] Reformers were usually 'new' men, either ennobled like Scharnhorst, who was the son of a sergeant, or from a younger generation, facing a long wait for promotion under the principle of seniority, like Boyen, born in 1771 and a product of Königsberg's military school, or Grolman, born in 1777 and one of Scharnhorst's own pupils at Berlin's *Kriegsakademie*. Such men were unsuccessful in introducing the election of officers into the army of the line, but they did manage to establish the practice in *Jäger* detachments, which were formed in 1813 from propertied and educated one-year volunteers, and in the *Landwehr*, whose officers were to be men of property nominated by the civilian government of the *Kreis* and elected by the other officers of their unit, according to Boyen's *Wehrgesetz* of September 1814. As officers were killed in the campaigns of 1813–15, both the *Jäger* and the *Landwehr*—a 'happy union of the warrior and civilian society', in Blücher's estimation—provided the regular army with replacements.[172]

Changes within the officer corps and within the rank and file, however incomplete, seemed to Prussian reformers to prepare the way for necessary tactical and strategic revisions. Better educated, more motivated, 'patriotic' officers and soldiers were expected to act, like their French counterparts, with greater independence. Influenced by integrated *corps d'armée*, permanent self-contained brigades were formed, combining artillery, cavalry, and infantry, which allowed them to train together and to manoeuvre more freely in battle and during marches. Like the redrafted cavalry regulations, the new Prussian infantry manual was simplified, outlining straightforward tactics on the battlefield, which all higher-ranking officers could follow on their initiative, when necessary. It was 131 pages long, compared to the 546 pages of the 1788 regulations and the 300 to 400 pages of the French *Ordonnance* of 1791, the British *Rules and Regulations*, and the Austrian manual of 1807. It paid more attention to the role of skirmishers (*Jäger*), who could advance in front of regular units in order to disrupt the enemy through sniping, and to the use of attack columns (*Angriffskolonne*) rather than lines of infantry, to be deployed within the eight platoons of a battalion in narrow rows, two soldiers wide and four deep, in order to present less of a target. The third part of all line battalions was to be composed of skirmishers and all regular troops were to receive light infantry training, with a battalion of light infantry attached to each regiment of two battalions. The ratio of light and regular infantry increased from 1:19 in 1786 to just over 1:3 in 1812.[173] Light troops were easier to equip and supply and, critically,

---

[171] K. Hagemann, *Mannlicher Muth und teutscher Ehre*, 97.
[172] Cited in G. A. Craig, *The Politics of the Prussian Army*, 70.
[173] See P. Paret, *Yorck*, 269.

they were more mobile on and off the battlefield. Although supply trains and magazines continued to be important, especially during the invasion of Russia in 1812, where fodder and food were scarce, large armies of light troops, with fewer horses and a smaller supply train to feed, could more easily live off the land, which was necessary during all the Napoleonic Wars.[174] With lines of supply less important, fewer troops were needed to defend them and less attention had to be given to fortifications and sieges, since pockets of enemy soldiers behind campaigning armies constituted less of a threat. Instead, wars of movement, with mass armies marching quickly and concentrating their forces unexpectedly—in battle—at their opponents' weak points, had proved to be decisive in Italy in 1796–7 and 1799–1800, in Austria in 1805 and 1809, and in Saxony in 1806.

At the battles of Jena and Auerstädt, Prussia and Saxony seemed, in the opinion of reformers, to have demonstrated what would happen if the lessons of the revolutionary and Napoleonic Wars went unheeded. Brunswick, reducing the strength of his army by more than 50,000 troops in order to protect purportedly vital positions, decided to attack the French army before it could assemble its various units, but his two armies, 40,000 troops under Hohenlohe and 50,000 under his own command, were too slow to advance and were caught off guard by the three columns of the French army moving rapidly northwards. 'The completed march to Erfurt and Weimar was not likely to bolster soldiers' self-confidence', recalled Boyen: 'In indescribable leisureliness, the battalions and squadrons moved out of their old quarters and headed to new ones, surrounded by baggage, which could, in many units of troops, only elicit great concern in the real field soldier because of the travelling comforts of officers.'[175] Learning of Napoleon's movements, Brunswick turned back to Weimar and Jena, being overtaken by Davout in the East and being caught up by Lannes, Augereau, and Napoleon in the centre and to the West. Fearing that his lines to Magdeburg and Berlin would be cut as he was outflanked, the Prussian commander attempted, with his baggage train already failing to keep up, to fall further back, leaving Hohenlohe on a plateau West of Jena to guard his retreat. The majority of troops—'the poor men'—had had nothing to eat apart from their remaining provision of hard bread, but they were prevented from taking food from surrounding farms.[176] The more contemplative officers were worried about their exposed position, 'wantonly brought upon ourselves', wrote Boyen with hindsight.[177] The main French army under Napoleon attacked Hohenlohe's forces near Jena before dawn on 14 October, driving them from their forward position on the plateau, before being driven back at 10 o'clock by Prussian infantry advancing in a line. Rather than following this advance with a bayonet charge, Hohenlohe elected to wait for reserves under Ernst von Rüchel, who brought his troops to the battlefield, only 6 miles away, marching in step, 'as

---

[174] Martin van Creveld has done most to qualify the notion of a transition from slow-moving supply trains and rapidly deployable armies living off the land, but without disproving that an important shift took place: M. v. Creveld, *Supplying War: Logistics from Wallenstein to Patton* (Cambridge, 1977).

[175] H. v. Boyen, *Denkwürdigkeiten*, vol. 1, 141.   [176] Ibid., 152.   [177] Ibid.

on parade', reported one onlooker.[178] While he waited, Hohenlohe kept his lines of infantry out in the open for two hours, while French skirmishers picked them off without offering a target themselves. When he finally arrived, five hours later, Rüchel—'a concentrated acid of pure Prussianism', in Clausewitz's phrase—attacked in straight lines and was destroyed by the enemy's concentric fire.[179] At Auerstädt, Brunswick's numerical superiority—50,000 troops against 27,300—was offset by the fact that his army was in retreat. Although they managed to stop Davout's attempt to outflank them, the Prussian troops' own advances were halted by aimed fire from infantry lying in the fields. In Boyen's opinion, looking back on the battle at Auerstädt, the Prussian cavalry was unable either to stop flanking movements or to engage the enemy until infantry units arrived. For its part, the infantry was hindered by the fact that 'our tactics at the time only knew of linear and not massed attacks'.[180] Strategically, in actions away from the battlefield, Prussia's armies had been outmanoeuvred, pushed into battles which they were poorly prepared, tactically, to fight. Many subsequent military reforms in Prussia, bitterly contested by conservative officers who blamed defeat on the mistakes of individual officers and the cowardice of the rank and file, were designed to redress these failings. In future, Prussian troops would fight much more like French soldiers.

Many of the changes which were effected in Prussia in reaction to France after 1806 were implemented in the states of the Confederation of the Rhine in anticipation of or in compliance with Napoleon's orders. The Kingdom of Westphalia, a Napoleonic construction ruled by the emperor's youngest brother, organized its army of 25,000 troops, composed of Hessian, Hanoverian, and other forces, in accordance with the French model of conscription and French military regulations and codes.[181] Likewise, Saxony and Baden adopted French tactics, rules, and, in the Badenese case, ranks, uniforms, and weapons.[182] All of France's German allies were forced to integrate into the *Grande Armée* and adopt its ways of fighting.[183] Wilhelm von Hochberg gave an unparalleled account of what such accommodation entailed, acting as a go-between for the Badenese contingent and the French military headquarters in the war against Austria in 1809 and as the commander of the Badenese troops in Russia in 1812 and Saxony in 1813.[184] The prevailing

---

[178] P. Paret, *The Cognitive Challenge of War*, 23. See also Karl von Suckow, *Aus meinem Soldatenleben* (Stuttgart, 1862), 63–9, who served under Rüchel.

[179] P. Paret, *The Cognitive Challenge of War*, 23.

[180] H. v. Boyen, *Denkwürdigkeiten*, vol. 1, 160.

[181] S. Fiedler, *Grundriss*, vol. 2, 226–7.

[182] Ibid., 228–9. P. Saurer, *Napoleons Adler*, 117. See also W. Meier, *Erinnerungen*, 4: 'experience of the new kind of war left much appear inadequate, patchy or impractical, so that it needed to be changed or abolished in future'.

[183] See, for instance, the account of Wilhelm von Woellwarth, the commander of Württemberg's cavalry in the 1812 campaign, in B. Hildebrand (ed.), *1812: Drei Schwaben unter Napoleon. Russlandberichte eines Infanteristen, eines Leutnants, eines Generals* (Aalen, 1967), 189–99; Georg Kirchmayer, *Veteranen-Huldigung oder Erinnerungen an die Feldzugsjahre 1813, 1814 und 1815* (Munich, 1846), 41, on Bavarian imitation of 'French' forced marches, even after October 1813; A. L. v. Ardenne, *Bergische Lanciers Westfälische Husaren Nr. 11* (Berlin, 1877), 6–10, on Berg.

[184] Wilhelm Markgraf v. Baden, *Denkwürdigkeiten*, vol. 1, 62–278. See also T. v. Barsewisch, *Geschichte des Grossherzoglich Badischen Leib-Grenadier-Regiments 1803–1871* (Karlsruhe, 1893), vol. 1, 64–92, and W. v. Conrady (ed.), *Aus stürmischer Zeit*, 180.

impression which he gave was of a war of movement, characterized by constant forced marches and frequent battles. In 1809, he saw his first fighting near Augsburg on 19 April and his first major battle near Landshut, 60 miles away, on 22 April, before marching through the night after the battle, without food or a coat, to Passau, on the Austrian border, by 27 April, and on to Salzburg in the South, after another all-night march, by 1 May.[185] Fighting took place at Esserding and battle was joined at Ebersberg, after which the troops began marching at night again, with further forced marches on 8 and 10 May, going without food for sixteen-hour stretches, until the troops reached the edge of Vienna, about 250 miles away from Augsburg, on 11 May. The French army entered Vienna on 13 May, crossed the Danube, and suffered a tactical defeat at Aspern-Essling on 21–22 May, before regrouping and defeating the Austrians at the battle of Wagram on 5–6 July. The fighting was brutal and the commanders ruthless, with Marshal André Masséna, to whom Wilhelm was attached as adjutant, not hesitating to throw his own injured troops off the bridge at Ebersberg—to their death—in order to attack the Austrian troops in the town on the other side of the river. The losses of the French army, of which the Badenese soldiers were a part, in the battles of Essling and Wagram were 'enormous', with the outcome perilously close.[186]

The 1812 campaign began in a similar fashion, with Baden's units (6,766 troops) placed in the Ninth Corps (31,000 men), as the 'colourful, converging masses of the French army' began at the start of May 'to divide themselves up in the usual way into different army corps'.[187] From then on, the pattern of marches, inadequate provisioning, living off the land, and ruthlessness was similar to that of 1809, degenerating steadily as supplies ran out and the weather worsened. The Badenese contingent, as part of the Ninth Corps, remained separate from the *Grande Armée* until late November, but it was present at the crossing of the Beresina on 26–29 November, at which the French lost between 30,000 and 45,000 dead or captured combatants and non-combatants, and it took over the rearguard in December. As the Ninth Corps shrank to 900–1,000 men, Hochberg was ordered to keep the rearguard intact, without food or ammunition.[188] The same practices, with the Badenese units placed under French or other allied commanders and expected to follow orders, continued in the campaign of 1813, albeit under different conditions, 'visibly [lacking] that confidence with which the French army was usually injected'.[189] The fact that Hochberg deliberately avoided contact with Napoleon during the final days at Leipzig, fearing an order to defend the city to the last, at once demonstrated a new mistrust of and a continuing subordination to the French leader's blood-curdling commands.

Unlike the states of the Confederation of the Rhine, the Habsburg monarchy, although defeated by France in 1797, 1801, 1805, and 1809, remained independent, ignoring even the limit of 150,000 troops imposed by the Peace of Schonbrünn on

---

[185] On the 1809 campaign, see G. E. Rothenberg, *The Emperor's Last Victory: Napoleon and the Battle of Wagram* (London, 2004).
[186] Wilhelm Markgraf v. Baden, *Denkwürdigkeiten*, vol. 1, 89.
[187] Ibid., 137.   [188] Ibid., 196–7.   [189] Ibid., 235.

14 October 1809. To Joseph Count Radetzky, who had reluctantly agreed to become chief of the Quartermaster-General Staff in July 1809, Austria was an intermediate power between the two Continental Great Powers, Russia and France. As such, the monarchy retained greater freedom of manoeuvre than Prussia after 1806, keeping in place some of the most significant elements of eighteenth-century warfare. Thus, Archduke Karl, who had reassumed command of the Habsburg army after Austria's and Russia's defeat at Austerlitz on 2 December 1805, reiterated long-established principles in his *Grundsätze der höheren Kriegskunst für die Generäle der österreichischen Armee* (1806), predicated on the existence of permanent laws of war, 'which shall always remain the same because they are based on irrefutable mathematical verities'.[190] Although stating that the 'real art of war is how to concentrate superior numbers at a decisive point', he continued to stress the importance of creating magazines along the main route of operations and to rule out strategies which threatened such a route.[191] In both the *Grundsätze* and a series of eight teaching manuals for officers, which were distributed to each battalion from 1806 onwards, Karl—together with other authors—maintained the importance of the line, as 'the ideal formation' for rapid fire, which was still preferred to aimed fire, and for bayonet charges, even against advancing cavalry.[192] When columns or 'battalion masses'—squares composed of densely packed columns—were used, they were to stay aligned and in close contact with each other, forming slowly from the right-hand side of the line and manoeuvring at 90–105 steps per minute.

Skirmishers were to be deployed more extensively than in the past, but 'one always must observe the basic rule that only a small portion of the troops may be employed as skirmishers while the main body must be kept as a reserve in closed order to decide the issue'.[193] Unlike in Prussia, there was no broad shift to light infantry. The organization of regiments was carried out in accordance with the model of 1769, with self-contained corps and more integrated artillery, infantry, and cavalry units only introduced hurriedly at the outbreak of war in 1809, leaving commanders no chance to get used to such large formations of combined arms. The very detail of the Austrian regulations, which were three times as long as their Prussian equivalent despite simplifying previous Habsburg codes, hinted at a persisting lack of initiative and an emphasis on drill. Soldiers were not expected to be freedom-loving patriots, as the *Dienst-Reglement* of 1807 made plain, but obedient servants: 'Love of his monarch and an honest life…', obedience, loyalty, resolution, these are the soldierly virtues', proclaimed the code: 'The confidence of a regiment in its capabilities, pride in its tradition, and the determination to safeguard its reputation constitute the *esprit de corps*. When such ideas have

---

[190] Cited in G. E. Rothenberg, *Napeoleon's Great Adversaries: The Archduke Charles and the Austrian Army, 1792–1814* (Bloomington, IN, 1982), 107. Karl v. Österreich, *Grundsätze der höheren Kriegskunst für die Generäle der österreichischen Armee* (Vienna, 1806), 89–91.

[191] Karl v. Österreich, *Grundsätze*, 8–9.

[192] G. E. Rothenberg, *Napeoleon's Great Adversaries*, 110.

[193] Karl v. Österreich, *Grundsätze*, 85–8. See also Karl v. Österreich, *Beyträge zum practischen Unterricht im Felde für die Officiers der österreichischen Armee* (Vienna, 1807), vol. 3, 89, which reiterates the fact that *tirailleurs* were used because of a lack of training in American and French revolutionary armies.

permeated to the common soldier...all duties and tasks will be carried out willingly.'[194] To Karl's mentor and his principal collaborator on the new military manuals, Karl Friedrich von Lindenau, the suggestion that social and technological transformations had altered the nature of warfare was 'sheer nonsense'.[195]

Nonetheless, Austrian officers were forced to adapt to French reforms, most notably by creating a larger army, in spite of the near bankruptcy of the Habsburg state. Attempts to increase recruitment during the 'first reform period' (1801–5) under Archduke Karl, when he had been given overall command of the army—at 29 years of age—after Austria's defeat at Hohenlinden on 3 December 1800, had met with only limited success, with the Hungarian Diet rejecting the introduction of conscription in 1802 and agreeing to increase its contingent in the standing army to 63,264, compared to 52,000 in 1798, for a period of three years. The new conscription law of 25 October 1804 regulated recruitment by appointing permanent officers in each district, but it contained many exemptions and applied merely to the Austrian lands, except the Tyrol, and to Bohemia and Galicia. No popular levy, reported one of the Archduke's advisors, whether called a

> militia, *Landsturm*, volunteers, *Cerniden*, *insurrectio*, or fencibles, in fact any armed force if it is not composed of trained troops, has any more hope of standing against our enemy than the papal soldiers or those of Cardinal Buffo—even if it were commanded by a Xenophon, Alexander, Turenne, Eugene, Montecuccoli, Condé, Friedrich or Bonaparte.[196]

As a consequence, Vienna failed in 1805 to muster the 320,000 troops pledged in its negotiations with London, in return for £400,000 per annum and a subsidy to defray the costs of mobilization—payments which were never made because of the speed of Austria's defeat. Karl Leiberich von Mack, having become *de facto* commander of Habsburg forces in 1805 after promising Emperor Franz I the quick mobilization of a large army, was unable to provide the 89,000 troops in Bavaria, 53,000 in Vorarlberg, and 142,000 in Italy envisaged in the joint Russian and Austrian plan of 16 July: the main army in Italy, under Karl, numbered 95,000 and the army in Germany about half that number initially, with further troops arriving from Italy and Switzerland. The chief of the Quartermaster-General Staff, admittedly acting in support of Karl's effort to avoid war, estimated that the Austrian army could count on 60,000 fewer infantry and 20,000 fewer cavalry than at the start of its last campaign.

The measures introduced by Karl during the 'second reform period' (1806–9) remedied such deficits, with the introduction by decree of two reserve battalions per line regiment on 12 May 1808, which were to be manned by previously unneeded 'conscripts', and the creation of a *Landwehr* by imperial patent on 9 June 1808, which made service compulsory for all men between 18 and 45, except for a smaller number of exemptions. Although the anticipated 180,000 Austrian and 50,000 Hungarian troops never materialized, *Landwehr* companies did assemble,

---

[194] G. E. Rothenberg, *Napoleon's Great Adversaries*, 118.
[195] Ibid., 110.   [196] Ibid., 73.

with some battalions fighting alongside the regiments of the regular army in 1809. Along with the fuller use of conscription, the creation of reserves, and a larger contingent from Hungary, which provided an extra 20,000 soldiers, the establishment of the *Landwehr* allowed the monarchy to form a battlefield force of 283,401 and a sedentary contingent of 310,815 in 1809.[197] After defeat at Wagram, Austria's force on the rolls fell to 259,918, with 171,066 immediately available. By early 1812, the army had been 'so extremely reduced and what remains of it is so badly paid, clothed and equipped that 60,000 men would be the most that the Government could at the present employ on active service', wrote the British agent in Vienna, John Harcourt King.[198] Yet the laws of conscription for the regular army, reserves, and *Landwehr* all remained in place, so that the Habsburg army could reconstitute itself in 1813, after Karl von Schwarzenberg had declared the neutrality of the Austrian corps on 30 January, having been cut off—with 7,000 killed in battle and 4,000 dying of illness or exposure to the cold—from the retreating *Grande Armée* in Poland. With Clemens von Metternich, the *Staatsminister* and Foreign Minister since 1809, wishing to come to terms with Paris and trying to balance the twin threats of Russia and France, Vienna maintained its neutrality until 27 June, when it joined Prussia, Russia, and Sweden, formally entering the war on 12 August 1813. In the meantime, it called up its conscripts from January onwards, reservists on 22 June, and the *Landwehr* on 6 July, assembling a total force of 479,000, with 298,000 combatants by the end of August. The monarchy eventually mobilized a total of 568,000 troops, making it the 'first power' of the Coalition, in Metternich's view, with the other powers 'auxiliaries'.[199]

Paradoxically, the size of the Coalition armies between 1813 and 1815 permitted their commanders to mimic the strategy of their eighteenth-century predecessors. Radetzky, the author of the allied Trachtenberg Plan adopted in July 1813, favoured 'a system of defence combined with offensive operations on a small scale over a general offensive movement, which might win much, but also might lose all'.[200] As in Russia in 1812, allied armies were to retire, if attacked by Napoleon, while the other Coalition forces arrived, wearing the French corps down through attrition and hemming them in, before a final concentric allied advance with superior numbers of troops. Such strategic manoeuvring took place in Saxony in the autumn of 1813, after early defeats inflicted on Blücher at Großgörschen (2 May), Peter von Wittgenstein at Bautzen (20–21 May), and Schwarzenberg at Dresden (26–27 August), with 335,000 troops of the Allies eventually facing 190,000 French-led soldiers at Leipzig (16–19 October). The strategy for the Coalition's invasion of France in early 1814 proceeded in a similar fashion: Schwarzenberg advanced cautiously with the army of Bohemia through Switzerland in order to avoid French forts to the north, before linking up with the army of Silesia in the Marne. Napoleon attacked Blücher near Brienne, but the Prussian commander withdrew

---

[197] Ibid., 126.   [198] Ibid., 175.
[199] Ibid., 180. See also O. Regele, *Feldmarschall Radetzky* (Vienna, 1957), 118.
[200] G. E. Rothenberg, *Napoleon's Great Adversaries*, 181.

until reinforced at La Rothière (29 January); he defeated Schwarzenberg at Montereau (17–18 February), but the Austrians retreated to Troyes in order not to risk being destroyed. Further assaults by Napoleon against the superior numbers of the army of Silesia, backed up by the army of the north, near Laon on 8–9 March— with 37,000 troops against Blücher's 85,000—and against the army of Bohemia at Arcis-sur-Aube on 20 March—with 30,000 against 100,000—were repulsed. As Napoleon marched east to threaten the Allies' lines of communication, the combined armies of the Coalition continued in the other direction with 200,000 men, occupying Paris by 30 March and prompting Napoleon's senior commanders to mutiny rather than supporting the emperor's last-ditch march back to the capital with 36,000 soldiers. Thus, although the Coalition had conducted a war of attrition and manoeuvre, it had done so with mass armies of raw conscripts, with under a third of Austrian soldiers fully trained—'peasants in uniform', in Radetzky's words—and the majority 'drenched to the bones, most of them without shoes, many without great coats', according to the report of the British military observer in August 1813.[201] In such circumstances, the Austrians had been obliged to simplify their tactics, to pay less attention to lines of supply, to live off the land to a greater extent, to keep their forces together, to escape from and catch up with the enemy—at a speed of 15 miles per day in pursuit of the French in late 1813— through forced marches, to accept large-scale losses, and to rely—with an overwhelming number of troops—on decisive battles.

Even in Austria, which remained the most independent of the German states, warfare had become broader in scope after 1792, with mass armies requiring more money and men, and it had become more intense, with a greater number of battles and higher rates of killing, compared to the conflicts of the eighteenth century. Arguably, battles of 'annihilation' (*Vernichtung*) and 'national' defence, combined with a revolutionary or Napoleonic redefining of territorial states and reordering of the European states' system, had brought into question the very existence of most German lands and, from many educated observers' point of view, a putative German nation. 'Austria faces a terrible crisis', Archduke Karl warned his brother, the emperor, after defeat at Austerlitz in 1805:

> Your Majesty stands alone at the end of a short but horrible war; your country is devastated, your treasury empty, your credit lost, the honour of your arms diminished, your reputation tarnished and the economic well-being of your subjects ruined for many years. The devotion of your people is shaky, you have no allies.[202]

In Prussia, to reformers such as Gneisenau, 'invasion' by the enemy was synonymous not merely with the 'annihilation' of an army in a decisive battle, but with the annihilation of the state.[203] If the French 'tyrant' had not yet toppled the

---

[201] Ibid., 179. R. Wilson, *Private Diary of Travels, Personal Services and Public Events during Missions and Employment with the European Armies in the Campaigns of 1812, 1813, 1814*, ed. H. Randolph (London, 1861), vol. 2, 89.

[202] G. E. Rothenberg, *Napoleon's Great Adversaries*, 104.

[203] Gneisenau to Hardenberg, 8 Aug. 1811, in A. W. A. N. v. Gneisenau, *Ausgewählte militärische Schriften*, 167.

throne of the Prussian monarch, 'we should thank the circumstance that Austria has not yet been subjugated and the plans of the French cabinet against Russia are not yet ready to be carried out', he had written in a memorandum of 1808: 'Sooner or later, we should expect to be removed from the ranks of independent peoples (*Völker*).'[204] Since the kingdom's standing army was not sufficient on its own to offer the prospect, or even the 'probability', 'of a successful outcome', it was necessary to contemplate 'sources of resistance which governments have until now neglected or feared'; namely, 'the arming of the people'.[205] The motto that 'You are either with us or against us', with any cooperation classified as 'high treason' and punished with execution, would have radically altered previous conventions, as would the orchestration of a 'popular uprising' (*Volksaufstand*) against an invading or occupying army, blurring the boundary between combatants and non-combatants, with the possibility that civilians would be killed like soldiers on the battlefield.[206] Militia units were to hide in the woods or mountains and to operate during the night, attacking and unsettling an occupying power. The named militia leaders were to be given, 'during an enemy invasion', 'the right over life and death, the goods and blood of the inhabitants for the purpose of the defence of the country'.[207] In the event, such plans were not put into effect, because when the war with France came, as Gneisenau and others were sure it would between 1807 and 1811, it occurred in concert with Austrian and Russian allies and after the collapse of the *Grande Armée* in 1812, making a military victory over Napoleon seem more likely and the necessity of a popular 'insurrection' more remote.[208] The fact that the leaders of the reformed Prussian army were willing to think in such terms, however, with the expressed aim of extending their plans to the 15 million inhabitants of the 'German nation', betrays *in extremis* the extent to which warfare had changed. No other German power countenanced this type of 'popular' uprising and conflict, but most had already accepted or adapted to the transition towards *Volkskriege* or 'people's wars'. The next chapter investigates how widespread and significant this understanding of warfare was amongst different sections of the people itself.

---

[204] Gneisenau memorandum, summer 1808, in A. W. A. N. v. Gneisenau, *Ausgewählte militärische Schriften*, 117.
[205] Ibid. On the background to this shift, see M. Rink, *Vom Partheygänger zum Partisanen. Die Konzeption des kleinen Krieges in Preußen 1740–1813* (Frankfurt, 1999).
[206] Gneisenau memorandum, 1808, in A. W. A. N. v. Gneisenau, *Ausgewählte militärische Schriften*, 118; Gneisenau to Hardenberg, 8 Aug. 1811, 163–89.
[207] Ibid., 180.   [208] Ibid.

2

Heroism and the Defence of the *Volk*

Three of the best-known philosophers in Germany—a country of poetic and thinking people according to the Romantic distortion of Germaine de Staël in 1810—showed how reactions to war differed during the two decades after 1792, and how they had changed.[1] Immanuel Kant produced the most famous treatise on 'Perpetual Peace' in 1795, criticizing the dynastic wars of absolutist regimes and praising the pacifism of republics, which listened to the frightened pleas of their own citizenry and the cautious counsel of commerce.[2] Republics had, 'as a result of their nature, to be inclined towards perpetual peace', wrote the Königsberg philosopher, alluding both to the moral imperatives which he had explored in his *Kritik der praktischen Vernunft* (1788) and to hopes which he continued to entertain of the revolutionary French republic.[3] War, it appeared, could be prevented by an internal political revolution, which had already given a voice to those most affected by war in France and, if the French model were followed, would do so elsewhere. Like Kant, who was his principal academic preceptor, the Swabian-born philosopher Georg Wilhelm Friedrich Hegel, teaching at the university of Jena between 1801 and 1807, admired the modernizing policies of French revolutionaries. He even extended such admiration to Napoleon, whose soldiers looted the university city after battle in October 1806, describing him as 'this soul of the world (*Weltseele*)' and marvelling at him 'raising his arm over the world and ruling it'.[4] Unlike Kant, Hegel maintained that war, which he claimed 'no one' had 'imagined' 'as we have seen it' in Jena, played a vital role in reinforcing the moral purpose of the state, which remained separate from the self-interested transactions of civil society and the altruistic limitations of families or nations.[5] Military conflict, wrote the philosopher in 1802, preserved 'the moral health of nations (*Völker*)', just 'as the movement of the wind' kept 'lakes from stagnation'.[6] Johann

---

[1] M. Wallenborn, *Deutschland und die Deutschen in Mme de Staëls De l'Allemagne* (Frankfurt, 1998).

[2] See V. Gerhardt, *Immanuel Kants Entwurf 'Zum ewigen Frieden'. Eine Theorie der Politik* (Darmstadt, 1995); and W. Beutin (ed.), *Hommage à Kant. Kants Schrift 'Zum ewigen Frieden'* (Hamburg, 1996).

[3] I. Kant, 'Zum ewigen Frieden', in I. Kant, *Gesammelte Schriften* (Berlin, 1900–83), vol. 8, 356.

[4] G. W. F. Hegel to F. I. Niethammer, 13 Oct. 1806, J. Hoffmeister (ed.), *Briefe von und an Hegel* (Hamburg, 1952), vol. 1, 120.

[5] Ibid., 126.

[6] G. W. F. Hegel, 'Über die wissenschaftlichen Behandlungsarten des Naturrechts' (1802), in G. W. F. Hegel, *Sämtliche Werke*, ed. H. Glockner (Stuttgart, 1927–30), vol. 1, 487–8. See also G. Drechsler and H. Jakubowski, 'Das Phänomen "Krieg" in Georg Wilhelm Friedrich Hegels Philosophie', in B. Bissmann (ed.), *Studien zur Kulturgeschichte, Sprache und Dichtung* (Jena, 1990), 78–93.

Gottlieb Fichte, a student of Kant and the predecessor of Hegel at the new University of Berlin, tended to agree, in this respect, more with the latter than with the former.

As an idealist, Fichte comprehended war within the framework of his 'theory of knowledge (*Wissenschaftslehre*)', which he defined as a 'pragmatic history of the human mind', designed to overcome—like Hegel in *Die Phänomenologie des Geistes* (1807)—Kant's distinction between subjects, faced by a phenomenal world of 'appearances', and objects, which were unknowable noumena or 'things-in-themselves'.[7] Whereas Kant had attempted to identify and justify a priori moral duties, Fichte recognized that the 'Nicht-Ich'—contrasted with the subjectivity of 'Ich' or 'I'—was not merely produced by subjects' unfolding and externalized consciousness, but was the result of a contingent history, not least because 'the majority of men would be more easily persuaded to take themselves for lumps of lava…than to consider themselves as egos'.[8] As such, Fichte's version of history was less closely tied than those of Hegel and Kant to philosophical premises, although his emphasis in *Reden an die deutsche Nation* (1808) on the 'educated classes in Germany' as 'the authors of this new creation' of a German nation derived, in part, from his overriding interest in the dualism of subject and object.[9] In accordance with changing conditions, the philosopher, who had considered offering his services as a lecturer to the French republic in the annexed territories of the left bank of the Rhine in the 1790s, altered his view of history, talking of perpetual peace and the harmonious coexistence of nations in a treatise on natural law as late as 1796–7 but turning to depictions of conflicting nations in later works dating from the Napoleonic period. 'Time is taking great strides with us more than with any other age since the history of the world began', he wrote in the lectures, referring back to *Die Grundzüge des gegenwärtigen Zeitalters* (1804–5): 'At some point [in the last three years] self-seeking has destroyed itself…, and since it would not voluntarily set itself any other aim but self, an external power has forced upon it another and a foreign purpose.'[10] The creation of a new German nation or national polity was hindered 'by that alien power [namely, the French First Empire] which governs its fate', but it could still be achieved: 'it is the aim of these addresses to show you its existence and its true owner, to bring before your eyes a living picture of it, and to indicate the means of creating it'.[11]

Throughout the revolutionary and Napoleonic years, Fichte assumed that nations were existing cultural entities and desirable political ones, claiming in the *Reden*, for instance, to 'speak for Germans simply, of Germans simply, not recognizing, but setting aside completely and rejecting, all the dissociating distinctions which for centuries unhappy events have caused in this single nation'.[12] The point of the lectures was, 'by means of the new education', 'to mould the Germans into a corporate body, which shall be stimulated and animated in all its individual members by a common interest'.[13] France's occupation of Germany had caused pain—'I know that pain'—but had also served as a 'spur' towards 'reflection, decision

---

[7] G. A. Kelly, 'Introduction', in G. A. Kelly (ed.), *Johann Gottlieb Fichte*, xix.   [8] Ibid.
[9] Ibid., 14.   [10] Ibid., 1.   [11] Ibid., 2.   [12] Ibid.   [13] Ibid., 12.

and action': 'it is only by means of the common characteristic of being German that we can avert the downfall of our nation which is threatened by its fusion with foreign peoples, and win back again an individuality that is self-supporting and quite incapable of any dependence upon others'.[14] Like the Germanic tribes under Arminius, who had 'assumed as a matter of course that every man would rather die than become half a Roman, present-day Germans could hope to bequeath "freedom to their children" only by resisting', imitating Arminius's followers' 'unyielding resistance, which the whole modern world has to thank for being what it now is'.[15] Nations were victorious when they renounced 'the way of thinking', typical of the eighteenth century, 'which regards war as a game of chance, where the stakes are temporal gain or loss, and which fixes the amount to be staked on the cards even before it begins the game—such a way of thinking is defeated even by a whim'.[16]

National wars were necessarily waged without fixed stakes, since there was an affinity between nations, states, and freedom which ensured that such conflicts endangered subjects' autonomy and identity, as well as government.[17] 'This much is clear, that an original people needs freedom, that this is the security for its continuance as an original people, and that, as it goes on, it is able to stand an ever-increasing degree of freedom without the slightest danger', wrote the philosopher, tying his earlier libertarianism via a continuing—and reinforced—belief in the nation to an instrumentalization and subordination of the state:

> This is the first matter in respect of which love of fatherland must govern the state, too. Then, too, it must be love of fatherland that governs the state by placing before it a higher object than the usual one of maintaining internal peace, property, personal freedom, and the life and well-being of all. For this higher object alone, and with no other intention, does the state assemble an armed force. When the question arises of making use of this, when the call comes to stake everything that the state, in the narrow conception of the word, sets before itself as object, viz., property, personal freedom, life, and well-being, nay, even the continued existence of the state itself; when the call comes to make an original decision with responsibility to God alone, and without a clear and reasonable idea that what is intended will surely be attained – for this is never possible in such matters—then, and then only, does there live at the helm of the state a truly original and primary life, and at this point, and not before, the true sovereign rights of government enter, like God, to hazard the lower life for the sake of the higher.[18]

There was no 'real true life' or 'original decision' required to maintain the constitution, laws, and 'civil prosperity' in normal times, in contrast to states of internal or external threat, 'when this regular course is endangered'.[19] 'The devouring flame of higher patriotism', which embraced 'the nation as the vesture of the eternal', ensured that 'the noble-minded man joyfully sacrifices himself'.[20] Such sacrifices were conceivable, in wars or revolutions, as the corollary of nationalism alone.

---

[14] Ibid., 3–4.   [15] Ibid., 123.   [16] Ibid., 124–5.
[17] In general, see H. Münkler, '"Wer sterben kann, wer will den den zwingen". Fichte als Philosoph des Krieges', in J. Kunisch and H. Münkler (eds), *Die Wiedergeburt des Krieges aus dem Geist der Revolution* (Berlin, 1999), 241–60.
[18] Ibid., 119–20.   [19] Ibid., 120.   [20] Ibid.

Recently, historians have questioned whether press and literary accounts of national wars of 'liberation' (*Befreiungskriege*) or 'freedom' (*Freiheitskriege*), which Fichte seemed at once to advocate and anticipate, were representative of a majority of subjects' views or, even, of 'public opinion'. Many scholars have taken issue with Otto Dann's thesis that widespread criticism of 'princes' wars' and support for 'perpetual peace', which had purportedly united the middling orders and the nobility in the late eighteenth century, was replaced after the turn of the century by patriotic backing of *Volkskriege* against France, as 'German citizens' (*deutsche Bürger*) became soldiers.[21] Fichte's lecture of 1813, in which he contrasts old, limited forms of dynastic warfare ('*Krieg der Herrscherfamilien*')—with citizens able to buy exemptions—and new types of 'wars of the nation' ('*Krieg des Volkes*') waged for 'the people's freedom and independence', is taken by Dann to be indicative of the transformation which had occurred.[22] Scholars have asked, first, how many patriotic soldiers there were, even within the iconic *Lützower* corps of volunteers, and how significant their role was.[23] Second, they have re-examined the assumption that civilians, affected by the traditional and new ravages of Revolutionary and Napoleonic Wars, made a distinction between different sides and conceived of such conflicts as patriotic or national struggles for survival and emancipation.[24] In particular, scholars have posited that Prussia constituted an exception, with its subjects—or those in the heartlands of Brandenburg—confronted by a unique programme of reform and experiencing an unusual pattern and type of wars, compared to the states of the Confederation of the Rhine and the lands of the South and West.[25] Third, they have linked the question of *Kriegsbilder* and experiences of war to the wider debate about the impact of nationalism in early nineteenth-century Germany, with some historians, such as Jörg Echternkamp, sceptical that

---

[21] O. Dann, 'Der deutsche Bürger wird Soldat', 61–84. Also, O. Dann, 'Vernunftfrieden und nationaler Krieg. Der Umbruch im Friedensverhalten des deutschen Bürgertums zu Beginn des 19. Jahrhunderts', in W. Huber and J. Schwerdtfeger (eds), *Kirche zwischen Krieg und Frieden. Studien zur Geschichte des deutschen Protestantismus* (Stuttgart, 1976), 169–224.

[22] O. Dann, 'Der deutsche Bürger wird Soldat', 74: the quotations are from Fichte. See also H.-M. Blitz, *Aus Liebe zum Vaterland. Die deutsche Nation im 18. Jahrhundert* (Hamburg, 2000).

[23] See, for instance, P. Brandt, 'Einstellungen, Motive und Ziele von Kriegsfreiwilligen 1813/14', 211–33; and P. Brandt, 'Die Befreiungskriege', 17–57; J. Echternkamp, '"Teutschland, des Soldaten Vaterland"', 181–203; M. Sikora, 'Desertion und nationale Mobilmachung', 112–40; K. Hagemann, 'Der "Bürger" als "Nationalkrieger"', 74–102.

[24] U. Planert, *Der Mythos*; U. Planert, 'Staat und Krieg an der Wende zur Moderne', 159–80; K. B. Aaslestad, 'Lost Neutrality and Economic Warfare', 373–94; K. B. Aaslestad, *Place and Politics*; K. B. Aaslestad, 'War without Battles: Civilian Experiences of Economic Warfare during the Napoleonic Era in Hamburg', in A. Forrest, K. Hagemann, and J. Rendall (eds), *Soldiers, Citizens, and Civilians: Experiences and Perceptions of the Revolutionary and Napoleonic Wars, 1790–182* (Basingstoke, 2008), 118–36; K. B. Aaslestad and K. Hagemann, '1806 and Its Aftermath: Revisiting the Period of the Napoleonic Wars in German Central European Historiography', *Central European History*, 39 (2006), 547–79.

[25] In addition to U. Planert, see T. C. W. Blanning, *The French Revolution in Germany*; M. Rowe, *From Reich to State*; U. Andrea, *Die Rheinländer*; G. Schuck, *Rheinbundpatriotismus und politische Öffentlichkeit*; P. Sauer, *Napoleons Adler*; H. Berding, *Napoleonische Herrschafts-*; J. Engelbrecht, *Das Herzogtum Berg*; M. Hamm, *Die bayerische Integrationspolitik in Tirol*. On so-called Prussian exceptionalism, see U. Frevert, *A Nation in Barracks: Modern Germany, Military Conscription and Civil Society* (Oxford, 2004).

a national awakening took place and others, like Karen Hagemann, emphasizing the breadth and significance of the movement, within a Prussian public sphere and sections of the Prussian *Bürgertum*, towards enduring, gendered, aggressive forms of nationalism during wartime.[26] Fourth, they have assessed the role of war—or belligerence—in the construction of national mythologies and the founding of nation-states.[27] Lastly, they have investigated the relationship between belligerence, nationalism, and the development of a public sphere (*Öffentlichkeit*), the press, political associations, and the social milieux which supported them.[28] The principal points of disagreement in such historical debates derive from scholars' different objects of study, with those who concentrate on ordinary citizens—especially outside the main cities—and on soldiers tending to qualify or deny the impact of patriotism or German nationalism during wartime, and those who examine an emerging public sphere tending to emphasize its impact. This chapter focuses on such a limited but expanding *Öffentlichkeit* in order to show how it altered contemporaries' attitudes to war.

'PUBLIC OPINION' AND THE STATE

Conceptions of war in the revolutionary and Napoleonic eras depended to a significant extent on discussions in newspapers, periodicals, pamphlets, almanacs, and other types of book, and on the relationship between the public sphere and the state. Such discussions took place within overlapping and changing historical understandings and symbolic representations of conflict, which remained closely tied to the self-image and projections of power of Germany's monarchical regimes.

---

[26] J. Echternkamp, *Der Aufstieg des deutschen Nationalismus*, 216, referring to Prussia; K. Hagemann, *Mannlicher Muth und Teutsche Ehre*. See the Introduction for further literature.

[27] Above all, see J. Leonhard, *Bellizismus und Nation. Kriegsdeutung und Nationsbestimmung in Europa und den Vereinigten Staaten 1750–1914* (Munich, 2008); and J. Leonhard, 'Nation-States and Wars', in T. Baycroft and M. Hewitson (eds), *What Is a Nation? Europe, 1789–1914* (Oxford, 2006), 231–54. Also, N. Buschmann and D. Langewiesche (eds), *Der Krieg in den Gründungsmythen europäischer Nationen und der USA* (Frankfurt, 2003); H.-U. Wehler, 'Nationalstaat und Krieg', in H.-U. Wehler, *Umbruch und Kontinuität* (Munich, 2000), 64–80; C. Tilly (ed.), *The Formation of Nation-States in Western Europe* (Princeton, 1975); D. Moran and A. Waldron (eds), *The People in Arms*; J. Kunisch and H. Münkler (eds), *Wiedergeburt*; M. Jeismann, *Das Vaterland der Feinde*.

[28] J. M. Brophy, *Popular Culture and the Public Sphere in the Rhineland, 1800–1850* (Cambridge, 2007); J. M. Brophy, 'The Common Reader in the Rhineland', *Past and Present*, 185 (2004), 119–58; J. M. Brophy, 'The Public Sphere', in J. Sperber (ed.), *Germany, 1800–1870* (Oxford, 2004), 185–208; R. Schenda, *Volk ohne Buch* (Munich, 1977); O. Dann, *Lesegesellschaften und europäische Emanzipation* (Munich, 1981); G. Jäger and J. Schönert (eds), *Die Leihbibliothek als Institution des literarischen Lebens im 18. und 19. Jahrhundert* (Hamburg, 1980); R. Engelsing, 'Zur politischen Bildung der deutschen Unterschichten 1789–1863', *Historische Zeitschrift* (1968), 337–69, also published in R. Engelsing, *Zur Sozialgeschichte deutscher Mittel- und Unterschichten*, 2nd edn (Göttingen, 1978). On political associations, see T. Nipperdey, 'Verein als soziale Struktur in Deutschland im späten 18. und frühen 19. Jahrhundert', in R. Engelsing (ed.), *Gesellschaft, Kultur, Theorie* (Göttingen, 1976), 174–205; O. Dann (ed.), *Vereinswesen und bürgerliche gesellschaft in Deutschland* (Munich, 1984); and C. Lipp, 'Verein als poltisches Handlungsmuster. Das Beispiel des württembergischen Vereinswesens von 1800 bis zur Revolution 1848–49', in E. François (ed.), *Sociabilité et société bourgeoise en France, Allemagne et en Suisse 1750–1850* (Paris, 1986), 275–96.

In museums, concert halls, and, to a more limited extent, theatres, rulers and administrations were able to shape or control the production and dissemination of works of art.[29] Some images and tropes of conflict were shared—the martial prince, a common stock of heroes, common histories of German and imperial armies, military uniforms, battle formations, the self-destruction of the Thirty Years' War—and others proved divisive, as military reformers, contending with burghers' critiques of standing armies, were aware. The subjects of the 350-odd Imperial Knights (350,000), the fifty-one Free Imperial Cities, the thirty-four ecclesiastical and sixty secular princes, and the forty or so monasteries and abbeys, although under the auspices of the imperial army, had little direct experience of the military, since their lands had, at most, largely ceremonial forces before the dissolution of the Holy Roman Empire in 1806. Even within the larger territories of the nine Electorates (Mainz, Trier, Cologne, Bohemia, Saxony, the Palatinate, Brandenburg, Bavaria, and Hanover), subjects had contrasting experiences, with some belonging to powerful states such as the Hohenzollern and Habsburg monarchies, boasting large armies and corresponding systems of recruitment, and with others belonging to virtual principalities such as the Electorate of Mainz, which had a population of 350,000 and an army of 2,800—respectively, twenty and a hundred times smaller than those of Prussia by the end of the eighteenth century. Against such a patchwork of reality, depictions of and discourses about war, however pervasive they seemed, were likely to contain differing sets of assumptions beyond 1806, when military reorganization and, to a lesser extent, experiences of combat began to converge.

The impact of 'public' discussions and opinion on historical and symbolic representations of conflict is difficult to gauge. In the absence of parties and parliaments in the absolutist systems of government of most German states, public debates were not connected straightforwardly to 'politics', but they did influence and inform the policies of state administrations.[30] Throughout the eighteenth century, the Holy Roman Empire had counted more newspapers than other European countries, with fifty to sixty in 1700—or more than the rest of Europe combined—and 200 in 1789, and with total readership increasing from about 250,000 to 3 million over the same period from a population of 29 million, or between 10 and 20 per cent of adults, exceeding by far the small educated middle class (*Bürgertum*), which constituted less than 5 per cent of the urban population.[31]

---

[29] See, for instance, J. J. Sheehan, *Museums in the German Art World from the End of the Old Regime to the Rise of Modernism* (Oxford, 2000), and T. C. W. Blanning, *The Culture of Power and the Power of Culture: Old Regime Europe, 1660–1789* (Oxford, 2003), 161–80.

[30] In addition to this chapter, see Chapter 1.

[31] M. Welke, 'Gemeinsame Lektüre und frühe Formen von Gruppenbildungen im 17. und 18. Jahrhundert. Zeitungslesen in Deutschland', in O. Dann (ed.), *Lesegesellschaften und bürgerliche Emanzipation* (Munich, 1981), 29. For the relevant population of the Holy Roman Empire, see P. H. Wilson, 'Bolstering the Prestige of the Habsburgs: The End of the Holy Roman Empire in 1806', *International History Review*, 28 (2006), 718; P. H. Wilson, *From Reich to Revolution: German History, 1558–1806* (Basingstoke, 2004), 364–77. On the urban educated middle class, see K. Hagemann, *Mannlicher Muth und teutscher Ehre*, 116. Rudolf Ibbeken, *Preussen*, 25, estimates that there were about 100,000 full participants in 'the cultural life of the nation' in the Holy Roman Empire and, therefore, about 25,000 in Prussia, based on Thomas Abbt's guess of 80,000 for the mid-eighteenth

The act of reading newspapers had, remarked Hegel, become the morning prayers of nineteenth-century men.[32] Such reading rested on an increase in literacy in the German lands from an estimated 10 per cent in 1700 to 25 per cent in 1800, with much higher rates for certain states (80–90 per cent of men and 40–45 per cent of women in Baden) and for cities (86.9 per cent of men and 60.4 per cent of women in Coblenz).[33] 'It really is the case that a new, universal and far more powerful reading fashion than any before has spread not just throughout Germany but throughout the whole of Europe too, attracting all classes and all strata of society, and suppressing almost every other kind of reading matter', wrote one observer in 1792: 'This is the reading of newspapers and political pamphlets.'[34] Although 'the smith on his anvil' and 'the cobbler on his stool' could be found reading newspapers by the 1790s, or having news read to them, most subscribers were educated and urban, betrayed by Christoph Martin Wieland's remark in 1791 that 'writers', 'the *real men of the nation*', were 'being read everywhere, their publications [penetrating] eventually into even the smallest towns'.[35] By the end of the eighteenth century, 24 per cent of Germans were living in towns, compared to 12 per cent a century earlier, and up to 94 per cent of property owners—in Berlin in 1782— could at least sign their names.[36]

Authors like Goethe recognized that they owed their position, despite accepting the patronage of the Duke of Saxe-Weimar after publishing the best-selling *Die Leiden des jungen Werther* in 1775, to a reading 'public', which extended to 'the middling sort [*einem gewissen Mittelstand*]... to which belong the people who live in the small towns, of which Germany boasts so many well-stocked examples', including 'all the officials great and small to be found there, the artisans, the manufacturers, and especially their wives and daughters, also all the rural clergy'.[37] Naturally, it would be misleading to pretend that such readers automatically formed part of a political nation or, even, a public sphere, since many of them were clearly seeking diversion or entertainment in the first instance, with 'the works of good and bad writers... to be found in the apartments of princes, and alongside the weaver's loom', as *Der Weltbürger* put it in 1791.[38] '*Belles lettres*' constituted 27.3 per cent of published titles in the German lands in 1800, compared to 2.8 per cent in 1700.[39] By the same token, however, works of history, politics, biography, geography, philosophy, science, commerce, and war made up 55 per cent at the end of the eighteenth century, compared to 30.8 per cent at its start. Previously, only academics had read books other than the Bible and catechisms, wrote Johann Gottfried Pahl, whereas, at the turn of the century, 'The various branches of

---

century, but he concedes that the audience of periodicals and books—with some contemporaries being read to or being informed of events by word of mouth—was much larger.

[32] K. Rosenkranz, *Georg Wilhelm Friedrich Hegels Leben* (Berlin, 1844), 543. T. C. W. Blanning, *The Culture of Power*, 158–9.

[33] H. J. Graff, *The Legacies of Literacy: Continuities and Contradictions in Western Culture and Society* (Bloomington, IN, 1987), 187; T. C. W. Blanning, *The Culture of Power*, 114.

[34] K. A. Ragotzky, cited in T. C. W. Blanning, *The Culture of Power*, 134.   [35] Ibid., 133–4.

[36] M. Erbe, *Deutsche Geschichte, 1713–1790* (Stuttgart, 1985), 26; T. C. W. Blanning, *The Culture of Power*, 114.

[37] T. C. W. Blanning, *The Culture of Power*, 132.   [38] Ibid., 133.   [39] Ibid., 146.

knowledge have ceased to be the possession of a specific estate and at least a super-ficial knowledge of them is deemed necessary for all educated people': 'This love of reading, now so widely diffused, has created the need for a large number of new books especially because the new breed of Germans do not read in the manner of their ancestors. ... We have got used to reading in a hurry.'[40] Readers consumed a more extensive range of works and periodicals, perhaps in a more superficial way. 'News' had come to constitute an important part of their diet.

It is difficult to assess with any certainty the impact of political treatises, national propaganda, and war reports in this expanding but ill-defined public sphere.[41] Even a successful publicist such as Ernst Moritz Arndt lamented, in the second part of *Geist der Zeit* (1809), that the 'fatherland', although able to count on 'bold and courageous hearts', lacked 'bold and courageous voices' willing to proclaim Germany's 'emergency and salvation with seriousness and love'.[42] What was more, when the Greifswald academic sought to address 'his *Volk*', he was unable to find it: 'how do I talk to you, German *Volk*? What are you and where are you?'[43] 'Writers' (*die Schreiber*), as he described his 'kin' or 'family' of academics and publicists, were usually too distant from 'life', as in the case of philosophers and historians, or, like journalists, they said nothing of substance or they 'flow thoughtlessly with the tide of the time'.[44] In an era of occupation and war, in which he feared that he might 'go under', 'to tell the truth is not easy', he went on in the first volume of *Geist der Zeit* (1806), shortly before being exiled in Sweden.[45] With states' 'resources overstretched', with 'the machinery of state, which moves people around', using its subjects like 'blindfolded mill-horses', and with 'old ine-qualities and injustices' resurfacing 'in the new order' through 'exceptions and privileges', the population had come to be characterized by a 'sense of slavery', with few links 'between citizens and the state'.[46] Prior to the revolutionary and Napoleonic periods, 'the artificiality and the machine-like nature of the regime of recent times' had permitted the gradual emergence of 'despotism', weighing down all subjects and creating 'a throng of suppliers, helpers' helpers and servants of power'.[47] Germany's despots had filled vacuums of power, in the same way that water and air followed 'eternal physical laws', according to the principle of 'I rule where I can': 'Governments have been able to do everything in the last centuries, republics have been destroyed, monarchies have for the most part become despot-isms.'[48] In the East, where 'the state machine ... goes about its business somewhat dumbly and cluelessly but also straightforwardly', this form of government had 'its advantages', needing fewer 'masters, helpers, leaders and improvers' than in the West, where 'despotism' was not 'a natural growth'.[49] In such circumstances, without institutional mechanisms to influence the exercise of power, publicists like Arndt sometimes felt powerless.

---

[40] E. Schön, *Der Verlust der Sinnlichkeit, oder die Verwandlungen des Lesers. Mentalitätswandel um 1800* (Stuttgart, 1987), 142.

[41] See J. J. Breuilly, 'The Response to Napoleon', 261.

[42] E. M. Arndt, *Geist der Zeit* (Berlin, 1806–9, 1813), vol. 1, 9.

[43] Ibid., vol. 2, 26.   [44] Ibid., vol. 1, 46, 10–47.   [45] Ibid., 14.

[46] Ibid., 62.   [47] Ibid., 56.   [48] Ibid., 54.   [49] Ibid.

Nevertheless, journalists and academics continued to publicize their opinions, perhaps believing along with Arndt, that nature gave people tears and speech in order to distinguish them from animals.[50] 'To tell the truth is not now easy', the essayist and poet continued, for 'I, too, can drown in this current', but 'education (*Bildung*) and all the arts' remained necessary, despite being threatened by 'the swords of soldiers', in order to prevent a return 'to the old barbarity'.[51] 'Contemporaries' (*Zeitgenossen*) had the feeling of living in a period of accelerated time, wrote Arndt: 'Whoever has lived through the last twenty years has lived for centuries.'[52] Although such a sentiment was 'only a reflection on time, and vanity at the same time', giving many 'the feeling of unusual misfortune', it gave citizens the impression of momentous transformation: 'The age is in flight and flashes its important pictures past in such rapid change.'[53] Contemporaries were frequently reduced to 'wondering spectators', feeling that they were at once faced by 'an endless length of time, opening out before them', and that they had 'no measure of time at all'.[54] For Arndt, the 'learned' or 'enlightened' eighteenth century, 'to which we all belong', had progressed 'restlessly' and 'one-sidedly', bringing 'the sciences and knowledge of the Europeans so far that they themselves marvelled more than once at the immeasurability of their oversight'.[55] The French Revolution had reinforced the tendencies of the closing century, provoking 'spiritual and moral revolutions of people in their inclinations and strivings', but leaving 'no trace, like a ship in the sea or a wing in the air', as the age broke with tradition after tradition 'without measure or feeling': 'The spirit of destruction is fresh; struggles are fiercest where they seem to be most tranquil; and the old order will crumble into rubble.'[56] The 'terrible revolutions' had begun well, with 'geniuses' hoping to effect 'a moderation and purification of the most noble minds of Europe' as a consequence of their 'spiritual education'.[57] The writer continued:

> The political—the overthrow of old thrones and constitutions, destructive wars, the exploitation and downfall of peoples—seemed to them [leaders or 'geniuses'], from their elevated point of view, merely petty, even useful for the great purpose of the period, as they used to say. ...Their error misled many and still misleads some'[,] [leading astray] the mob of blind fools and cowardly scoundrels who cannot see or seem not to be able to see what is as clear as day.[58]

In the end, such revolutionary 'one-sidedness' seemed to have brought about destruction for its own sake in France. It had, however, also elicited a necessary national reaction in Germany, in Arndt's view, permitting the 'social class (*Bürgerklasse*)' of writers to appeal to a broad reading public in a time of existential need.[59] Partly because of scepticism about revolutionary politics and partly to appeal to a wider public, Arndt addressed his readers, not in the manner of a political treatise but in the style of a religious sermon. Despite his contempt for the 'mob of fools', he assumed that his writings would reach and convince both

---

[50] Ibid., 10.   [51] Ibid., 14.   [52] Ibid., 49.   [53] Ibid.   [54] Ibid.
[55] Ibid., 26.   [56] Ibid., 50–1.   [57] Ibid., vol. 2, 7.
[58] Ibid.   [59] Ibid., vol. 1, 22.

policy-makers—he collaborated with Stein in government during 1813—and a German public.[60]

The various public spheres in Germany seem to have been characterized by fragmentation and discontinuity during the revolutionary and Napoleonic periods compared to those of the nineteenth and twentieth centuries, with few long-lived publications and a welter of different forms of publication, including newspapers, periodicals, almanacs, calendars, broadsheets, pamphlets, songs, poems, catechisms, and printed sermons competing for readers' attention. From a later standpoint, the boundaries between religious and political affairs, oral and written traditions, and popular and high culture frequently appear to have been indiscernible. In Stein's opinion, as he wrote to Hardenberg in August 1811,

> public spirit (*der öffentliche Geist*) can only be brought to life through institutions which awake, inflame and maintain religious feelings and through such political institutions which make use of all the forces of the nation. How this religious sense is awoken, led towards a single point, that of the love of the fatherland and defence, which liturgical arrangements to make, which instructions to give—the witty Professor Schleiermacher will be able to make suggestions about this.[61]

The Berlin theologian and writer seemed himself to be an embodiment of the close but inchoate relationship between the administration, politics, publicity, and religion, as a friend of Friedrich Schlegel and other Romantics and an acquaintance of Arndt, Stein, and Wilhelm von Humboldt, who encouraged his participation in the founding of Berlin University in 1810, where he subsequently taught. Such advisors, as well as civil servants like the head of the Prussian Department for Religion Georg Heinrich Ludwig Nicolovius, ensured that the kingdom's pulpits were used for the proclamation of official messages, most notably Friedrich Wilhelm III's address 'An Mein Volk' on Sunday 28 March 1813 and his second address 'to the assembled congregations' on 17 April 1815. 'We urge, in trust, all those to whom the care of souls is entrusted so that the great beginning succeeds and the correct spirit is awoken and maintained', wrote the minister in March 1813 to the 'clergy of the Prussian state': 'It is up to the clergy to make sure that the belief exists, in all parts of the fatherland, that no sacrifice for the general good is too great and that everything should be given for this with all good will and effort.'[62] In this way, it seemed possible to reach every 'son and brother' 'everywhere in the fatherland'.[63] It was, then, no coincidence that most widely circulated tracts in the Napoleonic era took the form of popular catechisms, such as Arndt's *Soldatenkatechismus* (1812 onwards), containing his most famous songs and poems, and Friedrich Ludwig Jahn's *Deutsche Wehrlieder*, which appeared in various editions in 1813–15. The third version of Arndt's *Katechismus für den teutschen Kriegs- und Wehrmann* (1813–15) went through ten editions and

---

[60] K. H. Schäfer, *Ernst Moritz Arndt als politischer Publizist. Studien zu Publizistik, Pressepolitik und kollektivem Bewusstsein im frühen 19. Jahrhundert* (Bonn, 1974).

[61] G. H. Pertz, *Das Leben des Ministers Freiherrn vom Stein* (Berlin, 1849–55, 6 vols), vol. 3, 14–15.

[62] Cited in K. Hagemann, *Mannlicher Muth und teutscher Ehre*, 144.   [63] Ibid., 144.

60,000–80,000 copies alone.[64] The form of these tracts differed from the factual or discursive structure of newspaper reports or philosophical arguments, replete with mournful or jubilant references to a 'dear fatherland', but it helped to guarantee a wide circulation and popular resonance for important official announcements and certain collections of war poems and other writings. Here, reading, singing, rituals, carnival, tumult and religion constituted overlapping forums, where news and ideas—about the wars, amongst other things—could be communicated and discussed.[65]

Sermons, songs, and almanacs, which reached wider audiences, were supplemented by newspapers and periodicals, which were read mainly by landowners, village notables, and the middling strata of the towns. Although the circulations of such publications were limited, they bore comparison with those of the mid-nineteenth century, with their actual readership probably between three and five times as large: Berlin's *Vossische Zeitung* (founded in 1721), which appealed to the capital's lower as well as middling orders, had 4,000 subscribers for its three weekly editions by 1813 and its principal competitor, the *Berlinische Nachrichten* (1740), which attracted more officials, nobles, educated burghers, and officers, counted 3,150; the *Hamburgische Correspondenten* (1724) had a circulation of 10,000, the *Leipziger Zeitung* (1665) 5,000, the *Deutsche Blätter* 4,000 (1813), and the *Rheinischer Merkur* (1814) up to 3,000.[66] Larger newspapers had an average circulation of about 1,000 in cities and smaller ones between 600 and 700 in less populous towns.[67] There were approximately 300 such newspapers, not including *Intelligenzblätter*, in the German lands at the start of the nineteenth century, encompassing most towns.[68] Virtually all sold most of their copies in the place where they were published, radiating out into the town's hinterland. This was even true of new political and historical journals such as the *Deutsche Blätter*, published by Friedrich Arnold Brockhaus and aspiring

> not to be a newspaper (*Zeitung*) but *a political paper of the people* (*Volksblatt*)—the word "Volk" understood in the higher and more noble sense here—a paper, which can be read, with participation, in *all* the lands of the German tongue, which in the case of a mere newspaper (*Zeitungsblatt*), which soon loses all interest at a certain distance, cannot be the case.[69]

---

[64] Ibid., 133.

[65] See especially J. M. Brophy, *Popular Culture and the Public Sphere*; J. M. Brophy, 'Carnival and Citizenship', *Journal of Social History*, 30 (1997), 873–904; J. M. Brophy, 'The Common Reader in the Rhineland', 119–58; J. M. Brophy, 'The Public Sphere', 185–208.

[66] E. Widdeke, *Geschichte der Haude- und Spenerschen Zeitung 1734 bis 1874* (Berlin, 1925), 104–5; O. Groth, *Die Zeitung. Ein System der Zeitungskunde* (Berlin, 1928), vol. 1, 245–7; H.-D. Fischer (ed.), *Deutsche Publizisten des 15. bis 20. Jahrhunderts* (Munich, 1971); H.-D. Fischer (ed.), *Deutsche Zeitungen des 17. bis 20. Jahrhunderts* (Munich, 1972); H.-D. Fischer (ed.), *Deutsche Zeitschriften des 17. bis 20. Jahrhunderts* (Munich, 1973); H.-D. Fischer (ed.), *Deutsche Presseverleger des 15. bis 20. Jahrhunderts* (Munich, 1975); K. Hagemann, *Mannlicher Muth und teutscher Ehre*, 151, 154.

[67] M. Welke, 'Zeitung und Öffentlichkeit im 18. Jahrhundert. Betrachtungen zur Reichweite und Funktion der periodischen deutschen Tagespublizistik', *Presse und Geschichte* (1977), 78.

[68] K. Hagemann, *Mannlicher Muth und teutscher Ehre*, 151.

[69] *Deutsche Blätter*, vol. 1, no. 31, 13 Nov. 1813.

In fact, the sales of the periodical were concentrated in Saxony and Thuringia, most of whose towns and larger villages had subscribers.[70] Of the fifty-seven political periodicals in Germany by 1815, thirty-eight of which had been founded since 1813, only the *Rheinischer Merkur* enjoyed a truly national circulation, with readers in Vienna, Berlin, Hamburg, Cassel, Göttingen, and Cologne, as well as in Coblenz, where it was edited by Joseph Görres.[71] Although subject to censorship, with Görres's publication banned in Baden, Bavaria, and Württemberg for instance, such periodicals and newspapers—typically containing local and general news, a section on commerce, and a '*Feuilleton*' on culture—were focal points of political discussion in cities and regions.[72] After the turn of the century, Berlin's two largest newspapers probably had an actual readership of between 20,000 and 35,000 out of a population of 175,000, comprising more than a third of the city's adults and extending well beyond the nobility and *Bürgertum*.[73] There are repeated references in contemporaries' diaries and correspondence to the press, even during periods of censorship.[74]

The relationship between such regional public spheres and politics had become closer between 1789 and 1815.[75] Public debate in a city like Leipzig had been connected in the eighteenth century to enlightened, religious, and academic controversies—with the majority of its fifty journals catering for small, learned circles before 1790—and to official news, disseminated by the state-backed *Leipziger Zeitung*.[76] The expansion of more articulate, reform-minded commercial and educated elites, which were separate from the traditional conservative elites of the city, and the political disruptions of the revolutionary and Napoleonic eras combined to transform the production of newspapers and periodicals, with the launching of commercial and fashion journals like the *Journal für Fabrik, Manufaktur, Handel und Mode* and the *Zeitung für die elegante Welt*, and with the eventual transfer of the *Leipziger Zeitung* to a pro-French reformer—who was compelled to take all the

---

[70] K. Hagemann, *Mannlicher Muth und teutscher Ehre*, 155.

[71] Ibid. Also, P. Czygan, *Zur Geschichte der Tagesliteratur während der Freiheitskriege* (Berlin, 1911), vol. 1, 338–40.

[72] See, for example, P. Ufer, *Leipziger Presse 1789 bis 1815. Eine Studie zu Entwicklungstendenzen und Kommunikationsbedingungen des Zeitungs- und Zeitschriftenswesens zwischen Französischer Revolution und den Befreiungskriegen* (Münster, 2000).

[73] H. v. Jordan, *Erinnerungsblätter*, 305, assumes that 'the Berlin newspapers' were being consulted by his correspondents.

[74] M. Prell, *Erinnerungen aus der Franzosenzeit in Hamburg 1806–1814*, ed. H. F. Beneke, 6th edn (Hamburg, 1911), 111–12; A. Adam, *Aus dem Leben eines Schlachtenmalers*, ed. H. Holland, (Stuttgart, 1886), 262, noted the arrival of news about 1812 in Bavaria, in spite of censorship. On censorship, see U. Eisenhardt, *Die kaiserliche Aufsicht über Buchdruck, Buchhandel und Presse im Heiligen Römischen Reich deutscher Nation* (Karlsruhe, 1970); H. Gisch, '"Preßfreiheit"—"Preßfrechheit". Zum Problem der Presseaufsicht in napoleonischer Zeit in Deutschland 1806–1818', in H.-D. Fischer (ed.), *Deutsche Kommunikationskontrolle des 15.–20. Jahrhunderts* (Munich, 1982), 56–74; D. Moran, *Towards the Century of Words: Johann Cotta and the Politics of the Public Realm in Germany, 1795–1832* (Berkeley, CA, 1990); W. Siemann, 'Ideenschmuggel. Probleme der Meinungskontrolle und das Los deutscher Zenoren im 19. Jahrhundert', *Historische Zeitschrift*, 245 (1987), 71–106.

[75] I. F. McNeely, 'The Intelligence Gazette (*Intelligenzblatt*) as a Road Map to Civil Society: Information Networks and Local Dynamism in Germany, 1770s to 1840s', in F. Trentmann (ed.), *Paradoxes of Civil Society: New Perspectives on German and British History* (New York, 2000), 135–56.

[76] P. Ufer, *Leipziger Presse*, 21–78.

publication's political news from the official French *Moniteur* after 1806—and the establishment of an outwardly apolitical but also reformist and 'local' *Leipziger Tageblatt* in 1807, supplemented in 1813–14 by anti-French periodicals such as the *Europäischer Aufseher* and the *Sächsischer Patriot*, which attempted to circumvent the strict censorship of the *Rheinbund* years. The timetable and impact of such changes, as they occurred across Germany, depended on the proximity of a territory to France, citizens' responses to the French Revolution, their experiences of occupation, the timing and incidence of the collapse of states and annexation of land, and the strength of subjects' reactions to defeat, invasion, and domination by French authorities. In most German states, however, there was, as a consequence, more political debate, especially at moments when censorship was loosened, as institutions and polities were dismantled and re-erected. It occurred, in part, within newspapers and within new political periodicals such as the *Preussische Correspondenten*; the *Tageblatt der Geschichte*, edited by Friedrich Lange in Berlin; *Der Wächter*, edited by Arndt in Cologne; the Hamburg-based *Deutsche Beobachter*, part-owned by the South German publisher Friedrich Cotta; *Nemesis*, edited by the Jena historian Heinrich Luden; and the *Teutschen Blätter*, created by the Freiburg historian Karl von Rotteck.

Political debate was produced by a growing cohort of 'writers', numbering 3,000 in 1766 according to one lexicon of '*Schriftsteller*', 8,000 in 1795, and 11,000 in 1806.[77] They came from a small educated minority—in one sample, 89 per cent had attended a *Gymnasium* or higher school, 55 per cent grew up within the *Bildungsbürgertum*, and 37 per cent went on to get a doctorate—and they were disproportionately young and 'philosophical', rather than graduates of law, theology, or medicine.[78] They were regularly accused of 'extraordinary impertinence', as in the Prussian censor and academic Friedrich von Raumer's denunciation of 'a numerous and intemperate class of writers of the day' to the Interior Minister in August 1815, and they were perceived as a threat to existing regimes by both the French and German authorities, with the sub-prefect of Cologne criticizing a Düsseldorf newspaper, thousands of copies of which were said to be circulating on the left bank of the Rhine in September 1800 for example, for 'continually sounding the alarm about the fate of our armies and about the domestic situation of the Republic' and for rekindling 'the hopes of the supporters of the old regime in these regions by its announcements that the old order is going to return': 'This paper achieves its large sales only by the falsehood of the news it prints. ... The newspapers of Frankfurt, Augsburg, and Neuwied, which are just as dangerous as that of Düsseldorf, are distributed throughout the department in the same profusion.'[79] A 'class' of writers, journalists, and publishers—with 500 bookshops and publishing houses across Germany by 1800—appeared to have consolidated its position and

---

[77] R. Wittmann, *Geschichte des deutschen Buchhandels* (Munich, 1991), 147.

[78] K. Hagemann, *Mannlicher Muth und teutscher Ehre*, 164. 'Philosophy' encompassed most humanities and social sciences.

[79] Cited in T. C. W. Blanning, *The French Revolution in Germany*, 199. Raumer is quoted in K. Hagemann, *Mannlicher Muth und teutscher Ehre*, 161.

evaded censorship, permitting and fomenting political discussion in spite—and perhaps because—of revolution, war, and occupation.[80]

The transfer and reception of the eclectic ideas about politics and war put forward within German public spheres proved to be haphazard but significant. Political elites within the German states, although 'their greater or lesser powers'—in Wieland's words—were 'limited on every side by laws, tradition and in many other ways', had been largely insulated from 'public opinion' by the structures and practices of absolutist rule.[81] To Arndt, who had been employed by Stein as his private secretary on the 1812 campaign on the Russian—not the Prussian—side and who later worked as a German propagandist after Stein was made head of the Allied Central Administration Authority (*Zentralverwaltungsbehörde*) in 1813, the social world and political circles of a former Prussian minister and *Reichsritter* such as Stein were unknown, until he was 'introduced into such ranks' by his master, who had 'become a great name' and who 'raised me from pettiness'.[82] Stein himself remained wary of public opinion, especially that of the 'upper classes', where 'the spirit of the times' was marked by 'pleasure-seeking, indolence, mischievousness and indifference to arguments and principles'.[83] Generals such as Scharnhorst and Gneisenau were much more critical, with the former referring to 'the small measure of loyalty to king and state' by 1810 and the latter to the 'abominable' state of opinion, characterized by a historical lack of patriotism—at least, of 'the genuine sort'—and 'no longer indifference, but open malevolence towards the government': there was 'no good will on the part of the *Volk*, with a division of political opinions here and a spirit of faction there'.[84]

Yet such criticism also showed how conscious Prussian and other German political elites had become of the public and how much, in their various programmes of reform and policies of consolidation, they had come to rely on it, making it a fulcrum of state-building or future resistance to France. Thus, Stein could still hope in 1810, despite 'the sense of slavery' which existed in Prussia, that the people, facing declining economic fortunes and insecurity, were beginning to see 'their position as alterable and subject to relentless change', prompting them to challenge the status quo and to free themselves from French domination: 'If there are, therefore, grounds to believe in a better future, in the nearing end of the slavery, in which we live, it is all the more our duty to steel and strengthen our souls by upholding powerful and noble principles.'[85] Like Stein, his successor in Berlin Hardenberg, who had been influenced by the British press—as a Hanoverian—after being cuckolded in London by the Prince of Wales in 1781, sought to monitor and lead public opinion as a means of educating the *Volk* and effecting necessary reforms. 'The new system, the only one by means of which our well-being can be

[80] W. v. Ungern-Sternberg, 'Medien', in K.-E. Jeismann and P. Lundgreen (eds), *Handbuch der deutschen Bildungsgeschichte* (Munich, 1987), vol. 3, 380–418.

[81] Cited in T. C. W. Blanning, *The Pursuit of Glory*, 284.

[82] E. M. Arndt, *Erinnerungen 1769–1815* (Berlin, 1985), 196.

[83] Stein memorandum, Mar. 1810, in G. H. Pertz, *Leben*, vol. 2, 423–5, vol. 3, 251–3.

[84] Cited in R. Ibbeken, *Preussen*, 310–11.

[85] G. H. Pertz, *Leben*, vol. 2, 423–5; vol. 3, 251–3.

grounded, rests on the fact that each inhabitant of the state, who is personally free, can also freely develop and use his own powers', declared the *Staatskanzler* to the Assembly of Notables gathered in his Berlin palace on 23 February 1811: '*one* national spirit, *one* interest and *one* purpose', achieved 'through education (*Erziehung*), through genuine religiosity and through every purposeful arrangement', could alone form the basis of 'our well-being and our security'.[86] In this sense, a reform-minded Chancellor such as Hardenberg in Prussia was no different from a less idealistic reformer like Maximilian von Montgelas in Bavaria or a reactionary like Clemens von Metternich in Austria: whatever their judgement of public opinion, all paid more attention to it than had their predecessors before 1789.[87]

WAR AND PEACE

Under public scrutiny, the nature of revolutionary warfare and the meaning of peace altered after 1792. To Friedrich II, who had wanted to conceal the very fact that the state was at war from his subjects, the distinction between war and peace was largely a diplomatic matter, to be decided by the monarch and his officials in accordance with *raisons d'état*. Military conflicts were instruments of policy designed to attain important goals which were assumed to outweigh the costs of combat, despite the possibility—evident during the Seven Years' War—of escalation. 'All wars whose sole design is to guarantee against usurpation, to maintain unquestionable rights, to guarantee the public liberty and to ward off the oppression and violence of the ambitious, are agreeable to justice', he maintained: 'When sovereign states engage in wars of this kind, they have no reason to reproach themselves with bloodshed; they are forced to it by necessity and in such circumstances war is a lesser evil than peace.'[88] Wars were part of a constant struggle on the part of states to defend, consolidate, and expand their territories and interests, acceptable in terms of their financial and human expenditure and justifiable on a number of grounds 'as a lesser evil than peace'. Pre-emptive strikes and other forms of aggression could be warranted in many instances, went on the Prussian monarch: 'Great men have always been successful when they make use of their forces before their enemies take such measures as tie their hands and suppress their power.'[89] The transition from 'peace' to 'war' to 'ceasefire' was marked by ambiguity in such circumstances. Peace treaties were regarded as 'little more than war-terminating instruments, mere cease-fires,... despite their flowering terminology of "perpetual amity" and concern for the "tranquillity of Europe"', in the opinion of one scholar.[90] Words such as 'Krieg' and 'Frieden' were certainly distinguished from each other by contemporaries, with some enlightened thinkers foreseeing and others denouncing the end of all war and the institution of a perpetual peace before the

[86] Cited in I. Herrmann, *Hardenberg. Der Reformkanzler* (Berlin, 2003), 294.
[87] E. Weis, *Montgelas* (Munich, 1971–2005), vol. 1, 184–94; vol. 2, 86–110, 371–87, 428–56, 640–7; E. E. Kraehe, *Metternich's German Policy* (Princeton, 1963), vol. 1, 65, 121–2, 213.
[88] E. Luard, *War in International Society* (London, 1986), 346–7.
[89] Ibid., 349.   [90] K. J. Holsti, *Peace and War*, 111.

French Revolution.[91] Nonetheless, the terms were widely perceived to encompass different forms of relation and conflict on a continuum of inter-state rivalry and competition.

Some historians contend that the distinction between war and peace was established fully only during the revolutionary and Napoleonic eras.[92] Others have argued that the threshold between 'peace'-time and the outbreak of military conflict had been lowered, as patriotic burghers began to justify war within the public sphere, not only as an act of self-defence, but also as a means, and a simpler one than via inter-state treaties and conventions, of creating a nation-state. 'With the establishment of revolutionary France as a political power, the parameters of the peace model of the Enlightenment were altered', claims Dann, pointing to the end of the putative compromise between the nobility and the *Bürgertum*, on which Kant's and other hopes of perpetual peace had been founded, with war commonly understood as a product of absolutism.[93] The realization of a 'modern civil society as a nation' in France demonstrated the potential of 'a political use of violence', in Dann's words, making revolutionary civil wars and national 'wars of freedom' into the most 'successful political recipes' of the nineteenth and twentieth centuries.[94] Even a conservative like the Prussian official and academic Jean-Pierre Frédéric Ancillon, who became the tutor of the Crown Prince—the future Friedrich Wilhelm IV—in 1810, had become convinced that 'A nation must never forget that there is a greater evil than war, namely the loss of its political independence and national existence.'[95] Within a broader Prussian public sphere, Friedrich Schleiermacher was already anticipating in 1807 that an anti-Napoleonic movement of resistance could be a 'palliative cure for much other evil', whereas Fichte could be found advocating a 'war against arbitrariness and autocracy' (*Alleinherrscherei*), not merely against external enemies.[96] The purpose of a 'true' war, continued Fichte in his defence of national warfare, 'Über den Begriff des wahrhaften Krieges in Bezug auf den Krieg im Jahre 1813' (1815), was the establishment of 'a true empire of law and right, such as has never existed in the world, in full enthusiasm for the freedom of the citizen..., founded on the equality of everything which has a human face'.[97] For such ends, it was legitimate to wage 'just wars', with the nation at once the beneficiary and the judge of the rectitude of a conflict.[98] Since a 'new model of peace on the basis of nation-states', which was required to stabilize diplomatic relations under these conditions, was 'nowhere to be seen in this epoch', in Dann's opinion, with the domination of Napoleon proving precarious, the reversion of statesmen to the principles of the *ancien régime* in 1814–15 could be perceived to be little more than a stop-gap, open to challenge and leaving international treaties 'fragile'.[99]

[91] J. Kunisch, 'Die Denunzierung des Ewigen Friedens. Der Krieg als moralische Anstalt in der Literatur und Publizistik der Spätaufklärung', in J. Kunisch and H. Münkler (eds), *Wiedergeburt*, 57–74.
[92] See, for instance, J. Dülffer (ed.), *Kriegsbereitschaft und Friedensordnung in Deutschland 1800–1814* (Münster, 1995), 2–3.
[93] O. Dann, 'Mitteleuropa im Zeichen der napoleonischen Herausforderung', in J. Dülffer (ed.), *Kriegsbereitschaft*, 16.
[94] Ibid.   [95] Cited in O. Dann, 'Der deutsche Bürger wird Soldat', 72.
[96] Ibid., 73.   [97] Ibid.   [98] Fichte wrote this in 1806, ibid.
[99] O. Dann, 'Mitteleuropa', 16.

There was a movement away from arguments for a perpetual peace in Germany's various public spheres during the 1790s. Even in the 1760s, 1770s, 1780s, and early 1790s, such arguments had been salient rather than dominant, opposed by authors writing after the Seven Years' War such as Thomas Abbt, who had sanctioned—in the words of his most famous work—'death for the fatherland' provided that the government of that land was 'enlightened' and its wars 'defensive'; Wilhelm Friedrich von Meyern, whose anti-military 'Indian' fiction *Dya-Na-Sore* (1787–91) had championed the notion of a patriotic war as a source of 'immortality'; and Johann Valentin Embser, who had aimed to replace the 'gods' of the 'philosophical' eighteenth century by starting with the 'first idol', namely *'ewiger Friede'*.[100] Looking back in 1788, the popular and academic historian Johann Wilhelm Archenholz was confident that his thesis about the transition from war as a purely state affair before 1756 to freedom-loving, patriotic, and national conflicts as sources of spiritual renewal after that date would find broad support: 'The culture of the age, and the type of freedom which resulted from it, had produced a patriotism, awoken by the admiration of Europe, amongst the inhabitants of North Germany, especially amongst those of the Prussian states, which had hitherto been alien in *Germania*.'[101] His history was designed to demonstrate 'to the Prussian patriot of every estate' the 'moral greatness of his people' and 'to the German patriot of other provinces' 'what can be achieved by the efforts of a whole nation [*Nation*], directed towards a single goal, under a wise government'.[102] Previously, conflicts had been perceived only as 'the piling up or distancing of new burdens', according to Archenholz, giving succour to the idea that they should be abolished altogether.[103] This hope, it seemed to many of the advocates of patriotic warfare, had become the framework of the debate about war and peace as a whole.

For Kant, whose 'Zum ewigen Frieden' (1795) found a comparatively wide readership and was reviewed in at least twenty publications, war had previously fostered the development of culture but it was now being replaced by the steady progress of humanity and by the expansion of trade, which demanded

---

[100] T. Abbt, *Vom Tode für das Vaterland* (Berlin, 1761); on Abbt, and on much of what follows, see J. Leonhard, *Bellizismus*, 193–7. On Meyern, see J. Kunisch, 'Die Denunzierung des Ewigen Friedens', 57–74. J. V. Embser, *Die Abgötterei unsers philosophischen Jahrhunderts. Erster Abgott: Ewiger Friede* (Mannheim, 1779); W. Janssen, 'Johann Valentin Embser und der vorrevolutionäre Bellizismus in Deutschland', in J. Kunisch and H. Münkler (eds), *Wiedergeburt*, 43–56. See also, J. F. Kazner, *Die Kriegskunst* (Berlin, 1760); G. D. von der Groeben, *Kriegs-Bibliothek, oder gesammelte Beyträge zur Kriegs-Wissenschaft* (Breslau, 1755–70); J. F. Beer, *Anfangs-Gründe in der Kriegskunst* (Frankfurt, 1771); K. F. W. Zincken, *Kurze und deutliche Einleitung zur Kriegesrechtsgelehrsamkeit in Deutschland* (Magdeburg, 1772); and K. F. W. Zincken and J. F. Eisenhardt, *Carl Wilhelm Friedrich Zinckens kruze Anleitung zur Kriegsrechts-Gelehrsamkeit* (Helmstädt, 1782); J. G. Nitzsche, *Die neue Kriegskunst in Vergleichung mit der Kriegskunst alter Zeiten* (Leipzig, 1782); J. G. Tielke, *Beyträge zur Kriegs-Kunst und Geschichte des Krieges von 1756–1783* (Vienna, 1786–7); L. Turpin de Crissé, *Versuche über die Kriegskunst* (Leipzig, 1787); H. W. Behrisch, *Litteratur jetztlebender militärischer Schriftsteller und der neuesten Kriegsbücher* (Magdeburg, 1789); G. F. Müller, *Das Krieges- oder Soldatenrecht in Preussen* (Berlin, 1789).
[101] J. W. v. Archenholz, *Geschichte des Siebenjährigen Krieges in Deutschland von 1756 bis 1763* (Frankfurt, 1793), 2 vols, in J. Kunisch (ed.), *Aufklärung und Kriegserfahrung. Klassische Zeitzeugen zum Siebenjährigen Krieg* (Frankfurt, 1996), 264.
[102] Ibid., 12, 15.   [103] Ibid., 463.

peaceful relations as a matter of individual and state self-interest.[104] To both the Königsberg philosopher and to critics such as Wilhelm Traugott Krug,

> The idea of peace is contained within the idea of law…Thus, the ultimate tendency of all pieces of writing which treat so-called natural law through the inclusion of the state and international law (*Völkerrecht*) necessary for it is none other than to demonstrate the viability of the idea of law in its greatest possible scope, which is then tantamount to coming up with a design for perpetual peace.[105]

Kant overturned the premise of natural law that the right to declare war could be derived from a state of nature, where contemporary states could be compared with earlier human beings, claiming instead that 'the state of peace amongst people living together is no state of nature (*status naturalis*), which is much more a state of war': a state of peace had 'to be *created*' by one neighbour for the other, 'which can only happen in a legal set of conditions'.[106] Although not attempting to rule out military conflict forever, the majority of proponents of natural law, too, had been anxious to limit and inhibit warfare.[107]

The limitations which advocates of natural law attempted to place on the waging of war—that conflicts required an injury or insult to justify their declaration, that they should serve to recreate peaceful and legal conditions, and that they should be conducted through means proportionate to the injury incurred—could themselves be seen to facilitate a barely distinguishable alternation of war and peace, typical of absolutist states.[108] Such states had, contended Kant, ignored their subjects' interests and availed themselves of standing armies, which 'threaten other states constantly with war, by their readiness always to appear to be armed for this', and which 'make use of people as mere machines and tools in the hands of another (of the state)'.[109] The establishment of republics in the place of absolutist monarchies, together with the institution of international law and a *Völkerbund*, as a 'federalism (*Föderalism*) of free states', would remove the root cause of war, the philosopher believed:

> Now, a republican constitution, the soundness of its origin apart, since it arose from the pure source of the concept of law and right, also has the prospect of attaining the desired result; namely, perpetual peace. The reason is this: if (which in this constitution cannot be otherwise), the consent of the citizens (*Staatsbürger*) is required in order to determine 'whether there should be war or not', nothing is more natural than that they should weigh the matter well before undertaking such a bad business, for in decreeing war they would be resolving to bring down all the miseries of war on themselves (that is, they must themselves fight; they must meet the costs of the war from their own property; they must do their poor best to make good the devastation which it leaves behind; finally, they have to accept a burden of debt, as a crowning ill, which

---

[104] D. Klippel and M. Zwanzger, 'Krieg und Frieden im Naturrecht des 18. und 19. Jahrhunderts', in W. Rösener (ed.), *Staat und Krieg*, 149.

[105] W. T. Krug, 'Allgemeine Uebersicht und Beurtheilung der Mittel, die Völker zum ewigen Frieden zu führen', *Leipziger Literatur-Zeitung* (1812), in W. Rösener (ed.), *Staat und Krieg*, 137.

[106] I. Kant, 'Zum ewigen Frieden', 22.

[107] D. Klippel and M. Zwanzger, 'Krieg und Frieden', 135–58.

[108] Ibid., 142.   [109] I. Kant, 'Zum ewigen Frieden', 8.

will embitter peace itself, and which they can never pay off because of always-impending new wars). By contrast, under a constitution where the subject is not a citizen, which is not in other words republican, it is the least serious thing in the world to wage war, because the ruler is not a fellow citizen but the owner of the state, and he does not in the least lose as a result of war, in the enjoyment of his table, hunts, pleasure palaces and feasts, and so forth. Rather, he can decide on war on unimportant grounds as if it were a game of pleasure, and he can—indifferently—leave any justification of it, for the sake of decency, to the ever-ready diplomatic corps.[110]

To other commentators such as Wilhelm von Humboldt, the role of the state was to safeguard the security of citizens, through a delegation of power to the judiciary and police at home and through the formation of a militia and the direct exercise of violence by the citizenry abroad, always ready to fight for its 'fatherland'.[111] Absolutist states and standing armies could not be entrusted with the powers needed for the defence of the nation, not least because they menaced the rule of law, domestic 'politics', and good governance. The breadth of support for a reform of the army bore witness to the unpopularity of 'absolutism'.[112]

For many subjects, war was a regular but distant occurrence in the eighteenth century. In pictorial terms, which were known to town-dwellers from prints and—more occasionally—museums, conflicts had been largely contained within long-range panoramas of troop formations on the battlefield, as well as in traditional, increasingly hollow symbols of martial grandeur and images of monarchs and commanders.[113] On the Baltic island of Rügen, Arndt, in his early twenties, barely registered the outbreak of war in 1792, despite his 'participation in world events' increasing 'from year to year' and his becoming 'not merely an eager public reader, but also an assiduous private reader of newspapers'.[114] As a student in Greifswald in 1793–4 and at Jena in 1794–6, he passed his time learning and living from hand to mouth, without remarking on the revolutionary campaigns in the West. He first acknowledged the existence of war during a year-and-a-half-long voyage in Austria and Italy, when he was 'surprised' by conflict 'breaking out again' in Tuscany in 1799 and was 'chased away' more quickly than he had anticipated, returning home via Nice, Marseille, Paris, Brussels, Cologne, Frankfurt, Leipzig, and Berlin.[115] Although troubled by 'every French victory against the Germans', despite being 'far from the scene and uproar' in Swedish Pomerania, Arndt recognized that French revolutionaries' aims were 'undeniably right and holy', creating turmoil in 'the hearts of half of Europe' and finding 'more friends than enemies' in the academic's '*Heimat*'.[116] Napoleon's defeat of Austria in 1805 and Prussia in 1806 purportedly altered the journalist's view definitively, persuading him 'to love

---

[110] Ibid., 23–4.

[111] W. v. Humboldt, *Ideen zu einem Versuch, die Gränzen der Wirksamkeit des Staats zu bestimmen* (1792), first published in Breslau in 1851, cited in J. Leonhard, *Bellizismus*, 221.

[112] D. Bald, 'Bürgerliche Militärreform—eine Chance zur Zivilisierung der Politik?', in J. Dülffer (ed.), *Kriegsbereitschaft und Friedensordnung*, 202–10.

[113] A. Jürgens-Kirchhoff, 'Der Beitrag der Schlachtenmalerei zur Konstruktion der Kriegstypen', in D. Beyrau et al. (eds), *Formen des Krieges*, 443–68.

[114] E. M. Arndt, *Erinnerungen us dem äusseren Leben*, ed. F. M. Kircheisen (Munich, 1913), 101.

[115] Ibid., 106.   [116] Ibid., 109, 112.

Germany', together with the Habsburg and Hohenzollern monarchies, 'with true love and to hate the "Welschen" with a true and loyal contempt'.[117]

Another North German academic, Barthold Georg Niebuhr, who had studied at the university of Kiel in the mid-1790s before entering the Danish civil service in 1796 and, again, in 1799, likewise paid little attention to the early revolutionary wars, continuing to harbour the hope of becoming a professor at the new *École normale* in Paris as late as November 1794 and prophesying 'great happiness and general enlightenment, which will serve to excuse much of what has happened' in France during the Jacobin 'terror'.[118] The first real impact of war came in 1798, he reported, as rumours of a French expedition against Hanover and Hamburg began to circulate, with the prospect of an extension of 'the terrible consequences of such an undertaking' into Holstein, which was 'the most valuable thing in the world' to him.[119] Niebuhr's desire was for 'the experience of a glorious war, combined with the abolition of privileges and the formation of a general militia with civilian officers who are partly elected', to dispel the people's 'fear of the military estate'.[120] The academic and administrator's conception of war, notwithstanding the fact that it seemed imminent, was still characterized by historical distance and disinterest. When he again was caught up in hostilities, as Britain prepared to bombard Copenhagen in 1801, 'it seems an object of wonderment to me to write to you of war and armaments, and of things which are quite alien to us', he wrote to his life-long confidant in Kiel, Dore Hensler.[121] It was only when Copenhagen was actually bombarded in April 1801, with thousands reportedly dead, that Niebuhr was faced with 'the terrible picture of a murderous struggle, which only experience gives us knowledge of'.[122] Such experiences meant that, when the wars of Austria and then Prussia against 'this terrible empire' of Napoleon and against 'French tyranny and outrage' took place in 1805–6, the banker and administrator portrayed the conflicts in much darker colours.[123] Entering the Prussian administration of Stein in the summer of 1806, he was confronted by a 'tragedy of horrors', after the kingdom's defeat in October.[124]

Even at that late date, however, other subjects elsewhere continued to welcome invasion and occupation by the French, as Heinrich Heine recalled in *Das Buch Le Grand*, which recounted his youth in Düsseldorf in half-fictional form. As well as a cipher for Napoleon, Le Grand was a drummer billeted in the Heine household, whose drumbeats told the writer that 'the Prussians had been dumb, dumb, dumb' and promised equality, fraternity, and to 'hang the

---

[117] Ibid., 114.

[118] B. G. Niebuhr to his parents, 16 Nov. 1794, in D. Gerhard and W. Norvin (eds), *Die Briefe Barthold Georg Niebuhrs* (Berlin, 1926–9), vol. 1, 67.

[119] Niebuhr to his parents, 2 Jan. 1798, ibid., 172–6.

[120] Niebuhr to his parents, 13 Feb. 1798, ibid., 185.

[121] Niebuhr to D. Hensler, 24 Mar. 1801, ibid., 250.

[122] Niebuhr to D. Hensler, 6 Apr. 1801, ibid., 263.

[123] Niebuhr to D. Hensler to A. Moltke, 17 Jan. 1806, ibid., 321–5.

[124] Niebuhr to D. Hensler to J. Gibsone, 17 Oct. 1806, ibid., 351.

aristocrats from the lamp-post'.[125] To such citizens, who constituted—if Heine is to be believed—the majority of the city's inhabitants, French wars, as late as 1806, remained a matter of enthusiasm and exhilaration, not fear or repulsion. Their responses arguably betray how far away military conflict had appeared in the late eighteenth century to the burghers of many German towns, whose opinions were at once formed and reinforced by depictions of the more or less capricious and self-interested armed disputes of princes and their standing armies.

Both the relative distance of late eighteenth-century warfare from civilian society and its greater impact after the turn of the century could be perceived in the writings of one of the few remaining advocates of a perpetual peace, the writer Jean Paul. Commenting after the defeats of 1805–6, the author, whose early novels in the 1790s had made him appear a literary equal of Goethe as he moved from Weimar via Berlin to Bayreuth in the early 1800s, was criticized for suggesting that German states should accept the imposed Peace of Tilsit (1807) as the basis of a new, French-dominated international order.[126] With his adopted city of Bayreuth occupied by French troops after 1806, having been taken by Prussia in 1791, Jean Paul saw defeat at Austerlitz (1805), Jena, and Auerstädt (1806) as proof that 'we had lost the old regime earlier than we had lost our battles': 'War exposed the weaknesses of our constitution rather than taking it from us.'[127] In some respects, the writer's critique of the old order was an extension of that of Kant and the late Enlightenment, depicting military conflict as the corollary of the 'bellicose disposition' of absolutist states and noting a 'growing insight' into the 'injustice' of war, which was a sign that 'the head always precedes the heart, amongst peoples, by centuries, as with the trade in negroes; even by millennia, as perhaps is the case with war'.[128] Over time, he hoped—in his Rousseauian discourse on education, *Levana oder Erziehlehre* (1806), which was written before Jena—there would be a movement, beyond sovereign states, towards a 'universal republic', which would make every conflict a destructive and avoidable 'civil war' (*Bürgerkrieg*) and which would be accompanied by the spiralling and inhibiting costs of warfare.[129]

In other respects, however, Jean Paul's *Levana, Friedens-Predigt* (1808), and *Dämmerungen für Deutschland* (1809) betrayed how publicists' attitudes to war had altered during the late-revolutionary and Napoleonic eras, as conflict came to seem like a more or less constant state, with deleterious consequences for civilian life. 'War', he wrote in 1806, 'is like a river of hell encircling and constraining the living earth.'[130] From this starting-point, the novelist attempted to shatter common

---

[125] H. Heine, *Ideen. Das Buch Le Grand* (1827), cited in P. Paret, *The Cognitive Challenge*, 37.
[126] Jean Paul, *Friedens-Predigt* (Heidelberg, 1808), 16.   [127] Ibid., 13.
[128] Jean Paul, *Levana oder Erziehlehre* (1806), cited in G. Niedhart, 'Jean Pauls "Kriegs-Erklärung gegen den Krieg"', in J. Dülffer (ed.), *Kriegsbereitschaft und Friedensordnung*, 97–8. See also O. Dann, 'Die Friedensdiskussion der deutschen Gebildeten im Jahrzehnt der französischen Revolution', in W. Huber (ed.), *Historische Beiträge zur Friedensforschung* (Stuttgart, 1970), 95–133.
[129] Cited in G. Niedhart, 'Jean Pauls "Kriegs-Erklärung gegen den Krieg"', 99–100.
[130] Ibid., 97. See also K. Hokkanen, *Krieg und Frieden in der politischen Tagesliteratur Deutschlands zwischen Baseler und Lunéviller Frieden 1795–1801* (Jyväskylä, 1975).

illusions in the press and literature that war was a test of manly virtues and that it was a source of reputation, glory, profit, and strength.[131] It was necessary to dispel 'press commonplaces' and popular misconceptions of heroism, which honoured the 'arsonist'—or general—more than those who had built the temple—namely, citizens—and which ignored the fact that heroic acts rested on 'mechanics', ranks of soldiers ('*die Sieger*' not '*der Sieger*'), and the common sense and reason of citizens during peacetime.[132] Whereas the duel of two individuals produced 'honour', the duel of millions, which should be proscribed by 'morality', resulted only in 'unhappiness': 'the misfortune of the earth until now rests on the circumstance that two people have decided on war and millions carried it out'; it would be better, 'although not good, if millions decided on it and two fought'.[133] The contrasting examples of representative government in Britain and the tyrannies of the East showed that internal order and peace could be extended, through the participation of citizens, to the relations of states, continued Jean Paul: 'The Orient lives at the same time in perpetual wars and perpetual powerlessness; England, by contrast, without land wars and without acts of cowardice.'[134] Yet the writer accepted, as the very form of his warnings made plain, that 'public opinion', urged on by 'big mouths' such as Arndt advocating wars of national defence, was still to be convinced of the case for peace, not least because, 'until now, the chapters of history were filled with war, between which peace placed a few footnotes'.[135] This '*perpetuum mobile* of the devil' remained in place in the Napoleonic period, like a 'machine of hell', perpetrating a 'history of annihilation' which had existed since the 'history of creation'.[136] In such conditions, defensive wars against Napoleon and 'death for the fatherland' were justified, notwithstanding the bloodiness of battle, it seemed by 1812.[137] Any transformation of popular conceptions of conflict and the order of states looked likely to be slow and uncertain.

Like other 'enlightened' publicists of the Napoleonic era, Jean Paul was aware of the proximity, destructiveness, and—at least momentary—inescapability of war, even though he never gave up the ultimate goal of peace.[138] Paradoxically, his raising of the possibility of perpetual conflict in *Friedens-Predigt* and of a 'war declaration against war' in *Dämmerungen für Deutschland* served to distinguish, more markedly than in the late eighteenth century, between war and peace as separate states of affairs, with the former relying on the latter for the accumulation of resources

---

[131] Jean Paul, *Dämmerungen für Deutschland* (Tübingen, 1809), 97–104, for a denial of the supposed '*Verweichlichung*' caused by peace.

[132] Ibid., 107–13.   [133] Ibid., 90.   [134] Ibid., 97.   [135] Ibid., 84.

[136] Ibid. For the reference to war as a 'machine of hell', ibid., 90.

[137] Jean Paul, *Die Schönheit des Sterbens in der Blüte des Lebens unter der Traum von einem Schlachtfelde* (1814), in G. Niedhart, 'Jean Pauls "Kriegs-Erklärung gegen den Krieg"', in J. Dülffer (ed.), *Kriegsbereitschaft und Friedensordnung*, 100.

[138] A. Klinger, 'Deutsches Weltbürgertum und französische Universalmonarchie: Napoleon und die Krise des deutschen Kosmopolitanismus', in A. Klinger, H.-W. Hahn, and G. Schmidt (eds), *Das Jahr 1806 im europäischen Kontext* (Cologne, 2008), 205–32, on the shifting position of other writers faced with Napoleon.

necessary for combat.[139] During the 1790s, many commentators had, at different points in time, repudiated the French Revolution and a French-backed peace. In Weimar, one of the pillars of German classicism, Wieland, had championed the French National Guard, the National Gendarmerie, and 'national soldiers of the line' in 1792 as 'particles of the sovereign', from whom 'shines a ray of original majesty (*Ur-Majestät*)' and who 'only obey whom, when and how they want to'.[140] By 1793, he was condemning the declaration by French revolutionaries of an international civil war for the alleged emancipation of oppressed peoples because it risked starting a conflict with 'all the kings and princes of the earth' at the same time as offering 'peace and brotherhood to all peoples'.[141] The following year, Wieland warned that 'bloody experiences should...finally convince us that violence can do little or nothing against this fanaticism for freedom and equality, by which the majority of the French nation is already possessed'.[142] War during the revolution seemed to have become more similar to the civil wars of the sixteenth and seventeenth centuries.[143]

In the Rhineland, the Catholic journalist and writer Joseph Görres—like Fichte, who changed his mind after 1797—took longer to distance himself from events in the neighbouring state, where 'a form of government, in which public opinion has a decisive weight', looked set gradually to rule out 'the proclivity towards war', as he put it in an essay on 'the ideal' of 'general peace' in 1798.[144] After a trip to the French capital between November 1799 and March 1800, the later editor of the *Rheinischer Merkur* outlined the 'Resultate meiner Sendung nach Paris' (1800), in which he alluded to the 'inevitable self-tearing-apart of popular sovereignty and absolute democracy'.[145] As a result, 'the emancipation of humanity' had not been achieved and French wars in its name were suspect.[146] In turn, 'the great idea of a perpetual peace in the world of states' had proved a deception, he wrote in 1802.[147] War, Görres later held, was a 'potent life force' with a positive function, akin to the 'destroying' element designed to determine and check 'every great life process in nature'.[148] Although still subject to many limitations, the use of force was warranted in defence of nations and their territories: 'No tribe has a claim on the possessions of another; none may drive their neighbour out of its territory.'[149]

---

[139] Jean Paul, *Friedens-Predigt*, 7; Jean Paul, *Dämmerungen für Deutschland*, 83–124.
[140] C. M. Wieland, in *Der neue teutsche Merkur*, Jan. 1792, cited in J. Leonhard, *Bellizismus*, 217.
[141] C. M. Wieland, 'Betrachtungen über die gegenwärtigen Lage des Vaterlandes' (1793), ibid.
[142] C. M. Wieland, 'Über Krieg und Frieden' (1794), in H. Günther (ed.), *Die französische Revolution. Berichte und Deutungen deutscher Schriftsteller und Historiker* (Frankfurt, 1985), 585–6.
[143] C. M. Wieland, 'Gespräche unter vier Augen' (1798), in C. M. Wieland, *Sämtliche Werke* (Leipzig, 1857), vol. 32, 52–4.
[144] J. Görres, 'Der Allgemeine Frieden, ein Ideal' (1798), in J. Leonhard, *Bellizismus*, 219.
[145] Cited in F. Boll, 'Joseph Görres: Vom ewigen Frieden zum kulturgeschichlich begründeten deutschen Hegemoniespruch', in J. Dülffer (ed.), *Kriegsbereitschaft und Friedensordnung*, 81–2.
[146] Ibid., 82.
[147] Cited in A. Portmann-Tinguely, *Romantik und Krieg. Eine Untersuchung zum Bild des Krieges bei deutschen Romantikern und 'Freiheitssängern'* (Freiburg, 1989), 114.
[148] Ibid., 86–7.
[149] J. Görres, 'Die Verhältnisse der Rheinländer zu Frankreich', *Rheinischer Merkur*, vol. 25, 11 Mar. 1814.

Since Napoleonic France was acting aggressively, German states had 'the higher right of defence and retaliation' in a 'holy crusade' by 1814.[150] 'A nation (*Volk*) should never let itself be ridiculed and injured in an unpunished fashion', he asserted in May of the same year, implicitly criticizing Germany's passivity in the past vis-à-vis its neighbour.[151] What was more, 'hellish powers have again found their centre in France, where Lucifer has returned and everything is moving and running in all haste to the taking up of weapons'.[152] Within a decade or so, Görres had passed from anticipation of a perpetual peace to the justification of military conflict against a national and religious enemy.

Friedrich Gentz, a former Prussian and later Austrian official and one of the most prominent publicists of the period, made the same transition. As an old student of Kant, his first articles in the *Berlinische Monatshefte* at the start of the 1790s were in support of natural rights, the Enlightenment, and the French Revolution, as 'the first practical triumph of philosophy', according to a letter of December 1790: 'It is our hope and comfort in the face of the multitude of old evils under which mankind sighs.'[153] Although Gentz became known as a conservative in 1793, after he translated Edmund Burke's *Reflections on the Revolution in France* (1790), he refused simply to repudiate natural rights, preferring to reinterpret them as part of the conjunction between the rule of law, normative principles and empirically describable institutions of the political order, and the idea of evolutionary progress, as outlined by the thinkers of the Scottish Enlightenment.[154] Thus, he opposed Fichte's notion of autarky as a means of creating peace, since it militated against the curiosity, competition, and strife which underpinned economic and cultural advances.[155] Since war could become purely destructive, as the revolutionary conflicts had demonstrated, the role of politics was to contain such violence, which remained inevitable and—in certain circumstances—necessary, in order to permit the development of European societies and economies. French revolutionaries had failed to curb violence at home, the countering of which was Gentz's priority until the turn of the century, and they had encouraged the unleashing of destructive conflicts abroad, prompting the publicist to concentrate on the relations between states during the 1800s and 1810s, before becoming one of Clemens von Metternich's main advisors at the Congress of Vienna in 1815:

> When a nation…suddenly severs all ties of duty, loyalty and subordination; when it declares its legal regent a usurper; when it suspends everything which can be called the highest power in the state by means of the same act of violence and declares, for our

---

[150] Ibid., vol. 29, 19 Mar. 1814.   [151] Cited in A. Portmann-Tinguely, *Romantik*, 97.

[152] *Rheinischer Merkur*, vol. 215, 30 Mar. 1815.

[153] Cited in G. Kronenbitter, '"The Most Terrible World War": Friedrich Gentz and the Lessons of the Revolutionary War', in R. Chickering and S. Förster (eds), *War*, 120.

[154] Ibid., 121. The term 'conservative' came into use in this period in English and French ('conservateur'), but entered into use in German later (the early 1830s) and remained contested: A. Schildt, *Konservatismus in Deutschland* (Munich, 1998), 23–62; M. Greiffenhagen, *Das Dilemma des Konservatismus in Deutschland* (Frankfurt, 1986), 41–61; K. Epstein, *The Genesis of German Conservatism* (Princeton, 1975).

[155] F. Gentz, 'Über den ewigen Frieden', in F. Gentz, *Gesammelte Schriften* (Hildesheim, 1999), vol. 5, 639.

benefit, a general interregnum of all laws for an unspecified time; when it recognises its own sovereignty, amidst this horrible and self-constituted anarchy, and, in order to fill this chasm of nonsense with something, allows an unauthorised assembly of demagogues, forty-thousand municipal tyrannies, a hundred-thousand clubs and four-million armed men rule in its name; when it abolishes all orders of rank, respects no type of property, destroys the freedom of every individual under the banner of a general freedom, renounces any form of payment and replaces the currency with a pile of worthless paper; when it leaves the worst misdemeanours unpunished and, a thousand times more aggravating, justifies and praises them daily in speeches and writing; when it publicly mocks religious ideas—the last hope of its victims of slaughter and the last dam against its own mischief—and treads under foot everything that was sacred to people: then the right of other nations to lead it back within the limits of social order are incontrovertibly established.[156]

In the *Historisches Journal*, which he edited and supplied with articles, Gentz openly opposed Kant's idea of a perpetual peace in 'Über den ewigen Frieden' (1800) with the claim that any attempt to impose a *Völkerbund* and rights without the agreement of the majority of states would provoke another war. France, with the help of a new type of warfare resting on the revolutionary zeal, defence of the republic, and love of glory of citizen-soldiers, had ignored the injunction that 'relations between states' should be regulated 'in the same ways as relations between individual members of civil society' and it had, instead, exported 'armed opinions' to territories—above all in Germany—defended by a badly organized, under-funded, sclerotic coalition, which 'forgot about the revolution'.[157] Although Gentz still entertained the possibility that Napoleon Bonaparte might reverse revolutionary changes in 1797–9, he conceded 'that the French Revolution has really happened', in a letter to the Romantic conservative Adam Müller in 1802: '"It is immortal, for it exists." Nothing on earth can make it un-happen.'[158] Napoleon's 'European federative system', which was nothing more than a bid for 'world domination' (*Weltherrschaft*) or an attempt to set up a 'universal monarchy' (*Universalmonarchie*), was an outgrowth of the interventionism and expansionism of the French Revolution, which was founded on the disruptive 'principle of so-called popular sovereignty', or 'the pivot around which the entire revolutionary system turns', as Gentz had declared to Metternich on 15 February 1814.[159] French revolutionaries had aimed to end war and create an alliance of nations, but they had succeeded only in precipitating the 'most terrible world war'.[160] Military conflict was necessary as a means of channelling human aggression and maintaining domestic order;

---

[156] F. Gentz, 1801, cited in J. Dülffer, 'Friedrich Gentz. Kampf gegen die Revolution und für das europäisches Gleichgewicht', in F. Gentz, *Kriegsbereitschaft und Friedensordnung*, 42. 'Universal-Monarchie' is associated by Gentz with Kant's perpetual peace, F. Gentz, 'Über den ewigen Frieden', 613.

[157] Ibid., 43; F. Gentz, *Über den Ursprung und Charakter des Krieges gegen die französischen Revolution* (Berlin, 1801), cited in G. Kronenbitter, '"The Most Terrible World War"', 127.

[158] F. Gentz to A. Müller, 13 Feb. 1802, in F. C. Wittichen (ed.), *Briefe von und an Friedrich von Gentz* (Munich, 1910), vol. 2, 88.

[159] F. v. Gentz to C. v. Metternich, 15 Feb. 1814, in J. Dülffer, 'Kampf', 43.

[160] Cited in G. Kronenbitter, '"The Most Terrible World War"', 130.

it was also required, in a new form but 'with regular troops alone', to counter the military threat of the revolutionary Napoleonic regime.[161]

The main way of controlling such war was not to revert to an eighteenth-century 'balance of power'—or 'anarchy, in the sense of international law', as he termed it in 'Über den ewigen Frieden'—with its constant warfare and misleading fiction of 'equality' of states, which had been easily overturned by France after 1792, but to institute 'an extensive social union…among the states in this part of the world, of which the essential and characteristic aim was the preservation and mutual guarantee of the well-won rights of each of its members'.[162] 'Men became aware that there were certain basic rules in the relationship between the strength of each individual part and the whole, without whose constant influence order could not be assumed', wrote the publicist in *Fragmente aus der neuesten Geschichte des politischen Gleichgewichts in Europa* (1806):

> not *how much power* one or the other possesses; but only whether he possesses it in such a way and under such limitations that he cannot with impunity deprive one of the rest of its own power—this is the question that must be decided in order to pass judgment at any given moment on the relation between individual parts or on the general proficiency of the edifice.[163]

The 'diverted, split forces of our great nation, channelled into weakly flowing streams, into foul swamps or illoyal, outflowing canals', had been responsible for much of the disorder of the revolutionary and Napoleonic periods: 'Europe fell because of Germany, and it must rise again through Germany.'[164] In order to end the 'slavery' of Germany and entrench a more stable international order, which might bring the regular conflicts of the eighteenth century and the constant warfare since 1792 to an end, the Allies needed to organize themselves for the decisive defeat of France.[165] In all such calculations, Gentz at once recognized and sought to control a different type of revolutionary conflict, necessitating a sharper and more effectively enforced distinction between war and peace.

Influential 'conservative' writers such as Adam Müller, Wilhelm and Friedrich Schlegel, and Achim von Arnim, many of whom were connected to overlapping circles of Romantics in Vienna (Müller, the Schlegels, Gentz, Beethoven), Heidelberg (Brentano, Eichendorff, Arnim, Loeben, the Grimms, Görres), and Berlin (Arnim, Kleist, Tieck, Schleiermacher, Schelling, Fichte), shared Gentz's opinion of war as part of a natural, historical order. For Friedrich Schlegel, who entered the Austrian civil service in 1809, Christian states were perceived to have prevented internal feuding, or a war of all against all, but they were not believed to be capable of eliminating a God-willed struggle of good against evil: military conflicts were an

---

[161] Ibid., 128; G. Kronenbitter, *Wort und Macht. Friedrich Gentz als politischer Schriftsteller* (Berlin, 1994), 308–9.

[162] F. Gentz, *Fragmente aus der neuesten Geschichte des politischen Gleichgewichts in Europa* (Leipzig, 1806), cited in G. Kronenbitter, '"The Most Terrible World War"', 132. On 'anarchy', see 'Über den ewigen Frieden', 606.

[163] Kronenbitter, '"The Most Terrible World War"', 132–3.

[164] F. v. Gentz, *Fragmente*, in J. Dülffer, 'Kampf', 46.   [165] Ibid., 54.

indication of the imperfections of humanity. Although, like Gentz, initially backing Kant's idea of a perpetual peace as 'brave and worthy', with 'universal and complete' republicanism as its prerequisite, the academic and poet quickly realized that the Revolutionary and Napoleonic Wars constituted an 'age of the violence of war', with the French as the 'Huns of the new times'.[166] Similarly, Arnim, despite earlier anticipating the 'political dissolution' of states as an obstacle 'to the spread of knowledge and the arts', came to see conflicts between states as a series of dichotomies of good and evil, being and appearance, spirit and matter, providing, in idealistic terms, the judgements of 'partial world courts': 'Whoever wins becomes the spirit of the world.'[167] Although they could appear to be little more than the 'common slaughter of people', with 'the individual appearing infinitely small compared to the mass' in the 'great events of war', requiring 'schnapps rather than heroic courage', battles could be seen to be exciting—'Nothing on earth is more fun than we hussars on the field, when we are in battle'—because they constituted part of a meaningful religious dialectic: any order 'in which war is merely calamitous' destroys itself, for 'this order is only a foreground, and leads via its own destruction, as its antithesis, to the synthesis of a higher truth, to world harmony, in which calamity stands in the service of salvation, and negative produces positive, evil creates good'.

Peace could not exist without war, Müller averred, as a constituent of his 'theory of opposites' and as an element of the natural order, 'where laws are shown in nature and its unending wars'.[168] Just as individual freedom was founded on restless and defensible activity, with 'every single character who belongs to the state as a whole' being 'able to create, argue and defend themselves in their own way', so nations and states had to be allowed to compete and fight for their own sets of values and goods: 'Wars are, from the standpoint of individual people, unpleasant things, which the living-side-by-side-with-one-another of individual peoples brings in its train', wrote the philosopher and administrator in 1809: they 'cannot be separated from the living-side-by-side-with-one-another of individuals'.[169] Whereas the 'old *Staatswissenschaften*' had looked on war as an exceptional state and had strived to attain perpetual peace, Müller saw such propositions as 'madness', 'as if wars between nations (*Völker*) were a suspension of law, i.e. illegal conditions, and the disputes of private persons within the same state were legal, because a real and effective judge exists for them'.[170] It was possible to achieve 'perpetual peace between peoples, i.e. *security from wars*', and 'perpetual peace within states, i.e. *security from revolutions*', by establishing a '*Weltpolizei*', but at the

---

[166] F. Schlegel, 'Versuch über den Begriff des Republikanismus', in E. Behler (ed.), *Kritische Friedrich-Schlegel-Ausgabe* (Paderborn, 1966), first series, vol. 7, 11–25; F. Schlegel, 'Gedanken' (1808–9), in E. Behler (ed.), *Kritische Friedrich-Schlegel-Ausgabe*, vol. 19, 282.

[167] A. v. Arnim, 'Das Wandern der Künste und Wissenschaften' (1798), in Portmann-Tinguely, *Romantik*, 188; A. v. Arnim, 'Todtenopfer' (1806) and 'Vorläufige Anzeige eines neuen Volksblattes "Der Preusse"' (1806), ibid., 196; A. v. Arnim to J. Grimm, 22 Oct. 1812, and 24 Jan. 1813, ibid., 197.

[168] A. Müller, 'Deutsche Wissenschaft und Literatur', A. Müller, *Kritische Schriften* (Neuwied, 1967), vol. 1, 75; A. Müller, *Die Lehre vom Gegensatze* (Berlin, 1804).

[169] A. Müller, *Die Elemente der Staatskunst* (Leipzig, 1809), vol. 1, 152–3, 80.

[170] Ibid., 173–5.

expense of 'the competitions of forces, true war, freedom, the good of all goods', which was unthinkable.[171] Conflict was part of the disputation necessary for life: 'Peace only becomes a living idea through war, the law only through freedom', he concluded.[172] Like his fellow Catholic-convert Friedrich Schlegel, Müller assumed that the moral and legal precepts generated by free disputes would, together with Christianity, limit war and prevent savagery.[173] Military conflicts, with the standing armies of absolutism in retreat, were not seen to endanger, but rather to constitute and maintain political and cultural life.

THE ART OF WAR

In literary and artistic circles, especially within those of the Romantics but also beyond them, war had become an important and acceptable theme, not least because it seemed to pose fundamental questions about human existence and death. In revolutionary France, artists' representations of battles and the other events of war quickly became a 'drama of the passions', with large allegorical and real figures occupying the foreground in struggles of principle and survival.[174] In Germany, the subjects and traditions of art changed less markedly and more unevenly, with some artists like Christian Gottfried Geissler producing detailed, realistic, unjudgemental studies of everyday life, as in his depiction of the colourful, ragged, pilfering *Französische Infanterie zieht in Leipzig* (1807) or his account of the delivery and protection of a baby by French troops in *Straßenszene in Lübeck* (1806–7), and with others such as Jacques François Swebach portraying, in a mixture of fantasy and nightmare, the realities of killing in *Der Tod des Prinzen Louis Ferdinand* (1807), where the French cavalry converge on the isolated, flailing, bareheaded Hohenzollern scion, in the middle of a corpse-strewn battlefield, in order to end his life.[175] This same sense of dream-like, subjective isolation could be found in the Romantic artist Caspar David Friedrich's painting of *Der Chasseur im Walde* (1813–14), in which a helpless, dismounted French cavalryman faces death, alone before a dark, snowbound forest (see Figure 2.1). Yet such depictions were rare, even if echoed in many of Friedrich's other portrayals of lone figures and motifs within a meaningful, sometimes foreboding, natural world. They were more common and better known within poems, prose, and plays.[176]

---

[171] Ibid.   [172] Ibid.   [173] A. Portmann-Tinguely, *Romantik*, 8–58, 117–55.

[174] E. Stolpe, 'Der Krieg als Drama der Leidenschaften. Paradigmawechsel in der militärischen Malerei des napoleonischen Zeitalters', in E. Mai (ed.), *Historienmalerei in Europa* (Mainz, 1990), 173–92.

[175] P. Paret, *The Cognitive Challenge*, 33–71.

[176] See E. Krimmer, *The Representation of War in German Literature from 1800 to the Present* (Cambridge, 2010), 19–64, which likewise concentrates on Schiller and Kleist. In addition to the plays examined here, see also Zacharias Werner's *Die Söhne des Tals* (Vienna, 1803–4), which treats the downfall of the Knights Templar, *Das Kreuz an der Ostsee* (Berlin, 1805–6), about the occupation and Christianization of 'old Prussia', *Attila, König der Hunnen* (Berlin, 1808), which details Attila's death, *Wanda, Königin der Sarmaten* (Tübingen, 1810), about the battle between the 'Polish' queen and Rüdiger, her Germanic suitor; Friedrich de la Motte Fouqué's *Nibelungen* trilogy, *Der Held des Nordens* (1808–10); and Heinrich Joseph von Collin's *Coriolan* (Berlin, 1804). On poetry, see Weber, *Lyrik der Befreiungskriege*, 145–281.

Figure 2.1. Caspar David Friedrich, *Der Chasseur im Walde* (1813–14)
Source: Private collection.

One of the most famous plays, although only staged in private before the 1820s, was Heinrich von Kleist's *Prinz Friedrich von Homburg* (1809–11), which referred obliquely to the death of Prince Louis Ferdinand von Preussen at the battle of Saalfeld (1806), four days before Jena and Auerstädt, and to the battle of Aspern (1809), which Kleist had witnessed.[177] Set in Brandenburg during the war of 1675, as the Elector's forces were attempting to push Swedish troops back to the Baltic, the plot turns on the sentencing of the Prince of Homburg to death, after he had attacked the retreating Swedish army too early—still in a trance, which he is unable to separate from reality—in defiance of his orders, allowing it to escape across a river. The Elector refuses to revoke the sentence in the name of the law, despite the fact that his general had attacked early in part because he had believed his ruler, who had switched horses, to have been slain. Yet he is opposed by his niece, Natalie, and his own officers, one of whom tells him, in direct reference to Prussia's defeats in 1806, that what matters is not rules but the vanquishing of the enemy. At first, when he learns of the Elector's decision and sees his own grave being dug, Homburg pleads for his own life at any price: 'Since I saw my grave, I want only to live, and won't ask whether honourably or not.'[178] He has been wrenched from his reverie and confronted with the finitude of existence. He subsequently rejects the offer of a pardon, declaring that 'to triumph over one's own weakness means more than gaining a cheap triumph in battle'.[179] As he declares from the scaffold, before being freed from the sentence at the last minute by his ruler:

> Now, immortality, you are all mine!
> Your light, as of a thousand suns,
> streams into my blindfolded eyes.
> My shoulders become wings,
> On which my spirit soars
> through boundless realms of silence.
> As from a ship, abducted by the wind,
> We see the busy harbour slip from sight,
> So does my life fade in the gathering dusk.
> Colours I still perceive, and shapes,
> And now fog covers all.[180]

Recovering from a faint, as his blindfold is removed, the prince asks 'Is it a dream?', to which an officer replies: 'What else?'[181] Simultaneously, other soldiers raise the cry 'to battle, to victory…; into the dust the enemies of Brandenburg!'[182] Amongst other things, the play examines the tension between law and military discipline and individual initiative and passion, and between reality and life and dreams and

---

[177] His account, like those of other contemporaries, betrays the two-way relationship between depictions of warfare and the wider aims of Romantics: see, for instance, R. Safranski, *Romantik* (Munich, 2007), 172–92.

[178] Act III, Scene 5, in H. v. Kleist, *Werke*, revised edn, ed. H. Gilow and W. Manthey (Berlin, 1900), vol. 3, 266. Translations from P. Paret, *The Cognitive Challenge*, 56–63.

[179] Act V, Scene 10, in Kleist, *Werke*, vol. 3, 294.   [180] Ibid., 295.   [181] Ibid.

[182] Ibid.

death, where Brandenburg's fate—or Prussia's in 1806—depends on a military encounter and the predicament of a soldier represents the choices, in a stark form, facing every subject.

The gap between war and peace is at once shortened and deepened in such works, as the audience learns of the humanity and exceptionality of soldiers' actions and fates. In the most celebrated plays of the period, Friedrich Schiller's trilogy *Wallenstein* (1798–9), war reveals truths which are obscured in peacetime. For Goethe, its historical subject matter was merely a thin cover for the purely human.[183] Albrecht von Waldstein or Wallenstein was an unknown Bohemian noble who became the commander of the principal Habsburg army in the first half of the Thirty Years' War and who was assassinated in 1632 with the consent of the Kaiser, as he contemplated switching to the side of the Protestant princes and bringing the war to an end through a compromise peace. The first play of the series, *Wallensteins Lager* (*Wallenstein's Camp*), focuses on the army itself, with the audience learning of Wallenstein's position, fearing the intrigue of the emperor and court and failing to keep control of his divided forces, from common soldiers, amidst the open spaces of the encampment, which Schiller conceives of as 'a small universe'.[184] Here, the leader and the mass of individual troops, who are not named, merge in a series of actions which will decide the fate of the empire and the religious settlement of Europe. Low-born men have been liberated from the conventions, corruptions, and distinctions of a society of estates through association with a successful general and they have been freed from the constraints of daily life, able to rob and to kill. Their courage also liberates them from a fear of death, which limits the lives of others, pointing to the paradox that external adversity and regimentation are compatible with inner freedom, as the closing song of the play spells out:

> Saddle up, comrades, to horse, to horse,
> On to war and to freedom.
> In war a man still counts,
> His heart is still weighed and valued.
> No one can take his place,
> He is on his own.[185]

'Freedom has passed from this world of lords and slaves. / ...Only the man who can look death in the face, / The soldier, is free!' continues the second verse, before the song ends with, 'And if you don't stake life, / You will never have gained life.'[186] As the action switches in the second and third plays to the enclosed chambers of castles, to the high politics and intrigues of his generals and figures from the court, and from informal German to the blank verse of nobles, the fortunes of the protagonists become tragic, caught within an accelerated sequence of what Schiller

---

[183] J. W. v. Goethe to F. Schiller, 18 Mar. 1799, in L. Sharpe, *Friedrich Schiller: Drama, Thought and Politics* (Cambridge, 1991), 249.

[184] F. Schiller, cited in L. Sharpe, *Friedrich Schiller*, 224.

[185] P. Paret, *The Cognitive Challenge*, 51.   [186] Ibid.

termed 'interlocking events'.[187] *Die Piccolomini* follows the deception of Octavio Piccolomini, one of Wallenstein's generals and a close friend, as he plots on behalf of the Kaiser, leaving his son Max, for whom the commander is a second father, to escape from the corruptions of his milieu through death in battle. Octavio's warning that Max has known only war and that he must accommodate himself to peace, prosperity, and tradition is undermined by the audience's awareness of the father's own civilian-inspired duplicity. The final play, *Wallensteins Tod*, shows how the soldiers refuse to betray the emperor and how power slips from the commander's hands. On one level, the trilogy anticipates the struggles of the revolutionary regimes and the emerging Napoleonic one, with the prologue of *Wallenstein's Camp* identifying the French general and later emperor—'You know him'—as 'the creator of strong armies, idol of the camp and scourge of many countries, the adventurous son of fortune'.[188] On another level, the works, which recreate Wallenstein's last days in what Hegel described as a horrific, unredeeming, and desolate—rather than tragic—way, reveal to spectators how the soldiers' lives, including that of their leader, illuminate and expose their own, by removing the hindrances and increasing the tempo and stakes of social existence.[189]

The soldier-poets of the 'wars of freedom', who achieved popularity in the 1810s, attempted to extend, aestheticize, and heroicize Schiller's intimation of soldiers' special knowledge, deriving from their proximity to death and their separation from civilian society. The Weimar playwright's account of warfare is certainly not heroic, with Wallenstein subject to overwhelming historical forces, yet responsible for his own actions, the consequences of which eventually lead to his death. By contrast, the poems of Max von Schenkendorf and Theodor Körner were heroic, resting on many of the new commonplaces about war—that it was inevitable and natural, that it should be waged by citizens not standing armies, that it was a moral, social, and political test rather than a danger—but radicalizing such tenets for the sake of soldiers' martyrdom. In Körner's posthumously published *Leier und Schwert* (1814), after he had been killed in combat in August 1813 at the age of 22, all except five of the thirty-seven poems are about dying and death, conceived of in valedictory terms, as the poet's dedication to the Lützower Corps, in which he had served, evinced: 'And should I be missing in the victory march home: / Don't cry for me, envy my good fortune! / For what, intoxicated, the *lyre* had sung, / The free act of the *sword* had already done.'[190] The war of 1813 was not merely a national necessity, it was a religious calling, as Körner explained to his father on volunteering in March:

Germany rise up; the Prussian eagle is awakening, through brave beating of its wings, the great hope of a German, at least a North-German, freedom. … Yes, dear father, I want to become a soldier…, in order to fight for a fatherland, even with my own blood. … Now, in God's name, it is a worthy feeling which drives me on, now it is the

---

[187] Cited in L. Sharpe, *Friedrich Schiller*, 220.
[188] P. Paret, *The Cognitive Challenge*, 49.
[189] G. W. F. Hegel, 'Über Wallenstein', in L. Sharpe, *Friedrich Schiller*, 248.
[190] M. Jeismann, *Das Vaterland der Feinde*, 34.

powerful conviction that no sacrifice is too great for the highest human good, for the freedom of one's *Volk*. ... no one is too good for the sacrifice of death for the freedom and for the honour of one's nation (*Nation*), but many are not good enough for this! ... Great times need great hearts ... That I risk my life is not much.[191]

To Körner, 'This is no struggle for the goods of this world, [since] we are protecting the most sacred thing with the sword'; 'This is no war that the kings of the earth lead', but a struggle led by the king of heaven; 'This is not war which crowns know of, it is a crusade, it is a holy war.'[192] Enemies were demonized in a war against 'hell', an 'edifice of lies'.[193] To Schenkendorf, Napoleon was 'satan', an anti-Christ, a 'wolf', a tyrant, and 'a prince of slaves', from whom—as a 'devil'—Germans should free themselves forever, after imploring the 'holy spirit' in accordance with 'the justified enmity of the majority'.[194] It was not evident how a conflict against such an enemy could be limited, especially when death was 'a mockery' and offered the promise of immortality: 'Let us inherit the earth, / You, eternal, true God... / This is a beautiful war / In such holy hatred'.[195] Action and death seemed to be linked to 'life', bringing poets such as Schenkendorf and Körner to long to die in a good cause. 'Tranquillity kills, only he who acts, lives, and I want to live, and will not die in front of death', intones Körner's Soliman, before dying.[196] In such romanticization of death, war is not only the opposite of peace, it is a means of reinvigorating life; it is no longer a distant and necessary event after the breakdown of peace, but a constant fantasy which citizens are encouraged to create and to make real in order to escape the 'tranquillity' and constraints of peacetime.

Most commentators, of course, did not perceive war in such terms. There were many ways to think of death, some religious and others not, which invoked fear and suffering rather than action, truth, and immortality. What was more, the relationship between military conflict, dislocation, violence, and death was a confused one. The characterization of war depended on its actual and purported impact and on its putative aims and justification. The following section investigates how and why the impact, aims, and justification of conflicts altered—or were believed to have altered—in the decades after 1792. The starting point of the majority of these debates in the public sphere was that war and peace were at once more clearly defined and more closely connected than in the past.

NATIONAL, PATRIOTIC, AND JUST WARS

In periodicals, newspapers, pamphlets, and treatises, many authors sought to justify war in national terms. By 1815, the Prussian censor Heinrich Renfner could

---

[191] T. Körner to his father, 10 Mar. 1813, cited in A. Portmann-Tinguely, *Romantik*, 327–8.
[192] T. Körner, 'Gebet während der Schlacht' (1813); 'Toni, 1812'; 'Aufruf, 1813', in T. Körner, *Werke*, ed. A. Stern (Stuttgart, 1890), vol. 1, 277, 90, 106.
[193] T. Körner, 'Gebet' (1813), in T. Körner, *Werke*, vol. 1, 277.
[194] Cited in A. Portmann-Tinguely, *Romantik*, 273.
[195] Schenkendorf, 'Die Leipziger Völkerschlacht', cited in A. Portmann-Tinguely, *Romantik*, 284.
[196] T. Körner, 'Zriny', in T. Körner, *Werke*, 413.

complain that articles such as Friedrich Rühs's 'Ueber die Einheit des teutschen Volkes', which proposed the introduction of uniform rights and a single legal code for all Germans before the eventual recreation of a German *Kaiserreich*, had become a monotonous national diet, constituting '*in toto et in parte* the same suggestions which we have already read in a hundred tracts and which we shall probably have to read *ad nausam usque* in future'.[197] Such observations had been articulated earlier, during the wars of Austria and Prussia against France and the dissolution of the Holy Roman Empire in 1805–6, with the well-known journal *Minerva* confirming in 1808 that 'many and varying things' had been written about 'Germany's regeneration' over the previous two years.[198] This contemporary testimony runs counter to the accounts of some historians, who have questioned the significance of nationalism between 1792 and 1815 and who have highlighted the difference between patriotism and national sentiment and between the opinions of writers and journalists and those of their readers and the majority of subjects effectively excluded from the reading public, despite admitting—in James Sheehan's words—that 'a small minority of Germans, especially German intellectuals', had 'helped to create a mythic image of the national past'.[199] In particular, the revolutionary and Napoleonic periods had witnessed bewildering exchanges of territory, with almost three-fifths of Germany's population gaining a new ruler; fundamental political changes, with the creation of coherent *Mittelstaaten*—Bavaria, Saxony, Württemberg, and Baden—and the appointment of reformist governments in Prussia and the Habsburg monarchy, all of which struggled to forge states that were able to survive in a French-dominated order; residual support for the old Reich and ambiguous attitudes to the Confederation of the Rhine and to the 'revolutionary' authorities and institutions of France; and a confusing variety of responses on the part of local corporations and communities, abandoned by their former rulers and subject to the depredations of the marching and occupying armies of both friend and foe.[200]

Nonetheless, ruling elites were frequently tempted to cast their efforts to build new states in a national light, however manipulatively, and their subjects, especially those belonging to the *Bürgertum*, often appear to have thought of themselves as 'Germans', as well as 'Prussians' or 'Bavarians', '*Kölsch*' or 'Frankfurters', Catholics, Calvinists, or Lutherans, referring back to the Holy Roman Empire as a political structure of German territories and populations.

> One cannot deny that the language, mores and ancient customs of the imperial cities [and] Prussian, Palatinate etc. countries…attaches them only to Germany; that notables

---

[197] H. Renfner, *Verzeichnis der im Monat Februar 1815 censierten historisch-politischen Schriften*, cited in K. Hagemann, *Mannlicher Muth und teutscher Ehre*, 204. Christian von Martens, *Vor fünfzig Jahren. Tagebuch meines Feldzuges in Sachsen 1813* (Stuttgart, 1863), vol. 2, 5, commented that 'a pile of pamphlets for the German cause appeared during this time' in 1813; Heinrich von Jordan, *Erinnerungsblätter*, 28, 162, noted the 'enthusiasm' and 'the love of the *Volk* for the king and his house' in Prussia, at least amongst the theatre-going public.

[198] *Minerva*, June 1808, vol. 2, 492, in A. Portmann-Tinguely, *Romantik*, 284, 207.

[199] J. J. Sheehan, 'State and Nationality', 48.

[200] See the introduction of this chapter for references to the literature.

unwillingly see themselves burdened by public duty or denied their petty sphere of power; that perhaps one does not count on the services of a native being provided with complete devotion; that indirect taxes cost an infinite amount; that one would like to be exempt from conscription and the National Guard; finally, that one would proba-bly prefer, above all in the cities, to return to that which one knew previously,

wrote one French prefect of the Rhineland in 1809, betraying the range and over-lapping nature of citizens' motives, even in a region known by Prussian officials for its 'large number of different sovereignties' and 'the resulting conflicting interests', which explained the unusual circumstance that 'no particular national character ever appeared'.[201] As a French commissioner general of police in Cologne reported in 1805, having 'devoted myself to knowing its public opinion' and having 'acquired the certainty that the majority of its inhabitants detest France and Frenchmen', the local inhabitants, although earlier disliking the sale 'of the property of the clergy' and the customs administration, had been compliant until the war with the Habsburg monarchy, which had rekindled 'all their hate' and had pushed them 'to harm the government', rejoicing in the arrival of the German powers, Austria and Prussia.[202] Throughout the official correspondence, there were indications that citizens distinguished between natives and 'foreigners'.[203] For many, such a distinc-tion meant more than affinity with insiders and suspicion or dislike of outsiders, at least under conditions of war and occupation, as one official on the left bank of the Rhine confirmed to another on the right bank in 1797:

> In general, it seems that the good genius of Germany once more inspires the hearts of all Germans on this side of the Rhine, too, with national pride, brings home to them the vileness of our inglorious French servitude, and arouses a lively desire for the return of peace and our old patriotic constitutions.[204]

'Germanness', for many subjects, was an affiliation and identity, although rarely the most important, not merely a geographical expression.

National sentiment and identification had a long history in Germany.[205] Nationalism as a political and intellectual movement or, at least, set of political ideas was much more recent, deriving from the debates, conflicts, civic activity, public improvements, litigation, commerce, and changing social distinctions of various sections of the *Bürgertum*, and more occasionally of other social strata, from the 1760s onwards.[206] According to Echternkamp, the civil servants, academics, journalists, lawyers, pastors, merchants, and other proponents of a German nation habitually participated in poorly defined but 'enlightened' public spheres and lit-erary markets, criticized the privileges and morals of the nobility, and opposed

[201] J. C. F. de Ladoucette, 12 Aug. 1809, cited in M. Rowe, *From Reich to State*, 127; J. D. F. Neigebaur, *Statistik der preussischen Rhein-Provinzen* (1817), cited in M. Rowe, *From Reich to State*, 118.
[202] Ibid., 125.   [203] J. D. F. Neigebaur, *Statistik*, 118.
[204] J. G. Kilian to Geheimrat Becker, 17 Sept. 1797, in T. C. W. Blanning, *The French Revolution in Germany*, 253.
[205] See especially T. C. W. Blanning, *The Culture of Power*, 185–265; E. Hellmuth and R. Stauber (eds), *Nationalismus vor dem Nationalismus* (Hamburg, 1998); L. Scales and O. Zimmer (eds), *Power and the Nation in European History* (Cambridge, 2005), 1–102, 315–32.
[206] J. Echternkamp, ' "Teutschland, des Soldaten Vaterland" ', 181–203.

what they perceived to be anachronistic authorities and the arbitrary exercise of power. Often their 'patriotism' was conceived of as benefiting 'humanity' and 'progress'—or the slightly different notion of steady '*Entwickelung*'—and, as such, it made no reference to national culture or political goals.[207] Yet, it was part of a wider movement of local political activity and cultural production and discussion, which provided many of the milieux and networks of nationalism before and during the Revolutionary and Napoleonic Wars.

The dissemination of long-standing symbols and myths, particularly of the 'Germanen', their 'Reich', and their language, together with the experience of cultural distance (exotic voyages overseas) and proximity (comparison with other European states, citizens, languages, and customs) through reading and travel, supplemented and complicated the cultural and historical outlook of much of the *Bildungsbürgertum*, helping to effect an incomplete semantic shift from a '*Volk*' understood as the organic product of climate and geography, which had been characteristic of the mid-eighteenth century, to the interchangeable concepts of '*Nation*' and '*Volk*' as linguistic and cultural communities in the late eighteenth century.[208] In Karl von Rotteck's *Allgemeine Geschichte vom Anfang der historischen Kenntnis bis auf unsere Zeiten* (1812–26) and Heinrich von Luden's *Allgemeine Geschichte der Völker und Staaten* (1814–24), the 'Germanen' were portrayed as the original ancestors of contemporary Germans, with free forms of social organization and successful traditions—most notably, under Arminius, or Hermann, against the Romans—of fighting and self-defence, waging '*National-Kriege*' only after the 'decision of the whole *Volk*' and through the sacrifices of 'all men capable of carrying a weapon'.[209] The potential conflict between the political and economic ideals, practices and interests, religious or humanist values, and 'German' culture of the *Bürgertum*, as an active, civic, and urban elite, on the one hand, and the 'Frenchified' decadence, exemptions, status, and power of nobles, courts, princes, and 'absolutist' systems of government, under the resented impositions, looting, and violence of French occupation and invasion, on the other hand, regularly served to reinforce German nationalism after 1792. However, it was also countered by shifting alliances, diverse experiences of warfare and of peace, loyalty to throne and altar, and competing affiliations and social differentiations within localities, making the '*Bürgertum*' itself—and its composite parts—anything but stable. Sometimes allegiances to localities, states, and 'Germany' overlapped, as in Prussia or Austria in 1805–6, 1809, and 1813–15, when even Metternich attempted to encourage national sentiment—by founding newspapers, paying for pamphlets, and threatening censorship—for the good of

---

[207] Ibid., 185–6.

[208] See, inter alia, J. Echternkamp, *Aufstieg*; D. Langewiesche, *Nation, Nationalismus, Nationalstaat*, and *Reich, Nation, Föderation*; W. Griep and H.-W. Jäger (eds), *Reise und soziale Realität am Ende des 18. Jahrhunderts* (Heidelberg, 1983); B. Struck, *Nicht West—nicht Ost. Frankreich und Polen in der Wahrnehmung deutscher Reisender zwischen 1750 und 1850* (Göttingen, 2006); R. A. Berman, *Enlightenment or Empire: Colonial Discourse in German Culture* (Lincoln, NE, 1998); S. Zantop, *Colonial Fantasies: Conquest, Family and Nation in Precolonial Germany, 1770–1870* (Durham, NC, 1997).

[209] K. v. Rotteck, *Allgemeine Geschichte vom Anfang der historischen Kentniss bis auf unsere Zeiten* (Freiburg, 1812–26), vol. 3, 124–5.

the Habsburg monarchy, and sometimes they clashed with each other, as was the case in most *Mittelstaaten* before October 1813, and in Prussia between 1807 and 1812.[210] In general, however, the combination of conflict, occupation, privations, political disorder, territorial reorganization, and the tightening and relaxation of censorship created conditions which fomented national sentiment and provoked nationalist activity on the part of a significant number of German subjects.

Publicists were much more emphatic in the articulation of national affiliations than were citizens. Their outpourings were rarely well defined, resting on contested terms alongside anti-aristocratic, proto-political, and local forms of patriotism, which were critical of existing, archaic, and absolutist institutions and polities, including those of the Holy Roman Empire of the German Nation.[211] The labels 'Nation', 'Volk', 'Vaterland', 'Land', and 'Patriotismus' were still used interchangeably on most occasions.[212] All the same, they were also deployed more extensively and precisely, referring to language and culture and portraying the 'nation'—after 1789—as a historical and political subject, as could be seen in the expanding entries of popular lexicons. Thus, in 1782, *Johann Hübeners Staats-Zeitungs- und Conversations-Lexicon*, which was one of the first publications to allude to language as a criterion of nationality, described the 'Nation' only briefly as 'any people (Volk) or land which has its own language, laws, morals or traditions'.[213] By 1817, Brockhaus's *Conversations-Lexicon* was devoting seven pages to the subject of 'Nation, Nationalität, Nationalcharakter' and insisting that 'nature founds many differences between people, which are first recognized as a higher culture is achieved and which are more and more freely developed'.[214] These traits were linked to 'descent' (*die Abstammung*) and to 'climate and geography', creating the 'national physiognomy' or 'family similarity of a nation' and helping to shape 'the nationality (*das Nationseyn*) or the life of people within the form and particularity of a nation, out of which national character, or the uniqueness of a nation, developing within the life and history of the nation, emerges'.[215]

There was little agreement about the political form of an existing or future German nation-state or other national entity, both because 'politics' remained vestigial within unrepresentative systems of government and because national traditions were believed, in accordance with the precepts of Montesquieu, Herder, and Burke, to vary, permitting the establishment of heterogeneous institutions. From this point of view, even 'the German Reich constitution, irrespective of its undeniable shortcomings and defects, is infinitely more bearable for the internal tranquillity and well-being of the nation as a whole, and better suited for its character and the level of nature at which it exists, than French democracy', wrote Wieland in the mid-1790s.[216] Whether Germany was to be unitary, federal, or confederal, as pro-Prussian commentators such as Wilhelm von Humboldt, Arnold Mallinckrodt,

[210] On Metternich, see J. Echternkamp, *Aufstieg*, 197. See also W. Meier on Austria's attempt to gain national support in 1809, even if unsuccessful in Baden: W. Meier, *Erinnerungen aus den Feldzügen*, 35.
[211] J. Echternkamp, *Aufstieg*, 50–5, 77–89.   [212] See the various citations in Chapters 1–3.
[213] K. Hagemann, *Mannlicher Muth und teuscher Ehre*, 224.
[214] Ibid., 234.   [215] Ibid.   [216] Cited in J. Echternkamp, *Aufstieg*, 158.

and even Fichte proposed, whether it was to be monarchical or republican, and whether it was to have a popular assembly, as Friedrich Christoph Dahlmann desired, or not, all remained open questions.[217] Correspondingly, when Arndt wrote in the first edition of *Der Wächter*, published in Cologne in 1815, that 'the time in which we live has encouraged us—we Germans—to become political people', he meant that 'all Germans see themselves as a *Volk*', not that they shared practical political goals, which he feared might be lost in a 'thoughtless' fatalism or a flight into mysticism.[218] In the Pomeranian publicist's opinion, as he looked back on the 1780s in *Geist der Zeit* (1806–9), the French Revolution, though politicizing the German population, had also divided it, slowing down a process of cultural nationalization which was already in train:

> It was a sense of a new and better epoch beginning that was being aroused by our better writers, a growing feeling of the *Volk*'s potential and of its value, which in turn led to a greater sense of community and common purpose, more perhaps than at any time in the past. People began to take a pride in the name 'German' and in German culture and the German way of life, and this pride would have cast invisible ties around the whole *Volk* and created a unity of consciousness if the French Revolution had not intervened.[219]

For such commentators, war seemed to have reinforced citizens' attachment to a German nation and politics to have undermined it.

The salience of debates about a German nation after the turn of the century was demonstrated by the advocates of the Reich and the *Rheinbund*, the majority of whom chose to depict the Holy Roman Empire and the Confederation of the Rhine in national colours, despite holding official or university posts in the 'particularist' states of the third Germany.[220] Consequently, only thoroughgoing defenders of the sovereignty of the *Mittelstaaten* such as the Bavarian reformer and publicist Johann Christian Freiherr von Aretin ignored German nationalism and prophesied the advent of a Napoleonic 'cosmopolitanism', using the term '*National-Repräsentation*' to refer to a popular assembly for an envisaged 'constitutional monarchy' in Bavaria.[221] For most commentators, like the conservative Reich 'patriot' Johannes von Müller, the structures imposed by Napoleon offered the chance to 'nationalize the *Bund*'.[222] Accordingly, both opponents of the old Reich and its supporters heralded the 'resurrection of the nation' in 1806, with the *Rheinbund* seeming to make 'German national unity into the predominant directive and into the pole star of all the individual German governments', as Karl Albert von Kamptz put it, while continuing to fear that 'Germany and a powerful German nation no longer exists', in contrast to the period before the dissolution of the Holy Roman

---

[217] Ibid., 254–90.

[218] Ibid., 255–6. See also W. Erhart and A. Koch (eds), *Ernst Moritz Arndt 1769–1860. Deutscher Nationalismus, Europa, transatlantische Perspektiven* (Tübingen, 2007).

[219] Translated in T. C. W. Blanning, *The Culture of Power*, 262.

[220] See Table, G. Schuck, *Rheinbundpatriotismus*, 223–5.

[221] J. C. v. Aretin, *Die Pläne Napoleons* (1809), in G. Schuck, *Rheinbundpatriotismus*, 285. On cosmopolitanism, see J. Echternkamp, *Aufstieg*, 184.

[222] Cited in G. Schuck, *Rheinbundpatriotismus*, 259.

Empire, leaving 'only Bavarians, only Württembergers, only Brandenburgers, only Saxons…, just as there were only Milanese, Parmanese, Mantuans, the inhabitants of Monacco and the Genovese etc. in Italy in the past'.[223] Authors like Johann Gottlob Furstenau saw the Confederation of the Rhine as an extension of the Reich, a 'new, not yet complete, but not unpleasant building, apparently [constructed] by a powerful builder following a grand plan', into which it was necessary for 'a part of the family' to move in order to save itself 'for the sake of the unity of the whole'.[224] Others such as Peter Adolf Winkopp perceived the *Rheinbund* as an unprecedented structure, necessarily under the protectorate of the French, however 'humiliating' it was 'for a brave *Volk*', which 'no longer has the necessary strength to defend itself against any external danger'.[225]

The uncontrollable events 'of the momentous times in which we live', wrote Friedrich Buchholz, had permitted the 'renaissance' of Germany:

> What used to be left to the hand of chance, the mind of man now dares to order with a free hand. Time, space and relations shrink together before him, and to the extent that they lose their aura and influence, he rises up and rises up over those things which he otherwise slavishly served. The gaping mass of humanity has risen up; like a long-sleeping volcano it has shaken the foundations of the Reich; some have collapsed and those which still stand are like undermined buildings which fall down with the first push.[226]

The 'political view of Germany' had been 'totally transformed', with much 'that had become worthy through familiarity with and love of the old' having been destroyed, declared the Giessen constitutional lawyers August Friedrich Wilhelm Crome and Karl Jaup in the first edition of their new journal *Germania* in 1808:

> What can and must we, as a *German nation*, save from this political shipwreck? What else but our firm, German sense of everything that is true, right, noble and good; what else but our language, our expansive scientific culture, our religion, our old German loyalty and honesty, as well as our simple mores, which safeguard our domestic happiness in spite of every storm outside; these must remain sacred and unchanged for us.[227]

The envisaged replacement for the *Kaiserreich*, which was defined by Wilhelm Josef Behr as a '*Völker-Staat*' designed to unite all its populations 'under a common high power', was a confederation—a '*Staatenbund*' or '*Völkerbund*'—which 'merely binds its parts with the band of a free association', allowing the coexistence of what Johann Gottfried Pahl called the 'self-contained and independent states' emerging from the 'feudal character' of the 'German state body' of the Holy Roman

---

[223] K. A. v. Kamptz, 'Aphorismen über die deutsche National-Einheit als Zweck des rheinischen Bundes', *Der Rheinische Bund* (1808), vol. 5, no. 15, 373, 371.

[224] J. G. Furstenau, 'Betrachtungen über die Souverainität', *Der Rheinische Bund* (1807), vol. 2, no. 6.

[225] P. A. Winkopp, 'Gedanken', *Der Rheinische Bund* (1807), vol. 3, no. 9, 455–6.

[226] F. Buchholz, 'Ueber die Gesichtspunkte', *Europäische Annalen* (1808), vol. 3, 227, cited in G. Schuck, *Rheinbundpatriotismus*, 281.

[227] A. F. W. Crome and K. Jaup, *Germania*, 1808, vol. 1, 3–4, in J. Echternkamp, *Aufstieg*, 176.

Empire.[228] In Pahl's view, the *Rheinbund* was the prelude to a 'German' *Bund.*[229] As the Hanoverian Ernst Brandes conceded, 'Germany no longer exists, but the *Volk* of the Germans is still extant.'[230]

Some commentators opposed such views and many more ignored them. In Württemberg, for instance, the monarch's and government's use of censorship and other threats seems to have been largely successful in preventing publicists and priests from supporting the national cause during the period of French tutelage after 1800, despite the earlier dissent of sections of the clergy and the majority of the *Land*'s estates, which had backed the French Revolution rather than their own state's participation in the Coalition.[231] According to Pahl, 'raw violence, on the one side, and cowardly and weak servitude in our fatherland of Württemberg, on the other, starved and suppressed the human right of the free expression of ideas'.[232] In sermons, the terms 'Germany' and 'German' were avoided and those such as 'fatherland', which was regularly deployed, referred ostensibly to individual states and their rulers, albeit in an ambiguous or a formulaic fashion on many occasions. In this sense, there was a continuity between the state church's injunctions to priests in the 1790s to instil in their parishioners the 'duty of giving everything to the defence and safeguarding of the fatherland', 'even with the sacrifice of [their] life', and the *Hofprediger*'s assertion, at the 1813 jubilee celebrations of King Friedrich I's accession to the throne, that 'the stormy times demand great efforts and heavy casualties' for the sake of an 'earthly fatherland' which 'uses its powers dutifully' and 'struggles against its tempestuous fate'.[233] 'Although we are required to increase the armies, with weapons in their hands, of our most gracious monarch', wrote one monk in the Badenese territories of the Habsburg monarchy, 'we are called on to support the power of Austrian armies through our public prayers'.[234] Loyalty towards the monarch and the fatherland, narrowly defined, was needed in wartime in order to bear the hardships of conflict: the beast of war 'bites with its teeth and froths with rage', with a sword in the right hand, 'from which steaming human blood drips', and with a torch in the left, 'whose flames seem to lick palaces and houses'.[235]

Some Catholic priests, such as Victor Zahn in Baden, went as far as to blame Austria rather than Napoleonic France for starting the various wars of the 1800s,

---

[228] W. J. Behr, 'Das teutsche Reich', *Der Rheinische Bund* (1808), vol. 7, no. 19, 111–12; J. G. Pahl, 'Bemerkungen und Bendenklichkeiten über einen Aufsatz in Winkopps Rhein. Bunde', *Chronik der Teutschen*, 4 Mar. 1808, vol. 15, 113–16, in G. Schuck, *Rheinbundpatriotismus*, 292–5.

[229] J. G. Pahl, 'Betrachtungen über den Rheinischen Bund', *National-Chronik der Teutschen*, 8 Oct. 1806, vol. 39, 305–10, in G. Schuck, *Rheinbundpatriotismus*, 291.

[230] Cited in J. Echternkamp, *Aufstieg*, 179.

[231] A. Gestrich, 'Kirchliche Kriegsmentalität in Württemberg um 1800', in J. Dülffer (ed.), *Kriegsbereitschaft*, 183–201.

[232] J. G. v. Pahl, *Denkwürdigkeiten aus meinem Leben und meiner Zeit*, ed. W. Pahl (Tübingen, 1840), 368.

[233] Instructions from 1794, cited in A. Gestrich, 'Kirchliche Kriegsmentalität', 189, and the *Hofprediger*'s sermon of 1 June 1813, ibid., 193.

[234] 'Rede über die allgemeine Anliegenheit des Krieges' (1793), U. Planert, *Mythos*, 510.

[235] Ibid., 512.

which had ensured that Baden had not 'enjoyed' peace.[236] There was little indication in such religious utterances, in which military conflicts were initially seen as
the punishment of God and later as a divine test, of a glorification of war.[237] Faced
by such changing policies and pronouncements in church, in the press, and elsewhere, contemporaries were frequently left with the impression that 'the world is
merely a theatre (or rather a lunatic asylum), so to say, for things happen today
which were exactly the opposite yesterday', in the words of one chemist in Erdingen
in 1813: 'Thus, the page turns.'[238] The succession of conflicts in the 1790s, 1800s,
and 1810s appeared to many observers to be the more or less meaningless twists
and turns of fate. Nonetheless, the majority of commentators felt compelled to try
to make sense of such turbulent and troubling events: arguably, more sought to do
so through reference to the values and character of 'Germany' than through an
appeal to the interests and affiliations of individual states. King Friedrich of
Württemberg's instruction to the Interior Ministry in October 1815 that the celebration of the battle of Leipzig 'could not be allowed in public', since 'the relations
of his royal Highness and of the kingdom do not permit of such', was itself an
admission that at least some subjects wanted to participate in and stage national
events.[239] The same was true of other states.[240]

Many, if not most, of the best-known journalists and writers of the late eighteenth and early nineteenth centuries deployed national arguments to justify war,
contending—along with Friedrich Perthes—that 'love of the fatherland, belonging
to a nation and sharing its fortune and misfortune', was 'so deeply embedded in
the soul of man that no relationship, no science, no universality, not even love and
God can comfort us over, and fill the place of, such a loss'.[241] Notoriously, 'the
freeing of Germany' had 'not yet become deeply rooted' in the mind of Goethe, a
64-year-old minister and literary deity in Weimar, but he nonetheless 'believes in
it seriously', recorded Wilhelm von Humboldt, tacitly acknowledging that the
writer was an exception by 1813.[242] According to Stein in 1814, journalists
required an 'adequate political and historical knowledge', so they could 'follow the
course of world events and the tendency of public opinion attentively', attached
'to a German fatherland with their heart and their mind'.[243] They included best-
selling authors such as Arndt and Jahn, academics-cum-publicists such as Fichte
and Schleiermacher, and editors or publishers of the principal political periodicals
like Görres, Luden, Cotta, and Rotteck.[244] The majority had initially welcomed

[236] Cited in ibid., 558.   [237] Ibid., 507–23.   [238] Cited in U. Planert, *Mythos*, 596.
[239] A. Gestrich, 'Kirchliche Kriegsmentalität', 194.
[240] The Prussian officer Wilhelm von Eberhardt reported to his mother on 31 Mar. 1813 that the
Prussian army was welcomed by the inhabitants of Saxony, in M. v. Eberhardt (ed.), *Aus Preussens
schwerer Zeit*, 124.
[241] F. Perthes to F. de la Motte Fouqué, 23 July 1815, in A. de la Motte Fouqué (ed.), *Briefe an
Friedrich Baron de la Motte Fouqué* (Bern, 1968), 289.
[242] W. v. Humboldt to his wife, 26 Oct. 1813, in F. Schulze (ed.), *Weimarische Berichte und Briefe
aus den Freiheitskriegen 1806–1815* (Leipzig, 1913), 205.
[243] Stein to the Generaldirektor of the Reichspost, 19 June 1814, in H. F. K. Freiherr vom Stein,
Briefe und amtliche Schriften, ed. W. Hubatsch (Stuttgart, 1964), vol. 5, 25–6.
[244] J. Leonhard, *Bellizismus*, 253–5, 261–4.

the French Revolution and criticized their own states for joining the Coalition against France in 1792.

They also numbered conservatives such as Gentz and Friedrich August von der Marwitz. In the opinion of the former, the utopian cosmopolitanism of the French revolutionaries had produced the most extensive war in history. By attempting 'to unite all the peoples of the earth in a great cosmopolitan federation', the revolutionaries had created 'the most gruesome world war which had ever shaken and torn apart society': 'A false system, which based the greatness and well-being of states on wars and conquests, pushed aside an enlightened, liberal, beneficent assessment of the real needs and true interests of nations.'[245] The revolution had extended the scope of war, but it had also made it 'easier, however contradictory this sounds, because it at least taught a nation the secret that it should no longer see it as a path towards exhaustion but as a means of extending its powers': 'War was popular, as at the start, and—in the sense of the revolution—genuinely national (*nazional*)', dispelling the earlier conviction of conservatives 'that a nation wrought by civilian unrest' could be defeated easily.[246] 'All the other nations' had been forced after 1789 to take account of the new, national reserves of strength available to their French opponent.[247] In the view of Marwitz, an old Prussian conservative, the German nation had come to take precedence over the Hohenzollern monarchy and other German principalities by 1813. Germany stood, as a 'nation of descent' (*Stamm-Nation*), in the middle of Europe, the focus of opposition to the 'principle of evil' incarnated in 'the French nation'.[248] War had emphasized the linguistic and geographical differences between nations, which should be defined and respected by the peace treaties signed after the Napoleonic conflicts, he went on, ending the previous practice of territorial compensation on dynastic grounds, irrespective of national belonging: the 'idea of a common German fatherland' had 'put down roots' which 'could not be destroyed'.[249] 'Whoever masters this idea will rule in Germany', he concluded.[250] Such conservative commentators, who remained steadfastly loyal to the crown and altar, betrayed how widespread the national idea had become within the Prussian and other German public spheres.

Johann Jakob Otto August Rühle von Lilienstern, a writer and Prussian officer, gave one of the most famous conservative pleas for national education in his 'Apologie des Krieges', first published in Friedrich Schlegel's *Deutsches Museum* in 1813 and later in revised form as a book entitled *Vom Kriege* in 1814. Rejecting Kant, in a work initially conceived in the late 1790s, he portrayed military conflicts as part of a wider set of struggles which gave meaning to life, pleasures, and possessions. 'A state of war in and of itself' was 'not as abhorrent as one-sided human reason is in the habit of believing', just as 'a state of peace in and of itself' was 'not

---

[245] F. v. Gentz, 'Über den ewigen Frieden' (1800), in K. v. Raumer (ed.), *Ewiger Friede* (Munich, 1953), 492–4.
[246] Ibid., 493–5; *Über den Ursprung*, ibid. 185–6.
[247] F. v. Gentz, 'Über den ewigen Frieden', 493–6.
[248] Cited in J. Leonhard, *Bellizismus*, 254–5.   [249] Ibid., 255.   [250] Ibid.

as desirable' as it was commonly held to be, he asserted.[251] Conflicts were intrinsic to nation-building, just as nations were an important element—perhaps the most important—of modern warfare:

> what history tells us...about the striving of peoples for national education (*nationale Erziehung*) [is that] it comes down to the military training of the male sex, and especially of male youth. What in respect of national education has not immediately had a belligerent purpose, history tells us, has had a religious proclivity, and if one is to give a truly clear account of the possible and necessary characteristics of all national education, one quickly finds that it can only derive from two poles; that of religion and that of the arming of the nation (*Nationalbewaffnung*).[252]

Combat was seen by Rühle as a test, not merely of individuals, but also of nations, which provided 'incontrovertible proof of [their] inner nobility and admirable national character' by demonstrating their 'honour and moral worth at war', removing 'all the poison of the freedom of peace', taming 'the wild and giving steel to the soft' in order to create 'a true, indissoluble national tie' under 'the extreme pressure of war' and 'to prepare a nation for peace by means of war':

> Just as it should be trained in war for peace, the nation should be trained in peace for war. Yet this is only possible insofar as...the army is nationalised and the nation is militarised: i.e. not only must...an internal army, made up of sons of the country take the place of a foreign army, merely external to the state, but the army and the *Volk* should also become one, with every creature and every piece of property being armed or, rather, itself becoming a weapon; every institution, branch of knowledge and disposition should at once be belligerent and peaceful. So it is when the state is understood to be in perpetual consciousness and enjoyment of itself, but also understood to be a perpetual safeguard for itself and in a constant state of self-defence: to strive for this is to prepare a nation militarily.[253]

For Rühle, as for other conservatives inside and outside of Prussia, war and the nation had become intimately connected during the revolutionary and Napoleonic eras.

The relationship between military conflict and nationalism in the writings of prominent German publicists derived from various sources, including the tribulations of occupation, long-standing anti-French stereotypes, domestic social and political struggles, the relaxation and tightening of censorship, the precarious position of writers, the dissolution and formation of states, different forms and degrees of state intervention, religious strife, and the sacralization of national sentiment. As a consequence, it is difficult to assess the significance of national ideas in contemporaries' understanding and waging of wars. It is possible to discern a 'nationalization of enmity' in the articles and treatises of some authors, which affected the way that they represented conflicts.[254] In certain cases, the extreme conditions of revolutionary

---

[251] Ibid., 258–9. J. J. O. A. Rühle von Lilienstern, 'Apologie des Krieges', *Deutsches Museum* (1813), vol. 3, 162. The essay has since been published as a book: Rühle von Lilienstern, *Apologie des Krieges* (Vienna, 1984).

[252] J. J. O. A. Rühle von Lilienstern, *Vom Kriege* (Frankfurt, 1814), 69.   [253] Ibid., 73–7.

[254] Michael Jeismann's *Das Vaterland der Feinde* remains the most suggestive account, convincing sceptics such as J. Echternkamp, *Aufstieg*, 222.

and Napoleonic warfare had served to radicalize journalists' attitudes towards perceived foes, with the German *Volk* embittered, in the words of one newspaper in 1813, by 'the weight, over many years, of French despotism' and left with the conviction that 'the remaining French corpses were not worthy of German soil, but should be left as food for the ravens'.[255] The reverse was also true, with the apprehension of conflicts in national terms itself exacerbating antipathies. The desire to create a set of 'German' values or attributes distinct from the German states' purportedly overbearing neighbour and in opposition to the Frenchified courts of self-interested princes and French-speaking milieux of aristocratic society helped to aggravate hostilities. 'I want hatred against the French, not merely for this war, I want it for a long time, I want it forever', wrote Arndt in a pamphlet on *Volkshass* in 1813: 'This hatred burns like the religion of the German *Volk*, as a holy madness in every heart and keeps us forever loyal, honest and courageous'.[256]

Partly, such injunctions to hate were intended to shock the publicist's readers, most of whom were less nationalistic, as indeed Arndt himself had been only a decade earlier, after a long stay in Paris during the summer of 1799: 'I love the French nation and believe that I know something about it; I don't hold everything it has done to be a crime, nor do I hold everything to be a virtue.'[257] Hatred was a necessary foundation of national identity, the former Swedish subject implied in his celebrated song 'Des Deutschen Vaterland', which described a German fatherland as a place 'Where every Frenchman is called a foe (*Feind*) / Where every German is called a friend (*Freund*).'[258] Yet it also seemed to derive from a 'hereditary historical enmity' or *Erbfeindschaft*, which—in the verdict of Friedrich Rühs—had 'always been inimical, as far back as history goes', from the godlessness and sinfulness of the French, with a second meaning of *Erbfeind* being 'the devil'; from their tyranny, symbolized by Napoleon, and their criminality, labelled 'a robber band of 500,000' by Görres for example; and from their artifice and superficiality, as Arndt put it in *Geist der Zeit*:

> When I say that I hate French carelessness, I despise French sensitivity, I disapprove of French loquacity and flightiness, I may pronounce a flaw, but it is a flaw that I share with all my people. ... Let us hate the French afresh, let us hate our Frenchmen, the dishonourers and destroyers of our power and innocence, all the more freshly, if we feel that they are softening and unnerving our virtue and strength.[259]

In such writings, 'Germans' were seen as a self-evident, political collectivity, morally superior to the 'French', who could be dismissed—for instance, by the poet

---

[255] *Feld-Zeitung*, 4 Nov. 1813, cited in M. Jeismann, *Das Vaterland der Feinde*, 92.

[256] E. M. Arndt, *Über Volkshaß und über den Gebrauch einer fremden Sprache* (Leipzig, 1813), 18–19.

[257] E. M. Arndt, *Germanien und Europa* (Altona, 1803), 249.

[258] E. M. Arndt, 'Des Deutschen Vaterland', in E. M. Arndt, *Werke* (Berlin, 1912), vol. 1, 127.

[259] F. C. Rühs, *Historische Entwickelung des Einflusses Frankreichs und der Franzosen auf Deutschland und die Deutschen* (Berlin, 1815), 5; J. v. Görres, 'Napoleon in Paris' (1815), in W. Frühwald (ed.), *Joseph Görres. Ausgewählte Werke* (Freiburg, 1978), vol. 1, 262; E. M. Arndt, *Geist der Zeit*, vol. 4, 148.

Friedrich Rückert—as wild animals and 'barbarians' and who, consequently, were to be destroyed by 'great acts of cruelty'.[260]

The stridency of such incitement of national hatred, it could be contended, betrayed an awareness on the part of national-minded agitators of their weak position. References to a German nation usually accompanied or supplemented other forms of 'patriotism', which denoted an attachment to an individual state or locality, rather than countering or contradicting them. In states such as Württemberg and Saxony, where local patriotism and German nationalism were potentially at variance, allusions to 'Germany' were generally restricted.[261] In Baden, Wilhelm, who had been in command of the Badenese troops in the disastrous Russian campaign of the *Grande Armée* in 1812, returned to Karlsruhe only to find that 'the *Karlsruher Zeitung* had not mentioned our march there with a single sentence' and had reported in November 1812, 'when it was going so badly for us, that everything was completely fine': together with a belated report in January 1813 about the crossing of the Beresina, 'that was all which was made known of the Badenese contingent'.[262] Returning a year later from the battle of Leipzig, which Baden had fought on the French side, Wilhelm found 'the mood…an unusual one', with the population estranged from France but not trusting themselves 'to allow their opinion to be articulated' and 'without enthusiasm for the so-called German business'.[263] In Bavaria and Prussia, in spite of strong disagreement about the states' policies towards France, patriotism and nationalism were more frequently linked, especially between 1813 and 1815, with the former more important than the latter. Thus, in his famous Breslau proclamation—issued in German and Polish—to 'my loyal *Volk*' on 17 March 1813, Friedrich Wilhelm III called on 'Brandenburgers, Prussians, Silesians, Pomeranians and Lithuanians' to fight 'for the fatherland and your own king' and he concentrated on past Prussian glories, including those of Friedrich the Great. Yet he also referred, amongst 'the holy goods' for which Prussian subjects were fighting, to the restoration of 'honour', 'because the Prussian and the German cannot live dishonourably':

> Great sacrifices are demanded of all orders, for *our* beginning is great, and the number and means of *our* enemies are not small. You will rather make them for the fatherland, for your born king, than for a foreign *ruler*. …Trust in God, stamina, courage and the powerful support of *our* allies will repay *our* honest endeavours with a successful reward. But whatever sacrifices might be asked of individuals, they will not outweigh the holy goods for which *we* are offering ourselves up, for which *we* are fighting and which *we* must win, if *we* do not wish to stop being *Prussians* and *Germans*.[264]

---

[260] F. Rückert, 'Geharnischte Sonnette', cited in M. Jeismann, *Das Vaterland der Feinde*, 91.

[261] A. Gestrich, 'Kirchliche Kriegsmentalität', in J. Dülffer (ed.), *Kriegsbereitschaft*, 183–201. See also the declaration by the King of Württemberg to his troops at the start of the war against Prussia in 1806, in which he exhorted them to fight for 'the fatherland and for your King' and for 'the honour of Württemberg', which was aligned 'for the first time with [the troops of] the other monarchs'; F. Schneider, *Erinnerungen aus den Feldzügen*, xvi.

[262] Wilhelm Markgraf v. Baden, *Denkwürdigkeiten*, vol. 1, 222.   [263] Ibid., 473.

[264] Friedrich Wilhelm III, 'Aufruf', in H. B. Spies (ed.), *Quellen zum politischen Denken der Deutschen* (Darmstadt, 1981), vol. 2, 254–5.

The king's subjects were facing a 'holy war' of life and death, which threatened both Prussia and Germany, it was implied: 'There is no outcome other than an honourable peace or a glorious downfall.'[265] Little distinction was made between Prussians and Germans, not least because Theodor Gottlieb von Hippel, the Prussian reformer who drafted the document, and Hardenberg, who amended it, wanted to encourage the other German states to join the war effort against Napoleon. What mattered more was the fact that a conservative monarch was attempting to mobilize all his male subjects in order to win a war of 'existence' and 'independence'.[266] This notion of shared sacrifice for the sake of the *Volk*, of which the king was part, was developed further in Friedrich Wilhelm III's proclamation of 18 June 1814, which was published in all Prussian newspapers after the capitulation of France.[267] The monarch's call to arms on 7 April 1815, at the start of the War of the Seventh Coalition, was more traditional.[268]

Two of the purportedly 'national' *causes célèbres* of the era—the death of Queen Luise of Prussia in 1810 and the insurrection of Major Ferdinand von Schill in 1809—evinced the extent and limits of nationalism. Both took place during Prussia's subjugation by French forces and drew on popular, anti-French sentiment. The former was an official event, after the unexpected death of Friedrich Wilhelm III's 34-year-old wife from an unidentified fourteen-day illness on 19 July.[269] Her demise was announced in all the kingdom's churches and the public acts of mourning lasted fourteen days. The public's response showed, in the opinion of the court preacher Friedrich Emanuel Sack, that the queen was 'deeply loved' and that her death was another 'bitter test' for the unfortunate country.[270] Yet although she quickly became a symbol of Prussia's resilience—famously, she had been convinced by her husband to beg for more lenient terms during a private audience with Napoleon at Tilsit in 1807—her death does not seem to have prompted public outpourings or popular demonstrations of grief outside the Hohenzollern monarchy. The latter event—the armed uprising initiated by Schill and his regiment of 550 hussars—did have ramifications outside Prussia, as the Prussian troops attacked the French vassal state of Westphalia on 28 April 1809 against the orders of Friedrich Wilhelm III, before being defeated—now 1,500 strong—on 31 May by French forces near Stralsund. The mutiny, which took place as Vienna attempted to launch a 'national' war against France on 10 April, seems to have occurred partly in protest at and partly in encouragement of the Hohenzollern monarch, who refused to become embroiled in the conflict.[271] Schill's revolt was covered extensively in the press and elicited popular support, leading Prussian officials to fear a revolution. 'I am beginning, from day to day, to become more and more fearful, if a decisive step is not taken soon', wrote the Berlin President of Police to the government in Königsberg on 2 May 1809:

---

[265] Ibid.   [266] Ibid.
[267] K. Hagemann, *Mannlicher Muth und teutscher Ehre*, 284.   [268] Ibid.
[269] P. Demandt, *Luisenkult. Die Unsterblichkeit der Königin von Preussen* (Cologne, 2003).
[270] Cited ibid., 368.
[271] S. A. Mustafa, *The Long Ride of Major von Schill: A Journey through German History and Memory* (Lanham, MD, 2008).

There is only one alternative. The coming of Hs. M. the King or war with Austria against France. ... For the *army is wavering*—and what can the authority of the individual authorities do then? It is a question of the tranquillity of the country—and of the throne of the monarch.[272]

Schill's actions had caused 'the greatest sensation', he had written a few days earlier, making it difficult 'to maintain public order': 'The shifts of mood are extraordinary and even our own participation in the war could not occasion greater emotion.'[273] However, it was evident to most observers that Schill attracted public sympathy in Prussia rather than active backing, revealing popular dissatisfaction with the unpatriotic subordination of the monarch to French authorities but also showing that 'dissolutions will never start from below', in the opinion of one official.[274] The king himself claimed that he did 'not fear the illegal unrest of my *Volk*' and that he would not be distracted 'by anarchic explosions in Berlin' from devoting himself 'to more important decisions'.[275] Indeed, 'if the higher authorities in Berlin had met the spirit of insolent unrest together, in unity and with force, instead of sighing and complaining and flattering the mob and the insane, these sort of unheard-of events would not have occurred', he asserted on 9 May.[276] Outside Prussia, the insurrection met with less interest in the press.[277]

Reportage of Schill's act of insubordination hinted at the extent to which public images of warfare had altered during the revolutionary and Napoleonic periods. Rather than war being dismissed or criticized as the affair of princes and the product of absolutism and standing armies, it was seen as a matter of public concern and, even, national honour, with the King of Prussia—the second most powerful prince in Germany—openly opposed because of his reluctance to go to war against Napoleon, despite the likely costs and sacrifices of such a conflict. As such, the justification of war had become a subject of domestic discussion, which was added to older concepts of 'just war' in Christian ethics and natural or international law.[278] Yet what would prevent states justifying all wars, as Kant had asked in 'Zum ewigen Frieden' in 1795, 'given the evil of human nature, which can be seen in an unconcealed form in the free relations of peoples with one another', in contrast to 'a state of civil legality', where human nature was 'substantially veiled as a result of state compulsion'?[279] If 'states as such stand under no communal, external compulsion', why would they limit either the grounds for the declarations of war or the means to which they were prepared to resort in order to win, since everything was now at stake?[280] In other words, were revolutionary and Napoleonic conflicts in the process of becoming a form of universal civil war, provoking fears of a reversion

[272] J. K. Gruner to H. L. A. zu Dohna, 2 May 1809, in H. Granier (ed.), *Berichte aus der Berliner Franzosenzeit 1807–1809* (Leipzig, 1913), 425.
[273] Gruner to Dohna, 29 Apr. 1809, in H. Granier (ed.), *Berichte aus der Berliner*, 414.
[274] Bardeleben to Beyme, 11 May 1809, cited in B. v. Münchow-Pohl, *Zwischen Reform und Krieg. Untersuchungen zur Bewusstseinslage in Preussen 1809–1812* (Göttingen, 1987), 156.
[275] Cited in U. Gaede, *Preussens Stellung zur Kriegsfrage im Jahre 1809* (Hanover, 1897), 94–5.
[276] Ibid.   [277] W. v. Conrady (ed.), *Aus stürmischer Zeit*, 177.
[278] D. Klippel and M. Zwanzger, 'Krieg und Frieden', 135–58.
[279] Ibid., 148.   [280] Ibid.

to the conditions of the Thirty Years' War?[281] The 'devouring force' of the French Revolution had, after all, transformed 'all the political conditions of Europe', blurring the distinction between domestic and foreign politics, after it had 'found no more sustenance inside France', if a conservative commentator such as Gentz were to be believed.[282]

From an opposing point of view, the liberal Friedrich Gottlieb Welcker—a philologist and older brother of Carl Theodor Welcker—argued in 1815 that there was 'no type of war more noble than that for civil freedom' (*bürgerliche Freiheit*).[283] 'True civil war' (*der echte bürgerliche Krieg*) was 'waged for an idea, for a spiritual good, for the sake of a holy purpose, free from greed and desperation'.[284] Most authors distanced themselves from the notion of a *Bürgerkrieg*, however, in the manner of the philosopher Wilhelm Traugott Krug—who became Kant's successor at Königsberg in 1805—in his summary of the period since 1792, *System der Kriegswissenschaften* (1815). War could be understood as a 'great legal conflict…between whole peoples or states' and was, therefore, to be distinguished from 'a duel, a feud or a so-called civil war (*Bürgerkrieg*)'.[285] National or patriotic wars were an extension of 'the legal and ethical principles by which war is made into a dispute of peoples (*Völkerstreit*)', since contemporary citizen-soldiers did 'not want to dishonour [their] elevated calling of defending the fatherland'.[286] In modern conflicts, where 'warriors and citizens' were 'one', a *Volk* could only safeguard its 'property and land, its self-worth and independence' if it was 'ready for a fight in its entirety, ready to defend its rights not only with the pen but also with a sword in hand, if it was ready to demand respect from every other neighbouring *Volk* not only for its education but also for its courage'.[287]

There seemed to be compelling reasons why modern conflicts—even if termed '*Revolutionskriege*' or '*Volkskriege*', as they had been from 1792 onwards, rather than '*Reichskriege*'—would not revert to the bloodletting of earlier civil wars. First, as Kant and many others had pointed out since the 1790s, conscription and popular participation in government, whether within a republic or not, placed constraints on statesmen's ability or willingness to declare war, since citizens would be the victims of any conflict, notwithstanding the perceived popularity of the wars of the French Revolution. Second, Johann Gottfried Herder's argument in favour of the peaceful coexistence of nations was widely believed. 'Cabinets may deceive each other; political machineries may be directed at each other', wrote the Weimar philosopher in a letter of 1795: 'Fatherlands do not clash with one another in this way…[rather] they stand by each other like families. The bloody struggle of fatherland against fatherland constitutes the worst barbarism in the language of humanity.'[288] The cultural differences of nations remained natural and incommensurable, militating against conquest and assimilation, and promoting progress and

---

[281] J. Leonhard, *Bellizismus*, 216, 227.   [282] F. v. Gentz, *Frieden*, 493–5.
[283] F. G. Welcker, 'Von ständischer Verfassung' (1815), in F. G. Welcker, *Von ständischer Verfassung und über Deutschlands Zukunft* (Karlsruhe, 1831), 19.
[284] Ibid.   [285] W. T. Krug, *System der Kriegswissenschaft und ihrer Literatur* (Leipzig, 1815), 3.
[286] Ibid., 15–16.   [287] Ibid., 118.
[288] J. G. Herder, *Sämtliche Werke*, ed. B. Suphahn (Berlin, 1881), vol. 17, 319.

peace, irrespective of 'the deceptive and thankless paths of their political and military histories', as each culture developed.[289] If most contemporaries eschewed Herder's criticism of wars per se, few perceived a connection between military conflict and nation-building. Third, states, usually founded on patriotic affiliation or national belonging, were held to be the principal guarantors of law and order, countering what the Saxon theologian Heinrich Gottlieb Tzschirner, in his influential work *Ueber den Krieg* (1815), portrayed as a Hobbesian state of nature, where each individual fought against every other. Whereas citizens had given powers to a sovereign to act on their behalf, nations (*Völker*) had not 'externalized the power of making judgments about their own rights', remaining at once 'a party to and a judge of' disputes and leaving 'neither of two conflicting peoples bound, in contentious cases of law, to subordinate its judgment to the judgment of another'.[290]

War was not only ineradicable, it was also a necessary foundation of national difference and state power, fostering the internal growth and external expansion of standing armies and other institutions. Instead of creating anarchy, however, such processes seemed to Tzschirner to consolidate societies, by ensuring 'that peoples come into being as societies distinct from one another and defined by their own characters', and that 'the fatherland becomes all the dearer to citizens the more they have tolerated it and fought and bled for it', rendering it 'all the worthier and more holy'.[291] States needed conflicts in order to develop, but they themselves then became the main moral and legal restraint on bellicose behaviour: 'The state is the condition of ethical and spiritual culture', he went on, 'and, thus, war, the founder of states, is a link in the chain of transformations which promote the education of humanity, a means chosen by nature itself for the attainment of its ends.'[292] Conflagrations such as those of the previous two decades, the memory of which would 'maintain national sentiment for centuries', were ultimately stabilizing, despite appearances:

> Through the dangers which it threatens and the acts which it gives rise to, war fills individual minds with love of the fatherland and enthusiasm, and raises them above the petty endeavours of acquisitiveness and pleasure-seeking; war undermines thrones, and princes believe that they will not be able to shore up the precarious ones with their own forces. ... War leads to events, the course of which human wisdom cannot foresee and human strength cannot direct. ... Thus, war, which extends its influence over the peoples, awakes in entire tribes a consciousness of their moral power and their dependence on God, and changes, in this way, the attitudes of whole epochs.[293]

In the public sphere at least, wars were frequently seen to be transformative but not destabilizing, partly because of a belief in culture or God, and partly because of enthusiasm for the state or nation, which itself was tied to demands for political reform and popular participation in government. For this reason, most commentators seem to have believed that Napoleon could be defeated and the era of wars

---

[289] Ibid., vol. 18, 137.
[290] H. G. Tzschirner, *Über den Krieg. Ein philosophischer Versuch* (Leipzig, 1815), 41, 47–8.
[291] Ibid., 71–2, 227–8.   [292] Ibid., 233–4.   [293] Ibid., 270–1.

beginning in 1792 could come to an end. Tzschirner, Herder, Welcker, Krug, Feuerbach, Fichte, Schleiermacher, Rühle, Gentz, Müller, the Schlegel brothers, Arnim, Körner, Schenkendorf, Görres, and Jean Paul all assumed that war would be followed by peace.[294] Most assumed that the longevity of the latter depended on the justice and decisiveness of the former.

Representations of conflicts changed between 1792 and 1815, as the nature of warfare altered and as a succession of wars, waged by seven separate coalitions, affected all the German lands. Most notably, long-established critiques of absolutism and hopes of a long-lasting or perpetual peace were eclipsed by new conceptions of 'revolutionary' conflict and wars of the '*Volk*'. Although their reports varied, the majority of commentators came to assume that greater popular participation in wars was required in order to defeat—or protect German states from—the revolutionary or Napoleonic regimes of France. Such mobilization of the *Volk* was often 'patriotic'—that is, linked to the defence of individual German states—rather than 'national', which required the conceptualization of a future German polity. Either type of mobilization, however, permitted the heroicizing of combat in the press, academic treatises, literature, and art.[295] War heroes, of course, had continued to exist in the eighteenth century, as in previous periods, from Achilles and Arminius to Gustavus Adolphus and Friedrich the Great, but they were joined from the 1790s onwards, influenced by French paintings of revolutionary figures which had individualized and allegorized warfare, by unnamed individuals—ordinary soldiers and citizens—engaged in heroic acts against a background of massed ranks, in which human forms merged in formation and movement.[296] In such acts, combatants and civilians were shown overcoming more powerful enemies, suffering nobly or making sense of the chaotic conditions of military conflict, with only stylized references to the agonies of death or with symbolic representations of unbloodied corpses.

The first images during the revolutionary campaigns of soldiers' heroic deaths or of civilians' suffering did not appear until 1794/5, after which the number of portrayals increased rapidly.[297] In works such as A. W. Küfner's *Tod des Oberstleutnants Graf von Forstenburg* (1795), *Causse: Es lebe die Republik* (1798), and *Gefecht bei Stanz* (1799), known and unknown soldiers on both sides were shown locked in battle in the foreground, with rows of bayonets and other symbols of anonymous ranks of soldiers behind.[298] In the same artist's *Grossmüthige Aufopferung einer*

[294] See especially, O. Dann, 'Der deutsche Bürger wird Soldat', in J. Dülffer (ed.), *Kriegsbereitschaft und Friedensordnung in Deutschland 1800–1814* (Münster, 1995), 39–126, 67–70; J. Leonhard, *Bellizismus*, 207–81, A. Portmann-Tingueley, *Romantik und Krieg*, 40–55, 84–113, 134–52, 191–226, 274–95, 325–50.

[295] See R. Schilling, *'Kriegshelden'. Deutungsmuster heroischer Männlichkeit in Deutschland 1813–1945* (Paderborn, 2002), 43–125; K. Hagemann, 'German Heroes: The Cult of Death for the Fatherland in Nineteenth-Century Germany', in S. Dudink et al. (eds), *Masculinities in Politics and War* (Manchester, 2004), 116–34.

[296] C. Danelzik-Brüggemann, *Ereignisse und Bilder*, 165–71. On Arminius and earlier heroes, see H. P. Hermann et al., *Machtphantasie Deutschland. Nationalismus, Männlichkeit und Fremdenhass im Vaterlandsdiskurs deutscher Schriftsteller des 18. Jahrhunderts* (Frankfurt, 1996), 32–79, 161–91.

[297] Ibid., 169, 183.   [298] Ibid.

Tochter für ihre Mutter zu Frankenthal (1795) and *Kindliche Liebe eines deutschen Mädchens zu Frankenthal* (1795), heroic scenes of self-defence, including women and children protecting their families from the brutality of soldiers, were staged and choreographed in a similar way.[299] The prints, which existed alongside traditional representations of battle formations, groups of soldiers in uniform, and royal commanders, revealed instances of courage or audacity on the part of ordinary people. They echoed the interest of artists, borrowing from their French counterparts, in the ordinary heroes—Danton, Marat, Robespierre, and Napoleon—of the French Revolution.[300] The later demonization of Bonaparte—as in J. M. Voltz's *Karikatur auf Napoleon* (1814), which imagined his head composed of corpses and skeletons insanely banging marching drums—was the culmination of the same fascination and the most extreme consequence of the sacralization of the warring nation or state.[301] During the 'wars of liberation', Napoleon had either been embodied as Satan or shown to be in league with the devil.[302] In one popular broadsheet, which gained international renown, the French ruler was represented as a child in the devil's arms, swaddled in the tricolour.[303] 'This is my beloved son, in whom I am well pleased', ran the caption, repeating Matthew 3:17. Such caricaturists' attempts to terrify their viewers remained an exception, however.

In spite of the injunctions of Arndt and others for citizens to hate their enemies, heroism, bravery, and bloodlessness, rather than terror, were characteristic of press and literary accounts of war, which generally avoided the worst consequences of military campaigns.[304] Thus, even Körner, who confronted death most directly in his poems and constantly used words to allude to the senses, referred only to '*der Tod*' as a 'duty of heroes' and to flesh and blood as elements of life, to which heroic acts gave meaning: 'That is my body, which I have given to you, that is my blood, which I have spilled for you. For your life, I go to my death.'[305] He envisaged 'corpses on corpses', 'hills of corpses', as well as 'floods' and 'earthly fires', as obstacles which it was necessary to traverse in the quest for a promised land: 'Through! There is the *Vaterland*!'[306] Death for the fatherland offered the chance of martyrdom 'in the temple of immortality', deriving from Christian and classical sources:

---

[299] C. Danelzik-Brüggemann, *Ereignisse*, 310–11. See also, H. M. Kaulbach, 'Männliche Ideale von Krieg und Frieden in der Kunst der napoleonischen Ära', in J. Dülffer (ed.), *Kriegsbereitschaft*, 127–41.

[300] On French models, see C. Prendergast, *Napoleon and History Painting: Antoine-Jean Gros's* La Bataille d'Eylau (Oxford, 1997); J. Träger, 'Kaiserliche Inkarnationen' and E. Stolpe, 'Der Krieg als Drama', in E. Mai (ed.), *Historienmalerei in Europa*, 135–92; T. Kirchner, 'Paradigma der Gegenwärtigkeit. Schlachtenmalerei als Gattung ohne Darstellungskonventionen', in S. Germer and M. F. Zimmermann (eds), *Bilder der Macht, Macht der Bilder* (Berlin, 1997), 107–24.

[301] C. Danelzik-Brüggemann, *Ereignisse*, 303.

[302] W. A. Coupe, *German Political Satires from the Reformation to the Second World War* (New York, 1987–93), vol. 2, untitled, 284, 286, 295–6, and 'Napoleons Traum', 285.

[303] Ibid., 294.

[304] See R. Schilling, '*Kriegshelden*', 43–125; K. Hagemann, 'German Heroes', 116–34.

[305] 'Nachtlied der Krieger', in T. Körner, *Werke*, ed. A. Stern (Stuttgart, 1890), vol. 1, 305; 'Das Abendmahl', in T. Körner, *Sämmtliche Werke*, ed. K. Streckfuss (Berlin, 1861), 90.

[306] 'Brutus' Abschied', in T. Körner, *Sämmtliche Werke*, 46–8.

'Calm kills, only he who acts lives, and I will live, I will not die in the midst of death.'[307] The poet was not waging a war 'of which crowns know', but a 'crusade', 'a holy war', against 'hell' as 'an edifice of lies' and for the salvation of 'justice, morals, virtue, belief and conscience'.[308] For Körner and other Romantics, the senses faced death in order to give meaning to it and to escape it. Although their outpourings have been described as 'fantasies of annihilation and bloodthirstiness', they rarely, in fact, ran out of control, despite their descriptions of sounds, sights, movements, emotions, and the body.[309] Accordingly, Körner's 'Song of Revenge' summoned up thunder and wild furies, dogs, hell, and the devil as it appealed for vengeful killing, but at the same time as acknowledging that it would be limited to soldiers ('all who carry a blade') and that it would require a religious demonology (with the enemy as 'the crop of hell's seed' and 'the devil's brood') to overcome his compatriots' reluctance to avenge their 'betrayed' brothers and to keep to their 'oath':

> Have at them! At them! the war trumpets blare!
> At them! the roar of thunder does command!
> Revenge calls out in storm and lightning's glare
> For Germany's avenging iron hand!
> Have at them, at them in the wild furies' dance!
> The toad yet lives and dares to swagger?
> At it, my brothers, with rifle, sword and lance!
> At it with poison and with dagger!
> What of the law of nations? Those pledged to night
> Are the crop of hell's seed.
> Where is the law these dogs have not defiled
> With murder and deceit?
> Avenge our blood with theirs! Kill all who carry a blade!
> They're all the devil's brood!
> Think of our oath, think of brothers betrayed
> And drink your fill of blood![310]

Here, in the drunkenness and fury of slaughter, as elsewhere in the representations of the early nineteenth century, there was little acknowledgement of the pain and meaninglessness of military killing.

Much of the historiographical debate about contemporaries' attitudes to war rests less on contested interpretations of press reports and literary depictions than on disputed assessments of the significance of such representations. Certainly, the majority of subjects had little knowledge of journalists', poets', and artists' accounts of military conflicts, which were, in any case, contradictory and haphazard. A reading 'public' in the German lands did have access to an increasing number of such accounts, however, as the wars succeeded one another, censorship was relaxed,

---

[307] 'Zriny', in T. Körner, *Werke*, vol. 2, 413.
[308] 'Toni' (1812), ibid., 277; 'Gebet' (1813) and 'Aufruf' (1813), ibid., vol. 1, 106, 90.
[309] M. Jeismann, *Das Vaterland der Feinde*, 76–94.
[310] I am grateful to Susanne Kord for her translation of these verses. The poem is cited in E. Klessmann (ed.), *Die Befreiungskriege in Augenzeugenberichten* (Düsseldorf, 1966), 129.

public spheres developed, and the possibility—or, even, need—of a coordinated national campaign against Napoleonic France arose, in Austria from 1809 onwards, Prussia from 1812, and most other German states from late 1813 onwards. For this section of society, which constituted the main constituency for the development of 'politics' in the first half of the nineteenth century, the notion of patriotic or national '*Volkskriege*' was associated, not only with new imperatives and necessities, but also with the possibility of reducing the number of conflicts and of instituting civilized laws of war. The next chapters investigate, from contemporaries' own points of view, how significant new, public representations of warfare were and whether they clashed with civilians' and combatants' actual experiences of conflict.

3

The Violence of Civilian Life

The extent to which contemporaries' conceptions of warfare altered during the revolutionary and Napoleonic periods depended, more than in the past, on their direct experience of military conflict. It is true that their exposure to war differed. Even a Rhinelander such as Karl August Varnhagen von Ense, born in Düsseldorf and travelling around western Germany in the 1790s, often appears to have felt detached from nearby events, recording in Aachen, for instance, that 'I learned almost nothing here of all the occurrences of war and revolution, which had been daily and hourly before my eyes and within earshot in Strasbourg'.[1] Having moved to Berlin to study medicine in 1800, he was still able to congratulate himself in 1803 on his 'blessed' circumstances of life, bound only by the 'highest feelings of freedom' and 'independence' and experiencing 'for the first time the full sensibility of being and acting' in the world.[2] The 'violent war between the French and the Austrians in South Germany' in 1805 was followed in Prussia with interest, not least because of the possibility of the Hohenzollern monarchy entering the conflict, but Varnhagen and his 'circle', although 'not indifferent', were not moved to a state of 'true political élan', even after the shock of Napoleon's victory.[3] How subjects experienced the Revolutionary and Napoleonic Wars was contingent on where they lived, whether they were burghers, peasants, or nobles, and whether they had been enlisted or conscripted.

Notoriously, Prussians had experienced an eleven-year peace between 1795 and 1806, which was without precedent in the eighteenth century. Nevertheless, in north Germany, too, the majority of people experienced military conflict for extended periods, with Prussia being defeated in 1806, many of its inhabitants living under French occupation until 1812, when a Prussian contingent of soldiers participated in the invasion of Russia, before the introduction of conscription in 1813, which resulted in 6 per cent of the population under arms. Conscription was introduced throughout the German lands, with up to 60 per cent of young men—in the French-occupied Rhineland—being recruited, compared to 55 per cent at the start of the First World War. The timing and impact of conflict were diverse, but its effects were widely felt. Inhabitants of most areas of Germany witnessed battles, the transit and billeting of soldiers, occupation, or the imposition of new political authorities and borders. Hamburg, which had been spared much of the fighting, has been aptly described as having witnessed a 'war without battles',

[1] K. A. Varnhagen v. Ense, *Denkwürdigkeiten des eignen Lebens* (Berlin, 1922–3), vol. 1, 40.
[2] Ibid., 104.   [3] Ibid., 169–71.

leaving its director of poor relief, returning to the city in September 1812, lamenting 'the ruin of earlier prosperity, stripped of its attributes, cloaked in the fog of a threatening future'.[4] 'How my heart bled', he concluded.[5] Varnhagen himself entered the Austrian army in 1809, being wounded at the battle of Wagram, and later took part in the wars against France between 1813 and 1815 in the Russian and Prussian armies. The following chapters investigate the consequences of such direct experiences of war.

CULTURES OF VIOLENCE AND DEATH

Scholars commonly contend that attitudes to suffering, pain, illness, violence, wounding, and death altered during the late eighteenth and early nineteenth centuries, but they disagree about the nature and causes of the change. Michel Foucault cites what has become the most famous case, the public execution in 1757 of the would-be assassin of Louis XV, Robert-François Damiens, which he contrasts with the purely disciplinary prison rules devised by Léon Faucher in 1838.[6] In the latter, the emphasis was on a minutely detailed daily regime administered behind prison walls to 'correct' the behaviour of the criminal; in the former, the spectacle demonstrated the power of the state, punishing and dismembering the body of Damiens in an act of retribution and deterrence, as the report of the *Gazette d'Amsterdam* indicated:

> The executioner dipped an iron in the pot containing the boiling potion, which he poured liberally over each wound. Then the ropes that were to be harnessed to the horses were attached with cords to the condemned man's body; the horses were then harnessed and placed alongside the arms and legs, one at each limb. ... The horses tugged hard, each pulling straight on a limb, each horse held by an executioner. After a quarter of an hour, the same ceremony was repeated and finally, after several attempts, the direction of the horses had to be changed, thus: those at the thighs towards the arms, which broke the arms at the joints. This was repeated several times without success.
>
> After two or three attempts, the executioner Samson and he who had used the pincers each drew out a knife from his pocket and cut the body at the thighs instead of severing the legs at the joints; the four horse gave a tug and carried off the two thighs after them, namely, that of the right side first, the other following; then the same was done to the arms, the shoulders, and the four limbs; the flesh had to be cut almost to the bone. The horses, pulling hard, carried off the right arm first and the other afterwards.[7]

To Foucault, the execution of Damiens was part of a transition from the 'staging' of punishment and suffering, in which the body was the 'major target of penal

---

[4] Caspar Voght, cited in K. B. Aaslestad, 'War without Battles: Civilian Experiences of Economic Warfare during the Napoleonic Era in Hamburg', in A. Forrest, K. Hagemann, and J Rendall (eds), *Soldiers, Citizens and Civilians*, 128.

[5] Ibid.   [6] M. Foucault, *Surveiller et punir* (Paris, 1975), 9–13.

[7] Translation of the *Gazette d'Amsterdam*, 1 Apr. 1757, in A. Giddens, *Sociology*, 2nd edn (Cambridge, 1993), 10.

repression' within a carnivalesque world of shared rituals and meanings, to a pervasive, discursive order of discipline, norms, and pathologies, as the judicial system redirected its attention from the body to 'the soul'.[8] Because he is most interested in the effects of self-discipline and relations of power in the nineteenth and twentieth centuries, Foucault pays less attention to experiences and toleration of violence in the eighteenth century.

Historical sociologists such as Norbert Elias and Anthony Giddens examine eighteenth-century forms of social organization and state power in greater depth, disagreeing with some of Foucault's arguments about their causes and consequences, yet concurring that overt acts and displays of violence had been incrementally removed from daily life. Elias maintains that the internal 'pacification' which took place in Europe between the early modern and modern eras was part of a broader 'civilizing process', closely connected to the formation of absolutist and national states, in which sexual, aggressive, and other 'animal-like' instincts were repressed. 'Once the monopoly of physical power has passed to central authorities, not every strong man can afford the pleasure of physical attack', he contends:

> Even in war in the civilized world, the individual can no longer give free rein to his pleasure, spurred on by the sight of the enemy, but must fight, no matter how he may feel, according to the commands of invisible or only indirectly visible enemy. And immense social upheaval and urgency, heightened by carefully concerted propaganda, are needed to reawaken instincts, the joy in killing and destruction that have been repressed from everyday civilized life.[9]

For Giddens, such pacification is not a sign 'that in the past people were more brutal, while we have become humane'.[10] Instead, 'punishment for crime became oriented towards creating the obedient citizen, rather than publicly displaying to the others the terrible consequences which follow from wrong-doing', with individuals—'not only criminals, but vagabonds, the sick, unemployed people, the feeble-minded and the insane'—'kept "locked away" from the outside world...as a means of controlling and disciplining their behaviour'.[11] The principal causes of these changes appear, to Giddens, to have been 'dull economic compulsion', connected to the spread of capitalist forms of production and exchange and to new types of discipline in industrial workplaces and within complex divisions of labour, and the gradual creation of nation-states, exercising monopolies of violence and disposing of more effective means of surveillance.[12] Urbanization, which accompanied the spread of capitalism and industrialization, helped to foster 'a "created environment", in which the transformation of nature is expressed as commodified time-space', making it into 'the *milieu* of all social action, no longer a distinct physical entity and social sector within a broader societal totality', and bringing into being 'those processes of time-space sequencing' required by modern organizations,

---

[8] M. Foucault, *Surveiller et punir*, 21, 14, 24.
[9] N. Elias, *The Civilizing Process* (New York, 1978), vol. 1, 202.
[10] A. Giddens, *Sociology*, 11.   [11] Ibid.
[12] A. Giddens, *The Nation-State and Violence* (Cambridge, 1985), 181–97.

including the nation-state, as the most prominent 'power-container'.[13] Within this temporal and spatial order, 'deviance'—including violence—and other phenomena causing distress and an interruption of the ordinary activities of daily life—including death itself—could be marginalized or 'sequestered', in Foucault's terms. 'In tribal and class-divided societies, tradition infuses routine and gives it moral sources through which day-to-day life connects to the existential parameters of human life, to the relations of human beings with nature, birth, sickness and death', Giddens concludes: 'The "existential contradiction" via which human beings live their lives—that they are part of inorganic nature, and relapse into it at death, yet are not of nature, insofar as they live also in consciousness of their finitude—is not separated from the organized dynamics of social life.'[14] One corollary of citizens ignoring this contradiction in modern states has been 'that the routinization of day-to-day life is precarious, resting upon a relatively shallow psychological base and not integrated with moral principles that provide means of meeting of existential dilemmas'.[15] The question here is not whether or why such processes occurred, which has arguably occasioned most scholarly debate, but how and when they had an effect.

Few historians deny that internal pacification took place in the eighteenth century, as a result, as Richard Evans rightly points out, of the ending of the post-Reformation wars of religion of the seventeenth century, depopulation and decreased competition for land, the growth of agricultural productivity and the slow rise of standards of living, as well as increases of state power and discussion of reform and civility in the public spheres of the Enlightenment.[16] The difficulty is how to assess the timing, degree, and nature of that pacification and its relationship to suffering, including the experience of pain, hunger, illness, and death. States' domestic use of violence declined. In Prussia, Friedrich II restricted the practice of torture to cases of treason and murder in 1740 and abolished it completely in 1754; in Württemberg, the last recorded case was in 1778 and it was abolished formally in 1809; in Hanover, it was last used in 1818, in Bavaria in 1806, in Hamburg in 1786, in Saxe-Weimar in 1783, and in Brunswick and Saxony in 1770; in Baden, abolition occurred in stages between 1767 and 1831, and in Austria between 1769 and 1776. By the time statistical records began in the early nineteenth century, there had already been a shift from corporal and capital punishment towards imprisonment, which was preferred in a large majority of cases. In Bavaria, ninety people were executed between 1801 and 1815, or between three and ten per year.[17] The introduction of the new Bavarian Criminal Code of Paul Anselm Feuerbach in 1813 had reduced and rationalized the number of corporal punishments and limited the means of execution to decapitation, to be applied to a smaller number of crimes. The model for this and other penal reform had been Prussia's General Law Code of 1794, which had replaced a welter of laws

---

[13] Ibid., 193.   [14] Ibid., 196.   [15] Ibid.

[16] R. J. Evans, *Rituals of Retribution: Capital Punishment in Germany, 1600–1987* (London, 1996), 120–1.

[17] See Table, ibid., 992.

and jurisdictions able to use corporal punishment by sentences of imprisonment proportional to graded categories of crime, intended in the words of one official to instil 'in the spirits of the lower classes of the people the sense of honour and self-respect, which in better organized natures is such a powerful influence in preventing many kinds of crime', but which was 'already weak' amongst the lower orders and was 'completely and utterly smothered and killed off by corporal punishments, especially by those which also dishonour the offender'.[18]

Nonetheless, corporal punishment continued to play an important role in the code, likewise graded according to the seriousness of the offence, and different forms of death penalty continued to apply, including burning at the stake (arson), decapitation with the sword (for infanticide, manslaughter, and lesser forms of treason), breaking with the wheel from the top down (murder, conspiracy to murder), breaking with the wheel from the bottom up (leading a conspiracy to murder, poisoning), exhibiting the corpse on the wheel after being broken from the bottom up (first-class treason), and 'the severest bodily and capital punishments' (high treason).[19] The right to use violence was sanctioned within the family (husbands against wives, children, and servants), the workshop (masters against apprentices), schools (teachers against pupils), and estates (landowners against serfs). Junkers, in particular, went on using demeaning punishments like the 'fiddle', 'Spanish cloak', and halters around the necks of offenders within their patrimonial jurisdictions, as well as iron collars and pillories, which were alluded to in the General Code, until at least 1810, when they were banned shortly after the abolition of serfdom. Gallows and ravenstones for displaying corpses, which were usually located in front of city gates, remained in place into the 1820s and beyond, serving as a reminder, in the words of one police chief in Landshut, Bavaria, of 'the ill-starred times of terrorism'.[20] Bodies were exhibited on them in Prussia until the practice was outlawed in 1811, after complaints from the authorities—for instance in Breslau in the same year—that 'the houseowners there had to live for several weeks with the terrible stink of the body displayed on the wheel'.[21]

There was little sign that most of the population of German towns took umbrage at such displays of state violence and individual death. Indeed, 'so many thousands of the local inhabitants had come for a look', went on the Police President of Breslau in 1811, that they had come to constitute a disturbance of the peace, leading a local newspaper to recommend, 'with ghastly wit, that a bar should be opened there to provide refreshments for the visitors'.[22] On 13 July 1812, Christoph Horst and Friederike Delitz, two arsonists who had killed at least ten people, were to be 'brought from life to death by fire', as the General Code put it, on the Jungfernheide on the northern edge of Berlin. The pair were dragged on an oxhide through the large crowd, in which there were many families, to the pyre, from where they were permitted to address the spectators. 'I've certainly led a dissolute life and

---

[18] R. Koselleck, *Preussen zwischen Reform und Revolution. Allgemeines Landrecht, Verwaltung und Soziale Bewegung von 1791 bis 1848* (Munich, 1989), 642.

[19] R. J. Evans, *Rituals of Retribution*, 135.

[20] Ibid., 225.   [21] Ibid., 226.   [22] Ibid.

deserve to be punished, but I'm too young a girl to deserve the death penalty!' cried Delitz, followed by Horst, who declared that he was a great criminal before he escaped from the chair he was being bound to, gave Delitz a last kiss, and 'went calmly back to his place', ran the report: 'After they had been bound tight, the condemned had their heads covered with the aforementioned hoods and the pyre was lit. The strong wind fanned the flames in a few minutes.'[23] Although the execution was the last instance of burning at the stake in Berlin, the practice was not stopped because of the horror of the public, but because many criminals no longer abided by the ritual of repentance and awe, the crowd often seemed to sympathize with them—to the point where some were in danger, it was held, of committing crimes merely to have such a good death—and there was a risk of public disorder. The riot after a notorious execution in Berlin in September 1800, in which a woman was broken with the wheel, initiated a similar course of events, with 'the crowds...so great that military assistance was already required the day before the execution to prevent disorder' and 'the crush of those who wanted to mount [the platform] either out of curiosity or for the purpose of buying some of the bloodied sand for supposed curing of epileptic fits, or for other superstitious uses', had become 'very heavy', recorded the official report.[24] Although they seem sometimes to have been moved by the humanitarian arguments of middle-class critics and reformers, the authorities were more regularly worried, in keeping with the well-known utilitarian arguments of Cesare Beccaria, that public executions were ineffective. 'The people rush with tremendous enthusiasm to watch a malefactor being led out and executed, just as to a play', wrote Kant in 1798:

> For the emotions and feelings which he expresses on his face and in his behaviour have a sympathetic effect on the spectators, and they leave—after these people have been frightened by the execution's power over their imagination (a power increased still further by its ceremoniousness)—a gentle but yet earnest feeling of fatigue, which makes them feel the pleasure in life which follows afterwards all the more strongly.[25]

Yet Kant remained in favour of the death penalty, like the majority of his contemporaries, including Hegel and Fichte, who argued respectively that retribution should match the crime and that criminals had broken the social contract and returned to a state of nature.[26]

The evidence suggests that there was widespread acceptance, or at least toleration, of acts of violence carried out in the name of the state against criminals, whose bodies were broken, dismembered, and destroyed in order to uphold the majesty of the law and to gain revenge for the relatives of the victim, who would otherwise be inclined to act on their own. However, official and middle-class reformers had also begun to react against such practices, motivated by a mixture of

---

[23] Cited ibid., 214.   [24] Ibid., 193–4.

[25] I. Kant, *Anthropologie in pragmatischer Hinsicht abgefasst* (Breslau, 1798), cited in R. J. Evans, *Rituals of Retribution*, 197.

[26] I. Kant, *Metaphysische Anfangsgründe der Rechtslehre*, 2nd edn (Breslau, 1798), 232–3; G. W. F. Hegel, *Grundlinien des Philosophie des Rechts* (Berlin, 1821), 72–9; B. Kreutziger, 'Argumente für und wider die Todesstrafe(n). Ein Beitrag zu Beccaria-Rezeption im deutschsprachigen Raum des 18. Jahrhunderts', in G. Deimling (ed.), *Cesare Beccaria* (Heidelberg, 1989), 99–125.

practical considerations concerning the superstitions and immorality of the 'mob' and a desire to maintain public order, on the one hand, and feelings of distaste and a belief in progress, on the other. 'Problematic though the utility of the death penalty may be, it is none the less certain that it can serve to deter others from committing serious crimes', noted one official after the Berlin execution riot of 1800: 'Yet the milder penal laws and the rarer pronouncements of death sentences by the courts indicate that it will gradually become unnecessary for non-military crimes with the progress of civilization.'[27] The authorities' eleven recommendations in the wake of the riots insisted that visits, the distribution of popular literature, the ceremonial public sentencing of the offender, their choice of apparel—particularly white clothes—and the slow procession of criminals to the place of execution were all to be prohibited. Executions were to take place at 5.00 a.m. in order to help prevent them becoming public spectacles. The measures were confirmed by decree in 1805 and subsequently extended to the whole of Prussia. They were part of an uneven movement across Germany away from public corporal and capital punishment, for the edification of spectators and the communities from which they came, to the punishment and sequestration of criminals within prisons and to executions in hushed conditions behind prison walls, away from the gaze of the public. As such, governments' preference for incarceration instead of public displays of violence seems to have been linked to upper- and middle-class subjects' fear of the instincts of the 'rabble', disgust at the sight and odour of mutilated and putrefying bodies, and an insistence of the privacy of death, which was often viewed as a natural act rather than a religious one, understood as a consequence of sin or the wrath of God.

THE SENSIBILITY OF SUFFERING

Contemporaries' reactions to violence and death were usually private or unrecorded, of course, not the result—or on the occasion—of state executions or punishment. Moreover, they rested on senses and emotions which are, in themselves, difficult to discover and interpret. 'Emotional utterances of the type "I feel afraid" or "I am angry"', remarks William Reddy, 'have (1) a descriptive appearance, (2) a relational intent, and (3) a self-exploring or self-altering effect', all of which make them impossible to 'prove'.[28] 'As descriptive statements, . . . emotion claims do not admit of independent verification', because 'the only way to determine the "accuracy" of an emotion claim such as "I am angry" is to notice the coherence of such a statement with other emotionally expressive utterances, gestures and acts—all of which make reference to something no one can see, hear or sense'.[29] Such statements of emotions are complicated by the fact that they frequently are 'part of (or appear to designate) specific scenarios or relationships', so that 'to say "I am afraid of you"

---

[27] The directors and counsellors of the Berlin city courts, cited in R. J. Evans, *Rituals of Retribution*, 196.

[28] W. M. Reddy, 'Emotional Liberty: Politics and History in the Anthropology of Emotions', *Cultural Anthropology*, 14 (1999), 268.

[29] Ibid.

may be a way of refusing to cooperate with someone or a request for a change in the relationship'.[30] Moreover, emotions often 'involve widespread activations of thought materials..., some of which may only be semi-conscious or imperfectly glimpsed and some of which may spill over into facial signals' so complex that they 'completely exceed the capacity of attention' or summary.[31] How late eighteenth-century Germans experienced acts of violence and the prospect of death depended on linguistic parameters ('emotion-rules'), their social and historical circumstances, and their physiological responses and reactions. Although 'there is no consistent visceral response to fear', writes Joanna Bourke,

> the emotional body nevertheless rapidly gives forth a multitude of signs: the heart pounds faster or seems to freeze, breathing quickens or stops, blood pressure soars or falls, and, sometimes, adrenalin is poured into the blood stream. ...The sensation of fear is not merely the ornament of the emotion: fear is 'what hurts'—the most irreducible 'real' of an individual's history.[32]

At some moments, such bodily functions seem to have overridden cognition, cultural categories and classifications, social context, relational intent, self-expression, and experimentation, yet usually they appear to have been combined with them. For this reason, it is necessary to beware of assumptions that contemporaries were used—and even hardened—to violence, pain, illness, blood, decay, and death, but also to avoid the contrary conceit that emotions are irreducible or unique and, therefore, incomparable and inexplicable.

In some respects, the reading public and courtly society of each German land had rarely been so attentive to their feelings as during the age of 'sensibility' and 'sentiment' of the late eighteenth century.[33] An older generation of writers doubted the genuineness of such outpourings of emotion. 'Today all our novelists pretend to have a sombre, lachrymose, and sentimental philosophy', Grimm had lamented in 1773: 'Have we become more philosophical or more sensitive? No, only weaker, more fainting, sadder.'[34] All the same, figures like Germaine de Staël made it their business to attend to their own and others' feelings, eliciting the mockery of her own mother, Mme Necker, who contended that her daughter's talk of 'love of country' and 'humanity' were mere 'vague terms empty of meaning that men invented to hide their insensitivity under the very veil of sentiment'.[35] De Staël's *De la littérature dans ses rapports avec les institutions sociales* (1800) outlined how stoicism had been overcome by Christianity and the free spirit of the northern peoples, followed by the modern novel's successful advocacy of 'man highest sentiment' in the form of a man's and a woman's 'friendship in love':

> Man's happiness grew with all the independence that the object of his tenderness had obtained; he could believe himself loved; a free being had chosen him; a free being

---

[30] Ibid.   [31] Ibid., 268–9.

[32] J. Bourke, 'Fear and Anxiety: Writing about Emotion in Modern History', *History Workshop Journal*, 55 (2003), 122–3.

[33] Frank Baasner, *Der Begriff 'sensibilité' im 18. Jahrhundert: Aufstieg und Niedergang eines Ideals* (Heidelberg, 1988).

[34] Ibid., 345.   [35] Cited in Ghislain de Diesbach, *Madame de Staël* (Paris, 1983), 90.

obeyed his desires. The perceptions of the mind, the nuances felt by the heart multiplied with the ideas and impressions of these new souls, who were trying out a moral
existence, after, for so long, having languished in life.[36]

Individuals' espousal of virtues such as love, gratitude, benevolence, and pity was
seen as the foundation of both morality and social ties, guarding against the vice of
passion and limiting selfishness: 'The same creative force that pumps the blood
toward the heart inspires courage and sensibility, two rights, two moral sensations
whose governance we destroy in attributing them to self-interest, just as you deface
the charm of beauty by analyzing it like an anatomist.'[37] De Staël was confident
that sentiment would curb self-interest in the realm of politics and state affairs,
having believed in 1789 that 'a sincere and disinterested enthusiasm inspired all the
French at that time; public spirit was everywhere, and, in the upper classes, the best
were those who desired most ardently that the nation's will count for something in
the direction of its affairs'.[38] Jacobinism was discounted as the consequence of the
masses' insensitivity, fostered by poverty and violence. Faced with the excesses of
Bonapartism, de Staël looked in *De l'Allemagne*, which she had finished writing in
1810 but was prevented from publishing in France until 1814, to the individual
German states as the repository of sentiment in politics, art, and philosophy. Not
all 'Romantics'—a movement which the Swiss writer had helped to found—were
so sanguine about the humanity of politics and the affairs of the state, in Germany
or elsewhere. They were, though, profoundly sensitive to the emotions aroused by
extremes of action and thought, suffering and death.

The connected imperatives of sentimentalism, education (*Bildung*), and morality were betrayed by the private blunderings of Georg Wilhelm Friedrich Hegel in
his courtship of Marie von Tucher, whom he married in 1811. Having been obliged
in 1807 to leave Jena, where he had taught at the university, after the city had been
damaged by French troops in 1806, causing most of the students to leave, Hegel
had briefly edited the *Bamberger Zeitung* before settling in Nuremberg in November
1808 in order to become the rector of the *Gymnasium*. Marie von Tucher was the
eldest daughter of one of the most notable of Nuremberg's patrician families. In
keeping with the usual etiquette, the philosopher's comportment was formal, letting Jobst Wilhelm Karl von Tucher, who was a member of the same literary club
('The Museum'), know of 'his wishes...to marry my daughter and to request an
opportunity to speak with the latter'.[39] In an informal but bluff tone, he had earlier
confessed to a friend, on arriving in Nuremberg, that 'I would also like to take up
and successfully conclude another business, namely to take a wife, or rather to find
one!'[40] Yet his entreaties to Marie herself were romantic, writing a love poem to
her on 13 April 1813 which evoked the ascent of a mountain, the redness of the

---

[36] Cited in W. M. Reddy, 'Sentimentalism and Its Erasure: The Role of Emotions in the Era of the
French Revolution', *Journal of Modern History*, 72 (2000), special issue, 109–52.

[37] Cited ibid., 146–7.

[38] Germaine de Staël, *Considérations sur la Révolution française*, ed. Jacques Godechot (Paris, 1983,
originally in 1818), 114–15.

[39] J. W. K. v. Tucher, April 1811, cited in T. Pinkard, *Hegel: A Biography* (Cambridge, 2000), 296.

[40] G. W. F. Hegel to F. I . Niethammer, cited in T. Pinkard, *Hegel*, 295.

sunrise, and nature's glory, at the same time as comparing the union of two people in a mutual emotional commitment to a phoenix, dissolving—as a metaphor for what divided lovers—and rising from its own ashes, as love recreated itself over and over again. When the 20-year-old Marie agreed to marriage shortly afterwards, Hegel wrote another verse about how a kiss said more than words could and how he envied the sad but beautiful song of the nightingale, ending with the image of souls flowing into one another.[41] For her part, his fiancée went further, chiding the rector, who was twenty years older than her, for writing to his sister that he expected to be happy in the marriage 'insofar as happiness belongs to my life's destiny'.[42]

In an attempt to justify himself, Hegel recalled how the couple had agreed the previous evening—perhaps in another lecture—that in 'non-superficial natures, every sensation of happiness is connected with sensation of melancholy', so that 'being contented' (*Zufriedenheit*), not happiness (*Glück*), was the foundation of conjugal love.[43] All the same, he continued in a more effusive, candid, and sentimental vein: 'Oh, how much more I could still write—about my perhaps hypochondriacal pedantry, which led me to insist so greatly on the distinction between "being satisfied" and happiness, a distinction which is once again so useless.'[44] He concluded by calling on Marie to be his 'healer' and to reconcile his 'inner self' with the external world.[45] He would not, he admitted after a later quarrel, be one of those husbands 'who torture their wives merely so that their . . . patience and love may be constantly tested', but he was reluctant, as a man, to compromise his principles on grounds of 'character' or to concede, as Marie claimed, that moral duty rested on feelings.[46] Rather, for the philosopher, sentiments, which could be glimpsed in his post-nuptial declaration to Friedrich Immanuel Niethammer that 'I have now reached my earthly goal', were always to be balanced by moral commitment, as he had explained to Marie before the marriage: 'love requires for its completion a still higher moment than that in which it consists merely in and for itself. What is perfect satisfaction, what is called being entirely happy, can only be completed by religion and a feeling of duty.'[47] Hegel, of course, was an exceptional suitor. Even he, though, paid lip service, detectable in his reference to 'what is called being entirely happy', to a prevailing sentimental discourse within the educated, middle-class circles of the German towns.

In this context of sentimentality, war seemed like a rupture of civilization:

When we observe this play (*Schauspiel*) of the passions, and look at the results of its violence, of its lack of reason, which is not only attached to [particular interests and needs], but also, and even especially, to good intentions and honest purposes, when we see the resultant evil, the wickedness, the fall of the most prosperous empires which human minds have ever brought forth, we can only be filled with sadness over this transience and end up, insofar as this fall is not merely a work of nature but of human will, with a moral grief, with the abhorrence of a good conscience, if we have one, over such a spectacle.[48]

[41] Ibid., 297.   [42] Ibid.   [43] Ibid., 298.   [44] Ibid.
[45] Ibid.   [46] Ibid., 298–9.   [47] Ibid., 302.
[48] G. W. F. Hegel, *Vorlesungen über die Philosophie der Geschichte*, 3rd edn (Stuttgart, 1961), 63.

One response to such 'misfortune, which even the greatest peoples, state forms and private virtues have suffered', wrote Hegel in the Introduction of his *Vorlesungen über die Philosophie der Geschichte* (1822–30), was to

> raise it up into the most terrifying picture (*Gemälde*) and increase one's sensitivity to the most profound, helpless mourning, which cannot be counterbalanced by any conciliatory outcome, and against which we can only steel ourselves, or from which we can only escape, by thinking: it has always been like this; it is fate; there is nothing that can be done to change it; and, then, we go back, in the boredom which any reflex of mourning can provoke in us, to our normal feelings for life, to the actuality of our purposes and interests—in short, we revert to selfishness, which lies on the quiet bank and enjoys the view of the confused mass of debris from a safe distance.[49]

The spectre of war which he evoked could appear overwhelming and seemed to owe much to Hegel's own experience of the Napoleonic Wars: 'By viewing history as this slaughter bench, on which the happiness of the nations, the wisdom of states and the virtue of individuals is sacrificed, the thought, and necessarily also the question, occurs as to whom, for which ends this greatest of sacrifices is being made.'[50] However, there was an alternative to fatalism, argued the philosopher, which was to act, as Napoleon—whom he continued to support until 1815—had done. 'What do we want with fate now?' the French emperor had asked Goethe during a meeting in October 1808, which Hegel took to citing in his lectures: 'Politics is our fate.'[51] The French had lost the 'fear of death', it seemed to the struggling Jena academic in January 1807, which had permitted France to wield 'the great power which she displays against others'.[52] Other nations, especially the Germans, were now being compelled to 'give up their indolence vis-à-vis actuality and to step out into it', which might allow them to 'surpass their teachers', he went on approvingly.[53] Although he had been present as the French army shelled Jena and he had come back from his refuge in the house of the family of a well-to-do student to find that 'knaves have, to be sure, messed up my papers like lottery tickets', he retained a distance from the events.[54] War was, from his point of view, still a 'play' or a 'spectacle'.

Hegel's continuing detachment was ambiguous, combined with apparent horror at the slaughter taking place. There seem to have been several reasons for it, including the fact that the philosopher himself had never served in the army and had not been a victim or a witness of military violence. He was accustomed to harshness, illness, and death, however, which ensured that the conditions of war were closer to those of peacetime than they were in the later nineteenth and early twentieth centuries. Like most of his contemporaries, he had experienced the death of a close relative by the time that he reached adulthood. In his case, the death of his mother when he was 13 years old appears to have placed strains on the family and to have dominated his later life, as he intimated to his sister Christiane at the

---

[49] Ibid., 63–4.   [50] Ibid., 64.   [51] Cited in T. Pinkard, *Hegel*, 231.
[52] Ibid., 243.   [53] Ibid.   [54] Ibid., 228.

age of 55 in 1825: 'Today is the anniversary of our mother's death, which I will hold forever in my memory.'[55] Although occasioning great sorrow, sickness and death were regular occurrences. In his memoirs, Arndt mentions the death of his wife during childbirth only in passing: 'My wife gave me the gift of a beautiful son in the summer of 1801, which cost her life.'[56] Others talked of their grief at greater length, but they also gave the impression that it comprised part of a natural cycle or a religious conception of the world, which made it bearable. To Theodor von Schön, a Prussian official, and his wife Amalie, the death of their son Bernhard in 1809 shortly after birth was followed by recurrent 'sad thoughts'.[57] Two years earlier in August 1807, Schön had learned of the demise of his first wife Lydia of typhus, together with two of his three children, pushing him to lament that 'all my happiness has gone and life has lost its value for me'.[58] 'Pain', he went on, 'overcomes me.'[59] After a year, however, he had remarried, having had 'the rare good fortune to find a second wife who constituted my life's happiness'.[60] It was an advantage that Amalie's aunt, who came from the Silesian nobility, had a prominent position at the court and kept him informed of its affairs. The death of the first son of his second marriage in 1809 interrupted such happiness, leaving Amalie, in poor health, unable to 'think of the saddest images of my life' but also unable to keep them from her mind.[61] On the anniversary of his first wife's death in August, Amalie wrote to her husband, away again with the peregrinating Prussian administration, that 'it pains me more than ever to know that you are alone today', for if they had been reunited 'our tears would flow together for this loving, pure being'.[62] Similar feelings were displayed by other contemporaries, including conservative Prussian officers like Friedrich August Ludwig von der Marwitz, who had lost his son in 1813 after a short illness. 'What impact this unexpected loss of our third, very healthy, strong and prospering child had on his mother... cannot be described', he recorded, as he prepared to go to war: 'For me, it was the hardest test that heaven could have sent me', even if, as he conceded in the next sentence, he was 'made' in such a way as 'to put house, home and family in the background in order to think only of the fatherland'.[63] In such cases, the language of sentiment or religion seemed to give meaning to the cycle of birth, sickness, and death.

The Romantic poet and Saxon noble Friedrich von Hardenberg, who was better known under his pseudonym of Novalis, evinced how a culture of sentiment extended beyond a *Bürgerwelt* which he, as a *Freiherr*, had first got to know as a student, as he had fallen in love with 'plain town girls' possessed of 'a hundred times more reason than the most noble'.[64] He also revealed how emotions were

---

[55] Ibid., 4.   [56] E. M. Arndt, *Erinnerungen*, 107.

[57] G. A. Klausa (ed.), '*Sehnlich erwarte ich die morgende Post'. Amalie und Theodor von Schöns Briefwechsel aus dem Befreiungskrieg* (Cologne, 2005), 11.

[58] Ibid., 5.   [59] Ibid.   [60] Ibid.   [61] Ibid., 11.

[62] Ibid.   [63] F. A. L von der Marwitz, *Aus dem Nachlasse*, 342.

[64] Novalis (F. v. Hardenberg), *Schriften. Die Werke Friedrich von Hardenbergs*, ed. R. Samuel (Stuttgart, 1975), vol. 4, 123.

connected intimately, even for a Romantic, not to fantasy, but to nature and morality, as he counselled his brother Erasmus in March 1793:

> You must not be impatient, for even the seemingly slow course of our education and development is the course of nature. To follow it faithfully, never to be impatient, always to acknowledge the good which we have and not to let oneself draw the parallels of an unhealthy sensitivity and fantasy, which are always extremely useless, damaging and untrue, not to refine as a result of one's sensitivity or situation, to suppress nothing which is a healthy, true feeling, to judge openly oneself and one's troubling moods, to be open to nature and to beware of exaggeration, that is all that we can do and it is truly enough. ... The moment does not exhaust the universal; the present does not contain our entire existence, if we don't want it to. *Pure force of will*, without the mist of refined feelings, is what we—alone—can live and act by. It is the element of man, without which he is not a man but half-castrated. It is the means by which we are and become healthy, for, certainly, only the harmony of our strengths, which is only possible by means of it, makes us into real people, to genuine beings in the ranks of things and the wonderful relations of the moral and physical world. Wherever there is sick fantasy, there is also sick sensitivity and sick reason. One is made healthy by the other, so that the health of the body and the soul reinforce each other, although the sickness of the body can never or very rarely have a deleterious effect on the spirit, if a pure, firm, eternal force of will is present.[65]

Life was made up, for Hardenberg, of moments to be seized, with 'my being' comprised 'of instances', but it also had a more profound meaning and continuity, requiring steadfastness, fortitude, and moral purpose.[66] Thoughts of Sophie, the 12-year-old girl whom he had met in 1794 and to whom he was betrothed a year later, could 'bestir his excitable fantasy' to such an extent that, in the end, he '*had to* suffer', with his body taking part but 'the main site of the evil his fantasy' itself; yet his exploration of such feelings was less an act of hedonism than a way of discovering his place in a natural order.[67] He wrote to his brother Karl in November 1795,

> How close to us, often, [is] the loss of all our happiness; how dangerous, therefore, [is] any speculation on happiness alone; and how much [is] enduring peace only to be found through the elevation of the soul above all strikes of fate and through the banishment of everything which stands under the power of chance.[68]

Experiencing and writing about emotions, which derived from pain as much as from joy, was the opposite of an escape into fantasy and remained closely connected to intimations of suffering.

Beset by illness or confronted by death, Hardenberg was largely matter-of-fact, eschewing 'fantasy' and 'hypochondria', despite his suffering. In January 1797, after Erasmus had fallen 'dangerously ill' as a consequence of a blood haemorrhage,

---

[65] F. v. Hardenberg to Erasmus von Hardenberg, 16 Mar. 1793, in Novalis, *Schriften*, vol. 4, 116–17.
[66] F. v. Hardenberg to Erasmus von Hardenberg, Aug. 1793, ibid., 122.
[67] F. v. Hardenberg to Caroline Just, Nov. 1794, ibid., 148.
[68] F. to Karl von Hardenberg, 30 Nov. 1794, ibid., 161.

the poet wrote to his brother that he was worried more about 'the indirect effects, the effects which pass through the medium of your fantasy': 'I was anxious that you would now suffer still more from hypochondria, that you would be incessantly worried.'[69] He took comfort that an acquaintance had recovered from a similar ailment. At the same time, a friend lay 'dangerously ill' because of a wound incurred in a duel and Sophie remained 'critical', with a stable fever and cough.[70] Hardenberg himself had had an accident, which had left him with 'pain and fever'.[71] Like Rahel Varnhagen and many other contemporaries, he appears to have viewed 'illness' as a regular but alien and life-threatening state, which was to be avoided at all costs.[72] In order to recover, 'cold blood and calmness' were required.[73] Nonetheless, recuperation was far from certain and reversals were common, condemning Sophie to death at the age of 15 in March 1797 and reducing Hardenberg to 'anxious indifference', 'despair', and 'disgust'.[74] 'My head is in the most wasted state—I can find nothing to help', he confided to Friedrich Schlegel: 'My disgust with life is terrible— and I see no end to it. I hoped that my studies would offer me a substitute—but everything here, too, is dead, wasteland, deaf, unmoving. Sleep is my only comfort—I sleep when I can. God knows how this will resolve itself.'[75] By 19 March, she was dead: 'After unspeakable suffering, which she bore exemplarily, she ended it.'[76]

She had suffered for a year and a half.

> Eight days before her death, I left her, with the firm conviction that I would not see her again—it was beyond my powers impotently to watch the terrible struggles of her declining blooming youth, the horrible anxieties of the heavenly creature. I have never feared fate—I first saw it threaten three weeks ago. It became dusk around me while I still looked at the sunrise. My mourning is boundless, like my love.[77]

As he wrote to Caroline Just, he had been faced with 'all the terrors of a lonely darkness', followed by a 'feeling of emptiness' and a 'hardening into stone', as 'pain' had 'lamed my memory'.[78] One month later, his brother Erasmus was also dead, passing 'into another world'.[79] Yet 'the death of Erasmus has had a beneficial rather than a disadvantageous effect', he wrote to Schlegel in April 1797: 'It has increased my strength rather than diminished it. He suffered indescribably.'[80] The death of Sophie and the proximity of her grave reinforced the idea that

> my autumn is here, and I feel myself so free, usually so strong—something can come of me. So much I can assure you, sacredly—that is already quite clear to me that her death has been heavenly fortune—a key to everything—a wonderfully becoming step.

[69] F. v. Hardenberg to Erasmus von Hardenberg, 20 Jan. 1797, ibid., 196.
[70] F. Hardenberg to F. Schlegel, 10 Jan. 1797, ibid., 194.
[71] F. Hardenberg to Erasmus von Hardenberg, 20 Jan. 1797, ibid., 195.
[72] R. Varnhagen to K. A. Varnhagen v. Ense, 23 May 1813, K. A. Varnhagen v. Ense and R. Varnhagen, *Briefwechsel zwischen Varnhagen und Rahel* (Berne, 1973), vol. 3, 95–6.
[73] Hardenberg to Erasmus, 20 Jan. 1797, in Novalis, *Schriften*, vol. 4, 196.
[74] F. v. Hardenberg to F. Schlegel, 14 Mar. 1797, ibid., 204.   [75] Ibid.
[76] F. v. Hardenberg to K. L. Woltmann, 22 Mar. 1797, ibid., 206.   [77] Ibid.
[78] F. v. Hardenberg to C. Just, 24 Mar. 1797, ibid., 207–8.
[79] F. v. Hardenberg to W. v. Thümmel, 13 Apr. 1797, ibid., 218.
[80] F. v. Hardenberg to F. Schlegel, 13 Apr. 1797, ibid., 220.

Only in this way could so much be resolved so purely, so much immaturity be removed. ... I am twenty-five years old and I have only lived for a half a year.[81]

Novalis took strength from the report that Sophie had not noticed the 'complete dissolution' of her body in her last days and that she had fantasized during her final night, stating that 'I feel it, I am mad—I am of no more use in this world—I must go.'[82] Although he appears to have found solace in religious premonitions of another world and in artistic sublimation, born of his 'power over death', the poet remained fearful of 'long illnesses—there is something terrible and something so useless about them—since only ideas, not bodily suffering, form one—especially when it is so serious that the mind can no longer find the courage to continue'.[83] Four years later, in March 1801, Hardenberg died of tuberculosis, which he had had since August 1800, at the age of 28.

It is not plausible to contend that Novalis or his contemporaries—those who have left written records, at least—were less sensitive to suffering, or less willing or able to express their feelings about it, than their late nineteenth- or early twentieth-century counterparts. It is possible, however, that regular exposure to illness, death, and, even, acts of violence, as part of an existence in which the odours, squalor, and deformity of the body—despite being covered—were often present, elicited different emotional responses on the part of contemporaries, abetted by religious and other sources of comfort, understanding, strength, and forbearance. Squeamishness and violence were more or less common in different social milieux, of course, whereas illness and death, although more public in some contexts than in others, were ubiquitous and affected virtually everyone from childhood onwards. For this reason, late eighteenth- and early nineteenth-century subjects seem to have been warier, as one British observer put it, of specific 'difficulties the most unanticipated, and trials the most unexpected', which differed from those facing their successors: namely, 'health cannot be calculated upon for a moment; friends may be suddenly snatched from our embrace; riches "make themselves wings, and fly away"; the deepest reverses, and the greatest elevations, are occurring in the daily history of men; and "in the midst of life, we are in death"'.[84] These fears, and the circumstances to which they corresponded, changed slowly and unevenly in the course of the nineteenth and twentieth centuries. Since they were applicable to the conditions of war as well as those of daily life, they served, with many exceptions, to mitigate the impact of mass warfare during the revolutionary and Napoleonic periods. The next section examines the effects of such warfare on civilians.

CIVILIANS AND THE BURDENS OF WAR

Historians such as Ute Planert have doubted whether civilians' experiences of military conflict differed fundamentally from those of their predecessors in the

---

[81] Ibid.   [82] F. v. Hardenberg to Woltmann, 14 Apr. 1797, ibid., 221.   [83] Ibid.
[84] John Jefferson, *An Antidote to Sudden Fear: Or, the Calmness in which Christians May Contemplate the Threatened Pestilence* (London, 1832), 3, cited in J. Bourke, 'Fear and Anxiety, 112.

eighteenth century. War overshadowed revolution in contemporaries' accounts of the period yet, since the revolutionary and Napoleonic campaigns are deemed to have been little more destructive than earlier conflicts and involved similar levels and types of civilian mobilization, Planert questions whether they brought about a transformation of subjects' attitudes to warfare.[85] The regularity of military conflict and civilians' exposure to hardship, illness, and death in the eighteenth century appeared to lessen the impact of warfare after 1792. Many citizens registered their disgruntlement at the burdens of war, including swingeing financial demands, looting, and conscription, but they frequently made little distinction between the forces of putative friend and foe.[86] Although there was a preponderant number of French officers 'who did not trouble themselves much about the conduct of their comrades', recorded one Swabian cleric, even these 'rested content when their own momentary needs were satisfied, and did evil to no person': many more

> deplored the extravagances of their comrades from the bottom of their hearts, bemoaned the evil consequences that arose thereby for the service and for the honour of the French name, and extended, often at risk to their person and with sacrifice, protection to those who had cause to fear pillage or maltreatment from others.[87]

What is most striking from Planert's examination of parish records and the accounts of ordinary subjects is the variability of contemporaries' reactions to warfare, depending on the unpredictable demands of occupiers and new authorities and on different conditions in each locality. When Napoleon travelled to Munich in late 1805, he was greeted along the route—as the 'universally adored idol of the mob', in the words of one noble—with peeling bells and volleys of celebratory gunfire, not least because he had defeated Austria, Bavaria's traditional enemy.[88] By contrast, many citizens in the old territories of Austria on the shores of Lake Constance, now belonging to Baden, rejoiced at the arrival of Austrian troops in 1813, expressing relief, like Maria Agatha Zimmermann from Villingen, that they had 'become imperial again'.[89] When the Tyrolean rebel leader Andreas Hofer fomented unrest in 1809, in the longest-lived and most extensive instance of resistance against French-led forces in the German lands, he was acting against Bavaria more than against France.[90] Such disparities make the effects of warfare on civilians difficult to gauge.

In his memoirs, Varnhagen von Ense—as a peripatetic civilian-turned-soldier—betrayed the diversity of contemporaries' experiences of warfare, but also the longer-term evolution of such experiences. He and his small, intellectual circle of friends in Hamburg and Berlin, including Kleist, Rühle, Schlegel, and Scharnhorst, were shocked by Austria's defeat in 1805, but still treated military conflict with a mixture of detachment and enthusiasm, confidently calling for a Prussian declaration

---

[85] U. Planert, 'Innovation or Evolution?', 69–84.
[86] U. Planert, '"Rette sich, wer kann". Konfliktstrukturen bei Rekrutierungsunruhen in Süddeutschland und Vorderösterreich', in U. Planert (ed.), *Krieg und Umbruch in Mitteleuropa um 1800* (Paderborn, 2009).
[87] U. Planert, 'From Collaboration to Resistance', *Central European History*, 39 (2006), 680.
[88] August von Platen, 1809, cited in U. Planert, 'From Collaboration to Resistance', 683.
[89] Ibid., 688.   [90] Ibid., 686.

of war, with little fear of the consequences, in 1806.[91] Initially, he was unable to believe that Prussia had been defeated at the battle of Jena in October: 'As the unhappy news of the lost battle reached and shot through the city [of Berlin], the first reaction was not to believe it, we ran from street to street, gathered in front of the houses where high officials lived…, we wanted news.'[92] Slowly, although the French proved not to be 'wild' and looting was not as bad as feared, the consequences of defeat and the pressures of occupation took their toll.[93] 'From day to day, the defeat of Prussia was shown to be greater and more humiliating', recorded Varnhagen of the immediate aftermath of battle:

> The misfortune of Prussia and the slender hopes which could be entertained of the continuing war were talked about over and over again, and—by way of contrast—the glittering circumstances and phenomena of Prussian military life before the terrible collapse. We couldn't fully comprehend the intervening change, we saw the consequences looming massively before us, and we couldn't believe them.[94]

By 1807, civilians in Berlin were struggling to survive, in the diarist's recollection, with 'peace' becoming indistinguishable from 'war'.[95]

'Resistance' under such circumstances could be compared to that of Spain, some of whose fighters—part of 'a greater and more open *Volkswiderstand*'—passed through the Prussian capital, having been taken prisoner by the French in 1808.[96] 'I have looked at the whole series of French bulletins on the war in Spain and I have seen more than they wanted to show', recorded Varnhagen one year later:

> Yet the news about the arming of Austria touched me more closely than these events. Everything there seems to be heading towards a genuine people's war (*Volkskrieg*), and enthusiasm and strength of every kind seems to be increasing. Here—and where is this not the case in Germany?—the government is allied with the French, but the people (*Volk*) is for Austria, with whose business German affairs are closely tied.[97]

After Prussia's defeat and three years of occupation, Varnhagen's attitude to conflict had changed, to the extent that his spirits had been greatly lifted by Austria's victory at the battle of Aspern, which had resonated 'throughout Germany', and he had come to assume that the failure of Austria in 1809 would mean, 'along with it, the failure of the German business'.[98] Hearing that every fourth man had been killed or wounded, Varnhagen now hastened to join the Austrian army in the name of a national cause and a Habsburg monarchy to which he had seemed indifferent before 1806 (see Map 3 for the territorial reconfiguration of Central Europe in this period). By 1812, after the 'retreat and destruction' of French forces, the writer was 'ready for anything'.[99] In the 'war camp' of Breslau, where much of the Prussian officer corps and many officials had gathered, 'élan inflamed everything, and the general desire was for weapons and a fight'.[100] Having entered the Russian army, Varnhagen was sent to Hamburg, where he was impressed by the pious patriotism

---

[91] K. A. Varnhagen v. Ense, *Denkwürdigkeiten*, vol. 1, 169–71, 190–9.
[92] Ibid., 197.   [93] Ibid., 202–3.   [94] Ibid., 227.   [95] Ibid., 231–2.
[96] Ibid., 272–3.   [97] Ibid., 298.   [98] Ibid., 299.
[99] Ibid., vol. 2, 135.   [100] Ibid.

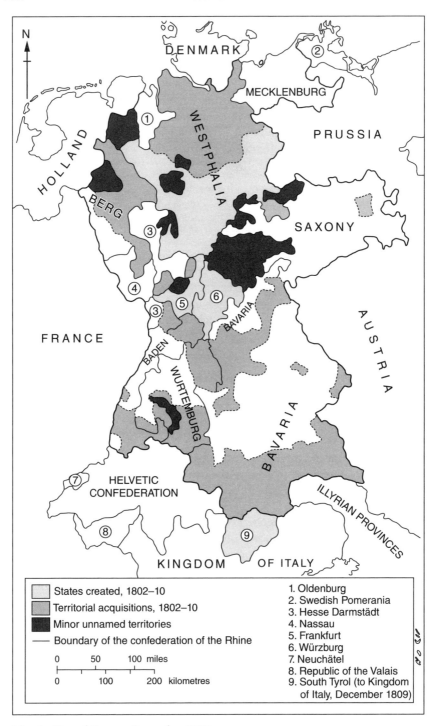

Map 3. Central Europe, September 1809

Source: C. Esdaile, *Napoleon's Wars: An International History, 1803–1815* (London, 2007), xxvii.

of locals, before he eventually served in the Prussian army.[101] As a civilian, his attitude to war had been transformed after 1806 by his assessment of the consequences of Prussia's defeat and the conditions of occupation. According to outside observers, this change of attitude was characteristic of much of the Prussian population.[102] Military conflict appeared to have become a national—or, at least, countrywide— and continuous state of affairs.

The burdens of such conflict were heavy and cumulative, as Joachim Kupferer, a bailiff from Erlach, noted of the previous twenty-five years in 1815:

> If we think about our time and conditions, compared to those in which we found ourselves before these wars, uprisings and invasions, we are overcome by a painful melancholy, for
>
> 1. instead of peace, tranquillity and unity, we have got war, unrest and division, partisanship and ruins, piles of debris and the graves of such dear family, friends and kin.
>
> 2. instead of our previous well-being: the destruction of households, poverty, the complete indebtedness and mortgages of citizens' and municipalities' wealth.
>
> 3. instead of old German loyalty, a long-lasting, cold lack of character.
>
> 4. instead of previous integrity, falsehood, intrigue and slyness.
>
> 5. instead of a man standing by his word, denial, breaking one's promises and false oaths.
>
> 6. instead of the old religion, coldness, contempt for religious practices, mockery, jokes and lack of belief.
>
> 7. instead of previous morality, abstemiousness and modesty, ugly indecency, licentiousness and bestial immodesty.
>
> 8. instead of the old probity, lying, dissemblance and hastiness.
>
> 9. instead of earlier brotherly love, hatred, rancour, intrigues and denigration.
>
> 10. instead of the old simple clothing, luxury, vanity and the apeing of fashion.
>
> 11. instead of child-like obedience, rawness, selfishness, curses, excesses and obstinacy and even abuse.
>
> Yes, dear later generations, these were the fruits, which were planted through the seeds of war, revolt and invasion.[103]

Although experiences varied, with some areas of textile production in the Rhineland prospering under the continental system, the overall effects of military conflict were deleterious and resented.[104]

---

[101] Ibid., 145.

[102] T. v. Barsewisch, *Geschichte des GrossherzoglichBadischen Leib-Grenadier-Regiments*, vol. 1, 93, prints a report of 4 Nov. 1811 from the Badenese contingent in Prussia, comparing the mood to that of 1806: 'Life and the people had noticeably changed since the regiment had passed through the same area five years ago. A great pressure weighed down on everyone.'

[103] U. Planert, *Der Mythos*, 114.

[104] The output of Aachen's woollen industry increased from 5 million francs per year in 1786 to 11 million francs in 1811, and its population grew from 24,000 in 1799 to 32,000 in 1814; M. Rowe, *From Reich to State*, 205. One good, if retrospective, account of how circumstances could change, from prosperity in the 1790s to impoverishment in the 1800s under the continental system and the impact of war, is given by Marianne Prell, *Erinnerungen aus der Franzosenzeit*, especially 58–65.

As the French had first arrived in southern Germany in 1796, 'freedom-loving, self-sacrificing, enlightened, tolerant people' had hoped for 'salvation' from the revolutionary forces, recorded one pastor in Erkheim, yet even they had soon come to see such forces 'in a different light', after welcoming parties had been plundered and threatened.[105] Partly as a consequence, 'rumours of war became more and more acute', filling inhabitants 'with anxiety and fear of the French'.[106] Violence, looting, requisitions, billeting, extra taxation, food shortages, disease, and conscription were all common in places which were close to the fighting or through which armies passed.[107] In Württemberg, what struck the statistician Heinrich Christoph Büttner, looking back in 1816, was the

> profoundly depressed state of the subjects...dejection—anxious yearning for better times—convulsions of biting pain over the heavy weight of burdens, which they have to bear, and over the pain of wounds, which the human loss of war, the loss of sons and fathers, war costs, harsh taxes, billeting, damage from hail, frost and floods have caused.[108]

At about the same time in a village near Ulm, one priest reported that people were eating forest roots, snails, and pigeons' heads, making it 'difficult to describe how weak man, woman, child and cattle became'.[109] From a minor official near Strasbourg in 1799 complaining that the 'burden weighed so heavily on me that my body and mind are in constant unrest' and would be the 'cause of an early death' to a Bavarian priest lamenting in 1809 'how little life is worth' between 'angst and terror', testimony of desperation was widespread during the war years.[110] Certainly, there were many exceptions to such suffering, but there is much evidence to suggest that the weight, extent, and duration of the burdens of war marked out the revolutionary and Napoleonic conflicts from eighteenth-century wars, prompting the Kühlsheim farmer and vintner Michael Schreck to comment laconically in 1814 that 'if peace (*der fride*) became with the french (*die franzhosen*) with the *Kaisser Von Oesterig* and with the *Kaißer Von rußland* the war (*der Krig*) has lasted 23 year (*sic*)'.[111] As one pamphleteer put it a year earlier, 'Europe's population has been turning itself into an army for the last twenty years, and its cities and villages have become one great camp'.[112] This sense of war as a more or less constant state of affairs seems to have been shared, if not uniformly, by the inhabitants of most German lands (see Figure 3.1).[113]

---

[105] U. Planert, *Der Mythos*, 134.   [106] Ibid., 137.

[107] On the effects in Göttingen and Braunschweig, see W. v. Conrady (ed.), *Aus stürmischer Zeit*, 199; A. Adam, *Aus dem Leben eines Schlachtenmalers*, 153, observed that 'the roads of Germany' were 'flooded' with troops in 1812.

[108] Cited in U. Planert, *Der Mythos*, 243.   [109] Cited ibid., 244.

[110] Ibid., 336–7.   [111] U. Planert, 'From Collaboration to Resistance', 691.

[112] Anonymous pamphlet, July 1813, cited in H.-B. Spies (ed.), *Die Erhebung gegen Napoleon 1806–1815* (Darmstadt, 1981), 304.

[113] Apart from U. Planert on the south and west, see K. Aaslestad, 'Paying for War: Experiences of Napoleonic Rule in the Hanseatic Cities', *Central European History*, 39 (2006), 641–75; K. Aaslestad, 'War without Battles', 118–36; D. Kienitz, *Der Kosakenwinter in Schleswig-Holstein 1813–14* (Heide, 2000), 26–30, 87–160; M. Rowe, *From Reich to State*, 158–212. See also H. Steffens, *Was ich erlebte*, ed. W. A. Koch (Leipzig, 1938), 168; C. v. Rotteck in *Teutschen Blättern* (1814), in C. v. Rotteck, *Gesammelte und nachgelassene Schriften* (Pforzheim, 1841–3), vol. 1, 129.

Figure 3.1. A. W. Küfner, *Grossmüthige Aufopferung einer Tochter für ihre Mutter zu Frankenthal* (1795)

Source: *Almanach der Revolutions-Charactere für das Jahr 1796* (Chemnitz, 1796).

Even the princely courts and administrations of the German states were affected profoundly by the recurrence of military conflict during the revolutionary and Napoleonic periods. In Baden, the court was sent to Ulm in 1792 along with the family silver and 'other valuable objects' in order to avoid the advancing Austrian army, returning to Karlsruhe in 1793 only to be faced with the prospect of a French attack.[114] After capitulating to the French at Mannheim in 1795, the Duke of Baden's family fled to Göppingen, Pforzheim, and elsewhere in the principality, before being forced into exile behind Prussian lines—in Heidelberg, then Ansbach—in 1796, as the French forces advanced across the Rhine. The rulers of the territory were reduced in such circumstances to contemplate what would happen if 'Schwaben' were turned into a republic, 'as was the case at the time in the lands conquered by the French in Italy', recorded one of the duke's sons retrospectively: 'My father appeared to have decided to found a free state in the South of Russia, where he hoped to gain a great stretch of land through his family ties.'[115] Despite signing a popular peace with France on 25 July 1796 at Stuttgart, at the price of 2 million livres, 1,000 horses, 25,000 *Zentner* of grain, 12,000 sacks of wheat, and 50,000 bales of hay, the court and administration continued to be menaced by the

[114] Wilhelm, Markgraf v. Baden, *Denkwürdigkeiten* (Heidelberg, 1906), vol. 1, 2.
[115] Ibid., 9.

movements of Austrian and French armies during the late 1790s, with the duke barricading his family in the royal palace and gardens as the two armies clashed near Karlsruhe in 1799.[116] Although Baden was a neutral state, doubling its territory in the decade of formal 'peace' between 1796 and the dissolution of the Holy Roman Empire in 1806, and expanding its territory again by another third after the Peace of Pressburg on 26 December, it remained in a state of undeclared war, unable to act 'against the will of the powerful emperor, brought to the highest transports of happiness by the victoriously concluded war'.[117] Throughout the war years, the principality's roads remained dangerous, as a consequence of banditry and combat, and the royal palace appeared temporary, so 'barely furnished' that the duchess had to put her own furnishings in the apartments designated for Napoleon, as he travelled through the Grand Duchy in 1806.[118]

Prussia avoided such dislocation until France's defeat of the monarchy in October 1806, when the administration and court fled Berlin for the eastern outpost of Memel, followed by chartered ships carrying state coffers.[119] Hardenberg described the disorder of the retreat, chancing upon the carriage of Queen Luise on her way to the fortress of Küstrin, where she was to meet the king, who was travelling separately.[120] 'The army', he wrote, 'was like a dispersed herd, pursued by wild animals, because it had no shepherd.'[121] Begged by Stein in December 1807 at least to return to Königsberg, Friedrich Wilhelm III replied that 'under the present pressing circumstances he preferred an outlying provincial town by far to a large, noisy city'.[122] Nevertheless, despite the fact that they had been forced into virtual exile—close to the territory of Russia—by war and occupation, members of the court and administration soon became accustomed to the new conditions of conflict, if the account of Theodor von Schön, a Prussian official working on the reform of municipalities under Stein and Hardenberg, is to be believed. The state had, he recorded, been reduced to a 'great skeleton', but the pulling up of 'state institutions by the roots', thus showing 'the people (*Volk*) that the government wanted to start a new life along with it', seems to have been welcomed by the administrator, with the summer of 1808 counting as 'the most wonderful, beautiful time'.[123] By the end of 1808 at the latest, the routine of work—'a thoughtless business after a thought-provoking time'—had been re-established, making him 'bad-tempered'.[124] In 1809, he returned to the quiet post of *Präsident* in Gumbinnen, in order to 're-establish' his *Heimat* after the war, where he remained until 1813, before joining Stein's *Zentralverwaltungsrat* as the Prussian delegate and proceeding to Breslau, Saxony, and Prague behind the Allied armies.[125]

[116] Ibid., 15.   [117] Ibid., 35.   [118] Ibid.

[119] H. Duchhardt, *Stein. Eine Biographie* (Münster, 2007), 157.

[120] I. Hermann, *Hardenberg*, 218–35.

[121] K. A. v. Hardenberg in Dec. 1806, in L. v. Ranke, *Denkwürdigkeiten des Staatskanzlers Fürsten von Hardenberg* (Leipzig, 1877), v. 3, 261.

[122] Stein, cited in T. Stamm-Kuhlmann, *König in Preussens grosser Zeit*, 285–6. Carl Ernst Wilhelm von Canitz und Dallwitz, *Denkschriften* (Berlin, 1888), vol. 1, 42, noted 'the great distance of the king', 'surrounded by an enemy power'.

[123] G. A. Klausa (ed.), '*Sehnlich erwarte ich die morgende Post*', 5.   [124] Ibid., 10.

[125] Ibid., 11.

During this period, Schön's tone was increasingly patriotic and portentous, recording in May 1813, for example, that 'the parties are starting to become disunited': 'We are facing troubling times: domestically, much will have to change before it gets better. No one thinks of what will become of Germany if we conquer it.'[126] Waiting in Saxony for the war with Napoleon's forces to recommence, the administrator wrote to his wife, who remained on the family estate in East Prussia, on 6 August 1813 that 'Things must become significantly different in the world for me to take joy in them. This will come but not immediately. We shouldn't want to fly. It is good, simply, that there is every indication that the war will continue. The war will bring everything in order.'[127] At home, his wife Amalie replied to his letters in similarly patriotic terms, noting in July that landowners were having to pay income tax and contributions to the *Landwehr* for 'the poor people' and that 'nerve fever [typhus] is apparently beginning to spread again', but also reporting that 'Everything here is, in general, good.'[128] In May, she had written that news of Prussia's victory in battle had occasioned 'general rejoicing' and had 'enthused everyone, right down to the lowest ranks, at least in my house':

> Thank you for the copy [of a report], which I have passed on to several people. It contains, indeed, quite a few more details than the newspaper report. The most interesting account of the battle can be read in the *Correspondent*. Praise be to God, who reinforces the courage and strength of our warriors![129]

To both Amalie and Theodor von Schön, even though he belonged to a temporary administration attached to the army in Saxony and Bohemia in 1813, war was still a distant affair of the state.

To Amalie, her husband was part of a heroic war effort. 'I heartily envy you now, being so close to the great events; that must make you very happy', she wrote in the early summer of 1813.[130] Schön himself was more measured, complaining at times of boredom and inactivity, but he seems to have shared his wife's attitude.[131] Although supplied with books by an acquaintance in order to fill the idle hours, 'the conjunction is so important and people are so excited that it is impossible to read', he noted in May: 'The armies are ready for battle and, hour by hour, we are waiting for the news here. . . . Just think of the agitation here. It is impossible to get down to any serious business; every hour there is something new.'[132] Nevertheless, the administrator remained detached from the killing and death of the battlefield and continued to depict events in heroic terms, even though his close relatives were involved in the fighting. His own son, Robert, and Amalie's nephews Wilhelm and Theodor all took part in the battles of 1813, with the latter dying in May. 'I learned of the death of Theodor from people in his company: he climbed down from his horse, as the attack started, and led his company, like a brave man, into the fire', he informed his wife: 'Then a bullet hit him in the head and he died the most beautiful

---

[126] Ibid., 25–6.   [127] T. to A. v. Schön, 8 Aug. 1813, ibid., 238.
[128] A. to T. v. Schön, 4 July 1813, ibid., 211.
[129] A. to T. v. Schön, 5 May 1813, ibid., 131.   [130] Ibid., 132.
[131] On his inactivity, see for example T. to A. v. Schön, 25 Apr. 1813, ibid., 103.
[132] T. to A. v. Schön, 3 May 1813, ibid., 110.

death without torment or suffering. If Robert dies like this, we would want, of course, to mourn his loss, but also to thank God that he let him die in this way.'[133] Amalie was 'particularly pained by the death of Theodor', making it 'a difficult task to tell the poor parents'.[134] She was proud of her brother because he 'belongs very pronouncedly to those few people who forcefully stand their ground, when many begin to waver. ... May God stand by him!'[135]

For both husband and wife, the war against the 'Frenchmen' (*Franzmänner*) was a test of the mettle of the German soldiers, with the 'Germans' being contrasted unfavourably with the 'English and the Spanish', supported and, when necessary, punished by God.[136] When the first battle was won in May, 'God' was to 'be praised': 'The struggle was hard, but our troops fought like lions.'[137] As the fighting approached Prussia's border, 'this does no harm': 'the king is as brave as ever, and the affair will cost many broken heads, but will go well'.[138] War in Silesia in June was even to be welcomed, not least as 'a justified chastisement' for the region's previous disloyalty, declared Schön: 'That Silesia suffers greatly is true, but God is just. ... My hopes are still high. We still have a 30,000-man, wonderful *Landwehr* here, which has not even seen the enemy yet. And our troops are full of courage.'[139] During the ceasefire in the summer, the administrator observed a 'general hope and desire for the outbreak of war once more', reiterating his conviction that, 'on the whole, all must go well, for God is with us and we have a just cause'.[140] When the fighting did start again in September and the French general Dominique Vandamme was 'destroyed', things seemed to be going 'so wonderfully that God's direction is unmistakeable'.[141] Throughout the campaign, Schön was sanguine, referring with apparent indifference to the 'annihilation' of entire French army corps and maintaining that it was 'really interesting to be so close' to events.[142]

'WAR-TIME'

Few civilians witnessed war at such close quarters as Schön. Many bore the burdens of military conflict and experienced the passage of armies through their territories between 1792 and 1815, leaving a significant number of citizens—even in northern Germany, which was spared much of the fighting until the period after 1806—with the impression of living in 'war-time'.[143] In Hamburg, Marianne

---

[133] T. to A. v. Schön, 16 May 1813, ibid., 134–5.
[134] A. to T. v. Schön, 26 May 1813, ibid., 147.   [135] Ibid.
[136] A. to T. v. Schön, 28 July 1813, ibid., 228.
[137] T. to A. v. Schön, 5 May 1813, ibid., 119.
[138] T. to A. v. Schön, 24 May 1813, ibid., 144–5.
[139] T. to A. v. Schön, 5 June 1813, ibid., 160.
[140] T. to A. v. Schön, 12 June and 1 July 1813, ibid., 168, 197.
[141] T. to A. v. Schön, 3 Sept. 1813, ibid., 265–6.
[142] T. to A. v. Schön, 26 May 1813, ibid., 145.
[143] This can be seen in the memoirs of those, like Arndt, who became enthusiastic supporters of 'wars of the people' and whose retrospective reflections are correspondingly unreliable, and in those

Prell, summoning up her childhood memories—and her relatives' accounts—of one of the city's notable families, remarked that

> what was terrible about these constant wars was the fact that the French not only took money and valuables with them from the conquered lands, but that they also led away all young people capable of bearing arms and lined them up in their armies, and that these had to head off with them in every climate, wherever the march led, irrespective of whether they were able to stand it or not.[144]

Although much of the fighting of the Napoleonic Wars took place elsewhere, notwithstanding the bombardment of Hamburg after the turn of the century and further military activity in 1807 and 1813, at least some of the inhabitants of the Hansa town believed that they were in a state of 'constant' war, tied to the fortunes of soldiers serving in Russia, France, Prussia, Saxony, and other parts of Germany. Such ties were not tantamount to witnessing combat directly, however, with news of victory at the battle of Leipzig itself only arriving 'drop-by-drop', 'so that genuine celebration did not even come into question'.[145] A similar distance and detachment appears to characterize the accounts of civilians who were much closer to the fighting. In Saxony, for instance, Amalie von Beguelin recalled how 'we heard' the battle of Bautzen on 20–21 May 1813 'by putting our ears to the ground': 'at the start, the cannon sounded between great pauses, then around midday it got quicker; at about 3 and 4 o'clock, the fighting was at its fiercest'.[146] Even for those next to the battlefields, combat was imagined rather than experienced, menacing, fascinating, and preoccupying, not disgusting, numbing, or life-changing. 'At this point, it went "ruck"—"ruck"—"ruck", until dusk and darkness brought an end to the terrible activity, and now only the wailing continued, we could imagine', continued Beguelin.[147] The act of imagining wailing soldiers hints at contemporaries' commonplace anxiety of war, which had arguably become more and more important to them after 1805–6. It does not, though, mean that many of them had a realistic conception of the conditions of combat.

In the small state of Sachsen-Weimar, the citizenry had been near to the fighting in 1806, after the battles of Jena and Auerstädt, and in 1813, at the time of the battle of Leipzig. During the former, the city had been set on fire, reported the writer Johanna Schopenhauer to her son Arthur on 19 October, but 'few dared to

---

of sceptics, like Varnhagen, and conservatives such as Gentz: E. M. Arndt, *Erinnerungen*, 106–66; K. A. Varnhagen v. Ense, *Denkwürdigkeiten*, vol. 1, 35–210; G. Kronenbitter, '"The Most Terrible World War"', 117–34. See also K. B. Aaslestad, 'Lost Neutrality and Economic Warfare', 373–94; K. B. Aaslestad, 'War without Battles', 118–22; K. B. Aaslestad, 'Paying for War', 646–9; H. Carl, 'Der Mythos des Befreiungskrieges. Die "martialische Nation" im Zeitalter der Revolutions- und Befreiungskriege 1792–1815', in D. Langewiesche and G. Schmidt (eds), *Föderative Nation* (Munich, 2000), 63–82.

[144] M. Prell, *Erinnerungen aus der Franzosenzeit*, 8.   [145] Ibid., 71.
[146] A. v. Beguelin, diary entry, 20 May 1813, in A. Ernst (ed.), *Denkwürdigkeiten von Heinrich und Amalie von Beguelin aus den Jahren 1807–1813* (Berlin, 1892), 269.
[147] Ibid.

come out of their houses', fearing the French soldiers.[148] 'There was terrible misery in the city', she went on, describing the aftermath of Prussia's defeat:

> The city was formally given over to plunder; the officers and cavalry remained free of the horror and did what they could to help and protect us. But what could they do against 50,000 raging people, who could do as they pleased here, since their leaders, at least negatively, allowed it![149]

Many houses, especially businesses and those abandoned by their owners, were 'completely plundered'.[150] During the latter period in 1813, the same burghers of Weimar—whose number still included Goethe, Wieland, and other prominent writers—feared 'a similarly violent catastrophe' to that of 1806, in the words of the diarist Johannes Falk, with Napoleon 'throwing himself on the city with more overwhelming force and giving it up to the flames out of a desire for revenge'.[151] Goethe himself was notoriously aloof from such events, recording the alternation of 'quiet' and 'disquieting' October days and nights in his diary.[152] He, too, accepted the centrality of national warfare, however, despite treating it—in Wilhelm von Humboldt's opinion—in a 'very relaxed and casual way', maintaining that 'world history must also have its fun'.[153] Indeed, 'the devastation wrought by the Cossacks, which is very bad, takes away all his joy in the fun': 'He maintains that the cure is worse than the malady; one will be free of servitude in order to go under.'[154] To Falk, it seemed that the menace of war had provoked a 'general fear and trembling' in Weimar in 1813, with 'the colourful events of war' changing as quickly as the languages of the allied armies.[155] Throughout Germany, a significant number of educated, largely urban subjects seem to have felt that they were at war—or immediately threatened by war—during the Napoleonic era, experiencing 'such extraordinary, surprising things that even youthful personalities, usually concentrating on everyday impressions, forgot the small concerns of the daily round', in the opinion of one adolescent in Baden.[156] For these contemporaries, war and occupation were not background facts of daily life, but defining features of existence.[157]

---

[148] J. Schopenhauer to A. Schopenhauer, 19 Oct. 1806, in F. Schulze (ed.), *Weimarische Berichte und Briefe aus den Freiheitskriegen 1806–1815* (Leipzig, 1913), 50.

[149] Ibid.   [150] Ibid.

[151] J. Falk, *Kriegsbüchlein* (Leipzig, 1911), 56.

[152] J. W. v. Goethe, diary, Oct. 1813, in F. Schulze (ed.), *Weimarische Berichte und Briefe aus den Freiheitskriegen 1806–1815*, 197–8.

[153] W. v. Humboldt to his wife, 26 Oct. 1813, ibid., 205.

[154] Ibid.   [155] J. Falk, *Kriegsbüchlein*, 56–7.

[156] F. v. Andlaw, *Mein Tagebuch; Auszüge aus Ausschreibungen der Jahre 1811 bis 1861* (Frankfurt a. M., 1862), 32. By the Napoleonic era, the painter Albrecht Adam was depicting 'years of peace' as the exception in Bavaria: A. Adam, *Aus dem Leben eines Schlachtenmalers*, 62.

[157] See, for example, W. Meier, *Erinnerungen aus den Feldzügen*, 28: 'The great school of education for people is life. But how different life is, whether moving in fixed tracks and in the usual order, or spurting forwards like a wild mountain torrent, ripping everything down, spilling over the banks and creating a new course. Richer experience, which people gain from stormy times, is of course bought at great expense, often at the cost of one's life... [but] how one rejoices over tests and dangers overcome,... on the way to the attained prize of the bloody struggle!'

Open opposition to France's wars and to French occupation remained rare, however, dispelling any notion of guerrilla warfare or underground resistance. Even in Prussia in 1812, when attacks against troops from the Confederation of the Rhine—on their way to Russia—were common, there was no possibility of a Spanish type of uprising, noted one officer from Frankfurt, since 'there are no mountains here...necessary for guerrillas'.[158] When French forces occupied the Rhineland in 1794–7, stationing between 136,000 and 187,000 troops there or one soldier for every ten inhabitants, the population cooperated, however reluctantly, with the occupying authorities, despite warnings from the rulers, usually in exile, that 'persons lacking German spirit and heart' would be treated as 'criminals against us, the German *Reich* and their fatherland', in the words of decrees issued by Emperor Franz II in December 1792 and April 1793.[159] Cities and lands initially reacted in different ways, depending on whether their elites had been destroyed or had fled (as in the former Hohenzollern territory of Cleves), whether they were divided (as in the imperial city of Aachen), or whether they were united (as in Cologne), but they all accepted French rule, which was formalized by the Treaty of Lunéville's extension of French law to the Rhineland on 9 February 1801. In these circumstances, declared the Elector of Cologne, 'It is far better [that the administration] should be in the hands of old established families than *sans-culottes*.'[160] When they took control of most of the Rhineland after the defeat of Napoleon in 1814, the Prussian authorities compiled reports on individual officials in the region, distinguishing between those who had remained 'German', those who had sullied their name by accepting a French honour, and those Bonapartists who were 'completely French'.[161] The implication of such reports was that much of the population had cooperated with the French regime. At most, some sections of society and the administration appear to have believed that 'Germany' or specific German states were at war or threatened by military conflict. They were not directly involved in warfare themselves. The same seems to have been true of other parts of western and southern Germany.[162]

It was also true of Prussia, even during the period of the occupation between 1807 and 1813, as military reformers such as Gneisenau began to contemplate the possibility of a popular uprising against the French. Certainly, the reformers themselves were not confident that the population—or sections of it—believed itself to be at war, as Clausewitz recorded in a memorandum of February 1812, designed to justify his withdrawal from the Prussian army:

> The view that France could be resisted has almost completely disappeared amongst us.
> One believes in the necessity of an unconditional alliance, of being at their mercy and,

---

[158] Cited in P. Holzhausen, *Die Deutschen in Russland. Leben und Leiden auf der Moskauer Heerfahrt* (Berlin, 1912), 11.

[159] Cited in M. Rowe, 'Resistance, Collaboration or Third Way? Responses to Napoleonic Rule in Germany', in C. J. Esdaile (ed.), *Popular Resistance in the French Wars: Patriots, Partisans and Land Pirates* (Basingstoke, 2003), 73.

[160] Ibid., 74.   [161] Ibid.

[162] See especially U. Planert, *Der Mythos*, 159–335, which examines the 'horrors of war' at the same time as showing how they remained within acceptable historical boundaries.

finally, of the renunciation of our own ruling dynasty. One submits to these gradations of evil with a shrug of the shoulders and, at most, blushes whilst lowering one's gaze. This is the general mood. Individuals still distinguish themselves by the impudence with which they insist on security and the quiet enjoyment of burghers' property, on sacrificing everything, the rights of the king, the honour of the king and also the security of the king.

This is public opinion (*die öffentliche Meinung*) with few exceptions. The way of acknowledging it, of following it, differs from one order to another and amongst individuals within a single order. The higher ranks are more corrupt, the court and state officials the most corrupted. ... The fact can't be kept secret, for all one's backing of the government, that lack of support for it is the primary source of the general despondency. The government itself shows just as little trust towards its subjects and, even, towards itself. This complete lack of trust in oneself and in others is the general cause of the public mood.[163]

Although the public mood seemed to be 'superficial', created by 'worthless, meaningless coincidences', this was not the case 'with public opinion, with support for the constitution and government, with the corruption of morals, with the loss of strength and everything which was founded deeper in a nation, which had been brought about earlier', Clausewitz continued: 'These things are not altered, admittedly, by insignificant causes.'[164] 'All these things' appeared to militate against 'a powerful resistance' (*Widerstand*).[165]

Civilian reformers such as Stein, who had lamented 'the readiness of public officials to meet the needs of the enemy's army and to inform them of the state's strengths' in November 1808, and commentators such as Niebuhr, who complained of the majority's lack of a sense 'of a public good' in the same year, had long subscribed to a similar view of popular opinion: 'Just as the well-disposed only make up a part and perhaps the minority of the actual public—not including the unspoiled *Volk*—so one hears much more regularly opinions of the utmost hopelessness being expressed with complete certainty'.[166] Likewise, the lower orders of the population beyond the sphere of the 'public', which publicists such as Arndt and Jahn saw as the repository of an increasingly heartfelt 'pride in the fatherland' from the turn of the century onwards, seem to have been unwilling to confront the occupying authorities with war-like acts of resistance. During the period of the war and its immediate aftermath between 1806 and the end of 1808, French military courts handed down only three death sentences in the *Kurmark*, at the heart of the new Prussia. Two of the accused were innocent.[167] Such passivity was all the more remarkable in the context of French expropriations and demands, which it has been estimated amounted—over a period of two years—to sixteen times Prussia's annual revenues.[168] In East Prussia, 350,000 troops had been deployed in 1806–7 within an area of 1,000 square miles. Prussian subjects there often found themselves close to the fighting.

[163] C. v. Clausewitz, *Politische Schriften und Briefe*, ed. H. Rothfels (Munich, 1922), 80–2.
[164] Ibid.   [165] Ibid.
[166] G. H. Pertz, *Das Leben des Ministers Freiherrn vom* Stein (Berlin, 1849–55), vol. 2, 288; B. G. Niebuhr, cited in R. Ibbeken, *Preussen*, 98.
[167] R. Ibbeken, *Preussen*, 100.   [168] Ibid., 92.

Civilians, even if they were close to the fighting, rarely witnessed its consequences and, when they did, were arguably less profoundly affected by them than were their counterparts in the later nineteenth century. Many appear to have been used to the prospect of death and violence.[169] Thus, as the armies of Prussia and Russia approached the city of Dresden in August 1813, E. T. A. Hoffmann remained nonchalant. 'Should I write about war and peace?' he asked his publisher:

> Ah, dearest! It's war!—wicked, evil war! The emperor with the garden went off last Sunday, and since that time the street has not been empty of troops—like a perpetual procession, artillery, cavalry, and infantry go up and down the *silesische Strasse*.—To date, we don't know whether a battle has taken place or not; but everything is very tense, and God knows what will happen to us! We trust entirely in chance and Napoleon's weapons, otherwise we are done for.—I'm moving into the city incidentally, since my little house—extremely agreeably—is in the firing line of an entrenched position.[170]

'Of one's life here, in the midst of war, you most honourable Bambergers have no idea!' he concluded.[171] Yet, when fighting began, Hoffmann continued to show little concern, even in the private pages of his diary. On the 21st, 'a countless load of injured on wagons' began to come into the city, but the writer made no further comment. On the 25th, he himself was caught up in an exchange of fire as he was walking in the city with an actor he knew. 'The line of French tirailleurs was standing only 50 paces in front of us,' he recounted:

> 300 paces further on individual Cossacks rode quietly up and down and took no notice at all of the firing of the French. I saw how one got off and tightened the saddle of his horse. Suddenly, Russian sharpshooters came through a bush, and now the firing became more and more lively—many French dropped dead, and others came back bloody and screaming. French batteries came into formation, and a battery of four cannons was set up; before this began to tune up, however, enemy bullets came over from a battery that I hadn't noticed, and now I also saw how a black line was moving down from the mountains. Since the bullets were falling close to the [Pirnaer] *Schlag*, we thought it was advisable, with much haste, to rush home through the Wilsdrufer Tor.—Night brought an end to the action (the first that I've seen in such proximity).[172]

As the fighting got worse on the 26th, Hoffmann remained unabashed, escaping through a back garden to his friend's house in the Neumarkt in order get a drop of wine or rum, which he had been appalled not to find in the house where he was staying. Having managed to get through the war-torn streets,

> we were looking out of the window in very good cheer, with a glass of wine our hands, when a grenade landed and exploded in the middle of the market—at the same

---

[169] This was particularly true of doctors, but also of many others: W. Meier, *Erinnerungen aus den Feldzügen*; W. Krimer, *Erinnerungen eines alten Lützower Jägers 1795–1819*, ed. A. Saager, 2nd edn (Stuttgart, 1913).
[170] Hoffmann to Kunz, 19 Aug. 1813, cited in E. Klessmann (ed.), *Die Befreiungskriege in Augenzeugenberichten*, 133.
[171] Ibid.   [172] Ibid., 134–5.

moment, a Westphalian soldier, who was pumping water, dropped dead with a smashed head—and, quite a long way from him, a respectably dressed burgher.[173]

The actor dropped his glass, but Hoffmann 'drank up and declared: "What is life? Not even able to withstand a bit of glowing iron. Human nature is weak!"'[174] Laden with rum, which he had been given by a merchant next door, the writer made his way home. Throughout, even after having seen the battlefield on 29 August, full of dismembered bodies and the groaning of the abandoned wounded, the writer maintained an unaffected tone, notwithstanding very occasional allusions to 'an atrocious sight'.[175] His descriptions of carnage are direct and factual, giving little indication that the author was shocked or sickened.

Other civilians like Arndt who witnessed killing were more obviously affected than was Hoffmann, but not profoundly enough to abandon their heroic conception of conflict. Following the Russian army as Stein's publicist in 1812, he wrote from the destroyed town of Vilnius in December to a friend in Württemberg, that he had been stuck for two days in the 'murderous hole', watching 'the transport of prisoners, with faces of death, some dying on sleighs, corpses lying naked here and there on the way, like cattle'.[176] Near Vilnius, there was 'more horror', as 'we rode over human remains through the outskirts of the city, with human corpses, dead horses, oxen, dogs and waifs...on both sides'.[177] The other day, he went on,

I saw sleighs piled up with 40 to 50 naked corpses, some with waifs or with a cap and cockade as their only clothing; all stacked up on one another haphazardly, with heads below legs, which were sticking up on top, or vice versa, as if one were dragging chopped-down willows or withered hedges, however withered and dried-up, to a meal—everything, shortly beforehand still swelling with defiance and opulence, now going forth in peaceful and dreadful stillness.[178]

The uncomfortable juxtaposition of terms such as 'peacefulness' and 'dreadfulness', animals and humans, betrayed Arndt's own horror and disgust at the consequences of war. It is likely that such experiences informed and reinforced the publicist's penchant for earthy, uncompromising descriptions of conflict and his full-blooded support of national hatred.[179] It did not, however, lead him to renounce war, or the nations which waged war. Even in Vilnius, sitting—like the dead—'still in this hole', Arndt preferred to turn 'to the living'.[180] Leaving aside 'the great losses which have been suffered', he remained 'well' and refused to allow his 'head [to] drop', as he declared to Georg Andreas Reimer in January 1813 from Königsberg.[181] Thus, after the battle of Großgörschen on 2 May 1813, he rejoiced from Dresden that 'it is not a defeat, but a bloody victory, and our honour is becoming uppermost'.[182] After the battle of Leipzig on 16–19 October, he wrote from Görlitz that 'my heart

[173] Ibid., 139.   [174] Ibid.   [175] Ibid., 141.
[176] E. M. Arndt to K. B. Trinius, 12 Dec. 1812, in E. M. Arndt, *Briefe*, ed. A. Dühr (Darmstadt, 1972–5) vol. 1, 235.
[177] Ibid.   [178] Ibid., 235–6.   [179] See Chapter 2.
[180] E. M. Arndt, *Briefe*, vol. 1, 236.
[181] E. M. Arndt to G. A. Reimer, 29 Jan. 1813, ibid., 237.
[182] E. M. Arndt to J. Motherby, 4 May 1813, ibid., 268.

is joyful', since 'we have . . . won a battle which frees Germany and the world. Last year, the first act was played out; this is the second; and the third will be on the Rhine'.[183] As he confessed to his intimate friend Johanna Motherby, the violence and unpredictability of the Napoleonic Wars left him 'in the flux of a fleeting and unsteady life', barely able to work out 'where I was and what I was', yet 'my heart swims in joy', having 'won a victory which will free the fatherland': 'We are free, our children are free; let us pray, Furina, be very pious and loving, my sweet child.'[184] To Arndt, who had seen much more of war than had most civilians, military conflict was at once destabilizing, meaningful, and redemptive.

Although few subjects conceived of warfare in such stark terms, many alluded to its dual character, hinting in turn that it had come to play a more central part in their lives and in 'politics'. Most civilians were insulated from the violence of warfare. Thus, when columns of emaciated and blood-soaked troops returned to East Prussia and other areas of Germany after the failed invasion of Russia in 1812, they seemed to be 'true figures of horror and misery', according to one chronicler.[185] In south-west Germany, the writer Helmina von Chézy reported how 'the distant peels of thunder in the North, whose tremors—unheard—also shook the world, crushed our spirits': 'The bitterest blows of the war fell on the Bavarian contingent. The whole of Bavaria was in mourning, the whole of Hesse cried over the victims of the battles. Young sons, loving husbands, fathers and brothers; every letter brought death notices.'[186] One young woman, who had heard that her husband had died near Smolensk, had wanted to go to recover and bury his remains; another 'young mourner thought of her orphaned children and found her will to live again, since she had to provide them with a mother'.[187] Although such mourning underlined the cost of war, it appears to have been incorporated by observers and, even, by relatives into a common cycle of life and death, whereas the sight and smell of disfigured and dead soldiers seems to have been more difficult to accept, as the 'first wagon of the wounded rolled through Darmstadt's streets' in 1813, after the war had reached the 'heart of Germany';[188] 3,000 seriously ill, wounded, and dying troops arrived in the city, 'many in a very sad state', risking having their clothes ripped off and being thrown into the street as they died, 'with their corpses still warm'.[189] As the soldiers and officers told stories of 'the murderous battle', 'we listened to them, shivering with fright'.[190] Yet, for Chézy at least, these glimpses and stories of killing and dying appear to have been qualitatively different from actual experience of battle. Having moved to Frankfurt, she recalled in a matter-of-fact tone and without further comment how the masses of Russian troops marching west crossed the path of 'wagons of corpses, which were carrying the victims of the prevailing nerve fever to their last resting place'.[191] In the next sentence, she

---

[183] E. M. Arndt to K. B. Trinius, 22 Oct. 1813, ibid., 322.

[184] E. M. Arndt to J. Motherby, 22 Oct. 1813, ibid., 320–1.

[185] Eberstein, *Aus dem Leben im Gumbinnen*, cited in G. A. Klausa (ed.), '*Sehnlich erwarte ich die morgende Post*', 17.

[186] H. v. Chézy, *Unvergessenes. Denkwürdigkeiten* (Leipzig, 1858), vol. 2, 59.

[187] Ibid.   [188] Ibid., vol. 2, 69–70.   [189] Ibid., 70.   [190] Ibid., 71.

[191] Ibid., 86.

recorded how 'The young *Tscherkessen* made the greatest impression on the masses of spectators, in their snow-white uniforms with silver and crimson lapels, their steel helmets, partly in gold and partly in silver, white and red like girls, with sparkling eyes and a strong bearing.'[192] 'We shall see them again, but not in such a poetic form and posture', she concluded.[193] Death and grandeur existed side by side in such accounts.

When soldiers did experience the violence of battle, they frequently kept their feelings and their suffering to themselves. In 1809, as Varnhagen rushed to join the Habsburg army, the writer and society hostess Rahel Levin, his future wife, gave full expression to her fears, hopes, admiration, and disapproval:

> Be courageous and brave! Think of me when you are being attacked: you know that I am fearful, but I would still prefer an unknown death, if I were there by choice; and don't waver. You are now above the common men; spur them on with the sound of your voice—intoxication helps—if they want to give in. Make yourself loved and known by them beforehand. It was thus that Bribes advanced at Austerlitz; his captain fell; he held the people (*Volk*) together by shouting and offering encouragement; they did not capitulate; he became captain and received the [iron] cross. You know what I think of war and these things. War is not for educated people. Those who don't know that their body is a person can let it be shot at; otherwise, one should only defend oneself if one is being attacked and if anger and revenge are torn away![194]

Before battle, Varnhagen replied in kind, confident that 'the enthusiasm [for war] is greater and more general than one could have imagined':

> Whenever it is going badly, I think of you, dearest Rahel, I immediately feel you beating with my heart. ...You, my dear angel, my fatherland, the blessed water for me, a flying fish! If you had already taken me in, without wounds, without anything else apart from common misfortune, I would hardly have deserved it![195]

When he was injured at the battle of Wagram in July 1809, he continued in a similar vein:

> My inwardly loved, sweet, dear, unique Rahel! My body is wounded, but my heart beats, without injury, for you! Even before the battle, of which I had given up all hope, since I could only see peace, I felt such yearning for you, spilled such tears because you are so far away, that I could think of nothing but our goodbyes.[196]

Although he hinted that he was not well, reassuring Rahel that, 'whatever happens, know that I am your friend, your intimate friend', Varnhagen's tone was breezy:

> The surgeon says that the bone has been damaged, but he hasn't confirmed it. I have been completely fresh and cheerful, and I have thought to myself that I only have to

---

[192] Ibid.   [193] Ibid.; H. v. Jordan, *Erinnerungsblätter und Briefe*, 329–31.
[194] R. Levin to K. A. Varnhagen v. Ense, 8 July 1809, in K. A. Varnhagen v. Ense and R. Varnhagen, *Briefwechsel zwischen Varnhagen und Rahel*, vol. 1, 8.
[195] Varnhagen to Rahel, 20 and 25 June 1809, in K. A. Varnhagen v. Ense and R. Varnhagen, *Briefwechsel zwischen Varnhagen und Rahel*, vol. 1, 3, 6.
[196] Varnhagen to Rahel, 4 Aug. 1809, in K. A. Varnhagen v. Ense and R. Varnhagen, *Briefwechsel zwischen Varnhagen und Rahel*, vol. 1, 12.

jump up and go into the liberating, fresh air under the trees which I can see from my window; but it will take a while before this happens, after all![197]

In his diary, however, which formed the basis of his later memoirs, Varnhagen was far less optimistic. As the battle began, all he noticed was the noise:

> This enormous sound of repeatedly renewed fire and still much more the endless sound of iron amidst the handling of more than twenty-thousand flints in such proximity and such a narrow space...everything, even the thunder of the numerous guns made little impression beside the thunderous roar of so-called small arms, these weapons by means of which our new battles habitually become murderous.[198]

'During the enemy's first attack, a shot hit me in the thigh and I could from now on only be an idle witness of the distant events which the battlefield presented', he went on: 'As I took the shot in the thigh, I felt only a hard hit at first, which went through me; I saw immediately, however, as I lifted up my tunic, two streams of blood pouring out, where the bullet had gone right through.'[199] As the armies wheeled around, 'I had to muster my last bit of strength in order not to be left behind. Two soldiers grabbed me under the arms and, half carried and half walking, I went back towards our camp.'[200] Left just behind the battle lines, as the soldiers returned to the fighting, Varnhagen was eventually dragged further back and then loaded onto an ammunitions wagon with other wounded troops. He recalled,

> The shuddering of the cart caused me great pain; the blood, which had flowed copiously at the start and had filled my boot, now congealed, and my knee and thigh became cold and numb; I suffered, just like the others, from terrible thirst, and the cold of the night, too, was very painful.[201]

After finally being seen briefly by a surgeon, he sank into a deep sleep. 'At daybreak, the noise woke me', he continued: 'My wounds had bled the entire night, I couldn't sit up,...and I gave myself up to fate.'[202] Forced to move again, fleeing capture by the French army, he 'even felt the pain of the wounds less and at times sank into pleasant dreams', before being 'all too often interrupted by the cry of pain, which each pull of the horses or unevenness of the road provoked'.[203] Billeted in a civilian household, he succumbed to fever: 'for twenty-four hours, I suffered the greatest pains, during which I did not conceal from myself that a serious turn could easily occur'.[204] With his dressings unchanged and his leg burning, he was taken to the hospital on the fourth day, where he was told that his femur was broken:

> For me, this was a kind of death sentence, for my medical knowledge told me that in such circumstances it could be held to be necessary to cut off the leg, that this would scarcely be possible so high up and that in the best case the painful and still risky recuperation could last six, eight or more months.[205]

---

[197] Ibid.   [198] K. A. Varnhagen v. Ense, *Denkwürdigkeiten*, vol. 1, 316.
[199] Ibid., 321.   [200] Ibid.   [201] Ibid.   [202] Ibid., 322.   [203] Ibid., 322–3.
[204] Ibid., 323.   [205] Ibid., 323–4.

Few of these experiences were detectable in Varnhagen's correspondence with Rahel. On 4 August, he wrote rhetorically that he had 'presented his life openly to death', with the result that 'death' had come 'between me and my old circumstances', but he went on to reassure his fiancée in the same letter that 'my wounds are nearly healed', which was a fabrication.[206] Although both became more accustomed to the absences and dangers of battle, their correspondence continued until 1815, with Varnhagen passing on patriotic anecdotes and Rahel responding in kind, although fearing her husband's imminent death.[207] Only rarely did civilians gain an insight into the true conditions of war. By contrast, a growing number of soldiers did experience battles, altering their perceptions of military conflict. The next chapter investigates their accounts.

[206] K. A. Varnhagen to R. Levin, 4 Aug. 1809, K. A. Varnhagen v. Ense and R. Varnhagen, *Briefwechsel zwischen Varnhagen und Rahel*, vol. 1, 18.
[207] K. A. Varnhagen v. Ense and R. Varnhagen, *Briefwechsel zwischen Varnhagen und Rahel*, vol. 2, 281–309 vol. 3, 1–223; vol. 4, 122–207.

4

The Lives of Soldiers

It is tempting to assume that the traumas of twentieth-century wars, resulting in well-documented psychiatric conditions such as mutism, were produced by the unparalleled destructiveness of such conflicts. Yet it is worth re-examining such an assumption. In terms of their scale, the revolutionary and, especially, Napoleonic campaigns, which began with the invasion of Italy in 1796 and culminated in what German historians later called the 'wars of liberation' between 1813 and 1815, were extraordinarily bloody. Between 1800 and 1815, just under a million French soldiers—or about 40 per cent of those in arms—died or disappeared.[1] Up to 400,000 from vassal states and allies, including many Germans, were also lost on the French side.[2] Alone the *Grande Armée*'s invasion of Russia in 1813 might have resulted in a million deaths.[3] At the battle of Borodino during that campaign, about 70,000 were killed from a total of 250,000 on the field. At Austerlitz, 35,000 out of 163,000 were killed, at Preussisch-Eylau 48,000 were left dead or wounded from 125,000, and at Waterloo 54,000 dead or wounded from 193,000. The chances of survival in such battles differed little from those in the First World War and were worse than those of other nineteenth-century conflicts. Death would usually occur during close combat, through untreated wounds, or unsuccessful amputations, disease, or freezing. With poor medical treatment and lack of provisioning, it is arguable that conditions were as bad as or worse than during twentieth-century wars.

WAR STORIES

Our understanding of soldiers' reactions to such conditions depends to a great extent on the interpretation of combatants' own accounts in the form of

---

[1] G. Best, *War and Society in Revolutionary Europe, 1770–1870* (London, 1982), 114. The figures are contested: see, for instance, Owen Connelly's criticism, in *The Journal of Military History*, 71 (2007), 921, of David Bell's claim that the French had lost 1 million soldiers killed in action: 'the French lost only 86,500 *killed in action*, not one million, which is the *casualty* figure, including killed, wounded, deserters, captured and missing. By contrast, in World War I, in four years, 1,400,000 French were *killed in action*.' Many more soldiers and civilians died in the revolutionary and Napoleonic periods of wounds, war-related diseases, and freezing, complicating direct comparisons of this kind.

[2] G. Best, *War and Society*, 114.

[3] S. Förster, 'Der Weltkrieg, 1792–1815: Bewaffnete Konflikte und Revolutionen in der Weltgesellschaft', in J. Dülffer (ed.), *Kriegsbereitschaft und Friedensordnung*, 22–3. Also for the figures following.

correspondence, diaries, memoirs, and other descriptions of battles and campaigns. These sources are often inaccurate, as Carl von Plotho, who went on to become one of the principal military writers of the Napoleonic Wars, made plain in 1811: 'so many different views and judgements of [military conflict] arise that falsehood and untruth establish themselves more and more firmly'.[4] What made any measure of the 'completeness of my work' doubtful was the fact that 'every individual, or every class of readers, makes a different judgement, has different opinions, and therefore makes different demands of the work, not counting those who perhaps merely want to enjoy the pleasure of criticism itself'.[5] All that Plotho could do was to acknowledge the 'incompleteness of the work' and to 'offer it to the public (*das Publikum*) with great modesty'.[6] The majority of memoirists were less modest, with the record of even the most famous—the Prussian staff officer Carl von Müffling—being discounted by one scholar as the 'self-serving' version of 'a vain man'.[7] Compared to letters, which form the basis of Alan Forrest's seminal study of the soldiers of the revolution and empire, 'the evidence of memoirs and reflections published after the event may be very different', allowing 'for so much more conceit and literary flourish; they may be seen as a man's own memorial to the years he had spent in the army, and that memorial is often carefully scripted'.[8] Whereas personal letters, which themselves often passed on false information from official bulletins and gave a misleading account from a particular point of view, were 'hastily composed and despatched in time for the next post', memoirs 'necessarily lack spontaneity', being 'the product of mature reflection, with all the advantages and shortcomings which reflecting implies'.[9] It is notable, however, that many contemporaries' testimony, of various types, gives a similar account of combatants' experience of warfare, especially of exposure to violence and killing, despite disagreement about events and their meaning.[10] Thus, although many authors challenged Plotho's ability 'to put right falsehood and untruth', with one Bavarian critic pitting a 'return-recollection' against his Prusso-centric memory of events, they coincided unexpectedly in other respects, putting forward a limited range of descriptions and narratives of their feelings, thoughts, and actions during campaigns, even though they fought on different sides.[11] In part, this convergence

---

[4] C. v. Plotho, *Tagebuch während des Krieges zwischen Russland und Preussen einerseits und Frankreich andrerseits in den Jahren 1806 und 1807* (Berlin, 1811), iv. See M. Hewitson, '"I Witnesses"', 310–25, for further literature.

[5] C. v. Plotho, *Tagebuch*, v.

[6] Ibid., iii. Even unpublished memoirists such as Otto Sauerborn, who wrote up his recollections in 1827, were conscious of the difficulties of writing 'history': his jottings 'can only serve as raw material for the history of war', he conceded. Otto Sauerborn, 'Waffentat eines Husaren-Wachtmeisters im Feldzuge von 1813', *Kriegsbriefe* Archive, Universitäts- und Landesbibliothek Bonn.

[7] G. E. Rothenberg's review in *Journal of Military History*, 62 (1998), 396. On the unreliability of memoirs, see also T. S. Anderson, 'Memoirs of the Wars of the French Revolution and Empire', *Journal of Modern History*, 2 (1930), 288–92.

[8] A. Forrest, *Napoleon's Men: The Soldiers of the Revolution and Empire* (London, 2002), 23.

[9] Ibid., 23–4.

[10] This includes private letters and diaries; see, for instance, the *Kriegsbriefe* Archive, Universitäts- und Landesbibliothek Bonn, or the collections of letters and other material used by Leighton S. James, *Witnessing the Revolutionary and Napoleonic Wars*.

[11] C. v. Plotho, *Tagebuch*, v. For a Bavarian 'reply', see anon., *Rück-Erinnerungen an die Jahre 1813 und 1814* (Munich, 1818).

Table 4.1. First Editions of Autobiographies and Memoirs by Publication Date

Up to 1829	1830–49	1850–69	1870–89	1890–1909	1910–15	Total
19	61	66	37	43	38	269

Source: derived from data in K. Hagemann, *Revisiting Prussia's Wars against Napoleon: History, Culture and Memory* (Cambridge, 2015), 304.

can be explained by the novelty and urgency of the situations in which they found themselves, suffering from hunger and confronting death. In part, it was the result of the vestigial, heterogeneous character of military reportage, testimony, and histories, leaving many memoirists, like the octagenarian Jean Garnier, able to 'do no more than draw upon some of the jottings I made at the time'.[12] In contrast to later wars, which inspired a flurry of writing, the Revolutionary and Napoleonic Wars were reported initially in diaries and correspondence, and only later in a gradually increasing flow of memoirs (see Table 4.1).[13]

Although contemporary observers noted an increase in the number of 'tales', 'stories', and 'histories' of military campaigns during the early nineteenth century, war literature constituted a minority interest and pursuit, with fewer conventions than during the period after the 1860s. Writers appear to have drawn on different literary genres and traditions, including the military reporting and regimental histories of battles, manoeuvres, and marches, which were adapted and popularized by Plotho. Here, technical descriptions of the movements of mass armies were combined with portrayals of the heroic or inglorious actions of commanders. August von Thurn und Taxis, an officer in the Bavarian army, provided a typical instance of this type of account, reducing even the retreat from Moscow in 1812 to a series of military details. On 11 December, he recorded, camp was struck at 2.00 in the morning, with the Bavarian contingent marching to join the corps of Marshall Ney at Evio, where they were ordered to help the rearguard:

> All kinds of defence measures were now taken in that place, although I freely confess that both its position and the condition of our men (most unfortunately had fingers so stiff that it was, so to say, physically impossible for them to cock their guns) did not seem to me to be conducive to tenacious resistance.[14]

During the afternoon, 'the first Cossacks appeared on this side of a wood before our front', followed by cavalry, which simply left the main road and went round

[12] J. Garnier, *Souvenirs de guerre en temps de paix*, in A. Forrest, *Napoleon's Men*, 25. Examples of German memoirs based on contemporaneous notes are F. Mändler, *Erinnerungen aus meinen Feldzügen 1809–1915*, ed. F. J. A. Schneidawind (Nuremberg, 1854); R. v. Meerheim (ed.), *Erlebnisse eines Veteranen der Grossen Armee während des Feldzuges in Russland* (Dresden, 1860); F. Steger, *Der Feldzug von 1812* (Essen, 1985), first published in 1845; L. v. Wolzogen, *Memoiren* (Leipzig, 1851); W. Meier, *Erinnerungen aus den Feldzügen*, 93, who simply stopped his account at the point when his papers had been confiscated.

[13] See the various published letters and *Tagebücher*. Regimental histories drew on these sources, too, together with contemporaneous official reports of battles and manoeuvres.

[14] A. v. Thurn und Taxis, *Aus drei Feldzügen 1812–1815. Erinnerungen* (Leipzig, 1912), 114.

the village, 'so that we soon ran the risk of being cut off'.[15] Since 'we, so to say, had no cavalry at all, we couldn't attack the enemy's', leading the Bavarian commander Carl Philipp von Wrede to advise a withdrawal but pushing Ney to attack—at the risk of death—'in order to produce élan through his own example'.[16] Finally, 'after the enemy artillery began to create more damage', Ney reluctantly gave the order to retreat, which was carried out 'in good order'.[17] The next day, camp was struck at 3.00 in the morning and the movement of the army continued in the same fashion until Thurn und Taxis met Wrede again on 17 December and delivered his report, after which 'nothing interesting' happened.[18] For many authors, the return to Germany and the survival of an ordeal was the climax of the story, but for Thurn and Taxis it had no military significance. The majority of officers, particularly high-ranking ones, produced variations on this military theme of a war of movement. Even Plotho, who gave himself greater licence to use colourful adjectives and to depict the heroic actions of battle, continued to concentrate on the attacks and counter-attacks which brought about victory or defeat. Accordingly, from his description of the opening battle of 1813 in Großgörschen on 2 May, during which 'they had pushed forward in the most violent and bloodiest fighting, conquered several villages and already forced the enemy to retreat', to his summation of the last day of fighting at the battle of Leipzig on 19 October, which was followed immediately by 'rapid marches' after the fleeing French forces, the Prussian military writer focused on the heroic actions of entire armies.[19]

The other principal type of account was also heroic, but it was concerned largely with the adventures of individual soldiers. Such 'reminiscences and fragments' were frequently marked, in the opinion of one officer and memoirist from Braunschweig, by 'such a romantic stamp that they have served rather to entertain than to teach'.[20] Typically, they followed the fortunes of the protagonist from country to country and army to army in the form of a travelogue. Thus, Wilhelm Freiherr von Schauroth, in 'the regiment of the *Rheinbund*', travelled from Coburg to Salzburg and into the Tyrol (1809), before embarking for Spain (1809–10), returning to his *Heimat* (1810–11), laying siege to Hamburg (1811–12), setting off for Russia (1812), passing through Königsberg on his way home (1812–13), and marching back to Magdeburg (1813), where he was taken prisoner by Russian forces.[21] The hardy 'heroes' of these tales were regularly buffeted by one set of adverse circumstances and then by another, as they accumulated experiences of foreign countries and unusual conditions. Their reports home were couched, whether deliberately or not, in the long-established conventions of the picaresque. One Prussian officer's account of the battle of Borodino, the worst battle of the 1812 campaign, was characteristic, revealing at the same time the extent to which soldiers were inured to the hardships and suffering of war at the turn of the nineteenth century. Having been

[15] Ibid., 14.   [16] Ibid., 15.   [17] Ibid.   [18] Ibid., 117.

[19] C. v. Plotho, *Der Krieg in Deutschland und Frankreich in den Jahren 1813 und 1814* (Berlin, 1817), vol. 1, 105–23; vol. 2, 422.

[20] E. Heusinger, *Ansichten, Beobachtungen und Erfahrungen* (Braunschweig, 1825), 1.

[21] W. v. Schauroth, *Im Rheinbund Regiment während der Feldzüge in Tirol, Spanien und Russland 1809–1813* (Berlin, 1905), 1–291: each chapter heading indicated a new stage on his journey.

present at Prussia's defeat at the battle of Auerstedt in 1806, in which he was shot, he vowed to continue the fight for his country's resurrection, sailing to Britain, before going on to Spain with the Duke of Wellington.[22] When Napoleon invaded Russia, he joined the forces of the latter, notwithstanding Prussia's agreement to contribute troops to the *Grande Armée*. Only the most hardened soldiers, he remarked, were present at Borodino, since the weaker ones had died en route. 'It could be predicted with certainty that the 7th September 1812 would be one of the bloodiest that the history of modern warfare had known, and many thousands of the warriors gathered here would cover the ground as stiff corpses or as forever dismembered wounded', he gloated retrospectively. During the battle, 'as the fighting raged more and more terribly' as if 'hell had opened its gates', the officer had his cheek ripped open and his earlobe chopped off by a Polish cavalryman, yet he continued to fight, commenting that 'this was really not very dangerous, but bled very copiously and left such a nasty scar that I henceforth could make no further claims to beauty'.[23] 'I must have been a hideous sight, my left ear hanging off in shreds, my cheek gaping open, and everything covered with a runny crust of blood and dirt', he went on: 'But I didn't have much time to do my toilette.'[24] It is difficult in such accounts to separate military bravado from insensitivity to violence. It is also true that victory at Borodino, which was hailed as 'a day of honour for the entire Russian army for all time', seemed to make suffering worthwhile, in spite of the cavalryman's own injuries and at least 40,000 dead or wounded on the Russian side.[25] However, the officer's tone in his diary is consistently matter-of-fact or nonchalant throughout, whether experiencing defeat or victory in the armies of Prussia, Britain, or Russia. It was redolent of a heroic adventure.

Despite incorporating repeated motifs and articulating common attitudes, the content and form of different types of testimony were surprisingly open, betraying the inchoate nature of this field of publishing. Plotho was not alone in lamenting that the 'wars of freedom' lacked a Schiller, unlike the Thirty Years' War.[26] Many authors seem to have been influenced, at least indirectly, by the conventions of the epic, embodied in eighteenth-century works such as Goethe's *Hermann und Dorothea* (1798), in which a hero struggles against fate within a chronicle serving as 'a "book of the tribe", a vital record of custom and tradition, and at the same time a story-book for general entertainment'.[27] 'The double relation of epic, to history on the one hand and to everyday reality on the other', had become more pronounced within war reports as a result of patriotic mobilization and popular representations of warfare.[28] As in the *Iliad* and *Beowulf*, the predicament of the hero in many accounts of the revolutionary and Napoleonic Wars appears to be external, as the soldier fights against impersonal opposing forces in the same way that individuals struggle against nature and, by their actions, against their own

---

[22] F. M. Kircheisen (ed.), *Wider Napoleon!*, vol. 1.   [23] Ibid., vol. 2, 137.
[24] Ibid., 139.   [25] Ibid., 142.
[26] K. v. Raumer, *Karl von Raumer's Leben von ihm selbst erzählt* (Stuttgart, 1866), 186. Also, H. v. Jordan, *Erinnerungsblätter*, 28, on the use of Schiller's verses in Wallenstein during the Napoleonic wars.
[27] P. Merchant, *The Epic* (London, 1971), 1.   [28] Ibid. See Chapter 2.

limitations.[29] Heroism, it could be held, resides in these accounts in the historical reputation—or eternalization—of the protagonist, as he defends the greater good of the tribe even at the risk—as in the cases of Achilles, Hector, and Beowulf—of his own extinction.[30] The notion of a wandering, introspective romantic hero, from the romances of the Middle Ages to the novels of the late eighteenth century, is overshadowed in the majority of accounts by that of an active one.

Many witnesses of combat also referred to battles as a 'drama' or *Schauspiel* and as a painting, with action staged or framed, occurring on a grand scale and intelligible only to an outside observer. Here, the incomprehensibility and repulsiveness of the spectacle seem to have provoked contradictory feelings of distance and fascination. Thus, for Christian von Martens, in Württemberg's contingent of the *Grande Armée*, the battle for Smolensk in 1812 was characterized by one 'storm' after another, 'with great loss and, for a long time, without success': 'the cries of the attackers, the ever increasing thunder of artillery and the constant fire of small arms, beside the thick cloud of gunpowder, made a cruel drama of the battlefield, strewn with corpses'.[31] On reaching Moscow, Martens saw 'the immeasurable city before us', 'still and silent, like a dead painting'.[32] The perceived significance or emotional immediacy of the events confronting commentators—mostly officers but also some civilians, on opposing sides and from different lands—provoked various responses, which went beyond the norms of a literary genre and revealed, however imperfectly, the sentimental, intellectual, and psychological dispositions of combatants.

HARD FACTS

Compared to later reportage, the letters, diaries, and memoirs of the soldiers of the revolutionary and Napoleonic Wars seem matter-of-fact. As in earlier eighteenth-century chronicles, a practical attitude to killing appears to have been combined with a heightened sense of military honour during the 1790s in accordance with the established practices of the main German armies. 'On the move!' wrote the young Hessian officer Wilhelm von Conrady in 1792 in his diary:

> What magical words these are for every soldier, and especially for the young cavalry officer! The perpetual solitude of peacetime service in the garrison is over, the boredom of days which all seem the same is over. . . . Reputation and honour beckon; in glorious attacks and bold patrols, one can show that one's arms are strong and one's eyesight is acute! No one thinks of death or wounding, illness and imprisonment, and it is good like this.[33]

---

[29] The classic analysis of this interpretation, contrasted with the heroes of romance, is W. P. Ker, *Epic and Romance* (London, 1896).

[30] Ferdinand von Varnbuler, *Beitrag zur Geschichtedes Feldzugs vom Jahr 1796*, 241, concluded that the campaign of 1796, which had 'again ended gloriously for the German army', had bestowed 'immortality' on 'the universally loved commander Grand Duke Karl of Austria'.

[31] C. v. Martens, *Vor fünfzig Jahren*, 104.   [32] Ibid., 133.

[33] W. v. Conrady, *Aus stürmischer Zeit*, 9. See also C. Klein to his father, 1 July 1794, *Kriegsbriefe* Archive, Universitäts- und Landesbibliothek Bonn: 'many Franks have been sent to another republic other than France in these last four days'.

The young Prussian officer Ludwig von Reiche, born in Hanover in 1775, left a similar record:

> One can easily imagine with what jubilation we greeted the first news of the happy victories of our arms, the capture of Longwy and Verdun! In our minds, we saw our troops on a victory parade before the gates of Paris. We only regretted that we, so close to the scenes of war, were not with them.[34]

Such elation disappeared as Reiche realized that the advance of the Coalition armies had been halted, with wounded soldiers starting to come back across the Rhine from Champagne: 'It was a pitiful sight to see those unfortunates in their lamentable condition.'[35] 'The sad course of the campaign of the Allies in Champagne in 1792 is well-known', wrote Conrady: 'Persistently bad weather; the disunity of the leaders; lack of care—of the worst sort—and maladies soon left the troops of the Allies in such a condition that they had to come back from Chalons via Trier and Coblenz and to cross the Rhine again as quickly as possible.'[36]

When Conrady's regiment had gone to war in 1792, 'I, too, dreamt of reputation and honour, promotion and decoration, without suspecting that this war would merely bring me, like so many others, endless punishments and disappointments', he noted: 'But anticipated military honours failed to come into being.'[37] Once the prospect of victory and glory had receded, soldiering reverted to a routine carrying out of duties and advancement, as another Prussian officer wrote home to his wife between 1794 and 1797, in the hope that 'this business will soon be over'.[38] 'God be praised that we have brought this year to an end, too', he declared on 31 December 1797:

> What can be a source of comfort for us in this is the fact that we don't have to look back on our actions in shame, but rather every one of us can stand forward proudly and without hesitation. One can only live happily in the reliable fulfilment of one's duties, and this, of course, is our communal desire, the fulfilment of which is closer to my heart than anything else.[39]

In these laconic reports of the 1790s, honour—and, indeed, a lack of honour—became a mundane affair and military manoeuvres a regular activity. Little mention was made of suffering, killing, and death. 'My strong body had overcome all trials successfully, but the depressing events of the last months had impressed themselves on my spirit', recorded Conrady simply.[40] After being taken prisoner by the French, he experienced 'the heavy burdens' of war and succumbed to a 'severe fever', losing consciousness and believing, 'in lucid moments, that the end

---

[34] L. v. Reiche, *Memoiren*, ed. L. v. Weltzien (Leipzig, 1857), 43.   [35] Ibid.
[36] W. v. Conrady, *Aus stürmischer Zeit*, 10.   [37] Ibid.
[38] M. v. Eberhardt (ed.), *Aus Preussens schwerer Zeit*, 13.
[39] Ibid., 15. Another business-like account of the revolutionary wars can be found in C. C. Zimmermann, *Geschichte des 1*, vol. 1, 16–85. Doing one's duty and not letting down relatives—especially fathers—at home were common motivations, as one official's son made plain in a letter home in 1794: C. Klein to his father, 12 Dec. 1794, *Kriegsbriefe* Archive, Universitäts- und Landesbibliothek Bonn.
[40] W. v. Conrady, *Aus stürmischer Zeit*, 10.

was near', yet he passed over this period of physical suffering, too, without further comment.[41]

The majority of the depictions of the wars of 1805 and 1806 diverged little from earlier narratives and descriptions.[42] One Prussian cavalry officer, who fought at Auerstädt, recalled how his father had taken leave of him in 1792, 'as if an inner premonition told him that he would find his death in this campaign'.[43] Having shed tears, despite never tolerating 'crying, even amongst children', his father nonetheless went on to tell his 'boy' to 'be brave' and 'become, if I should not see you again, a virtuous soldier who brings honour to our name'.[44] Military service at that time, reflected the officer in the mid-nineteenth century, 'was hard and strict, and one knew nothing of the luxury and softening, such as that which unfortunately is threatening to work its way increasingly into the army, too, in our times, was unknown at that time'.[45] Junkers, in particular, were brought up severely and sent off to the army, 'without the slightest thing being overlooked or excused'.[46] Correspondingly, during his first military action in 1806, skirmishing with French hussars, 'an unusual feeling pressed against my chest, as I now suddenly found myself opposite an enemy of much greater strength', but it 'lasted only a few seconds, then I drew my sabre and called to my own hussars: "Forwards, finally we have the Frenchmen we have been wanting", and so it went, under the jubilant cry of "Long live the King of Prussia", against the equally surprised enemy'.[47] In contrast to morale in the infantry, where some regiments had already witnessed 'critical levels of desertion' before the battle of Auerstädt, 'the mood in our cavalry regiment, indeed in the entire cavalry of Blücher's corps, was still good and bellicose'.[48]

In the battle itself, the 'thunder of heavy guns', mixed with that of rifles, 'increased our desire to fight', albeit counteracted by anxiety at 'the prevailing disorder'.[49] With some Prussian infantry in flight, the officer's regiment was ordered to attack French *tirailleurs*, 'whose bullets were already beginning to pester us':

> We surged forward at a gallop. The French sharpshooters shot down some amongst us and wounded several horses, but we pushed them back and struck down several dozen men. Several cavalrymen were so angry that they didn't think of granting pardons.[50]

In the next attack, the Prussians were shot down by French *carrés*, leaving 'the feeble remains of our squadrons in a wild flight' and 'the whole field around me full

---

[41] Ibid., 104. There were many examples of stoicism: C. Klein to his father, 12 Dec. 1794, *Kriegsbriefe* Archive, Universitäts- und Landesbibliothek Bonn: 'I prefer to bear my fate with patience and look forward to a happy future.'
[42] See M. v. Eberhardt (ed.), *Aus Preussens schwerer Zeit*, 61–3; C. v. Plotho, *Tagebuch*; C. C. Zimmermann, *Geschichte des 1*, 96–133; T. v. Barsewisch, *Geschichte des Grossherzolgich*, vol. 1, 1–60; W. v. Conrady, *Aus stürmischer Zeit*, 131–69; A. v. Blumröder, *Erlebnisse im Krieg und Frieden in der grossen Welt und in der kleinen Welt meines Gemüths* (Sondershausen, 1857), 23–31; L. v. Reiche, *Memoiren*, vol. 1, 166; K. v. Wedel, *Lebenserinnerungen 1793–1810* (Berlin, 1911), vol. 1, 32–47; G. v. Diest, *Aus der Zeit der Not und Befreiung Deutschlands in den Jahren 1806 bis 1815* (Berlin, 1905), 16–18, citing the diary of General v. Cardell.
[43] F. M. Kircheisen, *Wider Napoleon!*, 10.   [44] Ibid., 10.   [45] Ibid., 43.
[46] Ibid.   [47] Ibid., 90.   [48] Ibid., 91.   [49] Ibid., 93.   [50] Ibid., 95.

of dead or wounded men and horses'.[51] Tears streamed down the officer's cheeks: not out of pity for the dead, which were not referred to again, but 'out of anger' at the disorder of the Prussian army, which created within him a 'mood of desperation'.[52] This narrative coincided with others such as that of the young Prussian officer Karl von Suckow, who had also looked forward anxiously in 1806 to his 'baptism of fire', wanting 'to earn his spurs before the enemy':

> we wanted to show that we were worthy of serving in the ranks of an army which, under its great king, had so often fought for glory and victory; and no one doubted, at least amongst the younger generation, enthusiastic for the cause of Prussia, that this would finally be the result of this day, too.[53]

After the battles of Auerstädt and Jena were lost, panic ensued, as the remnants of the army streamed northward, plundering Prussian villages along the way and gathering in Magdeburg, where a 'very unappealing agitation' occurred, which was comparable to scenes at Vilnius during the retreat of the *Grande Armée* in 1812.[54] For officers at least, who remain the principal commentators, it was not the losses or, even, defeats of 1806 which were most galling, but the disorder of defeat. Wounding, killing, and dying seem to have been accepted as the normal activities of war: what caused distress to many officers was that they had not been carried out well.

The accumulation and escalation of the Napoleonic Wars of 1809, 1812, 1813–14, and 1815 moved many onlookers to alter their opinion of military conflict. Many soldiers, especially officers, continued to view combat as an honourable, sometimes heroic, but also as a technical, practical, and unexceptionable activity. Having entered the Bavarian army as a conscript in 1808, Friedrich Mändler left a typical record, based on contemporaneous notes, of his first fighting near the Danube in 1809:

> This fighting was the start of my life of actual war and struggle, and the first moment in which I stood opposite a killing abyss of fire. I openly acknowledge that I was unable to avoid, at this first taste, an anxious, if also only temporary, apprehension. A similar feeling affects everyone on their first contact or fighting with the enemy— something that truth-loving old men of war and comrades in arms would not deny. In addition, it is a fatal position for a soldier to be in when, as in this case at the edge of a wood, he remains immobile as cover for a battery and stands there, so to speak, serving merely as a target for the enemy, so that he hears—and has to hear—every bullet of the enemy. This affects the courage of an otherwise brave man in a quite different way from sorties on the training ground or on manoeuvres.[55]

The 17-year-old Wilhelm von Hochberg, the second son of the Grand Duke of Baden, gave a similar account of his first fighting in 1809, when he served as Masséna's adjutant. His tone was unemotional and his reporting supposedly factual, although written up—using his diary and other sources—in the decades after 1815. He experienced combat near Augsburg and then Landshut in late April, recording without further elaboration that 'the fighting began very violently' and

---

[51] Ibid., 97.   [52] Ibid., 101.   [53] K. v. Suckow, *Aus meinem Soldatenleben*, 64.
[54] Ibid., 69.   [55] F. Mändler, *Erinnerungen*, 6.

'the enemy's bullets struck us in thick volleys'.[56] As the French cavalry pushed forward and attacked, Hochberg noted that they left 'many a brave man' on the battlefield, but he passed over them to conclude that 'many soldiers gained rich pickings' from the 'machines of war' which had been left behind in this 'last struggle, which ended with the defeat of the enemy army'.[57] His detached reporting of events started to give way to expressions of feeling—above all, pity and repulsion—as the fighting continued and the casualties increased during May, June, and July, but his memoir remained a military history, interlaced with introspective recollections. It ended with a description of fighting on 9 July at Hollabrunn, which 'was taken after a bloody engagement', with Badenese troops playing a 'glorious part' despite 'considerable losses', and with a final attack by Austrian troops on 11 July, during which 'a cannonball ripped off the head of my neighbour, so that his brain sprayed me in the face': 'Since no gun would fire because of the rain, the [Austrian] battalion of grenadiers was soon taken prisoner, and the cavalry pushed on to Znaim', where they heard that a ceasefire had been declared.[58]

Such apparent indifference to wounding and death can be found in most accounts of 1809, including that of the Prussian writer and officer Rühle von Lilienstern, who had been forced to accompany the French forces against Austria, since he was the tutor of the King of Saxony's son. After a straightforward description of the battle of Wagram on 5–6 July, he recounted the death of a friend, injured during the fighting: '"Thank God", he said, "that I see you still standing . . . Who would have thought that I would die from indigestion; yet two bullets are too much even for the best stomach."'[59] 'However deeply the loss of a true friend and companion shook me', continued the writer, 'I was, at this moment, too affected by everything which was going on around me and I was too exhausted bodily to be able to give myself over, undivided, to a single mood.'[60] Rühle's depiction of the war went on unabated.

Reports of the 'ordeal' of 1812 were more mixed than those of previous wars, yet many were still matter-of-fact for the most part (see Map 4).[61] Although most diarists and memoirists paid tribute to the 'suffering' and 'horrors' of the battlefield, they did so only in passing. A good example was the young Mecklenburg officer, Otto von Raven, who barely mentioned combat at all in his letters to his wife, despite having just returned from the gruelling campaign in Russia in 1812. Most of his regiment had not returned, as he noted in a joint letter to the Duke of Mecklenburg:

As the small residue of the Mecklenburg contingent returned to the fatherland last year from the wasteland of the dead in Russia, it was still possible to entertain the faint

---

[56] Wilhelm, Markgraf v. Baden, *Denkwürdigkeiten*, vol. 1, 71.   [57] Ibid., 72.
[58] Ibid., 95, 97.
[59] J. J. O. A. Rühle von Lilienstern, *Reise mit der Armee 1809*, ed. J.-J. Langendorf (Vienna, 1986), 161.
[60] Ibid., 163.
[61] A good unpublished example is the 'Reisebuch' of Johann Wichterich, from Poppelsdorf, *Kriegsbriefe* Archive, Universitäts- und Landesbibliothek Bonn, who commented simply after finally meeting the 'enemy' (Russian troops): 'we were very hungry and looked at the dead bodies'.

hope that at least a part of those left behind would return one day. A full fifteen months have passed, however, and no one has appeared.[62]

'All—all have been stolen by that distant blood-curdling grave, which has swallowed thousands and hundreds of thousands', concluded the letter.[63] Yet, even in the privacy of his diary entries, Raven expressed very little disgust or complaint about his lot. On 7 December 1812, as the routed *Grande Armée* fled before the advancing Russian and allied forces, the officer was approached unexpectedly by a young man in civilian clothing who rubbed snow violently in his face in order to stop his nose getting frostbite. Raven's 'disgust' (*Entsetzen*) was directed at himself for failing, as a soldier, to notice his own plight.[64] He rushed back to the monastery where he had been staying, only to find its aisles full of dying soldiers whose clothes and shoes had been looted by their fellow soldiers. His comments were laconic: 'the frozen and starved were lying piled high on one another, partly having been brought in from adjacent rooms, partly having given up the ghost in front of the doors towards which they had struggled with the last effort of their expiring lives'.[65]

Throughout the invasion of Russia, in both summer and winter, the officer's diary entries were of a similar tenor, remarking at the siege of Vilno in August, for instance, that four 'robbers' and 'murderers' had been summarily executed by his own regiment, or recording at Valutina-Gora in October that the regiment had set up camp in the middle of the battlefield, surrounded by corpses, including that of 'a French field officer who had given up the ghost during an amputation', with the removed stump of his leg 'simply lying there'.[66] Corpses on the road generally showed the way to the advancing troops, with dead horses and humans 'in such a pile that they polluted the air'.[67] During the retreat, Raven commented detachedly that one of the first dead bodies which the troops had seen was a Polish lancer in a blue and red uniform: 'a powerful blow had cut the poorly fastened *Czapka* in two and had split the skull down to the mouth'.[68] As the Cossacks and other Russian troops attacked, 'we suffered a lot', he wrote on 21 November, 'but we could also stand a great deal, for we were already used to hardship'.[69] Raven's sole acknowledgement of discomfort was 'the sight of steaming cartridge cases coming out of the bodies' of executed opponents, which he found 'repugnant' (*widerlich*).[70] The rest of his diary is consistent with his later letters to his wife, in which he wrote—immediately after the blood-soaked battle of Leipzig in October 1813—that 'everything is going very well', apart from having to stand in 'terrible enemy fire' for three hours.[71] He was, he ended, proud to enjoy 'the friendship and trust of all his comrades'.[72]

---

[62] K.-U. Keubke (ed.), *Otto Gotthard Ernst von Raven: Tagebuch des Feldzuges in Russland im Jahre 1812* (Rostock, 1998), 177.

[63] Ibid.   [64] Ibid., 156.   [65] Ibid., 156–7.   [66] Ibid., 104 and 121.

[67] 20 and 21 July, ibid., 99.   [68] 23 Nov. 1812, ibid., 137.   [69] Ibid., 136.

[70] Ibid., 104.

[71] Benno von Knobelsdorff-Brenkenhoff, *Briefe aus den Befreiungskriegen. Ein Beitrag zur Situation von Truppe und Heimat in den Jahren 1813/14* (Zurich, 1998), 192.

[72] Ibid.

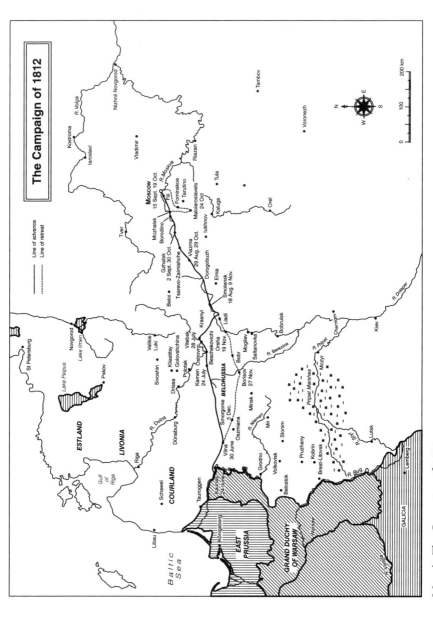

Map 4. The Campaign of 1812

Source: D. Lieven, *Russia against Napoleon: The True Story of the Campaigns of War and Peace* (London, 2010), xviii–xix.

Such testimony, which seemed to betray hardiness or even indifference to suffering and violence, remained common until 1815 and beyond.[73] It derived from several sources, including the harsh conditions of life in *ancien régime* armies. Most officers accepted unsentimentally that war involved losses and death. The majority of their reports alternated between tactical details and references to killing, in the manner of Gneisenau's correspondence about the 'wars of liberation', which praised the 'courage of our troops' at the same time as noting that the fighting had 'cost a lot of blood'.[74] Karl von Wedel's description of the campaign of 1806 was similar, notwithstanding an often-perceived distinction between victory in 1813 and defeat seven years earlier. At Auerstädt, his horse was shot in the mouth, leaving the Prussian officer to make his way back between the two armies, 'on which dangerous route a *tirailleur* stabbed me through my tunic and undergarments, without really wounding me' and, 'finally, a cannonball, which caught my hat and plume, deafened me and ripped me from my horse'.[75] Returning to another battalion, he was put in charge of 'a crowd of assorted people, from different regiments and in flight', who were asked to cover the flank of another attack.[76] 'This attack, however, went badly, and the battalion was repelled with such great losses that it did not think of carrying out a second one', he continued: 'My people, who had likewise lost many, again fled in different directions.'[77] Returning to his own brigade, 'I heard with pain that my father and brother had been brought back fatally injured', leaving him to start the retreat with a 'remorseful heart', yet he went on immediately to record the number of dead and wounded of the battle in formulaic terms, not the death of his closest relatives, with the defeat described as 'this terrible news'.[78]

It was common in such reports to turn, without comment, from descriptions of violence to mundane details of a campaign. Thus, the Bavarian Major-General Maximilian von Preysing-Moos wrote in his diary on 20 August 1812 that he had to march through Smolensk, 'where I saw nothing but smoking ruins and thousands of dead and dismembered corpses', before going on in the same sentence to remark that he had crossed the River Dneipr and continued on his way.[79] Two days earlier, at Polozk, another Bavarian officer, Joseph Maillinger, had talked in similarly unexpansive terms of a battlefield 'strewn with dead and wounded from both sides', before proceeding to note drily that the battle had lasted from four o'clock to half-past nine and then revealing that 200 guns had been trained on a small area

---

[73] See, for example, H. v. Brandt (ed.), *Aus dem Leben*; Louis von Weltzien (ed.), *Ludwig von Reiche. Memoiren*; Joachim Kannicht, *Und alles wegen Napoleon. Aus dem Kriegstagebuch des Georg von Coulon, 1760–1815* (Coblenz, 1986).

[74] 3 and 7 Oct. 1813, in J. v. Pflugk-Hartung (ed.), *Briefe des Generals Neidhardt von Gneisenau 1809–1815* (Gotha, 1913), 131–2.

[75] K. v. Wedel, *Lebenserinnerungen*, 43. Ordinary soldiers like Wichterich, 'Reisebuch', *Kriegsbriefe* Archive, Universitäts- und Landesbibliothek Bonn, gave similar accounts.

[76] K. v. Wedel, *Lebenserinnerungen*, 44.   [77] Ibid.   [78] Ibid., 46.

[79] M. v. Preysing-Moos, 'Tagebuch des Generalmajors Graf von Preysing-Moos, Fuehrer der Bayerischen Kavallerie-Division im Felzuge nach Russland 1812', *Darstellungen aus der Bayerischen Kriegs- und Heeresgeschichte*, 21 (1912), 32.

with 'murderous' effect.[80] Although this type of juxtaposition is characteristic of diaries, it also suggests that the violence of battle was unexceptionable, even if unusual. Accordingly, the autobiographical records of the seventeenth and eighteenth centuries had rarely mentioned wounding at all.[81] As one young Prussian officer, serving in France's army in Spain, put it: in battle, 'one can only be shot or wounded'.[82] 'In war, where human life has such a low value, one pays little attention to it and often treats it lightly', wrote another after the battle of Leipzig in October 1813.[83]

In many instances, senior officers appeared less concerned by the prospect of wounding and death than their juniors, despite being much closer to combat than their counterparts in later conflicts.[84] Many were killed, including Gerhard Johann Scharnhorst and the Duke of Brunswick (*Braunschweig*). When the former—Carl von Müffling's own superior—had died after the battle of Großgörschen in May 1813, the memoirist had 'seen him in the evening after the battle for the last time; he considered his wounds of no consequence and hoped soon to rejoin the army'.[85] Scharnhorst's insouciance had not been justified and he had died shortly afterwards in Prague. At the death of the latter, Müffling was also present: 'For me was reserved the heart-rending meeting with the Duke on his bed in Braunschweig, with bloody bandages over his sightless orbits, and the equally melancholy sight of his body on the day of his death in Ottensen', recorded Müffling, who was serving in the royal headquarters: 'With deep pain I viewed the remains of a Prince who, since the Seven Years' War, had played such an important part in the history of the world, who possessed many great and excellent qualities, and deserved a better fate.'[86] But Müffling's melancholy was arguably prompted by the Prussian army's loss of a great commander more than by the Duke's suffering per se. Certainly, this was the impression given by one of Brunswick's successors in the 'wars of freedom', General Gebhardt Leberecht von Blücher, who was injured in May 1813, but who was more concerned that the French forces had been defeated. 'Whatever news you have received, please don't worry, for although I got three bullets and also had my horse shot from under me, it is not dangerous, and I am and remain fully active', he wrote to his wife shortly afterwards: 'I have satisfaction enough that I attacked Herr Napoleon two times and both times pushed him back. The battle was so murderous that both sides were exhausted and both lacked ammunition. ... I got a shot in the back, which is very painful. I'll bring you the bullet.'[87] Thus, although

---

[80] J. Maillinger, 'Tagebuch des Hauptmannes Jospeh Maillinger im Feldzug nach Russland 1812', *Darstellungen*, 97.

[81] M. Dinges, 'Soldatenkörper in der Frühen Neuzeit. Erfahrungen mit einem unzureichend geschützten, formierten und verletzten Körper in Selbstzeugnissen', in R. van Dülmen (ed.), *Körper-Geschichten* (Frankfurt, 1996), 89.

[82] H. v. Brandt (ed.), *Aus dem Leben*, vol. 1, 281.   [83] L. v. Reiche, *Memoiren*, 345.

[84] A. Adam, *Aus dem Leben eines Schlachtenmalers*, 185, comments that even Prince Eugène de Beauharnais, Napoleon's adopted son and heir to the Kingdom of Italy, could be found in the thick of the fighting in 1812.

[85] C. v. Müffling, *The Memoirs of Baron von Müffling: A Prussian Officer in the Napoleonic Wars* (London, 1997), 32.

[86] Ibid., 18.   [87] W. Capelle (ed.), *Blüchers Briefe* (Leipzig, n. d.), 41.

they were involved in the thick of the fighting, officers like Blücher were prepared to countenance large-scale loss of life, even if this also included their own. None of the officers made many references to common soldiers, other than to say that they would desert or flee, if conditions were bad.[88] There is little indication that either generals or statesmen took much notice of the vast bulk of their armies, much of which had been recruited from amongst the poor and the powerless.

The reactions of ordinary soldiers to violence are difficult to judge, given the dearth of written evidence, but they were likely to have been at least partly conditioned by the harshness of life and the severity of discipline within the various armies. The introduction of new articles of war in Prussia in 1808 was heralded as an act of humanity, but the articles continued to sanction corporal punishment, 'severe arrest', and a range of death penalties. There would always be a place, declared Gneisenau, for 'sensitive disciplining'.[89] Before 1808, and in other armies, 'invective, beatings in the stocks and other harsh corporal punishments' remained in place.[90] Thus, when the Bavarian commander Wrede lamented

> that it is not the right moment to train soldiers in times of war, that one cannot demand the peasant becomes a soldier immediately, even if you put a soldier's tunic on him, give him a musket to carry on his back and make him march, and that such people can neither be made to put up with exhaustion nor be receptive to feelings of honour, patience and hardship

he was acknowledging that such disciplining, which distinguished the military from the civilian sphere, occurred routinely within armies under normal conditions.[91] One soldier, who joined the Prussian army voluntarily during peacetime and initially served in the ranks after the turn of the century, noted that he 'adapted to the unaccustomed compulsion', with 'habit' making 'the many hardships and limitations of natural freedom, which soldiery inevitably brings with it, less oppressive'.[92] To Joseph Schrafel, conscripted against his will into the ranks of the Bavarian army in 1807, the soldier's life, which was greeted as 'a strike of lightning', meant that 'all sustenance, every expectation of future well-being, all sweet hopes, in which we indulged, were at once destroyed'.[93] 'What sudden deprivation after—for someone from my estate (*Stand*)—a happy, even overflowing, way of life', he went on:

> And what a terrible prospect before me. At that time, military institutions were not as humane as they are now. Ordinary soldiers were almost entirely at the mercy of crude, often cruel NCOs. The regulations were extremely severe. Barely a day passed without corporal punishment. Not infrequently, it was used for quite inconsequential infractions, which would now be punished only with a warning. Thus, the terror and anxiety of the people for the life of the soldier was universal. One imagined the evil to be even greater than it really was. I thought of myself as a condemned criminal.

[88] See, for instance, F. M. Kircheisen (ed.), *Wider Napoleon!*, 91.
[89] G. Förster and C. Gudzent (eds), *Gneisenau. Ausgewählte militärische Schriften*, 116.
[90] J. F. v. Koenen report, 26 May 1808, in R. Vaupel (ed.), *Die Reorganisation*, part 2, vol. 1, 431.
[91] Wrede, 9 Nov. 1812, cited in J. Murken, *Bayerische Soldaten im Russlandfeldzug 1812*, 143.
[92] A. v. Blumröder, *Erlebnisse im Krieg und Frieden*, 23.
[93] J. Schrafel, *Merkwürdige Schicksale*, 6.

Outwardly, I behaved calmly and quietly, but an indescribable feeling of anxiety, a dull melancholy, which moved me to apathy, had gained control of me internally.[94]

Discipline was strictly enforced, with one general threatening the Swabian officer Christian von Martens with arrest in late July 1812 during the disastrous campaign in Russia because one of his men, suffering from dysentery, had not tightened his belt.[95] Usually, soldiers refrained from showing their emotions, despite their 'fears of death' and 'of coming things'.[96] One corporal admitted to his wife that 'tears and suffering are my daily bread', but he also remarked that he was 'no longer' ashamed of such displays of feeling, 'for you and my children are fully worthy of them'.[97] Toughness and taciturnity were arguably more typical. 'We were scarcely down there when it started again—boom, boom, boom—and the cannon shots greeted us so regularly that I had soon had enough, I was so hungry', wrote the Rhenish soldier Johann Wichterich phlegmatically in his 'travel diary' in 1812: 'But there were some amongst us who had had quite enough, when their heads flew in the air and their legs danced around on the floor. I thought I had eaten my last bit of army bread there, but I hadn't.'[98] One Austrian soldier, who had been 'half forced' into the army in 1809, gave an insight into how combatants mourned their dead after the battle of Aspern: 'The conversation at the fire of the watch turned partly on the dangers overcome and was partly devoted to the commemoration of missing comrades, with each making an observation about how this or that comrade had found his death or, as a wounded soldier, had left the ranks of combatants.'[99] 'These reminiscences were the only commemoration of the dead which we could bring ourselves to mount for our fallen brothers', he concluded.[100] Even though the fallen were like 'brothers', the soldiers' response to their death, perhaps because of exhaustion or the frequency of mourning, was matter-of-fact.

The rank and file of German armies were still seen to be expendable, as the increased levels of killing of the Napoleonic Wars had demonstrated. Napoleon himself, who combined the toughness of a career officer with the hierarchical attitudes of the *ancien régime*, had boasted of the numbers of troops which he was prepared to sacrifice in his struggle for supremacy. In Germany and elsewhere, reports of war losses routinely distinguished between commanders, who were usually named, officers, who were sometimes named and always treated as a separate group, and 'men', whose losses—frequently in the thousands—were merely counted or not mentioned at all. In regimental histories and in the individual accounts on which such histories rested, troops were a military resource, often enumerated in the same sentence as horses and pieces of artillery.[101] Friedrich Giesse, a 24-year-old junior

---

[94] Ibid., 6–7.   [95] C. v. Martens, *Vor fünfzig Jahren*, vol. 1, 81.
[96] Grasmann, *Tagebuch*, 20 Oct. 1812, and Layrer to his wife, 19 May 1812, cited in J. Murken, *Bayerische Soldaten*, 140.
[97] Layrer to his wife, 1 Mar. 1812, ibid., 144.
[98] Johann Wichterich, 'Reisebuch', *Kriegsbriefe* Archive, Universitäts- und Landesbibliothek Bonn.
[99] F. A. Brandner, *Aus dem Tagebuch eines österreichischen Soldaten im Jahre 1809* (Löbau, n. d.), 65.
[100] Ibid.
[101] Johann David von Dziengel, *Geschichte des Koeniglichen Zweiten Ulanen-Regiments* (Potsdam, 1858), 343, on the losses of the battle of Leipzig.

officer in the Westphalian army in 1812, provided insights into the way in which ordinary soldiers were viewed, noting laconically on 20 August that there were 8,000 casualties on the Russian side, along with 1,200 prisoners taken, 5,000 on 'this side', together with 400 prisoners.[102] At the battle of Borodino in early September, Giesse reported that the Westphalian contingent, which was '12,200 men strong', was composed of an 'infantry of 9,870 men, a cavalry of 1,530 men, foot artillery of 474 artillerymen, a mounted artillery of 56 artillerymen, 229 supply soldiers and 493 horses' and it went on to sustain a 'loss of nearly 500 dead and 3,500 wounded', including '18 officers killed, amongst whom were Generals Lepel and Damas', and 146 officers wounded, amongst whom were Generals Tharreau, Hammerstein, and Borstel, 'of whom many had since died of their wounds'.[103]

Likewise, the Swabian officer Christian von Martens, who proved in his diary entries to be particularly close to his men, remarked that the 'French' forces had lost 'at least 15,000 men' and 'the enemy' 'at most 10,000 men' in three days of fighting at Smolensk in August 1812:

> Generals Friant, Dolton, Grandjean and Zajonschek were wounded, Grabowski remained on the field. From ours [Württemberg's contingent], Captain v. Herwig and Lieut. v. Rüdt; General v. Koch, Lieut.-Colonel v. Bartruff and v. Bauer, Major v. Seybold, Captains v. Notter, v. Schaumberg and v. Woldenfels, die Lieuts. v. Rottenhof, v. Dobeneck, v. Parrot und v. Wächter—the last died several days later. The loss of NCOs and soldiers amounted to 684 men. The enemy lost 2 generals and several were wounded.[104]

As the Russians withdrew, the losses on either side from continued fighting were 'roughly the same', with 6,000 dead and wounded.[105] Martens again listed the names of all Württemberg's wounded officers but omitted to give the number of dead and wounded troops.[106] A similar tally was provided after Borodino. By the time of the 'victory' parade in Moscow on 20 September, which the officer conceded was no cause for pride, only 1,000 men from Württemberg's initial contingent of 16,000 were present, yet Martens had made few allusions to such a depletion of forces and he passed over the harrowing statistics on this occasion without further comment.[107] Such apparent callousness was consistent with the strict division between largely noble officers and 'men'. Under the special conditions of the retreat from Moscow in October, November, and December 1812, this division broke down, with Napoleon's order that only officers and armed soldiers be allowed to cross the pontoon bridge at Beresina on 27 November proving unenforceable. After that point, Martens continued,

> we dragged ourselves laboriously through great forests and over fields of snow, the entire brotherhood of arms; every feeling of humanity and pity disappeared before the

[102] F. Giesse, *Kassel—Moskau—Kuestrin 1812–1813*, ed. Karl Giesse (Leipzig, 1912), 109.
[103] Ibid., 123. K. v. Wedel, *Lebenserinnerungen*, 44–6, gives a similar account for the Prussian army, listing dead and wounded officers at the battle of Auerstädt but not giving the number of casualties amongst the rank and file.
[104] C. v. Martens, *Vor fünfzig Jahren*, vol. 1, 101.   [105] Ibid., 105.   [106] Ibid.
[107] Ibid., 142.

instinctive drive for survival; one saw only faces bearing the marks of hunger, cold and the smoke of the camp fire; many generals and higher officers were lost in the mass and were pleased to be able to warm themselves before the bivouac fires of the soldiers and to be able to find protection from the barbarities of the Cossacks amongst them.[108]

Normally, though, officers had not been part of the mass, as the Swabian officer had hinted at the start of the 1812 campaign, when he had been billeted in burgher's houses, the castles of Polish aristocrats, and even in hotels, complete with *table d'hôte*.[109] By 1813, the distinction between officers and men had been re-established.[110]

The expendability of ordinary soldiers derived in part from the distance between ranks in eighteenth- and early nineteenth-century societies. This sense of distance was most evident within royal courts and state governments, whose willingness to dispose of and sacrifice their subjects' lives surpassed that of the officer corps. Carl Bodo von Bodenhausen, who had been a courtier of the Queen of Westphalia between 1807 and 1811 before becoming a servant of the king and an officer, left a telling record of how insulated such circles were from the suffering of combatants. Having followed Jérôme, the new King of Westphalia, to Moscow in 1812, the courtier observed the retreat from the Russian city from the vantage point of his carriage, although walking during the day to save his horses. Thus, when he described 'the attacks of the Russians almost every day from all sides', causing the army to lose, 'through frost and hunger, as well as in constant fighting, all of its equipment and its horses', he was speaking as an outsider, who spent 'the nights by a bivouac fire or in my carriage, wrapped in several furs which I had bought. I was lucky enough to buy several poor-quality items of food and also received some in the imperial headquarters.'[111] At the river crossing at Beresina in late November, as the entire *Grande Armée* was trapped by the river, Bodo von Bodenhausen finally had to leave his carriage and his servants, crossing the bridge on foot with all his gold and some beans to eat. Just before his departure, he reported detachedly how 'a cannonball landed between me and the cook and tore off his lower leg'.[112] The cook had had 'the courage to ask for his kitchen knife...in order to cut off his destroyed leg completely'.[113] The crush to get over the bridge was so great that the courtier had had to wade through the freezing water and then ask a French guard— 'very politely'—to be allowed to cross.[114] Once on the other side, he had found the other Westphalian forces, having bought and plundered food, and he had prevailed on the commander, a relative, to allow him to travel in advance of the main army, together with a Westphalian officer and a Polish soldier, who could translate for them. They left the army on 3 December, avoided the poorly policed Russian lines, and travelled on French courier horses, paying for nights in individuals' houses and inns. Having procured a carriage in Vilnius, they made their way with

---

[108] Ibid., 209, 218.   [109] Ibid., 6–39.

[110] Amongst many sources, this can be seen in the second volume of C. v. Martens, *Vor fünzig Jahren*.

[111] C. Bodo von Bodenhausen, *Tagebuch eines Ordonnanzoffiziers von 1812–1813*, ed. B. v. Cramm (Braunschweig, 1912), 27–8.

[112] Ibid., 30–1.   [113] Ibid.   [114] Ibid., 32.

three horses and supplies of food to Warsaw, where, because 'we were all extremely tired', they 'rested for five to six days in a guesthouse'.[115] They then rode to Berlin by 28 December in another carriage acquired in Warsaw. The picture which the courtier painted of life behind the Russian lines was tranquil and comfortable, in contrast to the horrific conditions within the retreating *Grande Armée*, from which Bodo von Bodenhausen had been protected, with the exception of the crossing of the Beresina itself. Although physically close to the suffering of soldiers, the courtier remained socially detached.

CITIZEN-SOLDIERS

Not all onlookers were as indifferent to the fate of ordinary soldiers as Bodo von Bodenhausen. National-minded soldiers from the middling strata, a number of whom joined units of volunteers such as the Lützower corps, were more conscious of the fate of the ranks. In contrast to regular troops, these 'volunteers' (*Freiwillige*) came preponderantly from towns, not the countryside, with manual workers and journeymen making up 40 per cent of their number and the 'educated orders' 12 per cent.[116] It is possible that just under half of all Prussian students had joined units of volunteers—constituting 5 per cent of the total—by the summer of 1814, when *Freiwillige* comprised 30,000 troops of Prussia's total force of 280,000.[117] It is likely that educated sections of society were similarly over-represented amongst Bavaria's 6,000 volunteer soldiers and 230 volunteer officers, who enlisted in late 1813 and early 1814.[118] Although such soldiers carried out peripheral military duties, they enjoyed significant public support and played a significant symbolic role, prompting Napoleon to order troops from Württemberg to attack the Lützow corps during the summer ceasefire of 1813 and provoking one of the troops' German commanders to protest, ultimately in vain, that 'it is not right to move against these people in hostility'.[119] Certainly, Prussian officials talked of the volunteer corps without further explanation, for the benefit of a wider 'public', as part of the army.[120] The corps were supplemented by the recruitment of 12,000 cavalry (*Jäger*) and by the formation of the *Landwehr*, which came to number 120,000 conscripts in Prussia. By the end of the Napoleonic Wars, many other German states had created similar forces, albeit with varying functions and in different states of readiness. Bavaria, for instance, already had a National Guard of 10,000 men in late 1813.[121]

---

[115] Ibid., 39.
[116] P. Brandt, 'Das Freikorps Lützow', in J. Dülffer (ed.), *Kriegsbereitschaft und Friedensordnung*, 214.
[117] Ibid.   [118] U. Planert, *Der Mythos*, 600.
[119] O. Gerhardt, *Die Württemberger*, 63. They were later forced to attack the Lützow corps anyway, ibid., 67–9.
[120] T. to A. v. Schön, 1 May 1813, in G. A. Klausa (ed.), *'Sehnlich erwarte ich die morgende Post'*, 113 (Cologne, 2005).
[121] See Chapter 1. On the readiness of the Bavarian *Landwehr*, see G. Kirchmayer, *Veteranen-Huldigung*, 65–6.

The conditions in these units were often chaotic, relying on the recruitment of old soldiers and officers, whose methods were ten to twenty years out of date and whose training often amounted to little more than 'a military manner and a mechanical, once-inculcated, rudimentary capability', in the words of Wilhelm von Knobelsdorff, who was responsible for raising a cavalry squadron in the Prussian Neumark during the summer of 1813.[122] The *Landwehr* lacked money to pay the troops, material to manufacture their uniforms, manual labour, surgeons, guns, shell cases, and pots and pans, he continued: 'And yet, gradually, they succeeded.'[123] Knobelsdorff sometimes felt like a pawn, being moved around northern Germany in 1813, but he eventually took part in the battle of Leipzig, where he won an iron cross, which 'brought me great joy'.[124] Although he had persuaded former officers out of retirement and had recruited 'day labourers, tailors and carpenters etc.' who had already served in the army, he had also had to muster a much wider range of men, who—like conscripts in the regular army—came from most sections of society.[125] Some of these new recruits saw the wars of 1813–15 in a patriotic or national light. Even those disillusioned with the *Freiwillige* such as Friedrich Rückert, who—after earlier support—had come to denounce the Lützow corps as the 'crashed toy of the *Burschen*' and to declare himself merely 'for the Franks' and not for Prussia by May 1815, continued to consider it their duty to join the *Landwehr*, remaining in contact with and speaking on behalf of ordinary soldiers and citizens.[126]

For a vocal minority of combatants, war seemed to offer the possibility of patriotic or national regeneration through the necessity of much wider participation and mobilization.[127] Henrich Steffens, a Norwegian who had been to university in Germany and had become a professor at the University of Halle, gave a good, if contested, impression of new attitudes to and conditions of war which such participation had caused. Like many of his contemporaries, the physicist was 'not indifferent to the political conditions of Europe' during the late 1790s and early 1800s, sympathizing with the Jacobins, but he remained oblivious 'of a political present which would demand action', viewing politics as 'doctrine, theory, principle and future'.[128] Prussia's defeat by French forces in 1806 altered his view, proving that the state was the repository of power and an expression of popular will. Until then, the violence of the state, despite being 'the most vital source of enthusiasm', had resembled 'sources which have no outlet and, hidden by the mountain, stay on the inside'.[129] 'A belligerent, national feeling' had been 'the burgeoning source of life

---

[122] B. v. Knobelsdorff-Brenkenhoff, *Briefe aus den Befreiungskreigen*, 32.   [123] Ibid.
[124] Ibid., 90.   [125] Ibid., 32.
[126] F. Rückert to F. Schubart, 2 May 1813, in F. Rückert, *Briefe* (Schweinfurt, 1977), vol. 1, 72.
[127] Their sentiments were shared by at least some private correspondents and were not merely a matter of 'publicity'. Johann Gottlieb Carl Krahnert, 'Tagebuch', *Kriegsbriefe* Archive, Universitäts- und Landesbibliothek Bonn, was not unusual in talking of 'Germany, especially Prussia, [which] had sighed for long years under the forced rule of the French Kaiser.' 'Napoleon's continuing, planned oppression had no end, he placed no limits on his demands. Thus, the desire to become free of the slaves' shackles had sunk deep into the breast of every German.'
[128] H. Steffens, *Was ich erlebte*, 163.   [129] Ibid.

of the people (*Volk*)', he went on, but 'it had lost all higher significance' within succeeding regimes:

> The national, belligerent feeling, which was not to be articulated, became more and more powerfully pressing, more and more elastic, under external pressure, and a calm awareness emerged that the popular-belligerent sense would also have to infuse and revive the military one, if the state were to be regenerated by a new enlivening form out of the existing discredited one. Each true Prussian citizen began to realise that all higher spiritual and material interests were tied directly to a belligerent spirit.[130]

A national campaign led by Prussia in the name of Germany made war 'holy' for Steffens, helping to offset his greater sensitivity to and lack of knowledge of combat: 'From now on, it became, as it were, an axiom of my civilian (*bürgerlich*) life, the most sacred thing to me, that Germany in the most eminent sense could only be saved by the Prussian state.'[131] Thus, when he did become acquainted with war, as French troops entered the sleepy Prussian town of Halle in 1806, Steffens remained certain that the events had a greater purpose. 'It is, in my opinion, unfair to pay so little attention to the manifestations of civilian life when it is pressed by the circumstances of war', he wrote:

> The game of war in recent times has, in its harsh form, excluded all poetry, but the excited emotions of the oppressed nation (*Volk*) visible on many thousands of countenances, the rapid transition from fear to hope and back again, ... allow signs of the most secret life to come to light and have, we should believe, themselves an historical significance.[132]

'The terrible collapse of the country and the irreversible destruction, so it seemed, of everything which was sacred and dear to us loomed before our souls like a dark mass of the most diverse, sinister imaginings', helping to transform subjects' opinions of war and the state.[133] By his own reckoning, Steffens was one of many educated burghers to alter their estimation of 'the Prussian soldier, this slave-like hireling', who had enjoyed 'no respect amongst the people'.[134]

Steffens's response to the 'particular, anxious feeling' of subjugation 'to a foreign power' was to form a unit of volunteers, sanctioned by Scharnhorst and the King of Prussia.[135] Thousands, according to his own recollection, tried to join.[136] Unlike Jahn, who was recruiting the Lützower corps at the same time in Breslau, where the Norwegian academic had taken up a post, Steffens avoided 'utterances about the future shape of Germany', which were 'doubly suspect because they were being expressed—not rarely—by the most noble, courageous and daring men', and he recruited soldiers for the *Landwehr* as part of the regular army, 'even though I was not ignorant of the value of this free element' of the *Freiwillige*.[137] 'It was not difficult for me to make our youth believe that they would be closer to the most important events serving in the regular army (*in dem grossen Heere*)', he continued: 'I believed ... that my age and position allowed ... me to turn to where the great, ordered masses, led by outstanding army commanders, had to decide the momentous

---

[130] Ibid., 163–4. [131] Ibid., 164. [132] Ibid., 168. [133] Ibid., 174.
[134] Ibid., 165. [135] Ibid., 166. [136] Ibid., 333. [137] Ibid., 334.

fate of the peoples.'[138] A regular army was more likely to win, he calculated. Nevertheless, Steffens and others like him were convinced that German armies and German public opinion had changed, becoming national, patriotic, or, at least, popular:

> For the first time, as the pressure of an enemy, rightly vanquishing its slaves, as institutions were affected, threatened to thwart that burgeoning national idea, that anticipation of a special civic freedom in the innermost core of the soul, the original character of the *Volk* close to collapse, began to oppose the pressure, elastically, with a counter-pressure. The war was not one which—entered into superficially by a ruler—was fought out by an unwilling group of men: it was decided on by every honourable man; it was borne many thousands, after every one had declared it self-evident. How the internal moral struggles of every person oscillate uncertainly so that the combatant is uncertain about where to turn, and enemies remain concealed from one's own camp, until the point comes when the question forces itself upon him as to whether he can be saved morally or whether he should give up. ... So, the moment of a great, pure opposition became manifest; the question which confronted everyone was strict, clear and decisive, but the answer also had to be the same. It is well-known that a large part of Germany was still allied to Napoleon, that Germans fought against Germans still, encouraged and dominated by France, as during the disastrous Thirty Years' War: but how very different things were now. What could never become clear in the fatefully murky, internally confused conditions of the ruined German Reich now manifested itself very decisively: the opposition between France and Germany was no longer in doubt.[139]

The 'historical greatness' of Napoleon, wrote Steffens, rested on the fact that he had obliged 'every German' to decide whether he wanted to prostrate himself completely before French forces or maintain his independence.[140] 'This moral, even religious, civic renaissance would not, admittedly, be an absolutely purifying one, even if obstacles were successfully overcome', he concluded: 'But a national transformation had taken place.'[141] Although its course and outward aims often appeared contradictory, a war 'only had a meaning for me insofar as it was animated by that which inspired me internally'.[142] It was too early, in Steffens's opinion, to wage war for explicitly and narrowly national aims, but it was necessary to recognize 'what I would call the legitimate mass of war'.[143] The struggle against France had become a matter of concern to the mass of the people, with burghers serving as soldiers for the first time. Thus, 'I regarded it as an excellent, fortunate circumstance of the great era in which we lived that the more educated youth of the higher orders mixed with those of the lower orders', he recalled: 'the latter felt themselves honoured in this way, and a morally formative element, as I hoped, was bound to enter into the mass of warriors, albeit slowly, and raise them up'.[144] Everyone wore the same uniform and considered themselves equal 'throughout the whole war'.[145] From this point of view, the experiences and the lives of ordinary soldiers had become more visible and more valuable.

---

[138] Ibid., 334–5.   [139] Ibid., 341.   [140] Ibid.   [141] Ibid., 342.
[142] Ibid.   [143] Ibid., 334.   [144] Ibid., 333.   [145] Ibid.

The available accounts of volunteers suggest that they were motivated to fight, but also that they were profoundly affected by the actual conditions and violence of combat. Heinrich Bolte, a student of theology from Fehrbellin near Berlin, was a volunteer in a *Jäger* detachment of fusiliers. His diary of 1813 reveals his early excitement at the prospect of following 'the call of my besieged fatherland' (23 February), leaving his beloved family with a heroic 'Lebt wohl'.[146] 'What were his thoughts', he asked rhetorically as he rode over his first battlefield on 6 March: 'Oh, I shall experience the bloody erasure of the name of Auerstädt from the annals of Prussia! How many of my brothers will have fallen by that time!'[147] Despite being homesick, he still welcomed the spilling of blood, rejoicing in his metamorphosis from civilian to soldier: 'How the times have changed! Earlier destined by fate to be a herald of peace, now I am seeking to do everything to spill blood in abundance' (8 April). The commencement of fighting, reported verbally to his regiment, was greeted excitedly—'Now the course is set'—and seen, once more, as an opportunity to 'wipe the stain of shame of Jena from the bloody table of history' (11 April).[148] Bolte was prepared to put up with worsening homesickness—'I have never felt such a longing for my *Heimat* as I have during the last days' (14 April)— and to endure 'all these hardships' (15 April), including forced marches, for the sake of his 'loved ones back home'.[149] Thus, when his regiment was told 'that it would certainly come down to battle today', 'All welcomed this news with joy.'[150] His experience of the battle of Groß-Görschen on 2 May, after coming under fire at two o'clock, began to alter his opinion of warfare, however:

> The major ordered an attack on the burning village of Klein-Görschen, where the French were defending themselves like desperate men. We took it and now shot at fences and graves, in the process of which I received three shots through my clothing. The rain of bullets was terrible. ...At about 5 o'clock we left the village again and gathered in a wood behind a small rise, with only 30 men remaining. The terrible bullets had raged to such an extent. The field was covered with corpses and wounded men. We Prussians have few dead, but many injured; the French, the reverse. Here, I received another two shots, which did no damage, but I got another in my right foot, during another advance, which wounded me. I limped forwards slowly now and met a Russian battalion, whose chief embraced me and told me to be brave in broken German. In this way, I fled from danger. With rock-steady trust in you, my God, I went into the fire. I wasn't mistaken. I have not yet seen your protecting hand with greater wonderment. It is a wonder that I'm alive. God, I thank you with an inflamed heart. How my parents will rejoice when they hear from me. How anxious and troubled they will be until they learn of it.[151]

Battle had been so shocking that only a strong faith in God, previously unmentioned, gave it meaning. Bolte rarely mentioned his fatherland after this point,

---

[146] H. Lem von Zieten (ed.), *Tagebuch von Heinrich Bolte, Adjutant Blüchers 1813–14* (Berlin, n. d.), 14. See also W. Krimer, *Erinnerungen eines alten Lützower Jägers*, vol. 2, 27–69, and C. E. V. Krieg (ed.), *Vor fünfzig Jahren. Tagebuch eines freiwilligen Jägers der Jahre 1813 und 1814* (Wesel, 1863), who give similar accounts.
[147] H. Lem von Zieten (ed.), *Tagebuch*, 14.   [148] Ibid., 15.   [149] Ibid., 16.
[150] Ibid., 25.   [151] Ibid., 25–6.

other than as an object of pity and lament: 'The road was covered with the wounded and with troops. Five Russian cavalry regiments went by, God knows where to. I am in a terrible state of unrest. My poor, poor fatherland, will you be betrayed again or be lost? I could not survive your fall' (4 May).[152]

From his first experience of battle onwards, Bolte's tone was melancholic. At Bautzen on 9 May, 'I could not staunch my tears at the sight of these powerful young people who were to be sacrificed to death.'[153] When fighting recommenced in August, he professed to be 'curious about the coming campaign', but wondered immediately whether tonight would 'not cost many a bride bitter tears' (11 August).[154] As the campaign proceeded, he became more and more pessimistic, irrespective of the outcome of the war, which was now overshadowed—although not completely obscured—by the spectre of the killing and the brutality of life in the army:

> 28 August: Everywhere, war had left behind the most terrible traces, which made me shiver, seen at such close quarters. Truly, the most terrible thing about war is not the battles, with their horrors; it is the raging soldiery (*Soldateska*). Even when one wants to help with an honest will, one is not always able to do so on the low military rung, on which I am standing. This is something that I have felt and regretted deeply. How happy I would feel if I could, in the circumstances of a civilian, no longer be a witness of things which disgust my feelings. ... Oh, sweet times, when I lived in my *Heimat* in the Johannistal; how bitter you have become. And all these thousands of sacrifices don't help at all, or at least they seem, once again, to have been in vain!

> 29 August: I rushed in [where looting was taking place] and saw the horror of the very greatest devastation. The Austrians distinguished themselves outstandingly by their savagery. I helped, where I could, giving beatings bravely and limited this dreadful state of affairs, where I could, but mostly came too late, unfortunately. Oh, how the touching thankyou of these unfortunates made my heart well. Ah, father and my good mother, today I don't feel completely unworthy of you. An ugly act must have taken place here in this city. A fusilier—if one is thinking horrific thoughts—came forward with a smoking human foot, which he had found in the chimney. Perhaps the superstition of the brewer has led to the smoking of the human foot!

> 1 September: There was a dead person after every tenth step. ... In the burned-down mill, I saw a half-burned cadaver. Numerous corpses were already black and had begun to rot. The stench was disgusting.

> 8 September: God, a heart full of feelings is often appalled during wars. How devastating war is now, compared to earlier times! ... When will this dreadful war end; I am very much longing for it. If only I were with my own family. In the moment of strain, the life of the soldier is a peculiar thing. Once the moment is over, however, life also shows its wonderfully appealing sides.[155]

War had become fascinating to a volunteer such as Bolte because it permitted a 'view of danger' and a 'proud fearlessness of the soul', 'bending the world' towards its own purposes, but only after injuring, repelling, and re-educating him.[156]

---

[152] Ibid., 26.   [153] Ibid., 28.   [154] Ibid., 29.   [155] Ibid., 41–50.
[156] Ibid., 50.

Given the relative scarcity of such contemporaneous reports, it is difficult to determine how representative Bolte's reactions were. The responses of other civilians to the conditions of combat during the Napoleonic era suggest that many volunteers and other conscripts, particularly the significant minority coming from the educated sections of Germany's towns, probably experienced similar feelings of fervour and revulsion. Certainly, artists, writers, and doctors, who accompanied the armies but were not soldiers, seem to have been profoundly disillusioned by the Napoleonic conflicts.[157] Many would have agreed with the Badenese doctor Wilhelm Meier that 'the richer experiences which people gain in tempestuous times are bought at a high price'.[158] Like others, the painter Albrecht Adam, who witnessed the campaigns of 1809 and 1812 with the Bavarian army, set off for Russia in 1812 in a sanguine mood, taking 'a very heroic...leave of his fiancée': 'It was in the air at the time. Before I mounted my horse, I extended my hand to her again and said, "In eight months, if I am still alive, I am coming back."'[159] Adam had already been shocked by the killing in a series of engagements near Regensburg in late April 1809, as 'the first wounded came from the battle' and 'elicited my pity in the highest degree'.[160] 'Amongst many seriously wounded I came across a group which was aesthetically pleasing but looked dreadful', he continued:

> Two men and two horses lay in a tangle; they had been standing behind one another and had been blown up by a cannonball, which hit their ranks from a Bavarian battery. This had ripped off the hip of the first man and the left leg of the second, and had mortally wounded the one horse on the neck and the other on the chest and shoulder. The whole group literally swam in blood.[161]

The man who had lost his leg, which was still hanging on by 'strips of flesh', had the 'presence of mind to cut it off with a knife'.[162] Having no liquor, he had ridden away to find some, even though he was sure that the soldier with the hip injury 'would scarcely make it to the evening'.[163]

In the 1812 campaign, such scenes became much more common. Lice, heat, squalor, mud, disease, and disorder had already depleted the Bavarian forces by the time that they arrived at the battle of Smolensk on 17–18 August. Thus, although the burning city presented 'magical effects of light' and 'an outwardly beautiful spectacle', there 'was nothing pleasant to say' about it: 'the fire debris, which was still smoking, and the stink of carrion of the many dead horses and bodies, which were all still lying there unburied and were, in the terrible heat, all black within twenty-four hours and had started to rot, polluted the air'.[164] Adam noted later that 'one gets used to things in war from which one would turn away with a shudder and in disgust in normal life', but he revealed at the same time that he was

[157] Examples of doctors are Wenzel Krimer, *Erinnerungen*, and Wilhelm Meier, *Erinnerungen aus den Feldzügen*; J. J. O. A. Rühle von Lilienstern was a writer and Prussian officer who took part in the campaign of 1809 on France's side as the governor of Prince Bernhard of Weimar, in J.-J. Langendorf (ed.), *Rühle von Lilienstern. Reise mit der Armee 1809* (Vienna, 1986).
[158] Wilhelm Meier, *Erinnerungen*, 28.
[159] A. Adam, *Aus dem Leben eines Schlachtenmalers*, 153.   [160] Ibid., 62.
[161] Ibid., 63.   [162] Ibid.   [163] Ibid.   [164] Ibid., 178.

deeply affected by such sights, as 'the suffering and the sad consequences of this war of destruction' continued to mount.[165] At the battle of Borodino in September, he looked at the 'terrible picture' of the field 'with shudders': 'Between dismembered corpses and severed limbs, the wounded struggled with death, groaning in their own blood. ... Nobody cared about the others, for each was preoccupied with his own suffering.'[166] What was worse, the painter went on, was the feeling of isolation, dying 'in a desolate land so far from one's *Heimat* and one's dear and loved ones': 'However great a hero one is, in such a deathly silence such feelings weigh down on him. In the turmoil of battle, they disappear; one doesn't have time to reflect.'[167] War accustomed soldiers to much hardship and suffering, so that 'they even go to their death courageously and with a bold countenance', yet it also altered them.[168] Adam himself confessed that 'the transition from the life that I led for such a long time back to the narrow constraints of daily life was not as easy as I had initially thought'.[169] 'It required a lot of time until I had again got used to a more comfortable life', retaining 'until old age' 'a decided aversion to anything soft', he concluded.[170]

Many officers, despite recent experience of combat, shared the experiences of civilians and volunteers. The Prussian officer and military writer Rühle von Lilienstern, who was travelling with the French and Saxon armies as a civilian observer in 1809, seemed to perceive warfare as both an outsider and an insider. He admitted that war was a 'tragedy', yet he went on defending war—'this rich harvest of death'—as a sign of 'the undevastatable life force of human will'.[171] Moreover, his gaze was unflinching and his nerves intact:

> I have meanwhile found a great truth confirmed here once again. All pain and all discomfort that people suffer on earth do not become increasingly unbearable in the same proportion as their incidence and duration are multiplied. Time and reason assuage all mental discomfort and, even for bodily pain, there seems to be a specific measure, not too great, beyond which consciousness, and with it sensitivity, disappears—partly also [because] the nervous system can only retain the original irritability up to a certain point, or up to a certain degree of pain. ... In the same way, thousands of people dead in a pile make for an almost less horrifying sight than a single person on a hospital bed whose soul has already departed. Granted, reflection, distraction, preoccupation, exaltation and other spiritual and moral powers do their bit to produce a completely different mood from the start on a battlefield than that in a hospital ward, but I won't be talked out of believing that the repeated and multiplied view of lifeless forms mitigates one's instinctive aversion to them, and makes the phantom of the fear of death disperse, in that it lowers it to the status of something quite usual and quotidian, which makes our animal nature tremble because of its rarity. It is precisely those most seized by timidity before death and the dead who have looked death in the eye most rarely. The common soldier, who has grown old in the tumult of battles, the sailor, who as a cabin boy has already been rocked by the most horrific waves, go with

---

[165] Ibid.   [166] Ibid., 195.   [167] Ibid., 188.
[168] Ibid.   [169] Ibid., 261.   [170] Ibid.
[171] Cited in J.-J. Langendorf, 'Der Krieg als schöne Kunst betrachtet', in J. J. O. A. Rühle von Lilienstern, *Reise mit der Armee 1809*, ed. J.-J. Langendorf (Vienna, 1986), 258; Ibid., 145.

unreflecting indifference in the face of dangers the very thought of which makes the blood of the peaceful burgher run cold.[172]

Like many officers, Rühle quickly overcame his aversion to killing and examined physical suffering with a detached curiosity. Nonetheless, he also reflected at length on death and suffering. His account of the aftermath of battle betrayed his own emotional involvement in the soldiers' deaths:

It is scarcely possible to give you a comprehensive description of the suffering that we came across on this stretch [of the road] alone, and of the dreadful prospect which a battlefield like this one offers. Think of a great, mile-wide plain covered with parched straw and perhaps twenty-thousand corpses, villages turned into piles of rubble and ash, with all the inhabitants having fled, no tree or water far and wide, in the burning heat of the dogs' time of day—and in the middle of this Libyan, plague-infested desert perhaps a couple of hundred fatally wounded people languishing for three days in ignominious loneliness and helplessness, without company, without food and drink, without a human sound other than the distant wailing cries of similar despair from fallen brothers, and instead of the hope of imminent salvation, nothing but the certain prospect of a slow, suffering and tortured death.[173]

A significant number of officers reacted to the killing of the Napoleonic Wars in a similar fashion. In retrospect, battles such as Borodino became scenes of horror: 'It presented a vision so terrible that it was as if, not people had fought here, but rather cannibals had murderously torn themselves into pieces.'[174] 'Limbs without flesh, devoured skulls stuck out of the earth here and there, completely exhumed, in truth whole hills of the dead with weapons and machines thrown one on top of the other, fronts of corpses leaned against sheer walls of earth in rows', recalled the same Saxon officer in the mid-nineteenth century: 'here and there, a skeleton, which could no longer be called human, crawled out of the half-decayed residence of a horse's stomach and stammered mad words'.[175] The *Grande Armée* had resembled a swarm of locusts, 'which—after it had eaten everything in its vicinity—had once more to consume itself', recalled one Badenese soldier after the event.[176] At the time, too, scenes from the 1812 campaign had seemed to resemble 'hell', in the words of one former Prussian officer, who had joined the army of Württemberg after defeat in 1806.[177] Borodino was a 'murder-battle' (*Mordschlacht*) which had secured the victory of 'the dictator of Europe', but which had been 'bought with such sacrifices of human lives' that it was seen as a defeat: 'About twenty-thousand corpses covered this side of the battlefield alone.'[178] Under these conditions, soldiers became de-sensitized:

It is extraordinary how lacking in feeling we had become, I would like to say through habit, in tolerating the most horrible scenes indifferently and in quietly meting out the most objectionable treatment. Here are just a few examples, a greater number of

[172] Ibid., 171–2.   [173] Ibid., 169–70.
[174] R. v. Meerheim (ed.), *Erlebnisse eines Veteranen*, 222.   [175] Ibid.
[176] C. F. C. Pfnor, *Der Krieg, seine Mittel und Wege, sowie sein Verhältniss zum Frieden, in den Erlebnissen eines Veteranen* (Tübingen, 1864), 67.
[177] K. v. Suckow, *Aus meinem Soldatenleben*, 176.   [178] Ibid., 197.

which I could cite. Thus, I recall how, waking up by the bivouac fire, I once quite carelessly caught my head on a dead Frenchman, who had already lain close by my side before going to sleep. Certainly, the poor creature, albeit very different shortly beforehand, had not slipped himself under my head, for he was dead, but rather I had used him as a pillow, drunk with sleep and therefore unconscious.[179]

Such passages did not show that soldiers lacked emotion, but that they were conscious of and affected by what they had seen and how they had come to feel. In contrast to earlier eighteenth-century reports, many officers' narratives gave frank descriptions of tears and homesickness—'Many tears flowed on my side, but only because of the separation from my dear ones', as another, young, Prussian officer put it—and of fears and disillusionment, as a consequence of the hardship, suffering, and violence of Napoleonic warfare.[180] For Martens, an officer in one of Württemberg's contingents in 1812, the sight of Moscow burning on 18 September was symptomatic of the campaign in its entirety, 'a drama of horror and grandeur'.[181] The carnage of the battle of Borodino a few days earlier, as 'corpses fell over corpses', was said to be indescribable: 'Who can describe the destruction and suffering, which unfolded before my eyes', he asked as he surveyed the battlefield:

> The nearer I came to the redoubt, the more the pile of corpses on the field increased; I could easily recognize the hill attacked by our people by the dead, who lay around—there, the corpses of friend and foe lay on top of and beside one another peacefully, and the deathly silence of this blood-soaked, sickening field was only disturbed here and there by the groans of the dying.[182]

In this context, authors like Martens were repelled by what confronted them but not deterred from describing it: their frequent doubting of whether anyone could describe such scenes accurately and completely resulted from their dogged attempts to do so.

SURVIVING INVASION AND LIBERATION

There is evidence to suggest that some soldiers' perceptions of and attitudes to war were altered by the conditions and violence of combat during the Napoleonic era. These perceptions corresponded to overlapping narratives which referred to the escalation of conflict after 1805, culminating in the ordeal of 1812 for the soldiers of the Confederation of the Rhine and in the 'wars of freedom' in 1813–14 for those of Prussia and Austria. Although later histories often depicted the campaign in Russia as the nadir and that in Saxony, Bohemia, and France as the zenith of the German states' military fortunes, few—if any—combatants offered such a reading of events. Those soldiers who fought in both 1812 and 1813, such as the Bavarian officer Friedrich Mändler, usually described the campaigns as part of a series—in this case, the war against Austria (1809), the invasion of Russia (1812), and the

---

[179] Ibid., 234.   [180] H. v. Jordan, *Erinnerungsblätter*, 17.
[181] C. v. Martens, *Vor fünfzig Jahren*, vol. 1, 139.   [182] Ibid., 121, 125–6.

war against France (1813–14)—and they treated the transition from one to the next as inevitable: after the long march home from Moscow, 'we can only have been in Innsbruck eight to ten days when the order arrived that all officers at the post who were fit for service should present themselves to the new field division immediately', he recorded.[183] Such observers also barely commented on the *Rheinbund* states' switching of sides in October 1813.[184]

Those soldiers in the Prussian and Austrian armies who either did not participate in the Russian campaign or were part of Habsburg and Hohenzollern forces guarding the rear of the *Grande Armée* frequently viewed the wars of 1813 and 1814 as threatening—rather than redeeming—events, from which officers like Heinrich von Jordan implored God to be returned safely, and as an extension of a period of hostility which had begun in 1805 (Austria) or 1806 (Prussia).[185] As one volunteer cavalry officer put it, prior to his departure in the spring of 1813:

> My father suppressed a tear by saying: 'God be with you.'...My mother complained, turning to me: 'I have already struggled so hard to keep my eldest son from entering the military...and now I have to see you being taken away to descend in the blossom of youth into a grave. ...Your grave on the battlefield will leave no trace.'[186]

A few weeks later, only 86 out of 200 or so of the volunteer's comrades remained. Although such losses did not shake his conviction that 1813 was a 'time of patriotism' and that it was an 'honour' to camp on the battlefield of Leipzig, he conceded that soldiers 'broke like a bent blade of grass as soon as [the] noises of war fell silent or [they] had to leave the fighting'.[187] Others who fought at the battle of Leipzig were struck by 'the terrible losses' which had been incurred: 'It was truly horrific how everything had melted away.'[188]

Narratives of 1813 were regularly laced with such laments and were rarely unambiguously heroic.[189] Some Prussian authors had switched sides after 1806 and had fought in 1812 with French or Russian forces, going on to fight in Saxony in 1813 after a gruelling campaign in the winter of 1812 in Russia and Poland.[190] A larger number had heard—in Carl Ernst Wilhelm von Canitz und Dallwitz's opinion—'all kinds of rumours', which were later confirmed as the remnants of the *Grande Armée* reached Prussia in December 1812, that 'Napoleon's project' had failed in terrible

---

[183] F. Mändler, *Erinnerungen*, 104.

[184] Ibid., 126–8. Ordinary soldiers often simply referred to 'the enemy', without specifying what that enemy was: for instance, Wichterich, 'Reisebuch', *Kriegsbriefe* Archive, Universitäts- und Landesbibliothek Bonn, who was fighting—as a Rhinelander—for the French in 1812, only mentions a specific opponent when he encounters 'Cossacks'. He comments later in his diary, in 1815, that he was 'forced' by the Prussians to serve in a Silesian battalion, which he then did without further complaint.

[185] H. v. Jordan, *Erinnerungsblätter*, 162.   [186] C. E. V. Krieg (ed.), *Vor fünfzig Jahren*, 9.

[187] Ibid., 35.   [188] F. M. Kircheisen (ed.), *Wider Napoleon!*, 227.

[189] K. Hagemann, '"Unimaginable Horror and Misery": The Battle of Leipzig in October 1813 in Civilian Experience and Perception', in A. Forrest, K. Hagemann, and J. Rendall (eds), *Soldiers, Citizens and Civilians* (Basingstoke, 2009), 157–78.

[190] The officer portrayed by Kircheisen joined the Duke of Wellington in Spain after Prussia's defeat and went on to fight for Russia in 1812; Ibid., vol. 2, 131–42. Heinrich von Brandt had fought for France; H. v. Brandt (ed.), *Aus dem Leben*, 280–485.

circumstances.[191] The majority of these officers had been secret or public opponents of France in the period before 1813. As a result, few accounts of the 'wars of freedom' were triumphal. Even Plotho's 'historical' description of 'the battle of the peoples' (*Völkerschlacht*) at Leipzig, which was held 'clearly' to constitute 'a turning-point in the history of the world', admitted that 'great misfortune and painful experiences' had been produced.[192] Such conclusions derived at once from an immediate reaction to the changed conditions of warfare and from an extended narrative of military campaigns during the Napoleonic era.

For German soldiers belonging to the Confederation of the Rhine, the decisive campaign was that of 1812.[193] Many troops had already fought in Prussia in 1806, Spain in 1808, and Austria in 1809.[194] In each instance, from the forced marches and rapid collapse of Prussia, via 'the horror of the war' in Spain, marked by guerrilla warfare and civilian casualties, to the battles and killing of the conflict with Austria, with any 'description of the battle' of Wagram—the largest in history until that point—bound to occasion 'mourning', soldiers had experienced different forms of combat and slaughter, but nothing which compared to those incurred during the failed invasion of Russia in 1812.[195] Most accounts of the ordeal of 1812, as it was widely portrayed, were composed of separate parts, encompassing the massing, departure, and early adventures of the *Grande Armée* in the spring and early summer, the horrific battles of Smolensk and Borodino in August and September, and the retreat from Moscow in October, November, and December. Because of the toll of earlier campaigns and resentment of French demands in some cases, the mood of departing troops varied. 'I have never gone to war with so little enthusiasm and, even, without hope', remarked one veteran Westphalian officer, his anguish heightened by his recent marriage to a young wife.[196] As Badenese regiments passed through Prussia, the hard-pressed residents had 'prophesied disaster and unavoidable destruction for them from the coming Russian campaign'.[197] Nevertheless, in spite of fatigue and forebodings, the majority of military observers appear still to have been sanguine, with the Badenese soldiers themselves, according to one of their commanding officers,

---

[191] C. E. W. v. Canitz und Dallwitz, *Denkschriften*, vol. 1, 85.

[192] C. v. Plotho, *Der Krieg in Deutschland und Frankreich*, vol. 2, 424.

[193] Sixty-seven of Hagemann's 129 German-language military memoirs published before 1875 and dealing with the Napoleonic wars concentrated on the Russian campaign in 1812: two-thirds of them (forty-five) were written by members of the armies of the Confederation of the Rhine: K. Hagemann, *Revisiting Prussia's Wars against Napoleon*, 311.

[194] See, for instance, W. v. Conrady (ed.), *Aus stürmischer Zeit*; A. v. Blumröder, *Erlebnisse*; F. Mändler, *Erinnerungen*; A. L. v. Ardenne, *Bergische Lanciers Westfälische Husaren*; K. v. Suckow, *Aus meinem Soldatenleben*; H. v. Brandt (ed.), *Aus dem Leben*; Jakob Walter in B. Hildebrand (ed.), *Drei Schwaben unter Napoleon*, 9–94.

[195] G. Muhl, *Denkwürdigkeiten*, 68, on Spain; J. J. O. A. Rühle von Lilienstern, *Reise mit der Armee 1809*, 257, on Austria. K. Hagemann, *Revisiting Prussia's Wars against Napoleon*, 311: 26/129 military memoirs concentrate on the war in the Iberian peninsula, 23/129 on 1806–7, four on Schill and three on the uprising in the Tyrol, both in 1809.

[196] W. v. Conrady (ed.), *Aus stürmischer Zeit*, 196. Others barely mention their departure: for instance, F. Giesse, *Kassel—Moskau—Kuestrin 1812–1813*, 4–5; J. Schrafel, *Merkwürdige Schicksale*, 44.

[197] T. v. Barsewisch, *Geschichte des Grossherzoglich Badischen Leib-Grenadier-Regiments*, vol. 1, 93.

looking forward to 'winter balls in Moscow or St Petersburg'.[198] In Bavaria, 'the departure was celebratory and touching, as if the people suspected that scarcely one half of the third part of this truly handsome regiment would return', wrote one officer from Nuremberg with hindsight.[199]

In neighbouring Württemberg, 'from the highest to the youngest soldier everything was in cheerful suspense; nearly all were already familiar with service in the field, but few thought how very differently this imminent campaign against Russia could turn out, compared to earlier campaigns', noted Martens: 'it occurred to no one to compare those fertile lands of Austria, which the soldier had traversed in 1809 with the desolate steppelands of the frozen North'.[200] Officers like Martens appear to have viewed much of the rest of the march into Poland and Russia during the early summer as a voyage to a foreign land, for which they adopted some of the conventions of travel-writing, referring to the weather, topography, agriculture, towns, villages, and people along the way.[201] Ordinary soldiers seem to have been less inclined to enjoy the landscape as they left Frankfurt an der Oder, 'where the German language stopped and where *mores* and culture made a peculiar impression', for 'adversity and hunger increased from day to day' from that point onwards, in the words of one Swabian combatant.[202] Before they arrived at Smolensk in August, the rank and file had experienced 'hardships', which 'were increasing daily'.[203] 'People became weaker and weaker and the companies daily became smaller', reported the same soldier in July: 'Marches were continued day and night, and one man after another lay down dead tired on the ground; most of them died over several hours and some of them suddenly collapsed to the ground dead.'[204] Heat and lack of food and water had already had a severe effect on the condition and morale of the troops—if not of the officers—of the *Grande Armée* before they went into battle.

The principal battle of the 1812 campaign, which was joined at Borodino on 7 September, seemed to many combatants to be different from earlier military encounters. The battle of Smolensk on 16–18 August, which many like Martens estimated to have left 15,000 dead or wounded on the French and 10,000 on the Russian side, had already produced sights, if not numbers of casualties, which provoked awe and disgust amongst survivors.[205] Wounded soldiers were burned alive 'in a sea of flames', leaving the rest of the troops after the battle to step 'over piles of debris and ash, over glowing rubble and the skeletons of burned corpses', identifiable only by the insignia of their helmets, which had not been burned and through which 'we learned with pain that those half-charred remains were our comrades of war'.[206] The battle of Borodino, with at least 70,000 casualties in a single day's fighting, seemed to the Saxon officer Ludwig von Meerheim to be an event without precedent 'over the millennia', which was 'bloody, great and unique

[198] Ibid.
[199] F. v. Furtenbach, *Krieg gegen Rußland und russische Gefangenschaft* (Nuremberg, 1912), 21.
[200] C. v. Martens, *Vor fünfzig Jahren*, vol. 1, 6.   [201] For instance, ibid., vol. 1, 760.
[202] Jakob Walter in B. Hildebrand (ed.), *Drei Schwaben unter Napoleon*, 38–9.
[203] Ibid., 41.   [204] Ibid., 44.   [205] C. v. Martens, *Vor fünfzig Jahren*, vol. 1, 101.
[206] Ibid., 101–2.

in the military history of the world'.[207] The slaughter was such that even the
Bavarian commander Wrede lacked words to describe for the king 'the pain over
the loss of so many brave men, which both army corps have suffered in these
bloody days'.[208] While the general was comforted by the thought that 'the glory'
which 'Your Highness's army has gained' and 'the successful, illustrious outcome of
this bloody battle, which alone can dry the tears that we shed for our fallen comrades in arms', could compensate for the losses, many other commentators arrived
at a less forgiving verdict.[209] Meerheim was typical of officers in describing his
excitement and the honour of battle, which were gradually overwhelmed by the
scale of the killing:

> It must have been about seven o'clock when the battle, which had already become a
> general one, tested us, too. ... Here, the first bullets began to strike our ranks; at the
> same time, we had the advantage of having the entire battle of the centre in view,
> although everything, enveloped in the thickest pall of gunpowder, was only apparent
> as the movement back and forth of tightly closed masses against enemy heights, under
> the roaring of several hundred throats of fire and, now, very audible small-arms
> fire. ... We ... suffered greater and greater losses the nearer we came to the enemy's
> position.
>
> As we found ourselves right in the middle of the area of case-shot fire, we saw the
> milling crowd of the French infantry in the depression before us become much
> more animated, and what the smoke of the gunpowder concealed, the wild cries of
> the combatants betrayed: that hand-to-hand fighting with the enemy was taking
> place. ... Terrible fire from all sorts of guns told us that we were now the sole target
> of the enemy. ... Nothing could constrain the rage burning within us and we
> rushed without stopping through the highly dangerous site of the fire towards the
> enemy, which was already waiting for us with its favoured bayonets. ... Scarcely
> through it, we found ourselves in the middle of the enemy, which was attacking us,
> and the bloodiest massacre began in mutual, embittered rage. The bayonets
> snatched away many of our people, but our sabres ensured that they paid three
> times the price. One enemy *Karree* was barely knocked down, when another was
> once more so near that we had to keep at our uninterrupted, murderous work of
> killing (*Mordarbeit*). ... The struggle was terrible! ... in the inner space of the
> redoubt, we saw in the most horrible milling crowd cavalry and infantry, inflamed
> with the rage of killing (*Mordwut*), colourfully mixed with one another, strangling
> each other and tearing each other to pieces.
>
> The duration of this murder scene was not to be measured in moments, since the
> enemy, which was far superior in number, used all means possible and, even, those
> pieces which were now falling silent to exact revenge, with its last breath, for its
> inevitable death.[210]

---

[207] R. v. Meerheim (ed.), *Erlebnisse eines Veteranen der Grossen Armee*, 212.
[208] Cited in J. Murken, *Bayerische Soldaten*, 146.
[209] Ibid. See also M. v. Preysing-Moos, 'Tagebuch', *Darstellungen*, vol. 21, 36–7, for a similar
account by a senior Bavarian officer.
[210] Cited in P. Holzhausen, *Die Deutschen in Russland*, 92–101.

For Martens, who saw the day as one of 'groaning and horror', all the corps of the French army 'had been completely victorious in themselves', but 'the army had not achieved a complete victory or many trophies':

> The Russian army, beaten with such great losses but not destroyed, retreated slowly and ready for battle, and the victors, instead of the promised successes, surpluses, good winter quarters and an imminent return to the fatherland, found after the battle the same shortages as before, they found Moscow, the prize of the battle, in flames and a pile of ash, and they found during the march back, for the most part, death on the snow fields of Russia, succumbing to cold and hunger.[211]

The soldiers' suffering at Borodino was so great that Martens broke with his habit of reporting events contemporaneously and gave his readers—for the first time—a glimpse of the disastrous end of the campaign.

Such an end was caused by the manner of the *Grande Armée*'s retreat from Moscow during the autumn and winter of 1812. After the battle of Borodino and the fire of Moscow in September, no German diarist was sanguine about the prospects of the invasion of Russia. 'With the destruction of Moscow, our last hope disappeared; whilst the enemy armed itself for a new campaign, our strength increasingly dwindled', wrote Martens with hindsight.[212] The march back to Germany began in mid-October, shortly after the first snowfall on the 13th. It was the first time that 'Napoleon saw the need to begin a retreat, which at once was destined to become the most unfortunate and most terrible in the entire history of the world.'[213] The main French army, wrote the Westphalian infantry officer Friedrich Giesse, had 'penetrated deep into the heart of Russia and [was] provided with a single supply road', in what could be compared to 'a desert'.[214] Marching back along that road, soldiers were unable to venture out into the hinterland in search of food: those who did, 'as occurred daily', found either 'the most torturing death' or 'the most degrading imprisonment' at the hands of the pursuing Russian army.[215] 'The repetition and multitude of such fighting, with all its other entanglements, resembled a picture of a *kleiner Krieg*, which only rarely passed without blood flowing', recorded Giesse: 'The result of this, with the attacked mounting a defence, was always a struggle of life and death.'[216] Throughout, the weakest or most exposed were picked off by Russian cavalry, with 'the mere call of "Cossacks"' making 'whole columns get a move on' by the end of the march, when 'all defence had stopped'.[217] The term 'Cossacked' came to denote a state of panic and terror,

---

[211] C. v. Martens, *Vor fünfzig Jahren*, vol. 1, 122–3.

[212] Ibid., 135. See also W. Meier, *Erinnerungen*, 87, who called the fire a foretaste of the army's 'downfall'.

[213] C. v. Martens, *Vor fünfzig Jahren*, 167. Also, F. Peppler, *Schilderung meiner Gefangenschaft vom Jahre 1812 bis 1814* (Darmstadt, 1834), 6–7.

[214] F. Giesse, *Kassel—Moskau—Kuestrin 1812–1813*, 167.

[215] Ibid., 167.   [216] Ibid., 179.

[217] Ibid., 242. Also, W. Meier, *Erinnerungen*, 92–3; C. v. Martens, *Vor fünfzig Jahren*, vol. 1, 180, 197; K.-U. Keubke (ed.), *Otto Gotthard Ernst von Raven: Tagebuch des Feldzuges in Russland im Jahre 1812*, 133–6; M. v. Preysing-Moos, 'Tagebuch', *Darstellungen*, vol. 21, 48; Wilhelm Markgraf v. Baden, *Denkwürdigkeiten*, 202, 219.

hinting at the isolation of the French and German troops and their confrontation with an unknown and supposedly barbaric enemy.[218]

The crossing of the Beresina became the symbol of the soldiers' isolation and exposure, with the *Grande Armée* pushed by the advancing Russian army against a half-frozen river on 26 November, which it needed—but was unable—to cross in order to get home: the incident, claimed Suckow, had become a byword for the horror of war, recounted repeatedly over the following fifty years.[219] Between 30,000 and 45,000 troops and others in the baggage train were killed or captured on the French side, unable to cross the makeshift bridges erected by military engineers. 'From the overview which we had from our camp at the time of the valley, the river and the two bridges, one was confronted only with unpleasant images', wrote Giesse, describing the disordered 'mass' of 'people, horses and carriages, colourfully entangled'.[220] Pushing towards the bridges with his four friends, he was caught in

> a turbulent ebb and flow, coming from behind to the front, from left to right, where in the most favourable case one could arrive at one's desired destination, but in another case one would be led away from it and be pushed back, if one remained standing at all and was not trampled underfoot.[221]

This reduction to survival at the expense of comrades, with approximately 40,000 managing to cross in time, became emblematic of much of the march home, with soldiers plundering carriages, removing clothing from fallen comrades, and eating horse-meat. Starving in cold temperatures, troops simply fell by the roadside and died in their sleep: 'Each morning, one saw bivouacs turned into fields of corpses.'[222] In these circumstances, the chaos and social levelling of the final stage of the retreat merged with fantasy, as the ordered world of the army metamorphosed into the upside-down world of a carnival:

> What shocked me most was the realization that this kind of forgetting, which had already revealed itself to me a while ago in a different form, was purely a result of the lifelessness and shattering of my bodily and mental strength, and shuddered before the consequences which this could have for me! For thousands in the army, such a mental weakness had already reached its zenith and manifested itself in each person in strange ways. One witnessed scenes which no pen could describe! The whole mass of the army was without weapons and its procession was the most adventurous and bizarre that human fantasy has ever imagined. Most, lacking shoes, had bound their feet with rags, torn pieces of tablecloths, bits of fleece or hat-felt, held together with threads of straw or knitting. To protect themselves against the horrendous cold, many had covered their hollowed-out, vermin-eaten bodies with sacks or straw mats, furs or fleeces of all kinds, women's dresses, shawls of all colours, rags of cloth, horse covers or freshly

---

[218] See, above all, C. v. Plotho, *Die Kosaken, oder Geschichte derselben von ihrem Ursprunge bis auf die Gegenwart* (Berlin, 1811). Wilhelm von Hochberg was accused of using the methods of 'Cossacks' in 1814: T. v. Barsewisch, *Geschichte des Grossherzoglich Badischen Leib-Grenadier-Regiments*, vol. 1, 160.

[219] K. v. Suckow, *Aus meinem Soldatenleben*, 278.

[220] F. Giesse, *Kassel—Moskau—Kuestrin 1812–1813*, 222.

[221] Ibid., 221.   [222] Ibid., 177.

slaughtered animal hides. Under fur hats and head decorations of the most unusual composition, hollow-eyed, pale, haggard faces, covered in dirt and blackened by smoke, grinned out. ...With arms hanging down, sunken heads and profoundly shrouded faces, officers and soldiers went along beside each other, all similarly costumed, sighing at their terrible fate in a dull daze, without caring for one another, since hardship had long ago removed all rank. ...The army resembled an extended, ragged band of refugees from the land, provoking horror and disgust.[223]

Pictorially, the end of the campaign of 1812 was represented by masses of entangled bodies in the manner of well-known Renaissance paintings of biblical scenes or it was portrayed in the form of small groups struggling to survive in empty landscapes. *Übergang über die Beresina* (28 November) by Christian Wilhelm von Faber du Faur, an officer and official artist of the Württemberg contingent of the *Grande Armée*, depicted corpses, injured soldiers on the ground, a woman with a child beside a high-ranking officer, and cavalry and infantry of all ranks and in all kinds of clothing jostling for salvation.[224] Unlike in religious images of suffering and salvation, in which believers look up and climb towards the light of heaven, the painting showed imploring soldiers separated from each other by snow and gazing upwards towards a leaden grey, stormy, winter sky. The same theme of isolation and helplessness was examined in *Zwischen Dorogobusch und Mikalewka* (7 November), which showed soldiers in full military garb around a fire and against a backdrop of blackened masses of limping troops; in *Biwak bei Mikalewka* (7 November), which envisaged two soldiers uncovering the frozen, snow-covered, peaceful bodies of a bivouac; in *In der Gegend von Bobr* (23 November), which displayed an officer transporting his wife amongst the wreckage of their sleigh with a handful of other soldiers, defending themselves against circling Cossacks on a snow-covered plain; and in *Bei Evé* (11 December), which revealed a group of troops huddled together in the foreground, with their muskets aimed haphazardly at an unseen enemy, in front of a column of anonymous comrades filing into the distance.[225] The contrast between these scenes, which were dominated by featureless expanses of white and grey, and the bucolic impressions of the start of the campaign, which could be seen in *Am Niemen* (25 June), was stark: in June, the soldiers and their commanders were depicted on a hill overlooking the river, in a verdant, classical landscape framed by lush, old trees.[226] This vision of a pastoral campaign was repeated in *In der Gegend von Jenolani* (12 July), which sketched soldiers loading sheep and geese onto a horse, with the farmer, dressed in a kaftan, looking peacefully on, and it was continued in works such as *Vor Polotzk* (25 July), *Bei Beschenkowitschi* (28 July), and, even, in *Vor Smolensk* (18 August), which made reference to human civilization—often in the form of classically proportioned churches—within an ordered landscape.[227]

---

[223] Ibid., 241–2.
[224] C. W. v. Faber du Faur, *Napoleons Feldzug in Russland 1812* (Leipzig, 1897), 302.
[225] Ibid., 266–322. A similar written account is given by Friedrich Mändler, *Erinnerungen*, 95.
[226] C. W. v. Faber du Faur, *Napoleons Feldzug*, 3–130.   [227] Ibid.

As Faber du Faur's composition of 18 August demonstrated, with its background of smoke filling the sky, the battle of Smolensk marked a break between romantic visions of an adventure in a rural idyll and darker premonitions of a menacing, sometimes fantastical, at other times man-made, world of destruction and suffering. Thus, *An den Mauern vor Smolensk* (18 August) represented a cannon surrounded by artillerymen, in front of a watchtower and a high, obliquely angled, city wall, which faded into nothingness on the right-hand side of picture.[228] 'An den Mauern vor Smolensk' (ten p.m., 18 August) showed the same tower and wall within a much wider panorama of the city, with clouds of smoke emanating from the distant buildings and forming a swirling pattern of dark clouds, which loomed over the viewer.[229] A few weeks later, a burning Moscow was portrayed in an almost identical smoke-filled or ethereal light, juxtaposed now—for example, in *Moskau* (24 September)—with razed houses and rubble, burghers, and soldiers.[230] These images were interspersed with unblinking representations of killing and death in *Auf dem Schlachtfelde an der Moskwa or Semenowskoi* (7 September), which showed a disordered assemblage of individual and grouped soldiers slaughtering each other, and in *Auf dem Schlachtfelde an der Moskwa* (17 September), which displayed the piles of bodies left on the field after the battle.[231] At around the same time, Faber du Faur's most explicit depiction of death, *An der grossen Strasse von Moshaisk nach Krymskoje* (18 September) (see Figure 4.1), portrayed a group of soldiers huddling behind the shelter of a destroyed house, surrounded by skeletons and decaying corpses.[232] All such images of the cold ordeal of the march home contrasted with the light and warmth of *Lichtensteins Kaffehaus* (7 December), which represented a return to the comforting familiarity of German culture.[233]

The effects of the disastrous campaign of 1812 in Germany are disputed. The majority of soldiers died, preventing them from telling of their experiences directly. Within the German armies, however, memories of the campaign seem to have played an important role in shaping the attitudes of new recruits. 'In the entire regiment, only a few officers were familiar with service in the field', recorded Martens of Württemberg's reconstituted army: 'the dreadful facts of the campaign in Russia, which we have just survived, has made such a deep impression that our young, for the most part newly recruited unit is not leaving its *Heimat* in as happy a mood as our long-serving soldiers used to do'.[234] In other *Rheinbund* states such as Bavaria, soldiers seem to have had similar attitudes, as a non-commanding officer like Georg Kirchmayer made plain, commenting in August 1813 on the establishment of a new force of 36,000 troops:

The constitution of this army took place for the sake of the internal security of the fatherland, because increasingly unfavourable news was coming in about the great

---

[228] Ibid.   [229] Ibid.   [230] Ibid., 224–6.
[231] Ibid., 130–223.   [232] Ibid.
[233] Ibid., 316. The coffee-shop was in Vilnius, from which the French forces were expelled by Russian troops shortly afterwards.
[234] C. v. Martens, *Vor fünfzig Jahren*, vol. 2, 6.

An der grossen Strasse von Moshaisk nach Krymskoje, den 18. September 1812.

Figure 4.1. Christian Wilhelm von Faber du Faur, *An der grossen Strasse von Moshaisk nach Krymskoje*
Source: C. W. v. Faber du Faur, *Napoleons Feldzug in Russland 1812* (Leipzig, 1897), 316.

Napoleonic army, which fought in Russia and within which 30,000 valiant Bavarian soldiers were incorporated, out of which the majority, partly as a result of the cold, partly as a result of murderous fighting, were wiped out.[235]

There is evidence that the circumstances of France's defeat in 1812 had consequences beyond the armies of the Confederation of the Rhine, affecting public opinion and wider society in southern and western Germany.[236]

In Baden, wrote one abbot in February 1813, the authorities had already started to recruit a new army, given that 'only 400 are left from 6,000 Badenese troops', but most states were beginning to waver as a consequence of the losses and costs of the war:

In Germany, people seem to be taking fright in many places. It appears that the princes themselves no longer trust. It is said that Württemberg is refusing to put further troops at the disposal of the French outside the country. In Hesse and Hanau etc., things are very unsettled; in Berlin, it has come to actual conflicts.[237]

By April 1813, the scale of Napoleon's defeat was beginning to reach a reading public: 'For several weeks, a piece called "Retreat of the French from Moscow" has

[235] G. Kirchmayer, *Veteranen-Huldigung oder Erinnerungen*, 13.
[236] U. Planert, *Der Mythos*, 578–612.
[237] Diary entry, 5 Feb. 1813, U. Engelmann (ed.), *Das Tagebuch von Ignaz Speckle. Abt von St Peter im Schwarzwald* (Stuttgart, 1965), vol. 2, 417–18.

been circulating, in which the horrific defeat of the French army is depicted by an eye witness; [the army] was actually destroyed in battle and by hunger and cold, so that scarcely a single man escaped.'[238] As such rumours turned into realities, with most communities affected directly by the losses, many subjects of the *Rheinbund* states appear to have been influenced by the new vision of war presented by most myths of 1812. In Austria and Prussia, the same rumours circulated, but with more varied effect. A significant number of returning German soldiers in the *Grande Armée* had been attacked by Prussian peasants.[239] Nonetheless, the conditions and types of warfare encountered by troops in 1812 seem to have been widely known in the Hohenzollern and Habsburg monarchies, especially within military circles. Partly as a consequence, subjects' and soldiers' expectations of the Prussian and Austrian campaign against France in 1813 appear to have been mixed.[240]

Such doubts and fears are not salient in the testimony of commanding Prussian and Austrian officers in 1813.[241] Their anxieties were concealed by a desire to carry out their patriotic duties and to remove the dishonour of previous defeats. 'Setting off to fight for our independence, we do not wish to oppress a neighbouring people which speaks one and the same language as us, [and] feels the same hatred against the foreign oppressor', ran Blücher's proclamation to the Prussian corps under his command in the spring of 1813: 'Be gentle and humane to this *Volk* and view the Saxons as friends of the holy cause of German independence, for which we have picked up our weapons, and see them as future allies.'[242] The fight for Germany against a foreign occupier appeared to supersede other enmities and to banish fears about new forms of warfare. Even Clausewitz, who had resigned from the Prussian army—along with about a quarter of all officers—in protest at the terms of the Hohenzollern monarchy's alliance with France in February 1812, remained an enthusiastic supporter of a war in 1813, despite having witnessed the death and killing of the 1812 campaign as an officer in the Russian army.[243] Thus, the Prussian officer had seen 'nothing other than burned-out sites', including Moscow, which was 'turned into ashes', after the Russian command had decided to pre-empt the actions of the French advanced guard, which had taken 'a cannibalistic pleasure' in setting alight villages: 'Under these conditions, the burdens of the campaign were extraordinarily great for both sides; a lot of bloody battles came on top; both

[238] Ibid., 422.

[239] J. Maillinger, 'Tagebuch', *Darstellungen*, vol. 21, 145, claims that 'every day' he met those who had been attacked and that his own party was confronted by 'maltreatment' in 'almost every village'.

[240] For instance, C. v. Clausewitz to his wife, 29 Nov. 1812, in K. Linnebach (ed.), *Karl and Marie von Clausewitz. Ein Lebensbild in Briefen und Tagebuchblättern* (Berlin, 1917), 305: he had seen the 'corpses and dying men among smouldering ruins' with his own eyes, reporting to his wife in November 1812 that 'thousands of ghost-like men pass by screaming and begging and crying for bread in vain'.

[241] K. Hagemann, *Revisiting Prussia's Wars against Napoleon*, 311: 63/129 German-language military memoirs concentrate on 1813–14, with nearly two-thirds written by Prussian authors.

[242] Cited in T. Crepon, *Gebhard Leberecht von Blücher. Sein Leben, seine Kämpfe* (Rostock, 1999), 222.

[243] G. A. Craig, *The Politics of the Prussian Army*, 58.

sides have suffered enormous losses in this way.'[244] Nonetheless, he continued—in October 1812—to long for 'action in the German fatherland', which was perhaps 'closer than we think'.[245] Clausewitz was an unusual though not unique case, faced with the confiscation of his property because of his allegedly treasonous decision to fight on Russia's side against Prussia, leading him to defend his patriotic motives in a long 'Bekenntnisdenkschrift' in February 1812:

> I believe and profess that a *Volk* can acknowledge nothing higher than the worth and freedom of its own existence…
>
> That the stain of a cowardly subordination can never be removed.
>
> That this drop of poison in the blood of a *Volk* will be passed on in succeeding generations and will lame and undermine the strength of later kin.
>
> That the honour of the king and government is one with the honour of the *Volk* and the sole safeguard of its well-being. That a *Volk* cannot be overcome in the courageous struggle for freedom.
>
> That even the downfall of this freedom after a bloody and honourable struggle secures the renaissance of the *Volk*.[246]

The majority of commanding Prussian officers in 1813 had either left their posts in 1812—with Boyen travelling to Vienna and St Petersburg and Gneisenau to London, for instance—or they had sympathized with Yorck's signature of the Convention of Tauroggen in December 1812, which had 'neutralized' the Prussian corps and saved it from Russian attack without the permission of Friedrich Wilhelm III.[247] On 13 January, Yorck had written to the military Governor-General in East and West Prussia, Friedrich Wilhelm von Bülow, advising him that

> the time is now or never to regain our freedom and honour. With a bloody heart, I am tearing up the bonds of loyalty and conducting war by my own hand. The army desires a war against France. The *Volk* desires it and the king desires it, but the king does not have a free will. The army must give him a free will.[248]

Bülow in turn wrote to the king, backing Yorck's claims and contending that 'this will become the cause of the nation; the greatest sacrifices will be made voluntarily; and sources will appear which one had long believed to have run dry'.[249] Many officers had already congregated in the Silesian capital of Breslau, from where—according to the Austrian envoy—'the military and the heads of different sects have taken complete control of the reins of government under the mask of patriotism' and under the 'unlimited influence' of Scharnhorst.[250]

---

[244] C. v. Clausewitz to A. N. v. Gneisenau, 16 Oct. 1812, in C. v. Clausewitz, *Schriften, Aufsätze, Studien, Briefe*, ed. W. Hahlweg (Göttingen, 1990), vol. 2, 134.

[245] C. to M. v. Clausewitz, 15 Oct. 1812, in K. Linnebach (ed.), *Karl and Marie von Clausewitz*, 127.

[246] Cited in C. v. Clausewitz, *Schriften, Aufsätze, Studien, Briefe*, ed. W. Hahlweg (Göttingen, 1966), vol. 1, 688–9.

[247] For example, H. v. Boyen, *Denkwürdigkeiten und Erinnerungen*, vol. 2, 222–3.

[248] Cited in K. Hornung, *Scharnhorst. Soldat—Reformer—Staatsmann* (Munich, 1997), 267.

[249] Ibid., 267–8.   [250] Ibid., 269.

Whether such officers were 'patriotic' was a moot point: they certainly wanted to restore Prussian honour and independence, which was seen to be compatible with the interests of 'Germany'. Like Clausewitz, they argued in favour of a patriotic war—Prussian and German—against France and they viewed France's defeat as a military opportunity for the Hohenzollern monarchy rather than as a warning. 'All the news which I receive from the Russian army says that the French army is almost completely disbanded', wrote Gneisenau to Hardenberg on 17 December 1812: 'The present moment is unique for liberation; don't let it go unused! It might not reoccur in such a fashion. ...National honour, which has suffered so terribly, must be restored by something glorious.'[251] On his way to St Petersburg from Austria, Boyen witnessed the consequences of the 1812 campaign for himself, but his observations were entirely strategic, concluding that Napoleon had become preoccupied with frontal attacks at the expense of manoeuvres and that he had been stranded in Russia with too small an army.[252] 'Large areas' of Moscow 'scarcely contained traces of the buildings that had once covered them', wrote the general:

> From Moscow the route to Kiev passed through a section of the military road, along which the French army had retreated and on which the Russian army had chased it, and so there were new signs at every moment—the wounded, wagons of prisoners, destroyed bridges and the like—that a great act of war was reaching its final act.[253]

The cost and bloodletting of Napoleonic conflicts had not deterred a significant proportion of Prussia's military leaders, who came to power in 1813, from waging war. They had, however, convinced those leaders, in the words of Scharnhorst and Gneisenau's memorandum for Hardenberg on 8 April, that 'A war like the present one is not a normal war':

> [it was] not fought, for instance, for a province, but for the security of the throne, for the independence of the nation, for the holiest goods of life, for liberation from a disgraceful yoke, which destroys the entire well-being of the nation, demands the nation's blood for the subordination of foreign peoples, deprives the same of all noble culture and takes them back to a state of savagery.[254]

Similarly, Austrian officers, a smaller number of whom had resigned in protest at the Habsburg monarchy's alliance with France in March 1812, were convinced that war against Napoleon in 1813 was a 'holy war', as Radetzky called it, on which Austria's 'future life or its downfall' depended.[255]

Even reforming officers doubted that the 'public' shared their conception of the 'wars of freedom' or 'liberation'. 'In such a struggle, the greatest effort must be made', Scharnhorst and Gneisenau continued in their memorandum of 8 April 1813:

---

[251] A. N. v. Gneisenau to K. A. v. Hardenberg, 17 Dec. 1812, in G. Thiele (ed.), *Gneisenau. Eine Chronik* (Berlin, 2007), 158.

[252] H. v. Boyen, *Denkwürdigkeiten und Erinnerungen*, vol. 2, 201–10.   [253] Ibid.

[254] G. v. Scharnhorst and A. N. v. Gneisenau, memorandum, 8 Apr. 1813, in G. Thiele (ed.), *Gneisenau*, 173.

[255] O. Regele, *Feldmarschall Radetzky*, 117. On officers' resignations, see G. E. Rothenberg, *Napoleon's Great Adversaries*, 176.

'Each citizen (*Staatsbürger*), whether he belongs to the army or not, must participate, whether in an indirect or direct way. ...However, it seems as though not every citizen shares such a view.'[256] In the course of the spring and early summer, many Prussian officers—in contrast to their Austrian counterparts, who were more sceptical—altered their opinion, as a large number of volunteers came forward.[257] Scharnhorst welcomed the fact that 'the success of the recruitment [of *Freiwillige*] has certainly exceeded all expectations'.[258] 'The king called', rejoiced Gneisenau, 'and all, all came.'[259] Many who came seem to have looked forward, albeit fearfully, to the campaign of 1813 and to have seen themselves as representing a Prussian or German people. 'The *Volk* knew against which enemy this general levy of the nation (*Nation*) was directed, even if no name was mentioned', recorded one volunteer of Prussia's call for *Freiwillige* in February 1813:

> The holy fire, produced in the halls of science, nourished in the hearts of the youth, burst into bright flames; the *Volk*, full of vitality and rich in actions, rose up, awakened by the trumpeting mood of the battles, and everyone gathered resolutely together in order to pass jubilantly through the German homelands (*die deutschen Gaue*), to follow the call of the king, to free the fatherland from the weight of foreign domination.[260]

Like their commanding officers, such Prussian volunteers were convinced of the magnitude and significance of the war against Napoleon, continuing to talk of their patriotic duty and heroic actions throughout the campaign. Having left 'the *Weltstadt*' of Paris behind in 1814, the same volunteer trekked with 'imperishable memories back into a beloved fatherland'.[261] 'Like returning conquerors, like beloved compatriots (*Landsleute*), we were welcomed here with kindness, even with jubilation', he wrote of the troops' reception in Elberfeld, in contrast to that in the pro-French cities of Aachen and Düsseldorf.[262] In Berlin, the soldiers took part in a 'celebration, the likes of which have not been seen since'.[263] As in Saxony during the previous year, 'it needs no repeating that enthusiasm for a general uprising, in this era of patriotism, manifested itself in all strata of the populations of most German lands', he recollected.[264]

In combat, soldiers' patriotic conceptions of warfare were challenged and modified. For some volunteers, the perceived momentousness of the war against Napoleon in 1813 was linked to an awareness of different norms in the civilian and military spheres—with the 'spilling of human blood' only acceptable in the latter— and to fears of the slaughter occasioned by new forms of warfare.[265] Nervousness about violence was characteristic of the first weeks of the campaign, with one

---

[256] G. Thiele (ed.), *Gneisenau*, 173.
[257] Officers' commentary in Austria seems to have focused on the lack of preparedness of their troops in 1813; O. Regele, *Radetzky*, 114–18.
[258] Cited in K. Hornung, *Scharnhorst*, 270.
[259] In T. Crepon, *Gebhard Leberecht von Blücher*, 217.
[260] C. E. V. Krieg (ed.), *Vor fünfzig Jahren*, 9.   [261] Ibid., 163.
[262] Ibid., 169.   [263] Ibid., 171.
[264] Ibid., 79. See also Jordan, *Erinnerungsblätter*, 28, 328–31.
[265] H. Lem von Zieten (ed.), *Tagebuch von Heinrich Bolte*, 13.

detachment of *Freiwillige* shocked by 'close fire' on 8 April, only to find that the French were still 8 miles away.[266] Correspondingly, volunteers' accounts of fighting betrayed anxiety—'the fire which confronted the battalion was terrible'—combined with self-aggrandisement:

> in a short period of time, at least six of my neighbours had disappeared from my side [and]...one of my people in front, v. Sch., was shot in the head and fell down dead on the spot. We barely noticed all that, however, with no wounded man making a sound, and the village was taken with a loud hurrah.[267]

As one young Prussian soldier's sister recalled, in a report based on conversations with him, her brother had 'distinguished himself with glory' at the battle of Groß-Görschen, after which he had been made an officer, but he 'had also been in great danger'.[268] 'Oh, God! What experiences my dear brother had in this short period!' she went on: 'When you hear how his life was in danger a thousand times over, how he always dived into the greatest vortex and how 1000s of bullets whistled around him,...then we can drop onto our knees and thank the Almighty God whole heartedly for the preservation of our dear one.'[269] The brother himself could also be found praying for 'a quick, good outcome of the affair'.[270] Battle was always different from representations of it 'in descriptions and paintings', 'which never do justice to reality by far', wrote the academic and volunteer Karl von Raumer, before adding that 'I was so captivated by the drama that I quite forgot myself.'[271] On 26 August, he regretted not being able to go into battle.[272] Once there, however, he was confronted by sights that remained with him:

> On the battlefield near Wartenburg, I found a handsome Neapolitan soldier, whom a flint bullet had hit directly on the temple so that his brain was hanging out. His pale face, his desperate, pained look, with which he seemed to beg us to take pity on him and put an end to his torture—I will never forget that.[273]

In combat, wrote another volunteer, death 'piled up terribly', in victory as well as in defeat.[274] The suffering of those who were injured was 'dreadful', he went on.[275]

Because of such ambiguous recollections of conflict, the report which volunteers gave of the battle of Leipzig on 16–19 October 1813 differs markedly from those of later historians. By the time it was over, 'we had had no food for five days', wrote one member of the Lützower *Jäger*: 'in fact, it was a sad day after such a glorious victory'.[276] Earlier, events had turned quickly from the acts of a magnificent spectacle to scenes of horror: 'The clash of the two sides was imposing. At a considerable distance, one could feel the earth shake as if in an earthquake. The Hungarian cavalry began the dance; here, one saw what these troops could do.'[277] Soon, confusion and disorder started to dominate the picture, succeeded by the

[266] Ibid., 14.   [267] C. E. V. Krieg (ed.), *Vor fünfzig Jahren*, 32.
[268] H. v. Jordan, *Erinnerungsblätter*, 72.   [269] Ibid., 73.   [270] Ibid., 162.
[271] K. v. Raumer, *Karl von Raumer's Leben*, 169.   [272] Ibid., 171.   [273] Ibid., 180.
[274] W. Krimer, *Erinnerungen eines alten Lützower Jägers*, 45.   [275] Ibid., 46.
[276] Ibid., 67.   [277] Ibid., 63.

inescapable realities of conflict: 'The whole soon consisted of one great tangle, with everything mixed together colourfully. This mad rush did not last long; the French began to tear themselves away, and soon the flight was general, the bloodbath terrible.'[278] Only 'a small number escaped', continued the volunteer: 'whoever wasn't chopped down or shot was taken prisoner': 'The defeat was decisive', but it did not feel like a victory.[279] After the battle, 'one saw the horrifying consequences of the over-hasty retreat of the enemy and the premature demolition of the bridge over the Elster': 'Overall, destruction, laying waste, death and desperation. Hundreds of emaciated, starving opponents lay with death all around them; hundreds of corpses swam down the Elster—an immeasurable field of death.'[280]

Steffens's description of the aftermath of fighting at Möckern, near to Leipzig, was similar:

> I crossed the battlefield and had trouble getting any further, for the bodies were piled up. ...I had a horrifying feeling; in increasingly compressed piles, the spirits of the fallen surrounded me, and involuntarily I saw myself in the middle of the waiting families, who were anxiously following each of their steps in the great struggle.[281]

In pursuit of fleeing French troops after the battle of Leipzig, where he came across many combatants dying in bushes at the side of the road, the academic confessed 'that I wanted to be far away, that this misery appeared more horrific than the greatest defeat in the fiercest conflict'.[282] The 'killing spirit' of temporary military hospitals and the plague of typhus, which prevailed 'in all the areas behind the army', as well as the actual killing of battle, meant that Steffens's earlier expectations of the 'war of freedom' were now 'strangely mixed with mourning', as were those of other survivors: this feeling 'set the innermost reaches of the soul into vital movement and it could only make sense of itself through profound religious contemplation'.[283] 'The small remainder of Yorck's corps' was held to typify a more general sentiment: 'evening prayers took place, and as important as the victory was, the great losses nevertheless summoned up a quiet, troubled mood'.[284] For volunteers such as Raumer, 'complaints about the fallen were combined with joy that their blood had not flowed in vain, and we had won'.[285] Yet 'our joy was, admittedly, bought at great cost'.[286] The fact that 'the struggle was dreadful' was not lost from view, even after the event.[287] For German soldiers on the side of the French, the cost of the campaign was arguably more obvious, since it was not offset by a patriotic victory. To one Swabian participant, the human consequences of the battle of Leipzig were comparable to those of Borodino.[288]

The suffering of ordinary soldiers during the campaigns of 1813–15 entered the official and popular historical records of the conflicts, but it was marginalized by a narrative of Prussia's, Austria's, and 'Germany's' heroic victory over Napoleon and

---

[278] Ibid., 64.   [279] Ibid.   [280] Ibid., 69.   [281] H. Steffens, *Was ich erlebte*, 357.
[282] Ibid., 368.   [283] Ibid., 355.   [284] Ibid., 354.
[285] K. v. Raumer, *Karl von Raumer's Leben*, 189.   [286] Ibid., 188.
[287] Ibid., 187.   [288] C. v. Martens, *Vor fünfzig Jahren*, vol. 2, 145.

France.[289] Plotho's story of the battle of Leipzig was at once symptomatic and influential. He concluded his description, interrupting a long history of the war, with an evaluation of the event's world-historical significance:

> And history will place the *Völkerschlacht* near Leipzig, which grounded—after a four-day struggle—the freedom of the Germans (which had withstood so many attacks from the *Hermannschlacht* to Napoleon) perhaps for centuries once more, on an equal footing with those great battles of the past, by means of which great states were overthrown or maintained; and the reputation of the monarchs, commanders and armies, which have fought here, will not be forgotten. The battle itself was fought on both sides with every tactical effort and with the most persistent bravery, and in the midst of its fire a German *Volksgeist* was purified, and the eternal law was proven that peoples of one descent and language should be tied, in the transfer of most German fighters to the German army.
>
> And its consequences were still more important, and will be so in future, for they constitute a turning-point of world history.[290]

The rest of Plotho's narrative gives a vivid depiction of the events of the conflict, paying more attention to their strategic and historical importance than to their impact on individual soldiers, as his account of the end of the battle on 19 October demonstrates:

> Although the retreat of the French army had already begun yesterday, very many troops, a lot of artillery and baggage had been left behind until today, and all of this now crowded together into the narrow streets of Leipzig, on the narrow route to Lindenau, and blocked all the exits for those who were fleeing. Everything ran into everything else in terrible confusion, with every individual seeking salvation. Since Emperor Napoleon left the city—it was 10 o'clock in the morning—after completing a visit to the King of Saxony, he wanted to leave through the *Ranstädter Thor*, but he, too, could no longer get out and needed to clear a way out for himself to the *Petersthor*. And as he had crossed the bridge with his entourage..., he blew it up behind him; thus, as always, he indifferently sacrificed all the others, only thinking of himself, with unpardonable cruelty. An emergency bridge constructed in the *Richterschen Garten* collapsed under the weight of those in flight, and so all the troops were left without a means of escape, and in the hands of the victors. The victors pushed forward relentlessly in great masses from all sides. A defence was unthinkable, but the fleeing soldiers still hoped to escape through Leipzig park and common over the conjunction of the Pleisse and the Elster; here, thousands met their death in the water and through the unfailing pursuit of sharpshooters from all sides and through the heavy artillery fire of the Allies....All who were not drowned had to give themselves up to the victorious arms of the allied armies. ...
>
> Everywhere, forced marches were ordered, single shots were fired, and Prussians, Russians, Austrians and Swedes descended on the *Transädter Steinweg*; and before the *Ranstädter Thor*, there lay countless dead and wounded men and horses. ...

[289] Even 'patriotic' ordinary soldiers like Johann Gottlieb Küpper, 'Marschroute und Tagebuch', *Kriegsbriefe* Archive, Universitäts- und Landesbibliothek Bonn, who had recorded that he was fighting for 'our king' at the start of his diary, showed little ardour in their description of the actual events, noting that he had been dealt with, after capitulating in battle, in an 'indescribable' way.

[290] C. v. Plotho, *Der Krieg in Deutschland und Frankreich*, 424.

And the anxious inhabitants, who a few moments earlier had feared for the fate of a city conquered by storm, found their expectations of a pardon on the part of great-hearted monarchs, and of the humanity of their brave troops, exceeded by far; all property was protected and every citizen found his life and goods secure. Order was quickly restored and anxiety and fear turned into joyous nostalgia.

Thus, the hard work of the blood was done, victory fought for. The superiority of Germany over France had been decided from now onwards, and the foundation stone of the new edifice of European freedom was laid.[291]

In this and in other similar accounts, the human suffering, killing, and death of the Napoleonic Wars is portrayed in passing, as part of an epic, historical struggle of states, armies, and peoples. The tone and meaning of such representations ran counter to the recorded experiences of a large number of soldiers. These experiences were largely drowned out during the post-war era.

---

[291] Ibid., 420–2.

5

War Memories

The question of how the revolutionary and Napoleonic Wars were remembered and understood remains an unexpectedly open one. Recent scholarship has shown that memories of conflicts varied from one region to another, given the different alliances and policies of individual states, and that there was often a disparity between official and popular commemorations and recollections.[1] Historians still know comparatively little, however, about such popular forms of remembrance and about how significant they were, how they were perpetuated, and whether they were continuous or not.[2] They also remain uncertain of the degree of coalescence and conflict between differing conceptions of warfare; not merely between official and popular ones, but between varying images of war within states—on the part of ministers, diplomats, courtiers, and generals—and within different sections of society and emerging political milieux.[3] Did contemporaries' views of military conflict coincide in important respects and, if so, with what effects? How did contemporary Germans fit their experiences of and assumptions about the Revolutionary and Napoleonic Wars into a broader understanding of wars, ranging from anthropological readings of groups' struggle to exist to historical accounts of ancient, early modern, and nineteenth-century types of combat?[4] In light of recent events, how was war defined, and was it primarily an object of menace and fear, which could be glimpsed for instance in

---

[1] Regional variation did not just exist between north and south Germany, or between Prussia and the rest, but within the south, as Ute Planert, *Der Mythos*, 620–41, demonstrates. On the disparity between official and popular memories, see Chris Clark, 'The Wars of Liberation in Prussian Memory: Reflections of the Memorialization of War in Early Nineteenth-Century Germany', *Journal of Modern History*, 68 (1996), 550–76.

[2] This situation has been improved by the publication of Karen Hagemann's excellent account of history, culture, and memory, *Revisiting Prussia's Wars against Napoleon*. See also W. Burgdorf, 'Der Kampf um die Vergangenheit. Geschichtspolitik und Identität in Deutschland nach 1813', in U. Planert (ed.), *Krieg und Umbruch in Mitteleuropa um 1800*, 333–58. M. Jeismann, *Das Vaterland der Feinde*, 27–102, provides a suggestive interpretation of the development of enmity and a cult of the dead between 1792 and 1815, but he gives little indication of how such ideas were transmitted and transformed between 1815 and 1870. For more detailed, yet disparate, accounts, see R. Koselleck and M. Jeismann (eds), *Der politische Totenkult. Kriegerdenkmäler in der Moderne* (Munich, 1994).

[3] The fullest account is Jörn Leonhard's *Bellizismus und Nation*, 419–55, 571–644, but this work deliberately concentrates on the writings of academics and publicists. See also F. Akaltin, *Die Befreiungskriege im Geschichtsbild der Deutschen im 19. Jahrhundert* (Frankfurt, 1997).

[4] At present, it is not clear, for instance, how nineteenth-century Germans' differing interpretations of the Thirty Years' War, examined by Kevin Cramer in *The Thirty Years' War and German Memory in the Nineteenth Century*, relate to their conceptions of more recent wars.

Carl von Clausewitz's *Vom Kriege* (1832/4), or heroism and hope?[5] The following chapter investigates these questions.

1813: FESTIVALS OF FREEDOM, LIBERATION, AND SACRIFICE

After twenty-four years of war, sometimes sporadic and at other times relentless, peace in Germany and Europe arrived haltingly and interruptedly. Even after the final surrender of Napoleon on 15 July 1815, having been defeated at the battle of Belle Alliance (Waterloo) on 18 June, and on the eve of the signing of the Treaty of Paris on 20 November 1815, German officers returning from France voiced their doubts to a receptive domestic audience that the peace would last.[6] A year-and-a-half earlier, on 11 April 1814, the Allies had signed the Treaty of Fontainebleau and established the Congress of Vienna to agree the terms of the post-war order, only to witness the deposed French Emperor's escape from exile on Elba and his triumphant march from the south of France to Paris in March 1815. Varnhagen von Ense, who had been present as an officer in the French capital during the spring of 1814 and who was attending the Congress of Vienna as Napoleon escaped a year later, recounted how the mood of ruling elites, some of whom had initially reacted with equanimity, quickly turned to 'horror and angst, madness and disappointment' as the full extent of the reverse had sunk in: 'We might well say that history has nothing more astonishing, more fantastical and, in its effect, more violent to show for itself than this journey of Napoleon's from Cannes to Paris.'[7] At home in the individual German states, officials, soldiers, and civilians seem to have responded in a similar, dismayed fashion.[8] Few diaries and later memoirs pay as much attention to the 1815 campaign as to that of 1812 or 1813–14.[9]

Despite the lack of a definitive and unambiguous moment of victory, however, the majority of contemporaries seem to have felt relief and joy at the news that the war was over. Understandably, such rejoicing was especially heart-felt amongst soldiers, if also mixed with other feelings. In this respect, the better-known views of German military leaders, particularly those of Prussia, give a misleading impression. Most were matter-of-fact, proud that their strategies and valour in the

---

[5] C. v. Clausewitz, *Vom Kriege* (Berlin, 1832–4), was published posthumously. See R. Schilling, 'Kriegshelden', 43–125; K. Hagemann, 'German Heroes', 116–34.

[6] Diary entry, 15 Nov. 1815, in U. Engelmann (ed.), *Tagebuch*, vol. 2, 521.

[7] K. A. Varnhagen v. Ense, *Denkwürdigkeiten*, vol. 2, 335.

[8] See Ignaz Speckle's response, for example: U. Engelmann (ed.), *Tagebuch*, vol. 2, 74.

[9] The majority of soldiers' accounts concentrate solely on the 1812 or 1813 campaigns. For sections on 1815 in the longer, overarching accounts, see Wilhelm, Markgraf v. Baden, *Denkwürdigkeiten*, vol. 1, 386–420; W. Meier, *Erinnerungen aus den Feldzügen*, 140–52; W. v. Conrady (ed.), *Aus stürmischer Zeit*, 410–18; A. v. Blumröder, *Erlebnisse im Krieg und Frieden*, 92–9; Friedrich Mändler, *Erinnerungen*, 145–61; G. Kirchmayer, *Veteranen-Huldigung oder Erinnerungen an die Feldzugsjahre*, 66; M. v. Eberhardt (ed.), *Aus Preussens schwerer Zeit*, 153–5; T. v. Barsewisch, *Geschichte des Grosherzoglich*, vol. 1, 165–8; C. C. Zimmermann, *Geschichte des 1*, vol. 1, 200–5.

field had been vindicated but wary that Europe's diplomats would waste the positions which had been gained in battle. 'The faster that events moved forward in the last month of the war, the less that the world of affairs does the same', lamented Prussia's Quartermaster-General Gneisenau on 19 May 1814.[10] In his 'secret history of the campaign', sketched out in a letter to Carl von Clausewitz on 28 April, he had accused governments and diplomats more bluntly of 'asking…, finally begging, for peace' without good reason and prophesying 'the most terrible misfortune' in an attempt to prohibit necessary military risk-taking.[11] On the defeat of Napoleon, he had written simply to his wife on 31 March:

> Paris is ours. Yesterday, we attacked the enemy in its position here and completely destroyed it. Today, we moved in here. We are now throwing the tyrant from the throne. He is still running around with about 50,000 men. We have cut him off from the capital in the last few days. The people were enthusiastic today; the white cocarde was put up. The troops have again fought magnificently.[12]

A few days later, wrote his adjutant, 'the joy had disappeared from his face and, often, he sat mutely or complained sighingly that the most diverse interests, with their various intrigues, were being listened to and that the prize of victory would not be equal to the great amount of blood which it had cost'.[13] Blücher, the commander of the Prussian armies and Gneisenau's immediate superior, wrote in similar terms to Friedrich Wilhelm III in the same month, enjoying 'the short period of happiness' and 'the present which has been fought for so splendidly', 'at a moment of bloodily-achieved peace', at the same time as warning against throwing away the 'inheritance' of the army (territorial expansion and the place of the military in the state), the creation of which has been 'a holy duty for me'.[14]

Prussian leaders' 'passion for revenge and retaliation', in Clausewitz's words, which found expression *inter alia* in Gneisenau's wish to 'blow up the victory columns on the Place Vendôme and the bridges of Austerlitz and Jena', was usually overridden by the need to salvage and bolster the position of the army and the Hohenzollern monarchy.[15] Shockingly, from the point of view of ordinary soldiers and civilians in Prussia, Gneisenau, the Prussian War Minister Hermann von Boyen, and the Chief of the General Staff Karl Wilhelm von Grolman had actually drawn up plans in late 1814 for a war with Austria in order to secure the annexation of Saxony.[16] When these plans were overtaken by events in early 1815, with Napoleon's escape from Elba, the same generals, together with Hardenberg, had rejoiced at the spectre of another war: 'This is the greatest piece of good

---

[10] A. W. A. Neidhardt v. Gneisenau to J. Gruner, 19 May 1814, cited in G. Thiele (ed.), *Gneisenau*, 262.
[11] Gneisenau to C. v. Clausewitz, 28 Apr. 1814, in A. W. A. Neidhardt v. Gneisenau, *Ausgewählte militärische Schriften*, ed. G. Förster and G. Gudzent (Berlin, 1984), 329.
[12] Gneisenau to his wife, 31 Mar. 1814, ibid., 257.
[13] T. F. v. Stosch, early, Apr. 1814, ibid., 258.
[14] G. L. v. Blücher to Friedrich Wilhelm III, Apr. 1814, in T. Crepon, *Blücher*, 287.
[15] C. v. Clausewitz to his wife, 12 July 1815, cited in P. Paret, *Clausewitz and the State*, 253; A. W. A. Neidhardt v. Gneisenau, in H. Otto, *Gneisenau. Preussens unbequemer Patriot* (Bonn, 1979), 349.
[16] G. A. Craig, *Politics of the Prussian Army*, 66–7.

fortune that Prussia could encounter', declared the chief minister in the middle of the night on 8 March, 'his face shining with joy': 'now the war is starting afresh and the army will again make good all the mistakes made in Vienna'.[17] Blücher's conviction that 'civil war' had broken out in France in the spring of 1815, with the likelihood that 'the states will be brought into turmoil and eaten up again', did not detract from his desire to use the conflict to Prussia's advantage and, possibly, to establish a lasting 'order of peace for the nations (*Völker*)', or for that matter— in the next sentence—to enjoy the 'incomparable' weather, with 'everything in the most beautiful bloom'.[18] In general, military and civilian leaders in the Hohenzollern monarchy were willing to contemplate and use war as an instru- ment of policy—albeit a 'patriotic' and potentially radical one—in 1814 and 1815. In other states, there is evidence—for example, in the accounts of an Austrian commander such as Radetzky or a Badenese one such as Wilhelm von Hochberg—that military conflicts were viewed in a more routine way than in Prussia.[19]

Such matter-of-fact narratives of the Napoleonic Wars and the defeat of the French in 1814 and 1815 contrast with the reactions of lower-ranking officers and common soldiers, who betrayed feelings of fear, foreboding, hope, and, above all, joy and relief. When the courier announced that Napoleon had been defeated in April 1814, the troops' 'calls of "Hurrah" and the volleys of victory by the artillery batteries seemed like they would never end', reported the Swabian officer Christian von Martens from Strasbourg, where his regiment was still laying siege to the city.[20] For the Hessian officer Ludwig Wilhelm von Conrady, serving in the Prussian army by 1815, the Coalition's defeat of the French army at Belle Alliance on 18 June, in which he participated, 'will always remain the most important and most beautiful day of my military life'.[21] On their return home, such troops were feted as heroes. When the young Prussian soldier Heinrich von Jordan arrived back from the campaign with Blücher on 29 August ('I shall never forget this 29 August as long as I live', recorded his sister), he was greeted by three carriages full of family members, including 'his beloved old grandmother from Bodzanowitz'.[22] As he came into sight, everyone shouted, 'They are coming! They are coming!': 'Ah, how our hearts were beating—full of inexpressible joy.'[23] Before his carriage had reached them, he had jumped out, 'and now we lay in each other's arms, in speechless joy', continued his sister: 'My pen is too weak to paint more of this scene.'[24] Forty years

---

[17] A. v. Nostitz, diary entry, 8–9 Mar. 1815, in G. Thiele (ed.), *Gneisenau*, 276–7.

[18] Cited in T. Crepon, *Blücher*, 307–8.

[19] Radetzky noted that Austrian commanders were seen to be too 'methodical' and cautious in 1814 and 1815, as were their eighteenth-century predecessors, cited in O. Regele, *Feldmarschall Radetzky*, 164–78; Wilhelm von Hochberg only referred in passing to the fact that the war had ended in 1815, in Wilhelm, Margraf v. Baden, *Denkwürdigkeiten*, vol. 1, 418.

[20] Christian von Martens, *Vor fuenzig Jahren*, 160.

[21] W. v. Conrady (ed.), *Aus stürmischer Zeit*, 418.

[22] H. v. Jordan, *Erinnerungsblätter und Briefe eines jungen Freiheitskämpfers aus den Jahren 1813 und 1814*, ed. Ludwig von Jordan (Berlin, 1914), 328–9.

[23] Ibid., 329.   [24] Ibid.

after the event, she recalled the strength of the family's feelings and the extent to which their son was honoured:

> We could not see too much of our warmly loved one, who had become so well, so blooming and handsome, who had grown so much and become so strong. Who would have seen in him the punishments of war which he had overcome? How great God is in his all-powerfulness and goodness! We had only tears of thanks and joy in our eyes, but we could say nothing. After a short while, the beloved son had to sit in father's carriage, and we followed. Still, we had not got far when another wagon train came to us. It was our friends and neighbours, with the *Landrat* in front. ... The good people could not stop welcoming the young warrior home...and they accompanied us to Schönwald. At the edge of our property, everyone got out, for the first gate of honour had been erected here, with the inscription, 'Earth of the *Heimath*, bless him!' Behind it, [Jordan, very surprised] saw the entire population of the village of Schönwald, with the schoolchildren and teacher at the front, all dressed in festive clothing, the girls with crowns of laurels on their heads. The schoolteacher came forward and gave a wonderful speech to the feted one and gave three cheers at the end, accompanied by trumpets and drums. ... The girls now encircled the young hero and sang a gentle melody, and the whole village and all present joined in the song. [Jordan] was so surprised that he could only thank all the good people, with tearful eyes, and shake their hand. In a triumphal procession, with the musicians in front, then the girls etc., we now continued on the way to our house on foot, and here the people and all our friends split off from us, and we had our Heinrich all alone, and we celebrated our reunion according to our hearts' desire.[25]

The next day, more than a hundred guests turned up to continue the celebrations.[26] Two months later, he went back to the barracks in Potsdam, where he spent much of the next twenty-five years as an officer.[27]

Victory over France in 1814—recounted here in family lore—seems to have constituted a critical juncture in the lives of such soldiers, affecting the way in which they viewed war. Frequently, the joyful, self-aggrandizing, or relieved sentiments associated with victory coexisted alongside mourning for the dead and an unspecified fear of being injured or dying, as Varnhagen testified. In the winter of 1813/14, he wrote, 'the consequences of the battle of Leipzig developed more and more marvellously from day to day', with 'the numerous armies' waltzing along 'all roads, forwards into the liberated lands', gaining strength from the advance of 'enormous streams'.[28] As a result, 'all the lands between the Elbe and the Weser, the coast of the North Sea down to Holland, and the entire bank of the Rhine up to Switzerland, saw with joyful alarm the old fetters, in which they had languished for so long, fall off'.[29] The soldiers were 'heroic' and 'courageous', in sight of a victory which was, 'this time, a fact brought about by a thousand blessings'.[30] With Danish forces still fighting in north Germany and French soldiers behind the Coalition's lines, often in fortresses, the dangers of war were still obvious in 1814, but the defeat of Napoleon and the massing of troops in Paris nonetheless offered 'the warriors of

---

[25] Emilie Jordan's *Gedenkschrift*, 1852, ibid., 329–30.   [26] Ibid., 330.
[27] Ibid., 331.   [28] K. A. Varnhagen v. Ense, *Denkwürdigkeiten*, vol. 2, 204.
[29] Ibid.   [30] Ibid.

nearly all peoples…, as well as the most powerful rulers', the prospect—arising 'from their victory and more distant alliance'—of 'a new shaping of the world'.[31] In 1815, wrote the Badenese army doctor Wilhelm Meier, 'calm appeared to have been given back to humanity, after years of long and bloody conflicts'.[32] Although it was common, as another veteran noted, to dwell on the horrors and suffering of war and to neglect the happiness of peace, it seems that many combatants and civilians celebrated the end of the conflict in 1814 and 1815 in this manner, marking out the war as a painful yet significant, worthwhile, controllable, and terminable event.[33]

There was a great willingness amongst a wider public in most German lands to celebrate the end of the war. Such celebrations were most conspicuous in Prussia, where reformers within the state and army had done most to court popular sup- port for the campaign against France after 1813. Accordingly, the arrival of Russian troops on 11 March had been welcomed by enthusiastic crowds of Berliners. 'The popular throng surged to meet the victors, the saviours, as far as Weissensee', recorded one pamphlet: 'Nothing can be compared to the jubilation, the rejoicing which manifested itself in the city.'[34] The occasion was both an official and a spontaneous one:

> the most solemn moment was undoubtedly when the General-in-Chief stood at the side of the brother of our monarch on the Schlossplatz, surrounded by all the generals and officers of his General Staff under the gaze of the royal princesses and amidst the never-ending 'Hurrahs' of the people, as his triumphal procession marched past with the band playing and the banners flying.[35]

Without any official prompting, the city was lit up ceremoniously during the evening, with the citizenry continuing to celebrate with the Russian troops into the night. The same thing occurred two weeks later, as the Prussian troops entered the city under the leadership of General Johann David Ludwig Yorck von Wartenburg, who had signed a ceasefire with the Russians on 30 December 1812 (the Convention of Tauroggen) without Friedrich Wilhelm III's permission. In a similar spirit of officially sponsored popular celebration, festivals of victory and thanksgiving took place throughout Prussia on Sunday 24 October, with the king—returning specially from Leipzig—being greeted by peels of bells through- out Berlin before riding through the Brandenburger Tor to the Domkirche for an official service, with a full array of ministers, civil servants, and magistrates present. An open-air service for soldiers and the public was also held in the Opernplatz, brought to a close with a 101-gun salute. In the evening, the monarch, regaled with the *Lied* 'Heil Dir im Siegerkranz', attended a festival performance in the opera house, together with the city's elites.

---

[31] Ibid., 210, 243.   [32] W. Meier, *Erinnerungen*, 140.

[33] A. v. Blumröder, *Erlebnisse im Krieg und Frieden*, 99.

[34] *Russlands Triumpf 1812 oder das erwachte Europa* (1813), cited in K. Hagemann, *Mannlicher Muth und teutscher Ehre'*, 457.

[35] Ibid.

Smaller versions of the festival, with services, balls, and collections for the sick and injured, took place in the majority of Prussian towns and many villages, involving much of the population. In ritualized form, they were repeated after the news of the Coalition's victory over France in April 1814, when soldiers and regiments returned to Germany during the summer of the same year and on 18 and 19 October, as 'German national festivals', referred to variously as 'teutsche Nationalfeste', 'Nationalfeste der Teutschen', 'Feste aller Teutschen', and 'Geburtsfeste teutscher Nation', were staged throughout the German lands on the first anniversary of the battle of Leipzig.[36] In the Hohenzollern monarchy, 19 October was declared an official 'Feiertag', with festivals staged throughout Brandenburg, Vorpommern, and the Rhineland and in the larger cities, including Breslau and Königsberg, but rarely in East and West Prussia and Silesia, which were less well connected, and had more disparate networks of educated burghers and larger non-German populations. In Berlin, the celebrations had begun on Sunday 16 October with a great parade along Unter den Linden. After further parades on 18 October, there were both official events, attended by the court and the 'hero' Blücher, and popular ones, taking place on the training ground of the capital's gymnasts (the Hasenheide) and culminating in a huge bonfire of oak trees and a beacon lit on top of the 22-metre-high climbing tower of the gymnasts in honour, as the cheers and toasts made plain, of 'the king, then of all the brave men who fought at Leipzig'.[37] On the following day, there was a religious service of thanksgiving and a collection for assembled war widows, orphans, and wounded soldiers in the morning and a 'memorial for the battle of salvation of Leipzig', which counted members of the royal family among the 10,000 or so spectators. In the evening, a specially commissioned spectacle, 'Die hundertjährigen Eichen, oder das Jahr 1914' by August von Kotzebue, with a score by Carl Maria von Weber, was performed in the Royal Opera House.

In October 1814, 780 major national festivals of remembrance took place all over Germany, according to the ledger compiled by the Rödelheim *Justizrat* and close collaborator of Jahn and Arndt, Karl Hoffmann, in *Des Teutschen Volkes feuriger Dank- und Ehrentempel* in 1815. Many more events took place in smaller towns and villages. The centre of activity was West Germany—outside of Prussian territory—around Frankfurt and the Rhine and Main Rivers. From here, recorded Arndt in the second edition of his tract *Ueber die Feier der Leipziger Schlacht* (1815), 'as I stood on the summit of the Taunus, the mountain of the battle, along with several thousand happy people on 18 October', it was possible to see 'the heavens around, near and far, turned red by more than 500 fires'.[38] The hilltop bonfires were the novel part of a ritual of national celebration, along with the planting of oak trees, which was deliberately grafted onto the conventions of

---

[36] D. Düding, 'Das deutsche Nationalfest von 1814: Matrix der deutschen Nationalfeste im 19. Jahrhundert', in D. Düding et al. (eds), *Öffentliche Festkultur. Politische Feste in Deutschland von der Aufklärung bis zum Ersten Weltkrieg* (Hamburg, 1988), 67–8.

[37] K. Hoffmann (ed.), *Des Teutschen Volkes feuriger Dank- und Ehrentempel* (Offenbach, 1815), 685–91.

[38] E. M. Arndt, *Ueber die Feier der Leipziger Schlacht* (Frankfurt, 1815), 3–4.

traditional festivals, involving processions, feasts, balls, and fireworks, still remembered from the courtly occasions of the baroque era.[39] Prompted by Jahn—the founder of the gymnastics movement—to incorporate an outline of national festivals in his popular publications, after a meeting convened at Rödelheim by Hoffmann in early May 1814 (at which Karl and Theodor Welcker, amongst other 'patriots', were also present), Arndt had gone on to provide a blueprint for national celebrations, which were reprinted in sections of the press (the *Rheinischer Merkur* and *National-Zeitung der Deutschen*) and which were adapted by local organizers in October.

Critically, Arndt accepted only one of Jahn's suggested dates for national festivals—the anniversary of the battle of 'Hermann' (Arminius) in the Teutoburger Wald but not that of the battle of Heinrich I against the Magyars (933 AD) or the Augsburg religious settlement (25 September 1555)—and added two of his own: the death of Andreas Hofer, the leader of the Tyrolean uprising in 1809 (20 February 1810), and the battle of Leipzig (18 October 1813). His pamphlet *Ein Wort über die Feier der Leipziger Schlacht*, 7,500 copies of which were printed and distributed in September 1814, specified what should be done on each of the four days of battle (16–19 October) which were to be celebrated: on 18 October, which was to be a day of the 'Volk', fires were to be lit on mountain tops, hills, and towers and to be tended until midnight as a symbol for adjoining regions—in addition to connoting the wartime communication of 'the oldest peoples' and 'the flames and rubble of Zaragoza and Moscow' in recent years—of the 'community and harmony' reigning amongst 'all German people', the expression of '*one* sentiment and *one* idea'; on 19 October, which was the 'great festival day' because it was 'also held and treated as such by the authorities of all places', the morning was to be devoted to official processions and religious services and the afternoon to 'temporal pleasures and celebrations', 'so that it fulfills two aims at the same time, to fill all hearts with joy and deeply to impress on them the memory of what has happened'.[40] Arndt's advice was to wear German national costume ('*eine teutsche Volkstracht*'), to assemble all soldiers from the wars in uniform and in their regiments, to collect funds for the wounded, and to honour those who fought in 1813 and 1814.[41] His aim was to create a festival—together with children's games designed to encourage future generations—'as a great German *Volksfest* throughout the entire fatherland for all time'.[42] He would be satisfied 'when all Germans feel what they are, and what they can be, what their *Volk* is worthy of as a people', he concluded: 'Then, in future, battles would never have to be waged in the heart of Germany, which would have to celebrated, like the battle of Leipzig.'[43] Arndt's festival was thus conceived of as a fillip for national unity and as a warning of what could happen—and had just happened—as a consequence of national weakness.

---

[39] D. Düding, 'Das deutsche Nationalfest von 1814', in D. Düding et al. (eds), *Öffentliche Festkultur*, 83.

[40] E. M. Arndt, *Ein Wort über die Feier der Leipziger Schlacht* (Frankfurt, 1814), 10–11, 13.

[41] Ibid., 16–17.   [42] Ibid., 18.   [43] Ibid., 19.

Many of the commemorative national festivals in October 1814, only some of which were inspired by Arndt and Jahn, took place in states—Bavaria, Baden, Saxony, Berg, and Westphalia—which had not fought on the side of the Coalition at the battle of Leipzig. Usually, as Friedrich Rückert noted, the awkward facts were overlooked, as national events were celebrated or remembered vicariously. What did 'the shooting, noises etc. mean'? asked the poet's sister on 18 October 1814.[44] 'Because the French received a beating by the Prussians', came the reply.[45] The local ceremony, with speeches by the mayor to the civil guard and a toast to the Allies, bordered on parody, Rückert went on, but this circumstance did not seem to undermine the solemnity of the occasion: 'How the Bavarians can accommodate such jubilation', given that they had only switched sides in October 1813, 'no one seems, in their great joy, to think about'.[46] It is true that the incidence and form of celebrations differed from state to state. In Württemberg, celebrations were outlawed. In Saxony, where the king was still imprisoned and the land remained under the control of Russian authorities with an uncertain future, events centred on religious services, thanking God for the establishment of peace and the unity of Europe's monarchs, and they were largely restricted to Dresden and Leipzig. Nonetheless, they also included the gathering of a large crowd on the battlefield, a speech by the editor of the *Leipziger Zeitung*, and a series of other celebrations organized by the newly founded, middle-class *Verein zur Feier des 19. Oktobers*, which helped to ensure that the day's activities were—in the words of the *Allgemeine Zeitung*—'as happy and celebratory as they could be under the circumstances'.[47] In Baden, the journalist and academic Carl von Rotteck recorded in an article on 'Das Jahr 1813' in the *Teutschen Blätter* that many had 'accepted the defeats of their own sons with joy because freedom could only blossom again from these sources'.[48]

Local networks of burghers and notables were often instrumental in coordinating festivities in October 1814, particularly in cases where the state had not called on officials and the clergy to take part. As was to be expected, other subjects—small farmers, farm labourers, journeymen, and artisans—were less prominent in associations and circles of organizers, continuing to complain about the practicalities of life and the burdens of war, with states such as Württemberg and Baden providing more soldiers for the Coalition in 1814 (24,000 and 10,000, respectively) and 1815 (35,000 and 23,000) than in 1812 (15,800 and 7,166) for the French.[49] Many of them do seem to have attended festivals in October 1814, though, and to have given thanks, like one steward in Erlach (Württemberg) after

[44] F. Rückert to C. Hohnbaum, 18 Oct. 1814, in F. Rückert (ed.), *Briefe*, 43. Bavaria changed sides just before the actual battle, but Rückert ignores this.

[45] Ibid.   [46] Ibid., 44.

[47] 'Die Feier des 18. und 19. Oktobers in Sachsen', *Allgemeine Zeitung*, 1814, cited in S. L. Hoffmann, 'Mythos und Geschichte. Leipziger Gedenkfeiern der Völkerschlacht im 19. und frühen 20. Jahrhundert', in E. François, S. Hannes, and J. Vogel (eds), *Nation und Emotion* (Göttingen, 1995), 116.

[48] C. v. Rotteck, *Gesammelte und nachgelassene Schriften*, vol. 1, 131.

[49] See M. Hewitson, 'Princes' Wars, Wars of the People or Total War? Mass Armies and the Question of a Military Revolution in Germany, 1792–1815', *War in History*, 20 (2013), 452–90, and P. Sauer, *Napoleons Adler*, 287–9.

the battle of Leipzig in 1813, that the war had ended and Napoleon had been defeated: 'in the whole of Europe a roar in the air' went on

> for an hour like a powerful clap of thunder or the collective firing of many hundreds of pieces of cannon, which had all gone off together. This event was taken by everyone as if it were a pronouncement of God himself on the fall of the destroyer of people, the Emperor Napoleon.[50]

It was a cause of rejoicing that there was, as a coppersmith in Gunzenhausen (Bavaria) had put it in April 1814, 'Peace! Peace! Peace!', freeing a 'hostaged humanity!'[51] Likewise, to a shoemaker in Schwenningen (Württemberg), it was necessary, above all, just to 'wish for peace and no war'.[52] That such subjects regularly framed their expressions in religious and local, not national, terms was to be expected.[53] Correspondingly, peace had not met 'the expectations of the German nation' and had not brought about the anticipated return of the Breisgau to Austria, leaving local hopes 'unfulfilled', in the opinion of Ignaz Speckle, an abbot in the Black Forest (Baden) in December 1814, yet the past year would 'stay in the mind forever because of its great events':

> The domination of Napoleon, against whom all the peoples of Europe and many from Asia had united, came to an end; the Bourbons were put back on the French throne; Germany was freed from French domination; an unprecedented union of peoples and regents was brought into being; peace was created in Europe and the greatest and most beautiful hopes were justified.[54]

It was the popularity and profundity of the belief that the end of the war constituted an important juncture which account for the widespread nature of 'national festivals' in October 1814, in spite of the differing histories and policies of individual German states and the diverse outlooks of German subjects.[55] It has been estimated that hundreds of thousands might have celebrated, with—according to Hoffmann—4,000 in Siegen, over 5,000 in Heidelberg, more than 8,000 in Marburg, and many more than 10,000 in Berlin.[56]

There were fewer, less well-attended festivals in October 1815. Planert claims that this decline in activity revealed 'how little the day of remembrance was anchored in a collective memory'.[57] Yet there was less cause for celebration in 1815, given the unexpected recommencement of hostilities and renewed conscription in March of that year. With few associations firmly established enough to continue the practice of mass festivals of remembrance on their own, only active

---

[50] Cited in U. Planert, *Der Mythos*, 606.   [51] Ibid., 613.   [52] Ibid.

[53] These suppositions counter the case made by Ute Planert, *Der Mythos*, 596–619.

[54] I. Speckle, diary entry, 27 May and 31 Dec. 1814, in U. Engelmann (ed.), *Das Tagebuch von Ignaz Speckle*, 469, 489.

[55] This was true even of the Rhineland: U. Schneider, *Politische Festkultur im 19. Jahrhundert. Die Rheinprovinz von der französischen Zeit bis zum Ende des Ersten Weltkrieges 1806–1918* (Essen, 1995), 49–65.

[56] K. Hoffmann (ed.), *Des Teutschen Volkes*, 638–91. The figure of 100,000s comes from K. Hagemann, *Mannlicher Muth und teutscher Ehre*, 486.

[57] U. Planert, *Der Mythos*, 619.

support from individual states would have allowed the invention of an enduring tradition, but such support was rare. Hoffmann himself, whose survey of events in 1814 was published in September of the following year with the hope of founding an annual act of celebration and commemoration, betrayed doubts—in the form of a call to prove the contrary—that princes would be unable to overcome their 'mistrust of the loyalty of the peoples' and that they would hesitate to grant them 'the rights which had been promised to them'.[58]

For liberal periodicals such as the *Rheinischer Merkur*, this change of mood explained why the second anniversary of the battle of Leipzig lacked 'the bright light of enthusiastic hope typical of the previous year', for 'the inner firmament of the nation was much too disturbed' by the lack of political progress and plans for 'the building of the future'.[59] Other publications, including official ones like the *Amts-Blatt der königlich kurmärkischen Regierung*, were less concerned by the alleged political disappointments of the post-war order, noting that 18 October 1815 had been celebrated 'in a very festive manner in all circles of the province and by all its inhabitants', which had demonstrated the existence—without the prompting or coordination of the authorities—of a 'general, united will' in the territories around Berlin, 'as in other areas of the German fatherland'.[60] The *Berliner Nachrichten* and *Vossische Zeitung* reported similar events occurring in Aachen, Dessau, Düsseldorf, Frankfurt an der Oder, Hamburg, Cassel, Cologne, Cracow, Oldenburg, Potsdam, Salzburg, and Thorn, amongst other places.[61]

In the Prussian capital itself, 700 gymnasts participated in a 'memorial celebration' on the Hasenheide on 18 October and performed in front of a significant crowd, albeit a smaller one than in 1814, on the next day. The occasion came in the wake of public rejoicing at 'the final victory' in June, with the royal family meeting a 'packed, jubilant people in the square in front of the royal palace', in Niebuhr's contemporaneous account.[62] Although the civil servant and academic had lost his wife and father in the previous two months, he remained optimistic that his son was growing up in 'a better generation than the old ones of our age': 'God meanwhile is manifest more and more wonderfully in our land and in our people.'[63] Official events only took place on Sunday 22 October in conjunction with the celebration of the 400th jubilee of the Hohenzollern monarchy, which at once overshadowed the anniversary of 1813 and began to cast it in a deliberately Prussian light, with the king leading the resistance to France and his people—and those of other states—following.[64] Popular feeling, though, showed no sign of dimming, with burghers' celebrations in the capital in October 1816 exceeding those of 1815.

---

[58] K. Hoffmann (ed.), *Des Teutschen Volkes feuriger Dank- und Ehrentempel*, 5.

[59] 'Die zweyte Oktoberfeyer', *Rheinischer Merkur*, vol. 325, 6 Nov. 1815.

[60] *Amts-Blatt der königlich kurmärkischen Regierung*, 29 Mar. 1816, cited in Hagemann, *Mannlicher Muth und teutscher Ehre*, 493.

[61] Ibid.

[62] B. G. Niebuhr to T. v. Schön, 30 June 1815, in B. G. Niebuhr, *Die Briefe*, ed. D. Gerhard and W. Norvin (Berlin, 1926–9), vol. 1, 593.

[63] Ibid., 595.   [64] Ibid., 493–4.

THE POLITICS OF MEMORY

It is true that the cult of the *Freiwilligen*, which was established from 1813 onwards through poems, songs, memoirs, and paintings, sometimes contained implicit criticism of official commemorations (or their absence) and, even, of the regular army. The works of Romantic painters such as Caspar David Friedrich and Georg Friedrich Kersting, who served in the Lützower corps, often depicted figures in *altdeutsche Tracht* (for example, Friedrich's *Zwei Männer in Betrachtung des Mondes*, 1819) and volunteers' uniforms (Kersting's *Auf Vorposten*, 1827), reclining casually with their weapons in a manner distinct from that of the army.[65] In *Auf Vorposten*, which Kersting painted in 1815, Theodor Körner, Karl Friedrich Friesen, and the artist Ferdinand Hartmann were portrayed in the loose-fitting black uniforms and distinctive floppy hats of the Lützow volunteers, resting watchfully and confidently in a forest glade.[66] In *Huttens Grab* (1823–4) by Friedrich, a soldier in a similar uniform is shown leaning on a fictional monument to the sixteenth-century 'patriot' (see Figure 5.1). The gothic church, in which the monument is located, is in ruins, neglected by the painter's contemporaries. On the monument, visible but obscure, are inscribed the names of Arndt and Jahn, whose continuing imprisonment was challenged by the painting. However, Scharnhorst's name was also carved on the monument, testifying to the fact that the legacy of the Prussian army and state, as sites of both restoration and reform, was worth contesting, in Friedrich's view.

Accordingly, many of the artistic representations of the period, including works by Kersting himself, juxtaposed and merged the traditions of the volunteers, *Landwehr*, and regular army in Prussia and other German states. There was a broad shift from battle scenes, observed from above with the commanding officers in the foreground, to episodes of battle and soldiers' lives, which could be seen in paintings by Albrecht Adam (born in Mannheim, trained in Prussia, and working in Bavaria), Franz Krüger (Prussia), Adolph Northen (Prussia), Dietrich Monten (Bavaria), Peter von Hess (Bavaria), Johann Baptist Pflug (Bavaria), Johann Baptiste Seele (Württemberg), Johann Peter Krafft (Austria), and Friedrich Treml (Austria). All displayed different types of soldier in close proximity, part of a mass of individual fighters rather than an anonymous element of clearly defined regiments. Adam and Christian Wilhelm Faber du Faur, in particular, were well known for their pictorial chronicles of the daily life (and death) of ordinary soldiers in the south German units of the *Grande Armée*, which they published as series in the late 1820s and 1830s.[67] In lithographs such as *An der grossen Strasse von Moshaisk nach Krymskoje, den 18. September 1812*, and in watercolours such as *Die Überquerung der Beresina, 20. November 1812* (1827–30), Faber du Faur, who was serving as an officer in Württemberg's army, displayed officers and simple soldiers huddled

[65] W. Schnell, *Georg Friedrich Kersting 1785–1847* (Berlin, 1994); W. Hofmann, *Caspar David Friedrich* (New York, 2000).

[66] C. Clark, 'The Wars of Liberation in Prussian Memory', 567–76, on Kersting and Friedrich; K. Hagemann, *Mannlicher Muth und teutscher Ehre*, 510–17.

[67] S. Parth, *Zwischen Bildbericht und Bildpropaganda. Kriegskonstruktionen in der deutschen Militärmalerei des 19. Jahrhunderts* (Paderborn, 2010), 252–6.

Figure 5.1. Caspar David Friedrich, *Huttens Grab* (1823–4)
Source: Klassik Stiftung Weimar; Weimar, 18 May 2016.

together to survive the cold and attacks by the Russian army.[68] It is in this wider context of struggles for a vaguely defined 'freedom', in which the actual enmity of different German soldiers—Swabian, Bavarian, Saxon, Prussian, and Austrian—was overlooked, that the reverential treatment of volunteers—visible in Otto Donner von Richter's *Die Lützower an der Leiche Theodor Körners in Wöbbelin am 27. August 1813* (1848)—should be understood.[69] Certainly, what struck educated contemporaries was the commonality of the struggle, given the previous divisions of the German states.

Veterans' organizations, which might have maintained traditions of remembrance in spite of official hostility or indifference, were formed across the German lands, but belatedly. In states such as Hamburg, the existence of local associations, a civic militia, and more receptive authorities allowed the participation of citizens in the public commemoration of 1813 throughout the post-war era; notably, 'holy Alexander days' celebrating the Russian Tsar as a liberator, occasions marking the temporary raising of the French siege on 18 March 1813 and the anniversary of 18 October, which was made the main official festival by the Senate in 1817.[70] In the south, the first veterans' associations seem to have been set up in the mid-1820s and to have collaborated with friends and families of dead soldiers in erecting war memorials from the late 1820s onwards. During the 1830s and 1840s, states started to respond to such commemoration, partly out of a desire to recast their dynastic histories in an era of politicization. In Bavaria, which led the way, an obelisk was erected in Munich to mark the twentieth anniversary of the battle of Leipzig on 18 October 1833, after various plans to honour the dead of 1812 had circulated amongst soldiers and, especially, officers in the 1810s and 1820s.[71] The 30,000 soldiers to whom it was dedicated, in accordance with the wishes of King Ludwig I, were said in the inscriptions of the monument to have 'also died to liberate the fatherland', in a task 'completed on 18 October 1813', despite the fact that they had died on France's side in 1812, which was not mentioned.[72] Like other monuments erected by the Bavarian monarch, most notably the *Feldherrnhalle* (likewise in Munich, with a foundation stone laid on 18 October) and the *Walhalla* near Regensburg (planned by Leo von Klenze in 1821 and built between 1830 and 1842), the 'fatherland' referred to denoted both Bavaria and Germany. In Ludwig's own words, describing his time as Crown Prince during the Napoleonic Wars, he

---

[68] Ibid., 280–1.   [69] M. Jeismann, *Das Vaterland der Feinde*, 98–9.

[70] K. Aaslestad, *Place and Politics*, 324–8. There are also indications, from later records, that veterans' organizations had existed for a long time in Saxony, with their outlook fixed by the 'days of great acts' (1813–15): E. Trox, *Militärischer Konservatismus. Kriegervereine und 'Militärpartei' in Preussen zwischen 1815 und 1848/49* (Stuttgart, 1990), 43.

[71] U. Planert, 'From Collaboration to Resistance: Politics, Experience and Memory of the Revolutionary and Napoleonic Wars in Southern Germany', *Central European History*, 39 (2006), 695–6. See also J. Murken, 'Von "Thränen und Wehmut" zur Geburt des "deutschen Nationalbewußtseins". Die Niederlage des Russlandfeldzugs von 1812 und ihre Umdeutung in einen nationalen Sieg', in H. Carl (ed.), *Kriegsniederlagen. Erfahrungen und Erinnerungen* (Berlin, 2004), 107–22.

[72] W. Schmidt, 'Denkmäler für die bayerischen Gefallenen des Russlandfeldzuges von 1812', *Zeitschrift für bayerische Landesgeschichte*, 49 (1986), 303–26; T. Nipperdey, 'Nationalidee und Nationaldenkmal im 19. Jahrhundert', *Historische Zeitschrift*, 210 (1968), 529–85.

had first conceived of the idea of realizing 'the fifty most gloriously exceptional German sculptures in marble', which included Scharnhorst, Blücher, Gneisenau, and Schwarzenberg and which were later incorporated into the design of the *Walhalla*, during 'the days of Germany's deepest humiliation' in 1807.[73] Except in the Bavarian Palatinate, where soldiers had put up a monument to Napoleon in Mainz, there was little indication that this elision of 1812 and 1813—and of Bavaria and Germany—was contradicted by veterans themselves.[74]

In Baden and Württemberg, veterans' associations were created later than in neighbouring Bavaria, from the late 1830s onwards, but they went on to lobby the Grand Duke and king to honour all combatants and to award them medals, irrespective of rank, to which the heads of state acceded, respectively, in 1839 (with the exception of Badenese soldiers who had fought before 1805) and 1840 (for all Württemberg's soldiers who had fought 'for king and fatherland').[75] As Crown Prince, Wilhelm I of Württemberg had fought for the Coalition against French forces, including those of his own Swabian homeland, making him 'really the focal point' (Robert von Mohl), as king, of the anti-French refashioning of the state's recent 'German' history in the 1830s and 1840s, just as Ludwig I, who had opposed the Wittelsbach kingdom's stance during the Napoleonic Wars, had become the main object of Bavaria's 'national' history.[76] The slow shift of historical position over which they presided seems to have corresponded to memories of the wars of 'freedom' or 'liberation' which had been kept alive by veterans, their families, and other civilians. Thus, the Victory Column unveiled in Stuttgart in 1841, on the twenty-fifth anniversary of Wilhelm I's accession, had been paid for in part by a collection organized by members of the *Ständekammer* (Chamber of Estates) and it was inaugurated by a procession of the army, veterans, and subjects of all strata and occupations, extending several miles. As in Munich, the monument's reliefs referred only to battles against Napoleon, after Württemberg switched sides in October 1813. For their part, veterans only wore the uniforms and bore the flags of 1814–15.[77]

In the Hohenzollern monarchy, it seemed initially that popular and official memories of 1813 could coalesce. As elsewhere, veterans' associations, volunteer clubs, and funeral associations were formed in the 1830s and 1840s to organize meetings and to provide funds for the ceremonial burial, including uniformed pall-bearers, of *Freiwilligen* and other soldiers. Eckhard Trox has

---

[73] Ludwig I of Bavaria, *Walhalla's Genossen* (Munich, 1842), v. See also K. B. Murr, '"Treue is in den Tod". Kriegsmythen in der bayerischen Geschichtspolitik im Vormärz', in N. Buschmann and D. Langewiesche (eds), *Der Krieg in der Gründungsmythen* (Tübingen, 2002), 138–74.

[74] U. Planert, *Der Mythos*, 630–2. The elision was supported tacitly by popular sources, such as the *Rheinisches Conversations-Lexikon*, which treated the invasion of Russia in 1812 as a French disaster, with no mention of German troops: *Rheinisches Conversations-Lexikon oder encyclopädisches Handwörterbuch für gebildete Stände* (Cologne, 1824–30), vol. 2, 757.

[75] C. Väterlein (ed.), *Baden und Württemberg im Zeitalter Napoleons* (Stuttgart, 1987), vol. 1, 465.

[76] R. v. Mohl, *Lebenserinnerungen von Robert von Mohl 1799–1875* (Stuttgart, 1902), 17. See also A. Green, *Fatherlands: State-Building and Nationhood in Nineteenth-Century Germany* (Cambridge, 2001), 62–70.

[77] See U. Planert, 'From Collaboration to Resistance', 700–1.

discovered fifty-five *Kriegsvereine* of this type in most of the larger cities (Berlin, Münster, Crefeld, Elberfeld, Duisburg, Essen, Bochum, Dortmund, Neuwied, Cologne, Trier, Merseburg, Magdeburg, Halberstadt, Potsdam, Frankfurt an der Oder, Memel, and Breslau), in addition to associations of active soldiers (Minden, Düsseldorf, Aachen, Trier, Magdeburg, Frankfurt an der Oder, Kottbus, Königsberg, Potsdam, Marienwerder, and Danzig) and older burial societies and 'Schützengilden', some of which dated back to the Seven Years' War.[78] In the immediate aftermath of the Napoleonic Wars, groups of gymnasts and student fraternities (*Burschenschaften*) had perpetuated and adapted the rituals of remembrance.

The *Turnbewegung*, as it was commonly described, had been founded by Jahn in 1811 in Berlin, extending to a network of 150 clubs and about 12,000 members—mainly in central and northern Germany—by 1818. It was closely connected to the Lützow corps of *Freiwilligen*, for which Jahn and his followers had recruited volunteers, using a hotel near Prussia's *de facto* civil and military headquarters, in Breslau in 1813. Although the young middle-class *Turner* were critical of Germany's princes and their 'lackeys', cultivating a deliberately civilian form of physical fitness and organization, their preparations and points of reference, which encompassed the re-enactment of battles on carefully chosen training grounds, only made sense in the context of past and future wars against a French enemy.[79] As such, they were reconcilable with official accounts of Prussia's struggle against Napoleon. Thus, Friedrich Lieber's loving description of Jahn's visit to the battlefields of Silesia with a group of gymnasts in 1818, despite mockery of Austrian and Prussian royalty, was designed, above all, to ensure that 'the memory of the wars of liberation, which some of them had experienced personally, should never be submerged'.[80] Similarly, the very clothing of the gymnasts, which had come to be known through Jahn's own example as a patriotic uniform or *altdeutsche Tracht* consisting of a loose black jacket and grey, unbleached, linen trousers, were a conscious counterpoint to the decoration and frivolity of the court and the army, but it also continued to refer to the costumes of the *Freiwilligen* and the wars of 1813–15. 'The light and austere, unpretentious and thoroughly functional linen costume of the *Turner* is unsuited to red, blue and green braids, aiguillettes, armbands, dress swords and gauntlets on the leaders of processions etc.', wrote Jahn in *Deutsche Turnkunst* (1816): 'The earnest spirit of the fighter (*der Wehrmannsernst*) is thereby transformed into idle play.'[81] Unlike Greek athletics, which were competitive, 'German' *Turnen* was

---

[78] E. Trox, *Militärischer Konservatismus*, 44–53.

[79] D. Langewiesche, '…"Für Volk und Vaterland kräftig zu würken…"': Zur politischen Rolle der Turner zwischen 1811 und 1871', in D. Langewiesche, *Nation, Nationalismus, Nationalstaat*, 103–31.

[80] F. Lieber, *Die Fahrt nach Schlesien in 1818* (Berlin, 1818), cited in D. Düding, *Organisierter gesellschaftlicher Nationalismus in Deutschland 1808–1847. Bedeutung und Funktion der Turner- und Sängervereine für die deutsche Nationalbewegung* (Munich, 1984), 85–6. The account here diverges from that of Chris Clark, though remaining indebted to it: Chris Clark, 'The Wars of Liberation in Prussian Memory', 560–1.

[81] F. L. Jahn, *Deutsche Turnkunst*, 2nd edn (Berlin, 1847), 97. The translation is from Chris Clark, 'The Wars of Liberation in Prussian Memory', 563.

believed to be cooperative and civil, 'an enduring site for the building of fresh, sociable virtues...of a sense of decency and law, [of a feeling for] cheerful obedience without prejudice to freedom of movement and cheerful independence'.[82] Nevertheless, its purpose was tied, too, to military defence, according to Jahn, 'to develop a manly and orderly spirit' amongst the nation's youth.[83]

The emancipatory and military goals of the *Turnbewegung*, linked explicitly to the 'wars of freedom', were elaborated by Johann Christoph Friedrich GutsMuths, one of the founders of the movement, in his *Turnbuch für die Söhne des Vaterlandes* (1817) and other works. Exercises—turning, bending, swinging, and singing—were intended to reverse the inactivity and 'stiffness' of modern citizens. Town-dwellers, in particular, were characterized by an imbalance between body and spirit, with the former having 'given its strength' to the latter as a corollary of poor air, a lack of space 'to tumble around in the open', repetitive occupations which only exercised specific muscles, and a more fundamental isolation from nature.[84] Amongst 'the higher, exquisitely educated classes, the sickliness of the European can be observed, sometimes less so, sometimes more so', exacerbated by the temptations of wealth such as 'indulgence, pleasure-seeking, softness and an almost innate yearning for comfort and sensual well-being', GutsMuths complained.[85] As a result of a 'strict upbringing', those from the land were stronger and tougher, but their bodies, too, became 'stiff, heavy-limbed and unsuited to rapid, agile movement' and their minds became inflexible.[86] By teaching boys from their fourteenth year onwards (with the participation of those aged 10 to 13) to march, jump, skip, turn, pole vault, climb, wrestle, swim, throw, and shoot, the leaders of the gymnasts aimed not merely to counter the decadence of modern urban life, but also to shape future soldiers, with exercises 'seen from a patriotic point of view' as 'a necessary pre-schooling of those becoming defenders of the fatherland':

> If, in the counsels of the German governments, general arming has been decided on, if they want genuine defenders, they should and must direct the education of the sons of the fatherland towards these great goals. If they enthused them with love for the fatherland, *Volk* and noble princes, if they increased the strength and the suppleness of the body, it will be easy for them to adapt quickly to military exercises, and in this way the...inner goodness of the army will be powerfully met, for a person who has gained the true pre-requisites of audacity and courage, namely strength and suppleness, this person can only be a good fighter: the virtue of the individual, however, creates the virtue, the value of the army. I am remembering the year of the battle of Leipzig. Enthusiasm for Germany drove thousands towards salvation. Have you counted those, however, who—with the same level of enthusiasm but fettered by bodily weakness—had to stay behind?[87]

The year 1813 was used as both an example and a warning. 'Freedom and independence need to be defended', GutsMuths went on: 'Only an enslaved soul can

[82] F. L. Jahn, *Deutsche Turnkunst*, vii, cited in Chris Clark, 'The Wars of Liberation in Prussian Memory', 562.

[83] F. L. Jahn, *Die Deutsche Turnkunst* (Berlin, 1816), vol. 1, 3.

[84] J. C. F. GutsMuths, *Turnbuch für die Söhne des Vaterlandes* (Frankfurt, 1817), xxi.

[85] Ibid., xxii.   [86] Ibid., xxix–xxx.   [87] Ibid., xiv–xxxiv.

ask for proof of this sentence—to every genuine German, it stands as a self-evident truth.'[88] Yet such independence was to be protected by German armies, just as 'noble' princes continued to be worthy of enthusiastic support. Given its position 'at the centre of this part of the world', 'bedded down in a dangerous bed since primordial times', 'the German tribe' (*der deutsche Stamm*) was exposed to storms from all directions but it could defend itself, if the entire population remained strong, supplementing standing armies rather than replacing them, as had been shown by the *Landwehr* and volunteers at Leipzig:

> There are events, particularly in the situation of the tribe of Germans, in which standing armies no longer suffice. We have already experienced them—for this reason, the resort to weapons has become general; everyone should be a defender of the fatherland; the prince and the *Volk* want this, as does reason.[89]

'The warrior' was not to be treated as a 'machine', even 'in our current form of warfare' typified by loading and firing guns, since hand-to-hand and other types of combat called for flexibility and resilience, which could not be attained by 'purely military exercises'.[90] All the same, the exercises culminated, in the final part of the *Turnbuch*, in 'war', with simulations of battles taking place on carefully chosen 'battlefields' (*Kampfplätze*), on sandy ground 200 feet long and 100 feet wide, and with popular festivals exalting the life of the individual, 'warming his heart for the sake of the state and demanding a sense of community' through the evocation of past heroism and the commemoration of the dead.[91]

The *Turnbewegung* was part of a middle-class, predominantly urban, and disproportionately youthful political sphere after 1815, in which the 'wars of freedom' constituted an important point of reference, even if the claim by the *Zentraluntersuchungskommission* in Mainz that there was a widespread, coherent network of agitators and associations was an exaggeration.[92] In the absence of political parties and representative assemblies, gymnastic associations, *Burschenschaften*, circles of academics, secret societies, masonic lodges, and 'Deutsche Gesellschaften' (German societies) provided institutional means of 'commemorating' 1813 by means of collective, public rituals and gatherings.[93] Their members comprised a significant section of the *Bildungsbürgertum*, which became central to the development in the nineteenth century of 'public opinion' and a German public sphere (*Öffentlichkeit*). Nearly all of them had been to *Gymnasium*—of which there were just ninety-one in the whole of Prussia in 1818—or to another higher school, which together were attended by about 1.5 per cent—or 14,826 pupils—of the relevant age group in Prussia and by 6–7 per cent of 14 to 19 year olds in Berlin. Many had been to—or were still at—one of Germany's universities or similar institutions, of which there were over thirty, accommodating about 9,000 students (1810) and including the newest and largest universities of Berlin (founded in 1809), Breslau

---

[88] Ibid., xv. [89] Ibid. [90] Ibid., xxix. [91] Ibid., 200–3, iv.
[92] K. Luys, *Die Anfänge der deutschen Nationalbewegung von 1815 bis 1819* (Münster, 1992), 265.
[93] Conservative critics such as Friedrich de la Motte Fouqué, *Etwas über den deutschen Adel, über Ritter-Sinn und Militär-Ehre* (Hamburg, 1819), 26, were anxious to show, against such a widely held belief, that the '*Bürgerstand*' could not simply be equated with the '*Volk*'.

(1811), and Bonn (1818).[94] The intellectual elite who attended secondary schools and universities was mixed in origin—with some 43 per cent of pupils of *Gymnasien* in western Germany in the first half of the nineteenth century coming from lower middle-class groups, according to one estimate—and it dominated the critical political milieux of the towns, which together made up less than 10 per cent of the population of the German lands but which comprised the majority of the membership of associations and readership of the press.[95] It was also closely connected to the campaigns of 1813–14 and 1815, with about half of all students joining the *Freiwilligen*, the *Landwehr*, or the regular army.[96] Since a large proportion of students—half of the total in Jena and perhaps a third of all students, or about 3,000 in the German Bund—joined *Burschenschaften*, which had been set up after 1815 to replace regional *Landsmannschaften*, and other associations such as *Geheimbünde*, the Freemasons, and the gymnastics movement, memories of the war remained vivid and played a central role in societies' activities and programmes, along with other aspects of patriotic and national reform.[97]

Such memories seem to have been fundamental to the generations, identified by Jörg Echternkamp, who had been born in the 1760s and 1770s and had come to adulthood during the instability of the 1790s and 1800s (characterized by the French Revolution, war, the dissolution of the Holy Roman Empire, and territorial changes), and those who had been born between 1785 and 1805, experiencing the Napoleonic era during the conscious years of childhood, adolescence, and young adulthood, frequently influenced by teachers from the first generation.[98] This 'German youth, which has been my joy and consolation for eight years', wrote the Jena historian and co-founder of the '*Urburschenschaft*' Heinrich Luden (born in 1778) in the 1840s, would soon be replaced by another generation, 'which has had a completely different past'.[99] Until then, though, previous generations had had a living memory of 'that time of very violent unrest, when everyone felt that the well-being and fortunes of the nation would be in the balance forever', as the Prussian official and pedagogue Gerd Eilers (b. 1788) put it in his memoirs, published in the 1850s.[100] 'Germany felt itself free, after it had borne the heavy yoke of servitude for years', he continued: 'Germany had become free through the

[94] A. W. Daum, '*Wissenschaft* and Knowledge', in J. Sperber (ed.), *Germany, 1800–1870* (Oxford, 2004), 139–40. Wolfgang Hardtwig, 'Studentische Mentalität – Politische Jugendbewegung – Nationalismus. Die Anfänge der deutschen Burschenschaft', in Wolfgang Hardtwig, *Nationalismus und Bürgerkultur in Deutschland*, 139, gives a lower estimate of 6–8,000.

[95] T. Nipperdey, *Deutsche Geschichte 1800–1866*, 6th revised edn (Munich, 1993), 112, 459–60.

[96] J. Echternkamp, *Aufstieg*, 359.

[97] Ibid.; H. Lönnecker, 'Politische Lieder der Burschenschaften aus der Zeit zwischen 1820 und 1850', *Lied und populäre Kultur*, 48 (2003), 85.

[98] J. Echternkamp, *Aufstieg*, 366–77.

[99] H. Luden, *Rückblicke in mein Leben* (Jena, 1847), 216–17. The '*Urburschenschaft*' was the first *Burschenschaft*, founded in Jena in 1815. See also K. Ries, 'Zwischen Wissenschaft, Staat und Gesellschaft. Heinrich Luden als politischer Professor der Universität Jena', in H.-W. Hahn et al. (eds), *Bürgertum in Thüringen. Lebenswelt und Lebenswege im frühen 19. Jahrhundert* (Jena, 2001), 27–52.

[100] G. Eilers, *Meine Wanderung durchs Leben. Ein Beitrag zur inneren Geschichte des ersten Hälfte des 19. Jahrhunderts* (Leipzig, 1856), vol. 1, 224–5.

voluntarily-given blood of sacrifice, which had flowed in torrents.'[101] Understandably, the 'wars of freedom', in conjunction with the wider political and existential instability of 'a very agitated age', were frequently formative, constituting 'the foundations', in the words of the jurist Heinrich Karl Hofmann (b. 1795), which 'have proved their worth to me in joy and suffering' during 'the long years of isolation from everything that is dear and holy to a person'.[102] Even for Heinrich Leo (b. 1799), the son of an army chaplain and later a conservative historian, the *Freiheitskriege* had made 'German and Christian interests' popular, allowing 'the goals which Jahn had planted in my soul as the aims of my striving' to dominate all else and leaving 'nothing in the world at all ... except the German *Volk* or, rather, the ideal of the German *Volk*'.[103] From the point of view of students such as Leo, the 'wars of freedom' were intimately linked to the political aspirations and hopes of an entire generation. A third generation, born after 1805, had no memory of the Napoleonic Wars but they also had little reason to challenge already-established images of the conflicts.

As a result of such intergenerational support (or lack of opposition), memories of the wars were integral to the aims of the 'Verfassungs-Urkunde der allgemeinen teutschen Burschenschaft', decided at the second meeting of an all-German umbrella organization on 18 October 1818: namely, to achieve the 'Christian, German marshalling and training of every mental and bodily resource for the service of the fatherland', at the same as maintaining the 'unity, freedom and equality of all *Burschen* amongst themselves'.[104] They were visible, too, in the *altdeutsche Tracht* or black clothing of students (like that of the '*schwarze Schar*' of Lützow), the black, red, and gold flag (likewise the banner of the Lützower corps but now with the inscription 'Deutschlands Wiedergeburt' on it), and the regular references of *Burschen* to the 'humiliation', 'defence', and 'rising up' of Germany. 'We have all seen the great year 1813', wrote the Jena students who had participated in the Wartburg festival in 1817 at the suggestion of Luden: 'And would we not be contemptible before God and the world if we had not tended and sustained such thoughts and feelings? We have tended and sustained them and [we] return to dwell on them again and again and will never forsake them.'[105] At the festival itself, which took place on 18 October at the Wartburg—where Martin Luther had lived and worked—in celebration of the 400th anniversary of the Reformation and the fourth anniversary of the battle of Leipzig, 400–500 *Burschenschafter* had gathered

---

[101] Ibid., 225.

[102] H. K. Hofmann (ed.), *Beiträge zur Erörterung vaterländischer Angelegenheiten* (Darmstadt, 1831), iii.

[103] Ibid., 372; C. v. Maltzahn, *Heinrich Leo 1799–1878: Ein politisches Gelehrtenleben zwischen romantischen Konservatismus und Realpolitik* (Göttingen, 1979), 21.

[104] Joachim Leopold Haupt Altenburg, *Landsmannschaften und Burschenschaften. Ein freies Wort über die geselligen Verhältnisse der Studierenden auf den teutschen Hochschulen* (Leipzig, 1820), 257.

[105] 'Grundsätze und Beschlüsse der Wartburgfeier, den studierenden Brüdern auf anderen Hochschulen zur Annahme, dem gesamten Vaterlande zur Würdigung vorgelegt von den Studierenden in Jena' (December, 1817), cited in C. Clark, 'The Wars of Liberation in Prussian Memory', 565.

to recall the past and discuss the future.[106] Past wars were linked unthinkingly to a German nation and a future German polity.

Such discussions and commemorations were restricted or prohibited during the 'restoration'.[107] There is little to suggest that they would not have continued, if the authorities had not suppressed them after 1819/20—a fact intimated *inter alia* by the retention of the symbols of 1813 by associations in favour of Greek and Polish independence in the 1820s and by events at the time of the French revolution of 1830, most notably the Hambach *Fest* attended by 30,000 national-minded liberals and democrats in 1832. The German states agreed unanimously at the Austrian spa resort of Carlsbad on 20 September 1819 to clamp down on the *Burschenschaften* and other 'political' associations, after the theology student Karl Sand, who had been both a *Burschenschafter* and a volunteer in the war, had assassinated the famous conservative playwright and Russian spy August von Kotzebue on 23 March. The decrees were implemented in 1820. Yet, although Sand's suicide note announced that 'the renewal of our German life' had begun 'during the last twenty years, and particularly during the holy time of 1813', and it imagined 'the most disgraceful dishonour, if all the beautiful things that thousands joyfully gave up were to…die away with no lasting consequences', there is little evidence to suggest that German governments were worried primarily by the national legacy of the 'wars of freedom'.[108]

The Prussian *Staatskanzler* Hardenberg had been obliged, as he wrote in his diary on 13 December 1817, to lodge a formal complaint about 'the excesses of the press of Saxe-Weimar' at the time of the Wartburg festival and he was critical of the fact that '15 and 16 year-olds are misled into playing the part of senators and fathers of the *Vaterland*', yet he remained convinced that it was necessary to take account of 'world events' such as the recent wars, which had meant that 'history comprises a constant series of changes'.[109] Hardenberg's reactionary opponents in Prussia, who were dominant at court and in government by 1819 and who had ensured that the Hohenzollern monarchy took the lead in establishing the Confederation's apparatus of political police, were not persuaded by the Chancellor's call for a constitution to accommodate the transformations which had occurred over the last three decades but they, too, concentrated on the domestic designs of revolutionaries, not on their belligerent nationalism, labelling Wartburg a 'nonsense' which 'attacks all the princes, great and small' through the practice of 'terrorism, intolerance and the despotism of demagogues', in the estimation of Carl von Mecklenburg, the reactionary half-brother of Queen Luise.[110]

---

[106] P. Brandt, 'Das studentische Wartburgfest vom 18./19. Oktober 1817', in D. Düding (ed.), *Öffentliche Festkultur*, 89–112.

[107] Otto Wigand's *Conversations-Lexikon der neuesten Litteratur-, Völker- und Staatengeschichte* (Leipzig, 1841–5), vol. 1, depicted the return of 'a phalanx of heroes of freedom, who were used to speaking and acting as freely as they thought', to private lives and public circumstances which seemed 'the burden and result of dominant arbitrariness to their military and patriotic spirit'.

[108] Cited in C. Clark, 'The Wars of Liberation in Prussian Memory', 565.

[109] I. Herman, *Hardenberg*, 360, 373.

[110] C. v. Mecklenburg to Friedrich Wilhelm III, 3 Nov. 1817, cited in T. Stamm-Kuhlmann, *König in Preussens großer Zeit*, 426. W. Siemann, *'Deutschlands Ruhe, Sicherheit und Ordnung'. Die Anfänge der politischen Polizei 1806–1866* (Tübingen, 1985), 76–7.

Compared to his Prussian counterparts, the Austrian Foreign Minister Metternich had seemed more anxious about what he termed a dangerous enthusiasm for the 'fatherland' in warnings to German capitals in 1817.[111] However, his principal concern, after receiving reports from the Austrian minister in Dresden that the Wartburg meeting had been a 'Jacobin orgy', was for 'the principles of public order', which had been undergirded at Carlsbad by 'a group of anti-revolutionary measures' (censorship, surveillance of universities, a Central Commission to monitor political activity) that he had wanted to bring into being 'since 1813', when the Habsburg monarchy had first regained ascendancy in the German lands and Franz I had had the opportunity—not realized until 1819/20—of becoming *de facto* 'Emperor of Germany'.[112]

HISTORIES OF LIBERATION AND THE POST-WAR ORDER

The principal intellectual apologist of what became Metternich's 'system' was Gentz, who had made the transition from being a cautious supporter to an opponent of the French Revolution in the 1790s. Although it has been claimed that the publicist contributed to 'the revitalization of a pre-revolutionary paradigm of war', designed as a 'strategy of stabilization of the monarchical state' (in Jörn Leonhard's words), he began from the premise that warfare and diplomacy had altered fundamentally and irreversibly since 1792, ruling out the types of conflict and the regular alternation between war and peace which had characterized the eighteenth century.[113] The European powers were resolved, even after Napoleon's escape from Elba in 1815, to show the world that 'the basic principles of 1813 and 1814 have not wavered for one moment' and that 'anyone who wanted to threaten the general peace of Europe through new revolutions or new wars' would be treated as 'a communal enemy' and fought 'with weapons borne in common'.[114] The problem confronting the powers was no longer the French Emperor, who 'can no longer make Europe tremble', but 'the spirit animating this new, wicked deed', which 'should never be overlooked in contempt', warned Gentz in 1815.[115] Those calling for German populations and states to follow the lead of their Greek counterparts and to rise up for the sake of their 'independence' against Austria and Russia, whose 'dominance over Germany (*Teutschland*)' was allegedly safe until that point, were to be ridiculed, wrote the conservative journalist seven years later.[116] Their claim

---

[111] Cited in A. Palmer, *Metternich* (London, 1972), 170.

[112] Austrian Minister in Dresden to C. v. Metternich; F. Gentz in the *Österreichischer Beobachter* in 1817; C. v. Metternich to E. v. Metternich, 1 Sept. 1819, all cited in A. Palmer, *Metternich*, 170, 185. The Final Act of the Ministerial Conference to Complete and Consolidate the Organization of the German Confederation was signed in May 1820.

[113] J. Leonhard, *Bellizismus*, 423, hints in his treatment of Georg Wilhelm Valentini, for instance, that this was the case for at least some conservative authors.

[114] F. v. Gentz, 'Über die Deklaration der 8 Mächte gegen Napoleon', in G. Schlesier (ed.), *Schriften von Friedrich von Gentz* (Mannheim, 1838–40), vol. 2, 398.

[115] Ibid., 397.

[116] F. v. Gentz, 'Bemerkungen zu der Schrift "Über die gegenwärtige Lage von Europa"' (1822), ibid., vol. 5, 227. The article was first published in the *Allgemeine Zeitung*, 16 Oct. 1822.

that 'the fetters of the political system' were supposedly 'broken', with 'the uprising of the Greeks' held to be preparing 'the way for the uprising of the Germans' (since 'the present conjuncture is suited to an undertaking of this kind') was 'madness'.[117] Nonetheless, Metternich's fear, first raised by the combination of 'revolutions and wars' during the period after 1792, was that national insurrections in Germany, as in Greece, could overturn the existing political order, risking a descent into barbarism. 'The political system, which constitutes the last anchor of the social order in Europe, the last defence of the civilized world against the influx of barbarians, is still standing, firm and unshaken', he affirmed in the same article.[118] Although the European system and the German Confederation seemed secure for the moment, such threats were to be treated as 'significant' and 'instructive', for the danger—as the French Revolution and the Napoleonic Wars had proven—was real.[119] Like other conservative writers and publicists such as the Swiss historian Carl Ludwig von Haller and the Prussian philosopher and later Austrian official Adam Müller, Gentz believed that revolutions themselves, given the lessons of 1789, were closely tied to the transformation of warfare: 'total revolutions', which had occurred in France and the United States, had led to internal 'war', he had already declared in 1793, which 'cannot be explained in the usual way' and which was likely to escalate because both sides were convinced that they were right and because 'the yardstick for right and wrong' had been 'destroyed'.[120] For the Allies, the war against France after 1792 could be considered a 'self-perpetuating war of defence', which pro-longed the revolution (or the main cause of the war in the first place) and which staved off the annihilation of the losing side in the domestic civil war, making the conflict more difficult to end.[121] These mechanisms were quite different, in Gentz's opinion, from those of previous, limited wars.[122]

The political balance of power devised by Gentz to guard against the nefarious effects of revolutionary warfare was predicated on the idea of strong sovereign states. No state should be powerful enough, he held, to be certain of dominating the others, as France had been during the Napoleonic era:

> What we normally call the political balance of power (balance de pouvoir) is that constitution of contiguous and more or less well-connected states such that none of them can damage the independence or take away significant rights of another without incurring effective resistance from the other side and, as a consequence, without risk to itself.[123]

---

[117] Ibid.   [118] Ibid., 230.   [119] Ibid., 231.

[120] F. v. Gentz, 'Über die Moralität in den Staatsrevolutionen', in F. v. Gentz, *Ausgewählte Schriften*, ed. W. Weick (Stuttgart, 1836–38), vol. 2, 43, 49. See also C. L. v. Haller, *Restauration der Staats-Wissenschaft oder Theorie des natürlich-geselligen Zustands der Chimäre des künstlich-bürgerlichen entgegengesetzt* (Winterthur, 1820–25), vol. 1, 228–59; A. Müller, *Die Elemente der Staatskunst*, vol. 1, 3–69; P. P. Müller-Schmid, 'Adam Müller (1779–1829)', in B. Heidenreich (ed.), *Politische Theorien des 19. Jahrhunderts* (Berlin, 2002), 109–38.

[121] F. v. Gentz, *Über den Ursprung*, in F. v. Gentz, *Ausgewählte Schriften*, vol. 2, 273–5.

[122] Ibid., 274.

[123] F. v. Gentz, 'Fragmente aus der neuesten Geschichte des politischen Gleichgewichts in Europa' (1806), Ibid., vol. 4, 39.

Although the publicist rarely referred to nations on the French model, they informed his concept of sovereignty and equilibrium. 'There is neither an executive nor a judicial power between independent nations (*Völker*)', he continued in a seminal essay of 1806: 'to try to create one or the other through an external organization was always and remains a fruitless, pious wish'.[124] Whereas the 'security of the citizen of a state rests on the unity of its legal system and administration', with laws all emanating 'from the same central point' and being maintained 'by one and the same power', 'the law which binds states together merely lies in their mutual treaties', which were the result of a 'multiplicity of conditions', ruling out—'by the very nature of their origin—any higher, communal sanction in the stricter sense of the word'.[125] A balance of power was required because the 'social linkage' of 'states of this part of the world', despite being unusually developed, was not strong enough to prevent war on its own.[126] The following maxims were therefore necessary:

> That, if the states' system of Europe was to exist and to be maintained by communal efforts, none of the participants should ever be so powerful that all of the rest are not able to force it to comply;
>
> That, if the system is not merely to exist but should also be maintained without constant and great danger and violent shocks, each individual state which contravenes it must not only be forced to comply by the totality of all the others but also by any majority (if not by an individual state);
>
> But, to avoid the contrary danger of an uninterrupted series of wars or capricious subjugation of weaker states in every short interlude of peace, the fear of communal resistance or communal revenge for the other party must be sufficient to keep everyone within their limits; and
>
> That, if any European state were to desire to raise itself up to become a power by unjust undertakings...or to be able to defy an association of the whole, such a state should be treated as the common enemy of all the community; by the same token, if a similar power appears anywhere on the scene, as a result of a chance concatenation of circumstances without any illegal act on the part of the beneficiary, no means afforded by state wisdom should be spared to weaken it.[127]

In the last resort, sovereign states were to be dissuaded from waging war by an opposing majority within a balance of power. The balance, too, was to be maintained, if necessary, by force and the threat of war. 'The current federative system of Europe', which had been formed 'in 1813 for the dissolution of the Napoleonic empire', did not have 'the character of an actual alliance in the old diplomatic sense', wrote Gentz in 1819, 'but that of an armed coalition for the re-establishment of independence'.[128] The spectre haunting such a system was Napoleon's attempt to seize hegemony, which had been thwarted by a coalition of the other states and brought to an end only by military conflict.

---

[124] Ibid., 42. [125] Ibid.. [126] Ibid. [127] Ibid., 42–3.
[128] F. v. Gentz, 'Von Pradt's Gemälde von Europa', ibid., vol. 5, 268–9. The article appeared in the *Wiener Jahrbücher der Literatur*, Jan.–Mar. 1819.

Conservatives such as Gentz who helped to shape the post-war order were affected by the successful and unsuccessful campaigns of the Napoleonic era. On the one hand, war was perceived to be legitimate, leading to the defeat of France and the reversal of the effects of the French Revolution.[129] 'The war which the European powers conducted against the French Revolution was, for and in itself, indisputably a necessary war', Gentz had admitted in 1801: 'War is, if also immeasurably momentous, not a pure evil, despite all of its sad consequences.'[130] Since revolution itself was believed by many conservatives to be the primary cause of military conflict in the 1790s, 1800s, and 1810s as a corollary of the ineluctable escalation of a revolutionary civil war, a military intervention to quash the revolution appeared justifiable:

> There is only one case where the fundamental principle of the balance of power, properly understood, can make it the duty of the entire confederation of states (*Staatenbund*) to exercise an immediate influence on the internal affairs of a *Reich*; namely, where the complete destruction of entire areas of life of such a *Reich* obtains and a political collapse ensues, even if only momentary, through the violent overthrow of the government and through the dissolution of civil ties.[131]

Haller agreed, reducing the French Revolution to a 'threefold war—external, internal and civil'—before going on to show 'how war necessarily brought about its fall', after destroying 'natural' hierarchical ties between subjects, laying the French army and state open to the dictatorship of one man and ushering in 'ten years of the most terrible and bloody struggles'.[132] The war against revolutionary war was at once legitimate and different in kind from previous types of conflict. On the other hand, the new order of the 'restoration' was intended to prevent the recurrence of this form of warfare, in part because of its destructiveness. What had just ended was, claimed Gentz, 'a war of such an extraordinary type' that the usual conventions of peace-making were inapplicable.[133] For this reason, Metternich's advisor would not countenance the calls of 'patriots' like Görres to maximize German states' gains (including Alsace-Lorraine becoming a German territory) on the grounds that such demands would endanger the peace.[134] His priority in 1815 was to ensure that the 'existing relations between the great powers' were maintained, so that 'what has happened in the last two years' did not happen again, since a 'large war (*Hauptkrieg*) in Europe can only be caused by one of those violent revolutions which we see no reason to worry about', opening up 'the prospect

---

[129] Friedrich de la Motte Fouqué, *Etwas über den deutschen Adel, über Ritter-Sinn und Militär-Ehre*, 3, 48, talked of the campaign of 1813, as the removal of a 'yoke'. He also alluded to the heroism of volunteers.

[130] F. v. Gentz, *Über den Ursprung und Charakter des Krieges*, in F. v. Gentz, *Ausgewählte Schriften*, vol. 2, 276, 288.

[131] F. v. Gentz, 'Von dem Verfall des politischen Sinnes während des Revolutions-Krieges', ibid., vol. 4, 72.

[132] C. L. v. Haller, *Restauration der Staats-Wissenschaft*, 242–6, 260–3.

[133] F. v. Gentz, 'Betrachtungen über den Pariser Frieden' (1815), in F. v. Gentz, *Ausgewählte Schriften*, vol. 4, 330.

[134] Ibid., 331–3.

of a new golden age'.[135] Other conservatives such as Haller and the Gerlach brothers, writing in the *Evangelische Kirchenzeitung* in the 1830s, were more confident of the moral constraints on states' conduct, supposedly embodied in the Holy Alliance, than was Gentz but few thought that these would be sufficient on their own to prevent the outbreak of war or revolution. Their main concern was to maintain the vigilance and readiness of the powers to counter these combined threats.[136]

The idea that wars were an ineluctable, though controllable, corollary of the power and sovereignty of states in an uncertain states' system was common amongst 'liberal' or 'progressive' commentators and academics as well as conservative ones.[137] To Luden, who wrote his *Handbuch der Staatsweisheit oder der Politik* in 1811 and went on to become an influential editor (of *Nemesis*, until 1818), the regulation of inter-state relations by treaty did not prevent states from being 'tempted constantly to break through the barrier of law as soon as it is not to their disadvantage to do so'.[138] States themselves existed to protect individuals' rights from the incursions of others: 'the state is nothing more than an association of people who want to strive amongst themselves for a form of relations such that their general rights—or their common freedom—should be realized with the force of all against each infraction'.[139] Since the 'aims of the state and the aims of life' were 'one and the same', states had a duty to protect individuals and vice versa, for 'freedom and culture are conditional on its [the state's] independence'.[140] Because the enforcement of treaties between states in international law, or the 'law of peoples' (*Völkerrecht*), was 'not possible', the state was left to 'seek guarantees for the surety of its laws and rights *in its own power*': 'free autonomy (*Selbständigkeit*) is not the highest goal that is striven for but the necessary means, without which a people cannot attain a goal, whatever it is'.[141] Other states were therefore necessarily 'enemies', threatening the domestically safeguarded rights of citizens.[142] Moreover, the more people were imbued with 'the feeling of civility', the more clearly they recognized the link between civility and culture, rendering the words 'foreign' (*fremd*) and 'foe' (*Feind*) 'identical'.[143] In these circumstances, a balance of power only results from the competition of inimical states as they struggle to become 'equal' to their most powerful neighbours in order to guarantee their citizens' 'independence'.[144] Wars were legitimate insofar as they stimulated and consolidated national culture: 'The human race must work from savagery towards culture;

[135] Ibid., 344.
[136] H.-C. Kraus, 'Leopold und Ernst Ludwig von Gerlach', in B. Heidenreich (ed.), *Politische Theorien des 19. Jahrhunderts*, 2nd edn (Berlin, 2002), 173–5; Haller, *Restauration*, vol. 1, 304–8.
[137] The terms 'liberal' and 'conservative' were only established during the 1820s, 1830s, and 1840s.
[138] H. Luden, *Handbuch der Staatsweisheit* (Jena, 1811), 54.
[139] Ibid., 10.   [140] Ibid., 11, 16.
[141] Ibid., 52; H. Luden, *Einige Worte über das Studium der vaterländischen Geschichte* (Jena, 1810), 14.
[142] H. Luden, *Handbuch*, 54.   [143] Ibid., 55.
[144] See K. Goebel, 'Heinrich Luden, sein Staatsbegriff und sein Einfluss auf die deutsche Verfassungsbewegung', in K. Stephenson and A. Scharff (eds), *Darstellungen und Quellen zur Geschichte der deutschen Einheitsbewegung im neunzehnten und zwanzigsten Jahrhundert* (Heidelberg, 1970), 74–5.

the mind only senses its powers through resistance, and a common danger brings people together', making 'war necessary beside peace' because of 'the benefit which culture derives from war'.[145]

Military conflicts were also justified by the need of cultured, national states to become stronger and to fight for their independence within a balance of power or 'states' system' (*Staatensystem*):

> The reproaches which have been made in respect of the old balance-of-power system can be summarized as follows. It has a) not only caused wars but has made the wars of two states those of all, and b) it has ended the bloodiest wars by means of a peace through which things were left as they had been before. It has resulted c) in countless negotiations and a risible ceremonial through which wars, the misfortune of the peoples, were indescribably lengthened. It has led d) to the terrible burden, to the immeasurable increase of the standing military; and therefore not only i) made more and more new taxes necessary, but also ii) led to the temptation to adopt all sorts of means to increase power artificially, e.g. through paper money; and finally iii) has not achieved its aim. These reproaches obviously do not touch on the idea of the balance of power but at most on the previous realization of the same. Most disadvantages derive from the fact that the system was constructed out of emergency and need, and it was understood by very few statesmen. ... Yet most reproaches can be, if not disproven, then qualified considerably: a) wars broke out and became general; but was war an accident or generality? The former is difficult to stop; the latter cannot be less the case, when *one* state is too powerful. The proof lies before our eyes, if we don't shut them. And if the struggle for independence on the part of the nations (*Völker*)—on which our happiness rests—is a more noble struggle than that for a bit of land, so wars before the balance-of-power system were certainly pettier than those under that system. ... b) Such wars were, it is true, not able to yield the results which were possible under the ascendant power of *one* state; in the latter case, it was possible to discard one *Reich* every year, and have a different-looking map after each war. The consequences, however, which must follow from these wars is perhaps more significant and harder to gauge: it is not easy to prove that it is better to destroy *Reichs* than it is to keep them in mutual dependency. And is it not strange that such great changes are expected from wars when, on the one hand, one also wants to prohibit them and, therefore, all change? Negotiations have demonstrably promoted culture to an unusual degree; many ideas about nation, fatherland, rights and laws have developed in this way. Ceremony, though, necessarily derived from the same independence of states, which were defending their honour, and can only be risible for those who have lost their feeling of independence. In addition, wars are not lengthened by this means; ceremony only became relevant when one did not yet want peace, and, as such, long negotiation indisputably created ties between enemies who wanted war, which moderated the horrors of war. c) As far as standing armies etc. go, we are not going to address the question whether everything has somehow been better after the collapse of the balance-of-power system, but merely remark that wars were not conducted in earlier times without costs and that a military power could not be maintained free of charge.[146]

For 'enlightened' commentators such as Luden and his teacher Arnold Hermann Ludwig Heeren, whose *Handbuch der Geschichte des Europäischen Staatensystems*

---

[145] H. Luden, *Handbuch*, 65.   [146] Ibid., 72–3.

und seiner Colonien (1809) was in its third edition by 1819, the balance of power permitted a distinction to be made between 'inhuman, disgusting and mad' conflicts and justifiable wars for the independence of states and citizens, which guarded against the perpetual hegemony of one power alone, as had happened before 1813.[147]

From this starting point of a coalition of sovereign states using war legitimately to end the hegemony of the Napoleonic regime, liberal and conservative authors alike tended to minimize the risks of military conflict within a restored balance of power. As such, the wars against Napoleon and the French Revolution were comparatively uncontroversial, even if contemporaries' memories of them differed.[148] Thus, there were points of similarity in historical narratives of the wars, as there had been in ritualized forms of remembrance in the immediate aftermath of the conflict.[149] There were few echoes of the divisions of the German states and soldiers' and civilians' unsettling experiences of war and killing. According to Carl von Rotteck in his popular nine-volume *Allgemeine Geschichte vom Anfang der historischen Kenntniss bis auf unsere Zeiten* (1813–27), which had already been reissued nine times by 1833, Napoleon had had a 'plan for world domination', overturning the 'balance of several powers' which had acted as a 'safeguard of public law and rights'.[150] The Coalition's wars against France and its allies, including the states of the *Rheinbund*, were legitimate. Despite a desirable weakening of the aristocracy and improvements in 'the organization and administration of the state', 'Germany lived through an eternally humiliating and pitiable period in the days of the Confederation of the Rhine', the Freiburg academic and liberal editor of the *Staatslexikon* went on.[151] Matter-of-factly, he reported the defeat of Austria in 1805 at the battle of Austerlitz, 'with 30,000 men fallen on both sides' and 15,000 taken prisoner: 'a more destructive blow than that at Marengo'.[152] For its part, Prussia suffered the 'most comprehensive, insuperable defeat' in 'recent history' at Jena and Auserstädt, with the Prussian army losing 'more than 50,000 men on this terrible day' alone, having awoken 'from its disastrous blindness too late' and having realized that 'war was the slogan'.[153] Vienna was right to go to war again in 1809: even though eventually vanquished, Habsburg forces had shown at Esslingen that 'Napoleon can be beaten' and, though losing at Wagram, had ensured

---

[147] Cited in K. Goebel, 'Heinrich Luden, sein Staatsbegriff und sein Einfluss', 75. A. H. L. Heeren, *Handbuch der Geschichte des Europäischen Staatensystems und seiner Colonien* (Göttingen, 1819).

[148] See, for instance, the liberal *Conversations-Lexikon der neuesten Litteratur-, Völker- und Staatengeschichte* (Leipzig, 1841–5), vol. 1, 461, edited by Otto Wigand, repeating the common legend of national awakening on the battlefield in 1813: 'After a long wait and unprecedented patience, Germany in most recent times – ten or twenty years ago, or since those days when, on a bloody battlefield, it was shown a different path, for the third time for European civilization and in the history of the world – awoke from its lethargy'.

[149] K. v. Rotteck himself was a witness—as a journalist—of the events and then wrote about them as an historian; see, for instance, 'Das Jahr 1813', in K. v. Rotteck, *Gesammelte und nachgelassene Schriften*, vol. 1, 129–46.

[150] C. v. Rotteck, *Allgemeine Geschichte vom Anfang der historischen Kentniss bis auf unsere Zeiten* (Freiburg, 1826), vol. 9, 717–18.

[151] Ibid., 593.   [152] Ibid., 565–6.   [153] Ibid., 597, 595.

that 'the victorious army had more dead and wounded than the defeated one', which prompted Rotteck to rejoice.[154]

The losses during the 1812 campaign in Russia, 'which drew in over 100,000 German men—as the mercenaries of Napoleon—from the *Rheinbund* alone', occasioned more commentary about the 'terrible murder' at the battle of Borodino and the 'barbaric and desperate' act of burning down Moscow, but the faithfully recorded rumour 'that 300,000 human corpses' had been burned at the start of the following year was still only mentioned in passing, subordinated to 'the moral and political effects of such misfortune', from Napoleon's point of view.[155] By contrast, 'the Prussian war' against France in 1813 was marked by a 'numbingly quick turnaround' and the promise of 'the rebirth of an honourable *Reich*', in keeping with the 'primordial spirit of the German *Volk*'.[156] In this 'poetic era', encouraged by the pledge of a constitution and unity, 'thousands and thousands of youths and men from all the valleys of Germany rushed to sacrifice themselves for the worthy rebirth of a beloved fatherland', Rotteck declared: 800,000 armed men stood 'in a vast line from the Baltic to Italy' before 500,000 French soldiers, ready to wage a '"holy war"…for the great matter of the freeing of the world'.[157] Although Napoleon lost 80,000 men and the Coalition 50,000 'in the terrible four-day battle' of Leipzig in 1813, with Vienna subsequently stymieing 'the possibility of a German *Reich* or national unity', the 'liberation (*Befreiung*) of Germany' outweighed the losses and disappointments, it was implied.[158] 'The German nation (*die teutsche Nation*), full of jubilation over the great victory, over emancipation from a foreign yoke, soothed itself with wonderful dreams of a glorious future and looked at once trustingly and solicitously towards Vienna, from where the new order of things would come', only to be deceived.[159] 'Never was a victory more glorious, more decisive', he had written at the time.[160] The peace was lost, in Rotteck's opinion, but the wars were glorious.

The idea of 'wars of liberation' was popular even amongst 'democratic' liberals—indeed, even radicals such as Moses Hess used the term '*Befreiungskrieg*'—in the 1830s, 1840s, and 1850s.[161] Thus, the Heidelberg historian Georg Gottfried Gervinus, whose publication of *Einleitung in die Geschichte des neunzehnten Jahrhunderts* (1853) had led to his successful prosecution in Baden—revoked on appeal—for 'high treason', remained confident that 'The wars of the people (*Volkskriege*) in Spain, Russia, and Germany announced the new era in each place

---

[154] Ibid., 726, 728.   [155] Ibid., 761, 773.
[156] Ibid., 777–8.   [157] Ibid., 778, 781.
[158] Ibid., 788–90. At the time, in 1814, he had referred to Leipzig as a battle 'which should determine the fate of the world': 'Never was a victory more glorious, more decisive than that which crowned the Allies here.' See C. v. Rotteck, 'Das Jahr 1813', in C. v. Rotteck, *Gesammelte und nachgelassene Schriften*, vol. 1, 142–3.
[159] C. v. Rotteck, *Allgemeine Geschichte*, 855.
[160] C. v. Rotteck, *Gesammelte und nachgelassene Schriften*, vol. 1, 143. The article appeared in the *Teutschen Blättern*, edited by C. v. Rotteck, in 1814.
[161] M. Hess, 'Die europäische Triarchie' (1841), in M. Hess, *Philosophische und sozialistische Schriften*, ed. W. Mönke, 2nd edn (Vaduz, 1980), 147.

beyond France and, over time, beyond the duration of French domination.'[162] When he looked back as a historian—he was born in 1805—to the start of the French Revolution, he saw it as an 'immeasurable advance', which at once extricated France from the 'political sloth' and 'moral bog' typical of other 'Romance' countries like Spain and Italy and which completed the 'revolution' of society and politics that had started—but not ended—in seventeenth-century England.[163] Napoleon took on the mantle of the French Revolution, bringing 'good deeds and improvement to the conquered peoples', but he did so in a wider quest to establish the 'universal rule of the French'.[164] Although he was almost successful in this quest ('No universal ruler before him went further than he did at the time of his quasi-destruction of Prussia [and] complete weakening of Austria'), he also provoked a series of national reactions through his 'oppression of the peoples' which simultaneously shook the various peoples out of their 'docile habits...under the rule of monarchy' and pushed them to resist a foreign power, making the ideas of domestic 'freedom' (*Freiheit*) and external 'liberation' (*Befreiung*) seem interchangeable.[165] The French dictator had hoped to appeal to the pride of the peoples of Europe 'against the pride of England' but he had merely succeeded in eliciting 'the indignation of all nations against his own over-ambition and blind ruthlessness': 'The pressure placed on national freedom and the policy of de-nationalization (*Entnationalisirung*) excited, in the form of a natural reaction, feelings of their own self-worth on the part of the nations, which, indeed, signalled their political awakening.'[166]

The 'tearing up of the tribes through the erection of new Napoleonic vassal-states' also constituted an attack on history and, therefore, 'the roots of monarchy' as well as on 'national consciousness'.[167] As a consequence, monarchs were able to harness national, popular support and transform a series of military conflicts, which were otherwise burdensome and bloody, into '*Befreiungskriege*', '*Freiheitskriege*', and '*Volkskriege*', which authors like Gervinus deployed as synonyms:

> The weapons of the monarchs themselves became democratic; the struggle against tyrants was carried out in the name of the freedom of the peoples by armies in which the idea of the nation and politics was alive and well; and it was carried out more for the moderate principles of the revolution than against them.[168]

The Napoleonic Wars had led to the conscription of 3 million men and the 'sacrifice' of almost a sixth of that total 'for the ambition of one', as the historian acknowledged at the start of his *Geschichte des neunzehnten Jahrhunderts seit den Wiener Verträgen* (1855), but they had precipitated, too, the national wars and political awakening of 1813, after which 'the "great empire" of Napoleonic rule over Europe had collapsed in the wake of the battle of Leipzig'.[169] Although Gervinus—one of seven Göttingen professors removed from their posts in 1837

---

[162] G. G. Gervinus, *Einleitung in die Geschichte des neunzehnten Jahrhunderts* (Leipzig, 1853), 149.
[163] Ibid., 137.   [164] Ibid., 146.   [165] Ibid., 147–8.
[166] Ibid., 149.   [167] Ibid., 148.   [168] Ibid., 149.
[169] G. G. Gervinus, *Geschichte des neunzehnten Jahrhunderts* (Leipzig, 1855), vol. 1, 7, 3.

in protest at a constitutional 'coup' in Hanover—became one of the principal critics of the Congress of Vienna and the terms of the subsequent peace, which had been agreed amidst the resplendent balls of Viennese society at a time of great hardship for most of the population of Europe, his treatment of the wars of liberation remained positive.

The myth of the wars of liberation became an important element of 'Borussian' or pro-Prussian historiography in the 1850s, 1860s, and beyond, but important components of the legend of a national struggle for independence from France had already been established in the decades after 1813.[170] What happened in the intervening period, declared Heinrich von Sybel—Germany's principal expert on the French Revolution, whose five-volume *Geschichte der Revolutionszeit* was published between 1853 and 1879—in a lecture on 'Europe's Uprising against Napoleon I' from 1860, was that new evidence had emerged, altering the emphasis placed on events and the guilt attributable to different parties. 'Our knowledge of few stretches of world history has expanded to such a degree (and has almost been completed) as has that of the first great epoch of the first French Revolution and the Napoleonic domination of the world which it brought about', after 'an unsurveyable mass of rumours, illusions, myths and lies [had] filled the first historical accounts', he began: 'Many of the most decisive relations lay buried, therefore, deep in the darkness of the cabinets and archives, and so it came to be that anything but the truth about the most important moments of human development were widely believed by an entire generation.'[171] The new historical reading of the period between 1792 and 1815, which Sybel's own research had helped to create, rested on the revolutionary era— with France being exposed as the aggressor in 1792 and after, not Austria, Prussia, and Britain—and on the years during which the Holy Roman Empire collapsed and the Confederation of the Rhine was established, with Napoleon originally perceived to be a 'military champion of republican freedom' and states such as Bavaria as pursuers of their own 'self-interest', opening up the south of Germany to the French, but later believed to have had little choice, faced with a 'domineering, glory-seeking, calculating' French dictator.[172] In contrast to their studies of the revolutionary era, Sybel's and other scholars' accounts of the wars of liberation changed little. In earlier studies of the campaigns, according to the Munich historian, Napoleon had 'become the master of the European continent until he was finally overpowered in the wars of liberation (*Befreiungskriege*) by a fixed, fundamental and many-sided harmony of the powers, and freedom was given back to the world'.[173] In later studies, the 'harmony of the powers' had been replaced by a recognition of

---

[170] One sign of the consolidation of the myth was the growing number of entries under 'Battle of Leipzig' and other headings in popular encyclopedias: for instance, F. A. Brockhaus (ed.), *Kleineres Brockhaus'sches Conversations-Lexikon* (Leipzig, 1854–7), vol. 3, 445–6: 'world-historical consequences were involved in Napoleon's defeat at Leipzig – very sad ones for Saxony. ... In Leipzig itself, an association founded in 1843 has been active in preserving the memory of the "*Völkerschlacht*" in as true a form as possible for posterity and in collecting all writings on the subject.' See also *Rheinisches Conversations-Lexikon*, vol. 7, 229–36.

[171] H. v. Sybel, 'Die Erhebung Europa's gegen Napoleon I.', in H. v. Sybel, *Kleine historische Schriften* (Munich, 1863), 245.

[172] Ibid., 246–7.   [173] Ibid.

the loose, divided nature of the 'alliance of the governments', which were split 'from beginning to end' into 'two, constantly fighting parties'.[174] Now, it seemed, 'the war of 1813 was imbued on the side of the *Völker* with a singular, unprecedented enthusiasm': 'the sentiment of the masses, the heart of the peoples, the spirit of the nations had, at that time, led the leaders, ruled the rulers and vanquished those who had overcome the world'.[175]

Although it appeared misleading to the Berlin historian and forty-eighter Johann Gustav Droysen (whose work on Yorck von Wartenburg had constituted an important part of recent archival research) to label the campaigns 'wars of freedom', since they did not permit the establishment of 'freer political conditions domestically', it remained acceptable to call them 'wars of liberation', 'since the great *Volkskrieg* against Napoleon' had brought about the end of 'foreign rule'.[176] Even at this stage, Droysen's distinction between '*Freiheit*' and '*Befreiung*' had not entered into common usage, with Brockhaus's *Conversations-Lexikon* continuing to deploy the label '*Freiheitskrieg*' to 'the North American struggle for freedom in 1773–83,…the war on the Pyrenean peninsula against France in 1808–13 and, especially, the Russian–German war of 1812–15'.[177] This treatment—blurring the distinction between internal and external freedom—corresponded to that of Sybel, who emphasized the endeavours of 'unequivocal patriots' such as Yorck, Blücher, Gneisenau, Stein, and Arndt—'an image and expression of his people (*Volk*)'—to counter the 'profound fatalism and moral dissoluteness' of the Prussian court and the scheming, ambivalent, anti-revolutionary 'iciness' of Metternich to unleash popular patriotic sentiment: 'it was the enthusiastic will of all individuals which pushed the government forwards'.[178] Within months in early 1813, Prussia had been able to mobilize more soldiers—including volunteers—than France under the *levée en masse* in 1794, despite the prior 'disaster' (*Unheil*) of 1806, a 'six-year period of oppression', the 'sacrifices and suffering of 1812', and the absence of a 'regime of terror and demagogy' in the Hohenzollern monarchy.[179] 'All strata in the same measure', accompanied by the 'powerful' 'patriotic feelings' evident in Austria, supported the war in 1813, making it into a 'vow of millions'.[180] Although leaders such as Stein and Yorck—whose signature of the Convention of Tauroggen

[174] Ibid., 247.   [175] Ibid., 247–8.

[176] Cited in W. Nippel, *Johann Gustav Droysen. Ein Leben zwischen Wissenschaft und Politik* (Munich, 2008), 177; J. G. Droysen, *Das Leben des Feldmarschalls*, 3 vols. Without good evidence, Droysen did most to create the myth that Yorck was descended from a family of Catholic English aristocrats who had gone into exile during the Civil War; hence, he should be called 'York'.

[177] 'Freiheitskrieg', in F. A. Brockhaus (ed.), *Kleineres Brockhaus'sches Conversations-Lexikon* (Leipzig, 1854–57), vol. 2, 562. The term 'Freiheitskrieg' had arguably been more common in the early period, although 'Befreiungskrieg' was also used: F. A. Rüder (ed.), *Hübner's Zeitungs- und Conversations-Lexikon*, 31st edn (Leipzig, 1824–8), vol. 2, 421, refers to the Napoleonic wars as 'Freiheitskriege', typified by 'moral strength and enthusiasm'.

[178] H. v. Sybel, 'Am Denkmal Arndt's in Bonn' (1865), in H. v. Sybel, *Vorträge und Aufsätze* (Berlin, 1874), 270; H. v. Sybel, 'Die Erhebung Europa's gegen Napoleon I.', in H. v. Sybel, *Kleine historische Schriften* (Munich, 1863), 314, 339, 332. The case against Metternich was in keeping with Sybel's broader claim that Austria should not be involved in German affairs and was not a true part of Germany: V. Dotterweich, *Heinrich von Sybel. Geschichtswissenschaft in politischer Absicht 1817–1861* (Göttingen, 1978), 211.

[179] H. v. Sybel, 'Die Erhebung', 322.   [180] Ibid., 322, 325, 337.

with Russia against the orders of the King of Prussia on 30 December 1812 was lauded as the seizure of the moment of liberation—were aware of the 'sacrifices and dangers' of war, the risks and costs were obviously worth countenancing, which served to minimize the bloodiness of combat.[181]

Few, if any, commentators took issue with the fundamental pillars of the myth of 1813, despite differences of emphasis.[182] Amongst academics, conservatives such as the Halle historian Heinrich Leo, who had participated in the Wartburg meeting of *Burschenschafter* in 1817 but who had gone on to become part of the Prussian right and a champion of the German Confederation from the 1820s onwards, saw Napoleon as the illegitimate heir of the French Revolution and he viewed the populations and governments of the Coalition as 'spiritual powers, who now loomed massively against Napoleon'.[183] Given 'the pious spirit of heroism' of 'these poor people' in the Prussian army, history 'scarcely contained other examples akin to this one', he wrote in his *Lehrbuch der Universalgeschichte* in 1844, which drew largely on military accounts of the campaign—including that of Carl von Clausewitz—as well as on the memoirs of Arndt (published in 1840) and Varnhagen von Ense (1838) and the correspondence of Niebuhr (1838).[184] Liberals such as Droysen, in addition to gaining access—eventually—to the archive of the General Staff for his biography of Yorck, also relied heavily on the insights of contemporaries such as the Prussian official Theodor von Schön, Gneisenau's General Staff officer Carl von Müffling, and Yorck's adjutant Gustav von Below, with all of whom the Berlin historian had regular correspondence. Although they often fell out, with Schön complaining that his portrait of Yorck as a scoundrel did not figure in Droysen's manuscript for example, historians and eye-witnesses tended to disagree over matters of detail and personality rather than their overall evaluation of the wars: thus, when Müffling's *Aus meinem Leben* appeared posthumously in 1851, Droysen denounced it for besmirching 'the glorious history of Prussia' but only because—in an attempt to bolster its author's own reputation—it had 'defamed' Gneisenau, who can 'no longer defend himself' and was unlikely to

---

[181] Ibid., 316, 327.

[182] This was even true of Rudolph Eickemeyer, *Abhandlungen über Gegenstände der Staats- und Kriegs-Wissenschaften* (Frankfurt, 1817), vol. 1, 136, who had served as a general in the French army but who was critical of Napoleon's tyranny and over-ambition: 'Our intention is not to rule over other peoples, but also not to be ruled by them. ... One diverged from this, Europe's peoples were tortured by every evil of terrible wars, the most beautiful lands were laid waste, states were deprived of people and money, and what were the consequences of all of this? In inordinately large empires, created by the violence of weapons, unhappiness reigns internally and mistrust externally: both endanger their long life.' See also the Saxon General-Lieutenant Carl von Gersdorff, *Vorlesungen üer militärische Gegenstände* (Dresden, 1827), 4, who had fought on the French side but reacted in a similar fashion, critical of Napoleon holding Europe 'hostage'.

[183] H. Leo, *Lehrbuch der Universalgeschichte* (Halle, 1844), vol. 6, 88.

[184] Ibid. He also lists P. F. Stuhr, *Die drei letzten Feldzüge gegen Napoleon kritisch-historisch dargestellt* (Lemgo, 1832); C. Friccius, *Geschichte des Krieges in den Jahren 1813 und 1814* (Altenburg, 1843); anon. ('von einem preussischen Offizier'), *General Bülow von Dennewitz in den Feldzügen von 1813 und 1814* (1843); anon. ('von einem höheren Offizier der preussischen Armee'), *Beiträge zur Geschichte des Jahres 1813* (1843).

be defended by others since they were nearly all dead, not because it had questioned the Coalition's goals and conduct during the wars of liberation.[185]

Some of the accounts used by historians came out contemporaneously—most famously those of Plotho—but most were published during the 1830s, 1840s, 1850s, and 1860s, along with nearly all the memoirs and correspondence relating to the revolutionary and Napoleonic conflicts (see Tables 4.1 and 5.1).[186] Such official histories and the testimony of witnesses were believed by professional historians to have played a secondary role in the expansion of 'our knowledge' remarked upon by Sybel in the 1850s. Nonetheless, they appear both to have coincided with and informed much of the historiography on the wars of liberation. In 1826, Rotteck had had to rely largely on French sources for his account of the period in his *Allgemeine Geschichte*.[187] By 1855, Leopold von Ranke had a much more extensive secondary literature at his disposal, which in turn rested partly on memoirs and correspondence: Friedrich von Raumer's eight-volume *Geschichte Europas seit dem Ende des 15. Jahrhunderts* (Leipzig, 1832–50), Leo's *Lehrbuch der Universalgeschichte* (1835–44), Karl Adolf Menzel's anti-revolutionary *Geschichte unserer Zeit seit dem Tode Friedrichs II.* (1828), and Friedrich Christoph Schlosser's six-volume *Geschichte des 18. Jahrhunderts und des 19. bis zum Sturz des französischen Kaiserreichs* (1836–48).[188] Ranke's own moderately conservative, supposedly scientific reading of events between 1813 and 1815, which he reproduced in his private lectures for the King of Bavaria in 1854, showed—in keeping with the conclusions of other works—the perception of French rule and the spread of the revolution in Germany under Napoleonic auspices as 'the overthrow of the earlier constitution' of the Holy Roman Empire and, 'at the same time, as the rule of the French emperor…, who, after the defeating of Austria and Prussia, played the part of the lord of Germany, founded the *Rheinbund* and would have quickly brought the rule of the German princes to an end, if he had remained master'.[189] The fact that he was dislodged was the fortuitous result of his disastrous invasion of Russia, which he had earlier hoped to court, and the decision of the Russians 'as half-barbarians' to burn down Moscow.[190] It was also the corollary of 'the awakening of new courage in Germany, most notably in Prussia, even though it had sunk into complete political insignificance by that time', and of 'the harmony of the Allies', which were able to 'bring Napoleonic rule to an end'.[191]

Although working at the University of Berlin, Ranke in the 1830s, 1840s, and 1850s stood between Prussia and the other German states, attached to 'Mother Thuringia'—he was born in Saxon Thuringia, which was incorporated into the

---

[185] Droysen cited in W. Nippel, *Droysen*, 174. K. v. Müffling, *Aus meinem Leben* (Berlin, 1851). Also, H.-J. Behr (ed.), *Karl Freiherr von Müffling. Offizier—Kartograph—Politiker, 1775–1851* (Cologne, 2003).

[186] See especially the sources listed for Chapter 4.

[187] C. v. Rotteck, *Allgemeine Geschichte*, 18–34.

[188] L. v. Ranke, *Aus Werk und Nachlass. Vorlesungseinleitungen*, ed. V. Dotterweich and W. P. Fuchs (Munich, 1975), vol. 4, 243–6.

[189] L. v. Ranke, *Aus Werk und Nachlass. Über die Epochen der neueren Geschichte*, ed. T. Schieder and H. Berding (Munich, 1971), vol. 2, 433.

[190] Ibid., 434.   [191] Ibid., 434–5.

Table 5.1. Accounts of the Revolutionary and Napoleonic Wars by Decade

J. J. O. A. Rühle von Lilienstern, *Bericht eins Augenzeugen von dem Feldzug* (Tübingen, 1807)
C. v. Plotho, *Tagebuch während des Krieges zwischen Russland und Preussen einerseits und Frankreich andrerseits in den Jahren 1806 und 1807* (Berlin, 1811)
C. v. Plotho, *Die Kosaken, oder Geschichte derselben von ihrem Ursprunge bis auf die Gegenwart* (Berlin, 1811)
C. v. Plotho, *Der Krieg in Deutschland und Frankreich in den Jahren 1813 und 1814* (Berlin, 1817), 2 vols
C. v. Plotho, *Der Krieg des verbündeten Europa gegen Frankreich im Jahre 1815* (Berlin, 1818)
F. C. F. v. Müffling, *Die preussisch-russische Campagne im Jahr 1813* (Breslau, 1813)
F. C. F. v. Müffling, *Geschichte des Feldzugs der englisch-hanövrisch-niederländisch-braunschweigischen Armee unter Herzog Wellington und der preußischen Armee unter dem Fürsten Blücher von Wahlstadt im Jahr 1815* (Stuttgart, 1817)
J. W. v. Goethe, *Aus meinem Leben* (Stuttgart, 1811–14)
C. v. Clausewitz, *Der Feldzug von 1813 bis zum Waffenstillstand* (Berlin, 1813)
C. Niemeyer, *Die Schlachten des Heiligen Krieges* (Leipzig, 1817)
Anon., *Rück-Erinnerungen an die Jahre 1813 und 1814* (Munich, 1818)

F. C. F. v. Müffling, *Betrachtungen über die grossen Operationen und Schlachten der Feldzüge von 1813 und 1814* (Posen, 1825)
E. Heusinger, *Ansichten, Beobachtungen und Erfahrungen* (Braunschweig, 1825)
Büttner, *Beschreibung der Schicksale und Leiden des ehemaligen Korporals Büttner* (Nennsling, 1828)
K. W. F. v. Funck, *Erinnerungen aus dem Feldzuge des sächsischen Corps* (Dresden, 1829)

C. v. Clausewitz, *Vom Kriege* (Leipzig, 1832)
A. Böck, *Leben und Schicksale des ehemaligen Musikmeisters* (Halle, 1832)
W. Krimer, *Erinnerungen eines alten Lützower Jägers* (Stuttgart, 1833)
F. Peppler, *Schilderung meiner Gefangenschaft vom Jahre 1812 bis 1814* (Darmstadt, 1834)
C. L. Marter, *Fünf Marter-Jahre: Schicksale eines deutschen Soldaten in Spanien und Sicilien* (Weimar, 1834)
J. Schrafel, *Merkwürdige Schicksale des ehelmaligen Feldwebels im königl. Bayer. 5ten Linien-Infanterie-Regiment* (Nuremberg, 1834)
J. Meyer, *Erzählung der Schicksale und Kriegsabenteuer des ehemaligen westfälischen Artillerie-Wachtmeisters Jakob Meyer* (Dransfeld, 1836)
H. Steffens, *Was ich erlebte* (Leipzig, 1838)
K. A. Varnhagen v. Ense, *Denkwürdigkeiten* (Berlin, 1838)

E. M. Arndt, *Erinnerungen* (Berlin, 1840)
F. de la Motte Fouqué, *Lebensgeschicthe des Barons de la Motte-Fouque* (Halle, 1840)
C. R. v. Schäffer, *Denkwürdigkeiten*, ed. G. Muhl (Pforzheim, 1840)
F. Bersling, *Der böhmische Veteran* (Schweidnitz, 1840)
F. Harkort, *Die Zeiten des ersten Westphaelischen Landwehrregiments. Ein Beitrag zur Geschichte der Befreiungskriege* (Essen, 1841)
K. Müchler, *Doppelflucht um den Verfolgungen der Franzosen zu entgehen* (Cottbus, 1841)
W. T. Krug, *Krug's Lebensreise in sechs Stazionen* (Leipzig, 1842)
K. A. Varnhagen v. Ense, *Denkwürdigkeiten des eigenen Lebens* (Leipzig, 1843)
C. v. Pichler, *Denkwürdigkeiten aus meinem Leben* (Vienna, 1844)
A. Vater, *Was wir erlebten im Oktober 1813* (Leipzig, 1845)
F. Steger, *Der Feldzug von 1812* (Essen, 1985), first published in 1845
G. Kirchmayer, *Veteranen-Huldigung oder Erinnerungen an die Feldzugsjahre 1813, 1814 und 1815. Wahre Schilderung von Leistung und Verdienst des Soldaten* (Munich, 1846)
W. L. V. Henckel von Donnersmarck, *Erinnerungen aus meinem Leben* (Zerbst, 1846)
W. v. Bismarck, *Aufzeichnungen des Genrallieutenants Friedrich Wilhelm Grafen von Bismarck* (Karlsruhe, 1847)
H. v. Luden, *Rückblicke in mein Leben* (Jena, 1847)
A. v. Keyserling, *Aus der Kriegszeit* (Berlin, 1847–55)

K. G. v. Raumer, *Erinnerungen aus den Jahren 1813 und 1814* (Stuttgart, 1850)

F. C. F. v. Müffling, *Aus meinem Leben* (Berlin, 1851)

L. v. Wolzogen, *Memoiren* (Leipzig, 1851)

F. A. L. von der Marwitz, *Lebensbeschreibung* (Berlin, 1852)

T. D. Goethe, *Aus dem Leben eines sächsischen Husaren* (Leipzig, 1853)

W. Meier, *Erinnerungen aus den Feldzügen 1806 bis 1815* (Karlsruhe, 1854)

M. Burg, *Geschichte meines Dienstlebens* (Berlin, 1854)

F. Mändler, *Erinnerungen aus meinen Feldzüge in den Jahren 1809 bis 1815* (Nuremberg, 1854)

G. F. Bärsch, *Erinnerungen aus meinem vielbewegten Leben* (Aachen, 1856)

L. v. Reiche, *Memoiren* (Leipzig, 1857)

H. v. Chézy, *Unvergessenes. Denkwürdigkeiten aus dem Leben von Helmina von Chézy* (Leipzig, 1858)

A. v. Blumröder, *Erlebnisse im Krieg und Frieden in der grossen Welt und in der kleinen Welt meines Gemüths* (Sondershausen, 1857)

J. D. v. Dziengel, *Geschichte des Koeniglichen Zweiten Ulanen-Regiments* (Potsdam, 1858)

F. L. A. v. Meerheim, *Erlebnisse eines Veteranen der Grossen Armee während des Feldzuges in Russland* (Dresden, 1860)

W. Mente, *Von der Pieke auf. Erinnerungen an eine neun und vierzigjährige Dienstzeit* (Berlin, 1861)

L. Rellstab, *Aus meinem Leben* (Berlin, 1861)

K. v. Suckow, *Aus meinem Soldatenleben* (Stuttgart, 1862)

C. E. V. Krieg (ed.), *Vor fünfzig Jahren. Tagebuch eines freiwilligen Jägers der Jahre 1813 und 1814* (Wesel, 1863)

M. Prell, *Erinnerungen aus der Franzosenzeit* (Hamburg, 1863)

C. v. Martens, *Vor fünzig Jahren. Tagebuch meines Feldzuges in Sachsen 1813* (Stuttgart, 1863)

L. v. Hoffmann, *Erinnerungen eines alten Soldaten und ehemaligen Freiwilligen* (Berlin, 1863)

C. F. C. Pfnor, *Der Krieg, seine Mittel und Wege, sowie sein Verhältniss zum Frieden, in den Erlebnissen eines Veteranen* (Tübingen, 1864)

Wilhelm, Markgraf von Baden, *Denkwürdigkeiten* (Karlsruhe, 1864)

H. v. Brandt (ed.), *Aus dem Leben des Generals der Infanterie z. D. Dr Heinrich von Brandt* (Berlin, 1868)

F. A. Brockhaus, *Brockhaus, Friedrich Arnold. Sein Leben und Wirken* (Leipzig, 1872–81)

E. v. Stockmar (ed.), *Denkwürdigkeiten aus den Papieren des Freiherrn Christian Friedrich von Stockmar* (Braunschweig, 1872)

J. v. Hüser, *Denkwürdigkeiten aus dem Leben des Generals der Infanterie von Hüser* (Berlin, 1877)

A. L. v. Ardenne, *Bergische Lanciers Westfälische Husaren Nr. 11* (Berlin, 1877)

L. v. Ranke (ed.), *Denkwürdigkeiten des Staatskanzlers Fürsten von Hardenberg* (Leipzig, 1877)

C. C. Zimmermann, *Geschichte des 1. Grossherzoglich Hessischen Dragoner-Regiments* (Darmstadt, 1878)

A. Adam, *Aus dem Leben eines Schlachtenmalers*, ed. H. Holland (Stuttgart, 1886)

C. E. W. v. Canitz und Dallwitz, *Denkschriften* (Berlin, 1888)

H. v. Boyen, *Erinnerungen aus dem Leben des Generalfeldmarschalls Hermann von Boyen* (Leipzig, 1889–90), 3 vols

Hohenzollern monarchy in 1815—and to 'Mother Germany' more than to the Prussian state.[192] He also stood between the conservative circles of the German courts, especially those of Prussia and Bavaria, and the liberal circles to which he had been attached, at the salons of Rahel Varnhagen and Bettina von Arnim, at the start of his career.[193] Like most of his colleagues, he believed that Germany was 'a

[192] Ranke's correspondence from 1822, cited in J. Toews, *Becoming Historical: Cultural Reformation and Public Memory in Early Nineteenth-Century Berlin* (Cambridge, 2004), 375.

[193] See R. Vierhaus, *Ranke und die soziale Welt* (Münster, 1957), 6–52.

historical nation' (*eine historische Nation*)—'since antiquity there has been no other nation which has exercised such influence over others'—and that the wars of liberation had helped to create a 'universal conviction' that some form of German political unification was necessary, reviving the feeling of Germany's 'essential unity', as he put it in an essay from 1832.[194] At the University of Leipzig until 1818, he had been a supporter of the student movement, in which his brother Heinrich was actively involved, and he had revered Jahn, whom he had met in a 'sacred' moment in 1819 and whose writing desk he had subsequently acquired (and which he used all his life).[195] In 1841, he was made official historiographer of the Prussian state as part of a conspicuous policy of recruitment and national regeneration under the new monarch Friedrich Wilhelm IV. Hermann von Boyen was appointed War Minister (after being forced into retirement from the army in the early 1820s), Johann Albert Friedrich Eichhorn (who had briefly been a volunteer in Schill's *Freikorps*) was given the *Kultusministerium*, and Arndt was restored to his professorship of history and elected rector of the University of Bonn. The termination of police surveillance of Jahn and the award of the Iron Cross for his services in 1813 and 1814, the appointment of the philosopher Friedrich Wilhelm Joseph Schelling, the philologists Jacob and Wilhelm Grimm, the 'historical-school' lawyer Friedrich Karl von Savigny, and the composer Felix Mendelssohn were all designed to demonstrate that Prussia had again become the champion of a 'Christian–German' culture and state, as it had been between 1813 and 1815.[196]

The policy was intended to signal a cultural shift, which was symbolized above all by the national festival in 1842 to mark the completion of Cologne cathedral, which had been left without portals since the Middle Ages. Yet, in the representation and commemoration of the wars of liberation, which constituted the heart of the revival of 1840, the cultural policies of the Prussian monarch seemed to point to continuities rather than ruptures, not least because they dated back to a 'patriotic', more reformist 'shadow ministry' associated with the Crown Prince during the 1820s and 1830s, including Stein, Wilhelm von Humboldt, Fichte, Niebuhr, Schleiermacher, Scharnhorst, Gneisenau, and Clausewitz, all of whom had died before Friedrich Wilhelm IV's accession. Their purpose was to foster 'the unity felt by princes and peoples' for the 'immediate future and thus also for the more distant future of Germany', as the new king expressed it in a letter to Metternich in January 1841, after the French-provoked Rhine crisis of 1840 had caused 'an uplifting and Germanic sensibility' to move 'through all the people of the German Confederation in a way which has not been seen since 1813–1814'.[197] That members of the new Prussian regime believed that they could use the wars of liberation in order to restore harmony and patriotic sentiment in the Hohenzollern monarchy, with Friedrich Wilhelm IV as a self-professed 'king of the people' or '*Volkskönig*', suggests that the

---

[194] L. v. Ranke, 'Ueber die Trennung und die Einheit von Deutschland', in L. v. Ranke, *Sämmtliche Werke* (Leipzig, 1867–90), vols 49–50, 134. See also E. Schulin, 'Universal History and National History, mainly in the Lectures of Leopold von Ranke', in G. G. Iggers and J. M. Powell (eds), *Leopold von Ranke and the Shaping of the Historical Discipline* (Syracuse, NY, 1990), 70–81.
[195] J. Toews, *Becoming Historical*, 381.   [196] See Ibid., 19–116.
[197] Friedrich Wilhelm IV to C. v. Metternich, 10 Jan. 1841, cited in K. Blasius, *Friedrich Wilhelm*, 97.

myth of 1813 was a common rather than a contested point of historical reference. Throughout the German lands, reported Brockhaus's popular *Conversations-Lexikon*—produced in Leipzig—in 1832, the wars of freedom had been 'years of decision', giving rise to Germany's 'rebirth'.[198] After the submission of 'all the *Völker* of the West' to the destructive greatness of Napoleon, leading to the catastrophic campaign of 1812 against Russia, claimed the same publication in 1841, 'the whole of Germany joined the Allies and demanded retribution on French soil' in 1813–14.[199]

In the period of 'restoration' after 1819, the German states took the lead in commemorating the wars of liberation, erecting a limited number of monuments, sponsoring regimental histories, and commissioning works of art. These representations existed alongside the popular prints, privately produced paintings, pamphlets, poems, songs, and stories which circulated in a wider public sphere. Certainly, there were disagreements about the relative significance of the volunteers and the people, on the one hand, and the regular army and governments, on the other, with Gentz maintaining in the aftermath of the Wartburg festival in 1817, against what seemed the 'majority' view, that 'the princes and their ministries' had defeated Napoleon:

> Not all the demagogues and pamphleteers of the world and of posterity can take that away from them. …They prepared the war, founded it, created it. They did even more: they led it, nourished it and enlivened it. …Those who today in their youthful audacity suppose that they overturned the tyrant couldn't even have driven him out of Germany.[200]

There were also disputes about the roles of the different states and about individuals within each state, as Schön demonstrated in 1822 on hearing that General Friedrich Wilhelm von Bülow was to be honoured with his own monument, asking 'If all the king's friends are to get statues, where is the limit?'[201] Instead, he went on, a statue should be dedicated to the member of the militia who had shouted 'lick my ass' when the general had ordered a retreat.[202] Such objections rarely, if ever, challenged the depiction of 1813 as a heroic, patriotic, and successful undertaking and they were not made public.[203]

Typically, monarchs and governments commissioned neo-classical rather than gothic monuments and buildings, with notable exceptions such as Karl Friedrich Schinkel's memorial to the wars of liberation on the Kreuzberg outside Berlin. Many architects—and artists such as Friedrich—had imagined grandiose, popular, 'Germanic' monuments in the gothic style, including Schinkel's plan for a huge *Befreiungsdom* during the 1810s and Wilhelm Stier's design for a national cathedral

---

[198] F. A. Brockhaus (ed.), *Conversations-Lexikon der neuesten Zeit und Literatur* (Leipzig, 1832), vol. 1, 663.

[199] 'Bonaparte', in F. A. Brockhaus (ed.), *Conversations-Lexikon* (Leipzig, 1837–41), vol. 1, 287, 291.

[200] Cited in C. Clark, 'The Wars of Liberation in Prussian Memory', 552.

[201] Ibid., 559. [202] Ibid.

[203] Schön's comments were made in private correspondence: R. Koselleck, 'Kriegerdenkmale als Identitätsstiftungen der Überlebenden', in O. Marquand and K. Stierle (eds), *Identität* (Munich, 1979), 269.

in the early 1840s, which adopted and exaggerated many elements from Schinkel, but few were built. Instead, Schinkel's redesigning of *Unter den Linden* during the 1820s and 1830s—the *Altes Museum*, the *Neue Wache* (new guardhouse), the *Schlossbrücke*, and the redesigned royal cathedral—deliberately adapted the balanced proportions and order of classicism and turned away from the 'destructive' struggle and striving of gothic architecture.[204] This shift was less dramatic than it seemed as a consequence of the widely held belief in the propinquity of 'original' Greek and German cultures which had been established by Johann Joachim Winckelmann and his successors from the late eighteenth century onwards.[205] Leo von Klenze's construction of the classical Walhalla on the banks of the Danube near Regensburg betrayed a similar movement in Bavaria yet the narrative inscribed on the panels of the temple was explicitly 'Germanic', with representations of the battle of Arminius or 'Hermann' in the *Teutoburger Wald*, the Christian 'early era' (*Frühzeit*), and the victory over Napoleon in the wars of liberation.[206] As in other Bavarian monuments from the same period, no mention was made of the alliance of Bavaria and France under the auspices of the Confederation of the Rhine. The proclivity of such works, which could also be found in Schinkel's painting of a 'Triumphal Arch' in 1817 and his plan for a memorial to Friedrich the Great in 1829, was to combine Prussian, Bavarian, or other state insignia with German and Greek symbols and legends, using them to summon up a common national struggle.

Much of the historical, military painting of the era attempted to do the same thing, adapting traditional motifs of the genre and depicting common soldiers and commanding officers side by side in episodes of battles—for instance, Dietrich Monten's *Die Schlacht bei Ligny, 16. Juni* 1815 (1842), which showed the wounding of Blücher—and manoeuvres (Wilhelm Camphausen, *Blüchers Rheinübergang bei Caub am 1. Januar 1814*, completed in 1860).[207] In general, in these works as in other literary forms, the earlier 'trials' of the Revolutionary and Napoleonic Wars—especially the defeats of 1805, 1806, 1809, and 1812, some of the horrors of which were shown in paintings such as Albrecht Adam's generic *Nach der Schlacht* from 1840, portraying a living horse amidst the corpses of its rider and other horses—led to the redemption of 1813–15.[208] Heinrich Heine mockingly wrote in 1835:

> When God, snow and the Cossacks had destroyed Napoleon's best forces, we Germans received orders from on high to free ourselves from the foreign yoke and we flamed up in manly wrath because of the servitude we had borne too long, and we thrilled to the

---

[204] Schinkel cited in J. Toews, *Becoming Historical*, 143.
[205] B. Vick, 'Greek Origins and Organic Metaphors: Ideals of Cultural Autonomy in Neohumanist Germany from Winckelmann to Curtius', *Journal of the History of Ideas*, 63 (2002), 483–500.
[206] U. Schlie, *Die Nation erinnert sich* (Munich, 2002), 28–9.
[207] S. Parth, *Zwischen Bildbericht und Bildpropaganda*, 178–87.
[208] Ibid., 85–7. Also, Otto Wigand (ed.), *Conversations-Lexikon*, vol. 1, 469, arguing that 'the German people' were the same throughout, from the low of 1806 to the highs of 1813 and 1815.

good melodies and bad verses of Körner's songs, and we conquered our freedom, ... for we do everything commanded by our princes.[209]

Memories of wars of 'liberation' were risible to the exiled poet, not least because they recalled campaigns which had not achieved 'freedom', yet they were also accepted, without further comment, as a popular point of reference and veneration.[210] In this respect, the divided memories and other divisions—between individual states and between governments and sections of their populations—which seem so obvious to later historians seemed less so to contemporaries.

---

[209] H. Heine, *Die Romantische Schule* (1835), cited in P. Gay, *The Cultivation of Hatred* (London, 1993), 101.

[210] R. Schilling, 'Die soziale Konstruktion heroischer Männlichkeit im 19. Jahrhundert. Das Beispiel Theodor Körner', in K. Hagemann and R. Pröve (eds), *Landsknechte, Soldatenfrauen und Nationalkrieger* (Frankfurt, 1998), 121–44.

Conclusion
A History of Remembering and Forgetting

The campaigns of 1809 and 1813–15 came to be known as national 'wars of free-dom' or 'liberation', yet the relationship between belligerence, military conflict, and nationalism, on which much of the recent historiography has concentrated, remains contestable.[1] Scholars such as Otto Dann, Michael Jeismann, and Jörn Leonhard emphasize the role of nationalism in the waging of war, and vice versa, whilst others such as Ute Planert and Jörg Echternkamp are more sceptical about nationalism's scope and significance.[2] Virtually all, though, continue to focus largely on research questions which are defined by the relationship between national allegiance (or a *lack* of nationalism) and warfare: 'it has become clear that most modern nation-states were the product and trigger of military conflicts', contends Karen Hagemann.[3] In this study, I have shown both that contemporaries' attitudes to war were frequently separable from their support for a German nation and that their linkage of patriotism, nationalism, and warfare, when it did occur, was often of secondary importance and was rarely perceived to be problematic. What was of greater significance was the fact that wars had become more threatening, lasting longer and entailing greater financial and human cost, and they had

---

[1] See M. Hewitson, 'Belligerence, Patriotism and Nationalism', 839–76, for the literature on this topic.

[2] Those stressing the significance of nationalism include M. Jeismann, *Das Vaterland der Feinde*; J. Leonhard, *Bellizismus*; O. Dann, 'Der deutsche Bürger wird Soldat', 61–84; O. Dann, *Nation und Nationalismus in Deutschland*; O. Dann and J. Dinwiddy (eds), *Nationalism in the Age of the French Revolution*; O. Dann (ed.), *Patriotismus und Nationsbildung am Ende des Heiligen Römischen Reiches* (Cologne, 2003); K. Hagemann, *Mannlicher Muth und teutscher Ehre*; R. Ibbeken, *Preussen, 1807–1813*; B. v. Münchow-Pohl, *Zwischen Krieg und Reform*; D. Düding, *Organisierter gesellschaftlicher*; D. Klenke, *Der singende 'deutsche Mann'*; W. Hardtwig, *Nationalismus und Bürgerkultur in Deutschland*, 70–148; T. Nipperdey, 'In Search of Identity', 1–16; E. Weber, *Lyrik der Befreiungskriege 1812–1815*; G. E. Mosse, *Fallen Soldiers*; G. E. Mosse, *The Nationalization of the Masses*; H. Kohn, *Prelude to Nation-States*. More sceptical, although still concentrating on the relationship between the military and belligerence (or war weariness), on the one hand, and nationalism, on the other, include U. Planert, *Der Mythos*; J. Echternkamp, *Der Aufstieg des deutschen Nationalismus*; H.-U. Wehler, *Deutsche Gesellschaftsgeschichte 1700–1815*, vol. 1, 506–30; U. Planert, 'Wann beginnt der "moderne" deutsche Nationalismus?', 25–59; J. J. Breuilly, 'The Response to Napoleon and German Nationalism', 256–83, and J. J. Breuilly, 'Napoleonic Germany and State-Formation', 121–52; D. Langewiesche, *Nation, Nationalismus und Nationalstaat*; D. Langewiesche, *Reich, Nation, Föderation*; M. Umbach, *Federalism and Enlightenment in Germany*; D. Rogosch, 'Das Heilige Römische Reich Deutscher Nation', 15–28; R. D. Billinger, Jr, 'Good and True Germans', 105–39; J. J. Sheehan, 'State and Nationality in the Napoleonic Period', 47–59.

[3] K. Hagemann, *Mannlicher Muth und teutscher Ehre*, 60.

become participatory in nature (or an affair of the *Volk*), requiring conscription or levies *en masse*.

NATIONAL, PATRIOTIC, AND MASS WARFARE

Patriotism and nationalism remained relevant within Germany's public sphere and in government circles from the Napoleonic Wars onwards, but they were not necessarily connected to war, even though military conflict altered the conditions in which patriotic and national sentiments and ideas were articulated. The realms of 'politics' and 'publicity' were limited but had increased in scope, albeit unevenly, during the long period of war and territorial reorganization between 1792 and 1815. The conflicts of the revolutionary and Napoleonic eras stimulated a thirst for 'news' which the press, broadsheets, almanacs, and other forms of publication in the overlapping public spheres of the German lands sought to satisfy. It is possible that up to a third of Berlin's adult population occasionally read newspapers.[4] Censorship and political upheaval regularly halted or interrupted publication yet most evidence suggests that published news reached a sizeable readership. Such news was frequently presented in a patriotic or national context, linked to the interests of an individual state, its ruling house, and army or to 'Germany' as an existing cultural and ill-defined political entity. Sometimes governments' actions, particularly of those belonging to the Confederation of the Rhine, were difficult to reconcile with policies or blueprints advanced by 'nationalists' elsewhere. In Prussia and Austria, too, conservatives often put their monarchy's interests first. The Great Powers, including the Habsburg and Hohenzollern monarchies, had combined militarily to defeat France, not German nationalists or a coalition of German states, proclaimed the Prussian and, later, Austrian publicist Friedrich von Gentz.[5] Yet he and other 'conservative' writers such as Wilhelm and Friedrich Schlegel and Adam Müller rarely, if ever, pitted Prussia against Germany. French revolutionaries had begun a war which was at once anarchic and national, threatening to run out of control, asserted the 'old Prussian' observer Friedrich August von der Marwitz: at the same time, this national, revolutionary conflict had highlighted the linguistic and geographical boundaries between the German nation—a '*Stamm-Nation*' (nation of descent) whose 'real needs and true interests' were now unambiguous— and a disruptive French nation, which had to be defeated by the joint action of German (and other) states.[6] The idea of a 'common German fatherland' had put down 'deep roots' during wartime which would not be extirpated in peacetime, concluded Marwitz.[7] The majority of defenders of the Holy Roman Empire and of

---

[4] J. Brophy, 'The Public Sphere', 185–208.
[5] F. v. Gentz, 'Bemerkungen zu der Schrift "Über die gegenwärtige Lage von Europa"' (1822), in F. v. Gentz, *Ausgewählte Schriften*, vol. 5, 227–31.
[6] F. Gentz, *Über den Ursprung und Charakter des Krieges*, on the way in which France's national war transformed the states' system. Also, F. Gentz, 'Über den ewigen Frieden' (1800), in K. v. Raumer (ed.), *Ewiger Friede*, 493–6. F. A. von der Marwitz is cited in J. Leonhard, *Bellizismus*, 254–5.
[7] J. Leonhard, *Bellizismus*, 254–5.

the *Rheinbund* under the auspices of Napoleon reproduced similar types of 'German' rhetoric, notwithstanding the fact that their states were at war with one or both of the German Great Powers during the period between 1805 and 1813. German national unity was, in the words of Karl Albert von Kamptz, the 'pole star' of all the individual German governments.[8] In such instances, national justifications for war were used to conceal actual conflicts between enemy states.

The obverse of German historians' focus on the relationship between nationalism and new types of war, it can be held, has been an emphasis on the continuity of combatants' and civilians' experiences of warfare and on the absence of nationalism.[9] Was there a 'caesura', asks Planert, in the Coalition's way of making war?[10] Her negative reply is not only intended to counter the arguments of those propagating myths of national 'liberation', but also those such as David Bell who have claimed that the Napoleonic Wars constituted the first 'total war' in France and, by extension, in other areas of Europe.[11] By contrast, this study emphasizes the transformation of warfare and military organization during the Napoleonic period. Most German states had accepted or conformed to the transition towards *Volkskriege* or 'people's wars'.[12] Such wars were not 'total' in the twentieth-century meaning of the word, but they had become 'popular' or participatory, differing fundamentally from periods of 'peace'.[13] The raising of mass armies of conscripts in revolutionary and Napoleonic France had compelled the majority of German states, either through compliance with French requests or through imitation, to adopt similar measures themselves, prompting a transformation of the ways in which wars were fought—and, therefore, experienced—and entailing fundamental political, social, and economic adjustments on the part of governments and most sections of the population during the period of the wars themselves and during

---

[8] K. A. v. Kamptz, 'Aphorismen über die deutsche National-Einheit als Zweck des rheinischen Bundes', *Der Rheinische Bund*, 1808, vol. 5, no. 15, 271–3.

[9] Historians have tended to focus on the limits of nationalism, of course. Their preoccupation with this question, however, has informed the ways in which they have conceived of war and its impact. For more on these emphases, see M. Hewitson, 'On War and Peace', 447–83.

[10] U. Planert, 'Innovation or evolution?', 69.

[11] D. A. Bell, *The First Total War*; R. Weigley, *The Age of Battles*, 290; T. C. W. Blanning, *The French Revolutionary Wars*, 101. See also R. Chickering, 'Total War: The Use and Abuse of a Concept', in M. F. Boemeke, R. Chickering, and S. Förster (eds), *Anticipating Total War: The German and American Experiences, 1871–1914* (Cambridge, 1999), 13–28. Chickering argues in the Introduction of *War in an Age of Revolution*, 3, that changes in combat 'laid the moral and ideological foundations' of total war. Dierk Walter, 'Reluctant Reformers, Observant Disciples', and Wolfgang Kruse, 'Revolutionary France and the Meanings of Levée en Masse', in R. Chickering, *War in an Age of Revolution*, 85–101, 299–312, agree with this position. On the conflation of the terms 'total war', implying a total mobilization of resources, and 'modern war', resting on 'the fruits of industrialization and technological innovation', see H. Strachan, 'Essay and Reflection', 351.

[12] Here, I disagree with Karen Hagemann's distinction between monarchic-conservative *Befreiungskriege* (wars of liberation), liberal and German national *Freiheitskriege*, and Marxist 'people's wars': K. Hagemann, *Revisiting Prussia's Wars against Napoleon*, 15. The term *Volkskrieg*, or people's war, was used throughout by commentators from different constituencies. There was also a more regular interchanging of the terms '*Befreiungskrieg*' and '*Freiheitskrieg*', which remained the most widely used term until beyond 1848, than this distinction implies.

[13] M. Hewitson, 'On War and Peace', 447–83; M. Broers, 'The Concept of "Total War" in the Revolutionary-Napoleonic Period', 247–68.

their immediate aftermath.[14] Although the impact of combat remained uneven, many onlookers—perhaps, even, most—had come to view 'war' as a new, enduring, and defining feature of their lives.

Mass warfare was more intense than previous types of combat, with a greater number of battles and higher rates of killing, compared to the conflicts of the eighteenth century. War was an everyday or recurring reality for many subjects, becoming a central part of their dealings with the state and other authorities. As one pamphleteer put it in July 1813, Europe's population seemed to have turned into an army during the course of the previous two decades and its cities and villages appeared to have become 'one great camp'.[15] The continuing conflicts had not merely become a more regular feature of subjects' daily lives, they had also become a more important one, defining conscripts' and civilians' very existence in many cases.[16] For such contemporaries, battles of 'annihilation' (*Vernichtung*) and 'national' or 'patriotic' defence, combined with a revolutionary or Napoleonic redefining of territorial states and reordering of the European states' system, had brought into question the very existence of most German states and, from many educated observers' point of view, the future of a putative German nation. Archduke Karl's warning to his brother, the kaiser, that Austria faced 'a terrible crisis' was repeated throughout 'Germany'.[17] In Prussia, to reformers such as Gneisenau, 'invasion' by the enemy was synonymous not merely with the 'annihilation' of an army in a decisive battle, but with the annihilation of the state.[18] The evidence suggests that, in the German lands at least, the advent, duration, and nature of conflict during the Napoleonic period had produced political effects which were difficult to foresee or control. These effects were largely the corollary of new types of mass warfare and conscription, forced on military and official elites, who often remained in power, by French victories. Military reforms were undertaken out of necessity, not because of a wider 'ideological' or 'political' dynamic and notwithstanding public support for reformed German military organizations and forces, which contrasted with earlier criticism of 'absolutist' standing armies.[19] The human costs and economic burdens which resulted from mass warfare were unexpectedly heavy, with more significant consequences than those described by Planert.

Contemporaries' experiences of the Napoleonic Wars altered the parameters within which nineteenth-century Germans understood military conflict. The conscription of a wider range of recruits and the worsening conditions of war, as a result of larger, more mobile, less adequately provisioned armies pursuing more ambitious

---

[14] For more on this question, see M. Hewitson, 'Belligerence, Patriotism and Nationalism', 839–76.

[15] Anonymous pamphlet, July 1813, cited in H.-B. Spies (ed.), *Die Erhebung gegen Napoleon*, 304.

[16] See, for instance, K. A. Varnhagen v. Ense, *Denkwürdigkeiten*, vol. 1, 104, 169–71, and vol. 2, 135.

[17] Rothenberg, *Napoleon's Great Adversaries*, 104.

[18] Gneisenau to Hardenberg, 8 Aug. 1811, in G. Förster and C. Gudzent (eds), *Gneisenau. Ausgewählte militärische Schriften*, 167.

[19] In this respect, Broers's criticism of Bell is justified: M. Broers, 'The Concept of "Total War" in the Revolutionary-Napoleonic Period', 247–68. Many commentators opposed both positions, of course.

aims, had led to resistance to the new demands of military conflict in many cases.[20] Although there is little evidence to suggest that opposition to war, resistance, or desertion had increased overall within the heartlands of Prussia, Bavaria, or other recently expanded or newly constructed states, there are many indications that early nineteenth-century publics—or significant sections of them—assumed that military conflict would be bloodier and costlier than its eighteenth-century predecessors, which in turn widened the gap between war and peace.[21] Civilians' and conscripts' views of conflict seemed to have altered the basis on which wars were waged. Publicists' and policy-makers' changing conceptions of military conflict had helped to promote the mobilization of more and more soldiers, the encouragement of greater 'public' support for military campaigns, an acceptance of self-referential patriotic or national justifications of war, the adoption of escalating or undefined war aims, recognition of fewer restraints on the conduct of warfare, and an acknowledgement of greater hindrances to the negotiation of an admissible peace, given the increased costs of conflict.[22] The opposing pressures created by citizens' inflated expectations of war—greater freedom for governments to act, but also heavier burdens, higher stakes, and a more pressing need to win—often appeared uncontrollable during the 1790s, 1800s, and 1810s. This new type of military conflict had long-term consequences in Germany, including for the 'reaction' of the restoration era.[23] Paradoxically, the distinction between war and peace had become clearer, not merely because conflicts were heroic or had gained public backing, but because the realities of war were unexpectedly difficult to bear and the achievement of peace had proved so elusive. The sensitivities of middle-class recruits and, more occasionally, noble officers to the violence and suffering of mass warfare, amidst an entangled web of more matter-of-fact or picaresque accounts of ordinary soldiers and military commanders, contributed to such a paradox, in accordance with the expectations of sociologists such as Elias, Giddens, and Collins.[24] The tensions between these and other representations and experiences of conflict, which first became visible between

---

[20] On the diverse causes of resistance, see C. J. Esdaile (ed.), *Popular Resistance in the French Wars: Patriots, Partisans and Land Pirates* (Basingstoke, 2005).

[21] Amongst other things, Ute Planert, *Der Mythos*, shows that complaints about the wars of the mid-1790s were just as widespread and vociferous in the South and West—and perhaps more so—than those of 1812–15; Michael Rowe, 'Resistance, Collaboration or Third Way?', 67–90, demonstrates that actual resistance to war remained the exception in Germany; M. Sikora, 'Desertion und nationale Mobilmachung', 112–40, suggests that desertion rates for Prussian *Freiwillige* as a whole were low, at between 1 and 5 per cent.

[22] These features overlap with David Bell's definition of 'total war', without justifying such a term: D. Bell, *The First Total War*, 1–20.

[23] The next volume in this series of studies deals with such consequences. On the terminology of 'reaction' and 'conservatism', see O. Brunner, W. Conze, and R. Koselleck (eds), *Geschichtliche Grundbegriffe* (Stuttgart, 1972), vol. 1, 243–342. Gentz, J. H. Maurer-Constant (ed.), *Briefe an Johannes von Müller* (Schaffhausen, 1839), vol. 1; and Adam Müller, *Die Elemente der Staatskunst*, vol. 1, 373, referred to a 'principle of preservation' in this period. See also K. Epstein, *The Genesis of German Conservatism*, 10; and R. M. Berdahl, *The Politics of the Prussian Nobility: The Development of a Conservative Ideology, 1770–1848* (Princeton, 1988), 158–81.

[24] See the references to N. Elias, *The Civilising Process: The History of Manners* (New York, 1978), vol. 1; N. Elias, *The Civilising Process: Power and Civility* (Oxford, 1982), vol. 2; R. Collins, *Violence: A Micro-sociological Theory* (Princeton, NJ, 2008); and A. Giddens, *The Nation-State and Violence* (Cambridge, 1985), in the Introduction of this volume.

1792 and 1820, were reproduced during the long nineteenth century and culminated in the destroyed hopes of the First World War.[25]

THE LEGACY OF GERMAN *VOLKSKRIEGE*

Given what one Westphalian infantry officer called the 'horror and disgust' of Napoleonic warfare, the most significant question—which differs from those posed by recent historiography—is why there was so little resistance to war in the German lands after the cataclysm of the years of conflict between 1792 and 1815.[26] One answer, favoured by Planert, is that there was no cataclysm—or such a cataclysm was accepted as a fact of eighteenth-century life—for many subjects, who were exposed to traditional, albeit resented, forms of warfare, and that there were, partly as a consequence, complicated reactions to the Revolutionary and Napoleonic Wars after 1815, with veterans forming associations in some areas but not in others.[27] Those veterans' and civilians' 'polyvalent interpretations of the meaning and memories of war' were only transformed slowly during the nineteenth century through the 'construction of public memory' by the German states and by 'a growing liberal-national movement'.[28] 'The diversity of the war experience poses a problem', Leighton James concludes: 'How can we generalize on the shifting sands of these multiple voices?'[29] His response, like that of many other historians, is to emphasize continuity, with autobiographical literature showing that 'older understandings of warfare survived in German Central Europe'.[30] The persisting propinquity of civilian and military life, with subjects in regular contact with soldiers, helped to ensure that war remained indistinct from peace, with troops at once familiar figures and occasional perpetrators—even those professing to be 'liberators'—of 'looting, theft, violence and extortion'.[31] The 'incomplete' nature of military reforms by 1815 meant that 'the German armies of the Napoleonic Wars were remarkably similar to those of the eighteenth century, despite the rhetoric surrounding the citizen-soldier', with German-speaking soldiers' letters, diaries, and memoirs all referring to 'the diverse origin of the soldiery'.[32] The composition of a state's army was a 'hodge-podge of different groups—long-standing subjects, former subjects, newly acquired subjects, prisoners of war and deserters'.[33] Significant residues of 'aristocratic warfare', together with the 'contractual approach' of common soldiers to their terms of service, remained characteristic of the Napoleonic era,

---

[25] For more on this, see M. Hewitson, 'Violence and Civilization: Transgression in Modern Wars', in M. Fulbrook (ed.), *Uncivilizing Processes? Excess and Transgression in German Society and Culture* (Amsterdam, 2007), 117–56, and M. Hewitson, 'German Soldiers and the Horror of War: Fear of Death and the Joy of Killing in 1870 and 1914', *History* (forthcoming).

[26] F. Giesse, *Kassel—Moskau—Kuestrin 1812–1813*, 241–2.

[27] U. Planert, 'From Collaboration to Resistance', 695–6. Also, K. Aaslestad, *Place and Politics*, 324–8; E. Trox, *Militärischer Konservatismus*, 43.

[28] U. Planert, 'From Collaboration to Resistance', 705.

[29] Leighton S. James, *Witnessing the Revolutionary and Napoleonic Wars*, 189.

[30] Ibid., 190.   [31] Ibid., 191.   [32] Ibid.   [33] Ibid.

according to James.[34] Codes of honour, regimental colours, casual brutality, mutilation, and torture all seemed to be a continuation of the practices of the eighteenth century.

It is striking, however, how many commentators from different states and social milieux talked of the Napoleonic Wars as a watershed. In part, their versions of events corresponded to combatants' own accounts of suffering, which differed markedly in 1805–6, 1809, 1812, 1813–14, and 1815 from those of earlier conflicts. In part, they reflected the particular anxieties and sensibilities of an increasing but still limited reading public. It was those who wrote for this public (Arndt's class of 'Schreiber') who—along with governments—shaped nineteenth-century conceptions of war. From a close reading of their works, essays, and reports, such commentators had altered their view of warfare in similar ways, under the force of extreme circumstances, notwithstanding their different 'ideological' or 'national' positions.[35] These commentators played an important part in ensuring that postwar attitudes to conflict, including myths of 1813, were fundamentally different from those of the eighteenth century, with heroic conceptions of war quickly overshadowing diverse private and publicly enacted memories of suffering.[36] What was more, their shared view of 'war' was a narrower one than in the past, resting to a considerable extent on an imagined essence of combat rather than the wider effects of warfare, even though most writers had not been conscripted and had no direct experience of fighting.[37] In such writers' and artists' images of conflict, which informed discourses after 1815, stories of economic hardship, political disruption, opposition to conscription, disease, and cooperation or conflict with 'foreigners' were regularly linked and subordinated to dominant narratives about violence, death, and heroism, qualifying—although not denying—the significance of 'the recognition' given by recent scholarship to 'the diversity of war experiences', in the approving judgement of Aaslestad and Hagemann.[38]

What united most commentators was a conviction that the nature of warfare had altered, shifting the parameters of wartime and, especially, post-war diplomacy, conscription, and military strategy, and making war 'constitutive' of 'processes of nation-building and the establishment of new nation-states', as Leonhard has rightly suggested, but not making nationalism necessary for the waging of wars.[39] Historians' continuing focus on the relationship between war and nationalism, which derives from a desire to debunk earlier scholars' creation of myths of national 'wars of liberation', frequently obscures the more fundamental point that representations of war and peace in the public sphere had changed as a result of

---

[34] Ibid., 192.

[35] For more on this, see M. Hewitson, 'On War and Peace', 447–83.

[36] The argument here tempers Chris Clark's arguments about competing memories, which certainly continued to exist but were eclipsed by a dominant narrative about 1813: C. Clark, 'The Wars of Liberation in Prussian Memory', 550–76.

[37] The centrality of battle in memoirs accounts has also been noted by historians of the wars of unification: T. Rohkrämer, *Der Militarismus der 'kleinen Leute'. Die Kriegervereine im Deutschen Kaiserreich 1871–1914* (Munich, 1990), 93.

[38] K. Aaslestad and K. Hagemann, '1806 and Its Aftermath', *Central European History*, 39 (2006), 553.

[39] J. Leonhard, *Bellizismus*, 6.

contemporaries' experiences of military conflict. Both 'enlightened' and 'conservative' commentators, from different backgrounds and with opposing views of politics and state policy, altered their conceptions of, and attitudes to, war during the years between 1792 and 1820, at least in part, it appears from a reading of their works and other writings, because of what they had seen and learned of military conflict.[40] War had come during the course of the revolutionary and Napoleonic campaigns—often without national legitimation or a demonization of enemies—to be accepted by most writers and artists, and probably by many of their readers and viewers, as a discrete, threatening, and necessary state of affairs. What to do about that necessary threat remained a matter of profound dispute, dividing advocates of 'national', Prussian, 'federal', 'confederal', 'reactionary', 'liberal', and other solutions.[41] Few nineteenth-century German commentators, however, denied that the threat existed.

Why did this shift of 'opinion', which was founded on the horrific experiences of combatants, not create doubts about the efficacy or acceptability of war in the nineteenth century? The implication of Ute Frevert's work is that, outside Prussia, middle-class groups remained sceptical of the army and inured to the risks of military conflict.[42] Since, under the system of substitution, they did not have to do military service, they tended to treat the army, the arming of the people, and preparations for war as largely rhetorical. This study has treated the rhetoric of belligerence more seriously, casting the relationship between perceptions of the military and war in a different light. Myths of 1813 were pervasive in the nineteenth century and informed army recruitment, organization, and strategy, even in the 'third Germany'. It is true that many contemporaries distinguished between the military monarchy of Prussia and the different systems of the *Mittelstaaten*. Moreover, the varying use of labels such as 'conscription', 'standing army', and 'militia' created confusion, on occasion giving the impression that Hohenzollern and other forces were different in kind. Nonetheless, most politicians and publicists considered all the German armies, with the exception of those of the small states, to be a combination of an army of the line and *Landwehr*, lying on a

---

[40] See W. Burgdorf, 'Der Kampf um die Vergangenheit', 333–58.

[41] This contention runs counter to the recent preoccupation with a 'federative nation', as outlined by D. Langewiesche, 'Föderativer Nationalismus als Erbe der deutschen Reichsnation: Über Föderalismus und Zentralismus in der deutschen Nationalgeschichte', in D. Langewiesche and G. Schmidt (eds), *Föderative Nation* (Munich, 2000), 215–44; Dieter Langewiesche, 'Reich, Nation und Staat in der jüngeren deutschen Geschichte', in D. Langewiesche, *Nation, Nationalismus, Nationalstaat*, 190–216; D. Langewiesche, 'Zentralstaat, Föderativstaat. Nationalstaatsmodelle in Europa im 19. und 20. Jahrhundert' and 'Das Alte Reich nach seinem Ende. Die Reichsidee in der deutschen Politik des 19. und 20. Jahrhunderts', in D. Langewiesche, *Reich, Nation, Föderation*, 180–93, 211–34. Many different versions of states or national polities emerged in the aftermath of the revolutionary and Napoleonic conflicts, tied to—or separate from—varying readings of those conflicts.

[42] U. Frevert, *A Nation in Barracks: Modern Germany, Military Conscription and Civil Society* (Oxford, 2004); W. Wette, *Militarismus in Deutschland. Geschichte einer kriegerischen Kultur* (Darmstadt, 2008), 39. Markus Ingenlath, *Mentale Aufrüstung. Militarisierungstendenzen in Frankreich und Deutschland vor dem Ersten Weltkrieg* (Frankfurt, 1998), 59–60, makes a similar point in respect of Prussia, going further than Frevert in this respect.

continuum between an absolutist standing army and a republican militia.[43] In these circumstances, an attachment to the army and to the necessity of mass— or, even, universal—conscription in wartime served to maintain the military trad- itions of 1805–15 throughout the German lands. The establishment of such traditions itself militated against the voicing of doubts about the human cost of mass warfare. Censorship, dynastic celebrations, the disparate nature of Germany's overlapping public spheres, the delayed publication of the majority of war mem- oirs, and the failure of a large number of soldiers to return from the Napoleonic campaigns—especially the most harrowing expedition of 1812—all ensured that nineteenth-century images of warfare were predominantly positive. The fact that many combatants were used in their daily lives, as Elias envisaged, to the condi- tions of warfare—acts of violence, disease, hardship, and death—also made the costs of the conflicts easier to bear, without removing the fundamental shock of mass warfare for many contemporaries, particularly those belonging to the 'cultured' strata of the *Bürgertum* and nobility.[44] The next volume explores the consequences of such optimism against the background of continuing conscription, an ambiguous but increasing public abhorrence of slaughter and a technological escalation of killing.

[43] 'Krieg', F. A. Brockhaus (ed.), *Bilder Conversations-Lexikon der neuesten Zeit und Literatur* (Leipzig, 1837–41), vol. 2, 669.

[44] See Introduction.

Select Bibliography

PRIMARY SOURCES

Newspapers and Periodicals
Allgemeine Zeitung
Deutsche Blätter
Deutsches Museum
Europäische Annalen
Minerva
Der Rheinische Bund
Rheinischer Merkur

Poems, Songs, Plays, and Other Literature
E. M. Arndt, *Fünf Lieder für deutsche Soldaten* (Berlin, 1813).
H. J. v. Collin, *Coriolan* (Berlin, 1804).
H. Heine, *Das Buch Le Grand* (Berlin, 1914).
F. L. Jahn, *Deutsche Wehrlieder* (Berlin, 1813).
H. v. Kleist, *Germania an ihre Kinder*, ed. E. v. Pfuel (n. p., 1813).
H. v. Kleist, *Prinz Friedrich von Homburg* (1809–11) in H. v. Kleist, *Werke*, revised edn, ed.
     H. Gilow (Berlin, 1900), vol. 3.
T. Körner, *Drei deutsche Gedichte* (Berlin, 1813).
T. Körner, *Zwölf freie deutsche Gedichte* (Leipzig, 1813).
T. Körner, *Gedichte vor und im heiligen Kriege* (n. p., 1814).
T. Körner, *Kriegslieder der preußischen Freischaaren* (Berlin, 1814).
T. Körner, *Leyer und Schwert* (Berlin, 1814).
F. de la Motte Fouqué, *Der Held des Nordens* (Berlin, 1808–10), 3 vols.
M. v. Schenkendorf, *Gedichte* (Tübingen, 1815).
F. Schiller, *Wallenstein* (Tübingen, 1800).
F. Schlegel, *Gedichte* (Berlin, 1809).
W. v. Schütz, *Lieder für die christlichen Krieger in Deutschland* (n. p., 1813).
F. L. Z. Werner, *Die Söhne des Tals* (Vienna, 1803–4).
F. L. Z. Werner, *Das Kreuz an der Ostsee* (Berlin, 1805–6).
F. L. Z. Werner, *Attila, König der Hunnen* (Berlin, 1808).
F. L. Z. Werner, *Wanda, Königin der Sarmaten* (Tübingen, 1810).

Diaries, Correspondence, and Memoirs
W. A. Adam, *Aus dem Leben eines Schlachtenmalers*, ed. H. Holland (Stuttgart, 1886).
W. Alexis, *Eine Jugend in Preußen. Erinnerungen* (Berlin, 1991).
C. G. S. Ammerbacher, 'Aus der Nördlinger Franzosenzeit', *Nördlinger Jahrbuch*, 10 (1925–6),
     129–60.
F. v. Andlaw, *Mein Tagebuch; Auszüge aus Ausschreibungen der Jahre 1811 bis 1861* (Frankfurt
     am Main, 1862).
J. B. M. v. Arand, *In Vörderösterreichs Amt und Würden. Die Selbstbiographie des Johann
     Baptist Martin von Arand 1743–1831*, ed. H. Waller (Stuttgart, 1996).
J. C. v. Aretin, *Vaterländische Erinnerungen* (Augsburg, 1819).

E. M. Arndt, *Erinnerungen aus dem äusseren Leben*, ed. F. M. Kircheisen (Munich, 1913).

E. M. Arndt, *Briefe*, ed. A. Dühr (Darmstadt, 1972–5), vol. 1.

L. Assing (ed.), *Aus dem Nachlass Varnhagens von Ense* (Leipzig, 1865).

W. Markgraf von Baden, *Denkwürdigkeiten*, ed. Karl Obser (Heidelberg, 1906).

F. Bader (ed.), 'Ein unveröffentlichtes Roggenburger Kriegstagebuch aus den Jahren 1800 und 1801', *Der Heimatfreund. Geschichtliche Heimatblätter des Museumsvereins Weissenhorn*, 1–2 (1934), 6–8.

F. Barth, *Blutrosen von Friedrich Barth, Königlich Preußischem Lieutenant* (Berlin, 1814).

H. Beguelin and A. Beguelin, *Denkwürdigkeiten aus den Jahren 1807–13*, ed. A. Ernst (Berlin, 1892).

A. Birle, 'Bericht ueber die Schlacht von Elchingen den 14. October 1805. Nach dem Manuscript eines Augenzeugen', *Zeitschrift des historischen Vereins für Schwaben und Neuburg*, 6 (1879), 51–69.

A. v. Blumröder, *Erlebnisse im Krieg und Frieden in der grossen Welt und in der kleinen Welt meines Gemüths* (Sondershausen, 1857).

C. Bodo von Bodenhausen, *Tagebuch eines Ordonnanzoffiziers von 1812–1813*, ed. B. v. Cramm (Braunschweig, 1912).

H. v. Boyen, *Denkwürdigkeiten und Erinnerungen 1771–1813* (Stuttgart, 1899), vol. 1.

F. A. Brandner, *Aus dem Tagebuch eines österreichischen Soldaten im Jahre 1809* (Löbau, n. d.).

H. v. Brandt (ed.), *Aus dem Leben des Generals der Infanterie z. D. Dr Heinrich von Brandt* (Berlin, 1868), vol. 1.

W. D. Brednich (ed.), *Lebenslauf und Lebenszusammenhang. Autobiographische Materialien in der volkskundlichen Forschung* (Freiburg, 1982).

J. P. Brunnemair, *Geschichte der königlichen Bairischen Stadt und Herrschaft Mindelheim im Zusammenhang mit anderen wichtigen Weltbegebenheiten* (Mindelheim, 1821).

F. L. Burk, *Das Tagebuch es Friechrich Ludwig Burk. Aufzeichnungen ein Wiesbadener Bürgers und Bauern 1806–1866*, ed. J. Dollwet and T. Weichel (Wiesbaden, 1994).

C. E. W. v. Canitz und Dallwitz, *Denkschriften* (Berlin, 1888), vol 1.

W. Capelle (ed.), *Blüchers Briefe* (Leipzig, n. d.).

H. v. Chézy, *Unvergessenes. Denkwürdigkeiten aus dem Leben von Helmina von Chézy* (Leipzig, 1858), 2 vols.

C. v. Clausewitz, *Schriften, Aufsätze, Studien, Briefe* (Göttingen, 1966/90), 2 vols.

C. v. Clausewitz and M. v. Clausewitz, *Ein Lebensbild in Briefen und Tagebuchblättern*, ed. K. Linnebach (Berlin, 1917).

W. v. Conrady (ed.), *Aus stürmischer Zeit. Ein Soldatenleben vor hundert Jahren* (Berlin, 1907).

J. E. Dewald, 'Biedermeier auf Walze. Aufzeichungen und Briefe des Handwerkburschen Johann Eberhard Dewalt 1836–1838', in W. Fischer (ed.), *Quellen zur Geschichte des deutschen Handwerks* (Göttingen, 1957), 123–35.

G. v. Diest (ed.), Aus *der Zeit der Not und Befreiung in den Jahre 1806 bis 1815* (Berlin, 1905).

C. F. Dizinger, *Denkwürdigkeiten aus meinem Leben und meiner Zeit* (Tübingen, 1833).

M. Dugrillon (ed.), *Joachim Kupferer. Der Vogt zu Erlach* (Mösbach, 1998).

M. v. Eberhardt (ed.), *Aus Preussens schwerer Zeit. Briefe und Aufzeichnungen meines Urgrossvaters und Grossvaters* (Berlin, 1907).

J. Freiherr von Eichendorff, *Sämtliche Werke. Briefe* (Stuttgart, 1992), vol. 12.

K. F. Eichhorn, *Briefe* (Bonn, 1881).

G. Eilers, *Meine Wanderung durchs Leben. Ein Beitrag zur inneren Geschichte des ersten Hälfte des 19. Jahrhunderts* (Leipzig, 1856), vol. 1.

W. Emmerich (ed.), *Proletarische Lebensläufe* (Reinbek, 1974), vol. 1.

R. Engel, *Lebensbeschreibung der Wittwe des Obrist Florian Engle* (Zurich, 1821).

R. Engel, *Memoiren einer Amazone in napoleonischer Zeit* (Zurich/Munich, 1977).

C. W. Faber du Faur, *Blätter aus meinem Portefeuille im Laufe des Feldzuges 1812 in Rußland*, ed. F. v. Kaussler (Stuttgart, 1831–43).

C. W. Faber du Faur, *Napoleons Feldzug in Russland 1812* (Leipzig, 1897).

J. Falk, *Kriegsbüchlein* (Leipzig, 1911).

F. Förster, *Erinnerungen aus dem Befreiungskriege* (Stuttgart, 1840), vol. 1.

E. v. Frauenholz, *Infanterist Deifl. Ein Tagebuch aus napoleonischer Zeit* (Munich, 1939).

K. v. Freystadt, *Erinnerungen aus dem Hofleben*, ed. K. Obser (Heidelberg, 1902).

F. v. Furtenbach, *Krieg gegen Rußland und russische Gefangenschaft* (Nuremberg, 1912).

P. Gebhart, 'Kempten in den Kriegen der Franzoesischen Revolution', *Allgäuer Geschichtsfreund*, 40 (1937), 1–80; 41 (1937), 1–50.

O. Gerhardt, *Die Württemberger im deutschen Befreiungskampf 1813–1815* (Stuttgart, 1938).

F. Giesse, *Kassel—Moskau—Kuestrin 1812–1813*, ed. Karl Giesse (Leipzig, 1912).

N. v. Gneisenau, *Briefe* (Gotha, 1913).

N. v. Gneisenau, *Ein Leben in Briefen* (Leizpig, 1939).

J. v. Görres, *Gesammelte Briefe*, in M. Görres (ed.), *Gesammelte Schriften von Joseph von Görres* (Munich, 1874), vol. 8.

H. Granier (ed.), *Berichte aus der Berliner Franzosenzeit 1807–1809* (Leipzig, 1913).

K. Griewank (ed.), *Königin Luise. Briefe und Aufzeichnungen* (Leipzig, 1925).

F. W. Hackländer, *Bilder aus dem Soldatenleben im Kriege (1816–77)* (Nabu, 2010).

F. W. Hackländer, *Krieg und Frieden. Erzählungen und Bilder* (Nabu, 2010), vols 1–2.

G. A. L. Hanstein, *Die ernste Zeit* (Berlin, 1814/15).

F. Haus, *Chronik der Stadt Aschaffenburg oder der lustige Zeitvertreib* (Aschaffenburg, 1855).

E. Heusinger, *Ansichten, Beobachtungen und Erfahrungen* (Braunschweig, 1825).

B. Hildebrand (ed.), *1812: Drei Schwaben unter Napoleon. Rußlandberichte eines Infanteristen, eines Leutnants, eines Generals* (Aalen, 1967).

B. Hildebrand (ed.), '"Mit welcher Rührung betet Detuschland" Fürbitte des Pfarrers von Trochtelfingen für Napoleon', *Nordschwaben. Zeitschrift für Landschaft, Geschichte, Kultur und Zeitgeschehen*, 5 (1977), no. 4, 178–80.

P. Holzhausen, *Die Deutschen in Russland. Leben und Leiden auf der Moskauer Heerfahrt* (Berlin, 1912).

K. S. Hosang, *Aus der sogenannten guten alten Zeit. Kleine Geschichten aus Regensburgs Vergangenheit* (Regensburg, 1932), 2 vols.

A. Hupfer, 'Eine alte Hofer Chronik aus den Jahren 1798-1821', *Veröffentlichungen des Nordoberfränkischen Vereins für Natur-, Geschichts-, und Landeskunde*, 9 (1928), 14–21.

J. H. G. H. Hüser, *Denkwürdigkeiten aus dem Leben des Generals der Infanterie v. Hüser* (Berlin, 1877).

F. L. Jahn, *Die Briefe* (Leipzig, 1913).

F. L. Jahn, *Unbekannte Briefe* (Oberwerries, 1990).

J. Jerg, *Chronik des Bleichers Johannes Jerg 1771–1821. Ein Heimatbuch der Stadt Ebingen* (Balingen, 1953).

J. M. Jochner, 'Kriegerische Vorgänge im Markt Krumbach', *Zeitschrift des historischen Vereins für Schwaben und Neuburg*, 4 (1878), no. 3, 330–66.

H. v. Jordan, *Erinnerungsblätter und Briefe eines jungen Freiheitskämpfers aus den Jahren 1813 und 1814*, ed. Ludwig von Jordan (Berlin, 1914).

J. Kannicht, *Und alles wegen Napoleon. Aus dem Kriegstagebuch des Georg von Coulon, 1760–1815* (Coblenz, 1986).

K. P. Kayser, *Aus gärender Zeit. Tagebuchblätter des Professors Karl Philipp Kauser aus den Jahren 1793 bis 1827*, ed. F. Schneider (Karlsruhe, 1927).

J. Kermann (ed.), *Pfälzer unter napoleons Fahnen. Verteranen erinnern sich* (Neustadt, 1989).

F. M. Kircheisen, *Wider Napoleon! Ein deutsches Reiterleben 1806–1815* (Stuttgart, 1911), 2 vols.

G. Kirchmayer, *Veteranen-Huldigung oder Erinnerungen an die Feldzugsjahre 1813, 1814 und 1815* (Munich, 1846).

E. Klessmann (ed.), *Die Befreiungskriege in Augenzeugenberichten* (Düsseldorf, 1966).

B. v. Knobelsdorff-Brenkenhoff, *Briefe aus den Befreiungskriegen. Ein Beitrag zur Situation von Truppe und Heimat in den Jahren 1813/14* (Bonn, 1981).

K. A. Köhler, *1813/14. Tagebuchblätter eines Feldgeistlichen* (Berlin, 1912).

C. G. Körner, *Deutschlands Hoffnungen* (Leipzig, 1813).

T. Körner, *Briefwechsel* (Berlin, 1910).

J. K. Krais, *Tagebuch über diejenigen Begebenheiten, welche die Reichsstadt Biberach während des französischen Krieges vom Jahr 1790 bis zum Jahr 1801 erfahren hat* (Biberach, 1801, 1822), 2 vols.

G. Kreuzer (ed.), *Die autobiographischen Aufzeichnungen des Pfarrers Johann Nepomuk Kriehofer 1770–1836* (Günzburg, 2005).

C. E. V. Krieg (ed.), *Vor fünfzig Jahren. Tagebuch eines ehemaligen freiwilligen Jägers der Jahre 1813 und 1814* (Wesel, 1863).

W. Krimer, *Erinnerungen eines alten Lützower Jägers 1795–1819*, ed. A . Saager, 2nd edn (Stuttgart, 1913), 2 vols.

C. A. Krollmann (ed.), *Landwehrbriefe 1813* (Danzig, 1913).

M. H. Kügelen, *Ein Lebensbild in Briefe* (Stuttgart, 1900).

F. Lange (ed.), *Die Lützower-Erinnerungen, Berichete, Dokumente* (Berlin, 1953).

C. F. Laukhard, *Leben und Schicksale* (Leipzig, 1797).

H. Lem von Zieten (ed.), *Tagebuch von Heinrich Bolte, Adjutant Blüchers 1813–14* (Berlin, n. d.)

K. Lietzmann (ed.), *Freiwilliger Jäger bei den Totenkopfhusaren* (Berlin, 1909).

H. Luden, *Rückblicke in mein Leben* (Jena, 1847).

Joseph Maillinger, 'Tagebuch des Hauptmannes Joseph Maillinger im Feldzug nach Russland 1812', *Darstellungen aus der bayerischen Kriegs- und Heeresgeschichte*, 21 (1912), 57–155.

Friedrich Mändler, *Erinnerungen aus meinen Feldzügen 1809–1815*, ed. F. J. A. Schneidawind (Nuremberg, 1854).

J. C. v. Mannlich, *Ein deutscher Maler und Hofmann. Lebenserinnerungen 1741–1822*, ed. E. Stollreither (Berlin, 1910).

C. v. Martens, *Vor fünfzig Jahren. Tagebuch meines Feldzuges in Sachsen 1813* (Stuttgart, 1863), 2 vols.

F. A. L. von der Marwitz, *Aus dem Nachlasse. Lebensbeschreibung* (Berlin, 1852), vol. 1.

F. A. L. von der Marwitz, *Ein märkischer Edelmann im Zeitalter der Befreiungskriege*, ed. F. Meusel (Berlin, 1908/13), 2 vols.

R. v. Meerheim (ed.), *Erlebnisse eines Veteranen der Grossen Armee während des Feldzuges in Russland* (Dresden, 1860).

W. Meier, *Erinnerungen aus den Feldzügen 1806 bis 1815* (Karlsruhe, 1854).

A. Mintner, 'Auszug aus dem Tagebuch des Pfarrers Mintner', in Franz Xaver Kerer (ed.), *Von der Steinzeit bis zur Gegenwart. Die Geschichte eines Bauerndorfes* (Munich, 1907).

R. v. Mohl, *Lebenserinnerungen von Robert von Mohl 1799–1875* (Stuttgart, 1902).

A. de la Motte Fouqué (ed.), *Briefe an Friedrich Baron de la Motte Fouqué* (Bern, 1968).

F. de la Motte Fouqué, *Lebensgeschichte* (Halle, 1840).

C. v. Müffling, *The Memoirs of Baron von Müffling: A Prussian Officer in the Napoleonic Wars* (London, 1997).

G. Muhl, *Denkwürdigkeiten aus dem Leben des Freiherrn C. R. von Schäffer* (Pforzheim, 1840).

F. L. v. Mühlenfels, 'Ein Lützower Reiter', *Grenzboten*, 20 (1861), 481–500.

A. Müller, *Lebenzeugnisse*, ed. J. Baxa (Munich, 1966), 2 vols.

F. Müller, 'Lebenserinnerungen', in U. Wendler (ed.), *Pulverdampf und Kriegsgeschrei. Krieg und Alltag um 1800* (Engen, 2001), 121–249.

F. v. Müller, *Erinnerungen aus den Kriegszeiten 1806–1813* (Braunschweig, 1851).

B. G. Niebuhr, *Briefe und Schriften*, ed. L. Lorentz (Berlin, 1918).

B. G. Niebuhr, *Die Briefe*, ed. D. Gerhard and W. Norvin (Berlin, 1926–9), 2 vols.

J. Niemeyer (ed.), *Scharnhorst Briefe an Friedrich von der Decken 1803–1813* (Bonn, 1987).

Novalis (Friedrich von Hardenberg), *Schriften. Die Werke Friedrich von Hardenbergs*, ed. R. Samuel (Stuttgart, 1975–1981) vols 2–4.

K. F. v. Obermüller, *Aus der Zeit der Fremdherrschaft und der Befreiungskriege* (Karlsruhe, 1913).

F. Ohnesorgen, *Kriegsbilder aus dem Jahre 1812* (Berlin, 1837).

J. G. v. Pahl, *Denkwürdigkeiten zur Geschichte von Schwaben während beiden Feldzüge* (Nördlingen, 1802).

J. G. v. Pahl, *Denkwürdigkeiten aus meinem Leben und meiner Zeit*, ed. W. Pahl (Tübingen, 1840).

A. Perthes and W. Perthes, *Aus der Franzosenzeit in Hamburg* (Hamburg, 1910).

A. Perthes and W. Perthes, *Karoline Perthes. Im Briefwechsel mit ihrer Familie und ihren Freunden*, ed. R. Kayser (Hamburg, 1926).

J. B. Pflug, *Erinnerungen eines Schwaben 1780–1830*, ed. M. Gerster (Ulm, 1936).

J. B. Pflug, *Aus der Räuber- und Franzosenzeit Schwabens. Die Erinnerungen des schwäbischen Malers aus den Jahren 1780–1840*, ed. Max Zengerle (Weissenhorn, 1966).

J. v. Pflugk-Hartung (ed.), *Briefe des Generals Neidhardt von Gneisenau 1809–1815* (Gotha, 1913).

C. F. C. Pfnor, *Der Krieg, seine Mittel und Wege, sowie sein Verhältniss zum Frieden, in den Erlebnissen eines Veteranen* (Tübingen, 1864).

M. v. Poschinger, 'Eigenhändige Aufzeichnung des Martin von Poschinger', in M. Forster (ed.), *Die Franzosen vor München im Jahr 1796* (Munich, 1896).

K. G. Prätzel, *Zeitklänge* (Hamburg, 1815).

M. Prell, *Erinnerungen aus der Franzosenzeit in Hamburg 1806–1814*, ed. H. F. Beneke, 6th edn (Hamburg, 1911).

M. v. Preysing-Moos, 'Tagebuch des Generalmajors Graf von Preysing-Moos, Führer der Bayerischen Kavallerie-Division im Felzuge nach Russland 1812', *Darstellungen aus der bayerischen Kriegs- und Heeresgeschichte*, 21 (1912), 1–35.

L. v. Ranke (ed.), *Denkwürdigkeiten des Staatskanzlers Fürsten von Hardenberg* (Leipzig, 1877), vol. 3.

P.-E. Rattelmüller, *Dirndl, wo hast denn dein Schatz, juhe…Bayerische Soldatenlieder und vaterländische Gesänge aus dem 19. Jahrhundert* (Rosenheim, 1977).

K. v. Raumer, *Karl von Raumers Leben von ihm selbst erzählt* (Stuttgart, 1866).

O. G. E. v. Raven, *Tagebuch des Feldzuges in Rußland im Jahre 1812*, ed. K.-U. Keubke (Rostock, 1998).

L. v. Reiche, *Memoiren*, ed. L. v. Weltzien (Leipzig, 1857), 2 vols.

M. Rief, *Chronik oder journale der französischen Revolution und daraus entstandnem blutigsten Kriege in ganz Europa. Die Aufzeichungen des Magnus Rief, Pfarrer in Dürrenwaldstetten 1789–1814*, ed. B. Geiger (Konstanz, 2003).

J. F. Riesch, *Merkwürdige Lebensgeschichte des Veteranen Jakob Friedrich Riesch, welcher in den Feldzügen 1812, 1813, 1814 und 1815 für das Vaterland kämpfte* (Vaihingen, 1844).

H. v. Roos, *Mit Napoleon in Rußland*, ed. P. Holzhausen, 3rd edn (Stuttgart, n. d.).

F. Rückert, *Briefe* (Schweinfurt, 1977–82), 3 vols.

F. v. Rühl (ed.), *Briefe und Aktenstücke* (Leipzig, 1899–1902), 3 vols.

F. v. Rühl (ed.), *Aus der Franzosenzeit* (Leipzig, 1904).

J. J. O. A. Rühle von Lilienstern, *Bericht eines Augenzeugen von dem Feldzug* (Tübingen, 1807).

J. J. O. A. Rühle von Lilienstern, *Reise mit der Armee 1809*, ed. J.-J. Langendorf (Vienna, 1986).

J. A. Sack, *Briefwechsel mit Stein und Gneisenau 1807–17* (Stettin, 1931).

J. D. G. v. Scharnhorst, *Briefe* (Munich, 1914).

J. D. G. v. Scharnhorst, *Ausgewählte Schriften*, ed. U. v. Gersdorff (Osnabrück, 1983).

W. v. Schauroth, *Im Rheinbund Regiment während der Feldzüge in Tirol, Spanien und Russland 1809–1813* (Berlin, 1905).

T. v. Scherer, *Aus dem Tornister eines Soldaten der Revolutionsarmee. Charakter—und Sittengemälde aus der französischen Schreckenszeit* (Frankfurt, 1857).

A. W. Schlegel, *Briefe* (Zurich, 1930).

F. Schleiermacher, *Kleine Schriften und Predigten*, ed. H. Gerdes and E. Hirsch (Berlin, 1969).

F. Schleiermacher, *Aus Schleiermachers Leben. In Briefen*, ed. W. Dilthey (Berlin, 1970), 4 vols.

A. Schmitt, *Chronik der Stadt Kitzingen* (Kitzingen, 1873).

A. Schmitthenner, *Das Tagebuch meines Urgroßvaters 1790–1799* (Freiburg, 1908).

F. Schneider, *Erinnerungen aus den Feldzügen der Württemberger. 1806 und 1807 in Schlesien* (Stuttgart, 1866).

A. v. Schön and T. v. Schön, *'Sehnlich erwarte ich die morgende Post'. Amalie und Theodor von Schöns Briefwechsel aus dem Befreiungskrieg*, ed. G. A. Klausa (Cologne, 2005).

J. Schrafel, *Merkwürdige Schicksale des ehemaligen Feldwebels im königl. Bayer. 5ten Linien-Infanterie-Regiment* (Nuremberg, 1834).

J. Schrafel, *Des Nürnberger Feldwebels Joseph Schrafel im Krieg gegen Tirol, im Feldzuge gegen Rußland und in der Gefangenschaft 1812–1814* (Nuremberg, 1913).

W. Schrör, *Zur Erinnerung fuer seine Waffenbrüder* (Koenigsberg, 1814).

F. Schulze (ed.), *Weimarische Berichte und Briefe aus den Freiheitskriegen 1806–1815* (Leipzig, 1913).

F. v. Smitt (ed.), *Zur näheren Aufklärung über den Krieg von 1812* (Leipzig, 1861), 437–88.

Ignaz Speckle, *Das Tagebuch von Ignaz Speckle* (Stuttgart, 1966), 2 vols.

H. B. Spies (ed.), *die Erhebung gegen Napoleon 1806–1814/15* (Darmstadt, 1981).

F. A. v. Stägemann, *Erinnerungen an die preußischen Kriegsthaten in den Jahren 1813 bis 1815* (Halle/Berlin, 1818).

H. Steffens, *Was ich erlebte*, ed. W. A. Koch (Leipzig, 1938).

H. F. K. Freiherr vom Stein, *Briefe und amtliche Schriften*, ed. W. Hubatsch (Stuttgart, 1959–72), vols 1–5, 8.

K. v. Suckow, *Aus meinem Soldatenleben* (Stuttgart, 1862).

G. Thiele (ed.), *Gneisenau. Eine Chronik* (Berlin, 2007).

A. v. Thurn und Taxis, *Aus drei Feldzügen 1812–1815. Erinnerungen* (Leipzig, 1912).

F. v. Varnbuler, *Beitrag zur Geschichte des Feldzugs vom Jahr 1796* (Altona, 1797).

K. A. Varnhagen v. Ense, *Denkwürdigkeiten des eignen Lebens* (Berlin, 1922–3), 2 vols.

K. A. Varnhagen v. Ense und R. Varnhagen, *Briefwechsel zwischen Varnhagen und Rahel* (Berne, 1973), 6 vols.

R. Vaupel (ed.), *Die Reorganisation des Preussischen Staates unter Stein und Hardenberg* (Leipzig, 1938).

J. Wackenreiter, *Nachtrag zur Erstürmung Regensburgs am 23. April 1809* (Regensburg, 1866).

S. Walter, *Erinnerungen aus meinem Leben* (Dillingen, 1843).

K. v. Wedel, *Lebenserinnerungen 1793–1810*, ed. C. Tröger (Berlin, 1911), vol. 1.

J. A. P. Weltrich, *Erinnerungen für die Einwohner des ehemaligen Fürstentums Bayreuth aus den Jahren der französischen Okkupation 1806–1810* (Kulmbach, 1819).

F. von der Wengen, *Der Feldzug der Großherzoglich Badischen Truppen unter Oberst Freiherrn Karl von Stockhorn gegen die Vorarlberger und tiroler 1809*, ed. O. V. Stockhorn (Heidelberg, 1910).

H. O. Wesemann (ed.), *Kanonier des Kaisers. Kriegstagebuch des Heinrich Wesemann 1808–1814* (Cologne, 1971).

R. Wilson, *Private Diary of Travels, Personal Services and Public Events during Missions and Employment with the European Armies in the Campaigns of 1812, 1813, 1814*, ed. H. Randolph (London, 1861), 2 vols.

F. C. Wittichen (ed.), *Briefe von und an Friedrich von Gentz* (Munich, 1910), vol. 2.

L. v. Wollzogen, *Memoiren* (Leipzig, 1851).

Pamphlets, Treatises, Encyclopedias, and Histories

T. Abbt, *Vom Tode für das Vaterland* (Berlin, 1761).

J. L. H. Altenburg, *Landsmannschaften und Burschenschaften. Ein freies Wort über die geselligen Verhältnisse der Studierenden auf den teutschen Hochschulen* (Leipzig, 1820).

J. W. v. Archenholz, *Geschichte des Siebenjährigen Krieges in Deutschland von 1756 bis 1763* (Berlin, 1793).

A. L. v. Ardenne, *Bergische Lanciers Westfälische Husaren Nr. 11* (Berlin, 1877).

E. M. Arndt, *Germanien und Europa* (Altona, 1803).

E. M. Arndt, *Fragmente über die Menschenbildung* (Altona, 1805).

E. M. Arndt, *Geist der Zeit* (Berlin, 1806–9, 1813).

E. M. Arndt, *Kurze Katechismus für teutsche Soldaten* (St Petersburg, 1812).

E. M. Arndt, *Aufruf an die Deutschen zum gemeinschaftlichen Kampfe gegen die Franzosen* (Königsberg, 1813).

E. M. Arndt, *Das preußische Volk und Heer im Jahre 1813* (Leipzig, 1813).

E. M. Arndt, *Grundlinien einer teutschen Kriegsordnung* (Leipzig, 1813).

E. M. Arndt, *Über Volkshaß und über den Gebrauch einer fremden Sprache* (Leipzig, 1813).

E. M. Arndt, *Ansichten und Aussichten der Teutschen Geschichte* (Leipzig, 1814).

E. M. Arndt, *Ein Wort über die Feier der Leipziger Schlacht* (Frankfurt, 1814).

E. M. Arndt, *Entwurf einer teutschen Gesellschaft* (Frankfurt, 1814).

E. M. Arndt, *Noch ein Wort über die Franzosen und über uns* (Leipzig, 1814).

E. M. Arndt, *Über Sitte, Mode und Kleidertracht* (Frankfurt, 1814).

E. M. Arndt, *Über die Feier der Leipziger Schlacht* (Frankfurt, 1815).

E. M. Arndt, *Die deutsche Wehrmannschaft* (Leipzig, 1818).

T. v. Barsewisch, *Geschichte des Grossherzoglich Badischen Leib-Grenadier-Regiments 1803–1871* (Karlsruhe, 1893), vol. 1.

J. F. Beer, *Anfangs-Gründe in der Kriegskunst* (Frankfurt, 1771).

E. Behler (ed.), *Kritische Friedrich-Schlegel-Ausgabe* (Paderborn, 1966).

H. W. Behrisch, *Litteratur jetztlebender militärischer Schriftsteller und der neuesten Kriegsbücher* (Magdeburg, 1789).

P. F. Boost, *Über die National-Ehre der Deutschen. Eine historisch-philosophische Untersuchung* (Wiesbaden, 1812).

F. A. Brockhaus (ed.), *Conversations-Lexikon* (Leipzig, 1815–19), 10 vols.

F. A. Brockhaus (ed.), *Conversations-Lexikon der neuesten Zeit und Literatur* (Leipzig, 1832), vol. 1.

F. A. Brockhaus (ed.), *Conversations-Lexikon* (Leipzig, 1837–41), vol. 1.

F. A. Brockhaus (ed.), *Kleineres Brockhaus'sches Conversations-Lexikon* (Leipzig, 1854–7), vols 1–3.

A. H. D. v. Bülow, *Lehrsätze des neueren Krieges oder reinen und angewandte Strategie* (Berlin, 1805).

C. v. Clausewitz, *Politische Schriften und Briefe*, ed. H. Rothfels (Munich, 1922).

C. v. Clausewitz, *Schriften, Aufsätze, Studien, Briefe*, ed. W. Hahlweg (Göttingen, 1966–90), vols 1–2.

C. v. Clausewitz, *On War* (Princeton, 1976).

F. Cotta, *Über den Titel des Kaisers von Österreich* (Weissenburg, 1810).

J. G. Droysen, *Das Leben des Feldmarschalls Grafen York von Wartenburg* (Berlin, 1851–2), 3 vols.

J. D. v. Dziengel, *Geschichte des Königlichen Zweiten Ulanen-Regiments* (Potsdam, 1858).

F. Ehrenberg, *Der Charakter und Bestimmung des Mannes* (Elberfeld, 1806/9).

F. Ehrenberg, *Das Volk und seine Fürsten* (Leipzig, 1815).

R. Eickemeyer, *Abhandlungen über Gegenstände der Staats- und Kriegs-Wissenschaften* (Frankfurt, 1817), vol. 1.

J. V. Embser, *Die Abgötterei unsers philosophischen Jahrhunderts. Erster Abgott: Ewiger Friede* (Mannheim, 1779).

A. Feuerbach, *Über die Unterdrückung und Wiederbefreiung Europens* (Munich, 1813).

A. Feuerbach, *Die Weltherrschaft, das Grab der Menschheit* (Nuremberg, 1814).

J. G. Fichte, *Reden an die deutsche Nation* (Berlin, 1808).

J. G. Fichte, *Über den Begriff des wahrhaften Krieges in Bezug auf den Krieg im Jahre 1813* (Tübingen, 1815).

J. G. Fichte, *Schriften zur Revolution* (Opladen, 1967).

C. Friccius, *Geschichte des Krieges in den Jahren 1813 und 1814* (Altenburg, 1843).

T. H. Friedrich, *Deutsche Volkstracht* (Berlin, 1815).

T. H. Friedrich, *Satyrischer Feldzug in einer Reihe von Vorlesungen* (Berlin, 1815).

W. Frühwald (ed.), *Joseph Görres. Ausgewählte Werke* (Freiburg, 1978), vols 1 and 5.

F. v. Gentz, *Über den Ursprung und Charakter des Krieges gegen die Französische Revoluzion* (Berlin, 1801).

F. v. Gentz, 'Fragmente aus der neuesten Geschichte des politischen Gleichgewichts in Europa' (1806), 'Betrachtungen über den Pariser Frieden' (1815), and 'Von Pradt's Gemälde von Europa' (1819), in F. v. Gentz, *Ausgewählte Schriften* (Stuttgart, 1836–8), vols 4–5.

F. v. Gentz, *An die Deutsche Fürsten, an die Deutschen* (n. p., 1813).

F. v. Gentz, 'Über die Moralität in den Staatsrevolutionen', in F. v. Gentz, *Ausgewählte Schriften*, ed. W. Weick (Stuttgart, 1836–8), vol. 2.

F. v. Gentz, 'Über die Deklaration der 8 Mächte gegen Napoleon' and 'Bemerkungen zu der Schrift "Über die gegenwärtige Lage von Europa"' (1822), in G. Schlesier (ed.), *Schriften von Friedrich von Gentz* (Mannheim, 1838–40), vol. 2.

F. Gentz, 'Über den ewigen Frieden', in F. Gentz, *Gesammelte Schriften* (Hildesheim, 1999), vol. 5, 603–82.

C. v. Gersdorff, *Vorlesungen über militärische Gegenstände* (Dresden, 1827).

G. G. Gervinus, *Einleitung in die Geschichte des neunzehnten Jahrhunderts* (Leipzig, 1853).

G. G. Gervinus, *Geschichte des neunzehnten Jahrhunderts* (Leipzig, 1855), vol. 1.

A. W. A. N. v. Gneisenau, *Ausgewählte militärische Schriften*, ed. G. Förster and C. Gudzent (Berlin, 1984).

J. v. Görres, *Politische Schriften* (Munich, 1854), vol. 1.

J. v. Görres, 'Napoleon in Paris' (1815), in W. Frühwald (ed.), *Joseph Görres. Ausgewählte Werke* (Freiburg, 1978), vol. 1, 259–63.

G. D. von der Groeben, *Kriegs-Bibliothek, oder gesammelte Beyträge zur Kriegs-Wissenschaft* (Breslau, 1755–70).

J. C. F. GutsMuths, *Turnbuch für die Söhne des Vaterlandes* (Frankfurt, 1817).

K. Hagen, 'Über die öffentliche Meinung in Deutschland von den Freiheitskriegen bis zu den Karlsbader Beschlüssen', in F. v. Raumer (ed.), *Historisches Taschenbuch* (Leipzig, 1846), 599–700.

C. L. v. Haller, *Restauration der Staats-Wissenschaft oder Theorie des natürlich-geselligen Zustands der Chimäre des künstlich-bürgerlichen entgegengesetzt* (Winterthur, 1820–5), vol. 1.

G. W. F. Hegel, *Grundlinien des Philosophie des Rechts* (Berlin, 1821).

G. W. F. Hegel, 'Über die wissenschaftlichen Behandlungsarten des Naturrechts' (1802), in G. W. F. Hegel, *Sämtliche Werke*, ed. H. Glockner (Stuttgart, 1927–30), vol. 1.

G. W. F. Hegel, *Vorlesungen über die Philosophie der Geschichte*, 3rd edn (Stuttgart, 1961).

J. G. Herder, *Sämtliche Werke*, ed. B. Suphahn (Berlin, 1881), vols 17–18.

M. Hess, 'Die europäische Triarchie' (1841), in M. Hess, *Philosophische und sozialistische Schriften*, ed. W. Mönke, 2nd edn (Vaduz, 1980).

H. K. Hofmann (ed.), *Beiträge zur Erörterung vaterländischer Angelegenheiten* (Darmstadt, 1831).

K. Hoffmann (ed.), *Des deutschen Volkes feuriger Dank- und Ehrentempel* (Offenbach, 1815).

J. Hoffmeister (ed.), *Briefe von und an Hegel* (Hamburg, 1952), vol. 1.

J. Hübener (ed.), *Zeitungs- und Conversations-Lexikon* (Leipzig, 1824–8), 4 vols.

F. Jacobs, *Deutschalnds Gefahren und Hoffnungen. An Germaniens Jugend* (Gotha, 1813).

F. Jacobs, *Deutschlands Ehre* (Gotha, 1814).

F. L. Jahn, *Deutsches Volksthum* (Luebeck, 1810).

F. L. Jahn, *Die Deutsche Turnkunst* (Berlin, 1816).

F. L. Jahn, *Deutsche Turnkunst*, 2nd edn (Berlin, 1847).

F. L. Jahn, *Werke*, ed. C. Euler (Hof, 1884–7), 3 vols.

Jean Paul, *Friedens-Predigt* (Heidelberg, 1808).

Jean Paul, *Dämmerungen für Deutschland* (Tübingen, 1809).

J. C. G. Jörg, *Ahndungen für Deutsche bei Eröffnung des Feldzuges von 1814* (Leipzig, 1814).

I. Kant, *Metaphysische Anfangsgründe der Rechtslehre*, 2nd edn (Breslau, 1798).

I. Kant, 'Zum ewigen Frieden', in I. Kant, *Gesammelte Schriften* (Berlin, 1900–83), vol. 8.

J. F. Kazner, *Die Kriegskunst* (Berlin, 1760).

F. Kohlrausch, *Deutschlands Zukunft* (Elberfeld, 1814).

J. B. Krey, *Predigten in den Jahren 1813 und 1814* (Leipzig, 1815).

W. T. Krug, *System der Kriegswissenschaften und ihrer Literatur* (Leipzig, 1815).

J. Krünitz (ed.), *Öconomische Encyclopädie* (Berlin, 1773–1858).

H. Leo, *Lehrbuch der Universalgeschichte* (Halle, 1844), vol. 6.

L. A. F. Liebenstein, *Über stehende Heere und Landwehr* (Karlsruhe, 1817).

H. Luden, *Einige Worte über das Studium der vaterländischen Geschichte* (Jena, 1810).

H. Luden, *Handbuch der Staatsweisheit* (Jena, 1811).

F. S. Meidinger, *Der Verfall güter Sitten und überhandgenommener Ausgelassen unter dem schönen Geschlecthe: oder die bösen Folgen des Krieges* (Landshut, 1803).

F. de la Motte Fouqué, *Etwas über den deutschen Adel, über Ritter-Sinn und Militär-Ehre* (Hamburg, 1819).

A. Müller, *Die Lehre vom Gegensatze* (Berlin, 1804).

A. Müller, *Die Elemente der Staatskunst* (Leipzig, 1809), vol. 1.

A. Müller, 'Deutsche Wissenschaft und Literatur', in A. Müller, *Kritische Schriften* (Neuwied, 1967), vol. 1.

G. F. Müller, *Das Krieges- oder Soldatenrecht in Preussen* (Berlin, 1789).

J. D. F. Neigebaur, *Statistik der preussischen Rhein-Provinzen* (Cologne, 1817).

J. G. Nitzsche, *Die neue Kriegskunst in Vergleichung mit der Kriegskunst alter Zeiten* (Leipzig, 1782).

K. v. Österreich, *Grundsätze der höheren Kriegskunst für die Generäle der österreichischen Armee* (Vienna, 1806).

K. v. Österreich, *Beyträge zum practischen Unterricht im Felde für die Officiers der österreichischen Armee* (Vienna, 1807), vol. 3.

J. G. v. Pahl, *Materialien zur Geschichte des Kriegs in Schwaben im Jahre* (Nördlingen, 1797/8).

K. Pfaff, *Geschichte des Militärwesens in Württemberg* (Stuttgart, 1842).

A. Pfister, *Der Milizgedanken in Württemberg und die Versuche zu seiner Verwirklichung* (Stuttgart, 1883).

C. v. Plotho, *Die Kosaken, oder Geschichte derselben von ihrem Ursprunge bis auf die Gegenwart* (Berlin, 1811).

C. v. Plotho, *Tagebuch während des Krieges zwischen Russland und Preussen einerseits und Frankreich andrerseits in den Jahren 1806 und 1807* (Berlin, 1811).

C. v. Plotho, *Der Krieg in Deutschland und Frankreich in den Jahren 1813 und 1814* (Berlin, 1817), 2 vols.

L. v. Ranke, 'Über die Trennung und die Einheit von Deutschland', in L. v. Ranke, *Sämmtliche Werke* (Leipzig, 1867–90), vols 49–50.

L. v. Ranke, *Aus Werk und Nachlass. Vorlesungseinleitungen*, ed. T. Schieder, H. Berding, V. Dotterweich, and W. P. Fuchs (Munich, 1971–5), vols 2 and 4.

K. v. Rotteck, *Allgemeine Geschichte vom Anfang der historischen Kentniss bis auf unsere Zeiten* (Freiburg, 1812–26), vol. 3.

K. v. Rotteck, *Über stehende Heer und Nationalmiliz* (Freiburg, 1816).

K. v. Rotteck, *Gesammelte und nachgelassene Schriften* (Pforzheim, 1841–3), 5 vols.

J. O. A. Rühle von Lilienstern, *Kriegs-Katechismus für die Landwehr* (Breslau, 1813).

J. O. A. Rühle von Lilienstern, *Vom Kriege* (Frankfurt, 1814).

J. O. A. Rühle von Lilienstern, *Die Deutsche Volksbewaffnung* (Berlin, 1815).

J. O. A. Rühle von Lilienstern, *Apologie des Krieges* (Vienna, 1984).

F. C. Rühs, *Historische Entwicklungen des Einflusses Frankreichs und der Franzosen, Teutschland und die Teutschen* (Berlin, 1815).

F. Schlegel, 'Versuch über den Begriff des Republikanismus', in E. Behler (ed.), *Kritische Friedrich-Schlegel-Ausgabe* (Paderborn, 1966), first series, vol. 7, 11–25.

F. Schulze (ed.), *Urkunden der deutschen Erhebung* (Leipzig, 1913).

L. I. v. Stadlinger, *Geschichte des württembergischen Kriegswesens von der fruhesten bis zur neuesten Zeit* (Stuttgart, 1856).

G. de Staël, *Considérations sur la Révolution française*, ed. Jacques Godechot (Paris, 1983, originally in 1818).

L. v. Stein, *Die Lehre vom Heerwesen. Als Theil der Staatswissenschaft* (Stuttgart, 1872).

F. L. Streit, *Militairische Encyclopädie für künftige Offiziere* (Bad Honnef, 1982).

P. F. Stuhr, *Die drei letzten Feldzüge gegen Napoleon kritisch-historisch dargestellt* (Lemgo, 1832).

F. v. Suckow, *Nachklang der Waffen* (Berlin, 1816).

H. v. Sybel, 'Die Erhebung Europa's gegen Napoleon I.', in H. v. Sybel, *Kleine historische Schriften* (Munich, 1863).

H. v. Sybel, 'Am Denkmal Arndt's in Bonn' (1865), in H. v. Sybel, *Vorträge und Aufsätze* (Berlin, 1874).

C. A. Tiedge, *Denkmale der Zeit* (Leipzig, 1814).

J. G. Tielke, *Beyträge zur Kriegs-Kunst und Geschichte des Krieges von 1756–1783* (Vienna, 1786–7).

L. Turpin de Crissé, *Versuche über die Kriegskunst* (Leipzig, 1787).

H. G. Tzschirner, *Über den Krieg. Ein philosophischer Versuch* (Leipzig, 1815).

F. v. Varnbuler, *Beitrag zur Geschicthe des Feldzugs vom Jahr 1796 in besonderer Rücksicht auf das schwäbische Korps* (Altona, 1797).

F. G. Welcker, 'Von ständischer Verfassung' (1815), in F. G. Welcker, *Von ständischer Verfassung und über Deutschlands Zukunft* (Karlsruhe, 1831).

C. M. Wieland, 'Gespräche unter vier Augen' (1798), in C. M. Wieland, *Sämtliche Werke* (Leipzig, 1857), vol. 32.

C. M. Wieland, 'Über Krieg und Frieden' (1794), in H. Günther (ed.), *Die französische Revolution. Berichte und Deutungen deutscher Schriftsteller und Historiker* (Frankfurt, 1985).

O. Wigand (ed.), *Conversations-Lexikon der neuesten Litteratur-, Völker- und Staatengeschichte* (Leipzig, 1841–5), vol. 1.

F. L. Zacharias Werner, *Ausgewählte Schriften* (Berne, 1970).

A. Zarnack, *Preußens Erinnerung an 1813 und 1814* (Berlin, 1814).

C. C. Zimmermann, *Geschichte des 1. Grossherzoglich Hessischen Dragoner-Regiments* (Darmstadt, 1878).

K. F. W. Zincken, *Kurze und deutliche Einleitung zur Kriegesrechtsgelehrsamkeit in Deutschland* (Magdeburg, 1772).

K. F. W. Zincken and J. F. Eisenhardt, *Carl Wilhelm Friedrich Zinckens kurze Anleitung zur Kriegsrechts-Gelehrsamkeit* (Helmstädt, 1782).

SECONDARY LITERATURE

K. B. Aaslestad, *Place and Politics: Local Identity, Civic Culture and German Nationalism in North Germany during the Revolutionary Era* (Leiden, 2005).

K. B. Aaslestad, 'Remembering and Forgetting: the Local and the Nation in Hamburg's Commemorations of the Wars of Liberation', *Central European History*, 38 (2005), 384–416.

K. B. Aaslestad, 'Paying for War: Experiences of Napoleonic Rule in the Hanseatic Cities', *Central European History*, 39 (2006), 641–75.

K. B. Aaslestad, 'War without Battles: Civilian Experiences of Economic Warfare during the Napoleonic Era in Hamburg', in A. Forrest et al. (eds), *Soldiers, Citizens, and Civilians: Experiences and Perceptions of the Revolutionary and Napoleonic Wars, 1790–1820* (Basingstoke, 2008), 118–36.

K. B. Aaslestad, 'Lost Neutrality and Economic Warfare: Napoleonic Warfare in Northern Europe, 1795–1815', in R. Chickering and S. Förster (eds), *War in an Age of Revolution, 1775–1815* (Cambridge, 2010), 373–94.

K. B. Aaslestad and K. Hagemann, '1806 and Its Aftermath: Revisiting the Period of the Napoleonic Wars in German Central European Historiography', *Central European History*, 39 (2006), 547–79.

K. B. Aaslestad, K. Hagemann, and J. A. Miller (eds), 'Gender, War and the Nation in the Period of the Revolutionary and Napoleonic Wars', *European History Quarterly*, 37 (2007), special issue.

K. B. Aaslestad and J. Joor (eds), *Revisiting Napoleon's Continental System: Local, Regional and European Experiences* (Basingstoke, 2014).

K. Adel (ed.), *Joseph von Hormayr und die 'vaterländische Romantik' in Österreich* (Vienna, 1969).

F. Akaltin, *Die Befreiungskriege im Geschichtsbild der Deutschen im 19. Jahrhundert* (Frankfurt, 1997).

J. C. Allmayer-Beck and E. Lessing, *Das Heer unter dem Doppeladler. Habsburgs Armeen, 1718–1848* (Munich, 1981).

U. Andrea, *Die Rheinländer, die Revolution und der Krieg 1794–1798* (Essen, 1994).

J. Angelow, 'Die "belgisch-luxemburgische Krise" von 1830–1832 und der Deutsche Bund', *Militärgeschichtliche Mitteilungen*, 49 (1991), 61–80.

J. Angelow, *Von Wien nach Königgrätz. Die Sicherheitspolitik des Deutschen Bundes im europäischen Gleichgewicht 1815–1866* (Munich, 1996).

W. T. Angress, 'Der jüdische Offizier in der neueren deutschen Geschichte, 1813–1918' in U. Breymayer, Bernd Ulrich, and K. Wieland (eds), *Willensmenschen. Über deutsche Offiziere* (Frankfurt, 1999), 67–78.

F. Baasner, *Der Begriff 'sensibilite' im 18. Jahrhundert: Aufstieg und Niedergang eines Ideals* (Heidelberg, 1988).

P. Baumgart, B. R. Kroener, and H. Stubig (eds), *Die preussische Armee. Zwischen Ancien Régime und Reichsgründung* (Paderborn, 2008).

W. Baumgart, *Der Friede von Paris. Studie zum Verhältnis von Kriegsfuehrung, Politik und Friedensbewahrung* (Munich, 1972).

W. Baumgart, *Europäisches Konzert und nationale Bewegung. Internationale Beziehungen 1830–1878* (Paderborn, 1999).

E. D. Becker, *Schiller in Deutschland 1781–1970* (Frankfurt, 1972).

E. W. Becker, 'Zeiterfahrungen zwischen Revolution und Krieg. Zum Wandel des Zeitbewusstseins in dern napoleonischen Ära', in N. Buschmann and C. Horst (eds), *Die Erfahrung des Krieges. Erfahrungsgeschichtliche Perspektiven von der französischen Revolution bis zum Zweiten Weltkrieg* (Paderborn, 2001), 67–95.

D. A. Bell, *The First Total War: Napoleon's Europe and the Birth of Warfare as We Know It* (Boston, 2007).

D. A. Bell, 'The Limits of Conflict in Napoleonic Europe – and Their Transgression', in E. Charters, E. Rosenhaft, and H. Smith (eds), *Civilians and War in Europe, 1618–1815* (Liverpool, 2012), 201–8.

H. Berding, *Napoleonische Herrschafts- und Gesellschaftspolitik im Königreich Westfalen 1807–1813* (Göttingen, 1973).

H. Berding, 'Das geschichtliche Problem der Freiheitskriege 1813–1814', in K. O. v. Aretin and G. A. Ritter (eds), *Europa zwischen Revolution und Restauration 1797–1815* (Stuttgart, 1987), 201–15.

S. Berger, *Germany: Inventing the Nation* (London, 2004).

R. Bergien and R. Pröve (eds), *Spiesser, Patrioten, Revolutionäre. Militärische Mobilisierung und gesellschaftliche Ordnung in der Neuzeit* (Göttingen, 2010).

G. Best, *War and Society in Revolutionary Europe, 1770–1870* (London, 1982).

W. Beutin (ed.), *Hommage à Kant. Kants Schrift 'Zum ewigen Frieden'* (Hamburg, 1996).

O. Bezzel, *Geschichte des Königl. Bayerischen Heeres unter König Max I Joseph von 1806 bis 1825* (Munich, 1933).

R. D. Billinger, Jr, 'Good and True Germans: The "Nationalism" of the *Rheinbund* Princes, 1806–1814', in H. Duchhardt and A. Kunz (eds), *Reich oder Nation? Mitteleuropa, 1780–1815* (Mainz, 1998), 105–39.

G. Birtsch (ed.), *Patriotismus* (Hamburg, 1991).

T. Bitterauf, 'Zur Geschichte der öffentlichen meinung im Königreich Bayern im Jahre 1813 bis zum Abschluss des Vertrags von Ried', *Archiv für Kulturgeschichte*, 11 (1914), 31–69.

T. Bitterauf, 'Die Zensur der politischen Zeitungen in Bayern 1799–1825', in *Festschrift für S. Riezler* (Gotha, 1923).

J. Black, *A Military Revolution? Military Change and European Society, 1550–1800* (Basingstoke, 1991).

J. Black, 'Eighteenth-Century Warfare Reconsidered', *War in History*, 1 (1994), 215–32.

J. Black, *Warfare in the Eighteenth Century* (London, 1999).

D. Blackbourn, *Germany, 1780–1918* (London, 1997).

T. C. W. Blanning, *The French Revolution in Germany: Occupation and Resistance in the Rhineland, 1792–1802* (Oxford, 1983).

T. C. W. Blanning, *The French Revolutionary Wars, 1787–1802* (London, 1996).

T. C. W. Blanning, *The Culture of Power and the Power of Culture: Old Regime Europe, 1660–1789* (Oxford, 2003).

T. C. W. Blanning, *The Pursuit of Glory: The Five Revolutions That Made Modern Europe, 1648–1815* (London, 2007).

W. K. Blessing, 'Staatsintegration als soziale Integration. Zur Entstehung einer bayerischen Gesellschaft im frühen 19 Jahrhundert', *Zeitschrift für bayerische Landesgeschichte*, 41 (1978), 633–700.

W. K. Blessing, 'Umbruchskrise und "Verstörung". Die "Napoleonische" Erschütterung und ihre sozialpsychologische Bedeutung', *Zeitschrift für bayerische Landesgeschichte*, 42 (1979), 75–106.

W. K. Blessing, *Staat und Kirche in der Gesellschaft. Institutionelle Autorität und mentaler Wandel in Bayern während des 19 Jahrhunderts* (Göttingen, 1982).

H.-M. Blitz, *Aus Liebe zum Vaterland. Die deutsche Nation im 18. Jahrhundert* (Hamburg, 2000).

H. Boersch-Supan and L. Griesebach (eds), *Karl Friedrich Schinkel* (Berlin, 1981).

J. Bourke, 'Fear and Anxiety: Writing about Emotion in Modern History', *History Workshop Journal*, 55 (2003), 111–33.

P. Brandt, 'Das studentische Wartburgfest vom 18/19 Oktober 1817', in D. Düding, P. Friedemann, and P. Münch (eds), *Öffentliche Festkultur* (Hamburg, 1988), 89–112.

P. Brandt, 'Einstellungen, Motive und Ziele von Kriegsfreiwilligen 1813/14: Das Freikorps Lützow', in J. Dülffer (ed.), *Kriegsbereitschaft und Friedensordnung in Deutschland 1800–1814* (Münster, 1995), 211–33.

P. Brandt, 'Die Befreiungskriege von 1813 bis 1815 in der deutschen Geschichte', in M. Grüttner, R. Hachtmann, and H.-G. Haupt (eds), *Geschichte und Emanzipation* (Frankfurt, 1999), 17–57.

K. Breitenhorn and J. H. Ulbricht (eds), *Jena and Auerstedt: Ereignis und Erinnerung in europäischer, nationaler und regionaler Perspektive* (Dössel, 2006).

J. J. Breuilly, 'Sovereignty and Boundaries: Modern State Formation and National Identity in Germany', in J. Fulbrook (ed.), *National Histories and European History* (London, 1993), 94–140.

J. J. Breuilly, 'Napoleonic Germany and State-Formation', in M. Rowe (ed.), *Collaboration and Resistance in Napoleonic Europe: State-Formation in an Age of Upheaval, c.1800–1815* (London, 2003), 121–52.

J. J. Breuilly, 'The Response to Napoleon and German Nationalism', in A. Forrest and P. H. Wilson (eds), *The Bee and the Eagle: Napoleonic France and the End of the Holy Roman Empire, 1806* (Basingstoke, 2009), 256–83.

P. Brock, *Freedom from War: Non-Sectarian Pacifism, 1814–1914* (Toronto, 1991).

M. Broers, *Europe after Napoleon: Revolution, Reaction and Romanticism, 1814–1848* (Manchester, 1996).

M. Broers, *Napoleonic Imperialism and the Savoyard Monarchy, 1773–1821* (Lampeter, 1997).

M. Broers, *The Napoleonic Empire in Italy, 1796–1814: Cultural Imperialism in a European Context?* (Basingstoke, 2005).

M. Broers, *Politics and Religion in Napoleonic Italy: The War against God, 1801–1814* (London, 2007).

M. Broers, 'The Concept of "Total War" in the Revolutionary-Napoleonic Period', *War in History*, 15 (2008), 247–68.

M. Broers, *Napoleon's Other War: Bandits, Rebels and Their Pursuers in the Age of Revolutions* (New York, 2010).

J. M. Brophy, 'Carnival and Citizenship', *Journal of Social History*, 30 (1997), 873–904.

J. M. Brophy, 'The Common Reader in the Rhineland', *Past and Present*, 185 (2004), 119–58.

J. M. Brophy, 'The Public Sphere', in J. Sperber (ed.), *Germany, 1800–1870* (Oxford, 2004), 185–208.

J. M. Brophy, *Popular Culture and the Public Sphere in the Rhineland, 1800–1850* (Cambridge, 2007).

T. Bruder, *Nürnberg als bayerische Garnison von 1806 bis 1914* (Nuremberg, 1992).

G.-F. Budde, *Auf dem Weg ins Bürgerleben. Kindheit und Erziehung in deutschen und englischen Bürgerfamilien 1840–1914* (Göttingen, 1994).

W. Burgdorf, *Ein Weltbild verliert seine Welt. Der Untergang des alten Reiches und die Generation von 1806* (Munich, 2006).

W. Burgdorf, 'Der Kampf um die Vergangenheit. Geschichtspolitik und Identität in Deutschland nach 1813', in U. Planert (ed.), *Krieg und Umbruch in Mitteleuropa um 1800* (Paderborn, 2009), 333–58.

J. Burkhardt, 'Alte oder neue Kriegsursachen? Die Kriege Bismarcks im Vergleich zu den Staatsbildungskriegen der frühen Neuzeit', in L. Walther and V. Dotterweich (eds), *Deutschland in den internationalen Beziehungen des 19. und 20 Jahrhunderts* (Munich, 1996), 43–69.

J. Burkhardt, 'Kriegsgrund Geschichte? 1870, 1813, 1756 – historische Argumente und Orientierungen bei Ausbruch des Ersten Weltkrieges', in J. Burkhardt, *Lange und kurze Wege in den Ersten Weltkrieg* (Munich, 1996), 9–86.

J. Burkhardt (ed.), *Krieg und Frieden in der historischen Gedächtniskultur* (Munich, 2000).

O. Büsch, *Military System and Social Life in Old Regime Prussia, 1713–1807: The Beginnings of the Social Militarization of Prusso-German Society* (Atlantic Highlands, NJ, 1997).

N. Buschmann and C. Horst (eds), *Die Erfahrung des Krieges. Erfahrungsgeschichtliche Perspektiven von der französischen Revolution bis zum Zweiten Weltkrieg* (Paderborn, 2001).

N. Buschmann and D. Langewiesche (eds), *Der Krieg in den Gründungsmythen europäischer Nationen und der USA* (Frankfurt, 2003).

J. Calliess (ed.), *Gewalt in der Geschichte* (Düsseldorf, 1983).

R. C. Canevali, 'The "False French Alarm": Revolutionary Panic in Baden, 1848', *Central European History*, 18 (1985), 119–42.

H. Carl, 'Der Mythos des Befreiungskrieges. Die "martialische Nation" im Zeitalter der Revolutions- und Befreiungskriege 1792–1815', in D. Langewiesche and G. Schmidt (eds), *Föderative Nation* (Munich, 2000), 63–82.

H. Carl, '"Der Anfang vom Ende". Kriegserfahrung und Religion Belgien während der Französischen Revolutionskriege', in D. Beyrau, M. Hochgeschwender, and D. Langewiesche (eds), *Formen des Krieges* (Paderborn, 2007), 86–110.

J. C. Chesnais, *Histoire de la violence en Occident de 1800 à nos jours* (Paris, 1981).

R. Chickering, 'Total War: The Use and Abuse of a Concept', in M. F. Boemeke, R. Chickering, and S. Förster (eds), *Anticipating Total War: The German and American Experiences, 1871–1914* (Cambridge, 1999), 13–28.

R. Chickering and S. Förster (eds), *War in an Age of Revolution, 1775–1815* (Cambridge, 2010).

C. Clark, 'The Wars of Liberation in Prussian Memory: Reflections of the Memorialization of War in Early Nineteenth-Century Germany', *Journal of Modern History*, 68 (1996), 550–76.

C. Clark, *Iron Kingdom: The Rise and Downfall of Prussia, 1600–1947* (London, 2007).

S. E. Cooper, *Patriotic Pacifism: Waging War on War in Europe, 1815–1914* (New York, 1991).

A. Corbin, 'L'Histoire de la violence dans les capagnes francaises au xixème siècle', *Ethnologie Française*, 21 (1991), 224–35.

A. Corbin, *Das Dorf der Kannibalen* (Stuttgart, 1992).

G. A. Craig, *The Politics of the Prussian Army, 1640–1945* (Oxford, 1955).

K. Cramer, *The Thirty Years' War and German Memory in the Nineteenth Century* (Lincoln, Nebraska, 2007).

T. Crepon, *Gebhard Leberecht von Blücher. Sein Leben, seine Kämpfe* (Rostock, 1999).

M. van Creveld, *Supplying War: Logistics from Wallenstein to Patton* (Cambridge, 1977).

M. van Creveld, *Die Zukunft des Krieges* (Munich, 1998).

M. van Creveld, *The Rise and Decline of the State* (Cambridge, 1999).

H. Cyrus, 'Von erlaubter und unerlaubter Frauenart, um Freiheit zu kämpfen – Freiheitskämpferinnen im 19. Jahrhundert und die Freie Hansestadt in Bremen', in H. Grubitzsch (ed.), *Grenzgängerinnen* (Duesseldorf, 1985), 19–69.

E.-O. Czempiel, Friede und Konflikt in der Gesellschaftslehre', *Aus Politik und Zeitgeschichte*, 20 (1974), 13–24.

U. Daniel and W. Siemann (eds), *Propaganda. Meinungskampf, Verfuehrung und politische Sinnstiftung, 1789–1989* (Frankfurt, 1994).

U. Daniel and W. Siemann (eds), *Augenzeugen. Kriegsberichterstattung vom 18. zum 21. Jahrhundert* (Göttingen, 2006).

O. Dann, 'Die Friedensdiskussion der deutschen Gebildeten im Jahrzehnt der französischen Revolution', in W. Huber (ed.), *Historische Beiträge zur Friedensforschung* (Stuttgart, 1970), 95–133.

O. Dann, 'Vernunftfrieden und nationaler Krieg. Der Umbruch im Friedensverhalten des deutschen Bürgertums zu Beginn des 19. Jahrhunderts', in W. Huber and J. Schwertfeger (eds), *Kirche zwischen Krieg und Frieden* (Stuttgart, 1976), 169–224.

O. Dann, *Lesegesellschaften und europäische Emanzipation* (Munich, 1981).

O. Dann (ed.), *Vereinswesen und bürgerliche Gesellschaft in Deutschland* (Munich, 1984).

O. Dann 'Der deutsche Bürger wird Soldat', in R. Steinweg (ed.), *Lehren aus der Geschichte* (Frankfurt, 1990), 61–84.

O. Dann, *Nation und Nationalismus in Deutschland 1770–1990* (Munich, 1993).

O. Dann (ed.), *Schiller als Historiker* (Stuttgart, 1995).

O. Dann (ed.), *Patriotismus und Nationsbildung am Ende des Heiligen Römischen Reiches* (Cologne, 2003).

O. Dann and J. Dinwiddy (eds), *Nationalism in the Age of the French Revolution* (London, 1988).

P. Demandt, *Luisenkult. Die Unsterblichkeit der Königin von Preussen* (Cologne, 2003).

K. Demeter, *Das deutsche Offizierkorps in Gesellschaft und Staat 1650–1945*, 2nd edn (Frankfurt, 1962).

C. Diemel, *Adelige Frauen im buergerlichen Jahrhundert. Hofdamen, Stiftsdamen, Salondamen 1800–1870* (Frankfurt, 1998).

P. Dieners, *Das Duell und die Sonderrolle des Militärs* (Berlin, 1992).

G. de Diesbach, *Madame de Staël* (Paris, 1983).

C. Dipper, 'Über die Unfähigkeit zum Frieden. Deutschlands bürgerliche Bewegung und der Krieg 1830–1914', in *Frieden und Geschichte und Gegenwart*, ed. Historischen Seminar der Universität Düsseldorf (Düsseldorf, 1985), 88–110.

E. Dorn Brose, *German History, 1789–1871* (Providence, RI, 1997).

A. Dörner, 'Die symbolische Politik der Ehre. Zur Konstruktion der nationalen Ehre in den Diskursen der Befreiungskriege', in L. Vogt und A. Zingerle (eds), *Ehre. Archäische Momente in der Moderne* (Frankfurt, 1994), 78–95.

A. Dörner, *Politischer Mythos und symbolische Politik. Sinnstiftung durch symbolische Formen am Beispiel des Hermannsmythos* (Opladen, 1995).

V. Dotterweich, *Heinrich von Sybel. Geschichtswissenschaft in politischer Absicht 1817–1861* (Göttingen, 1978).

G. Drechsler and H. Jakubowski, 'Das Phänomen "Krieg" in Georg Wilhelm Friedrich Hegels Philosophie', in B. Bissmann (ed.), *Studien zur Kulturgeschichte, Sprache und Dichtung* (Jena, 1990), 78–93.

H. Duchhardt, *Stein. Eine Biographie* (Münster, 2007).

H. Duchhardt, *Vom Nachleben, von der Stilisierung und von der Instrumentalisierung des preußischen Reformers* (Göttingen, 2008).

H. Duchhardt and A. Kunz (eds), *Reich oder Nation? Mitteleuropa 1780–1815* (Mainz, 1998).

D. Düding, *Organisierter gesellschaftlicher Nationalismus in Deutschland 1808–1847* (Munich, 1984).

D. Düding, P. Friedemann, and P. Münch (eds), *Öffentliche Festkultur. Politische Feste in Deutschland von der Aufklärung bis zum Ersten Weltkrieg* (Hamburg, 1988).

S. Dudink, K. Hagemann, and J. Tosh (eds), *Masculinities in Politics and War* (Manchester, 2004).

R. Dufraisse (ed.), *Revolution und Gegenrevolution 1789–1830. Zur geistigen Auseinanderseitzung in Frankreich und Deutschland* (Munich, 1991).

J. Dülffer (ed.), *Parlamentarische und öffentliche Kontrolle von Rüstung in Deutschland 1700–1970* (Düsseldorf, 1992).

J. Dülffer (ed.), *Kriegsbereitschaft und Friedensordnung in Deutschland 1800–1814* (Münster, 1995).

J. Dülffer, *Im Zeichen der Gewalt. Frieden und Krieg im 19. und 20. Jahrhundert* (Cologne, 2003).

P. G. Dwyer (ed.), *Napoleon and Europe* (London, 2001).

P. G. Dwyer, 'New Avenues for Research in Napoleonic Europe', *European History Quarterly*, 33 (2003), 101–24.

P. G. Dwyer and A. Forrest (eds), *Napoleon and His Empire, 1804–1814* (London, 2007).

J. C. Eade (ed.), *Romantic Nationalism in Europe* (Canberra, 1983).

J. Echternkamp, *Der Aufstieg des deutschen Nationalismus 1770–1840* (Frankfurt, 1998).

J. Echternkamp, '"Teutschland, des Soldaten Vaterland". Die Nationalisierung des Krieges im frühen 19. Jahrhundert', in W. Rösener (ed.), *Staat und Krieg. Vom Hochmittelalter bis zur Moderne* (Göttingen, 2000), 181–203.

J. Echternkamp, '"Religiöses Nationalgefühl" oder "Frömmelei der Deutschtümler"? Religion, Nation und Politik im Frühnationalismus', in H.-G. Haupt and D. Langewiesche (eds), *Nation und Religion in der deutschen Geschichte* (Frankfurt am Main, 2001), 142–69.

J. Echternkamp, 'Die "Architektur" der Nation im Krieg. Patriotismus, Kultur und Radikalisierung der Gewalt zur Zeit Karl Friedrich Schinkels', in A. Dorgerloh, M. Niedermeier, and H. Bredekamp (eds), *Klassizismus—Gotik. Karl Friedrich Schinkel und die patriotische Baukunst* (Munich, 2007), 43–57.

J. Echternkamp, 'La Formation de l'ennemi français dans l'Allemagne des guerres anti-napoléoniennes. Nationalisme, mobilisation en masse et la représentation de l'autre au début du XIXe siècle', *Francia*, 34 (2007), 1–17.

J. Echternkamp, '"Wo jeder Franzmann heißet Feind…"? Nationale Propaganda und sozialer Protest im napoleonischen Deutschland', in V. Veltzke (ed.), *Napoleon. Trikolore und Kaiseradler über Rhein und Weser* (Cologne, 2007), 411–28.

J. Echternkamp et al. (eds), *Perspektiven der Militärgeschichte. Raum, Gewalt und Repräsentation in historischer Forschung und Bildung* (Munich, 2010).

W. Eckermann, *Ferdinand von Schill. Rebell und Patriot* (Berlin, 1963).

C. Eifert, *Paternalismus und Politik. Preussische Landräte im 19 Jahrhundert* (Münster, 2003).

U. Eisenhardt, *Die kaiserliche Aufsicht über Buchdruck, Buchhandel und Presse im Heiligen Römischen Reich deutscher Nation* (Karlsruhe, 1970).

J. Engelbrecht, *Das Herzogtum Berg im Zeitalter der Französischen Revolution. Modernisierungsprozesse zwischen bayerischem und französischem Modell* (Paderborn, 1996).

R. Engelsing, 'Zur politischen Bildung der deutschen Unterschichten 1789-1863', *Historische Zeitschrift*, 206 (1968), 337–69.

K. Epstein, *The Genesis of German Conservatism* (Princeton, 1975).

W. Erhart and A. Koch (eds), *Ernst Moritz Arndt 1769–1860. Deutscher Nationalismus, Europa, transatlantische Perspektiven* (Tübingen, 2007).

C. J. Esdaile, *The Wars of Napoleon* (London, 1995).

C. J. Esdaile (ed.), *Popular Resistance in the French Wars: Patriots, Partisans and Land Pirates* (Basingstoke, 2005).

C. J. Esdaile, *Napoleon's Wars: An International History* (London, 2007).

C. J. Esdaile, 'Recent Writing on Napoleon and His Wars', *Journal of Military History*, 73 (2009), 209–20.

R. J. Evans, *Rituals of Retribution: Capital Punishment in Germany, 1600–1987* (Oxford, 1996).

W. Faulstich, *Die bürgerliche Mediengesellschaft 1700–1830* (Göttingen, 2002).

E. Fehrenbach, 'Die Ideologisierung des Krieges und die Radikalisierung der Französischen Revolution', in D. Langewiesche (ed.), *Revolution und Krieg. Zur Dynamik historischen Wandels seit dem 18. Jahrhundert* (Paderborn, 1989), 57–66.

E. Fehrenbach, *Vom Ancien Régime zum Wiener Kongreß*, 4th edn (Munich, 2001).

G. Fesser, *1813. Die Völkerschlacht bei Leipzig* (Jena, 2013).

S. Fiedler, *Grundriss der Militär und Kriegsgeschichte* (Munich, 1976), vol. 2.

S. Fiedler, *Kriegswesen und Kriegsführung im Zeitalter der Kabinettskriege* (Coblenz, 1986).

S. Fiedler, *Heerwesen der Neuzeit. Taktik und Strategie der Revolutionskriege 1792–1848* (Augsburg, 2002), vol. 3.

H.-D. Fischer (ed.), *Deutsche Publizisten des15. bis 20. Jahrhunderts* (Munich, 1971).

H.-D. Fischer (ed.), *Deutsche Zeitungen des 17. bis 20. Jahrhunderts* (Munich, 1972).

H.-D. Fischer (ed.), *Deutsche Zeitschriften des 17. bis 20. Jahrhunderts* (Munich, 1973).

H.-D. Fischer (ed.), *Deutsche Presseverleger des 15. bis 20. Jahrhunderts* (Munich, 1975).

P. Fleck, 'Konskription und Stellvertretung. Die Behandlung der Kriegsdienstpflicht im hessen-darmstädtischen Landtag von 1820 bis 1866', *Archiv für hessische Geschichte und Altertumskunde*, 43 (1985), 193–228.

R. G. Foerster (ed.), *Die Wehrpflicht. Entstehung, Erscheinungsformen und politisch-militärische Wirkung* (Munich, 1994).

A. Forrest, *Napoleon's Men: The Soldiers of the Revolution and Empire* (London, 2002).

A. Forrest, K. Hagemann and J. Rendall (eds), *Soldiers, Citizens, and Civilians: Experiences and Perceptions of the Revolutionary and Napoleonic Wars, 1790–1820* (Basingstoke, 2008).

E. Frauenholz, *Die Entwicklung des Geankens der allgemeinen Wehrpflicht im neunzehnten Jahrhundert* (Munich, 1925).

U. Frevert, *Ehrenmänner. Das Duell in der bürgerlichen Gesellschaft* (Munich, 1995).

U. Frevert, 'Nation, Krieg und Geschlecht im 19. Jahrhundert', in M. Hettling and P. Nolte (eds), *Nation und Gesellschaft in Deutschland* (Munich, 1996), 151–70.

U. Frevert, 'Soldaten, Staatsbürger. Überlegungen zur historischen Konstruktion von Männlichekeit' in T. Kühne (ed.), *Männergeschichte—Geschlechtergeschichte* (Frankfurt, 1996), 69–87.

U. Frevert, 'Das jakobinische Modell. Allgemeine Wehrpflicht und Nationsbildung in Preussen Deutschland', in U. Frevert (ed.), *Militär und Gesellschaft im 19. und 20. Jahrhundert* (Stuttgart, 1997), 17–47.

U. Frevert (ed.), *Militär und Gesellschaft im 19. und 20. Jahrhundert* (Stuttgart, 1997).

U. Frevert, 'Herren und Helden. Vom Aufstieg und Niedergang des Heroismus im 19. und 20. Jahrhundert', in U. Frevert (ed.), *Die Erfindung des Menschen. Schöpfungsräume und Körperbilder* (Cologne, 1998), 323–44.

U. Frevert, *Kasernierte Nation. Militärdienst und Zivilgesellschaft in Deutschland* (Munich, 2001).

U. Frevert, *Vergängliche Gefühle* (Göttingen, 2013).

E. Frie, 'Preussische Identitäten im Wandel 1760-1870', *Historische Zeitschrift*, 272 (2001), 353–75.

Johannes Fried, 'Der Löwe als Objekt. Was Literaten, Historiker und Politiker aus Heinrich dem Löwen machten', *Historische Zeitschrift*, 262 (1996), 673–93.

A. Funk and N. Pütter, 'Polizei und Miliz als Bürgerorgane', in A. Lüdtke (ed.), *Sicherheit* (Frankfurt, 1992), 37–64.

J. Gagliardo, *Reich and Nation: The Holy Roman Empire as Idea and Reality, 1763–1806* (Bloomington, IN, 1980).

M. Gailus, *Strasse und Brot* (Göttingen, 1990).

M. Gailus, 'Hungerunruhen in Preussen', in M. Gailus and H. Volkmann (eds), *Der Kampf um das tägliche Brot* (Opladen, 1994).

A. Gat, *War in Human Civilization* (Oxford, 2006).

A. Gat, 'What Constituted the Military Revolution of the Early Modern Period?', in R. Chickering and S. Förster (eds), *War in an Age of Revolution, 1775–1815* (Cambridge, 2010), 21–48.

P. Gay, *The Cultivation of Hatred* (London, 1993).

A. Geisthoevel, *Eigentumlichkeit und Macht. Deutscher Nationalismus 1830–1851. Der Fall Schleswig-Holstein* (Wiesbaden, 2003).

W. Gembruch, 'Krieg und Heerwesen im politischen Denken des Freiherrn vom Stein', *Militärgeschichtliches Mitteilungen*, 10 (1971), 27–54.

W. Gembruch, 'Bürgerliche Publizistik und Heeresreform in Preußen (1805–1808)', in J. Kunisch (ed.), *Staat und Heer* (Berlin, 1990), 334–65.

S. Georgi, '1812 in der Erinnerung. Die bayrische Monarchie und die Verteranen der Napoleonischen Kriege im Vormärz' (Magisterarbeit, Erlangen, 2001).

V. Gerhardt, *Immanuel Kants Entwurf 'Zum ewigen Frieden'. Eine Theorie der Politik* (Darmstadt, 1995).

S. Germer and M. F. Zimmermann (eds), *Bilder der Macht, Macht der Bilder. Zeitgeschichte in Darstellungen des 19. Jahrhunderts* (Munich, 1997).

A. Gestrich, 'Kirchliche Kriegsmentalität in Württemberg um 1800', in J. Dülffer (ed.), *Kriegsbereitschaft und Friedensordnung in Deutschland 1800–1814* (Münster, 1994), 183–201.

P. Geuniffey, *La Politique de la Terreur: essai sur la violence révolutionnaire 1789–1794* (Paris, 2000).

M. Geyer and H. Lehmann (eds), *Religion und Nation* (Göttingen, 2004).

H. Gisch, '"Preßfreiheit" – "Preßfrechheit". Zum Problem der Presseaufsicht in napoleonischer Zeit in Deutschland 1806–1818', in H.-D. Fischer (ed.), *Deutsche Kommunikationskontrolle des 15.–20. Jahrhunderts* (Munich, 1982), 56–74.

H. Glaser (ed.), *Krone und Verfassung: König Max Joseph und der neue Staat 1799–1825* (Munich, 1980).

H. Gollwitzer, 'Zur Auffassung der mittelalterlichen Kaiserpolitik im 19. Jahrhundert', in R. Vierhaus and M. Botzenhart (eds), *Dauer und Wandel der Geschichte* (Münster, 1966).

F. Göse, 'Der Kabinettskrieg', in D. Beyrau, M. Hochgeschwender, and D. Langewiesche (eds), *Formen des Krieges* (Paderborn, 2007), 121–47.

A. Grab, *Napoleon and the Transformation of Europe* (Basingstoke, 2003).

H. T. Graef, 'Reich, Nation und Kirche in der gross- und kleindeutschen Historiographie', *Historisches Jahrbuch*, 116 (1996), 367–94.

A. Green, *Fatherlands: State-Building and Nationhood in Nineteenth-Century Germany* (Cambridge, 2001).

W. D. Gruner, *Das bayerische Heer 1825 bis 1864* (Boppard, 1972).

K. Hagemann, 'Der "Bürger" als "Nationalkrieger". Entwürfe von Militär, Nation und Männlichkeit in der Zeit der Freiheitskriegen', in K. Hagemann and R. Pröve (eds), *Landsknechte, Soldatenfrauen und Nationalkrieger* (Frankfurt, 1998), 74–102.

K. Hagemann, *Mannlicher Muth und teutscher Ehre. Nation, Krieg und Geschlecht in der Zeit der antinapoleonischen Kriege Preussens* (Paderborn, 2001).

K. Hagemann, 'German Heroes: The Cult of Death for the Fatherland in Nineteenth-Century Germany', in S. Dudink. K. Hagemann, and J. Tosh (eds), *Masculinities in Politics and War* (Manchester, 2004), 116–34.

K. Hagemann, 'Gendered Images of the German Nation: The Romantic Painter Friedrich Kersting and the Patriotic-National Discourse during the Wars of Liberation', *Nations and Nationalism*, 12 (2006), 653–79.

K. Hagemann, '"Unimaginable Horror and Misery": The Battle of Leipzig in October 1813 in Civilian Experience and Perception', in A. Forrest, K. Hagemann, and J. Rendall (eds), *Soldiers, Citizens and Civilians* (Basingstoke, 2009), 157–78.

K. Hagemann, 'A "Valorous Nation" in a "Holy War": War Mobilization, Religion and Political Culture in Prussia, 1807 to 1815', in M. Broers et al. (eds), *The Napoleonic Empire and the New European Political Culture* (Basingstoke, 2011), 186–200.

K. Hagemann, *Revisiting Prussia's Wars against Napoleon: History, Culture and Memory* (Cambridge, 2015).

K. Hagemann and R. Pröve (eds), *Landsknechte, Soldatenfrauen und Nationalkrieger. Militär, Krieg und Geschlechterordnung im historischen Wandel* (Frankfurt, 1998).

M. Hamm, *Die bayerische Integrationspolitik in Tirol 1806–1814* (Munich, 1996).

H. Händel, *Der Gedanke der allgemeinen Wehrpflicht in der Wehrverfassung des Königreiches Preußen bis 1819* (Frankfurt, 1962).

W. Hansen, *Nationaldenkmaler und Nationalfeste im 19. Jahrhundert* (Luneberg, 1976).

W. Hardtwig, 'Von Preussens Aufgabe in Deutschland und Deutschlands Aufgabe in der Welt. Liberalismus und borussianisches Geschichtsbild zwischen Revolution und Imperialismus', *Historische Zeitschrift*, 231 (1980), 265–324.

W. Hardtwig, *Geschichtskultur und Wissenschaft* (Munich, 1990).

W. Hardtwig, *Nationalismus und Bürgerkultur in Deutschland, 1500–1914* (Göttingen, 1994).

J. F. Harrington and H. W. Smith, 'Confessionalisation, Community and State-Building in Germany, 1555–1870', *Journal of Modern History*, 69 (1997), 77–101.

J. F. Harris, 'Arms and the People: The Bürgerwehr of Lower Franconia in 1814 and 1849', in K. H. Jarausch and L. E. Jones (eds), *In Search of a Liberal Germany* (New York, 1990), 133–60.

F. Hauer and W. Keller (eds), *Schillers Wallenstein* (Darmstadt, 1977).

H. Haupt (ed.), *Quellen und Darstellungen zur Geschichte der Burschenschaft und der deutschen Einheitsbewegung* (Heidelberg, 1910–40), 17 vols.

H.-G. Haupt, 'Zur historischen Analyse der Gewalt', *Geschichte und Gesellschaft*, 3 (1977), 236–56.

H.-G. Haupt, M. G. Müller, and S. Woolf (eds), *Regional and National Identities in Europe in the Nineteenth and Twentieth Centuries* (The Hague, 1998).

J. A. W. Heffernan (ed.), *Representing the French Revolution: Literature, Historiography and Art* (Hanover, NH, 1992).

W. Heindl, 'Vom schwierigen Umgang mit (Helden-) Ahnen in der Zeit des Nationalismus', in C. Bosshart-Pfluger, J. Jung, and F. Metzger (eds), *Nation und Nationalismus in Europa* (Frauenfeld, 2002), 395–418.

E. Hellmuth and R. Stauber (eds), *Nationalismus vor dem Nationalismus* (Hamburg, 1998).

E. Henderson, *Blücher and the Uprising of Prussia against Napoleon, 1806–1815* (London, 1911).

H. Herbell, *Staatsbürger in Uniform 1789 bis 1961* (Berlin, 1969).

A. Herberg-Rothe, 'Die Entgrenzung des Krieges bei Clausewitz', in J. Kunisch and H. Münkler (eds), *Die Wiedergeburt des Krieges aus dem Geist der Revolution* (Berlin, 1999), 185–209.

A. Herberg-Rothe, *Clausewitz's Puzzle: The Political Theory of War* (Oxford, 2007).

J. Hermand, 'Dashed Hopes: On the Painting of the Wars of Liberation', in J. D. Steakley (ed.), *Political Symbolism in Modern Europe* (New Brunswick, NJ, 1982), 216–38.

I. Herrmann, *Hardenberg. Der Reformkanzler* (Berlin, 2003).

U. Herrmann (ed.), *Volk, Nation, Vaterland* (Hamburg, 1996).

W. Herzberg, *Das Hambacher Fest* (Leipzig, 1974).

M. Hettling (ed.), *Revolution in Deutschland? 1789–1989* (Göttingen, 1991).

M. Hettling (ed.), *Bürgerliche Feste. Symbolishe Formen politischen Handels im 19. Jahrhundert* (Göttingen, 1993).

M. Hettling (ed.), *Der bürgerliche Wertehimmel. Innenansichten des 19. Jahrhunderts* (Göttingen, 2000).

M. Hettling and P. Nolte (eds), *Nation und Gesellschaft in Deutschland* (Munich, 1996).

M. Hewitson, 'Violence and Civilization: Transgression in Modern Wars', in M. Fulbrook (ed.), *Uncivilizing Processes? Excess and Transgression in German Society and Culture* (Amsterdam, 2007), 117–56.

M. Hewitson, '"I Witnesses": Soldiers, Selfhood, and Testimony in Modern Wars', *German History*, 28 (2010), 310–25.

M. Hewitson, 'Black Humour: Caricature in Wartime', *Oxford German Studies*, 41 (2012), 213–35.

M. Hewitson, 'Belligerence, Patriotism and Nationalism in the German Public Sphere, 1792–1815', *English Historical Review*, 128 (2013), 839–76.

M. Hewitson, 'Princes' Wars, Wars of the People or Total War? Mass Armies and the Question of a Military Revolution in Germany, 1792–1815', *War in History*, 20 (2013), 452–90.

M. Hewitson, 'On War and Peace: German Conceptions of Conflict, 1792–1815', *Historical Journal*, 57 (2014), 447–83.

G. Heydemann, *Carl Ludwig Sand. Die Tat als Attentat* (Hof, 1985).

W. v. Hippel (ed.), *Freiheit, Gleichheit, Bruderlichkeit? Die Französischen Revolution im deutschen Urteil* (Munich, 1989).

L. Höbelt, 'Zur Militärpolitik des Deutschen Bundes. Corpseinteilung und Aufmarschpläne im Vormärz', in H. Rumpler (ed.), *Deutscher Bund* (Vienna, 1990), 114–35.

S.-L. Hoffmann, 'Mythos und Geschichte. Leipziger Gedenkfeiern der Völkerschlacht im 19. und 20. Jahrhundert', in E. Francois, H. Siegrist, and J. Vogel (eds), *Nation und Emotion* (Göttingen, 1995), 111–32.

A. Hoffmeister-Hunger, *Pressepolitik und Staatsreform. Die Institutionalisierung staatlicher oeffentlichkeitsarbeit bei Karl Augsut von Hardenberg 1792–1822* (Göttingen, 1994).

W. Hofmann, *Caspar David Friedrich* (New York, 2000).

P. Hohendahl, *Building a National Literature: The Case of Germany, 1830–1870* (Ithaca, 1989).

A. Hohlfeld, *Das Frankfurter Parlament und sein Kampf um das deutsche Heer* (Berlin, 1932).

R. Höhn, *Verfassungskampf und Heereseid. Der Kampf des Bürgertums um das Heer 1815–1850* (Leipzig, 1938).

R. Höhn, *Die Armee als Erziehungsschule der Nation. Das Ende einer Idee* (Bad Harzburg, 1963).

D. Hohrath, *Die Bildung des Offiziers in der Aufklärung. Ferdinand Friedrich von Nicolai (1730–1814) und seine enzyklopädischen Sammlungen* (Stuttgart, 1990).

D. Hohrath and K. Gerteis (eds), *Die Kriegskunst im Lichte der Vernunft. Militär und Aufklärung im 18. Jahrhundert* (Hamburg, 2000).

K. Hokkanen, *Krieg und Frieden in der politischen Tagesliteratur Deutschlands zwischen Baseler und Lunéviller Frieden 1795–1801* (Jyväskylä, 1975).

K. Holl, *Pazifismus in Deutschland* (Frankfurt, 1988).

S. Holsten, *Allegorischen Darstellungen des Krieges* (Munich, 1976).

K. J. Holsti, *Peace and War: Armed Conflicts and International Order, 1648–1989* (Cambridge, 1991).

D. M. Hopkin, *Soldier and Peasant in French Popular Culture, 1766–1870* (Suffolk, 2003).

D. M. Hopkin, 'Storytelling, Fairytales and Autobiography: Some Observations on Eighteenth- and Nineteenth-Century French Soldiers' and Sailors' Memoirs', *Social History*, 29 (2004), 186–98.

K. Hornung, *Scharnhorst. Soldat—Reformer—Staatsmann* (Munich, 1997).

M. Howard, *War in European History* (Oxford, 1976).

W. Huber and J. Schwerdtfeger (eds), *Historische Beiträge zur Friedensforschung* (Stuttgart, 1970).

W. Huber and J. Schwerdtfeger (eds), *Kirche zwischen Krieg und Frieden. Studien zur Geschichte des detuschen Protestantismus* (Stuttgart, 1976).

C. Hudemann-Simon, 'Réfractaires und déserteurs de la Grande Armée en Sarre 1802–1813', *Revue Historique*, 111 (1987), 11–45.

M. Hughes, *Nationalism and Society: Germany, 1800–1945* (London, 1988).

B. Hüppauf (ed.), *War, Violence and the Modern Condition* (Berlin, 1997).

H.-G. Husung, 'Zu einigen Problemen der historischen Protestforschung am Beispiel gemeinschaftlichen Protests in Norddeutschland 1815–1847', in H. Volkmann and J. Bergmann (eds), *Protest* (Opladen, 1984), 21–35.

P. Hüttenberger and H. Molitor (eds), *Franzosen und Deutsche am Rhein 1789–1945* (Essen, 1989).

R. Ibbeken, *Preussen, 1807–1813. Staat und Volk als Idee und Wirklichkeit* (Cologne, 1970).

G. G. Iggers, *The German Conception of History*, rev. edn (Middletown, CT, 1983).

G. G. Iggers and J. M. Powell (eds), *Leopold von Ranke and the Shaping of the Historical Discipline* (Syracuse, NY, 1990).

M. Jacobs, 'Die Entwicklung des deutschen Nationalgedankens von der Reformation bis zum deutschen Idealismus', in H. Zillessen (ed.), *Volk-Nation-Vaterland: Der deutsche Protestantismus und der Nationalismus* (Gütersloh, 1970).

F. Jäger, *Bürgerliche Modernisierungskrise und historische Sinnbildung: Kulturgeschichte bei Droysen, Burckhardt und Weber* (Göttingen, 1994).

G. Jäger and J. Schönert (eds), *Die Leihbibliothek als Institution des literarischen Lebens im 18. und 19. Jahrhundert* (Hamburg, 1980).

L. S. James, 'Travel Writing and Encounters with National "Others" in the Napoleonic Wars', *History Compass*, 7 (2009), 1246–58.

L. S. James, *Witnessing the Revolutionary and Napoleonic Wars in German Central Europe* (Basingstoke, 2013).

L. Jamieson and H. Corr (eds), *State, Private Life and Political Change* (Basingstoke, 1990).

C. Jansen (ed.), *Der Bürger als Soldat. Die Militarisierung europäischer Gesellschaft im langen 19. Jahrhundert* (Essen, 2004).

C. Jansen, L. Niethammer, and B. Weisbrod (eds), *Von der Aufgabe der Freiheit. Politische Verantwortung und bürgerliche Gesellschaft im 19. und 20. Jahrhundert* (Berlin, 1995).

C. Jany, *Geschichte der Königlich Preussischen Armee* (Berlin, 1933), vols 3–4.

M. Jeismann, *Das Vaterland der Feinde. Studien zum nationalen Feindbegriff und Selbstverständnis in Frankreich und Deutschland 1792–1918* (Stuttgart, 1992).

D. Jenson, *Trauma and Its Representations: The Social Life of Mimesis in Post-Revolutionary France* (Princeton, 2003).

O. Jessen, '*Preussens Napoleon'? Ernst von Rüchel 1754–1823* (Paderborn, 2007).

O. W. Johnson, *Der deutsche Nationalmythos* (Stuttgart, 1990).

C. Jones, 'The Military Revolution and the Professionalisation of the French Army under the Ancien Régime', in M. Duffy (ed.), *The Military Revolution and the State, 1500–1800* (Exeter, 1980), 29–48.

E. Jöst, 'Der Heldentod des Dichters Theodor Körner. Der Einfluss eines Mythos auf die Rezeption einer Lyrik und ihre literarische Kritik', *Orbis Litterarum*, 32 (1977), 310–40.

M. Junkelmann, *Napoleon und Bayern. Von den Anfängen des Königreiches* (Regensburg, 1985).

A. Jürgens-Kirchhoff and A. Matthias (eds), *Krieg, Kunst und Medien* (Weimar, 2006).

D. Kaiser, *Politics and War: European Conflict from Philip II to Hitler*, new edn (Cambridge, MA, 2000).

W. Kaschuba, *Lebenswelt und Kultur der unterbürglichen Schichten im 19 und 20 Jahrhundert* (Munich, 1990).

J. Katz, *Die Hep-Hep Verfolgungen des Jahres 1819* (Berlin, 1994).

S. Kaufmann, *Kommunikationstechnik und Kriegführung 1815–1945* (Munich, 1996).

H. M. Kaulbach, *Bombe und Kanone in der Karikatur* (Marburg, 1987).

H. M. Kaulbach, 'Männliche Ideale von Krieg und Frieden in der Kunst der napoleonischen Ära', in J. Dülffer (ed.), *Kriegsbereitschaft und Friedensordnung in Deutschland 1800–1814* (Münster, 1995), 127–41.

R. Kawa, *Georg Friedrich Rebmann 1768–1824. Studien zu Leben und Werk eines deutschen Jakobiners* (Bonn, 1980).

F. Keinemann (ed.), *Westfalen im Zeitalter der Restauration und der Juli-Revolution, 1815–1833* (Münster, 1987).

G. A. Kelly (ed.), *Johann Gottlieb Fichte: Addresses to the German Nation* (New York, 1968).

E. Kessel, *Militärgeschichte und Kriegstheorie in neuerer Zeit* (Berlin, 1987), ed. J. Kunisch.

D. Kienitz, *Der Kosakenwinter in Schleswig-Holstein 1813/14* (Heide, 2000).

S. Kienitz, *Sexualität, Macht und Moral. Prostitution und Geschlechterbeziehungen am Anfang des 19. Jahrhunderts in Württemberg* (Berlin, 1995).

T. Kirchner, 'Paradigma der Gegenwärtigkeit. Schlachtenmalerei als Gattung ohne Darstellungskonventionen', in S. Germer and M. F. Zimmermann (eds), *Bilder der Macht, Macht der Bilder* (Berlin, 1997), 107–24.

W. Klein, *Der Napoleonkult in der Pfalz* (Munich, 1934).

D. Klenke, *Der singende 'deutsche Mann'. Gesangvereine und deutsches Nationalbewusstsein von Napoleon bis Hitler* (Münster, 1998).

A. Klinger, 'Deutsches Weltbürgertum und französische Universalmonarchie: Napoleon und die Krise des deutschen Kosmopolitanismus', in A. Klinger, H.-W. Hahn, and G. Schmidt (eds), *Das Jahr 1806 im europäischen Kontext* (Cologne, 2008), 205–32.

D. Klippel and M. Zwanzger, 'Krieg und Frieden im Naturrecht des 18. und 19. Jahrhunderts', in W. Rösener (ed.), *Staat und Krieg. Vom Hochmittelalter bis zur Moderne* (Göttingen, 2000), 135–58.

J. Kloosterhuis and S. Neitzel (eds), *Krise, Reformen und Militär. Preussen ovr und nach der Katastrophe von 1806* (Berlin, 2009).

M. Klug, *Rückwendung zum Mittelalter? Geschichtsbilder und historische Argumentation im politischen Katholizismus des Vormärz* (Paderborn, 1995).

H. W. Koch, *Die Befreiungskriege 1807–1815. Napoleon gegen Deutschland und Europa* (Berg, 1998).

J. Kocka and R. Jessen, 'Die abnehmende Gewaltsamkeit sozialer Proteste. Vom 18. zum 20. Jahrhundert', in P.-A. Albrecht and O. Backes (eds), *Verdeckte Gewalt* (Frankfurt, 1990).

P. Köding, *August von Kotzebue. Auch ein deutsches Dichterleben* (Stuttgart, 1988).

H. Kohn, *Prelude to Nation-States: The French and German Experience, 1789–1815* (Princeton, NJ, 1967).

P. Kondylis, *Theorie des Krieges. Clausewitz, Marx, Engels, Lenin* (Stuttgart, 1988).

R. Köpping, *Sachsen gegen Napoleon. Zur Geschichte der Befreiungskriege 1813–1815* (Berlin, 2001).

H.-M. Körner, *Staat und Geschichte im Königreich Bayern 1806–1918* (Munich, 1992).

R. Koselleck, 'Staat und Gesellschaft in Preussen, 1815–1848', in W. Conze (ed.), *Staat und Gesellschaft im deutschen Vormärz, 1815–1848* (Stuttgart, 1962), 94–105.

R. Koselleck, 'Kriegerdenkmäle als Identitätsstiftungen der Überlebenden', in O. Marquard and K. Stierle (eds), *Identität* (Munich, 1979), 255–76.

R. Koselleck, *Vergangene Zukunft* (Frankfurt, 1988).

R. Koselleck, *Preussen zwischen Reform und Revolution. Allgemeines Landrecht, Verwaltung und Soziale Bewegung von 1791 bis 1848* (Munich, 1989).

R. Koselleck, *Begriffsgeschichten* (Frankfurt, 2006).

R. Koselleck and M. Jeismann (eds), *Der politische Totenkult. Kriegerdenkmäler in der Moderne* (Munich, 1994).

E. E. Kraehe, *Metternich's German Policy* (Princeton, 1963), vol. 1.

D. Kramer, 'Folter als diskursgeneratives Moment in der Literatur der Romantik', in T. Weitin (ed.), *Wahrheit und Gewalt. Der Diskurs der Folter in Europa und den USA* (Bielefeld, 2010), 145–60.

F. Kramer, 'Bayerns Erhebung zum Königkreich', *Zeitschrift für bayerischer Landesgeschichte*, 68 (2005), 815–34.

H.-C. Kraus, *Ernst Ludwig von Gerlach* (Göttingen, 1994), 2 vols.

H.-C. Kraus, 'Leopold und Ernst Ludwig von Gerlach', in B. Heidenreich (ed.), *Politische Theorien des 19. Jahrhunderts*, 2nd edn (Berlin, 2002), 155–75.

A. Krause, *Der Kampf um die Freiheit. Die Napoleonischen Befreiungskriege in Deutschland* (Stuttgart, 2013).

E. Krimmer, *The Representation of War in German Literature from 1800 to the Present* (Cambridge, 2010).

E. Krimmer and P. A. Simpson (eds), *Enlightened War: German Theories and Cultures of Warfare from Frederick the Great to Clausewitz* (Rochester, NY, 2009).

E. Krippendorff, *Staat und Krieg. Die historische Logik politischer Unvernunft* (Frankfurt, 1985).

B. R. Kroener, 'Aufklärung und Revolution. Die preussische Armee am Vorabend der Katastrophe von 1806', in Militärgeschichtliches Forschungsamt (ed.), *Die Französische Revolution und der Beginn des Zweiten Weltkrieges aus deutscher und französischer Sicht* (Bonn, 1989).

B. R. Kroener, *Kriegerische Gewalt und militärische Praesenz in der Neuzeit* (Paderborn, 2008).

B. R. Kroener and R. Pröve (eds), *Krieg und Frieden* (Paderborn, 1996).

G. Kronenbitter, *Wort und Macht. Friedrich Gentz als politischer Schriftsteller* (Berlin, 1994).

G. Kronenbitter, '"The Most Terrible World War": Friedrich Gentz and the Lessons of the Revolutionary War', in R. Chickering and S. Förster (eds), *War in an Age of Revolution, 1775–1815* (Cambridge, 2010), 117–34.

G. Krumeich and S. Brandt (eds), *Schlachtenmythen. Ereignis—Erzählung—Erinnerung* (Munich, 2001).

W. Kruse, *Krieg und nationale Integration. Eine Neuinterpretation des sozialdemokratischen Burgfriedensschlusses 1914/25* (Essen, 1994).

W. Kruse (ed.), *Eine Welt von Feinden. Der Grosse Krieg 1914–1918* (Frankfurt, 1997).

W. Kruse, *Die Erfindung des modernen Militarismus. Krieg, Militär und bürgerliche Gesellschaft im politischen Diskurs der Französischen Revolution, 1789–1799* (Munich, 2003).

W. Kruse, 'Revolutionary France and the Meanings of *Levée en masse*', R. Chickering and S. Förster (eds), *War in an Age of Revolution, 1775–1815* (Cambridge, 2010), 299–312.

T. Kühne and B. Ziemann (eds), *Männergeschichte, Geschlechtergeschichte. Männlichkeit im Wandel der Moderne* (Frankfurt, 1996).

T. Kühne and B. Ziemann (eds), *Was ist Militärgeschichte?* (Paderborn, 2000).

J. Kunisch, *Der kleine Krieg. Studien zum Heerwesen des Absolutismus* (Wiesbaden, 1973).

J. Kunisch (ed.), *Staatsverfassung und Heeresverfassung in der europäischen Geschichte der früheren Neuzeit* (Berlin, 1986).

J. Kunisch, 'Von der gezähmten zur entfesselten Bellona. Die Umwertung des Krieges im Zeitalter der Revolutions- und Freiheitskriege', in J. Kunisch (ed.), *Fürst—Gesellschaft—Krieg. Studien zur bellizistischen Disposition des absoluten Fürstenstaates* (Cologne, 1992), 203–26.

J. Kunisch and Münkler (eds), *Die Wiedergeburt des Krieges aus dem Geist der Revolution* (Berlin, 1999).

C. Küther, *Räuber und Gauner in Deutschland* (Göttingen, 1987).

M. Lahrkamp, *Münster in napoleonische Zeit 1800–1815. Administration, Wirtschaft und Gesellschaft im Zeichen von Säkularisation und französischer Herrschaft* (Munster, 1976).

D. Langewiesche (ed.), *Revolution und Krieg* (Paderborn, 1989).

D. Langewiesche, ' "…für Volk und Vaterland kräfitg zu würken…" Zur politischen und gesellschaftlichen Rolle der Turner zwischen 1811 und 1871', in O. Grupe (ed.), *Kulturgut oder Körperkult. Sport und Sportwissenschaft im Wandel* (Tübingen, 1990), 22–61.

D. Langewiesche, 'Gewalt und Politik im Jahrhundert der Revolutionen', in W. Speitkamp and H.-P. Ullmann (eds), *Konflikt und Reform* (Göttingen, 1995), 233–46.

D. Langewiesche, 'Föderativer Nationalismus als Erbe der deutschen Reichsnation: Über Föderalismus und Zentralismus in der deutschen Nationalgeschichte', in D. Langewiesche and G. Schmidt (eds), *Föderative Nation* (Munich, 2000), 215–44.

D. Langewiesche, *Nation, Nationalismus und Nationalstaat in Deutschland und Europa* (Munich, 2000).

D. Langewiesche, 'Zum Wandel von Krieg und Kriegslegitimation in der Neuzeit', *Journal of Modern European History*, 2 (2004), 5–27.

D. Langewiesche, 'Liberalismus, Nationalismus und Krieg im 19. Jahrhundert', in H. Ehlert (ed.), *Militärisches Zeremoniell in Deutschland* (Potsdam, 2008), 59–74.

D. Langewiesche, *Reich, Nation, Föderation* (Munich, 2008).

K. Latzel, *Vom Sterben im Krieg. Wandlungen in der Einstellung zum Solatentod vom Siebenjaehrigen Krieg bis zum Zweiten Weltkrieg* (Warendorf, 1988).

K. Latzel, '"Schlachtbank" oder "Feld der Ehre"? Der Beginn des Einstellungswandels gegenüber Krieg und Tat 1756–1815', in W. Wette (ed.), *Der Krieg des kleinen Mannes* (Munich, 1992), 77–92.

K. Latzel, *Europa zwischen Restauration und Revolution 1815–1849*, rev. edn (Munich, 1993).

M. V. Leggiere, *Napoleon and Berlin: Franco-Prussian War in North Germany, 1813* (Norman, OK, 2002).

M. V. Leggiere, 'From Berlin to Leipzig: Napoleon's Gamble in North Germany, 1813', *Journal of Military* History, 67 (2003), 39–84.

M. V. Leggiere, *The Fall of Napoleon: The Allied Invasion of France, 1813–1814* (Cambridge, 2007).

M. V. Leggiere, *Blücher: Scourge of Napoleon* (Norman, OK, 2014).

M. V. Leggiere, *Napoleon and the Struggle for Germany: The Franco-Prussian War of 1813* (Cambridge, 2015).

F. Lenger, 'Die Erinnerung an die Völkerschlacht bei Leipzig im Jubilaeumsjahr 1863', in M. Hettling (ed.), *Figuren und Strukturen* (Munich, 2002), 25–41.

J. Leonhard, 'Nation-States and Wars', in T. Baycroft and M. Hewitson (eds), *What Is a Nation? Europe, 1789–1914* (Oxford, 2006), 231–54.

J. Leonhard, *Bellizismus und Nation. Kriegsdeutung und Nationsbestimmung in Europa und den Vereinigten Staaten 1750–1914* (Munich, 2008).

W. B. Lerg, 'Geschichte der Kriegsberichterstattung', *Publizistik*, 37 (1992), 405–22.

M. Levinger, *Enlightened Nationalism: The Transformation of Prussian Political Culture, 1806–1848* (Oxford, 2000).

A. N. Liaropoulos, 'Revolutions in Warfare: Theoretical Paradigms and Historical Evidence – The Napoleonic and First World War Revolutions in Military Affairs', *Journal of Military History*, 70 (2006), 363–84.

D. Lieven, *Russia against Napoleon: The True Story of the Campaigns of War and Peace* (London, 2010).

M. van der Linden and G. Mergner (eds), *Kriegsbegeisterung und mentale Kriegsvorbereitung* (Berlin, 1991).

C. Lipp, 'Verein als poltisches Handlungsmuster. Das Beispiel des württembergischen Vereinswesens von 1800 bis zur Revolution 1848–49', in E. François (ed.), *Sociabilité et société bourgeoise en France, Allemagne et en Suisse 1750–1850* (Paris, 1986), 275–96.

E. Luard, *War in International Society* (London, 1986).

A. Lüdtke, 'Militärstaat und "Festungspraxis" – Staatliche Verwaltung, Beamtenschaft und Heer in Preussen, 1815–1850', in V. R. Berghahn (ed.), *Militarismus* (Cologne, 1975), 164–85.

A. Lüdtke, 'Praxis und Funktion staatlicher Repression. Preussen 1815–50', *Geschichte und Gesellschaft*, 3 (1977), 190–211.

A. Lüdtke, 'Von der "tätigen Verfassung" zur Abwehr von "Störern". Zur Theoriegeschichte von "Polizei" und staatlicher Zwangsgewalt im 19 und frühen 20 Jahrhundert', *Der Staat*, 20 (1981), 201–28.

A. Lüdtke, '"Wehrhafte Nation" und "innere Wohlfahrt". Zur militärischen Mobilisierbarkeit der bürgerlichen Gesellschaft', *Militärgeschichtliche Mitteilungen*, 30 (1981), 7–56.

A. Lüdtke, *'Gemeinwohl', Polizei und 'Festungspraxis'. Staatliche Gewaltsamkeit und innere Verwaltung in Preussen 1815–1850* (Göttingen, 1982).

A. Lüdtke (ed.), *'Sicherheit' und 'Wohlfahrt'. Polizei, Gesellschaft und Herrschaft im 19 und 20 Jahrhundert* (Frankfurt, 1992).

M. Lurz, *Kriegerdenkmäler in Deutschland* (Heidelberg, 1985), 3 vols.

K. Lütsch, *'Jeder Krieg ist anders. Jeder Krieg ist gleich.' Eine Analyse des Kriegsbegriffes bei Carl von Clausewitz* (Potsdam, 2009).

K.-H. Lutz, *Das badische Offizierkorps 1840–1870/71* (Stuttgart, 1997).

K. Luys, *Die Anfänge der deutschen Nationalbewegung von 1815 bis 1819* (Münster, 1992).

J. A. Lynn, *The Bayonets of the Republic: Motivation and Tactics in the Army of Revolutionary France, 1791–1794* (Urbana, IL, 1984).

I. F. McNeely, 'The Intelligence Gazette (*Intelligenzblatt*) as a Road Map to Civil Society: Information Networks and Local Dynamism in Germany, 1770s to 1840s', in F. Trentmann (ed.), *Paradoxes of Civil Society: New Perspectives on German and British History* (New York, 2000), 135–56.

H. Maier, 'Gewaltdeutungen im 19. Jahrhundert. Hegel, Goethe, Clausewitz, Nietzsche', in H. Maier (ed.), *Wege in der Gewalt. Die modernen politischen Religionen* (Frankfurt, 2000), 54–69.

C. v. Maltzahn, *Heinrich Leo 1799–1878: Ein politisches Gelehrtenleben zwischen romantischen Konservatismus und Realpolitik* (Göttingen, 1979).

U. Marwedel, *Carl von Clausewitz. Persönlichkeit und Wirkungsgeschichte seines Werks bis 1918* (Boppard, 1978).

M. Maurer, *Die Biographie des Bürgers. Lebensformen und Denkweisen in der formativen Phasen des deutschen Bürgertums 1618–1815* (Göttingen, 1996).

M. Maurer, 'Nationalcharakter und Nationalbewußtsein. England und Deutschland im Vergleich', in U. Herrmann (ed.), *Volk, Nation, Vaterland* (Hamburg, 1996), 89–100.

M. Messerschmidt, 'Die preussische Armee', in Militärgeschichtliches Forschungsamt (ed.), *Handbuch zur deutschen Militärgeschichte* (Munich, 1976), vol. 2, 3–225.

M. Messerschmidt, 'Preussens Militär in seinem gesellschaftlichen Umfeld', in H.-J. Puhle and H.-U. Wehler (eds), *Preussen im Rückblick* (Göttingen, 1980), 43–88.

M. Messerschmidt, 'Grundzüge der Geschichte des preussisch-deutschen Militärs', in H.-J. Gamm (ed.), *Militärischen Sozialisation* (Darmstadt, 1986), 17–57.

K. H. Metz, *Grundformen historiographischen Denkens. Wissenschaft als Methodologie* (Munich, 1979).

K. H. Metz, *Geschichte der Gewalt. Krieg, Revolution, Terror* (Primus, 2010).

M. Middell (ed.), *Widerstände gegen Revolutionen 1789–1989* (Leipzig, 1994).

H.-E. Mittig and V. Plagemann (eds), *Denkmaler im 19. Jahrhundert* (Munich, 1972).

E. Mochmann and U. Gerhardt (eds), *Gewalt in Deutschland. Soziale Befunde und Deutungslinie* (Munich, 1995).

E. Mohr, *Heeres- und Truppengeschichte des Deutschen Reiches und seiner Länder 1806 bis 1918. Eine Bibliographie* (Osnabrück, 1989).

H. Möller, *Fürstenstaat oder Bürgernation. Deutschland 1763-1815* (Berlin, 1998).

W. J. Mommsen, *Bürgerliche Kultur und politische Ordnung. Künstler, Schriftsteller und Intellektuelle in der deutschen Geschichte 1830–1933* (Frankfurt, 2000).

W. J. Mommsen and G. Hirschfeld (eds), *Sozialprotest, Gewalt, Terror. Gewaltanwendung durch politische und gesellschaftliche Randgruppen im 19. und 20. Jahrhundert* (Stuttgart, 1982).

J. Mooser, 'Rebellion und Loyalität 1789–1848. Sozialstruktur, sozialer Protest und poltiisches Verhalten laendlicher Unterschichten im östlichen Westfalen', in P. Steinbach (ed.), *Probleme politischer Partizipation in der Modernisierungsprozess* (Stuttgart, 1982), 57–87.

D. Moran, *Towards the Century of Words: Johann Cotta and the Politics of the Public Realm in Germany, 1795–1832* (Berkeley, CA, 1990).

D. Moran and A. Waldron (eds), *The People in Arms: Military Myth and National Mobilisation since the French Revolution* (Cambridge, 2003).

D. H. J. Morgan, 'Theatre of War: Combat, the Military and Masculinities', in H. Brod and M. Kaufmann (eds), *Theorizing Masculinities* (London, 1994), 165–82.

K. Moritz, *Das Ich am Ende des Schreibens. Autobiographisches Erzählen im 18. und frühen 19. Jahrhunderts* (Würzburg, 1990).

G. L. Mosse, *The Nationalization of the Masses: Political Symbolism and Mass Movements in Germany from the Napoleonic Wars through the Third Reich* (New York, 1975).

G. L. Mosse, *Fallen Soldiers* (Oxford, 1991).

K. Müller-Salget, *Erzählungen für das Volk. Evangelische Pfarrer als Volksschriftsteller in Deutschland des 19 Jahrhunderts* (Berlin, 1984).

B. v. Münchow-Pohl, *Zwischen Krieg und Reform. Untersuchungen zur Bewusstseinslage in Preussen 1809–1812* (Göttingen, 1987).

H. Münkler, 'Staat, Krieg und Frieden. Die verwechselte Wechselbeziehung', in R. Steinweg (ed.), *Kriegsursachen* (Frankfurt, 1987), 135–44.

H. Münkler, 'Dialektik des Militarismus oder Hegung des Krieges. Krieg und Frieden bei Clausewitz, Engels und Carl Schmitt', in H. Münkler, *Gewalt und Ordnung* (Frankfurt, 1992), 54–79.

H. Münkler, *Gewalt und Ordnung. Das Bild des Krieges im politischen Denken* (Frankfurt, 1992).

H. Münkler, 'Instrumentelle und existentielle Auffassung des Krieges bei Carl von Clausewitz', in H. Münkler, *Gewalt und Ordnung* (Frankfurt, 1992), 92–110.

H. Münkler, 'Feindbilder – Bilder vom Feind', in H. Münkler, *Politische Bilder, Politik der Metaphern* (Frankfurt, 1994).

H. Münkler, *Die Deutschen und ihre Mythen* (Hamburg, 2010).

J. Murken, 'Von "Thränen und Wehmut" zur Geburt des "deutschen Nationalbewußtseins". Die Niederlage des Russlandfeldzugs von 1812 und ihre Umdeutung in einen nationalen Sieg', in H. Carl, H. H. Kortum, D. Langewiesche, and F. Lenger (eds), *Kriegsniederlagen. Erfahrungen und Erinnerungen* (Berlin, 2004), 107–22.

J. Murken, *Bayerische Soldaten im Russlandfeldzug 1812. Ihre Kriegserfahrungen und derer Umdeutung im 19 und 20. Jahrhundert* (Munich, 2006).

A. Mürmann, *Die öffentliche Meinung in Deutschland über das preussische Wehrgesetz von 1814 während der Jahre 1814–1819* (Berlin, 1910).

K. B. Murr, '"Treue is in den Tod". Kriegsmythen in der bayerischen Geschichtspolitik im Vormärz', in N. Buschmann and D. Langewiesche (eds), *Der Krieg in der Gründungsmythen* (Tübingen, 2002), 138–74.

S. A. Mustafa, *The Long Ride of Major von Schill: A Journey through German History and Memory* (Lanham, MD, 2008).

M. Naumann, *Strukturwandel des Heroismus. Vom sakralen zum revolutionären Heldentum* (Königstein, 1984).

E. Neubuhr (ed.), *Geschichtsdrama* (Darmstadt, 1980).

J. Niemeyer, *Das österreichische Militärwesen im Umbruch. Untersuchen zum Kriegsbild zwischen 1830 und 1860* (Osnabrück, 1979).

W. Nippel, *Johann Gustav Droysen. Ein Leben zwischen Wissenschaft und Politik* (Munich, 2008).

T. Nipperdey, 'Nationalidee und Nationaldenkmal in Deutschland im 19. Jahrhundert', *Historische Zeitschrift*, 206 (1968), 529–85.

T. Nipperdey, 'Verein als soziale Struktur in Deutschland im späten 18. und frühen 19. Jahrhundert', in T. Nipperdey, *Gesellschaft, Kultur, Theorie* (Göttingen, 1976), 174–205.

T. Nipperdey, 'In Search of Identity: Romantic Nationalism', in J. C. Eade (ed.), *Romantic Nationalism in Europe* (Melbourne, 1983), 1–16.

T. Nipperdey, *Deutsche Geschichte 1800–1866*, 6th rev. edn (Munich, 1993), vol. 1.

H. G. Nitschke, *Die preußischen Militärreformen 1807–1813* (Berlin, 1983).

P. Nolte, *Staatsbildung als Gesellschaftsreform. Politische Reformen in Preußen und den süddeutschen Staaten 1800–1820* (Frankfurt, 1990).

N. Öllers, *Schiller—Zeitgenosse aller Epochen. Dokumente zur Wirkungsgeschichte Schillers in Deutschland* (Frankfurt, 1970), 2 vols.

C. Opitz, 'Der Bürger wird Soldat – und die Bürgerin? Die Revolution, der Krieg und die Stellung der Frauen nach 1789', in V. Schmidt-Linsenhoff (ed.), *Sklavin oder Bürgerin? Französische Revolution und Neue Weiblichkeit 1760–1830* (Frankfurt, 1989), 38–55.

C. Opitz (ed.), *Gerhard von Scharnhorst. Vom Wesen und Wirken der preußischen Heeresreform* (Bremen, 1998).

G. Ortenburg, *Heerwesen der Neuzeit. Waffen der Revolutionskrieg* (Augsburg, 2002), vol. 4.

G. Papke, 'Von der Miliz zum stehenden Heer', in *Handbuch zur deutschen Militärgeschichte 1648–1939* (Munich, 1979), vol. 1, 154–235.

P. Paret, *Yorck and the Era of Prussian Reform, 1807–1815* (Princeton, 1966).

P. Paret, *Clausewitz and the State*, new edn (Princeton, 1985).

P. Paret, 'Napoleon and the Revolution in War', in P. Paret (ed.), *The Makers of Modern Strategy* (Princeton, 1986), 123–42.

P. Paret, *Art as History: Episodes in the Culture and Politics of Nineteenth-Century Germany* (Princeton, 1988).

P. Paret, *Imagined Battles* (Chapel Hill, 1997).

P. Paret, *The Cognitive Challenge of War: Prussia, 1806* (Princeton, 2009).

G. Parker, 'The Military Revolution, 1560–1660 – A Myth?', *Journal of Modern History*, 48 (1976), 195–214.

G. Parker, *The Military Revolution: Military Innovation and the Rise of the West, 1500–1800* (Cambridge, 1988).

S. Parth, 'Medialisierung von Krieg in der deutschen Militärmalerei des 19. Jahrhunderts', in A. Jürgens-Kirchhoff and A. Matthias (eds), *Krieg, Kunst und Medien* (Weimar, 2006), 45–65.

S. Parth, *Zwischen Bildbericht und Bildpropaganda. Kriegskonstruktionene in der deutschen Militärmalerei des 19. Jahrhunderts* (Paderborn, 2010).

E. Pelzer, 'Die Wiedergeburt Deutschlands und die Dämonisierung Napoleons', in G. Krumeich and H. Lehmann (eds), *'Gott mit uns'. Nation, Relgion und Gewalt im 19. und frühen 20. Jahrhundert* (Göttingen, 2000), 135–56.

L. Peter, *Romances of War: Die Erinnerung an die Revolutions- und Napoleonischen Kriege in Großbritannien und Irland 1815–1945* (Paderborn, 2012).

H.-W. Pinkow, *Der literarische und parlamentarische Kampf gegen die Institution des stehenden Heeres in Deutschland in der ersten Hälfte des 19 Jahrhunderts 1815–1848* (Berlin, 1912).

J. Plamper, *Geschichte und Gefühl. Grundlagen der Emotionsgeschichte* (Munich, 2012).

U. Planert, 'Staat und Krieg an der Wende der Moderne', in W. Rösener (ed.), *Staat und Krieg. Vom Hochmittelalter bis zur Moderne* (Göttingen, 2000), 159–80.

U. Planert, 'Wessen Krieg? Welche Erfahrung? Oder: Wie national war der Nationalkrieg gegen Napoleon', in D. Beyrau (ed.), *Der Krieg in religiösen und nationalen Deutungen der Neuzeit* (Tübingen, 2001), 111–39.

U. Planert, 'Zwischen Alltag, Mentalität und Erinnerungskultur. Erfahrungsgeschichte an der Schwelle zum nationalen Zeitalter', in N. Buschmann and H. Carl (eds), *Die Erfahrung des Krieges* (Paderborn, 2001), 51–66.

U. Planert, 'Wann beginnt der "moderne" deutsche Nationalismus? Plädoyer für eine nationale Sattelzeit', in J. Echternkamp and S. O. Müller (eds), *Die Politik der Nation. Deutscher Nationalismus in Krieg und Krisen 1760–1960* (Munich, 2002), 25–59.

U. Planert, 'Auf dem Wege zum Befreiungskrieg. Das Jubiläum als Mythenstifter', in W. Müller (ed.), *Das historische Jubiläum* (Münster, 2004), 195–219.

U. Planert, 'From Collaboration to Resistance: Politics, Experience and Memory of the Revolutionary and Napoleonic Wars in Southern Germany', *Central European History*, 39 (2006), 676–705.

U. Planert, *Der Mythos vom Befreiungskrieg. Frankreichs Kriege und der deutsche Süden 1792–1841* (Paderborn, 2007).

U. Planert, 'Die Kriege der Französischen Revolution und Napoleons: Beginn einer neuen Ära der europäischen Kriegsgeschichte oder Weiterwirken der Vergangenheit?', in D. Beyrau, M. Hochgeschwender, and D. Langewiesche (eds), *Formen des Krieges* (Paderborn, 2007), 149–62.

U. Planert, 'Innovation or Evolution? The French Wars in Military History', in R. Chickering and S. Förster (eds), *War in an Age of Revolution, 1775–1815* (Cambridge, 2010), 69–84.

U. Planert, 'Vom Reichspatriotismus zur dynastisch-nationalen Kriegsmobilisierung. Das Freiburger Bürgermilitär in den Kriegen der Französischer Revolution', in R. Bergien and R. Pröve (eds), *Spiesser, Patrioten, Revolutionaere. Militärische Mobilisierung und gesellschaftliche Ordnung in der Neuzeit* (Göttingen, 2010), 215–34.

A. Platthaus, *1813. Die Völkerschlacht und das Ende der Alten Welt* (Berlin, 2013).

A. Portmann-Tinguely, *Romantik und Krieg. Eine Untersuchung zum Bild des Krieges bei deutschen Romantikern und 'Freiheitssängern'* (Freiburg, 1989).

S. Poser, *Die Völkerschlacht bei Leipzig. 'In Schutt und Graus begraben* (Leipzig, 2013).

C. Prendergast, *Napoleon and History Painting: Antoine-Jean Gros's La Bataille d'Eylau* (Oxford, 1997).

V. Press, 'Warum gab es keine deutsche Revolution? Deutschland und das revolutionäre Deutschland', in D. Langewiesche (ed.), *Revolution und Krieg* (Paderborn, 1989), 67–86.

C. Prignitz, *Vaterlandsliebe und Freiheit. Deutscher Patriotismus von 1750 bis 1850* (Wiesbaden, 1981).

R. Pröve, '"Der Mann des Mannes": "Civile" Ordnungsformationen, Staatsbürgerschaft und Männlichkeit im Vormaerz', in K. Hagemann and R. Pröve (eds), *Landsknechte, Soldatenfrauen und Nationalkrieger* (Frankfurt, 1998), 103–20.

R. Pröve, *Stadtgemeindlicher Republikanismus und die 'Macht des Volkes'. Civile Ordnungsformationen und kommunale Leitbilder politischer Partizipation in den deutschen Staaten vom Ende des 18 bis zur Mitte des 19 Jahrhunderts* (Göttingen, 2000).

R. Pröve, *Militär, Staat und Gesellschaft im Neunzehnten Jahrhundert* (Munich, 2006).

M. Puschner, *Antisemitismus im Kontext der poltischen Romantik. Konstruktionen des 'Deutschen' und des 'Jüdischen' bei Arnim, Brentano und Saul Ascher* (Tübingen, 2008).

N. Ramsey, *The Military Memoir and Romantic Literary Culture, 1780–1835* (Aldershot, 2011).

W. M. Reddy, 'Sentimentalism and Its Erasure: The Role of Emotions in the Era of the French Revolution', *Journal of Modern History*, 72 (2000), special issue, 109–52.

W. M. Reddy, *The Navigation of Feeling: A Framework for the History of Emotions* (Cambridge, 2001).

D. A. Reder, *Frauenbewegung und Nation. Patriotische Frauenvereine im frühen 19. Jahrhundert 1813–1830* (Cologne, 1998).

O. Regele, *Feldmarschall Radetzky* (Vienna, 1957).

V. Regling, 'Grundzüge der Landkriegführung zur Zeit des Absolutismus und im 19. Jahrhundert', in Militärgeschichtliches Forschungsamt (ed.), *Handbuch zur deutschen Militärgeschichte 1648–1939* (Munich, 1979), vol. 5, 11–425.

P. H. Reill, *The German Enlightenment and the Rise of Historicism* (Berkeley, 1975).

H. Reinalter, 'Heinrich Ritter von Srbik', in H-U Wehler (ed.), *Deutsche Historiker* (Göttingen, 1982), vol. 8, 86–7.

K. Repgen, 'Kriegslegitimation in Alteuropa. Entwurf einer historischen Typologies', *Historische Zeitschrift*, 241 (1985), 27–49.

J. Requate, *Journalismus als Beruf. Entstehung und Entwicklung des Journalistenberufs im 19. Jahrhundert* (Göttingen, 1995).

J. Requate, 'Öffentlichkeit und Medien als Gegenstände historischer Analyse', *Geschichte und Gesellschaft*, 25 (1999), 5–32.

K. Ries, 'Zwischen Wissenschaft, Staat und Gesellschaft. Heinrich Luden als politischer Professor der Universität Jena', in H.-W. Hahn (ed.), *Bürgertum in Thüringen. Lebenswelt und Lebenswege im frühen 19. Jahrhundert* (Jena, 2001), 27–52.

D. Riesenberger, *Geschichte des Friedensbewegung in Deutschland. Von den Anfängen bis 1933* (Göttingen, 1985).

A. Rigney, *The Rhetoric of Historical Representation: Three Narrative Histories of the French Revolution* (Cambridge, 1990).

M. Rink, *Vom Partheygänger zum Partisanen. Die Konzeption des kleinen Krieges in Preußen 1740–1813* (Frankfurt, 1999).

M. Rink, 'Der kleine Krieg. Entwicklung und Trends asymmetrischer Gewalt 1740 bis 1815', *Militärgeschichtliche Zeitschrift*, 65 (2006), 355–88.

G. Ritter, *Staatskunst und Kriegshandwerk* (Munich, 1970), vol. 1.

M. Roberts, 'The Military Revolution, 1560–1660', in M. Roberts, *Essays on Swedish History* (Minneapolis, 1967), 195–225.

C. J. Rogers (ed.), *The Military Revolution Debate* (Boulder, CO, 1995).

D. Rogosch, 'Das Heilige Römische Reich Deutscher Nation und die Entstehung des deutschen Nationalgefühls', in H. Timmermann (ed.), *Die Entstehung der Nationalbewegung in Europa 1750–1849* (Berlin, 1993), 15–28.

H. N. Röhloff (ed.), *Napoleon kam nicht nur bis Waterloo. Die Spur des gestürzten Giganten in Literatur und Sprache, Kunst und Karikatur* (Frankfurt, 1992), 328–77.

S. Rohrbacher, *Gewalt im Biedermeier. Antijüdischer Ausschreitungen in Vormärz und Revolution 1815–1848/49* (Frankfurt, 1993).

K. A. Roider, *Baron Thugut and Austria's Response to the French Revolution* (Princeton, 1987).

B. V. A. Röling, Einführung *in die Wissenschaft von Krieg und Frieden* (Neukirchen-Vluyn, 1970).

P. L. Rose, *Revolutionary Antisemitism in Germany from Kant to Wagner* (Princeton, 1990).

H. Rosenberg, *Bureaucracy, Aristocracy and Autocracy: The Prussian Experience, 1660–1815* (Boston, 1966).

W. Rösener (ed.), *Staat und Krieg. Vom Hochmittelalter bis zur Moderne* (Göttingen, 2000).

G. E. Rothenberg, *Napoeleon's Great Adversaries: The Archduke Charles and the Austrian Army, 1792–1814* (Bloomington, IN, 1982).

G. E. Rothenberg, *The Napoleonic Wars* (London, 1999).

G. E. Rothenberg, *The Emperor's Last Victory: Napoleon and the Battle of Wagram* (London, 2004).

M. Rowe, 'Divided Loyalties: Sovereignty, Politics and Public Service in the Rhineland under French Occupation, 1792–1801', *European Review of History*, 5 (1998), 151–68.

M. Rowe, 'Between Empire and Home Town: Napoleonic Rule on the Rhine, 1799–1814', *Historical Journal*, 42 (1999), 643–74.

M. Rowe, *From Reich to State: The Rhineland in the Revolutionary Age, 1780–1830* (Cambridge, 2003).

M. Rowe, 'Resistance, Collaboration or Third Way? Responses to Napoleonic Rule in Germany', in C. J. Esdaile (ed.), *Popular Resistance in the French Wars: Patriots, Partisans and Land Pirates* (Basingstoke, 2003), 67–90.

F. Ruof, *Johan Wilhelm von Archenholtz: Ein deutscher Schriftsteller zur Zeit der Französischen Revolution und Napoleons (1741–1812)* (Berlin, 1915).

J. Rüsen, *Begriffene Geschichte. Genesis und Begründung der Geschichtstheorie J. G. Droysens* (Paderborn, 1969).

J. Rüsen, 'Die vier Typen des historischen Erzählens', in J. Rüsen, *Zeit und Sinn. Strategien historischen Denkens* (Frankfurt, 1990), 153–230.

R. Safranski, *Romantik* (Munich, 2007).

M. Salewski, 'Vom Kabinettskrieg zum totalen Krieg. Der Gestaltwandel des Krieges im 19. und 20. Jahrhundert', in U. Lappenküper (ed.), *Masse und Macht im 19 und 20. Jahrhundert* (Munich, 2003), 51–66.

P. Sauer, *Das württembergische Heer in der Zeit des Deutschen und des Norddeutschen Bundes* (Stuttgart, 1958).

P. Sauer, *Revolution und Volksbewaffnung* (Ulm, 1976).

P. Sauer, *Napoleons Adler über Württemberg, Baden und Hohenzollern. Südwestdeutschland in der Rheinbundzeit* (Stuttgart, 1987).

L. Scales and O. Zimmer (eds), *Power and the Nation in European History* (Cambridge, 2005).

K. H. Schäfer, 'Zur Frühgeschichte der Feldzeitungen', *Publizistik*, 18 (1973), 160–4.

K. H. Schäfer, *Ernst Moritz Arndt als politischer Publizist. Studien zu Publizistik, Pressepolitik und kollektivem Bewusstsein im frühen 19. Jahrhundert* (Bonn, 1974).

R. Schenda, 'Schundliteratur und Kriegsliteratur', in R. Schenda, *Die Lesestoff der Kleinen Leute* (Munich, 1976), 78–104.

R. Schenda, *Volk ohne Buch* (Munich, 1977).

T. Schieder, 'Die historische Krisen im Geschichtsdenken Jacob Burckhardts', in T. Schieder, *Begegnungen mit der Geschichte* (Göttingen, 1962).

A. Schildt, *Konservatismus in Deutschland* (Munich, 1998).

R. Schilling, 'Die soziale Konstruktion heroischer Männlichkeit im 19. Jahrhundert. Das Beispiel Theodor Körner', in K. Hagemann and R. Pröve (eds), *Landsknechte, Soldatenfrauen und Nationalkrieger* (Frankfurt, 1998), 121–44.

R. Schilling, 'Der Körper des "Helden" – Deutschland 1813 bis 1945', in S. Conze (ed.), *Körper macht Geschichte—Geschichte Macht Körper* (Bielefeld, 1999), 119–40.

R. Schilling, *'Kriegshelden'. Deutungsmuster heroischer Männlichkeit in Deutschland 1813–1945* (Paderborn, 2002).

G. Schmid, 'Die Gedenkjahre 1859 und 1905 als Brennpunkte bürgerlicher Schiller-Verehrung in Deutschland', in W. Dietze und W. Schubert (eds), *Berichte zur deutschen Klassik und Romantik* (Berlin, 1986), 90–114.

D. Schmidt, *Die preussische Landwehr* (Berlin, 1981).

M. Schmidt, 'Die Apotheose des Krieges im 18 und frühen 19 Jahrhundert im detuschen Dichten und Denken', in W. Huber and J. Schwerdtfeger (eds), *Kirche zwischen Krieg und Frieden* (Stuttgart, 1976), 130–66.

W. Schmidt, 'Denkmäler für die bayerischen Gefallenen des Russlandfeldzuges von 1812', *Zeitschrift für bayerische Landesgeschichte*, 49 (1986), 303–26.

W. Schmidt, *Eine Stadt und ihr Militär. Regensburg als bayerische Garnisonsstadt im 19 und frühen 20 Jahrhundert* (Regensburg, 1993).

H. Schnabel-Schüle, *Überwachen und Strafen im Territorialstaat* (Cologne, 1997).

E. Schneider, 'Revolutionserlebnis und Frankreichbild zur Zeit des ersten Revolutionskrieges', *Francia*, 8 (1980), 277–393.

E. Schneider, 'Das Bild der französischen Revolutionsarmee', in J. Voss (ed.), *Deutschland und die französische Revolution* (Munich, 1983).

F. Schneider, *Aufklärung und Politik. Studien zur Politisierung der deutschen Spätaufklärung am Beispiel A. G. F. Rebmanns* (Wiesbaden, 1978).

H. Schneider, 'Revolutionäre Lieder und vaterländische Gesänge', in U. Herrmann (ed.), *Volk—Nation—Vaterland* (Hamburg, 1996), 291–324.

U. Schneider, *Politische Festkultur im 19. Jahrhundert. Die Rheinprovinz von der französischen Zeit bis zum Ende des Ersten Weltkrieges 1806–1918* (Essen, 1995).

W. Schnell, *Georg Friedrich Kersting 1785–1847* (Berlin, 1994).

K.-H. Schodrok, *Militärische Jugend-Erziehung in Preussen 1806–1820* (Olsberg, 1989).

E. Schön, *Der Verlust der Sinnlichkeit, oder die Verwandlungen des Lesers. Mentalitätswandel um 1800* (Stuttgart, 1987).

D. Schönpflug, *Luise von Preussen. Eine Biographie* (Munich, 2010).

F. H. Schubert, 'Volkssouveränität und Heiliges Roemisches Reich', *Historische Zeitschrift*, 213 (1971), 91–122.

G. Schuck, *Rheinbundpatriotismus und politische Öffentlichkeit zwischen Aufklärung und Frühliberalismus. Kontinuitätsdenken und Diskontinuitätserfahrung in den Staatsrechts- und Verfassungsdebatten der Rheinbundpublizistik* (Stuttgart, 1994).

A. Schulz, 'Der Aufstieg der "vierte Gewalt". Medien, Politik und Öffentlichkeit im Zeitalter der Massenkommunikation', *Historische Zeitschrift*, 270 (2000), 65–97.

H. Schulze, *Der Weg zum Nationalstaat. Die deutsche Nationalbewegung vom 18. Jahrhundert bis zur Reichsgründung* (Munich, 1983).

H.-D. Schultz, 'Land, Volk, Staat. Der geographische Anteil an der "Erfindung" der Nation', *Geschichte in Wissenschaft und Unterricht*, 54 (2000), 4–16.

D. Schumann, 'Gewalt als Grenzüberschreitung: Überlegungen zur Sozialgeschichte der Gewalt im 19. und 20. Jahrhundert', *Archiv für Sozialgeschichte*, 37 (1997), 366–86.

K. v. See, 'Held und Kollektiv', *Zeitschrift für Altertum und deutsche Literatur*, 122 (1993), 1–35.

K. v. See, *Barbar, Germane, Arier* (Heidelberg, 1994).

H. Seier, *Die Staatsidee Heinrich von Sybels in der Wandlungen der Reichsgründungszeit 1862/1871* (Lübeck, 1961).

L. Sharpe, *Friedrich Schiller: Drama, Thought and Politics* (Cambridge, 1991).

J. J. Sheehan, 'Liberalism and the City in Nineteenth-Century Germany', *Past and Present*, 51 (1971), 116–37.

J. J. Sheehan, 'What Is German History?', *Journal of Modern History*, 53 (1981), 1–23.

J. J. Sheehan, 'The Problem of the Nation in Germany History', in O. Buesch and J. J. Sheehan (eds), *Die Rolle der Nation in der deutschen Geschichte und Gegenwart* (Berlin, 1985), 3–20.

J. J. Sheehan, *German History, 1770–1866* (Oxford, 1989).

J. J. Sheehan, 'State and Nationality in the Napoleonic Period', in J. J. Breuilly (ed.), *The State of Germany: The National Idea in the Making, Unmaking and Remaking of a Modern Nation-State* (London, 1992), 47–59.

J. J. Sheehan, 'Nation und Staat: Deutschland als "imaginierte Gemeinschaft"', in M. Hettling and P. Nolte (eds), *Nation und Gesellschaft in Deutschland* (Munich, 1996), 33–45.

J. J. Sheehan, *Museums in the German Art World from the End of the Old Regime to the Rise of Modernism* (Oxford, 2000).

D. E. Showalter, 'Weapons and Ideas in the Prussian Army from Frederick the Great to Moltke the Elder', in J. A. Lynn (ed.), *Tools of War: Instruments, Ideas and Institutions of Warfare, 1445–1871* (Chicago, 1990), 177–210.

D. E. Showalter, 'Hubertusburg to Auerstädt: The Prussian Army in Decline?', *German History*, 12 (1994), 25–50.

K. Siblewski, *Rittlicher Patriotismus und romantischer Nationalismus in der deutschen Literatur 1770–1830* (Munich, 1981).

B. Sicken (ed.), *Staat und Militär 1815–1914* (Paderborn, 1998).

M. Siebe, *Von der Revolution zum nationalen Feindbild. Frankreich und Deutschland in der poltisichen Karikatur des 19. Jahrhunderts* (Münster, 1995).

R. P. Sieferle and H. Breuninger (eds), *Kulturen der Gewalt. Ritualisierung und Symbolisierung von Gewalt in der Geschichte* (Frankfurt, 1998).

W. Siemann, 'Heere, Freischaren, Barrikaden. Die bewaffnete Macht als Instrument der Innenpolitik in Europa 1815–1847', in D. Langewiesche (ed.), *Die deutsche Revolution von 1848/49* (Darmstadt, 1983), 87–102.

W. Siemann, *'Deutschlands Ruhe, Sicherheit und Ordnung'. Die Anfänge der politischen Polizei 1806–1866* (Tübingen, 1985).

W. Siemann, 'Ideenschmuggel. Probleme der Meinungskontrolle und das Los deutscher Zenoren im 19. Jahrhundert', *Historische Zeitschrift*, 245 (1987), 71–106.

W. Siemann, *Vom Staatenbund zum Nationalstaat. Deutschland 1806–1871* (Munich, 1995).

M. Sikora, 'Verzweiflung oder Leichtsinn? Militärstand und Desertion im 18. Jahrhundert', in B. R. Kroener and R. Pröve (eds), *Krieg und Frieden. Militär und Gesellschaft in der Frühen Neuzeit* (Paderborn, 1996), 237–64.

M. Sikora, 'Desertion und nationale Mobilmachung. Militärische Verweigerung 1792–1815', in U. Bröckling and M. Sikora (eds), *Armeen und ihre Deserteure* (Göttingen, 1998), 112–40.

M. Sikora, 'Scharnhorst und die militärische Revolution', in J. Kunisch and H. Münkler (eds), *Die Wiedergeburt des Krieges aus dem Geist der Revolution. Studien zum bellizistischen Diskurs des ausgehenden 18. und beginnenden 19. Jahrhunderts* (Berlin, 1999), 153–83.

M. Sikora, 'Aneignung zur Abwehr. Scharnhorst, Frankreich und die preußische Heeresreform', in M. Aust (ed.), *Vom Gegner Lernen* (Frankfurt, 2007), 61–94.

M. Sikora, 'Scharnhorst. Lehrer, Stabsoffizier, Reformer', in K.-H. Lutz (ed.), *Reform, Reorganisation, Transformation* (Munich, 2010), 43–64.

J. Smets, 'Von der "Dorfidylle" zur preußischen Nation. Sozialdisziplinierung der linksrheinischen Bevölkerung durch die Franzosen am Beispiel der allgemeinen Wehrpflicht (1802–1814)', *Historische Zeitschrift*, 262 (1996), 695–738.

C. Sommerhage, *Caspar David Friedrich* (Paderborn, 1993).

J. Sperber, 'Echoes of the French Revolution in the Rhineland, 1830–1849', *Central European History*, 22 (1989), 200–17.

J. Sperber (ed.), *Short Oxford History of Germany, 1800–1870* (Oxford, 2004).

R. Speth, *Nation und Revolution. Politische Mythen im 19 Jahrhundert* (Opladen, 2000).

H.-B. Spies (ed.), *Die Erhebung gegen Napoleon 1806–1814/15* (Darmstadt, 1981).

S. A. Stargardter, *Niklas Vogt, 1756–1836: A Personality of the Late German Enlightenment and Early Romantic Movement* (New York, 1991).

P. N. Stearns and C. Z. Stearns, 'Emotionology: Clarifying the History of Emotions and Emotional Standards', *American Historical Review*, 90 (1985), 813–36.

H.-P. Stein, *Symbole und Zeremoniell in detuschen Streitkräften vom 18 bis zum 20 Jahrhundert* (Herford, 1984).

A. Stephens, 'Kleist's Mythicisation of the Napoleonic Era', in J. C. Eade (ed.), *Romantic Nationalism in Europe* (Canberra, 1983), 165–80.

W. v. Sternburg, *Fall und Aufstieg der deutschen Nation. Nachdenken über einen Massenrauch* (Frankfurt, 1993).

F. S. Steussy, *Eighteenth-Century Autobiography: The Emergence of Individuality* (New York, 1996).

H. v. Stietencron and J. Rüpke (eds), *Töten im Krieg* (Freiburg, 1995).

R. Stöber, *Deutsche Pressegeschichte* (Constance, 2000).

E. Stolpe, 'Der Krieg als Drama der Leidenschaften. Paradigmawechsel in der militärischen Malerei des napoleonischen Zeitalters', in E. Mai (ed.), *Historienmalerei in Europa* (Mainz, 1990), 173–91.

H. Strachan, 'Essay and Reflection: On Total War and Modern War', *International History Review*, 22 (2000), 341–70.

B. Struck, *Nicht West, nicht Ost. Frankreich und Polen in der Wahrnehmung deutscher Reisender zwischen 1750 und 1850* (Göttingen, 2006).

B. Struck, 'War, Occupation and Entanglements: The Napoleonic Era in German Perspectives', in C. Germond and H. Türk (eds), *A History of Franco-German Relations in Europe: From 'Hereditary Enemies' to Partners* (Basingstoke, 2008), 27–38.

H. Stübig, *Armee und Nation. Die pädagogisch-politischen Motive der preußischen Heeresreform 1807–1814* (Frankfurt, 1971).

H. Stübig, 'Die preußische Heeresreform in der Geschichtsschreibung der Bundesrepublik Deutschland', *Militärgeschichtliches Mitteilungen*, 48 (1990), 27–40.

H. Stübig, 'Die Armee als "Schule der Nation". Entwicklungslinien der sozialen Militarisierung im 19. Jahrhundert', in H. Stübig, *Bildung, Militär und Gesellschaft in Deutschland* (Cologne, 1994), 9–24.

H. Stübig, 'Die Wehrverfassung Preussens in der Reformzeit. Wehrpflicht im Spannungsfeld von Restauration und Revolution 1815–1860', in R. Foerster (ed.), *Die Wehrpflicht* (Munich, 1994), 39–53.

H. Szepe, 'Opfertod und Poesie. Zur Geschichte der Theodor-Koerner-Legende', *Colloquia Germanica*, 9 (1975), 291–304.

C. Tacke, *Denkmal im sozialen Raum. Nationale Symbole in Deutschland und Frankreich im 19. Jahrhundert* (Göttingen, 1995).

J. M. Thompson, *Napoleon Bonaparte* (Oxford, 1988).

C. Tilly (ed.), *The Formation of Nation-States in Western Europe* (Princeton, 1975).

R. Tilly, 'Unruhen und Proteste in Deutschland im 19 Jahrhundert', in R. Tilly, *Kapitalismus, Staat und sozialer Protest in der deutschen Industrialisierung* (Göttingen, 1980).

J. Toews, *Becoming Historical: Cultural Reformation and Public Memory in Early Nineteenth-Century Berlin* (Cambridge, 2004).

R. Töppel, *Die Sachsen und Napoleon. Ein Stimmungsbild 1806–1813* (Cologne, 2008).

A.-C. Trepp, 'The Emotional Side of Men in Late Eighteenth-Century Germany', *Central European History*, 27 (1994), 127–52.

A.-C. Trepp, 'Anders als sein "Geschlechtscharakter". Der bürgerliche Mann um 1800 – Ferdinand Beneke 1774–1848', *Historische Anthropologie*, 4 (1996), 57–77.

A.-C. Trepp, *Sanfte Männlichkeit und selbständige Weiblichkeit. Frauen und Männer im Hamburger Bürgertum zwischen 1770 und 1840* (Göttingen, 1996).

E. Trox, *Militärischer Konservatismus. Kriegervereine und 'Militärpartei' in Preussen zwischen 1815 und 1848/49* (Stuttgart, 1990).

E. Trox, 'Kriegerfeste, militärische Männerbunde und politisierte Offiziere', *Militärgeschichtliche Mitteilungen*, 51 (1992), 23–46.

H. Überhorst (ed.), *Friedrich Ludwig Jahn 1778/1978* (Munich, 1978).

P. Ufer, *Leipziger Presse 1789 bis 1815. Eine Studie zu Entwicklungstendenzen und Kommunikationsbedingungen des Zeitungs- und Zeitschriftenwesens zwischen Französischer Revolution und den Befreiungskriegen* (Münster, 2000).

M. Umbach, *Federalism and Enlightenment in Germany, 1740–1806* (London, 2000).

W. v. Ungern-Sternberg, 'Medien', in K.-E. Jeismann and P. Lundgreen (eds), *Handbuch der deutschen Bildungsgeschichte* (Munich, 1987), vol. 3, 380–418.

A. Uwe, *Die Rheinländer, die Revolution und der Krieg, 1794–1798* (Essen, 1994).

C. Väterlein (ed.), *Baden und Württemberg im Zeitalter Napoleons* (Stuttgart, 1987), vol. 1.

W. Vaughan, *German Romantic Painting* (New Haven, 1980).

V. Veltzke, *Für die Freiheit—Gegen Napoleon. Ferdinand von Schill, Preussen und die deutsche Nation* (Cologne, 2009).

B. Vick, 'Greek Origins and Organic Metaphors: Ideals of Cultural Autonomy in Neohumanist Germany from Winckelmann to Curtius', *Journal of the History of Ideas*, 63 (2002), 483–500.

R. Vierhaus, *Ranke und die soziale Welt* (Münster, 1957).

W. R. Vogt (ed.), *Militär als Lebenswelt* (Opladen, 1988).

H. Volkman, 'Kategorien des sozialen Protestes im Vormaerz', *Geschichte und Gesellschaft*, 3 (1977), 164–89.

H. Volkman, 'Protestträger und Protestformen in den Unruhen von 1830 bis 1832', in H. Volkman and Bergmann (eds), *Sozialer Protest. Studien zu traditioneller Resistenz und kollektiver Gewalt in Deutschland vom Vormärz bis zur Reichsgründung* (Opladen, 1984).

M. Wagner, 'Germania und ihre Freier. Zur Herausbildung einer deutschen nationalen Ikonographie um 1800', in U. Hermann (ed.), *Volk—Nation—Vaterland* (Hamburg, 1996), 244–67.

J. Wallach, *Kriegstheorien. Ihre Entwicklung im 19. und 20. Jahrhundert* (Frankfurt, 1972).

M. Wallenborn, *Deutschland und die Deutschen in Mme de Staëls De l'Allemagne* (Frankfurt, 1998).

D. Walter, *Preußische Heeresreformen 1807–1870* (Paderborn, 2003).

D. Walter, 'Reluctant Reformers, Observant Disciples: The Prussian Military Reforms, 1807–1814', in R. Chickering and S. Förster (eds), *War in an Age of Revolution, 1775–1815* (Cambridge, 2010), 85–101.

G. Wawro, *Warfare and Society in Europe, 1792–1914* (London, 2000).

E. Weber, *Lyrik der Befreiungskriege 1812–1815. Gesellschaftliche Meinungs- und Willensbildung durch Literatur* (Stuttgart, 1991).

E. Weber, 'Der Krieg und die Poeten. Theodor Körners Kriegsdichtung und ihre Rezeption im Kontext des reformpolitischen Bellizismus der Befreiungskriegslyrik', in J. Kunisch und H. Münkler (eds), *Die Wiedergeburt des Krieges aus dem Geist der Revolution* (Berlin, 1999), 285–325.

B. Wegner (ed.), *Wie Kriege entstehen. Zum historischen Hintergrund von Staatenkonflikten* (Paderborn, 2000).

H.-U. Wehler, *Deutsche Gesellschaftsgeschichte 1700–1815* (Munich, 1987), vol. 1.

H.-U. Wehler, 'Nationalstaat und Krieg', in W. Rösener (ed.), *Staat und Krieg. Vom Hochmittelalter bis zur Moderne* (Göttingen, 2000), 225–40.

H.-U. Wehler, 'Nationalstaat und Krieg', in H.-U. Wehler, *Umbruch und Kontinuität* (Munich, 2000), 64–80.

R. Weigley, *The Age of Battles: The Quest for Decisive Warfare from Breitenfeld to Waterloo* (Bloomington, IN, 1991).

E. Weis, *Montgelas* (Munich, 1971–2005), 2 vols.

E. Weis, 'Die aussenpolitischen Reaktionen der deutschen Staaten auf die französische Hegemonialpolitik: zwischen Widerstand und Anpassung', in K. O. v. Aretin and G. A. Ritter (eds), *Historismus und modern Geschichtswissenschaft* (Stuttgart, 1987), 185–200.

M. Welke, 'Zeitung und Öffentlichkeit im 18. Jahrhundert. Betrachtungen zur Reichweite und Funktion der periodischen deutschen Tagespublizistik', in E. Blühm (ed.), *Presse und Geschichte* (Munich, 1977), 71–99.

M. Welke, 'Die Presse und ihre Leser. Zur Geschichte des Zeitungslesens in Deutschland von den Anfängen bis zum frühen 19. Jahrhundert', in K. Beyrer and M. Dallmeier (eds), *Als die Post noch Zeitung machte* (Frankfurt, 1994), 140–7.

U. Wender, 'Bauerliche Gewalt und Widerstand gegen Soldaten – der Hegau 1796', in J. Deventer (ed.), *Zeitenwenden. Herrschaft, Selbstbehauptung und Integration zwischen Reformation und Liberalismus* (Muenster, 2000), 403–20.

W. Wette (ed.), *Der Krieg des kleinen Mannes. Eine Militärgeschichte von unten* (Munich, 1992).

J. Whaley, *Germany and the Holy Roman Empire, 1493–1806* (Oxford, 2012), 2 vols.

C. White, *The Enlightened Soldier: Scharnhorst and the 'Militärische Gesellschaft' in Berlin, 1801–1805* (New York, 1989).

E. Wienhoefer, *Das Militärwesen des Deutschen Bundes und das Ringen zwischen Österreich und Preussen um die Vorherrschaft in Deutschland 1815–1866* (Osnabrück, 1973).

S. Wilkinson, *The French Army before Napoleon* (Aldershot, 1991).

E. Willems, *Der preussisch-deutsche Militarismus. Ein Kulturkomplex im sozialen Wandel* (Cologne, 1984).

P. H. Wilson, *German Armies: War and German Society, 1648–1806* (London, 1998).

P. H. Wilson, 'European Warfare, 1450–1815', in J. Black (ed.), *War in the Early Modern World* (London, 1999), 177–206.

P. H. Wilson, 'Bolstering the Prestige of the Habsburgs: The End of the Holy Roman Empire in 1806', *International History Review*, 28 (2006), 709–36.

H. A. Winkler, *Der lange Weg nach Westen. Deutsche Geschichte vom Ende des Alten Reiches bis zum Untergang der Weimarer Republik* (Munich, 2000), vol. 1.

B. Wirsing, '"Gleichsam mit Soldatenstrenge". Neue Polizei in süddeutschen Städten', in A. Lüdtke (ed.), *Sicherheit* (Göttingen, 1992), 65–94.

R. Wirtz, '*Widersetzlichkeiten, Excesse, Crawalle, Tumulte und Skandale'. Soziale Bewegung und gewalthafter Sozialer Protest in Baden 1815–1848* (Berlin, 1981).

R. Wirtz, 'Bemerkungen zum "sozialen Protest" in Baden 1815–1848. Determinanten, Motive und Verhaltensmuster', in H. Volkmann and J. Bergmann (eds), *Protest*, (Opladen, 1984), 36–55.

M. Wishon, *German Forces and the British Army: Interactions and Perceptions, 1742–1813* (Basingstoke, 2013).

R. Wittmann, *Geschichte des deutschen Buchhandels* (Munich, 1991).

R. Wittram (ed.), *Das Nationale als europäisches Problem. Beiträge zur Geschichte des Nationalitätsprinzips vornehmlich im 19. Jahrhundert* (Göttingen, 1954).

R. Wohlfeil, 'Vom stehenden Heer de.s Absolutismus zur Allgemeinen Wehrpflicht 1789–1814', in H.-M. Wecker (ed.), *Handbuch zur deutschen Militärgeschichte 1648–1939* (Frankfurt, 1964), vol. 1.

R. Wohlfeil, *Vom stehenden Heer des Absolutismus zur Allgemeinen Wehrpflicht 1789–1814* (Munich, 1979).

R. Wohlfeil, 'Militärgeschichte. Zu Geschichte und Problemen einer Disziplin der Geschichtswissenschaft', *Militärgeschichtliche Mitteilungen*, 52 (1993), 323–44.

E. Wolfrum, *Krieg und Frieden in der Neuzeit* (Darmstadt, 2003).

B. S. Wright, 'An Image for Imagining the Past: Delacroix, Cromwell and Romantic Historical Painting', *Clio*, 21 (1992), 243–63.

A. Zamoyski, *Moscow 1812: Napoleon's Fatal March* (New York, 2004).

S. Zantop, 'Re-presenting the Present: History and Literature in Restoration Germany', *Modern Language Notes*, 102 (1987), 570–86.

Y.-L. Zhang, 'Ideales denken, um Reales zu begreifen. Die methodischen Aspekte des Absoluten Krieges bei Carl von Clausewitz', *Zeitschrift für Politik*, 42 (1995), 369–82.

B. Ziemann (ed.), *Perspektiven der historischen Friedensforschung* (Essen, 2002).

H. Zimmer, *Auf dem Altar des Vaterlands. Religion und Patriotismus in der deutschen Kriegslyrik des 19. Jahrhunderts* (Frankfurt, 1971).

T. Ziolkowski, *Berlin. Aufstieg einer Kulturmetropole um 1810* (Stuttgart, 2002).

Index

Aaslestad, Katherine 7
absolute democracy 94
absolute war 1–3, 6, 38
Abyssinia 17
Achilles 164
Adam, Albrecht 183–4, 215, 242, 245
Adorno, Theodor 12
Alexander I, Tsar of Russia 57
Alexander III (Alexander the Great), King of
    Macedon 68
Ancillon, Jean-Pierre Frédéric 87
animal 11, 15–17, 27, 70, 116, 127, 146, 154,
    184, 193
Archenholz, Johann Wilhelm 88, 259
Aretin, Johann Christian 109
aristocracy, *see* nobility
Arndt, Ernst Moritz 79–81, 84–5, 90, 93, 109,
    112, 115, 122, 136, 148, 152, 154–5,
    210–12, 215, 235–6, 240, 250
  and Geist der Zeit (1806–9) 79–80, 115–16
Arnim, Achim von 97, 121
Arnim, Bettina von 239
artillery 34–5, 39–41, 48, 62–3, 67, 153, 162,
    164, 174–5, 194, 202, 207
Auerstädt, battle of (1806) 33–4, 46, 49, 52,
    64–5, 92, 101, 149, 163, 166–7, 171,
    175, 181
August, Prince of Prussia 39
Auschwitz, *see* Holocaust
Austria 1, 5, 31–3, 36–40, 43–8, 51–8,
    63–71, 86, 90–1, 95, 97, 105–8, 111,
    118, 124–8, 140–1, 145–6, 164, 168,
    174, 182, 186–9, 196–202, 206–7,
    213, 215, 219, 224–6, 231, 233–7,
    245, 247, 283
autobiography 27–30

Baberowski, Jörg 9–11
Baden, Grand Duchy of 32–3, 45, 47–8, 52–8,
    65–6, 78, 83, 105, 108, 111–12, 116,
    128, 140, 143, 145–6, 150, 167–8, 183,
    185, 188, 191, 195, 205, 207, 209,
    212–13, 218, 232, 239, 242, 248
balance of power 97, 226–31
Bamberger Zeitung 133
barbarity 9–11, 80, 116, 119, 176, 192, 226,
    232, 237
Batavian Republic 31
Bauman, Zygmunt 11
Bautzen, battle of (1813) 69, 149, 182
Bavaria, Kingdom of 26–7, 32–3, 46, 48,
    54–5, 58–9, 65, 68, 77, 83, 86, 105,
    109–10, 116, 128–9, 140, 144, 150, 155,

160–2, 167, 171, 177, 183, 189–90,
    194–5, 212–15, 217–18, 232, 237
Beauharnais, Stéphanie de 56
Beccaria, Cesare 130
Becker, Frank 5
Beethoven, Ludwig von 97
Beguelin, Amalie von 149
Behr, Wilhelm Josef 110
Bell, David 6, 42, 159, 246–7
Below, Gustav von 236
Benjamin, Walter 14
Beowulf 164
Beresina, crossing of (1812) 66, 116, 175–7,
    192–3, 215
Berg, Grand Duchy of 32
Berger, Stefan 5
Berliner Nachrichten 214
Berlinische Monatshefte 95
Bernadotte, Jean-Baptiste 49
bio-politics 22
Blücher, Gebhardt Leberecht von 52, 63, 69–70,
    149, 166, 172–3, 196, 206–7, 210, 218,
    235, 242
Bodo von Bodenhausen, Carl 176–7
Bolte, Heinrich 181–2
Boring, E. G. 26
Borodino, battle of (1812) 159, 162–3, 175,
    184–6, 189, 191, 201, 232
Bourdieu, Pierre 14
Bourke, Joanna 17, 27, 132
Boyen, Hermann von 33, 37, 52, 63–5, 197–8,
    206, 240
Brandes, Ernst 111
Brandt, Peter 8
Brentano, Clemens 97
Breuilly, John 5
Britain 11–12, 31, 37, 91, 93, 163, 234
Broers, Michael 6–7, 247
Brunswick (Braunschweig), Karl Wilhelm
    Ferdinand, Duke of 34–5, 44, 49, 64–5,
    162, 172
Burschenschaft (student association) 178, 219,
    221–4, 236
Buschmann, Nikolaus 25–6
Bülow, Friedrich Wilhelm von 197, 241
Bürgertum (middle class) 29, 76–7, 83–4, 87,
    105–7, 221–2, 252
Büttner, Heinrich Christoph 144

cabinet 119, 234
cabinet war 34–43, 51–60, 71, 119
Camphausen, Wilhelm 242

Campo Formio, Treaty of (1797) 32–3, 46
Canitz und Dallwitz, Carl Ernst
    Wilhelm 187–8
cantonal system 37, 46–7, 50–1, 53–4
capital punishment 126–31
Carl, Horst 25–6
Catherine, Tsarina 46
Catholicism 55, 94, 99, 105, 111
cavalry 39–41, 48, 53, 55, 63, 65, 67–8, 99,
    150, 153, 161–4, 166, 168, 175, 177–8,
    182, 187, 190–1, 193, 200
Central Administration Authority
    (*Zentralverwaltungsbehörde*) 85
Chézy, Helmina von 155
Chickering, Roger 7
citizen 3, 12, 20, 22, 25, 45, 60–1, 72, 75–6,
    79–80, 84, 87, 89–93, 96, 103–9, 119–22,
    127–8, 140, 143, 148–9, 177–86, 199,
    203, 209, 217, 220, 229, 231
civil war 35, 43, 87, 92, 94, 118–19, 207, 226,
    228, 235
civilian 3, 6–8, 10, 12, 20, 27, 29, 33–5, 38–9,
    45, 51, 59, 61, 63, 71, 75, 91–2, 103,
    113, 121, 124–58, 177–86, 199, 205–7,
    209, 218–19, 231, 246–9
civilization 2, 10–11, 14–16, 21, 131, 134,
    193, 231
Clausewitz, Carl von 1–2, 25, 34–8, 42–3,
    51–2, 63, 65, 151–2, 196–8, 205–6,
    236, 238, 240
Cold War 2, 11–12, 23, 25
Collins, Randall 17–20
Colloredo-Waldsee, Franz de 46
combat 1, 5–6, 9–10, 13, 17–21, 25–31,
    33, 35, 38, 42, 45, 51, 55, 59, 66, 77,
    86, 94, 103, 114, 121, 124, 146, 149,
    159–204, 209, 218, 221, 236, 246–7,
    250–1
commemoration 174, 204, 214–15, 217, 221,
    224, 240
Communists 12
Condé, Louis de Bourbon, Prince of 68
Confederation of the Rhine 32, 40, 47–8, 54,
    57, 65–6, 75, 105, 109–10, 151, 186,
    188, 195, 231, 234, 242, 245
Conrady, Wilhelm von 164–5
conscription 2–3, 7–8, 23, 38, 43–5, 53, 58,
    60, 65, 68–9, 75, 106, 119, 125, 140,
    144, 213, 233, 245, 247, 250–2
corporal punishment 126–31
cosmopolitanism 109, 113
Cotta, Friedrich 84, 112
crime 13, 18–19, 23, 25, 115, 126–31,
    151, 156
Crimean War 13
Crome, August Friedrich Wilhelm 110
culture (*Kultur*) 15, 19, 29, 42, 49, 58–9,
    81–3, 88, 106–10, 120, 126–39, 189,
    194, 198, 229–30, 240, 242, 249, 252

Dahlmann, Friedrich Christoph 109
Damiens, Robert François 126
Dann, Otto 3, 5, 75, 87
Danton, Georges 122
Darwin, Charles 27
Davout, Louis Nicolas 49, 64–5
Delitz, Friederike 129
desertion 37, 42–3, 47, 53, 58–9, 166, 248
Deutsche Blätter 82
Dohna-Schlobitten, Alexander zu 49
Donner von Richter, Otto 217
Dresden, battle of (1813) 69
Drives 11, 14–16, 19, 21, 176
Dumouriez, Charles François 44

Echternkamp, Jörg 4, 8, 75, 114, 222, 244
ego documents, *see* autobiography and memoir
Egypt 31
Eichhorn, Johann Albert Friedrich 240
Eichmann, Adolf 24–5
Eilers, Gerd 222
Einstein, Albert 15
Elias, Norbert 15–17, 20–1, 25, 127, 248
    and *Über den Prozeß der Zivilisation*
    (1939) 21
Embser, Johann Valentin 85
emotions 9, 11, 13–14, 16, 18, 21, 26–30,
    118, 123–39, 164, 167, 174, 185–6, 212
epic 163–4, 203
Evans, Richard J. 128–9, 131
experience 25–6

Faber du Faur, Christian Wilhelm von 193–5,
    215
fairy tales 28
Falk, Johannes 150–1
Fanon, Frantz 24
Fichte, Johann Gottlieb 3, 73–5, 87, 94–5, 97,
    112, 121, 130, 240
    and *Grundzüge des gegenwärtigen Zeitalters*
    (1806) 73
    and *Reden an die deutsche Nation*
    (1808) 4–5, 73
First World War 15, 25, 29, 31, 40, 125,
    159, 249
Förster, Stig 7
forward panic 18–19
Foucault, Michel 22–3
    and *Volonté de savoir* (1976) 22
France 4, 6–7, 12, 31–4, 37, 39, 41–56,
    58–61, 65–9, 71–6, 80, 84–7, 91, 95–9,
    105–6, 111–13, 116–19, 124–6, 133–5,
    140–2, 145–6, 149–51, 164, 172, 180,
    183, 186–8, 195–8, 202–10, 217, 226–8,
    231–5, 242, 245–6
Franz I, Emperor of Austria (Franz II, Emperor
    of the Holy Roman Empire) 68, 151, 225
French Revolution 6–8, 12, 24, 28, 31, 41, 67,
    72, 80, 84, 87, 90, 94–6, 109, 111, 113,

119, 122, 222, 224–6, 228, 231, 233–4, 236, 244–6
Freud, Sigmund 14–15
  and *Das Unbehagen in der Kultur* (1930) 15
Friedrich I, King of Württemberg 53, 56, 58, 111–12
Friedrich II (Frederick the Great), King of Prussia 35–8, 62, 86, 116, 121, 128, 242
Friedrich, Caspar David 99, 215
Friedrich August I, King of Saxony 57, 168, 202
Friedrich Wilhelm III, King of Prussia 39, 42, 52, 81, 116, 146, 197, 206, 209
  and 'An Mein Volk' 81, 116–17
Friesen, Karl Friedrich 215
Fromm, Eric 15
Fukuyama, Francis 12
Furstenau, Johann Gottlob 110

Garnier, Jean 161
Gat, Azar 35, 41
Geissler, Christian Gottfried 99
Gentz, Friedrich von 95–8, 113, 119, 131, 149, 225–9, 241, 245
  and 'Über den ewigen Frieden' (1800) 96–7, 245
Gerlach, Ernst Ludwig von 229
Gerlach, Leopold von 229
German Confederation 3, 225–6, 236, 240
Gervinus, Georg Gottfried 232–3
Ghana 16
Giddens, Anthony 20, 127–8, 248
  and *The Nation-State and Violence* (1985) 20
Giesse, Friedrich 174–5, 191–2
Glenn, Russell W. 18
Gneisenau, August von 33–4, 52, 60–2, 70–1, 85, 151, 171, 173, 197–9, 206–7, 218, 235–6, 240, 247
Goethe, Johann Wolfgang von 44, 78, 92, 102, 112, 135
Goetzen, Friedrich Wilhelm von 50
Görres, Joseph 83–4, 94–5, 112, 115, 121, 228
Gravert, Julius von 39
Gray, John 12
  and *Black Mass* (2007) 12
Great Migrations 17
Great Power 2, 25, 35, 37, 67, 228, 245–6
Grimm, Friedrich Melchior von 132
Grimm, Jacob 97
Grimm, Wilhelm 97, 240
Grolman, Karl von 62–3, 206
Großgörschen, battle of (1813) 69
Gulf War 13
Gustavus Adolphus 40, 121
GuthsMuths, Johann Christoph 220–1
gymnastic associations 210–11, 214, 219–22

Habsburg monarchy, *see* Austria
Hagemann, Karen 76, 244
Haller, Carl Ludwig von 226

Hamburg 59, 82–3, 91, 125, 128, 140–1, 148–9, 162, 217
Hamburgische Correspondenten 82
Hanover, Kingdom of 38, 46, 59, 65, 77, 85, 91, 111, 118, 128, 165, 234
Hardenberg, Erasmus von 136–7
Hardenberg (Novalis), Friedrich von 136–9
Hardenberg, Karl August von 60, 81, 85–6, 117, 146, 198, 206, 224
Harrant, Valentin von 56
Hartmann, Ferdinand 215
Hector, Trojan prince 164
Heeren, Arnold Hermann Ludwig 230–1
Hegel, Christiane 135–6
Hegel, Georg Wilhelm Friedrich 72–3, 78, 103, 133–5
  and *Vorlesungen über die Philosophie der Geschichte* (1822–30) 135
Heine, Heinrich 91–2, 242
Heinrich I, King of East Francia (*Ostfrankenreich*) 211
Helvetic Republic 31
Hensler, Dore 91
Herder, Johann Gottfried 108, 119–21
Heβ, Moses 232–3
Hess, Peter von 215
Hesse 43, 65, 155, 164, 195, 207
  and Kurhessen 53
Heydrich, Reinhard 24–5
Hippel, Theodor Gottlieb von 117
Historisches Journal 96
History 225–43
Hobbes, Thomas 9–10, 120
Hofer, Andreas 140, 211
Hoffmann, E. T. A. 153–4
Hoffmann, Karl 210
Hofmann, Heinrich Karl 223
Hohenlinden, battle of (1800) 32, 47, 68
Hohenlohe, Friedrich Ludwig von 33, 49, 64–5
Holland, *see* United Provinces
Holocaust 10–11, 22–3, 25
Holy Roman Empire 32, 46, 77, 105, 108–9, 146, 222, 234, 237, 245
Horst, Christoph 129
Humboldt, Wilhelm von 81, 90, 108, 112, 150, 240
Hynes, Samuel 28

infantry 18, 39–41, 48, 53, 55, 59, 63–8, 166, 175, 190–1, 193, 249
Intelligenzblätter 82
international law 89, 97, 118, 229
Italy 7, 31–2, 40, 46, 64, 68, 90, 110, 145, 159, 172, 232–3
Italy, Kingdom of 31–2, 172

Jahn, Friedrich Ludwig 81, 112, 152, 179, 210–12, 219–20, 223
James, Leighton S. 249–50

Japan 12
Jaup, Karl 110
Jean Paul 92–4, 121
Jeismann, Michael 3, 5, 76
Jemappes, battle of (1792) 45
Jena 72, 90, 133–5, 222–3
Jena, battle of (1806) 33–4, 39, 46, 49, 52, 64,
    92, 101, 141, 149, 167, 181, 206, 231
Johann, Austrian Archduke 47
Jordan, Emilie 207–8
Jordan, Heinrich von 51, 83, 105, 187, 200,
    207–8
Joseph II 46

Kalckreuth, Wilhelm Heinrich Adolf von 39
Kamptz, Karl Albert von 109
Kant, Immanuel 72–3, 87–9, 92, 96, 113,
    118–19, 130
    and *Kritik der praktischen Vernunft* (1788) 72
    and 'Zum ewigen Frieden' (1795) 72, 88, 118
Karl, Austrian Archduke 32, 40, 47, 67–8,
    70, 247
Karl, Grand Duke of Baden (earlier Heir
    Apparent or 'Crown Prince') 56–7, 164
Karlsruher Zeitung 116
Kersting, Georg Friedrich 215
King, John Harcourt 69
Kirchmayer, Georg 194–5
kleine Kriege (mobile, limited wars) 38, 41, 191
Kleist, Heinrich von 97, 99, 101, 140
Klenze, Leo von 242
Knobelsdorff, Wilhelm von 178
Koenen, Johann Friedrich von 60
Körner, Theodor 103–4, 121–4
Kotzebue, August von 201
Krafft, Johann Peter 215
Krug, Wilhelm Traugott 89, 119, 121
Krüger, Franz 215
Küfner, A. W. 121–2
Kupferer, Joachim 143

Landsturm (home guard) 50, 68
Landwehr (national guard) 48, 50–2, 58, 63,
    68–9, 147–8, 177–9, 215, 221–2, 251
Lange, Friedrich 84
Leipzig, battle of (1813) 55, 58, 112, 116, 149,
    154, 162, 169, 172, 174, 178, 187, 200–2,
    208, 210–14, 217, 220, 223, 233–4
Leipziger Tageblatt 84
Leipziger Zeitung 82–3
Lenin, Vladimir 13
Leo, Heinrich 223
L'Estocq, Anton Wilhelm von 48
levée en masse 3, 5, 7, 43–51, 58, 68, 199,
    235, 245
Lindenau, Karl Friedrich von 68, 202
Loeben, Otto Heinrich von 97
Louis XIV, King of France 35
Louis XV, King of France 126

Louis Ferdinand, Prussian Prince 101
Luden, Heinrich 84, 107, 112, 222–3, 229–30
Ludwig I, King of Bavaria 218
Luise, Queen of Prussia 117, 146, 224
Lunéville, Treaty of (1801) 32–3, 47, 151

Mack, Karl Leiberich 68
Maillinger, Joseph 171–2, 196
Mainz, battle of (1793) 45
Malinckrodt, Arnold 108–9
Mann, Michael 20
Mao Tse-tung 23
Marat, Jean-Paul 122
Marengo, battle of (1800) 32, 231
Marshall, S. L. A. 18
Martens, Christian von 105, 164, 174–6, 186,
    189, 191, 194, 207, 230
Marwitz, Friedrich August von der 62, 113,
    136, 245
Marx, Karl 14, 24, 246
Masséna, André 66
Max Joseph, King of Bavaria 53–5, 58
Mändler, Friedrich 167–8, 187–8, 193, 205, 239
Mecklenburg, Carl von 224
Meerheim, Ludwig von 189–90
memoir 5, 28, 133, 136, 140, 148, 157,
    159–64, 166, 168, 171–2, 188, 196, 205,
    215, 222, 236–7, 249–50, 252
memory 37, 120, 136, 138, 149, 160–1, 194,
    199, 204, 211, 213, 215–25, 234, 239,
    241–3, 249–50
Mendelssohn, Felix 240
Menzel, Karl Adolf 237
Metternich, Clemens von 69, 86, 95–6, 107,
    225, 235, 240
Meyern, Wilhelm Friedrich 88
middle class, *see* Bürgertum
Militärische Gesellschaft (Berlin) 37
Military Reorganisation Commission 38, 49,
    52, 60–2, 77
military revolution 33–43
Mohl, Robert von 218
Moltke, Helmuth von, the Elder 35
Monten, Dietrich 215, 242
Montesquieu, Charles-Louis Secondat 108
Montgelas, Maximilian von 55, 86
monuments 215, 217–18, 241–2
Moscow 55, 161, 164, 175–6, 186–9, 191,
    194–6, 198, 211, 237
Motherby, Johanna 155
Müffling, Carl von 160, 172, 236–7
Müller, Adam 96–9, 245
Müller, Johannes von 109
Münkler, Herfried 9–10
mutiny 70, 117

Naples 37
Napoleon I, Emperor of France 1–8, 28, 31–3,
    37–8, 40–2, 45, 47–9, 51–8, 62, 64–6,

69–73, 75–6, 79, 81, 83, 87, 90–3, 95–9, 103–5, 107, 109, 111, 113–15, 117–18, 120–2, 124–6, 135, 139–42, 144–7, 149–51, 153, 155, 159–61, 163–7, 171–8, 180, 183, 185–9, 191, 193, 195–9, 201–8, 212–13, 217–19, 222–3, 225–8, 231–8, 241–2, 244–7, 249–52
National Socialists 12
nationalism 4–8, 72–124, 205–25, 244–51
natural law 73, 89
Ney, Marshal Michel 56, 161–2
Nicolovius, Georg Heinrich Ludwig 81
Niebuhr, Barthold Georg 39, 49, 91
Niethammer, Friedrich Immanuel 134
nobility 21, 33–5, 50–3, 58, 62–3, 75, 80, 82–3, 85, 87, 92, 102, 106–8, 110, 114–15, 119, 121, 125, 136, 140, 175–6, 179, 198, 220–1, 230–1, 235, 248–9, 252
Nothen, Adolph 215

occupation 49, 73, 79, 84–5, 91, 99, 106–8, 114, 125, 141, 143, 146, 150–1, 184, 218, 220, 246, 251
Ottoman Empire 32, 37

pacification 2, 20–1, 25, 127–8
Palestine 31
Paris 31, 33, 35, 43, 49, 55–6, 69–70, 82, 90–1, 94, 115, 165, 199, 205–6, 208
patriotism 7–9, 44–5, 51–60, 104–24, 196–202, 206–7, 220–4
peace 86–99, 102–7, 112–14, 119–21, 144–6, 153–4, 205–7, 212–13, 245–6, 249–50
Poland 32, 37, 48, 69, 187, 189
police 19, 22, 35, 90, 106, 117, 129, 176, 224, 240
power 2–3, 13–16, 19–26, 34–41, 76–9, 85–7, 93–7, 103–18, 128–30, 135–9, 178–84, 208–9, 225–36, 245–8
Pressburg, Peace of (1805) 32, 146
primitive, *see* barbarity
Prussia 1–2, 4–6, 31–71, 75–7, 84–92, 101–8, 112–18, 124–6, 128–9, 140–55, 160–79, 183–8, 196–215, 219–26, 231–42, 245–51
psychology/psychoanalysis 14–15, 18, 21, 23, 26, 29, 128, 164
public sphere 76–86, 151–2

Radetzky, Joseph von 67, 69–70, 198–9, 207
Ranke, Leopold von 146, 237, 239–40
Rastatt, Congress of (1798) 32
Raumer, Friedrich von 84, 200–1, 237
Raumer, Karl von 200
Raven, Otto von 168–9
Reddy, William 131–2
Reiche, Ludwig von 165
Reimer, Georg Andreas 154–5

religion 5, 26, 35, 80–1, 83, 95–6, 98, 102–4, 107, 112, 114, 123, 131, 136, 139, 143, 180, 193, 201, 210–13
Renfner, Heinrich 104–5
resistance 18–19, 23, 43, 57, 71, 85, 87, 140–1, 151–2, 161, 214, 226–7, 230, 248–9
Rheinischer Merkur 82–3, 94, 211, 214
Roberts, Michael 40
Robespierre, Maximilien 122
Rotteck, Karl von 84, 107, 112, 231–2, 237
Rüchel, Ernst von 49, 64
Rühle von Lilienstern, Johann Jakob Otto August 113–14, 168, 184
and *Apologie des Krieges* (1813) 113–14
Rühs, Friedrich 105, 115
Russia 2, 32–4, 37, 42–3, 46–53, 55–6, 67–9, 71, 85, 116, 125–6, 141, 145–6, 149, 151, 153–5, 159, 162–3, 168–9, 174–7, 181–3, 186–9, 191–2, 194–8, 202–9, 212, 217–18, 224–5, 232, 235–7, 241

Sack, Friedrich Emanuel 117
Sakharov, Andrei 25
Sand, Karl 224
Sardinia 37
savagery 2, 99, 182, 198, 229
Savigny, Karl von 240
Savoy 37
Saxe-Weimar 128, 224
Saxe-Weimar, Karl August, Duke of 78
Saxony, Kingdom of 48–9, 53, 57, 64–5, 69, 77, 83, 105, 112, 116, 128, 146–7, 149, 168, 186–7, 199, 202, 206, 212, 217, 234
Scharnhorst, Gerhard Johann David von 33–4, 37, 39–40, 45, 50–1, 59–60, 63, 85, 140–1, 172, 179, 197–200, 215, 218, 240
Schauroth, Wilhelm von 162
Schelling, Friedrich Wilhelm Joseph 97, 240
Schenkendorf, Max von 103–4, 121
Schill, Ferdinand von 117–18, 188
Schiller, Friedrich 99, 102–3, 163
Schinkel, Karl Friedrich 241–2
Schlegel, Friedrich 81, 97, 99, 113, 121, 138, 140, 245
Schlegel, Wilhelm 97, 121, 245
Schleiermacher, Friedrich 81, 87, 97, 112, 121, 240
Schlosser, Friedrich Christoph 237
Schön, Amalie von 136, 147–9
Schön, Robert von 147
Schön, Theodor von 136, 146–9, 236
Schopenhauer, Arthur 149–50
Schopenhauer, Johanna 149–50
Schrafel, Joseph 173
Schreck, Michael 144
Schwarzenberg, Karl von 47, 69–70, 218
Second World War 18, 27, 29

Seele, Johann Bapiste 215
sentiment, *see* emotions
Seven Years' War 37, 39, 41–2, 62, 86, 88,
    171–2, 219, 225
Sheehan, James 4, 12, 105
siege 35, 40, 64, 162, 169, 207, 217
Sikora, Michael 8
Silesia 1, 52, 58, 69–70
Smolensk, battle of (1812) 164, 171, 175, 183,
    188–9, 194
Sofsky, Wolfgang 9–11
Soviet Union 12
Spain 33, 53, 141, 162, 172, 187–8, 232–3
Speckle, Ignaz 195, 205, 213
sports 18
Staël, Germaine de 72
    and *De l'Allemagne* (1814) 133
state 1–13, 22–5, 31–76, 104–24, 127–8,
    130–5, 143–6, 149, 151–2, 155, 159,
    173, 176–9, 182, 187, 191, 194–6,
    198, 202–43
Stearns, Carol 30
Stearns, Peter 29–30
Steffens, Henrich 178–80, 201
Stein, Heinrich Friedrich Karl vom und
    zum 39, 49, 81, 85, 112, 146, 152,
    154, 202, 235, 240
Stier, Wilhelm 241–2
structural violence 13–14
subjective violence 13
subjectivity 13, 26–7, 73, 99
Suckow, Karl von 167, 192
Suvorov, Aleksandr 32
Swebach, Jacques François 99
Sybel, Heinrich von 234–7
symbolic violence 13–14, 19, 23
systemic violence, *see* structural violence

Talleyrand, Charles-Maurice de 48
Taussig, Michael 14
technology 6, 13, 24–5, 40
terror 10–14, 18, 24, 91, 122, 129, 138–9,
    144, 173, 191, 224, 235
terrorism 9–10, 18, 129, 224
Thirty Years' War 35–7, 40–1, 77, 102, 119,
    163, 180, 204
Thugut, Franz Maria von 45–6
Thurn und Taxis, August von 161–2
Tieck, Ludwig 97
total war 6–7, 9, 33–43, 246–8
Trachtenberg Plan (1813) 69
trauma 13, 27, 159
travel writing 28, 107, 162, 174, 189, 249–52
Tucher, Jobst Wilhelm Karl von 133
Tucher, Marie von 133–5
Tyrol 32, 58, 68, 140, 162, 188, 211
Tzschirner, Heinrich Gottlieb 120–1

United Provinces 31, 37, 208
United States 7, 11–12, 226

Valais Republic 31
Valmy, battle of (1792) 44–5
Vandamme, Dominique 56, 148
Vaquette, Jean-Baptiste 41
Varnhagen von Ense, Karl August 125–6, 138,
    140–1, 149
Varnhagen von Ense, Rahel (née Levin) 138,
    156–8, 239
Venice 37
Vienna, Congress of 95, 205, 234
Vietnam War 18, 23, 29
Volkskrieg (people's war) 43, 71, 141, 246
Voltz, J. M. 122
volunteers (*Freiwillige*) 29, 33, 44, 47, 50,
    58–9, 63, 68, 75, 103, 177, 179, 181,
    187, 199–201, 215, 217–19, 221, 224,
    228, 235, 240–1
Vossische Zeitung 82, 214

Wagram, battle of (1809) 55, 66, 69, 126, 156,
    168, 188, 231
War
    of 1792 59, 90, 94, 97, 113, 121, 145, 151,
        164–6, 226, 234
    of 1805 1, 32–3, 37, 40, 46, 48, 52, 59,
        64–71, 90, 92, 107, 125, 140, 149, 166,
        186–7, 231, 242, 250
    of 1806 1, 4–5, 8, 72, 75, 77, 79, 83–4, 87,
        90, 93, 97–9, 101–2, 109, 111–12, 116,
        141, 144, 146, 148–50, 152, 160, 163,
        166–7, 171, 178–9, 185, 187–8, 213,
        224–7, 235, 239, 242, 250
    of 1809 1, 4, 32–3, 47–8, 53–8, 64–7,
        106–9, 117–18, 124, 126, 128, 140–2,
        156, 162, 167–8, 174, 183–9, 211, 231,
        242, 244, 250
    of 1812 2, 32–3, 39, 42, 47–8, 50, 53,
        55–6, 63–6, 69, 71, 85, 93, 108, 116,
        124–6, 129, 141, 151, 154–5, 159,
        162–4, 167–9, 171, 174–7, 183, 185–9,
        191, 193–8, 205–6, 209, 212, 215,
        217–18, 232, 235–6, 241–2, 250, 252
war articles (*Kriegsartikeln*) 61–2, 173
war literature 28, 159–64, 249–52
Wars
    of the Austrian Succession (1740–48) 36
    of freedom 87, 103, 163, 172, 188, 198,
        220–4, 235, 241, 244
    of the Grand Alliance (1689–97) 36
    of liberation 5, 7, 9, 122, 159, 171, 204,
        215, 219–20, 223–4, 232, 234–5, 237,
        240–2, 246, 250
    of the Spanish Succession (1701–14) 36
Warsaw, Grand Duchy of 32, 49
Water, Majorie Van de 26
Waterloo (Belle Alliance), battle of (1815) 159,
    205, 207
weaponry 18, 23, 34–5, 39, 61, 65, 95, 192,
    196, 215, 221, 225, 233, 236
Weber, Carl Maria von 210

Weber, Max 19–20
Wedel, Karl von 171, 175
Welcker, Carl Theodor 19, 121, 211
Welcker, Friedrich Gottlieb 119
Wellington, Arthur Wellesley, Duke of 163, 187
Westphalia, Kingdom of 32, 54, 58, 65, 175–6,
 212, 249
Westphalia, Treaty of (1648) 35, 37
Wichterich, Johann 174
Wieland, Christoph Martin 78, 85, 94, 108, 150
Wilhelm, Markgraf von Baden 56, 167, 207
Wilhelm I, King of Württemberg 218
Winckelmann, Johann Joachim 242
Winkopp, Peter Adolf 110
Wittgenstein, Ludwig 30
Wittgenstein, Peter von 69

Wrede, Carl Philipp von 162, 173, 190
Wurmser, Dagobert Sigismund 46
Württemberg, Kingdom of 32–3, 47–8, 53–6,
 58, 65, 76, 83, 105, 110–12, 116, 128,
 144, 154, 164, 175, 177, 185–6, 189,
 193–5, 212–13, 215, 218

Xenophon 68

Yorck von Wartenburg, Johann David
 Ludwig 51–2, 62, 197, 201, 209, 235–6

Zahn, Victor 111
Zimmermann, Maria Agatha 140
Žižek, Slavoj 13–14
 and *Violence* (2008) 13–14